Inequality in Immunization 2023

Inequality in Immunization 2023

Editors

Ahmad Reza Hosseinpoor
M. Carolina Danovaro
Devaki Nambiar
Aaron Wallace
Hope L. Johnson

MDPI

Basel • Beijing • Wuhan • Barcelona • Belgrade • Novi Sad • Cluj • Manchester

Editors
Ahmad Reza Hosseinpoor
World Health Organization
Geneva, Switzerland

M. Carolina Danovaro
World Health Organization
Geneva, Switzerland

Devaki Nambiar
World Health Organization
Geneva, Switzerland

Aaron Wallace
Centers for Disease Control
and Prevention
Atlanta, GA, USA

Hope L. Johnson
The Vaccine Alliance
Geneva, Switzerland

Editorial Office
MDPI
St. Alban-Anlage 66
4052 Basel, Switzerland

This is a reprint of articles from the Special Issue published online in the open access journal *Vaccines* (ISSN 2076-393X) (available at: https://www.mdpi.com/journal/vaccines/special_issues/3VPV7OD2W5).

For citation purposes, cite each article independently as indicated on the article page online and as indicated below:

Lastname, A.A.; Lastname, B.B. Article Title. *Journal Name* **Year**, *Volume Number*, Page Range.

ISBN 978-3-0365-8152-1 (Hbk)
ISBN 978-3-0365-8153-8 (PDF)
doi.org/10.3390/books978-3-0365-8153-8

Cover image courtesy of WHO

Contents

About the Editors

Ahmad Reza Hosseinpoor

Ahmad Reza Hosseinpoor leads the Health Inequality Monitoring Team at the Department of Data and Analytics of the World Health Organization. He has conceptualized and coordinated the development of resources and tools in this area, including the Health Inequality Data Repository, the WHO global platform for disaggregated health data; the WHO Health Equity Assessment Toolkit (HEAT), a software application to explore and compare health inequalities; the WHO Handbook and step-by-step manuals on Health Inequality Monitoring, resources to strengthen and guide the development of health inequality monitoring; and a series of WHO thematic global inequality reports. Dr. Hosseinpoor is the lead author of a number of peer-reviewed articles quantifying inequalities in health, both at the national and global, as well as methodological articles such as decomposition and summary measures of health inequality. He holds an MD and a PhD in Epidemiology.

M. Carolina Danovaro

M. Carolina Danovaro has been working in immunization for over 20 years. She is part of the Immunization Analysis & Insights (IAI) team of the World Health Organization, where she participates in the production of global vaccination statistics and supports WHO Member States with immunization program monitoring and evaluation (M&E) activities. Before joining WHO headquarters, Carolina worked in the Pan-American Health Organization (PAHO) for over 10 years, leading the Immunization Strategic team and advancing the regional agenda on immunization data quality and electronic immunization registries, among other duties. She has co-authored over 100 articles in peer-reviewed journals, book chapters, and technical documents with a focus on vaccination epidemiology, surveillance, and service delivery in routine and conflict settings. She has also taught various Vaccinology courses and mentored young professionals in the course of her career.

Devaki Nambiar

Devaki Nambiar consults for the Health Inequality Monitoring Team at the Department of Data and Analytics of the World Health Organization. Based out of India, she has authored over 100 articles, book chapters, and technical reports on health equity, health for all, social determinants of health in local settings (in India), but also in regional and global contexts, partnering with individuals and organizations spanning the globe. She is passionate about health and social justice as well as mentorship, and has both run and designed coursework and supported mentorship programs related to inequality monitoring, equity research, health policy and systems research, and systems thinking. She is a Board Member of Health Systems Global and a Lancet Commissioner on Population Health Post COVID. She received her PhD in Public Health from the Johns Hopkins Bloomberg School of Public Health.

Aaron Wallace

Aaron Wallace has served as team lead for the Immunization Delivery Science Team within the Global Immunization Division at the US Centers for Disease Control and Prevention since 2019. He first joined GID/CDC in 2003 as a research fellow focused on examining the global evidence for integrated delivery alongside immunization services. Since joining GID full-time in 2007, he has supported and led several immunization-based research studies across multiple topics, including integration, urban immunization, missed opportunities for vaccination, vaccine acceptance, and synergies between routine and supplementary immunization activities. Aaron has a BS in biology from UC Berkeley and an MPH, MBA and PhD in epidemiology from Emory University.

Hope L. Johnson

Hope L. Johnson is currently the Director of Measurement, Evaluation & Learning at Gavi, the Vaccine Alliance. Dr. Johnson is responsible for overseeing the monitoring and evaluation of Gavi's strategy, programs, policies, priority initiatives, strategic information, and management of Gavi investments in immunization data strengthening and research. She is an infectious disease epidemiologist with more than 20 years working in global health focused on bridging the strategy to execution gap with information to accelerate access to lifesaving interventions to those that need them the most. Dr. Johnson is a graduate and former faculty of the Johns Hopkins Bloomberg School of Public Health. Her focus is on establishing the evidence base and building capacity for data-driven decision making to accelerate development and implementation of maternal and child health interventions with a specific focus on vaccine preventable diseases.

vaccines

Editorial

Inequality in Immunization: Holding on to Equity as We 'Catch Up'

Devaki Nambiar [1], Ahmad Reza Hosseinpoor [1,*], Nicole Bergen [1], M. Carolina Danovaro-Holliday [2], Aaron Wallace [3] and Hope L. Johnson [4]

1 Department of Data and Analytics, World Health Organization, 20 Avenue Appia, 1211 Geneva, Switzerland; nambiard@who.int (D.N.); bergenn@who.int (N.B.)
2 Department of Immunization, Vaccines, and Biologicals, World Health Organization, 20 Avenue Appia, 1211 Geneva, Switzerland; danovaroc@who.int
3 Global Immunization Division, US Centres for Disease Control and Prevention, Atlanta, GA 30329, USA; ccu7@cdc.gov
4 Measurement, Evaluation and Learning Department, Gavi, The Vaccine Alliance, 1218 Geneva, Switzerland; hjohnson@gavi.org
* Correspondence: hosseinpoora@who.int; Tel.: +41-22-791-3205

Citation: Nambiar, D.; Hosseinpoor, A.R.; Bergen, N.; Danovaro-Holliday, M.C.; Wallace, A.; Johnson, H.L. Inequality in Immunization: Holding on to Equity as We 'Catch Up'. *Vaccines* **2023**, *11*, 913. https://doi.org/10.3390/vaccines11050913

Received: 19 April 2023
Revised: 21 April 2023
Accepted: 24 April 2023
Published: 28 April 2023

1. Slowed Progress in Global Immunization Coverage

Immunization, hailed as one of the most successful public health interventions in the world, has contributed to major advancements in health as well as social and economic development [1]. Vaccines help to avert more than 20 life-threatening diseases and are responsible for preventing an estimated 3.5 to 5 million deaths each year [2]. Following the introduction of the Expanded Immunization Programme by the World Health Organization (WHO) in 1974 [3], there were dramatic gains in immunization coverage worldwide, bolstered by global collaborative efforts to increase coverage and expand immunization among under-vaccinated populations.

Yet, in recent years, progress has largely stalled and, in some cases, reversed. Although these trends were becoming evident prior to the COVID-19 pandemic [4], they have been greatly exacerbated since the onset of COVID-19 and associated disruptions in 2020. Childhood immunization programmes have lost ground, with an estimated 25 million children under the age of 1 not receiving a third dose of diphtheria-tetanus-pertussis-containing vaccine (DTP3) in 2021—the highest number for more than a decade; 18 million of these children did not even receive the first dose of DTP vaccine (zero-dose children) [5]. Between 2019 and 2021, there were decreases in global coverage of the first dose of Human Papillomavirus vaccine (HPV) among girls (from 20% in 2019 to 15% in 2021) [5], and coverage decreases were reported across many other WHO-recommended vaccines, including polio, pneumococcal, rotavirus, and measles-containing vaccines [6].

Against this backdrop of slowed progress, inequalities are an increasingly highlighted concern as certain population groups remain systematically at risk of being unvaccinated or under-vaccinated. More than 60% of unvaccinated or under-vaccinated children in 2021 lived in just 10 countries (India, Nigeria, Indonesia, Ethiopia, the Philippines, the Democratic Republic of the Congo, Brazil, Pakistan, Angola, and Myanmar) [5], and unvaccinated children remain disproportionately represented in impoverished, rural or urban slum areas, and situations of conflict or fragility [7]. Meanwhile, with recent disruptions to immunization programs, inequalities have emerged or become worse in many middle-income countries that have typically had high-performing programs [8].

2. Major Initiatives to Tackle Inequality in Immunization

As part of efforts to restore progress and tackle inequality, in 2020, the World Health Assembly endorsed the Immunization Agenda 2030 (IA2030) [9]. IA2030 sets forth an "ambitious, overarching global vision and strategy for vaccines and immunization for the decade 2021–2030" [9]. IA2030's third Strategy Priority places emphasis on coverage across subgroups of gender, age, location, or socioeconomic status and promotes principles of people-centredness and country ownership for processes that are premised on partnership and guided by data. Realizing the IA2030 vision—a world where everyone, everywhere, at every age fully benefits from vaccines for good health and well-being—is aligned with the Sustainable Development Goal (SDG) imperative of "leaving no one behind" [9]. Indeed, immunization is central to achieving the health-specific SDG (SDG3), and, furthermore, contributes to 14 of the 16 other SDGs [10].

Equity is a major priority area for Gavi, the Vaccine Alliance. Gavi, established in 2000 to improve access to vaccines among children in the poorest countries, has supported countries in the provision of vaccines to 981 million children in 77 countries through routine immunization programmes, and an additional 1.4 billion vaccinations through campaigns [11]. Gavi's current 2021–2025 strategy builds on this work, addressing within country equity as an organizing principle "with a high ambition to reduce the number of under-immunized children and an intensified focus on reaching the unreached" [12]. This includes additional support for countries such as the Identify–Reach–Monitor–Measure–Advocate (IRMMA) framework, a new Equity Accelerator Fund and Learning Hub [13].

Another noteworthy initiative is the Equity Reference Group for Immunization (ERG), an action-oriented thinktank consisting of senior experts in global health working with WHO, Gavi, the World Bank, the Bill and Melinda Gates Foundation, and UNICEF; academics in critical topics such as metrics, gender, and health systems development; and senior leaders from ministries of health. The ERG has four priority thematic areas: urban poor areas; remote rural areas; children affected by conflict; and gender-related inequities and barriers to immunization [14].

3. The Special Issue: Monitoring Inequalities and Understanding Drivers; Sharing Experiences and Impact of Equity-Focused Interventions

In this Special Issue, we bring together research and evaluation on Inequality in Immunization to contribute to growing evidence and insights on monitoring immunization inequalities and understanding drivers of coverage, as well as pathways towards enhancing and sustaining equity in immunization. The Special Issue features research, reviews, and commentaries that span a range of immunization topics and populations. While there is an emphasis on childhood vaccinations [15–18]—exploring inequalities in DTP and measles-containing vaccine (MCV) coverage [19–23] and patterns of inequality in unvaccinated or zero-dose children [24–29]—contributions also cover inequalities in adult immunization [30], including protection of pregnant women and their newborns against tetanus [31] and COVID-19 vaccination [32,33].

An encouraging observation while putting together this Special Issue has been the use of a variety of data sources to assess immunization inequalities. Studies have made use of traditional sources of immunization data like administrative data [19,23,32] and population surveys [18,21,22,27,29,30] (including Demographic and Health Surveys and/or Multiple Indicator Cluster Surveys [15,20,31]), while several other studies explored the potential of novel sources such as geospatial data [24,25], electronic immunization registries [34], dialogues [16], country appraisals and reports [35], and funding proposals [26]. Three review studies relied on synthesis and structured analyses drawing from a multitude of existing studies [17,33,36]. Indeed, the diversity of data sources represented across the articles of this Special Issue points to greater availability of data, and, critically, the innovative use of these data to delve more deeply into inequality analysis and inference. This is a practice that is welcome and will be key to generating new insights into immunization inequalities and progress in this area.

This collection of articles makes important contributions to understanding dimensions of immunization inequality—that is, the diverse demographic, socioeconomic, or geographical characteristics that define populations who are advantaged and disadvantaged, while also highlighting the frequent co-occurrence and compounding of multiple deprivations.

As dimensions of inequality present themselves and intersect in dynamic ways, our modes of understanding must keep up. Several studies in this Special Issue examined multiple dimensions of immunization inequality [18,19,21,27,29,31,33,36], while others focused on specific dimensions, such as gender barriers [20,34] or socioeconomic status [15,30,32].

There is an established and growing evidence base on exemplars of action on immunization equity, particularly among Gavi-supported countries, but also in other contexts with successful immunization programmes [26,35,37]. This research offers important insights into what strategies are being deployed to reduce inequalities ("the what") [35,37,38], while starting to shed light on how gains in immunization equity were achieved ("the how") [39,40]. There is, admittedly, a long way to go in expanding the evidence base in this latter "how" category and what is required to feasibly implement these strategies, including costs and drivers of sustained change.

Taken together, the articles in this Special Issue spotlight some of the most current and pressing areas of interest in the topic of inequality in immunization, though the absence of certain themes is notable. For instance, analyses pertaining to conflict or fragile state contexts were lacking. Several of the contributions to this Special Issue acknowledge the need for greater reliance on qualitative methodologies and longer-term engagement with affected populations. These approaches are vital to developing contextually tailored monitoring and planning mechanisms that foreground equity in the face of changing or worsening relationships of security or trust.

Our Special Issue launch in April 2023 is timed to coincide with the 2023 World Immunization Week, which this year focuses on the theme of 'The Big Catch-Up' [41]. This initiative calls for the year 2023 to be a coordinated, intensified period of vaccination catch-up—to close immunity gaps among persons missed during the pandemic—involving recovery and strengthening of immunization services. "The Big Catch-Up" is a concerted effort intended to be driven by communities and countries, regions working in partnership with IA2030 institutions and structures, to which equity is integral [42]. This requires vigilance to change local realities with more sensitive and flexible metrics and methods to understand the complex, intersectional and dynamic nature of inequities, alongside concerted collaboration, context-tailored, and community-driven responses that chip away at inequities. In short, it is crucial that we hold on to equity in immunization in our efforts to catch up on the IA2030 goals to realize the vision of a world where everyone, everywhere, at every age, fully benefits from vaccines to improve health and well-being [9].

Funding: The Special Issue was funded in part by Gavi, The Vaccine Alliance. Beyond the individual contribution of HLJ, who is a Gavi employee, the funder had no role in the writing of the editorial.

Institutional Review Board Statement: Not applicable.

Informed Consent Statement: Not applicable.

Data Availability Statement: Not applicable.

Conflicts of Interest: The authors declare no conflict of interest. The authors alone are responsible for the views expressed in this publication and they do not necessarily represent the views, decisions or policies of their institutions.

References

1. Bloom, D.E. The Value of Vaccination. In *Hot Topics in Infection and Immunity in Children VII*; Curtis, N., Finn, A., Pollard, A.J., Eds.; Springer: New York, NY, USA, 2010.
2. World Health Organization. Vaccines and Immunization. Available online: https://www.who.int/health-topics/vaccinesNewYork,USA-and-immunization#tab=tab_1 (accessed on 7 April 2023).
3. Henderson, R.H.; Sundaresan, T. Cluster Sampling to Assess Immunization Coverage: A Review of Experience with a Simplified Sampling Method. *Bull. World Health Organ.* **1982**, *60*, 253–260. [PubMed]
4. UNICEF Immunization Unit. *Immunization Coverage: Are We Losing Ground?* World Health Organization and UNICEF: New York, NY, USA, 2020.
5. World Health Organization. Immunization Coverage. Available online: https://www.who.int/news-room/fact-sheets/detail/immunization-coverage (accessed on 7 April 2023).

6. Lassi, Z.S.; Naseem, R.; Salam, R.A.; Siddiqui, F.; Das, J.K. The Impact of the COVID-19 Pandemic on Immunization Campaigns and Programs: A Systematic Review. *Int. J. Environ. Res. Public Heal.* **2021**, *18*, 988. [CrossRef] [PubMed]
7. Chopra, M.; Bhutta, Z.; Chang Blanc, D.; Checchi, F.; Gupta, A.; Lemango, E.T.; Levine, O.S.; Lyimo, D.; Nandy, R.; O'Brien, K.L.; et al. Addressing the Persistent Inequities in Immunization Coverage. *Bull. World Health Organ.* **2020**, *98*, 146–148. [CrossRef] [PubMed]
8. Lindstrand, A.; Cherian, T.; Chang-Blanc, D.; Feikin, D.; O'Brien, K.L. The World of Immunization: Achievements, Challenges, and Strategic Vision for the Next Decade. *J. Infect. Dis.* **2021**, *224*, S452–S467. [CrossRef]
9. World Health Organization. *Immunization Agenda 2030: A Global Strategy to Leave No One Behind*; World Health Organization: Geneva, Switzerland, 2020.
10. Gavi, The Vaccine Alliance. Sustainable Development Goals. Available online: https://www.gavi.org/our-alliance/global-health-development/sustainable-development-goals (accessed on 7 April 2023).
11. Gavi, The Vaccine Alliance. Facts and Figures. Available online: https://www.gavi.org/sites/default/files/programmes-impact/our-impact/Gavi-Facts-and-figures-2023.pdf (accessed on 7 April 2023).
12. Gavi, The Vaccine Alliance. The Equity Goal: Strengthen Health Systems to Increase Equity in Immunization. Available online: https://www.gavi.org/our-alliance/strategy/phase-5-2021-2025/equity-goal (accessed on 7 April 2023).
13. Gavi, The Vaccine Alliance. Zero-Dose Learning Hub. Available online: https://zdlh.gavi.org/ (accessed on 19 April 2023).
14. Equity Reference Group for Immunization. Summary. Available online: https://drive.google.com/file/d/1VpuVX85RWd_vq6FJ4lcmCnPOYJp1AhuM/view (accessed on 25 April 2023).
15. Patenaude, B.N.; Sriudomporn, S.; Odihi, D.; Mak, J.; de Broucker, G. Comparing Multivariate with Wealth-Based Inequity in Vaccination Coverage in 56 Countries: Toward a Better Measure of Equity in Vaccination Coverage. *Vaccines* **2023**, *11*, 536. [CrossRef]
16. Shearer, J.C.; Nava, O.; Prosser, W.; Nawaz, S.; Mulongo, S.; Mambu, T.; Mafuta, E.; Munguambe, K.; Sigauque, B.; Cherima, Y.J.; et al. Uncovering the Drivers of Childhood Immunization Inequality with Caregivers, Community Members and Health System Stakeholders: Results from a Human-Centered Design Study in DRC, Mozambique and Nigeria. *Vaccines* **2023**, *11*, 689. [CrossRef]
17. Dadari, I.; Belt, R.V.; Iyengar, A.; Ray, A.; Hossain, I.; Ali, D.; Danielsson, N.; Sodha, S.V. The Global Urban Immunization Working Group Achieving the IA2030 Coverage and Equity Goals through a Renewed Focus on Urban Immunization. *Vaccines* **2023**, *11*, 809. [CrossRef]
18. De Oliveira Roque e Lima, J.; Pagotto, V.; Rocha, B.S.; Scalize, P.S.; Guimarães, R.A.; de Lima, M.D.; da Silva, L.N.; da Silva Oliveira, M.D.; Moura, W.É.; Teles, S.A.; et al. Low Vaccine Coverage and Factors Associated with Incomplete Childhood Immunization in Racial/Ethnic Minorities and Rural Groups, Central Brazil. *Vaccines* **2023**, *11*, 838. [CrossRef]
19. Perry, M.; Cottrell, S.; Gravenor, M.B.; Griffiths, L. Determinants of Equity in Coverage of Measles-Containing Vaccines in Wales, UK, during the Elimination Era. *Vaccines* **2023**, *11*, 680. [CrossRef]
20. Johns, N.E.; Kirkby, K.; Goodman, T.S.; Heidari, S.; Munro, J.; Shendale, S.; Hosseinpoor, A.R. Subnational Gender Inequality and Childhood Immunization: An Ecological Analysis of the Subnational Gender Development Index and DTP Coverage Outcomes across 57 Countries. *Vaccines* **2022**, *10*, 1951. [CrossRef]
21. Tohme, R.A.; Scobie, H.M.; Okunromade, O.; Olaleye, T.; Shuaib, F.; Jegede, T.; Yahaya, R.; Nnaemeka, N.; Lawal, B.; Egwuenu, A.; et al. Tetanus and Diphtheria Seroprotection among Children Younger Than 15 Years in Nigeria, 2018: Who Are the Unprotected Children? *Vaccines* **2023**, *11*, 663. [CrossRef] [PubMed]
22. Yang, Y.; Kostandova, N.; Mwansa, F.D.; Nakazwe, C.; Namukoko, H.; Sakala, C.; Bobo, P.; Masumbu, P.K.; Nachinga, B.; Ngula, D.; et al. Challenges Addressing Inequalities in Measles Vaccine Coverage in Zambia through a Measles–Rubella Supplementary Immunization Activity during the COVID-19 Pandemic. *Vaccines* **2023**, *11*, 608. [CrossRef] [PubMed]
23. Saidu, Y.; Di Mattei, P.; Nchinjoh, S.C.; Edwige, N.N.; Nsah, B.; Muteh, N.J.; Ndoula, S.T.; Abdullahi, R.; Zamir, C.S.; Njoh, A.A.; et al. The Hidden Impact of the COVID-19 Pandemic on Routine Childhood Immunization Coverage in Cameroon. *Vaccines* **2023**, *11*, 645. [CrossRef] [PubMed]
24. Fullman, N.; Correa, G.C.; Ikilezi, G.; Phillips, D.E.; Reynolds, H.W. Assessing Potential Exemplars in Reducing Zero-Dose Children: A Novel Approach for Identifying Positive Outliers in Decreasing National Levels and Geographic Inequalities in Unvaccinated Children. *Vaccines* **2023**, *11*, 647. [CrossRef] [PubMed]
25. Haeuser, E.; Nguyen, J.Q.; Rolfe, S.; Nesbit, O.; Fullman, N.; Mosser, J.F. Assessing Geographic Overlap between Zero-Dose Diphtheria–Tetanus–Pertussis Vaccination Prevalence and Other Health Indicators. *Vaccines* **2023**, *11*, 802. [CrossRef]
26. Ducharme, J.; Correa, G.C.; Reynolds, H.W.; Sharkey, A.B.; Fonner, V.A.; Johri, M. Mapping of Pro-Equity Interventions Proposed by Immunisation Programs in Gavi Health Systems Strengthening Grants. *Vaccines* **2023**, *11*, 341. [CrossRef]
27. Nchinjoh, S.C.; Saidu, Y.; Agbor, V.N.; Mbanga, C.M.; Jude Muteh, N.; Njoh, A.A.; Ndoula, S.T.; Nsah, B.; Edwige, N.N.; Roberman, S.; et al. Factors Associated with Zero-Dose Childhood Vaccination Status in a Remote Fishing Community in Cameroon: A Cross-Sectional Analytical Study. *Vaccines* **2022**, *10*, 2052. [CrossRef]
28. Hogan, D.; Gupta, A. Why Reaching Zero-Dose Children Holds the Key to Achieving the Sustainable Development Goals. *Vaccines* **2023**, *11*, 781. [CrossRef]

29. Ishoso, D.K.; Danovaro-Holliday, M.C.; Cikomola, A.M.-W.; Lungayo, C.L.; Mukendi, J.-C.; Mwamba, D.; Ngandu, C.; Mafuta, E.; Lusamba, P.; Lulebo, A.; et al. "Zero Dose" Children in the Democratic Republic of Congo: How Many and Who Are They? *Vaccines* **2023**, *11*, 900. [CrossRef]
30. Singh, D.; Sinha, A.; Kanungo, S.; Pati, S. Disparities in Coverage of Adult Immunization among Older Adults in India. *Vaccines* **2022**, *10*, 2124. [CrossRef]
31. Johns, N.E.; Cata-Preta, B.O.; Kirkby, K.; Arroyave, L.; Bergen, N.; Danovaro-Holliday, M.C.; Santos, T.M.; Yusuf, N.; Barros, A.J.D.; Hosseinpoor, A.R. Inequalities in Immunization against Maternal and Neonatal Tetanus: A Cross-Sectional Analysis of Protection at Birth Coverage Using Household Health Survey Data from 76 Countries. *Vaccines* **2023**, *11*, 752. [CrossRef]
32. Choudhary, R.; Carter, E.; Monzon, J.; Stewart, A.; Slotnick, J.; Samayoa Jerez, L.L.; Rodriguez Araujo, D.S.; Zielinski-Gutierrez, E.; Suchdev, P.S. Sociodemographic Factors Associated with COVID-19 Vaccination among People in Guatemalan Municipalities. *Vaccines* **2023**, *11*, 745. [CrossRef]
33. Bergen, N.; Johns, N.E.; Chang Blanc, D.; Hosseinpoor, A.R. Within-Country Inequality in COVID-19 Vaccination Coverage: A Scoping Review of Academic Literature. *Vaccines* **2023**, *11*, 517. [CrossRef] [PubMed]
34. Siddiqi, D.A.; Iftikhar, S.; Siddique, M.; Mehmood, M.; Dharma, V.K.; Shah, M.T.; Setayesh, H.; Chandir, S. Immunization Gender Inequity in Pakistan: An Analysis of 6.2 Million Children Born from 2019 to 2022 and Enrolled in the Sindh Electronic Immunization Registry. *Vaccines* **2023**, *11*, 685. [CrossRef]
35. Ivanova, V.; Shahabuddin, A.S.M.; Sharkey, A.; Johri, M. Advancing Immunization Coverage and Equity: A Structured Synthesis of Pro-Equity Strategies in 61 Gavi-Supported Countries. *Vaccines* **2023**, *11*, 191. [CrossRef]
36. Patikorn, C.; Cho, J.-Y.; Lambach, P.; Hutubessy, R.; Chaiyakunapruk, N. Equity-Informative Economic Evaluations of Vaccines: A Systematic Literature Review. *Vaccines* **2023**, *11*, 622. [CrossRef]
37. Athiyaman, A.; Ajayi, T.; Mutuku, F.; Luwaga, F.; Bryer, S.; Giwa, O.; Mngemane, S.; Edwige, N.N.; Berman, L. Recovering from the Unprecedented Backsliding in Immunization Coverage: Learnings from Country Programming in Five Countries through the Past Two Years of COVID-19 Pandemic Disruptions. *Vaccines* **2023**, *11*, 375. [CrossRef]
38. Shaum, A.; Wardle, M.T.; Amponsa-Achiano, K.; Aborigo, R.; Opare, J.; Wallace, A.S.; Bandoh, D.; Quaye, P.; Osei-Sarpong, F.; Abotsi, F.; et al. Evaluation of Container Clinics as an Urban Immunization Strategy: Findings from the First Year of Implementation in Ghana, 2017–2018. *Vaccines* **2023**, *11*, 814. [CrossRef]
39. Shimp, L.; Ghosh, R.S.; Elkes, K. Addressing Immunization Inequity—What Have the International Community and India Learned over 35 Years? *Vaccines* **2023**, *11*, 790. [CrossRef]
40. Datta, S.S.; Martinón-Torres, F.; Berdzuli, N.; Cakmak, N.; Edelstein, M.; Cottrell, S.; Muscat, M. Addressing Determinants of Immunization Inequities Requires Objective Tools to Devise Local Solutions. *Vaccines* **2023**, *11*, 811. [CrossRef]
41. World Health Organization. World Immunization Week 2023. Available online: https://www.who.int/campaigns/world-immunization-week/2023 (accessed on 21 April 2023).
42. O'Brien, K. Member States Information Session—The Global Immunization "Big Catch-Up" Effort. Available online: https://apps.who.int/gb/MSPI/pdf_files/2023/03/Item1_24-03.pdf (accessed on 13 April 2023).

vaccines

Article

Inequalities in Immunization against Maternal and Neonatal Tetanus: A Cross-Sectional Analysis of Protection at Birth Coverage Using Household Health Survey Data from 76 Countries

Nicole E. Johns [1], Bianca O. Cata-Preta [2], Katherine Kirkby [1], Luisa Arroyave [2], Nicole Bergen [1], M. Carolina Danovaro-Holliday [3], Thiago M. Santos [2], Nasir Yusuf [3], Aluísio J. D. Barros [2] and Ahmad Reza Hosseinpoor [1,*]

1 Department of Data and Analytics, World Health Organization, 20 Avenue Appia, 1211 Geneva, Switzerland
2 International Center for Equity in Health, Federal University of Pelotas, Rua Mal Deodoro 1160, Pelotas 96020-220, Brazil
3 Department of Immunization, Vaccines, and Biologicals, World Health Organization, 20 Avenue Appia, 1211 Geneva, Switzerland
* Correspondence: hosseinpoora@who.int; Tel.: +41-22-791-3205

Citation: Johns, N.E.; Cata-Preta, B.O.; Kirkby, K.; Arroyave, L.; Bergen, N.; Danovaro-Holliday, M.C.; Santos, T.M.; Yusuf, N.; Barros, A.J.D.; Hosseinpoor, A.R. Inequalities in Immunization against Maternal and Neonatal Tetanus: A Cross-Sectional Analysis of Protection at Birth Coverage Using Household Health Survey Data from 76 Countries. *Vaccines* **2023**, *11*, 752. https://doi.org/10.3390/vaccines11040752

Academic Editor: Alessandra Casuccio

Received: 17 February 2023
Revised: 15 March 2023
Accepted: 16 March 2023
Published: 29 March 2023

Abstract: Substantial progress in maternal and neonatal tetanus elimination has been made in the past 40 years, with dramatic reductions in neonatal tetanus incidence and mortality. However, twelve countries have still not achieved maternal and neonatal tetanus elimination, and many countries that have achieved elimination do not meet key sustainability thresholds to ensure long-lasting elimination. As maternal and neonatal tetanus is a vaccine-preventable disease (with coverage of the infant conferred by maternal immunization during and prior to pregnancy), maternal tetanus immunization coverage is a key metric for monitoring progress towards, equity in, and sustainability of tetanus elimination. In this study, we examine inequalities in tetanus protection at birth, a measure of maternal immunization coverage, across 76 countries and four dimensions of inequality via disaggregated data and summary measures of inequality. We find that substantial inequalities in coverage exist for wealth (with lower coverage among poorer wealth quintiles), maternal age (with lower coverage among younger mothers), maternal education (with lower coverage among less educated mothers), and place of residence (with lower coverage in rural areas). Inequalities existed for all dimensions across low- and lower-middle-income countries, and across maternal education and place of residence across upper-middle-income countries. Though global coverage changed little over the time period 2001–2020, this obscured substantial heterogeneity across countries. Notably, several countries had substantial increases in coverage accompanied by decreases in inequality, highlighting the need for equity considerations in maternal and neonatal tetanus elimination and sustainability efforts.

Keywords: inequality; maternal and neonatal tetanus; immunization; vaccination; health disparities

1. Introduction

Maternal and neonatal tetanus (MNT) is a form of tetanus, an acute and potentially fatal disease caused by the bacterium *Clostridium tetani*. It affects women during pregnancy or within six weeks of the end of pregnancy and infants during their first 28 days of life [1]. MNT constitutes a major public health concern, as neonatal case-fatality rates are upwards of 80% and approach 100% when untreated [2]. Since the initial adoption of maternal and neonatal tetanus elimination (MNTE) goals by the World Health Organization (WHO) and global health partners in the late 1980s [3], the annual number of deaths due to neonatal tetanus has decreased substantially, from 787,000 in 1988 to 25,000 in 2018 [4]. MNTE, which is defined as less than one case of neonatal tetanus per 1000 live births in every district in a country each year (neonatal tetanus is considered a proxy indicator for maternal tetanus), has been achieved in 47 of the 59 priority countries targeted for MNTE as of December 2020 [5].

MNT is a vaccine-preventable disease [1,2]. Immunization is therefore a key strategy for achieving and sustaining its elimination, alongside clean birth and cord care practices, reliable surveillance, and use of data to identify areas and populations at risk for MNT [3]. To achieve life-long protection, the WHO recommends that national immunization programs provide six doses of tetanus toxoid containing vaccines (TTCV) administered in childhood and adolescence [2]. Pregnant women who are not vaccinated against tetanus, or for whom vaccination status is unknown, should receive at least two TTCV doses starting as early as possible during pregnancy. Pregnant women who are partially immunized with one to four doses should receive one dose before giving birth [2]. Thus, as populations increasingly receive the routine six doses during childhood and adolescence, fewer women will require TTCV during pregnancy.

MNT is associated with poverty and lack of access to adequate health services, and occurs most frequently in settings with weak health and immunization systems, largely in the worst performing districts in low- and lower-middle-income countries [1,2]. Therefore, MNT is inherently a health equity issue. Despite this, relatively few publications have examined predictors of and inequalities in maternal tetanus immunization, particularly relative to other child immunization outcomes. Prior research examining inequalities in childhood immunizations and using multi-national samples has found several factors which are significantly associated with disparities in coverage, including household wealth [6–9], maternal age [10], maternal education [8,9,11], and place of residence (urban/rural) [9,11–13]. A number of single-country studies have examined factors associated with tetanus vaccination uptake by pregnant women in, for example, Afghanistan [14], Bangladesh [15,16], Ethiopia [17,18], The Gambia [19], India [20], Kenya [21], Myanmar [22], Sierra Leone [23], and Sudan [24]. Across these studies, higher levels of maternal education and household wealth have often been found to be associated with increased TTCV uptake, and in some (but not all) contexts, there were also significant associations between uptake and maternal age and place of residence. Two multi-country studies within Africa found greater maternal age, education, and household wealth to be significantly associated with higher coverage of births protected against neonatal tetanus [25,26].

To date, no global multi-country analyses have explored the extent of inequalities in maternal tetanus immunization coverage. Though smaller-scale (e.g., country-level or subnational-area-level) analyses are important to understand context-specific determinants of maternal tetanus immunization coverage and inequalities, a multi-country examination such as this one provides the opportunity to assess whether broader trends in drivers of coverage and inequalities exist, by using consistent outcome and inequality dimension measures and methods. They also permit benchmarking (comparisons) between countries to identify different situations of inequality, and explore where lessons to address inequality can be learned or applied. Findings from multi-country analyses such as these are particularly useful for informing broad, multinational initiatives [27]. This study examines levels and trends in tetanus protection at birth by four dimensions of inequality (wealth, maternal age and education, and area of residence), and explores variations by country World Bank income level (low-, lower-middle-, and upper-middle income). Specifically, we hypothesize that factors shown to be associated with childhood immunization coverage (household wealth, maternal age, maternal education, and place of residence) will also be associated with MNT vaccination coverage across low- and middle-income country contexts. Quantifying and reporting inequalities in tetanus protection at birth can inform strategies and interventions to reach the goal of MNTE.

2. Materials and Methods

2.1. Data Sources

Data from this study come from 76 countries with a recent (2011–2020) Demographic and Health Survey (DHS) or Multiple Indicator Cluster Survey (MICS), which collected information on maternal tetanus immunization coverage during pregnancy [28,29]. DHS and MICS are nationally-representative household surveys that collect extensive information about health outcomes, interventions, and healthcare behaviors. The information analyzed here comes from interviews with women aged 15–49 years. DHS and MICS survey methodologies have been published elsewhere [30,31].

2.2. Study Outcome

We examine maternal tetanus immunization coverage via the standard measure Protection at Birth (PAB), the proportion of women whose most recent live birth was protected against neonatal tetanus [32,33]. A birth is considered protected from tetanus if the mother (a) received at least two doses of TTCV during the pregnancy for her most recent live birth; (b) received at least two doses of TTCV, the last one within 3 years of the most recent live birth; (c) received at least 3 doses of TTCV, the last one within 5 years of the most recent live birth; (d) received at least 4 doses of TTCV, the last one within 10 years of the most recent live birth; or (e) ever received at least 5 doses of TTCV at any time prior to the most recent live birth. This measure is based on women whose most recent live birth occurred in the 59 or 23 months prior to the survey for DHS or MICS, respectively. This difference in time frame is due to the data collection methodologies of the two survey families. Additionally, maternal tetanus vaccination is ascertained via recall in DHS, while maternal vaccination cards are requested for confirmation in MICS and recall is used only if no card is available.

2.3. Dimensions of Inequality

Based on drivers of inequality identified in previous publications on childhood vaccination as well as data availability in DHS and MICS, we examined the following four dimensions of inequality: household wealth (country-specific wealth quintiles) [6–9], maternal age (15–19, 20–49) [10], maternal education (none, primary, secondary or higher) [8,9,11], and place of residence (urban, rural) [9,11–13].

For a set of sub-analyses, we classified countries based on World Bank 2022 income groups: low-income, lower-middle income, or upper-middle income [34]. Only two high-income countries (Uruguay and Trinidad and Tobago) had available data, so they were excluded from these sub-analyses.

2.4. Statistical Analyses

We first present the latest situation of inequality in MNT vaccination coverage for each country (using the most recent survey available from 2011 to 2020) via disaggregated data and summary measures of inequality. For each of the four dimensions of inequality (household wealth, maternal age, maternal education, and place of residence), we calculated the following, based on the country-specific estimates:

1. Median coverage by subgroup of each inequality dimension, overall;
2. Median coverage by subgroup of each inequality dimension, by country income group;
3. Absolute inequality in coverage between the most and least advantaged subgroups of each inequality dimension, calculated using difference (e.g., highest wealth quintile coverage minus lowest wealth quintile coverage) and the slope index of inequality (SII), overall and by country income group;
4. Relative inequality in coverage between the most and least advantaged subgroups of each inequality dimensions, calculated using ratio (e.g., highest wealth quintile coverage divided by lowest wealth quintile coverage) and the relative index of inequality (RII), overall and by country income group.

For each median value estimated, we also present the 95% confidence interval (CI) of the median, calculated using the centile Stata command with default specifications. This uses a binomial-based method described in Mood and Graybill 1963 that makes no assumptions on the distribution of the coverage variable [35,36].

We also examined changes over time in coverage levels and coverage inequalities. For this analysis, we included countries with at least one survey in the period 2011–2020 and one in the period 2001–2010, where the two surveys were at least 5 years apart. When multiple surveys in a time range were available, the most recent survey that maintained a 5-year gap was used. To assess changes in inequality over time, we first examined annual absolute change in national coverage levels, calculated as the national coverage in the more recent survey minus the national coverage in the older survey divided by the number of years between surveys. We then calculated annual absolute excess change in coverage, which compares the annual rate of change in the least and most advantaged subgroups. This is calculated as (absolute annual change for least advantaged subgroup) minus (absolute annual change for most advantaged subgroup). Several patterns in coverage can lead to positive (pro-disadvantaged) or negative (pro-advantaged) excess change. For example, a positive excess change in coverage value can arise when both groups have increasing coverage but the increase in the disadvantaged group is faster than the increase in the advantaged group; when both groups have decreasing coverage but the decrease in the disadvantaged group is slower than the decrease in the advantage group; or when the disadvantage group increased (or had no change in) coverage while the advantage group had a decrease (or had no change in) coverage. Excess change in coverage has been previously used to portray change in inequality over time in diphtheria-tetanus-pertussis (DTP) immunization coverage and in other maternal health outcomes [7,37].

As an additional post hoc analysis, we examined whether trends in inequality differed substantially based on MNTE achievement status, assessing inequality metrics separately for countries who have achieved MNTE vs. those who have not achieved MNTE.

Relevant survey sampling designs were taken into account when calculating point estimates of disaggregated data and corresponding 95% CIs at the country level. Statistical significance was set at $p < 0.05$ for all comparisons, and 95% CIs are reported throughout.

We conducted all analyses in Stata 17, and we developed data visualizations using Tableau version 2022.1.1.

3. Results

3.1. PAB Coverage Medians

Median national PAB coverage among the most recent survey sample (N = 76) was 69.1% (95% CI 61.6–71.9%), ranging from 15.0% in Trinidad and Tobago to 91.8% in India. Median national PAB coverage was 71.0% (95% CI 58.2–79.3%) in low-income countries (n = 20), 71.3% (95% CI 66.1–76.1%) in lower-middle-income countries (n = 34), and 64.7% (95% CI 35.7–71.2%) in upper-middle-income countries (n = 20). PAB coverage differed by within-country populations subgroups for all examined dimensions of inequality (see Figure 1, Interactive Supplemental Table S1). Median PAB coverage increased monotonically with increasing wealth, from 61.6% (95% CI 51.4–70.2%) among the poorest quintile to 77.3% (95% CI 67.8–80.1%) among the richest. Children of younger mothers were less likely to have protection at birth, with median coverage increasing from 63.0% (95% CI 60.1–69.6%) among mothers aged 15–19 to 71.1% (95% CI 66.8–75.1%) among mothers aged 20–49. Maternal education was also associated with median PAB coverage, increasing from 63.1% (95% CI 52.5–69.2%) among mothers with no education, to 71.5% (95% CI 66.7–75.3%) among mothers with primary education, to 78.5% (95% CI 74.5–81.1%) among mothers with secondary or higher education. Finally, children in urban areas had higher median PAB coverage than children in rural areas (73.6% urban [95% CI 66.9–77.4%] vs. 66.0% rural [95% CI 59.1–72.7%]).

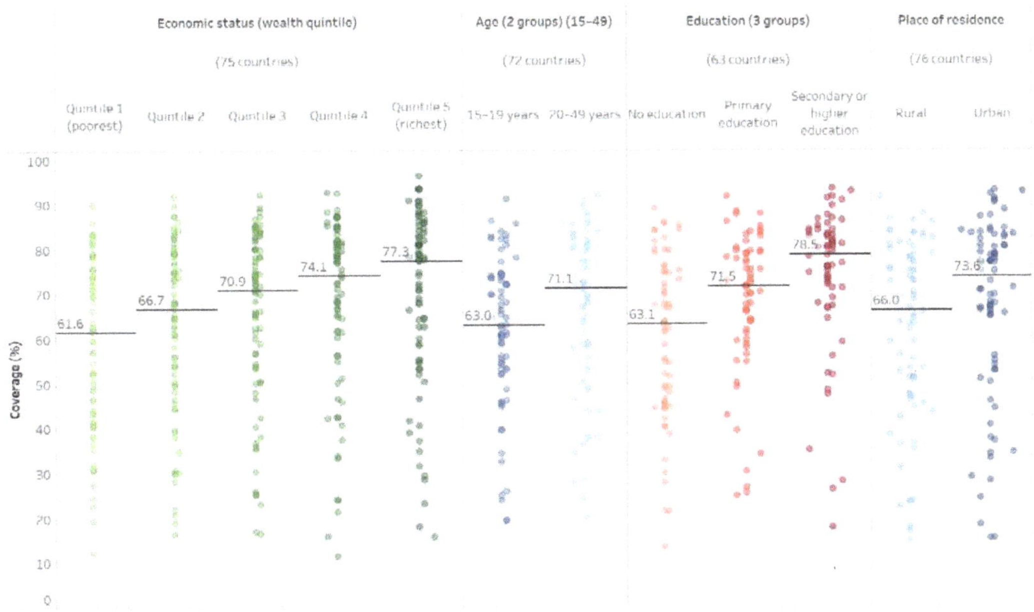

Figure 1. Latest situation of inequality in PAB coverage (DHS/MICS, 2011–2020).

These patterns in inequalities in PAB coverage are largely consistent across country income groupings, with two exceptions. Increasing wealth and increased maternal age are not associated with increased coverage for upper-middle-income countries (see Figure 2a,b). Increasing wealth and older maternal age are associated with increased coverage for low-income and lower-middle-income countries, however. Within all three income groupings, we see a consistent increase in coverage with increasing maternal education (see Figure 2c) and greater coverage in urban compared to rural areas (see Figure 2d).

3.2. Absolute and Relative Inequality in PAB Coverage

The median difference between PAB coverage in the richest wealth quintile and poorest wealth quintile among the most recent survey sample was 7.9 percentage points (95% CI 5.0–11.8), and the ratio in coverage between these quintiles was 1.12 (95% CI 1.08–1.19) (see Table 1, Interactive Supplemental Table S1). These measures differed by country income grouping; in low-income countries, the median difference was 15.2 percentage points (95% CI 5.7–24.7), lower–middle-income countries had a smaller gap of 10.9 percentage points (95% CI 7.2–16.7), and upper-middle-income countries had a small negative gap of −1.5 percentage points in coverage (95% CI −6.5–5.5). The median ratio of coverage between the richest and poorest wealth quintile followed a similar pattern: 1.21 (95% CI 1.09–1.66) among low-income countries, 1.16 (95% CI 1.10–1.32) among lower-middle-income countries, and 0.98 (95% CI 0.88–1.08) among upper-middle-income countries.

Differences by maternal age were also evident. Overall, the median difference between PAB coverage in children of mothers aged 15–19 and mothers aged 20–49 among the most recent survey sample was 4.5 percentage points (95% CI 2.9–6.1), and the ratio in coverage between these groups was 1.07 (95% CI 1.04–1.10). In low-income countries, the median difference in coverage was 4.8 percentage points (95% CI 1.9–8.4). Lower-middle-income countries had a slightly larger gap of 6.0 percentage points (95% CI 3.7–8.3), while upper-middle-income countries had a small gap of 1.1 percentage points (95% CI −3.0–5.0) in coverage. The median ratio of coverage between the children of older and younger mothers followed a similar pattern: 1.09 (95% CI 1.03–1.18) among low-income countries, 1.09 (95%

CI 1.06–1.14) among lower-middle-income countries, and 1.03 (95% CI 0.96–1.14) among upper-middle-income countries.

(**a**)

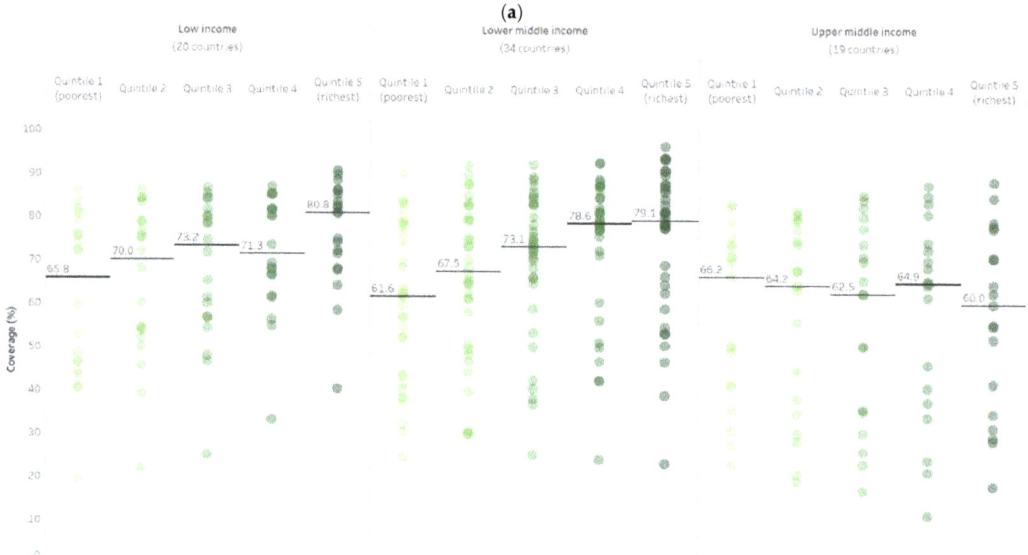

(**b**)

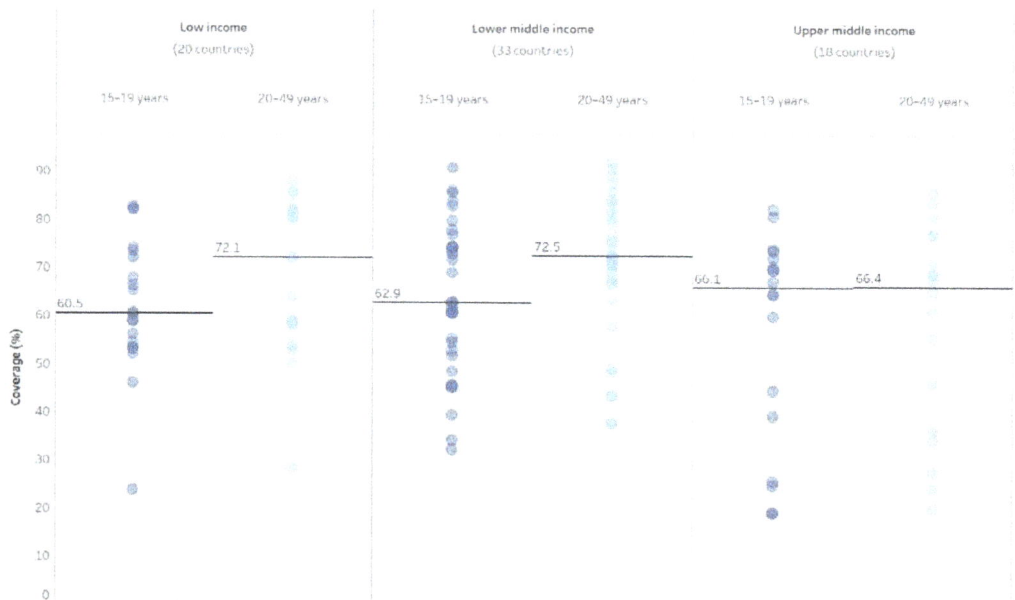

Figure 2. *Cont.*

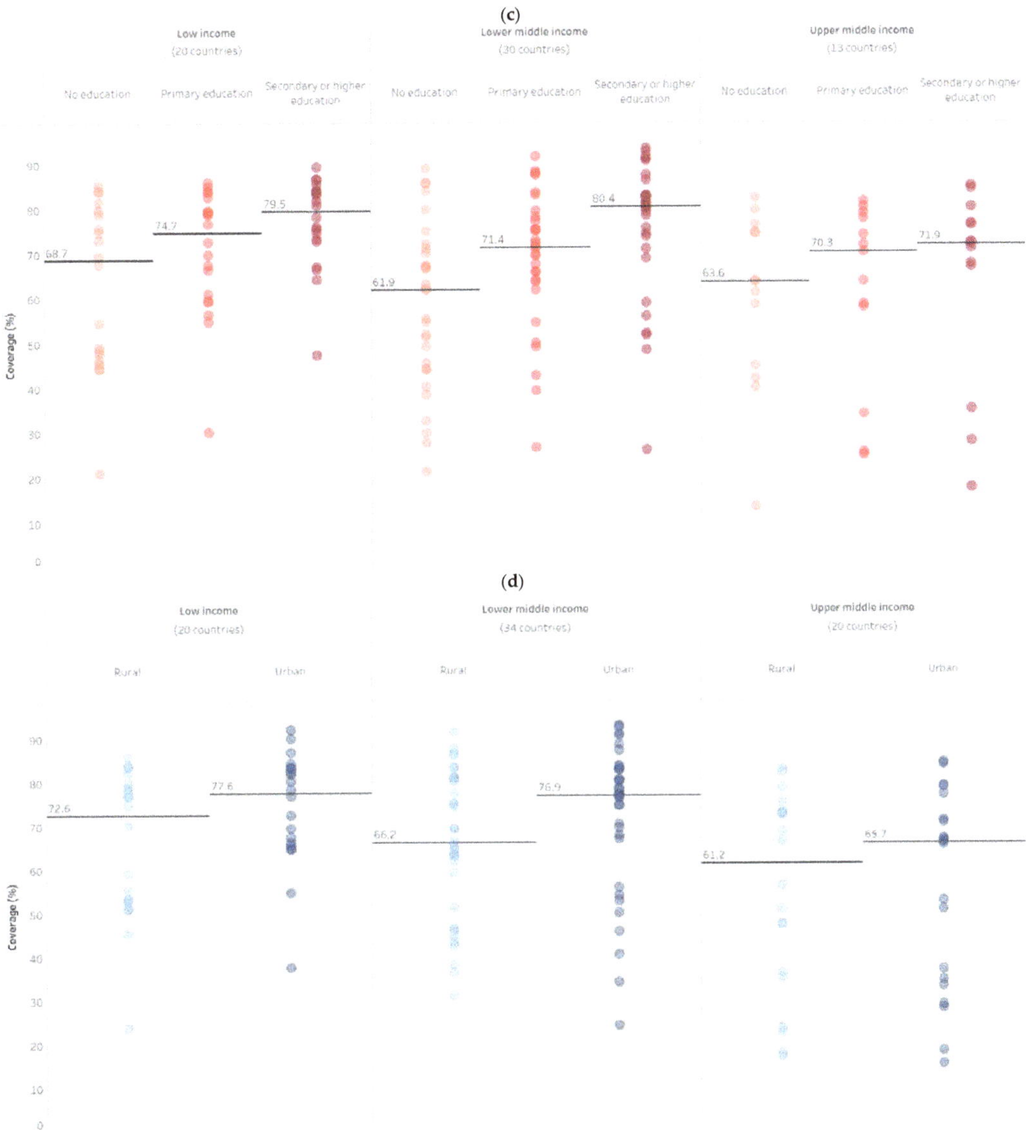

Figure 2. Latest situation of inequality in PAB coverage by World Bank income group (DHS/MICS, 2011–2020). (**a**) Wealth quintile; (**b**) maternal age; (**c**) maternal education; (**d**) place of residence.

The median difference between PAB coverage in children of mothers with secondary or higher education and mothers with no education was 11.6 percentage points (95% CI 8.4–15.7), and the ratio in coverage between these groups was 1.18 (95% CI 1.12–1.25). Differences in PAB coverage by maternal education were substantial across all country income groups. In low-income countries, the median difference between PAB coverage in children of mothers with secondary or higher education and mothers with no education was 15.6 percentage points (95% CI 4.3–25.2). Lower-middle-income countries had a gap of 13.1 percentage points (95% CI 10.0–25.9), while upper-middle-income countries had a gap of 7.3 percentage points (95% CI −3.3–9.5). The median ratio of coverage between the children of more and less educated mothers followed a similar pattern: 1.23 (95% CI 1.05–1.53) among low-income countries, 1.20 (95% CI 1.17–1.47) among lower-middle-income countries, and 1.11 (95% CI 0.96–1.15) among upper-middle-income countries.

The median difference between PAB coverage in urban areas compared to rural areas was 3.7 percentage points (95% CI 1.9–6.4), and the ratio in coverage between these groups was 1.05 (95% CI 1.03–1.10). In low-income countries, the median difference in coverage was 7.3 percentage points (95% CI 3.8–11.3). Lower-middle-income countries had a gap of 4.7 percentage points (95% CI 1.3–8.1), while upper-middle-income countries had a negligible gap of 0.2 percentage points (95% CI −1.7–2.9). The median ratio of coverage between the children in urban versus rural areas followed a similar pattern: 1.10 (95% CI 1.05–1.21) among low-income countries, 1.07 (95% CI 1.02–1.13) among lower-middle-income countries, and 1.00 (95% CI 0.94–1.05) among upper-middle-income countries.

We analyzed both simple and complex measures of inequality in PAB coverage for each of the four examined dimensions of inequality. As simple and complex measures demonstrated similar patterns of results, we focus on reporting the simple measures of inequality (difference and ratio) here. Complex measure findings can be found in Interactive Supplemental Table S1.

3.3. Change in Inequality in PAB Coverage over Time

We focus our change over time results on inequalities in household wealth; findings for other dimensions of inequality are available in Interactive Supplemental Table S2). The change over time analyses included 41 countries with data in both the periods 2001–2010 and 2011–2020.

Examining annual absolute change in national average PAB coverage (see Figure 3, x-axis; Interactive Supplemental Table S2), we find almost no annual change (median −0.04 percentage points, 95% CI −0.35–0.76) in overall PAB coverage across the examined countries from earlier (2001–2010) to more recent (2011–2020) time frames. There is substantial variation by country, however, ranging from an annual decrease in coverage of 2.0 percentage points in Suriname to an annual increase of 2.6 percentage points in Afghanistan. Twelve countries saw annual improvements in coverage of 1 percentage point or more (suggesting at least a 10-percentage point improvement in coverage over the examined 10-year time period), while three countries saw annual decreases in coverage of at least 1 percentage point (suggesting at least a 10-percentage point decrease in coverage over the examined time period). Of note, no countries with 80% or higher coverage at the earlier time period (n = 8) saw any improvements in national coverage.

Examining annual absolute excess change in the poorest compared to the richest wealth quintiles (Figure 3, y-axis; Interactive Supplemental Table S2), we find an annual excess change median value of 0.26 percentage points (95% CI 0.05–0.41), indicating slightly more favorable change over time for the poorest quintile over the examined time period. This measure also demonstrated heterogeneity by country, ranging from 2.4 percentage points annual excess change in Liberia to −1.9 percentage points annual excess change in Zambia. Ten countries had excess annual change of 1 percentage point or more (equivalent to 10 percentage points or more over the examined time period, favoring the poorest quintile), while six countries had excess annual change of −1 percentage point or less (equivalent to 10 percentage points or more over the examined time period, favoring the richest quintile).

Six of the examined countries had a substantial increase in national average of 15 percentage points over the 10-year time period (annual change of 1.5 percentage points increase or more)—Afghanistan, Cambodia, Namibia, Nepal, Senegal, and Togo. All six countries also had positive annual absolute excess change, indicating faster improvement among the poorest than the richest. Afghanistan and Cambodia saw the largest statistically significant annual excess change, equivalent to 23 percentage points excess improvement for the poorest relative to the richest in Afghanistan, and 13 percentage points excess improvement for the poorest relative to the richest in Cambodia over the examined 10-year time period. The Gambia, Lesotho, Liberia, and Nigeria also indicated statistically significant excess change in favor of the poorest quintile, all four with excess change of 15 percentage points or more over the 10-year time period. Only three countries—the Democratic Republic of the Congo, Egypt, and Zambia—saw statistically significant excess change in favor of the richest quintile of 15 percentage points or more over the 10-year time period; all three countries saw decreases in their average national coverage over the same time period.

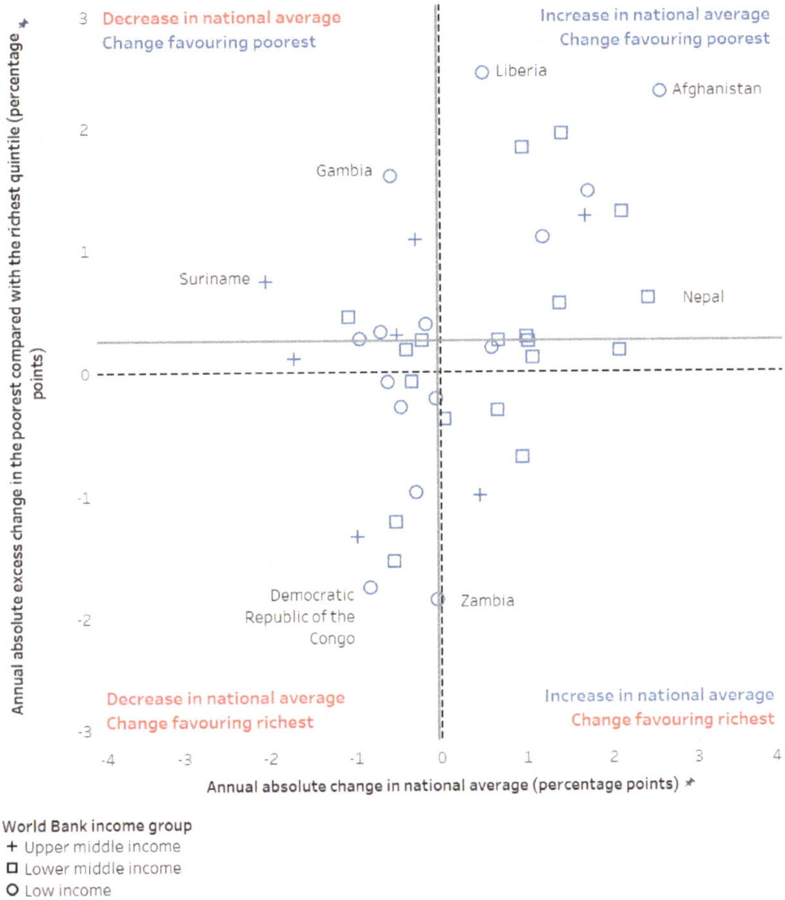

Figure 3. Change in national average and wealth-related inequality in PAB coverage (DHS/MICS, 2001–2010 and 2011–2020).

Examining the subset of 15 countries with data from the two most recent years of available data (2019–2020), we see substantial heterogeneity in change over time for coverage level and inequality by wealth quintile (see Figure 4). For example, Senegal had significant improvement in coverage levels for all wealth quintiles, but almost no changes in absolute inequality across levels of wealth. In contrast, Liberia had a negligible change in the national average coverage, but substantial reductions in inequality. Thus, while cross-national medians suggest little change for either coverage or inequality of PAB from 2001–2020, specific country patterns demonstrate meaningful changes over the time period.

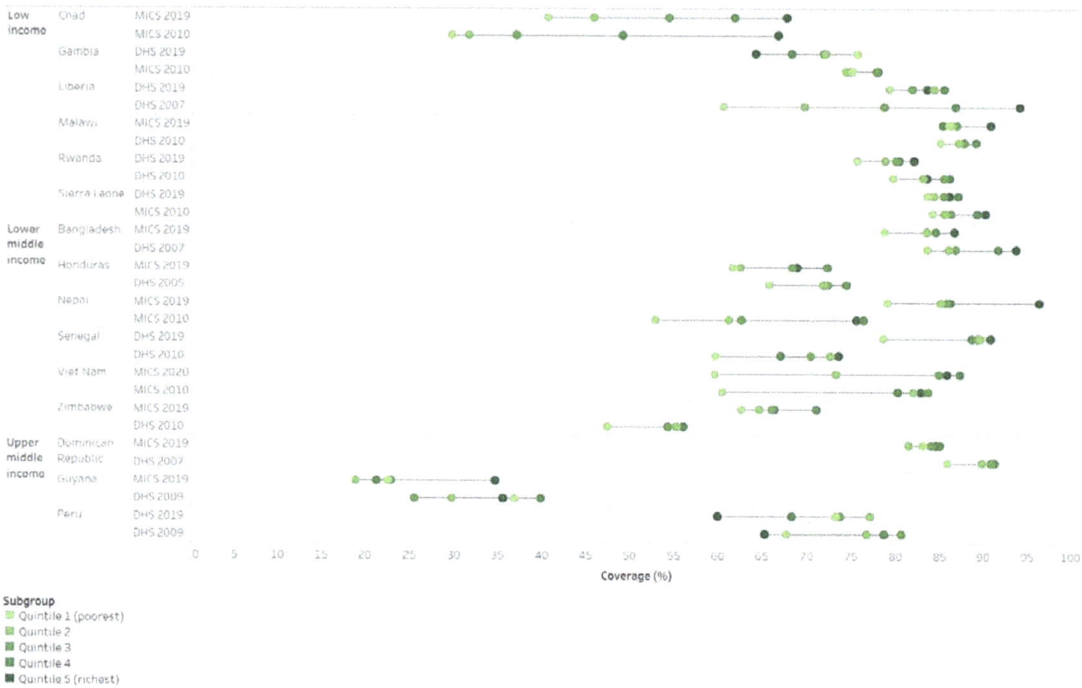

Figure 4. Change in inequality in PAB coverage (DHS/MICS, 2001–2010 and 2011–2020), countries with latest survey in 2019 or later.

3.4. PAB Coverage in Countries by MNTE Achievement Status

This study includes data from 10 of the 12 countries who have not achieved MNTE as of 2020: Afghanistan, Angola, Central African Republic, Guinea, Mali, Nigeria, Pakistan, Papua New Guinea, Sudan, and Yemen (Somalia and South Sudan have not met MNTE but did not have available data) [5]. All 10 countries demonstrated statistically significant inequality in PAB coverage across maternal education; nine had significant inequality in PAB across household wealth, nine had significant inequality in PAB across place of residence, and four had significant inequality in PAB across maternal age. Of the five countries for which we had data to examine change over time, three (Afghanistan, Nigeria, and Pakistan) demonstrated significant improvements in national average coverage over the examined time period, while two (Central African Republic and Mali) had stagnant coverage. Of these five, only Afghanistan and Nigeria had statistically significant excess change over time across any of the examined dimensions, indicating decreased inequality in PAB coverage by wealth in Afghanistan, and decreased inequality for all dimensions in Nigeria.

As a post hoc analysis, we also examined median inequality measures by MNTE achievement status (see Table 2, Supplemental Figure S1). We find that there is substantially larger inequality (as measured by difference and ratio) in household wealth, maternal education, and place of residence among countries which have not achieved MNTE compared to those which have achieved MNTE; no meaningful difference in inequality by MNTE status is observed for maternal age.

Table 1. Median difference and ratio in PAB coverage across four dimensions of inequality, overall and by World Bank income group (DHS/MICS, 2011–2020).

	Household Wealth Highest vs. Lowest Quintile		**Maternal Age Age 20–49 vs. Age 15–19**		**Maternal Education Secondary or More vs. No Schooling**		**Place of Residence Urban vs. Rural**	
	Difference (95% CI)	Ratio (95% CI)	Difference (95% CI)	Ratio (95% CI)	Difference (95% CI)	Ratio (95% CI)	Difference (95% CI)	Ratio (95% CI)
All Countries	7.9 (5.0–11.8)	1.12 (1.08–1.19)	4.5 (2.9–6.1)	1.07 (1.04–1.10)	11.6 (8.4–15.7)	1.18 (1.12–1.25)	3.7 (1.9–6.4)	1.05 (1.03–1.10)
Low-Income Countries	15.2 (5.7–24.7)	1.21 (1.09–1.66)	4.8 (1.9–8.4)	1.09 (1.03–1.18)	15.6 (4.3–25.2)	1.23 (1.05–1.53)	7.3 (3.8–11.3)	1.10 (1.05–1.21)
Lower-Middle Income Countries	10.9 (7.2–16.7)	1.16 (1.10–1.32)	6.0 (3.7–8.3)	1.09 (1.06–1.14)	13.1 (10.0–25.9)	1.20 (1.17–1.47)	4.7 (1.3–8.1)	1.07 (1.02–1.13)
Upper-Middle Income Countries	−1.5 (−6.5–5.5)	0.98 (0.88–1.08)	1.1 (−3.0–5.0)	1.03 (0.96–1.14)	7.3 (−3.3–9.5)	1.11 (0.96–1.15)	0.2 (−1.7–2.9)	1.00 (0.94–1.05)

Table 2. Median difference and ratio in PAB coverage across four dimensions of inequality, overall and by MNTE status (DHS/MICS, 2011–2020).

	Household Wealth Highest vs. Lowest Quintile		**Maternal Age Age 20–49 vs. Age 15–19**		**Maternal Education Secondary or More vs. No Schooling**		**Place of Residence Urban vs. Rural**	
	Difference (95% CI)	Ratio (95% CI)	Difference (95% CI)	Ratio (95% CI)	Difference (95% CI)	Ratio (95% CI)	Difference (95% CI)	Ratio (95% CI)
All Countries	7.9 (5.0–11.8)	1.12 (1.08–1.19)	4.5 (2.9–6.1)	1.07 (1.04–1.10)	11.6 (8.4–15.7)	1.18 (1.12–1.25)	3.7 (1.9–6.4)	1.05 (1.03–1.10)
Countries which have NOT achieved MNTE	30.6 (23.1–46.1)	1.89 (1.67–2.14)	2.0 (−1.7–8.0)	1.04 (0.97–1.17)	28.4 (23.8–37.4)	1.67 (1.52–2.17)	18.0 (11.3–26.0)	1.40 (1.21–1.56)
Countries which have achieved MNTE	6.4 (3.5–9.8)	1.10 (1.05–1.15)	4.7 (3.0–6.2)	1.07 (1.05–1.10)	9.1 (5.6–12.0)	1.15 (1.08–1.19)	3.0 (1.4–5.0)	1.04 (1.02–1.07)

4. Discussion

Findings from this study of 76 countries suggest that there is substantial inequality in maternal tetanus immunization coverage globally. In particular, we find substantial inequality in tetanus protection at birth coverage by household wealth quintile, maternal age, maternal education, and place of residence. Though previous studies have demonstrated inequalities in coverage in one or more of these inequality dimensions in single-country or single-continent contexts, this is the first study to examine inequalities in PAB coverage across all four of these dimensions utilizing a large, global sample of low-, lower-middle, and upper-middle income countries. As the burden of MNT is highest in the most vulnerable populations (including those with lower wealth, younger maternal age, lower maternal education, and rural residence) [1], the lower immunization coverage we observe in these groups is particularly concerning.

We find that greater maternal education and urban (compared to rural) residence are associated with greater PAB coverage, overall and for each country income grouping. This is consistent with prior research of other childhood vaccines, and with priority focus areas of major immunization initiatives, which include reducing gender-related barriers to immunization (such as maternal education) and reaching remote rural populations [12,27,38–42].

Older maternal age and higher household wealth are also associated with greater PAB coverage overall and for low- and lower-middle-income countries, similarly consistent with prior research and immunization targets. However, the upper-middle-income country group demonstrated approximately equitable coverage by maternal age and wealth. As MNTE has been achieved in all examined upper-middle-income countries, many for more than 20 years, tetanus toxoid vaccination efforts likely differ from those in low- or lower-middle-income countries, possibly resulting in alternate patterns of coverage [43].

With regard to age, upper-middle-income countries generally have higher and more equitable childhood vaccination coverage and have for the past several decades [7]—meaning more young mothers received the basic three doses of DTP vaccines and additional TTCV doses in childhood and adolescence, resulting in complete PAB coverage by the time of childbirth. We similarly expect inequalities in PAB coverage by maternal age to continue to narrow over time as childhood DTP3 and additional TTCV dose coverage increases. With regards to wealth, the fact that the lowest wealth quintile had the highest coverage was unexpected. Similarly, the observation of lower overall median PAB coverage across upper-middle-income countries (65%) compared to low- and lower-middle income countries (both 71%) was counter to hypothesized patterns based on other childhood vaccine coverages. These findings provide further evidence of differences in tetanus immunization strategies across country income groupings. This includes substantial supplementary immunization activities (SIAs) or campaigns in countries with the highest burden of maternal and neonatal tetanus, which are largely low- and lower-middle-income countries, and relatively few such activities in upper-middle-income settings [44]. Additionally, as MNTE has been achieved in all upper-middle-income countries analyzed, the disease is often no longer considered a priority public health issue, and immunization may be considered less necessary as there is near universal access to clean birth environments and adequate umbilical cord management practices [43]. Nonetheless, the findings regarding equitable PAB coverage by wealth within upper-middle-income countries, and relatively lower PAB coverage overall in these settings, warrant further exploration within country-specific contexts.

Differential patterns of PAB coverage across dimensions of inequality and country income grouping highlight the importance of examining multiple dimensions of inequality. However, this study examines only four potential factors which may influence PAB coverage. Additional factors, such as conflict-affected areas and intensity [24,45], or subpopulations defined by double disaggregation, such as urban poor [46,47], have been shown to be associated with lower PAB coverage. Future work using multi-country samples should examine these and other potentially related factors to better understand determinants of coverage levels and inequalities, and consider multivariate analyses to understand the relative importance of co-existing factors. For analyses of smaller geographic scope, examining factors which are as relevant and as specific to the context as possible will best enable targeted efforts to improve TTCV coverage and eliminate MNT [5].

Despite large strides in MNTE efforts over the examined time period, and success in achieving MNTE in 47 of 59 countries with MNT as of 2020, there has been little change in maternal tetanus immunization levels and inequalities over the study time period on aggregate. However, this hides significant heterogeneity in coverage levels and inequality across countries. We see significant improvements in PAB coverage of 15 percentage points or more over 10 years for six countries, all of which also demonstrated reductions in wealth-related inequality in PAB coverage over the same time period. Though we cannot determine the direction of this relationship in current analyses, efforts to improve coverage should simultaneously be oriented towards reducing inequality. Importantly, we see evidence of inequalities in PAB coverage for all ten examined countries which have not achieved MNTE, and only see improvements in coverage and inequality for two of these target countries. We also observe substantially greater inequalities in PAB coverage among countries which have not achieved MNTE compared to countries which have been successful in achieving MNTE for three of the four examined dimensions (wealth, maternal education, and place of residence) in the most recent data. Reductions in these inequalities in coverage will be crucial to achieve MNTE.

Efforts to improve PAB coverage and equity should thus remain a key aim of MNTE initiatives, including quality targeted supplementary immunization activities, increases in uptake by LMICs of TTCV booster doses along the life-course, improved antenatal care visit access and TTCV administration during antenatal care, and increased institutional deliveries and clean delivery practices [48–51]. Additionally, persistent inequalities in PAB coverage in those countries which have achieved MNTE suggest the need for ongoing efforts to ensure MNTE sustainability, such as periodic neonatal tetanus risk analyses and corrective measures to close immunity gaps [43]. Assessments of inequality such as this one may help inform the groups to be targeted in these MNTE sustainability efforts. Global initiatives, such as the Immunization Agenda 2030 (IA2030), also present opportunities to catalyze action to address inequalities in PAB [27]. Positioning maternal and neonatal tetanus as a tracer of inequality in health care provision will enable more visibility and enhanced resource mobilization for the global initiative to eliminate MNT.

This study relies largely on maternal vaccination self-report, which is subject to recall bias, particularly as childhood doses may have been received 20+ years prior [52]. No recent review has explored the reliability of recall for immunization coverage, but prior research suggests that it can be problematic for childhood vaccines [53]. In particular, older women and women with more children may be more susceptible to underreport prior doses, and maternal recall likely underestimates TTCV coverage generally [54]. However, TTCV immunization protocols indicate that women who do not remember if they received a dose—or who report that they have not received a dose—should be immunized; thus, successful TTCV immunization efforts should negate this bias. Increasing use of home-based records and digitalized personal health records will likely also lead to decreased recall bias, reduction in unnecessary doses, and improved coverage over time [55]. The complex nature of PAB definition requires surveyors to correctly and comprehensively collect information about past tetanus immunization, leading to potential underreporting of coverage if information is only partially collected. We do not have reason to think that such bias would differ by the dimensions of inequality examined, however. In particular, women with multiple prior pregnancies may have underreporting or inaccurate reporting of prior doses; limiting these analyses to first births only would help mitigate this potential bias. Though such analyses were outside of the scope of this manuscript, future work should consider examination of first births (single parity mothers) only. Despite limiting analyses to the most recent data available, we include surveys from 2011 to 2020, and the current situation in a country may have changed substantially in the time since. This is particularly a concern in light of the COVID-19 pandemic, which interrupted immunization efforts and healthcare access in many places. Conclusions from these analyses about specific country situations should therefore be interpreted with caution. Finally, the nature of this cross-sectional, aggregate analysis does not allow for conclusions about the relative importance of the examined dimension of inequality, a causal relationship between inequality and coverage levels, subnational inequalities in coverage, the relative contributions of immunization prior to versus during the most recent pregnancy, nor the most effective potential solutions for improving coverage and reducing inequalities. All of these areas would benefit from examination in future research.

Despite these limitations, findings from this work can be used to inform future research, policy, and clinical practice and to benchmark progress. The occurrence of maternal and neonatal tetanus is a marker of inequities as this disease affects the most vulnerable populations, thus, MNTE efforts should continue considering equity a priority to ensure sustained results. This includes regular data collection of PAB coverage along with sociodemographic data to be able to regularly perform disaggregated data monitoring and analysis. Findings from this routine monitoring then can and should be used to inform subpopulations which can be the targets of interventions to improve coverage including SIAs, additional ANC-based screening and vaccination opportunities, improved immunization documentation efforts, and tetanus awareness and education activities. These analyses also provide an initial set of potential priority groups (the lowest wealth quintile, lower maternal education, and rural populations) for vaccinations efforts, and provide a potential framework for identifying additional subpopulations of interest.

5. Conclusions

Maternal immunity against tetanus, measured as PAB coverage, is a key aspect of MNTE. Findings from this study of 76 countries suggest that substantial inequalities in PAB coverage exist for wealth, maternal age, maternal education, and place of residence, and that these inequalities exist globally across low-, lower-middle-, and upper-middle-income countries. Though global coverage changed little over the time period 2001–2020, several countries had substantial increases in PAB coverage accompanied by decreases in inequality, highlighting the need for continued equity considerations in MNTE efforts.

Supplementary Materials: The following supporting information can be accessed at: https://public.tableau.com/app/profile/katherine.kirkby/viz/Interactivetable-Inequalitiesintetanustoxoidprotectioncoverage/Interactivetables Interactive Supplemental Table S1: Latest situation of inequality; Interactive Supplemental Table S2: Change in inequality over time. The following supporting information can be downloaded at https://www.mdpi.com/article/10.3390/vaccines11040752/s1: Supplemental Figure S1: Latest situation of inequality in PAB coverage by country MNTE achievement status (DHS/MICS, 2011–2020).

Author Contributions: A.R.H. led the conceptualization and execution of the study and interpretation of results; N.E.J. led manuscript development; B.O.C.-P. and N.E.J. led data preparation and analysis; K.K., L.A. and T.M.S. contributed to data preparation and analysis; all authors had full access to the data in the study; B.O.C.-P., L.A., T.M.S. and A.J.D.B. had direct access to and verified the underlying data reported in the manuscript; K.K., N.B., A.R.H., M.C.D.-H., N.Y. and A.J.D.B. provided interpretation, text, and review of findings specific to inequalities and immunization; K.K. produced visuals. All authors have read and agreed to the published version of the manuscript.

Funding: This research was funded by Gavi, the Vaccine Alliance. The funders had no role in the design of the study; in the collection, analyses, or interpretation of data; in the writing of the manuscript, or in the decision to publish the results.

Institutional Review Board Statement: Not applicable.

Informed Consent Statement: Not applicable.

Data Availability Statement: All analyses were carried out using publicly available datasets that can be obtained directly from the DHS (dhsprogram.com) and the MICS (mics.unicef.org) websites. Data access is free and publicly available, but requires registration as a data user with the corresponding survey organization and submission of a request to access data for research purposes (https://dhsp

rogram.com/data/Access-Instructions.cfm; https://mics.unicef.org/visitors/sign-up). Datasets are continuously sourced and updated by the International Center for Equity in Health (equidade.org) as they are released. Analyses used the latest available dataset versions as of 18 December 2022.

Conflicts of Interest: The authors declare that they have no conflict of interest. The authors alone are responsible for the views expressed in this publication and they do not necessarily represent the views, decisions or policies of their institutions.

References

1. Roper, M.H.; Vandelaer, J.H.; Gasse, F.L. Maternal and neonatal tetanus. *Lancet* **2007**, *370*, 1947–1959. [CrossRef] [PubMed]
2. World Health Organization. Tetanus vaccines: WHO position paper—February 2017. *Wkly. Epidemiol. Rec.* **2017**, *92*, 53–76.
3. World Health Organization. *Protecting All against Tetanus: Guide to Sustaining Maternal and Neonatal Tetanus Elimination (MNTE) and Broadening Tetanus Protection for All Populations*; World Health Organization: Geneva, Switzerland, 2019.
4. World Health Organization. Maternal and Neonatal Tetanus Elimination. Available online: https://www.who.int/initiatives/maternal-and-neonatal-tetanus-elimination-(mnte) (accessed on 22 September 2022).
5. Kanu, F.A.; Yusuf, N.; Kassogue, M.; Ahmed, B.; Tohme, R.A. Progress toward Achieving and Sustaining Maternal and Neonatal Tetanus Elimination—Worldwide, 2000–2020. *MMWR Morb. Mortal. Wkly. Rep.* **2022**, *71*, 406–411. [CrossRef] [PubMed]
6. Bergen, N.; Cata-Preta, B.O.; Schlotheuber, A.; Santos, T.M.; Danovaro-Holliday, M.C.; Mengistu, T.; Sodha, S.V.; Hogan, D.R.; Barros, A.J.D.; Hosseinpoor, A.R. Economic-Related Inequalities in Zero-Dose Children: A Study of Non-Receipt of Diphtheria-Tetanus-Pertussis Immunization Using Household Health Survey Data from 89 Low- and Middle-Income Countries. *Vaccines* **2022**, *10*, 633. [CrossRef]
7. Hosseinpoor, A.R.; Bergen, N.; Schlotheuber, A.; Gacic-Dobo, M.; Hansen, P.M.; Senouci, K.; Boerma, T.; Barros, A.J. State of inequality in diphtheria-tetanus-pertussis immunisation coverage in low-income and middle-income countries: A multicountry study of household health surveys. *Lancet Glob. Health* **2016**, *4*, e617–e626. [CrossRef] [PubMed]
8. Acharya, K.; Dharel, D.; Subedi, R.K.; Bhattarai, A.; Paudel, Y.R. Inequalities in full vaccination coverage based on maternal education and wealth quintiles among children aged 12–23 months: Further analysis of national cross-sectional surveys of six South Asian countries. *BMJ Open* **2022**, *12*, e046971. [CrossRef]
9. Mutua, M.K.; Mohamed, S.F.; Porth, J.M.; Faye, C.M. Inequities in On-Time Childhood Vaccination: Evidence from Sub-Saharan Africa. *Am. J. Prev. Med.* **2021**, *60*, S11–S23. [CrossRef]
10. World Health Organization. *Explorations of Inequality: Childhood Immunization*; World Health Organization: Geneva, Switzerland, 2018.
11. World Health Organization. *State of Inequality: Childhood Immunization*; World Health Organization: Geneva, Switzerland, 2016.
12. Levine, O.; Lemango, E.; Befson, J.; Gurley, N.; Rowley, E.; McIlvaine, B. *ERG Discussion Paper 08: Tackling Inequities in Immunization Outcomes in Remote Rural Contexts*; Equity Reference Group for Immunisation: New York, NY, USA, 2018.
13. Adamu, A.A.; Uthman, O.A.; Sambala, E.Z.; Ndwandwe, D.; Wiyeh, A.B.; Olukade, T.; Bishwajit, G.; Yaya, S.; Okwo-Bele, J.M.; Wiysonge, C.S. Rural-urban disparities in missed opportunities for vaccination in sub-Saharan Africa: A multi-country decomposition analyses. *Hum. Vaccines Immunother.* **2019**, *15*, 1191–1198. [CrossRef]
14. Sherley, J.; Newton, S. The association between area of residence and sufficient antenatal tetanus vaccination in women ages 15–49 in Afghanistan: An analysis of the 2015 DHS dataset. *Glob. Health Res. Policy* **2020**, *5*, 51. [CrossRef]
15. Amin, M.B.; Roy, N.; Meem, A.E.; Hossain, E.; Aktarujjaman, M. Trends and determinants of taking tetanus toxoid vaccine among women during last pregnancy in Bangladesh: Country representative survey from 2006 to 2019. *PLoS ONE* **2022**, *17*, e0276417. [CrossRef]
16. Rahman, M.; Obaida-Nasrin, S. Factors affecting acceptance of complete immunization coverage of children under five years in rural Bangladesh. *Salud Publica Mex.* **2010**, *52*, 134–140. [CrossRef]
17. Thind, A. Determinants of tetanus toxoid immunization in pregnancy in rural Bihar. *Trop. Dr.* **2005**, *35*, 75–77. [CrossRef] [PubMed]
18. Liyew, A.M.; Ayalew, H.G. Individual and community-level determinants of poor tetanus toxoid immunization among pregnant women in Ethiopia using data from 2016 Ethiopian demographic and health survey; multilevel analysis. *Arch. Public Health* **2021**, *79*, 92. [CrossRef] [PubMed]
19. Barrow, A.; Barrow, S.; Jobe, A. Differentials in prevalence and correlates on uptake of tetanus toxoid and intermittent preventive treatment with sulfadoxine-pyrimethamine during pregnancy: A community-based cross-sectional study in The Gambia. *SAGE Open Med.* **2022**, *10*, 20503121211065908. [CrossRef] [PubMed]
20. Haile, Z.T.; Chertok, I.R.; Teweldeberhan, A.K. Determinants of utilization of sufficient tetanus toxoid immunization during pregnancy: Evidence from the Kenya Demographic and Health Survey, 2008-2009. *J. Community Health* **2013**, *38*, 492–499. [CrossRef]
21. Kidane, T. Factors influencing TT immunization coverage and protection at birth coverage in Tselemti District, Ethiopia. *Ethiop. J. Health Dev.* **2004**, *18*, 153–158. [CrossRef]
22. Tun, Z.M.; Ring, Z.; Tam, C.C. Factors associated with maternal tetanus vaccination in Myanmar: An analysis of demographic and health survey data. *Vaccine* **2022**, *40*, 1135–1142. [CrossRef]

23. Yaya, S.; Kota, K.; Buh, A.; Bishwajit, G. Prevalence and predictors of taking tetanus toxoid vaccine in pregnancy: A cross-sectional study of 8722 women in Sierra Leone. *BMC Public Health* **2020**, *20*, 855. [CrossRef]
24. Mohamed, S.O.O.; Ahmed, E.M. Prevalence and determinants of antenatal tetanus vaccination in Sudan: A cross-sectional analysis of the Multiple Indicator Cluster Survey. *Trop. Med. Health* **2022**, *50*, 7. [CrossRef]
25. Belay, A.T.; Fenta, S.M.; Agegn, S.B.; Muluneh, M.W. Prevalence and risk factors associated with rural women's protected against tetanus in East Africa: Evidence from demographic and health surveys of ten East African countries. *PLoS ONE* **2022**, *17*, e0265906. [CrossRef]
26. Yeshaw, Y.; Jemere, T.; Dagne, H.; Andualem, Z.; Akalu, Y.; Dewau, R.; Teshale, A.B.; Tesema, G.A.; Dagnew, B. Factors associated with births protected against neonatal tetanus in Africa: Evidences from Demographic and health surveys of five African countries. *PLoS ONE* **2021**, *16*, e0253126. [CrossRef] [PubMed]
27. World Health Organization. *Immunization Agenda 2030: A Global Strategy to Leave No One Behind*; World Health Organization: Geneva, Switzerland, 2020.
28. The DHS Program. The Demographic and Health Surveys Program. Available online: https://dhsprogram.com/ (accessed on 18 January 2023).
29. UNICEF. Multiple Indicator Cluster Surveys. Available online: https://mics.unicef.org/ (accessed on 18 January 2023).
30. The DHS Program. Methodology. Available online: https://dhsprogram.com/Methodology/ (accessed on 18 March 2022).
31. UNICEF. MICS Publications—Reports and Methodological Papers. Available online: https://mics.unicef.org/publications/reports-and-methodological-papers (accessed on 18 January 2023).
32. World Health Organization. Neonates Protected at Birth against Neonatal Tetanus (%). Available online: https://www.who.int/data/gho/indicator-metadata-registry/imr-details/3207 (accessed on 18 January 2023).
33. DHS Program. Tetanus Toxoid Injections. Available online: https://dhsprogram.com/data/Guide-to-DHS-Statistics/Tetanus_Toxoid_Injections.htm (accessed on 18 January 2023).
34. The World Bank. World Bank Country and Lending Groups. Available online: https://datahelpdesk.worldbank.org/knowledgebase/articles/906519-world-bank-country-and-lending-groups (accessed on 18 January 2023).
35. Conover, W.J. *Practical Nonparametric Statistics*, 3rd ed.; Wiley: New York, NY, USA, 1999.
36. Mood, A.M.; Graybill, F.A. *Introduction to the Theory of Statistics*, 2nd ed.; McGraw-Hill: New York, NY, USA, 1963.
37. World Health Organization; International Center for Equity in Health Pelotas. *State of Inequality: Reproductive, Maternal, Newborn and Child Health*; World Health Organization: Geneva, Switzerland, 2015.
38. Feletto, M.; Sharkey, A.; Rowley, E.; Gurley, N.; Sinha, A.; Champions, E.; Gupta, A.; Tolhurst, R. *A Gender Lens to Advance Equity in Immunization*; Equity Reference Group for Immunisation: New York, NY, USA, 2018.
39. World Health Organization. *Why Gender Matters: Immunization Agenda 2030*; World Health Organization: Geneva, Switzerland, 2021.
40. Gavi the Vaccine Alliance. Phase V (2021–2025). Available online: https://www.gavi.org/our-alliance/strategy/phase-5-2021-2025 (accessed on 18 March 2022).
41. Johns, N.E.; Santos, T.M.; Arroyave, L.; Cata-Preta, B.O.; Heidari, S.; Kirkby, K.; Munro, J.; Schlotheuber, A.; Wendt, A.; O'Brien, K.; et al. Gender-Related Inequality in Childhood Immunization Coverage: A Cross-Sectional Analysis of DTP3 Coverage and Zero-Dose DTP Prevalence in 52 Countries Using the SWPER Global Index. *Vaccines* **2022**, *10*, 988. [CrossRef] [PubMed]
42. Vidal Fuertes, C.; Johns, N.E.; Goodman, T.S.; Heidari, S.; Munro, J.; Hosseinpoor, A.R. The Association between Childhood Immunization and Gender Inequality: A Multi-Country Ecological Analysis of Zero-Dose DTP Prevalence and DTP3 Immunization Coverage. *Vaccines* **2022**, *10*, 1032. [CrossRef]
43. Yusuf, N.; Steinglass, R.; Gasse, F.; Raza, A.; Ahmed, B.; Blanc, D.C.; Yakubu, A.; Gregory, C.; Tohme, R.A. Sustaining Maternal and Neonatal Tetanus Elimination (MNTE) in countries that have been validated for elimination—Progress and challenges. *BMC Public Health* **2022**, *22*, 691. [CrossRef] [PubMed]
44. Dhir, S.K.; Dewan, P.; Gupta, P. Maternal and Neonatal Tetanus Elimination: Where are We Now? *Res. Rep. Trop. Med.* **2021**, *12*, 247–261. [CrossRef] [PubMed]
45. Okwo-Bele, J.-M.; Conner, R.; McIlvaine, B.; Rowley, E.; Bernson, J. *ERG Discussion Paper 06: Tackling Inequities in Immunization Outcomes in Conflict Contexts*; Equity Reference Group for Immunisation: New York, NY, USA, 2018.
46. Rahman, M. Tetanus toxoid vaccination coverage and differential between urban and rural areas of Bangladesh. *East Afr. J. Public Health* **2009**, *6*, 26–31. [CrossRef]
47. Nandy, R.; Reese, H.; Bernson, J.; Digre, P.; Rowley, E.; McIlvaine, B. *ERG Discussion Paper 07: Tackling Inequities in Immunization Outcomes in Urban Contexts*; Equity Reference Group for Immunisation: New York, NY, USA, 2018.
48. Pathirana, J.; Nkambule, J.; Black, S. Determinants of maternal immunization in developing countries. *Vaccine* **2015**, *33*, 2971–2977. [CrossRef]
49. Khan, A.A.; Zahidie, A.; Rabbani, F. Interventions to reduce neonatal mortality from neonatal tetanus in low and middle income countries—A systematic review. *BMC Public Health* **2013**, *13*, 322. [CrossRef]
50. Vouking, M.Z.; Tadenfok, C.N.; Ekani, J.M.E. Strategies to increase immunization coverage of tetanus vaccine among women in Sub Saharan Africa: A systematic review. *Pan Afr. Med. J.* **2017**, *27*, 25. [CrossRef]
51. World Health Organization. *Reaching Every District (RED), 2017 Revision*; WHO Regional Office for Africa: Brazzaville, Congo, 2017.
52. De Francisco, A.; Chakraborty, J. Maternal recall of tetanus toxoid vaccination. *Ann. Trop. Paediatr.* **1996**, *16*, 49–54. [CrossRef]

53. Dansereau, E.; Brown, D.; Stashko, L.; Danovaro-Holliday, M.C. A systematic review of the agreement of recall, home-based records, facility records, BCG scar, and serology for ascertaining vaccination status in low and middle-income countries. *Gates Open Res.* **2019**, *3*, 923. [CrossRef] [PubMed]
54. Deming, M.S.; Roungou, J.B.; Kristiansen, M.; Heron, I.; Yango, A.; Guenengafo, A.; Ndamobissi, R. Tetanus toxoid coverage as an indicator of serological protection against neonatal tetanus. *Bull. World Health Organ.* **2002**, *80*, 696–703. [PubMed]
55. Brown, D.W.; Bosch-Capblanch, X.; Shimp, L. Where Do We Go from Here? Defining an Agenda for Home-Based Records Research and Action Considering the 2018 WHO Guidelines. *Glob. Health Sci. Pract.* **2019**, *7*, 6–11. [CrossRef] [PubMed]

vaccines

MDPI

Article

Subnational Gender Inequality and Childhood Immunization: An Ecological Analysis of the Subnational Gender Development Index and DTP Coverage Outcomes across 57 Countries

Nicole E. Johns [1], Katherine Kirkby [1], Tracey S. Goodman [2], Shirin Heidari [2], Jean Munro [3], Stephanie Shendale [2] and Ahmad Reza Hosseinpoor [1,*]

1 Department of Data and Analytics, World Health Organization, 20 Avenue Appia, 1211 Geneva, Switzerland
2 Department of Immunization, Vaccines, and Biologicals, World Health Organization, 20 Avenue Appia, 1211 Geneva, Switzerland
3 Gavi, the Vaccine Alliance, Chemin du Pommier 40, Le Grand-Saconnex, 1218 Geneva, Switzerland
* Correspondence: hosseinpoora@who.int

Citation: Johns, N.E.; Kirkby, K.; Goodman, T.S.; Heidari, S.; Munro, J.; Shendale, S.; Hosseinpoor, A.R. Subnational Gender Inequality and Childhood Immunization: An Ecological Analysis of the Subnational Gender Development Index and DTP Coverage Outcomes across 57 Countries. *Vaccines* **2022**, *10*, 1951. https://doi.org/10.3390/vaccines10111951

Academic Editor: Davide Gori

Received: 11 October 2022
Accepted: 15 November 2022
Published: 18 November 2022

Abstract: The role of gender inequality in childhood immunization is an emerging area of focus for global efforts to improve immunization coverage and equity. Recent studies have examined the relationship between gender inequality and childhood immunization at national as well as individual levels; we hypothesize that the demonstrated relationship between greater gender equality and higher immunization coverage will also be evident when examining subnational-level data. We thus conducted an ecological analysis examining the association between the Subnational Gender Development Index (SGDI) and two measures of immunization—zero-dose diphtheria-tetanus-pertussis (DTP) prevalence and 3-dose DTP coverage. Using data from 2010–2019 across 702 subnational regions within 57 countries, we assessed these relationships using fractional logistic regression models, as well as a series of analyses to account for the nested geographies of subnational regions within countries. Subnational regions were dichotomized to higher gender inequality (top quintile of SGDI) and lower gender inequality (lower four quintiles of SGDI). In adjusted models, we find that subnational regions with higher gender inequality (favoring men) are expected to have 5.8 percentage points greater zero-dose prevalence than regions with lower inequality [16.4% (95% confidence interval (CI) 14.5–18.4%) in higher-inequality regions versus 10.6% (95% CI 9.5–11.7%) in lower-inequality regions], and 8.2 percentage points lower DTP3 immunization coverage [71.0% (95% CI 68.3–73.7%) in higher-inequality regions versus 79.2% (95% CI 77.7–80.7%) in lower-inequality regions]. In models accounting for country-level clustering of gender inequality, the magnitude and strength of associations are reduced somewhat, but remain statistically significant in the hypothesized direction. In conjunction with published work demonstrating meaningful associations between greater gender equality and better childhood immunization outcomes in individual- and country-level analyses, these findings lend further strength to calls for efforts towards greater gender equality to improve childhood immunization and child health outcomes broadly.

Keywords: immunization; vaccination; zero-dose children; diphtheria-tetanus-pertussis vaccine; determinants of immunization; health status disparities; gender equity; gender inequality

1. Introduction

Gender inequality is increasingly recognized as a key determinant of childhood immunization coverage and health equity [1–4]. Gender-related barriers to immunization have been shown to operate at the individual, interpersonal, community, and broader socio-structural levels [2]. These include barriers faced by (frequently women) caregivers, such as lower health education and literacy, travel restriction, and limited household decision-making influence; by health workers delivering services (who are disproportionately women), including gender pay gap, workplace harassment and inequitable exposures to health risks; and by policy-makers (where women are frequently under-represented), who enact laws and guidelines which may amplify or reinforce gender inequities [2,5]. Several recent studies have examined the relationship between childhood immunization coverage and measures of gender inequality empirically, at the individual [6,7] and national [8,9] levels. These studies consistently find significant and meaningful associations between greater gender inequality and lower immunization coverage.

Existing individual-level analyses use the survey-based women's empowerment (SWPER) index, a three-dimensional measure of women's empowerment comparable across time and geographies [10]. These studies find that children of women with greater empowerment (as measured by social independence [including such items as schooling attainment and access to information], decision-making control, and attitudes towards violence) were more likely to have received three doses of the combined diphtheria-tetanus-pertussis (DTP) vaccine and less likely to have received zero doses of DTP than children of women with lower empowerment [6,7]. Individual-level analyses have several advantages: mothers are frequently caregivers for their child, and their experiences are proximally related to their child's outcomes; confounding mother- and child-level information known to be associated with immunization coverage could be accounted for, including mother's education and child birth order; and unlike aggregated analyses, these methods can avoid the ecological fallacy and account for individual variation. However, individual measures of empowerment do not take into account broader gender norms, policies, and social climates that may contribute to gender inequality. Furthermore, it is difficult to assess empowerment or gender equity at the individual level given existing measures.

National level analyses that have examined gender barriers and immunization outcomes similarly find that countries with lower gender inequality have higher rates of DTP3 coverage and lower zero-dose DTP prevalence [8,9]. The advantages of national analyses include: readily available data and the ability to examine large numbers of geographies; standard measures of inequality that are comparable across countries and time; and the fact that national averages capture the broader state of women in a society, as laws, economics, health systems, and education are often determined and implemented at the national level. However, these analyses fail to account for individual variation and may reflect averages which obscure more important within-country inequality. They also fail to capture community factors at the subnational level, where there may be significant differences in regional policies or implementation of national practices and priorities.

Our current analysis expands on this previous work and fills an important gap by utilizing subnational data to examine the association between gender inequality and childhood immunization at the subnational region level. Although subnational analyses also cannot capture all levels at which gender inequality may affect child immunization, they do bridge the gap between existing national and individual level information. Subnational units may be particularly relevant for laws, health systems, government or nonprofit initiatives, as well as geographic variation in education, religion, wealth, industry, and other factors which may be associated with both gender equity and childhood immunization. Specifically, in this manuscript we test the hypothesis that the subnational gender development index will be associated with zero-dose DTP prevalence and DTP3 coverage at the subnational level.

2. Materials and Methods

2.1. Indicators and Data Sources

The data used in this study include up to 10 years of subnational region estimates of childhood immunization, indicators of gender inequality, and other demographic, economic, and social characteristics. Data were available for 702 subnational regions across 57 countries. We included the 10 most recent years of available data (2010–2019); all region years where estimates for subnational gender development and immunization outcomes were available were included, for a total of 1066 total region years of data.

2.1.1. Immunization Outcomes

We examined two outcomes based on subnational coverage of the DTP vaccine. First, the prevalence of zero-dose children (zero-dose DTP), defined as the percentage of surviving one-year old children in a subnational region who have not received the first dose of the DTP vaccine series. This indicator is a proxy for children who have missed immunization services entirely. Second, the prevalence of DTP3 immunization (DTP3), the percentage of surviving one-year old children in a subnational region who have received three doses of DTP vaccine. This indicator is a proxy for children who have accessed the full series of basic immunizations. Together, these are frequently used indicators of child health more broadly as they reflect regular and timely interaction with health services (DTP3) and health equity (zero-dose DTP) [11–13].

These estimates are derived from Demographic and Health Surveys (DHS) Program data, which uses a rigorous survey design to create representative samples at the subnational level. Substantial detail on the study design and methodology of the DHS has been published elsewhere [14].

2.1.2. Factors Associated with Immunization Coverage

We examined variables selected a priori based on prior national-level analyses, to make findings as directly comparable as possible [9]. These factors were chosen to account for demand and supply side factors that influence vaccination and might confound the association between immunization and gender inequality [15–19]. These included subnational estimates of percent of population under 15 years of age, percent of population living in urban areas, and a number of human development indicators (described below). We also utilized national estimates of average annual rate of population change; estimates corresponding to study subnational regions were not readily available.

To capture human development in adjusted models, we utilized the subnational human development index (SHDI). The SHDI is a summary measure of development in three dimensions, namely education, health, and standard of living, with an index normalized between 0 and 1 created for each dimension [20]. The education index based on mean expected years of schooling for children and mean years of schooling for adults ages 25 years and older, the health index is based on life expectancy at birth, and the standard of living index is based on gross national income per capita (2017 purchasing power parities [PPP] in USD). We utilized the three dimension-specific indices in analyses. Each of these indices are calculated both for the total population, as well as disaggregated by sex. All human development indicators were available at the subnational level.

2.1.3. Gender Inequality

Gender inequality was measured using the subnational gender development index (SGDI) [20,21]. The SGDI is the only readily publicly available metric of gender inequality available at the subnational level which is comparable across geographies and time.

SGDI captures gender inequalities in achievement in the three dimensions of development captured by the SHDI (items detailed above). The SGDI is the ratio of SHDI among men to SHDI among women within a subnational region; additional detail regarding the SGDI is published elsewhere [20]. We include both SGDI (the ratio of development between women and men) as well as the SHDI (the overall level of development) in adjusted models.

SGDI values below 1 indicate higher human development among men than women, a value equal to 1 indicates equality, and values above 1 indicate higher development among women than men. We created a binary analysis variable for SGDI based on quintiles of its sample distribution, dichotomized to higher gender inequality favoring men (highest quintile) versus lower gender inequality (quintiles 2–5). In analyses limited to the most recent year of data, we recreated the binary variable based on quintiles of the most recent year sample distribution. We present summary statistics for the continuous SGDI measure, but analyzed SGDI as a binary measure (higher versus lower gender inequality) in regression analyses for ease of interpretation.

2.2. Data Sources

All subnational estimates of outcomes, gender inequality, human development, and demographic characteristics came from the Global Data Lab [22]. Though the Global Data Lab produces SHDI estimates for subnational regions in 161 countries for all years from 1990–2019, we utilized only those country years in which a DHS survey was conducted, as subnational vaccination coverage was only available for these years. As a result, all data in this study is derived from DHS survey-weighted estimates and do not rely on interpolation. Full details on data sources for the indicators compiled, calculated, and distributed by Global Data Lab have been published elsewhere [20]. Estimates of national average annual rate of population change came from the World Development Indicators [23].

Table 1 presents a summary of indicators.

Table 1. Measures.

Category	Indicator
Outcomes	Zero-dose DTP prevalence
	DTP3 immunization coverage
Gender inequality	Subnational gender development index (SGDI)
Demographic/geographic characteristics	Average annual rate of population change (%) *
	Population <15 years (%)
	Urban population (%)
Human development	Subnational health index (0 to 1)
	Subnational education index (0 to 1)
	Subnational income index (0 to 1)

* All indicators at the subnational level with the exception of annual rate of population change, which is assessed at the national level due to data availability.

2.3. Analyses

We present descriptive statistics, bivariate comparisons of immunization outcomes and SGDI, and unadjusted outcome distributions by SGDI, for the most recent year of data available for each subnational region. We then present regression analyses to examine the association between childhood immunization and gender inequality using the full 10-year dataset. All region years with available data were included in analyses. All models were conducted using fractional logit specifications, as the outcomes are proportions with values between 0 and 1 [24,25].

Models were estimated with SGDI as a binary variable equal to 1 if subnational regions were in the highest gender inequality quintile, and 0 if regions were in any of the four lower inequality quintiles.

For each immunization outcome, we first estimated the unadjusted association between the outcome and SGDI, without controlling for any other factors. We then conducted adjusted analyses, including controls for annual population growth and age structure, percentage of urban population, and the three individual dimensional indices of the SHDI (health, education, and income).

Unadjusted and adjusted models accounted for non-parametric time trends via year fixed effects, and were estimated with standard errors clustered at the subnational region level.

To account for the geographically clustered nature of subnational regions within countries, we also conducted a series of analyses accounting for country-level clustering.

- First, we replicated the adjusted fractional logistic regression as described above with the addition of a covariate which was the country-year average zero-dose DTP prevalence or DTP3 coverage.

- Second, we retained only the most recent year of available data for each subnational region, and conducted the same adjusted fractional logistic regression, but with the clustered standard errors based on country, rather than region.
- Third, we included all available data but used a multi-level mixed effects linear regression approach, using nested random effects of subnational region within country, with covariate fixed effects as defined by the adjusted model above. For these models, we specified random intercepts for both country and region, and random slopes for region, with an identity variance-covariance structure; these specifications were selected based on model performance as assessed by AIC and BIC.
- Fourth, we replicated the mixed-effects linear regression approach using the most recent year of available data for each subnational region, and including only random intercepts for country.

Statistical significance was set at $p < 0.05$ for all comparisons including adjusted odds ratios (AORs); 95% confidence intervals (CIs) are reported throughout. All analyses were conducted using STATA 16.1 [26].

3. Results

3.1. Descriptive Analyses

In the most-recent-year sample, where each observation is one region, the mean value of SGDI was 0.90, ranging from a low of 0.51 to a high of 1.09. This mean value below 1 indicates that, overall, human development was lower among women than men in the analyzed subnational regions. Distributions of the SGDI for the pooled 10-year (Figure 1a) and most-recent-year (Figure 1b) samples are shown in Figure 1.

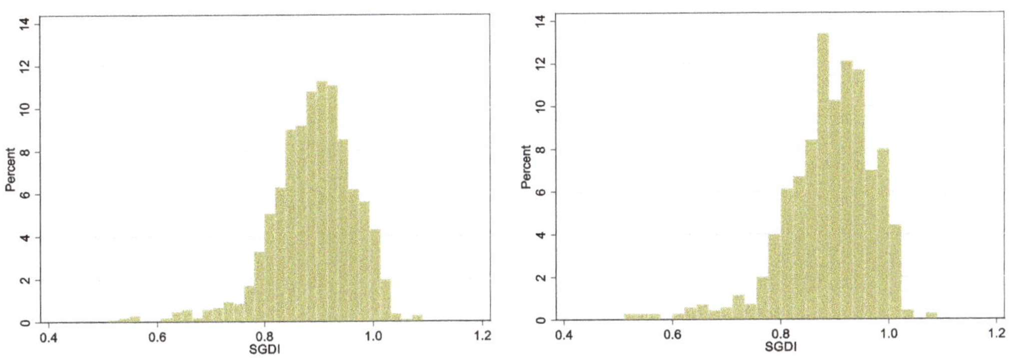

(**a**) Pooled 10-year sample (**b**) Most recent year of data sample

Figure 1. Distribution of Subnational Gender Development Index score.

In unadjusted comparisons, higher gender inequality was associated with higher prevalence of zero-dose DTP and lower DTP3 immunization coverage (Table 2, Figures 2 and 3). Examining the most recent year of available data sample, subnational regions with higher gender inequality (favoring men) as measured by the SGDI had 13.4 percentage points greater zero-dose prevalence (18.2% vs. 4.8%), and 21.6 percentage points lower DTP3 immunization coverage (86.0% vs. 64.4%) than regions with lower inequality.

Table 2. Prevalence of zero-dose DTP and DTP3 immunization coverage by SGDI category, most recent year of available data.

	Zero-Dose DTP (%)			DTP3 Immunization Coverage (%)			
	Median	Min	Max	Median	Min	Max	*N*
High gender inequality	18.2	0	96.6	64.4	2.6	98.1	*214*
Medium/low/negligible gender inequality	4.8	0	81.2	86.0	9.7	100	*852*
p-value	<0.001			<0.001			

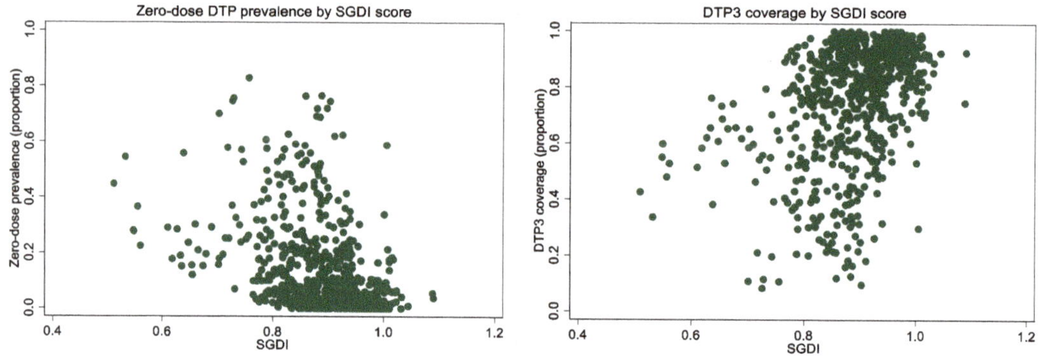

Figure 2. Prevalence of zero-dose DTP and DTP3 immunization coverage by continuous SGDI score, most recent year of available data.

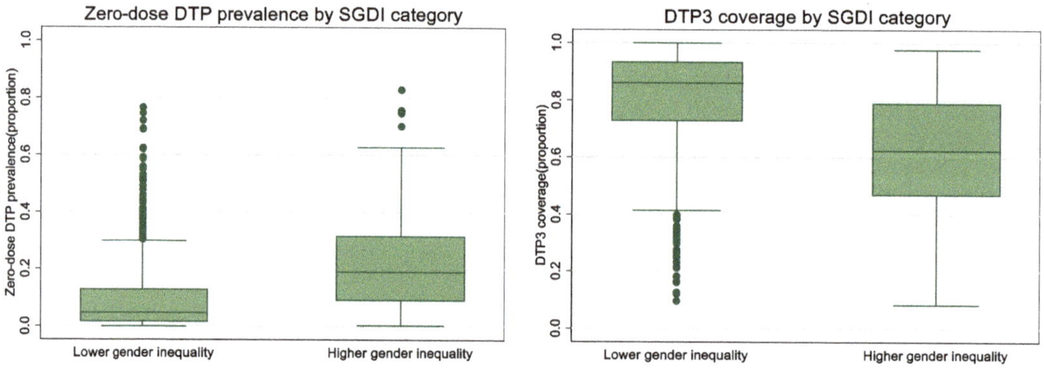

Figure 3. Prevalence of zero-dose DTP and DTP3 immunization coverage by SGDI category, most recent year of available data. Note that boxes show 25–75th percentile values, with 50th percentile (median) line inside box. Single dots are outlier values.

3.2. Regression Analyses

Higher inequality was significantly associated with lower zero-dose prevalence and higher DTP3 coverage in unadjusted and adjusted fractional logistic regression analyses (Table 3). In subnational regions with higher gender inequality, zero-dose prevalence odds were 1.7 times higher (AOR = 1.74, 95% CI: 1.38–2.19) compared to subnational regions with lower inequality. Consistently, the odds of DTP3 coverage were 39% lower (AOR = 0.61, 95% CI: 0.51–0.75) in regions with higher gender inequality relative to regions with lower inequality.

Table 3. Odds ratios for zero-dose DTP prevalence and DTP3 immunization coverage by SGDI category (702 subnational regions across 57 countries, 2010–2019).

	Unadjusted	Adjusted
Zero-dose children		
High gender inequality	2.637 ***	1.742 ***
95% CI	(2.122–3.275)	(1.384–2.193)
DTP3 immunization coverage		
High gender inequality	0.437 ***	0.614 ***
95% CI	(0.364–0.524)	(0.505–0.746)

*** $p < 0.001$.

We also estimated the average marginal effects of SGDI to indicate the average percentage point change in the outcome variable (zero-dose DTP or DTP3 coverage) by higher versus lower gender inequality (See Figure 4). A subnational region with higher inequality (favoring men) is expected to have 5.8 percentage points higher prevalence of zero-dose DTP relative to a region with lower inequality, increasing from 10.6% (95% CI 9.5–11.7%) for regions with lower inequality to 16.4% (95% CI 14.5–18.4%) for regions with higher inequality. A subnational region with higher gender inequality is expected to have 8.2 percentage points lower coverage of DTP3 immunization than a region with lower gender inequality, dropping from 79.2% (95% CI 77.7–80.7%) for regions with lower inequality to 71.0% (95% CI 68.3–73.7%) for regions with higher inequality.

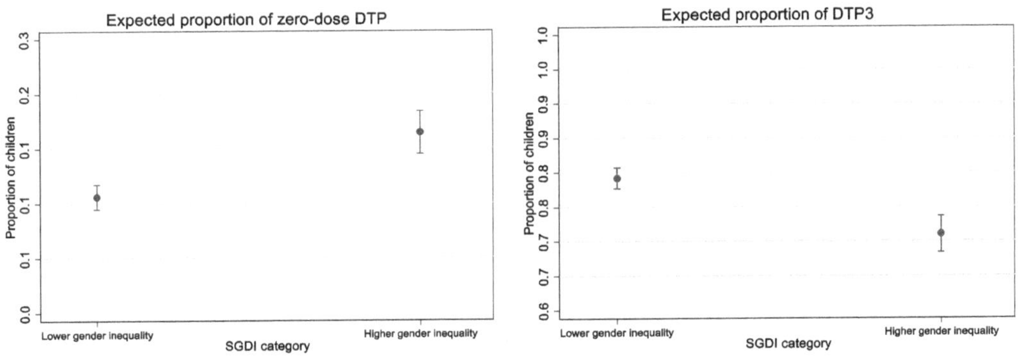

Figure 4. Adjusted * expected proportions of zero-dose DTP and DTP3 immunization coverage by SGDI category, 702 subnational regions across 57 countries, 2010–2019. Estimated proportions are adjusted for annual population growth and age structure (measured as the percentage of the population under 15 years of age), percentage of urban population, and the three individual dimensional indices of the SHDI (health index, education index, and income index).

Models Accounting for Country-Level Clustering

Consideration of country-level clustering reduced the observed associations between subnational gender inequality and immunization coverage outcomes. In the model additionally controlling for the average zero-dose prevalence or DTP3 coverage for the corresponding country-year, we find a significant association between gender inequality and both zero-dose DTP prevalence and DTP3 coverage. In the model limited to the most recent year of data available for each subnational region and clustering standard errors by country, we do not observe a significant association between gender inequality and immunization outcomes. In multilevel linear regression models accounting for nested random effects of subnational regions within country, we find significant associations between gender inequality and both zero-dose DTP prevalence and DTP3 coverage. Findings are similar when limited to the most recent year of data, utilizing a linear regression model with country random effects. To more directly compare findings between models, we present predicted marginal effects of higher versus lower gender inequality, e.g., the predicted percentage point difference in coverage between subnational regions with higher gender inequality compared to those with lower gender inequality (see Table 4). We first present the adjusted model that does not account for country clustering, as well as the four models discussed above. Though the direction of association remains constant across models, the magnitude and strength of association is reduced for the models that take into account country-level clustering.

Table 4. Predicted marginal effects [percentage point difference] for zero-dose DTP prevalence and DTP3 immunization coverage by SGDI category (702 subnational regions across 57 countries, 2010–2019).

	No Country Consideration (Fractional Logistic Model, Full Sample)	Fractional Logistic Model, Plus Country-Year Average Coverage	Fractional Logistic Model, Most Recent Year of Data Only, Country Clustered Standard Errors	Mixed Effects Linear Regression Model, Nested Random Effects	Mixed Effects Linear Regression Model, Most Recent Year of Data Only, Country Random Effect
N	*1066*	*1066*	*702*	*1066*	*702*
Zero-dose children					
High gender inequality	5.83 **	3.31 **	3.48	3.64 *	4.16 *
95% CI	(3.26–8.39)	(1.82–4.80)	(−1.04–8.00)	(1.36–5.91)	(1.57–6.75)
DTP3 immunization coverage					
High gender inequality	−8.20 **	−4.07 **	−5.16	−4.22 *	−5.30 *
95% CI	(−11.64 to −4.77)	(−6.06 to −2.09)	(−11.69–1.38)	(−7.00 to −1.45)	(−8.48 to −2.12)

* $p < 0.01$; ** $p < 0.001$.

4. Discussion

Findings from this study of 702 subnational regions across 57 countries suggest that greater gender equality, as measured by the SGDI, is associated with positive childhood immunization outcomes—higher DTP3 coverage and lower zero-dose prevalence. We find that, after adjustment, a subnational region with higher gender equality is expected to have 5.8 percentage points lower prevalence of zero-dose DTP and 8.2 percentage points higher coverage of DTP3 than a region with lower gender equality. To put this coverage difference in context, it took more than 10 years of concerted effort for global DTP3 coverage to improve by 8 percentage points—DTP3 coverage globally increased from 78% in 2006 to 86% in 2019 (prior to COVID-19-related declines) [27].

These findings align with prior work examining gender inequality and childhood outcomes, including child mortality and immunization coverage, using different analytic approaches including alternate measures of gender inequality and national or individual units of analysis [6–9,28–30]. These studies consistently find that gender equality, and the related construct of women's empowerment, are associated with improved immunization coverage, decreased child mortality, and other positive child health outcomes. Existing work has also demonstrated substantial subnational inequality in immunization, highlighting the relevance of subnational policies and outreach efforts, as well as intra-country variations in immunization access and resources [31,32]. Our study builds on this existing literature to demonstrate that within-country variation in gender inequality is associated with immunization coverage at the subnational level, and suggests that gender inequality may be one of many drivers of subnational inequalities in coverage.

Compared to national analyses, we find an even stronger association between immunization and subnational gender inequality [9]. For example, the same adjusted regressions suggests that at the national level, countries with higher gender equality have 4.6 percentage points higher DTP3 coverage than countries with lower gender equality, while we find that subnational regions with higher gender equality had 8.2 percentage points higher DTP3 coverage than subnational regions with lower gender equality. This larger (and statistically stronger) association highlights the importance of within-country variation in determinants of immunization. Nonetheless, we do find that the magnitude of these associations is reduced somewhat when we take into account the clustering of subnational regions within countries. This reduction in effect size suggests that national-level factors remain important and meaningful predictors of immunization.

Reaching zero-dose and under-immunized children means reaching the communities they are a part of; these 'missed communities' are not only a heightened risk for disease outbreaks, but often also suffer from a lack of basic services and face entrenched socio-economic marginalization [33]. Better understanding the drivers of subnational inequalities—such as subnational differences in gender inequality—can enable targeted and tailored approaches to improve not only gender equality, but also reach these missed communities to improve immunization coverage and equity.

Findings from this study should be viewed in light of its limitations. Firstly, these are ecological analyses, and hence does not imply causation. However, taken together, the consistent association between gender equality and better childhood immunization coverage across a range of individual, national, and subnational analyses lend strength to the assertion that gender inequality is a key determinant of immunization coverage and equity. Second, these data are available for low- and middle-income countries; high-income countries, which likely have stronger health systems, and other countries without available data may or may not exhibit the same patterns of association. Third, while these findings demonstrate an association between gender inequality and immunization coverage, they do not elucidate the pathways through which that association may be causal. Qualitative work is needed to better understand the contextual pathways through which restrictive gender norms and gender-related barriers hamper immunization efforts.

A growing body of evidence on gender as a determinant of health examines the ways in which gender inequality influences decision-making about health services, access to and affordability of health services, limitations on mobility and decision-making, and provider attitudes, among others [4,34,35]. Further work is needed to understand the ways in which interventions may operate across these pathways, and understand which interventions are effective in addressing and circumventing gender-related barriers to immunization. Addressing these factors in order to improve child immunization coverage and equity are strategic priorities of major international immunization initiatives including the Immunization Agenda 2030 (IA2030) and the Gavi Phase 5 strategy [36,37]. Ensuring gender transformative approaches and efforts to improve gender equality will not only have a benefit for childhood immunization coverage, but better health outcomes for all.

5. Conclusions

Our study of 702 subnational regions across 57 countries suggests that gender equality is positively associated with childhood immunization coverage at the subnational level. These findings fill a gap in the existing literature and strengthen findings of individual- and national-level analyses, which collectively show a robust and meaningful association between gender inequality and immunization coverage outcomes. Multi-sectoral gender-responsive and gender-transformative approaches are needed to ensure improvements in immunization coverage and equity.

Author Contributions: All authors meet the four criteria for authorship in the ICMJE Recommendations. Conceptualization, A.R.H.; Formal analysis, N.E.J.; Supervision, A.R.H.; Writing—Original draft, N.E.J., K.K. and A.R.H.; Writing—Review and editing, N.E.J., K.K., T.S.G., S.H., J.M., S.S. and A.R.H. All authors have read and agreed to the published version of the manuscript.

Funding: This research was funded by Gavi, the Vaccine Alliance. Beyond the individual contributions of J.M., who is a Gavi employee, the funders had no role in the design of the study; in the collection, analyses, or interpretation of data; in the writing of the manuscript; or in the decision to publish the results.

Institutional Review Board Statement: Not applicable.

Informed Consent Statement: Not applicable.

Data Availability Statement: Publicly available datasets were analyzed in this study. These data can be downloaded from the following locations: https://globaldatalab.org/ and https://databank.worldbank.org/source/world-development-indicators (both accessed on 30 August 2022).

Conflicts of Interest: The authors declare no conflict of interest. The authors alone are responsible for the views expressed in this publication and they do not necessarily represent the views, decisions, or policies of their institutions.

References

1. Feletto, M.; Sharkey, A.; Rowley, E.; Gurley, N.; Sinha, A.; Champions, E.; Gupta, A.; Tolhurst, R. *A Gender Lens to Advance Equity in Immunisation*; Technical Report for Equity Reference Group for Immunisation: New York, NY, USA, 2018.
2. Feletto, M.; Sharkey, A. The influence of gender on immunisation: Using an ecological framework to examine intersecting inequities and pathways to change. *BMJ Glob. Health* **2019**, *4*, e001711. [CrossRef] [PubMed]
3. Chopra, M.; Bhutta, Z.; Blanc, D.C.; Checchi, F.; Gupta, A.; Lemango, E.T.; Levine, O.S.; Lyimo, D.; Nandy, R.; O'Brien, K.L.; et al. Addressing the persistent inequities in immunization coverage. *Bull. World Health Organ.* **2020**, *98*, 146–148. [CrossRef] [PubMed]
4. *Why Gender Matters: Immunization Agenda 2030*; World Health Organization: Geneva, Switzerland, 2021.
5. *The Gender Pay Gap in the Health and Care Sector a Global Analysis in the Time of COVID-19*; World Health Organization and the International Labour Organization: Geneva, Switzerland, 2022.
6. Wendt, A.; Santos, T.M.; Cata-Preta, B.O.; Costa, J.C.; Mengistu, T.; Hogan, D.R.; Victora, C.G.; Barros, A.J.D. Children of more empowered women are less likely to be left without vaccination in low- and middle-income countries: A global analysis of 50 DHS surveys. *J. Glob. Health* **2022**, *12*, 04022. [CrossRef] [PubMed]
7. Johns, N.E.; Santos, T.M.; Arroyave, L.; Cata-Preta, B.O.; Heidari, S.; Kirkby, K.; Munro, J.; Schlotheuber, A.; Wendt, A.; O'Brien, K.; et al. Gender-Related Inequality in Childhood Immunization Coverage: A Cross-Sectional Analysis of DTP3 Coverage and Zero-Dose DTP Prevalence in 52 Countries Using the SWPER Global Index. *Vaccines* **2022**, *10*, 988. [CrossRef]
8. Arsenault, C.; Johri, M.; Nandi, A.; Rodriguez, J.M.M.; Hansen, P.M.; Harper, S. Country-level predictors of vaccination coverage and inequalities in Gavi-supported countries. *Vaccine* **2017**, *35*, 2479–2488. [CrossRef]
9. Vidal Fuertes, C.; Johns, N.E.; Goodman, T.S.; Heidari, S.; Munro, J.; Hosseinpoor, A.R. The Association between Childhood Immunization and Gender Inequality: A Multi-Country Ecological Analysis of Zero-Dose DTP Prevalence and DTP3 Immunization Coverage. *Vaccines* **2022**, *10*, 1032. [CrossRef]
10. Ewerling, F.; Raj, A.; Victora, C.G.; Hellwig, F.; Coll, C.V.N.; Barros, A.J.D. A Survey-Based Women's Empowerment Index for Low- and Middle-Income Countries: The SWPER Goes Global. *Int. J. Epidemiol.* **2021**, *50*, 168–193. [CrossRef]
11. Gavi the Vaccine Alliance. Measuring Our Performance: 2011–2015 Indicators. Available online: https://www.gavi.org/programmes-impact/our-impact/measuring-our-performance/2011-2015-indicators (accessed on 6 June 2022).
12. Sodha, S.V.; Dietz, V. Strengthening routine immunization systems to improve global vaccination coverage. *Br. Med. Bull.* **2015**, *113*, 5–14. [CrossRef]
13. Bergen, N.; Cata-Preta, B.O.; Schlotheuber, A.; Santos, T.M.; Danovaro-Holliday, M.C.; Mengistu, T.; Sodha, S.V.; Hogan, D.R.; Barros, A.J.D.; Hosseinpoor, A.R. Economic-Related Inequalities in Zero-Dose Children: A Study of Non-Receipt of Diphtheria-Tetanus-Pertussis Immunization Using Household Health Survey Data from 89 Low- and Middle-Income Countries. *Vaccines* **2022**, *10*, 633. [CrossRef]
14. The DHS Program. Methodology. Available online: https://dhsprogram.com/Methodology/ (accessed on 18 March 2022).
15. Streatfield, K.; Singarimbun, M.; Diamond, I. Maternal Education and Child Immunization. *Demography* **1990**, *27*, 447–455. [CrossRef]
16. Vikram, K.; Vanneman, R.; Desai, S. Linkages between maternal education and childhood immunization in India. *Soc. Sci. Med.* **2012**, *75*, 331–339. [CrossRef] [PubMed]
17. Abuya, B.A.; Onsomu, E.O.; Kimani, J.K.; Moore, D. Influence of Maternal Education on Child Immunization and Stunting in Kenya. *Matern. Child Health J.* **2011**, *15*, 1389–1399. [CrossRef] [PubMed]
18. Forshaw, J.; Gerver, S.M.; Gill, M.; Cooper, E.; Manikam, L.; Ward, H. The global effect of maternal education on complete childhood vaccination: A systematic review and meta-analysis. *BMC Infect. Dis.* **2017**, *17*, 801. [CrossRef] [PubMed]
19. Burroway, R.; Hargrove, A. Education is the antidote: Individual- and community-level effects of maternal education on child immunizations in Nigeria. *Soc. Sci. Med.* **2018**, *213*, 63–71. [CrossRef]
20. Smits, J.; Permanyer, I. The Subnational Human Development Database. *Sci. Data* **2019**, *6*, 190038. [CrossRef]

21. United Nations Development Programme. Gender Development Index (GDI). Available online: https://hdr.undp.org/en/content/gender-development-index-gdi (accessed on 10 March 2022).
22. Global Data Lab. Available online: https://globaldatalab.org/ (accessed on 30 August 2022).
23. The World Bank. World Development Indicators. Available online: https://databank.worldbank.org/source/world-development-indicators (accessed on 30 August 2022).
24. Papke, L.E.; Wooldridge, J.M. Panel data methods for fractional response variables with an application to test pass rates. *J. Econom.* **2008**, *145*, 121–133. [CrossRef]
25. Wooldridge, J.M. *Econometric Analysis of Cross Section and Panel Data*, 2nd ed.; MIT Press: Cambride, MA, USA, 2010.
26. StataCorp. *Stata Statistical Software: Release 16*; StataCorp LLC: College Station, TX, USA, 2019.
27. WHO/UNICEF. WHO UNICEF Immunization Coverage Estimates 2021 Revision. 2022. Available online: https://data.unicef.org/wp-content/uploads/2016/07/wuenic2021rev_web-update.xlsx (accessed on 30 August 2022).
28. Brinda, E.M.; Rajkumar, A.P.; Enemark, U. Association between gender inequality index and child mortality rates: A cross-national study of 138 countries. *BMC Public Health* **2015**, *15*, 97. [CrossRef]
29. Singh, K.; Bloom, S.; Brodish, P. Gender equality as a means to improve maternal and child health in Africa. *Health Care Women Int.* **2015**, *36*, 57–69. [CrossRef]
30. Thorpe, S.; VanderEnde, K.; Peters, C.; Bardin, L.; Yount, K.M. The Influence of Women's Empowerment on Child Immunization Coverage in Low, Lower-Middle, and Upper-Middle Income Countries: A Systematic Review of the Literature. *Matern. Child Health J.* **2016**, *20*, 172–186. [CrossRef]
31. *State of Inequality: Childhood Immunization*; World Health Organization: Geneva, Switzerland, 2016.
32. Kirkby, K.; Bergen, N.; Schlotheuber, A.; Sodha, S.V.; Danovaro-Holliday, M.C.; Hosseinpoor, A.R. Subnational inequalities in diphtheria-tetanus-pertussis immunization in 24 countries in the African Region. *Bull. World Health Organ.* **2021**, *99*, 627–639. [CrossRef]
33. Cata-Preta, B.O.; Santos, T.M.; Mengistu, T.; Hogan, D.R.; Barros, A.J.D.; Victora, C.G. Zero-dose children and the immunisation cascade: Understanding immunisation pathways in low and middle-income countries. *Vaccine* **2021**, *39*, 4564–4570. [CrossRef] [PubMed]
34. Phillips, S.P. Defining and measuring gender: A social determinant of health whose time has come. *Int. J. Equity Health* **2005**, *4*, 11. [CrossRef] [PubMed]
35. Sen, G.; Östlin, P. Gender as a social determinant of health: Evidence, policies, and innovations. In *Gender Equity in Health*; Routledge: London, UK, 2009; pp. 23–68.
36. *Immunization Agenda 2030: A Global Strategy to Leave No One Behind*; World Health Organization: Geneva, Switzerland, 2020.
37. Gavi the Vaccine Alliance. Phase V (2021–2025). Available online: https://www.gavi.org/our-alliance/strategy/phase-5-2021-2025 (accessed on 18 March 2022).

vaccines

MDPI

Article

Assessing Geographic Overlap between Zero-Dose Diphtheria–Tetanus–Pertussis Vaccination Prevalence and Other Health Indicators

Emily Haeuser [1], Jason Q. Nguyen [1], Sam Rolfe [1], Olivia Nesbit [1], Nancy Fullman [2] and Jonathan F. Mosser [1,3,*]

1 Institute for Health Metrics and Evaluation, University of Washington, Seattle, WA 98195, USA
2 Department of Global Health, School of Medicine and School of Public Health, University of Washington, Seattle, WA 98195, USA
3 Department of Health Metrics Sciences, School of Medicine, University of Washington, Seattle, WA 98195, USA
* Correspondence: jmosser@uw.edu

Abstract: The integration of immunization with other essential health services is among the strategic priorities of the Immunization Agenda 2030 and has the potential to improve the effectiveness, efficiency, and equity of health service delivery. This study aims to evaluate the degree of spatial overlap between the prevalence of children who have never received a dose of the diphtheria–tetanus–pertussis-containing vaccine (no-DTP) and other health-related indicators, to provide insight into the potential for joint geographic targeting of integrated service delivery efforts. Using geospatially modeled estimates of vaccine coverage and comparator indicators, we develop a framework to delineate and compare areas of high overlap across indicators, both within and between countries, and based upon both counts and prevalence. We derive summary metrics of spatial overlap to facilitate comparison between countries and indicators and over time. As an example, we apply this suite of analyses to five countries—Nigeria, Democratic Republic of the Congo (DRC), Indonesia, Ethiopia, and Angola—and five comparator indicators—children with stunting, under-5 mortality, children missing doses of oral rehydration therapy, prevalence of lymphatic filariasis, and insecticide-treated bed net coverage. Our results demonstrate substantial heterogeneity in the geographic overlap both within and between countries. These results provide a framework to assess the potential for joint geographic targeting of interventions, supporting efforts to ensure that all people, regardless of location, can benefit from vaccines and other essential health services.

Keywords: immunization; spatial overlap; DTP vaccine; integrated service delivery; geospatial modeling; zero-dose children; vaccination; vaccine coverage; geographic inequality

Citation: Haeuser, E.; Nguyen, J.Q.; Rolfe, S.; Nesbit, O.; Fullman, N.; Mosser, J.F. Assessing Geographic Overlap between Zero-Dose Diphtheria–Tetanus–Pertussis Vaccination Prevalence and Other Health Indicators. *Vaccines* **2023**, *11*, 802. https://doi.org/10.3390/vaccines11040802

Academic Editor: Pedro Plans-Rubió

Received: 16 February 2023
Revised: 17 March 2023
Accepted: 29 March 2023
Published: 5 April 2023

1. Introduction

Since the inception of the Expanded Programme on Immunisation (EPI) in 1974 [1], global efforts to expand access to lifesaving vaccines have produced tremendous public health benefits, with an estimated 50 million deaths averted by vaccination activities between 2000 and 2019 alone [2]. Over the past four decades, country immunization programs have overseen large gains in coverage for vaccines included in the original EPI program, alongside the global rollout and scale-up of newer vaccines.

However, since 2010, these gains have stalled or reversed in many countries, and global vaccination coverage has largely plateaued [3,4]. In addition, disruptions to immunization delivery efforts due to the COVID-19 pandemic have resulted in additional, persistent declines in global vaccine coverage, with the coverage of key vaccines such as diphtheria–tetanus–pertussis (DTP) falling in many countries to the lowest levels in decades [5,6].

The stagnation and backsliding of global vaccine coverage in recent years emphasizes the need for new approaches to vaccine delivery. The Immunization Agenda 2030 (IA2030)

aims to provide such a global strategy, coordinating and strengthening vaccination efforts around the world to ensure that "everyone, everywhere, at every age fully benefits from vaccines for good health and well-being" [7]. IA2030 also contains a strong strategic emphasis on the integration of vaccine delivery with other key health services [7], embedding immunization programs within the broader context of primary health care and global goals to achieve universal health coverage [8,9].

To achieve these ambitious goals, immunization programs must be equipped to reach "zero-dose" children—children who have never received a dose of a routine vaccine—including children and communities historically missed by immunization services. Operationally, "zero-dose" is generally proxied by "no-DTP"; that is, children who have never received a dose of a DTP-containing vaccine [10]. Recent work analyzing the complex paths from birth to full immunization in 92 countries emphasizes the importance of zero-dose children, as receipt of a first vaccine is strongly associated with additional vaccinations [11]. Furthermore, zero-dose children are more likely to have limited access to water, sanitation, and education [12] and live in poorer households [11]. A substantial number of zero-dose children also live in proximity to conflict [13]. Therefore, more deliberate provisioning of multiple interventions or services in contact with health systems or providers, including vaccination services, could be an efficient way to reach at-risk children and communities and reduce health inequalities.

To understand where and with which services integrated delivery could have the greatest impact for previously underserved communities, an understanding of the degree of overlap between no-DTP prevalence and other health gaps is needed. Numerous previous studies have assessed these relationships at an individual level, most commonly using data from household surveys [12,14–16]. At the population level, analyses of the spatial overlap between gaps in immunization coverage and other health services can complement these individual-level analyses. Spatial analyses conducted in recent years have emphasized the substantial degree of subnational inequality in vaccine coverage [13,17–23], as well as other key health services and indicators [22,24–31]. Fewer studies have assessed whether subnational distributions of zero-dose (or no-DTP) children are similar to those for other health indicators [32]. Some publicly available tools, such as the WHO Health Equity Assessment Toolkit [33], allow for powerful comparisons of health indicators within countries, although only for the years in which surveys have been conducted, and are limited to the geographic resolution of traditional survey methods (e.g., the first administrative level). Spatial overlap analyses can help to identify subnational areas and health services that may benefit most from integrated intervention.

Here, we propose a set of analyses that can be used to explore and quantify the degree of spatial overlap between populations of zero-dose children (proxied by no-DTP prevalence and counts) and gaps in vaccine coverage or other health-related indicators. Leveraging estimates of vaccination coverage from geospatial models and publicly available gridded estimates of other health indicators, we estimate patterns of spatial overlap in five example countries to demonstrate how these patterns may be explored both between and within countries, as well as over time. The approaches presented here can be expanded to other countries and health indicators and could serve as a resource when considering the possibility of joint intervention targeting.

2. Materials and Methods

2.1. Geospatial Estimation of Vaccination Coverage

For the purposes of this analysis, we used the prevalence of no-DTP (the proportion of children of the target age for vaccination who have not received any doses of a DTP-containing vaccine (DTPcv)) as a proxy for zero-dose children. We used a previously published geospatial modeling approach to estimate DTP vaccine coverage at the 5×5 km level [17], updating the approach to include more recent data and extending through 2019 (estimates were previously published for years 2000–2016).

To simplify the demonstration of these analyses, we selected the following five countries as examples for this analysis: Nigeria, Democratic Republic of the Congo (DRC), Indonesia, Ethiopia, and Angola. These countries were selected by ordering all the countries by the total number of estimated no-DTP children in 2019 [3], excluding countries for which spatial estimates were unavailable for two or more comparator indicators (Supplemental Table S1).

We searched the Global Health Data Exchange (GHDx) for household-based surveys containing information on DTP vaccination status between 2000 and 2019 [34]. We included surveys with information on DTP coverage information among children aged 12–59 months and excluded surveys that lacked subnational geographic information, had unrealistic coverage estimates, or contained areal data but were missing survey design variables that precluded the calculation of representative DTP coverage for each areal unit. From these five countries, we included data from 35 surveys with vaccination coverage information for 420,710 children from 11,047 GPS-located clusters and 2772 areal units. We calculated coverage at the most geographically granular level available for inclusion in the model. To better estimate the covariate effects and account for cross-border patterns of vaccine coverage, we modeled each country as part of a multi-country region (mirroring regions used to estimate MCV1 coverage by Sbarra et al. [18]), resulting in the inclusion of an additional 202 surveys including data for 1,200,877 children from other surrounding countries in the modeling process. A full list of included surveys can be found in Supplemental Table S2 and excluded surveys (with rationale for exclusion) in Supplemental Table S3.

We defined DTP1 coverage as the proportion of children who have received at least one dose of a DTPcv. At the most granular geospatial resolution possible for each survey, we calculated DTP1 coverage for each birth cohort. We then used a previously described Bayesian continuation ratio ordinal regression model-based geostatistical estimation framework to estimate DTP1 coverage [17], aggregated these estimates to the second administrative level using population estimates from WorldPop [35,36] and a modified version of the Database of Global Administrative Areas (GADM) shapefile [37], and then calculated no-DTP prevalence as 1—DTP1 prevalence. For analyses using counts of zero-dose children, we similarly converted no-DTP prevalence to counts by multiplying the estimates of children under 1 year of age for each second-level administrative unit and year derived from the gridded estimates from WorldPop. For brevity and consistency throughout this manuscript, we refer to second-level administrative units as "districts" hereafter, while acknowledging that the nomenclature for these units varies between countries (e.g., local government areas in Nigeria). Additional details of the geospatial modeling strategy can be found in the Supplemental Material (Supplemental Methods).

2.2. Spatial Estimates of Other Health Indicators

To assess the degree to which areas with a high prevalence or counts of zero-dose children may also exhibit gaps in other health services or outcomes, we identified and included the following five additional health indicators in our analyses: mortality among children under 5 years of age (U5M) [24], children with stunting [25], children with diarrhea who did not receive oral rehydration therapy (ORT) [38], prevalence of lymphatic filariasis (LF) [39], and individuals not sleeping with insecticide-treated bed nets (ITNs) [31]. These metrics were selected based on their persistent significance in the global health sphere, the role that subnational disparity plays in that persistence, and relationships to immunization that may give rise to potentially useful overlap analyses.

In addition to their significance in global health, these metrics were selected according to the availability of published estimates over time across multiple countries at a 5 × 5 km resolution. Estimates available in this format were most readily comparable to those produced for no-DTP prevalence. The estimation of these different metrics also employed geospatial modeling techniques that incorporated similar survey and other data sources and accounted for relationships with covariates, as well as correlations across space and time. The range of years with available estimates differed for each metric (Table 1). For each metric, we analyzed the overlap with no-DTP prevalence in the most recent year of data available, and for select analyses, we compared the overlap during the most recent year to that in the year 2000. Given their limited use in the country, missing ITN information was not available in Indonesia, but there was full coverage for all other indicators and countries.

Table 1. Details for health indicator estimates.

Indicator	Definition	Example Countries Available	Most Recent Year Available	Target Population Age Range	Citation
No-DTP	No-DTP prevalence rate	Angola, DRC, Ethiopia, Indonesia, Nigeria	2019	Under 1 year	Mosser, J.F. et al. [17] *
Stunting	Stunting prevalence rate	Angola, DRC, Ethiopia, Indonesia, Nigeria	2019	Under 5 years	Kinyoki, D.K. et al. [25]
U5M	Mortality probability and death counts	Angola, DRC, Ethiopia, Indonesia, Nigeria	2017	Under 5 years	Burstein, R. et al. [24]
Missed ORT	(1–ORT coverage) for children who had diarrhea	Angola, DRC, Ethiopia, Indonesia, Nigeria	2017	Under 5 years	Wiens, K.E. et al. [38]
Missed ITNs	(1–proportion of population that sleeps under an ITN)	Angola, DRC, Ethiopia, Nigeria	2019	All ages	Bertozzi-Villa, A. et al. [31]
LF	LF prevalence rate	Angola, DRC, Ethiopia, Indonesia, Nigeria	2018	All ages	Cromwell, E.A. et al. [39]

* Estimates updated to include additional years, geographies, and data sources.

2.3. *Analyses of Spatial Overlap*

For this analysis, we assessed the spatial overlap of no-DTP and these additional indicators in the context of assessing the degree to which the greatest burden for both no-DTP and the other indicators fell within the same districts. We fractionally aggregated the 5 × 5 km resolution pixel estimates for each metric to the same modified GADM shapefile [37]. Because prioritization decisions may be based not only on prevalence but also on total counts, we multiplied the respective prevalence estimates by the target population (Table 1) data available from WorldPop [35,36] to calculate the count estimates for each metric. For metrics with count data already available (i.e., for U5M, ORT, and LF), we used those values directly, although these were also based on WorldPop data. For both no-DTP and the health indicators, we assessed the overlap based on the mean estimates of prevalence or counts, without accounting for the uncertainty associated with all of these indicators.

In practice, decisions about prioritization for integrated service delivery are (and should be) made not only by considering the geographic patterns of the relevant indicators, but by accounting for a broad range of factors, including the available resources and data, and tailored by local expertise to each context [9]. For the purposes of this study, we used a highly simplified categorization scheme to illustrate the potential applications of spatial overlap analysis to contribute to the prioritization decisions. Similar analytic techniques, however, could easily be applied to other prioritization groupings. In this illustrative categorization approach, we assigned districts to population-weighted quartiles of burden for each metric, where districts with the highest values for each metric were in the top quartile and the districts with the lowest values for each metric were in the bottom quartile. Through population weighting, we ensured that the sum of target populations within each quartile were roughly equal. The scope of categorization needs and overlap assessment may vary between country-focused and global stakeholders. To explore the implications of these different frames of reference, we organized districts into quartiles both (1) within countries and (2) at a multi-national scale across countries. Similarly, we also categorized the districts into quartiles according to both (1) prevalence and (2) counts. To assess the full scope of overlap, we produced bivariate maps displaying overlap across all quartiles (Figure 1). We also produced simplified maps highlighting only those districts in the highest quartile for no-DTP, the respective comparator metric, or both. Finally, while we largely focused on comparing no-DTP categorization with each individual comparator metric, we also produced maps quantifying the number of metrics in the highest quartile in each district.

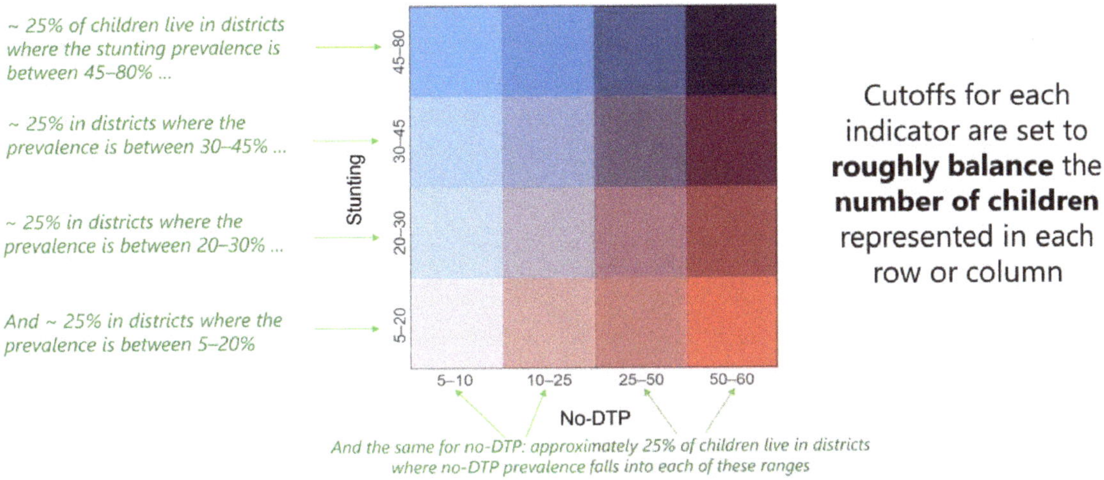

Figure 1. Example for a bivariate color legend used in maps to describe quartile classification overlap between no-DTP and the other health indicators (with stunting here as an example). For each of the two indicators, districts are distributed across four bins based on prevalence values such that the total target population value is roughly equal in each bin. Color bins along the diagonal (from bottom left to top right) indicate matching category assignments for the two indicators for a given district. Schema is used in figures representing all categorization quartiles.

We also aimed to quantify the overall degree of overlap between no-DTP and the other health indicators using the summary metrics to facilitate high-level comparisons. We calculated the proportion of districts in the highest quartile for no-DTP that were also in the highest quartile for the other indicators. Furthermore, we devised an additional measure that was not reliant on the quartile categorization schema. We envisioned a scenario where vaccination stakeholders might prioritize districts by aiming to reach the greatest number of no-DTP children in the fewest districts possible. If these same districts were also targeted for simultaneous interventions for our comparator health indicators, what proportion of that country's target groups for those indicators would be reached? We applied this hypothetical approach, serially targeting districts based on the number of no-DTP children, beginning with the targeting of the single district with the highest number of no-DTP children, then the two highest no-DTP districts, and so on. At each step, we calculated the cumulative proportion of individuals reached (for both no-DTP and the additional indicator), with each subsequent district targeted based upon the number of no-DTP children. By comparing these cumulative proportions between the two indicators for each set of serially targeted districts, we can calculate the area under the curve (AUC) to serve as a measure of overlap (Figure 2). This process is illustrated in step plots in Supplemental Figures S1–S23. As an example, an AUC of 0.5 indicates that geographic targeting based upon no-DTP reaches areas with equal proportions of no-DTP children and children with stunting. AUC values < 0.5 would indicate a smaller proportion of children with stunting reached, and AUC values > 0.5 would indicate greater proportions of children with stunting reached. We then analyzed AUC values between countries and indicators and over time, comparing AUC values in 2000 to those in the most recent year of available data.

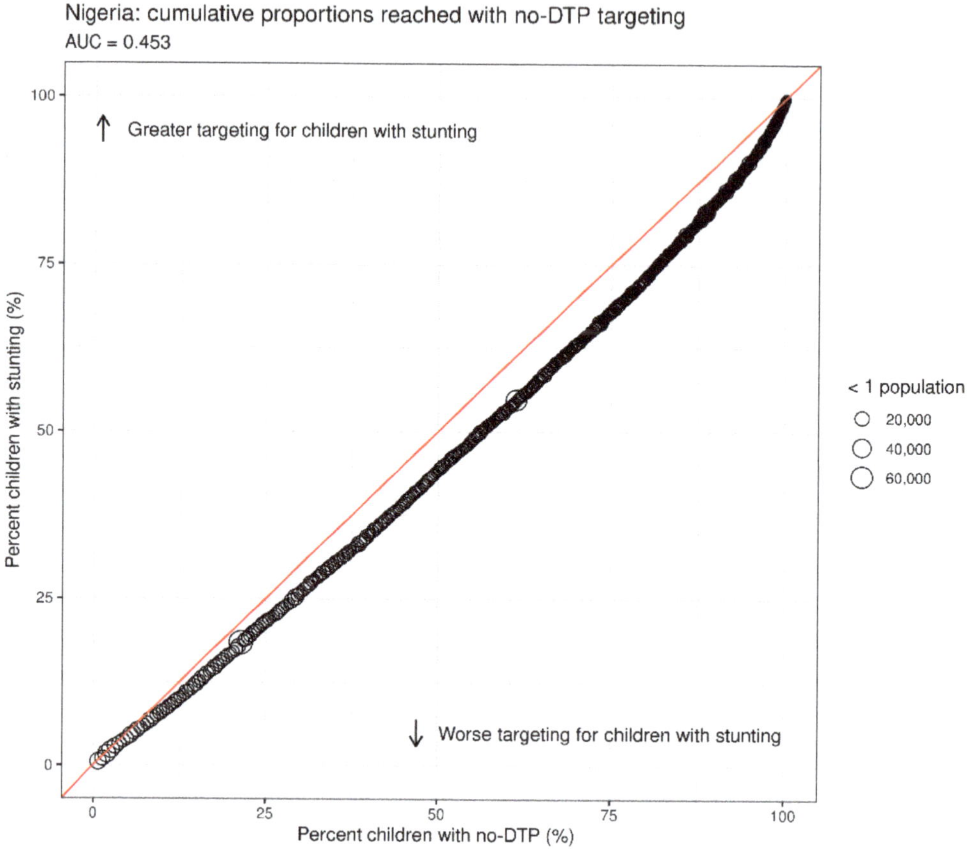

Figure 2. Area under the curve (AUC) scatter plot example. This example scatterplot visualizes how the area under the curve (AUC) can be used to quantify the proportion of children with stunting (Y axis) in Nigeria that could be reached through cumulative proportion targeting of districts for children with no-DTP (X axis). Individual points represent districts, ordered to begin with the district with the highest number of no-DTP children, then the second highest, until the cumulative proportion of no-DTP children reaches 100%. The red line represents AUC = 0.5, indicating equal proportions of children with stunting through cumulative no-DTP targeting. Curves below the red line are associated with AUC < 0.5 or smaller proportions of children with stunting, and curves above the red line are associated with AUC > 0.5, or greater proportions of children with stunting. Point size represents district population size of children under 1.

2.4. Ethical Approval and Reporting Guidelines

Data were not obtained from subjects for the Global Burden of Diseases, Injuries, and Risk Factors Study or related analyses such as this study. Instead, we used pre-existing, publicly available, de-identified datasets that include, but are not limited to, administrative and survey-based vaccine coverage reports. Data were identified through online searches, outreach to institutions that hold relevant data such as ministries of health, or individual collaborator references and identification. Most of the data used are publicly available. Therefore, informed consent was not required. This study was approved by the University of Washington's Human Subjects Division Study ID: STUDY00009060. Our study follows the Guidelines for Accurate and Transparent Health Estimates Reporting (GATHER; Supplemental Table S4).

3. Results

3.1. Mapping Overlap

3.1.1. Country-Specific Overlap by Prevalence

Figure 3A shows an example bivariate map that illustrates the spatial overlap between the population-weighted quartile classifications for no-DTP and stunting in Nigeria, based on the prevalence of each indicator. In this example, when categorizing by prevalence within Nigeria, based on the available geospatial estimates for both no-DTP and stunting, higher-prevalence districts tended to be more widely distributed through the northern regions of the country, while the southern regions had a lower prevalence for both indicators. Overlap between no-DTP and stunting categorization was high; nearly two thirds of all districts in Nigeria (488 of 774 districts, or 63.0%) were designated to the same population-weighted quartile for both no-DTP and stunting. Figure 4A shows a simplified representation of the same analysis, restricting the mapped districts to only the high-quartile areas for each indicator. Of the 207 districts in the highest quartiles for either no-DTP or stunting, half of those districts (49.0%, or 100 of 207 total) were in the highest quartile for both indicators.

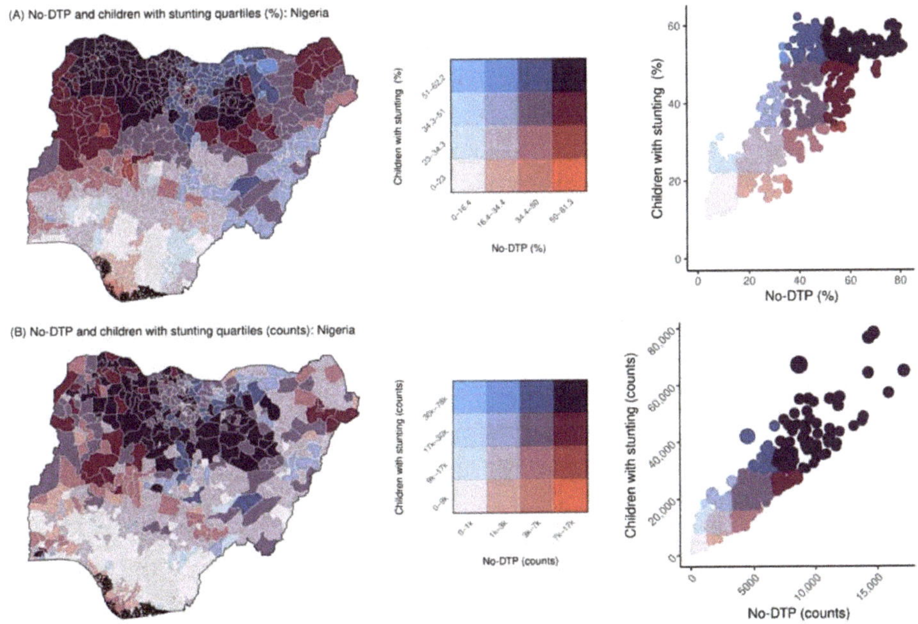

Figure 3. Country-specific Nigeria overlap for no-DTP and stunting, for all categorization quartiles. The top row (**A**) shows categorization based on prevalence, while the bottom row (**B**) shows categorization based on counts. Population-weighted quartile ranges for no-DTP and children with stunting are delineated in the bivariate color legends (center). District-level values are shown both as maps (left) and with scatterplots (right), with colors corresponding to quartile legend values. Point size in scatterplots reflects relative size of under-1 population in each district.

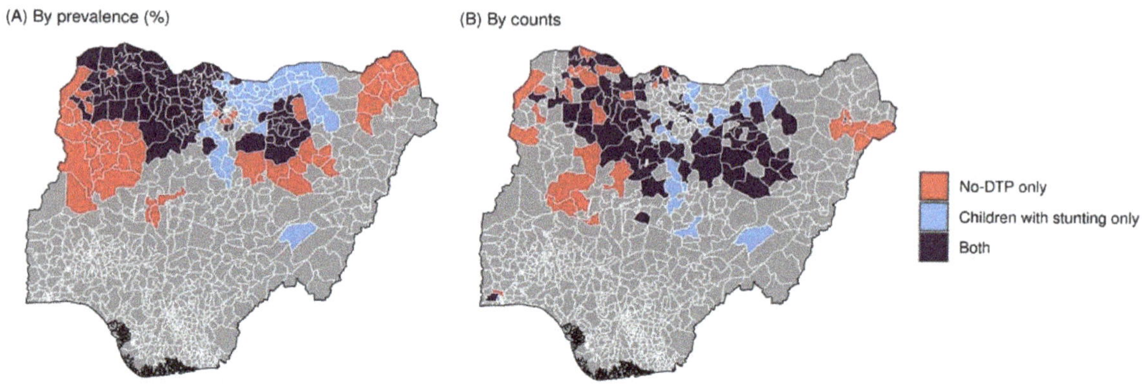

Figure 4. Country-specific overlap between no-DTP and stunting in Nigeria for highest category quartiles only. Districts in red are in the highest quartile for no-DTP only, blue are in the highest quartile for children with stunting only, and purple are in the highest quartile for both indicators. The map on the left (**A**) shows categorization based on prevalence, and the map on the right (**B**) shows categorization based on counts.

The spatial overlap between health indicators varies from indicator to indicator and country to country (Supplemental Figures S24–S69). In Ethiopia, for example, the locations with the highest no-DTP prevalence are located primarily in the east and south of the country (especially in the Afar and Somali regions) and are distinct from those with the lowest ITN coverage, which are located more centrally (for instance, in Amhara and Oromia) (Supplemental Figures S40a and S63a). In the Democratic Republic of the Congo, the geographic overlap between under-5 mortality and no-DTP prevalence is highly heterogeneous, with a mixture of high-prevalence areas for no-DTP, U5M, both, and neither indicator (Supplemental Figures S34a and S57a).

3.1.2. Country-Specific Overlap by Counts

As expected, when these same analyses are repeated using an example categorization approach based on counts rather than prevalence, the results tend to emphasize areas of large populations—although this pattern is not universal across indicators and countries.

For the overlap between no-DTP and stunting in Nigeria, for example, when categorization is based on counts rather than prevalence, higher-quartile districts still tended to be in the northern regions of the country, while southerly districts tended to be in the lower quartiles (Figure 3B). Compared to the prevalence-based approach, there was more concordance between count-based classifications, with more than three fourths of all districts (597 of 774 districts, or 77.1%) being designated to the same quartiles for both no-DTP and stunting. Fewer districts were classified into the highest quartiles for either metric based on counts compared to prevalence (125 vs. 207 districts), but a greater proportion were in the highest quartile for no-DTP and stunting (78 of 125 districts, or 62.4%). There were 44 districts categorized in the highest quartile for both no-DTP and stunting according to both prevalence and counts (Figure 4).

However, these patterns again varied between countries and indicators (Supplemental Figures S24–S69). For Indonesia, for instance, locations that might be targeted for joint targeting based on spatial overlap between no-DTP and missed ORT would vary broadly depending on whether decisions were informed by analyses of prevalence or counts (Supplemental Figures S45 and S68). In Angola, prevalence-based analysis of the overlap between no-DTP and ITN use identifies broad areas of the country that is potentially amenable to joint targeting (Supplemental Figures S31a and S53a). Due to the population distribution in the country, however, count-based analysis suggests that joint targeting opportunities might be focused upon relatively few locations (Supplemental Figures S31b and S53b).

3.1.3. Overlap for Multiple Indicators

For some stakeholders, it may be of interest not only to understand the degree of geographic overlap between no-DTP and other health indicators individually, but also to identify locations that may be amenable to integrated intervention across many indicators. We, therefore, produced country-specific maps that show the number of health indicators in the highest quartile in each district, using our population-weighted classification approach. Here, we continue to show results from Nigeria as an example, although results for other countries can be found in Supplemental Figures S70–S73.

According to both prevalence and counts, more indicators were classified in the highest quartile in northern and northwestern Nigeria (Figure 5). Districts in southern Nigeria were largely only in the highest quartile for one to two indicators (missed ITNs and/or LF), whereas districts in northern and northwestern Nigeria had many cases of the overlapping classification for no-DTP, stunting, U5M, and missed ORT.

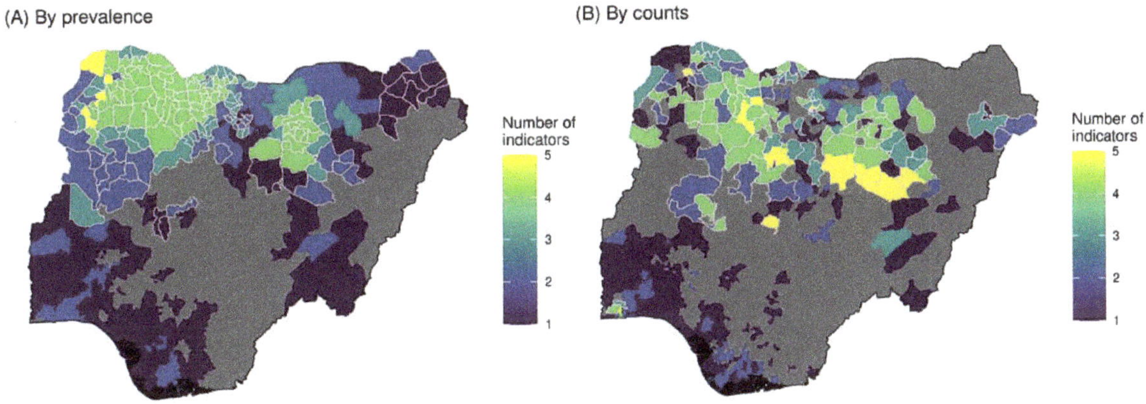

Figure 5. Country-specific multi-indicator overlap for Nigeria. Color given in each district reflects the number of indicators assigned to the highest quartile in that district. Districts outlined in white indicate those where no-DTP is among the indicators in the highest quartile. The map on the left (**A**) shows categorization based on prevalence, and the map on the right (**B**) shows categorization based on counts.

When classified by prevalence, high-quartile districts were relatively more concentrated across indicators in Nigeria compared to other countries (Figure 5A, Supplemental Figures S70–S73). More than two thirds of districts in Nigeria were categorized into the highest quartile for at least one of the six indicators analyzed (525 of 774, or 67.8%), but these proportions were even greater in all other countries, including 74.8% of districts in Indonesia (374 of 500), 81.1% of districts in DRC (194 of 239), 81.0% of districts in Ethiopia (64 of 79), and 87.7% of districts in Angola (143 of 163).

The opposite was true when categorizing the districts into population-weighted quartiles by counts. In this example, a much smaller proportion of districts—43.7%—were in the highest quartile for at least one indicator in Nigeria (338 of 774 districts; Figure 4B). This trend was consistent across other countries (Supplemental Figures S70–S73).

3.1.4. Multinational Overlap by Prevalence

The analyses above focus on describing the spatial patterns of no-DTP and other indicators, based upon within-country classification for each indicator. For global or regional decision-makers, however, examination of the degree of spatial overlap across countries may be of interest. We, therefore, repeated these analyses, but instead categorized districts as those with the highest prevalence or counts for each indicator across all five example countries included in these analyses, rather than within the countries separately. Given the limited number of countries and indicators used in this analysis, these example results are meant to be illustrative only, to demonstrate the magnitude of differences in the perceived overlap when looking across rather than between countries and are not meant as policy recommendations.

Categorizing by prevalence across our five focal countries combined, population-weighted quartile assignments for no-DTP and stunting were markedly similar (Figure 6). The quartile classifications for no-DTP and stunting exactly matched (i.e., districts in the lowest quartile for no-DTP were also in the lowest quartile for stunting, etc.) in nearly half of all districts (795 out of 1755 total; 45.3%). Districts in the highest quartile across all countries for no-DTP could be found in every country, as well as districts in the highest quartile for stunting (Figure 7). The districts where the highest-quartile categorization for no-DTP and stunting overlapped largely fell within Nigeria and Angola, with 27.0% of districts in Nigeria and 50.3% of districts in Angola being in the highest category for both indicators (209 of 774 in Nigeria and 82 of 163 districts in Angola). While significant portions of DRC and Ethiopia were in the highest quartile for one indicator or the other, there was little overlap between indicators in these countries, and none in Indonesia (Figure 7).

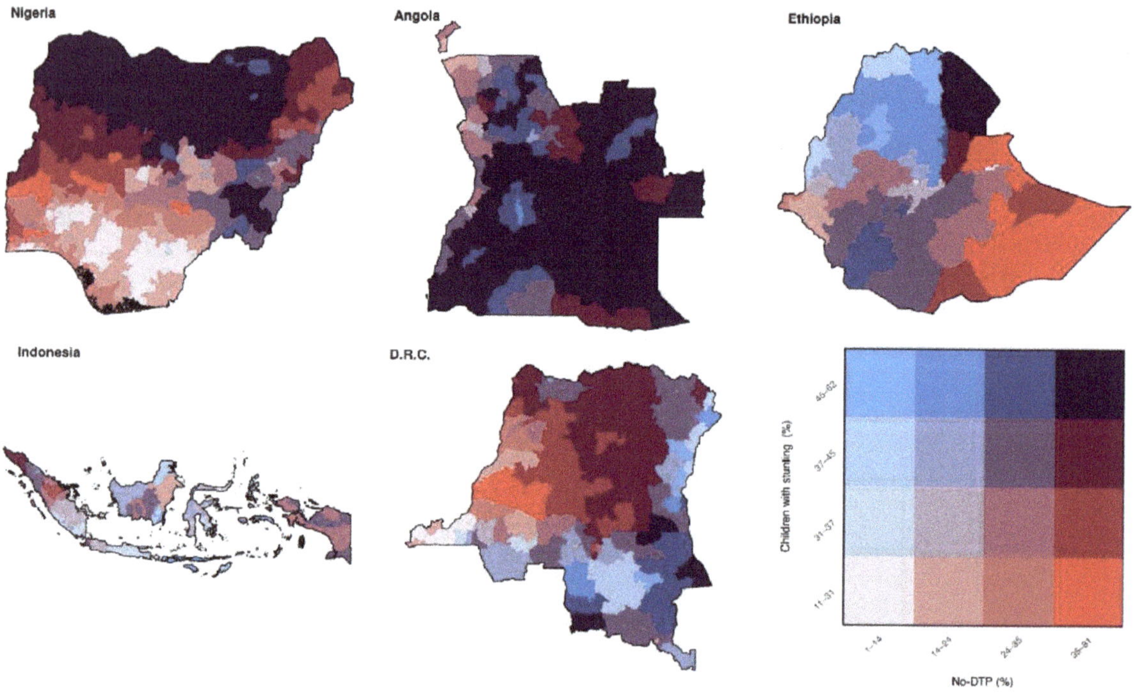

Figure 6. Multinational overlap between stunting and no-DTP for all categorization quartiles, based on prevalence. Ranges for population-weighted quartiles across the five example countries combined for no-DTP and children with stunting are delineated in the bivariate color legend (bottom right).

Different patterns were observed for other comparator indicators (Supplemental Figures S74–S81). For instance, when comparing categorization for no-DTP and ORT across all five countries to that for no-DTP and stunting, fewer districts in Nigeria and Angola were in the highest quartile for both indicators, whereas larger areas of Ethiopia and DRC were in the highest quartile for both (Supplemental Figure S80).

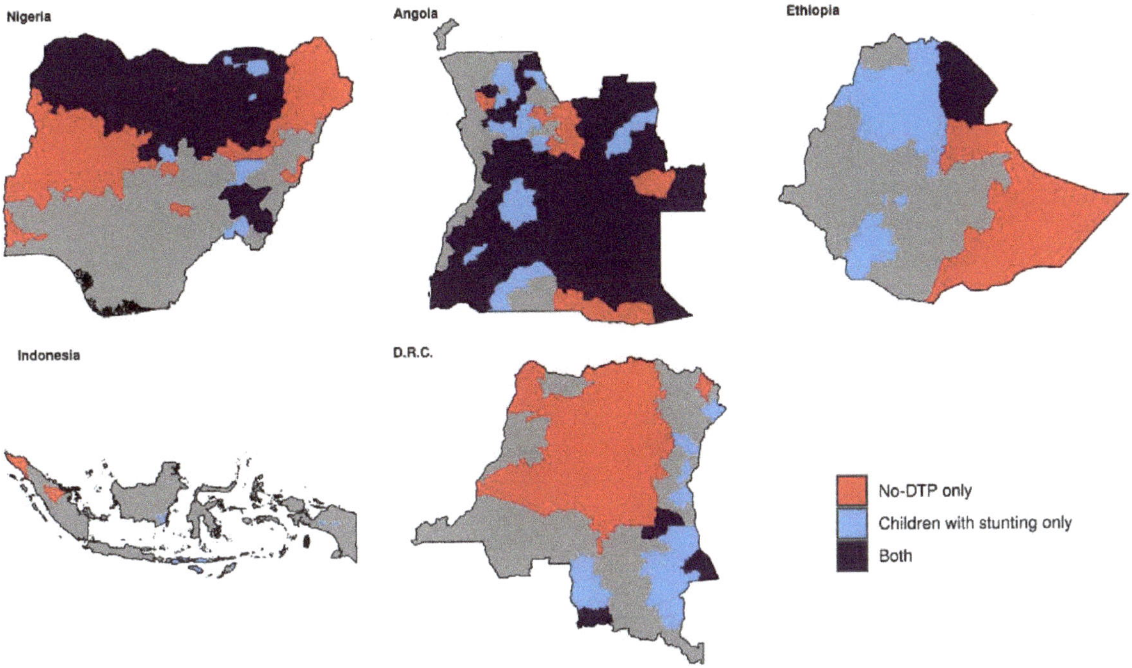

Figure 7. Multinational overlap between stunting and no-DTP for highest quartiles only, based on prevalence. Districts in red are in the highest quartile for no-DTP only, blue are in the highest quartile for children with stunting only, and purple are in the highest quartile for both indicators.

3.1.5. Multinational Overlap by Counts

Categorization at the multinational scale was even more closely aligned between no-DTP and stunting when classifying districts according to counts rather than prevalence (Figure 8). When categorizing by counts, quartile assignment matched exactly between no-DTP and stunting in 71.1% of all districts (1248 of 1755 total). Far fewer districts were in the highest quartile when considered in terms of counts—only 5.8% of districts were in the highest quartile for either indicator using counts, compared to 35.5% of districts when considered by prevalence (102 vs. 623 out of 1755 districts, respectively; Figures 8 and 9). In addition, the highest-quartile districts for either indicator fell largely in Ethiopia and DRC. The highest-quartile districts were scarce in the other three countries, making up <3% each for districts in Nigeria, Angola, and Indonesia. Only 49 districts were in the highest quartile for both no-DTP and stunting (2.7% of all districts), and more than half (28 of 49) were found in Ethiopia. This trend was largely consistent across all indicators (Supplemental Figures S82–S89).

3.2. *Quantifying Spatial Overlap*

District-level mapping, as in the analyses above, can help to identify subnational locations with potential for joint targeting. In some cases, however, it may be useful to quantify the degree of spatial overlap between no-DTP and another indicator in a single summary metric—i.e., to compare between countries or across comparator indicators. These summary metrics may help to determine the potential benefit of integrated services and delivery for some indicators compared to others, for instance.

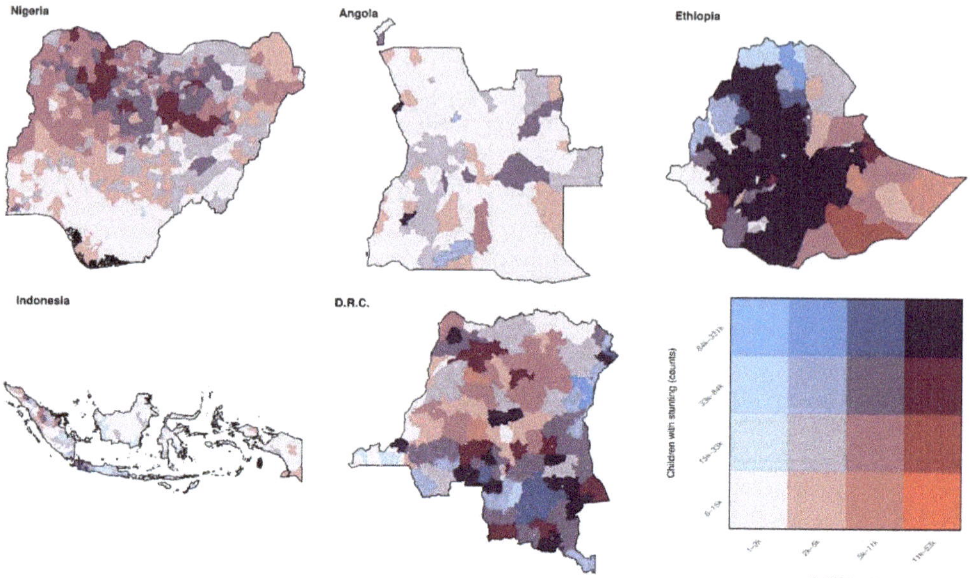

Figure 8. Multinational overlap between stunting and no-DTP for all categorization quartiles, based on counts. Ranges for population-weighted quartiles across the five example countries combined for no-DTP and children with stunting are delineated in the bivariate color legend (bottom right).

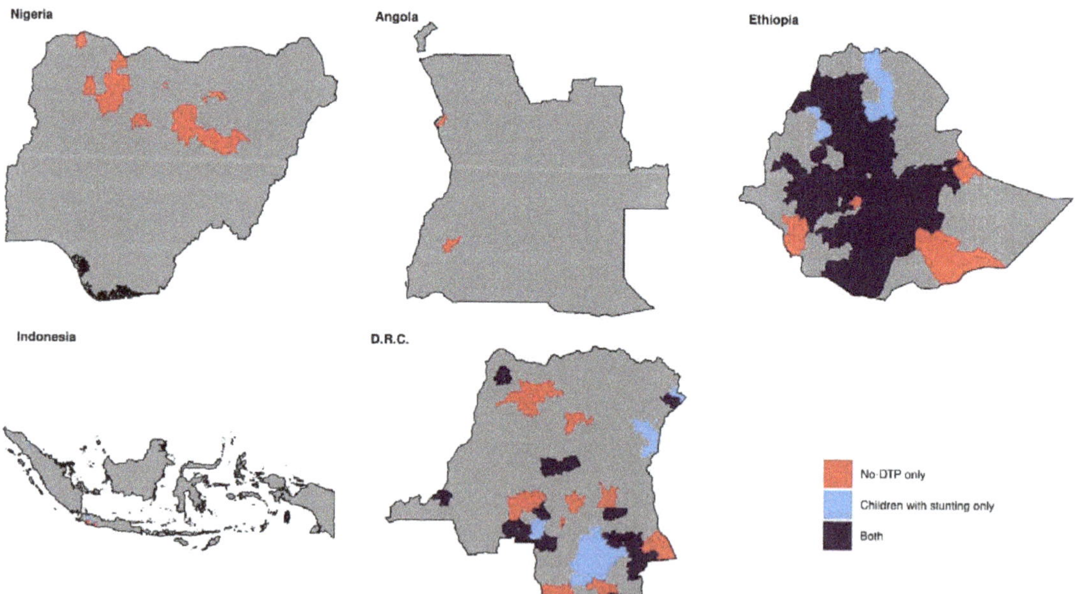

Figure 9. Multinational overlap between stunting and no-DTP for highest quartiles only, based on counts. Districts in red are in the highest quartile for no-DTP only, blue are in the highest quartile for children with stunting only, and purple are in the highest quartile for both indicators.

3.2.1. Percent Overlap of High-Quartile Districts

First, we identified all the districts in the highest quartile for no-DTP and calculated the proportion of those districts that were also categorized into the highest quartile for each of the other indicators. This proportion of overlap varied greatly between and within countries and indicators (Figure 10). The overlap was almost always higher when districts were classified based on counts rather than prevalence, with a few exceptions (e.g., overlap with LF or with ORT in several countries). For both prevalence- and count-based categorization approaches, the degree of overlap between no-DTP and other indicators tended to be lower in DRC compared to other countries; the proportion overlap was less than 50% for all comparator indicators except LF (where 66.2% of districts categorized in the highest quartile for no-DTP overlapped with LF highest-quartile categorization using prevalence, compared to 46.7% using counts).

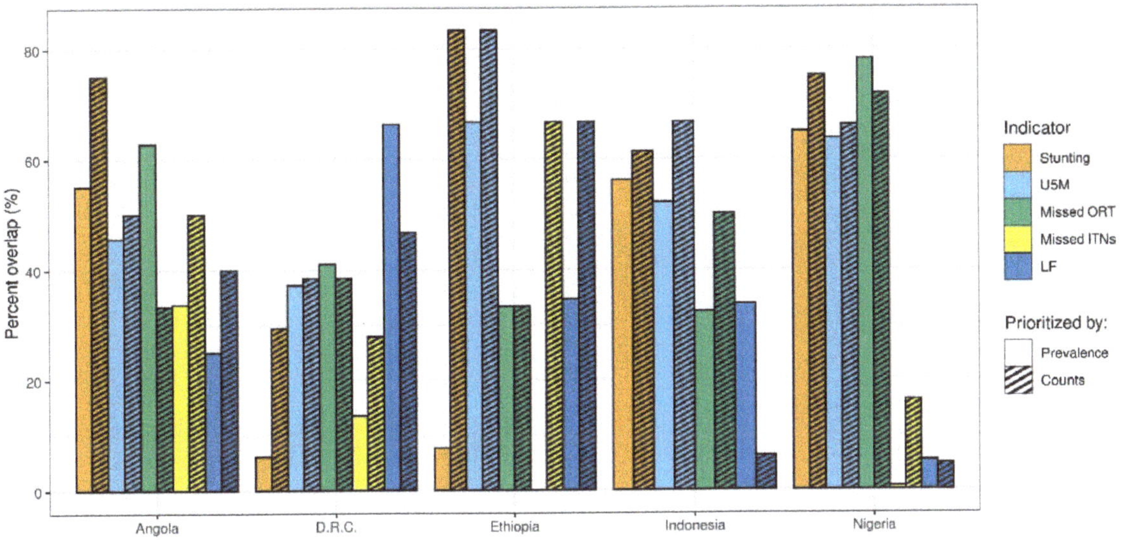

Figure 10. Overlap between districts in highest quartile categories for both no-DTP and comparator indicators, by country. Percent overlap indicates the proportion of districts in the highest quartile for no-DTP that are also in the highest quartile for the respective comparator indicators. Solid bars represent categorization based on prevalence, while striped bars represent categorization based on counts.

Although the ranges between the indicators tended to be broad, there was nevertheless variation in consistency within most countries. For example, for categorization based on prevalence, there was some degree of overlap with no-DTP for every comparator indicator in Angola; the proportions of overlap ranged from 25.0% for LF to 62.8% for missed ORT. In Nigeria, on the other hand, proportions ranged from extremely low overlap with missed ITNs (0.6%) to high overlap with missed ORT (77.9%).

3.2.2. AUC

In the more recent year of measurement, across countries and indicators, the median AUC was 0.43 (where AUC = 0.5 indicates equal proportions of the comparator indicator and no-DTP reached through no-DTP targeting, AUC < 0.5 indicates lower proportions of the population reached for the given indicator compared to no-DTP, and AUC > 0.5 indicates greater proportions of the population reached for the given indicator). The AUC for stunting in Nigeria was slightly above this value at 0.453 (Figure 2). The overall range of values for this measure was relatively narrow (Figure 11, Supplemental Figures S1–S23).

Two-thirds of the observations fall between 0.39 and 0.46, with all indicators in Ethiopia and DRC falling within that range. The AUC was higher in Angola compared to other countries overall; only in Angola did any indicators reach an AUC > 0.5 (stunting at 0.52, LF at 0.55, and missed ITNs at 0.58), indicating even greater proportions of those target populations reached (compared to no-DTP populations reached). This finding is possible when the degree of geographic concentration is greater for other indicators than for no-DTP.

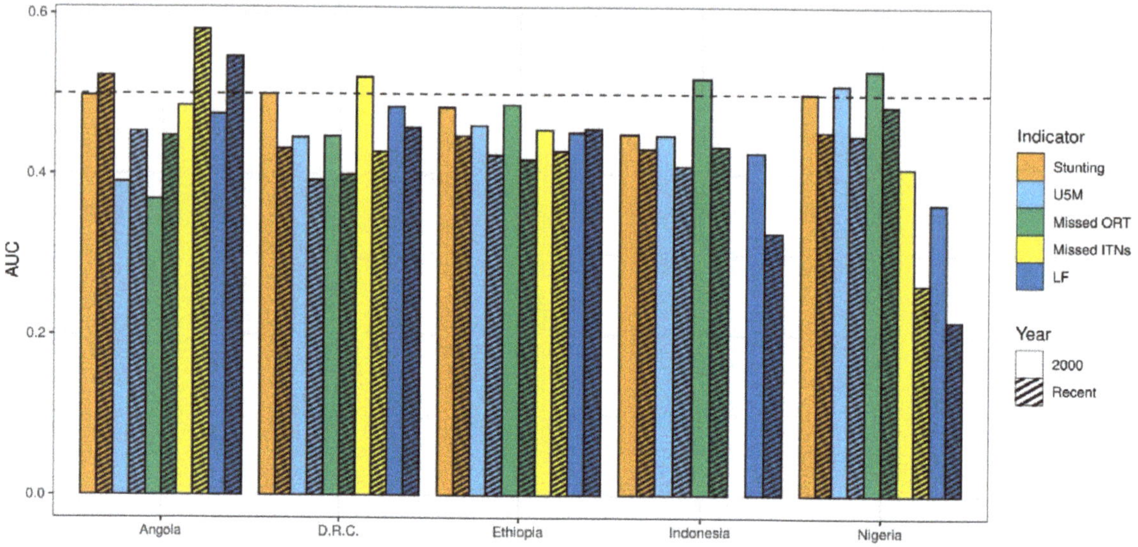

Figure 11. Comparison of AUC in 2000 and the most recent year of available data for each comparator indicator, by country. Solid bars represent values for the year 2000, while striped bars represent values for the most recent year of data available for the given metric (Table 1).

Based on AUC, across indicators, overlap with no-DTP was generally lower in 2000 compared to the more recent year measured in the countries included here, indicating broad reductions in spatial overlap over time (Figure 11). The largest decreases were for LF and missed ITNs in Nigeria, which were already lower than the other indicators in Nigeria in 2000 and these declined by 0.15 and 0.14, respectively. Angola was an exception to this trend, with a higher AUC in the more recent year across the indicators.

4. Discussion

In this study, we present a series of analyses of the distribution of no-DTP children and populations in need of other health interventions, using available subnational estimates of each indicator, and highlight their potential utility by applying these approaches to five example countries. These results demonstrate the substantial variation in joint geographic overlap between no-DTP and other health indicators, both between and within countries. In addition, the degree of spatial overlap and potential areas for joint geographic targeting vary depending on whether classification is based on prevalence or counts, and whether policy decisions are being made within or across countries. In general, the degree of spatial overlap between no-DTP and other indicators (measured by AUC) decreased over time for most comparisons and countries, with the exceptions of LF in Ethiopia and multiple indicators in Angola. For several of these analyses, we derived hypothetical categorization schemes for no-DTP children for illustrative purposes, such as population-weighted quartiles or serial targeting of districts based upon the estimated number of no-DTP children living in each district. We note, however, that these approaches could (and should) be tailored to reflect specific subnational prioritization plans under consideration in the future, while also expanding to include more countries and/or comparator indicators in the analysis. Taken together, the analytic approaches presented here form a foundation for future work to better understand the degree of geographic overlap between districts with high numbers of no-DTP children and those in need of other vital health services.

The comparator indicators presented here reflect a mixture of health service and health outcome measures, illustrating the different ways in which spatial overlap analyses might be applied. For instance, previous integration efforts have often included co-delivery of immunizations and ITNs [40], and areas with high LF prevalence and low immunization coverage may benefit from mass drug administration and immunization efforts. Reducing the disease burden of childhood diarrhea requires multifaceted approaches, such as preventive measures (including vaccination, i.e., for rotavirus) and access to treatment (including ORT) [41]. Malnutrition and immunization have complex interactions; malnourished children are at a higher risk for infectious disease mortality [42] and may benefit most from the protection of vaccines. Malnutrition may also affect immunologic responses to vaccination, and vaccination is an important component of multi-pronged interventions to reduce malnutrition [43]. Lastly, despite substantial progress, under-5 mortality in many countries is still significantly higher [44] than the stated Sustainable Development Goal (SDG) target of 25 or fewer deaths per 1000 live births by 2030 [8], and immunization is one of the cornerstones of efforts to reduce child mortality. Comparisons between gaps in vaccination coverage and these indicators, therefore, can illustrate a variety of potential uses for spatial overlap analyses.

For no-DTP children and communities that face barriers to accessing essential health services beyond immunization, integrating vaccine delivery with the delivery of other services could potentially provide substantial equity benefits. Integrated approaches also have the potential to increase the efficiency of health service delivery. As a result, integration has been a key theme of global immunization strategies over the past decades. The integration of immunization service delivery along with other public health interventions across one's life course is one of the strategic priority goals of IA2030 [7], formed one of the strategic focus areas of the Global Immunization Vision and Strategy (2006–2015) [45], and was one of the guiding principles of the Global Vaccine Action Plan (2011–2020) [46]. The World Health Organization has also published extensive guidance for the integration of immunization services across one's life course and within health systems [47].

Past efforts have focused on the integration of immunization services with other interventions in both campaign and routine immunization settings, including services such as ITN distribution, mass drug administration for deworming, vitamin A supplementation and nutritional services, family planning, HIV services, water and sanitation, and intermittent preventive therapy for malaria, among others [9,40]. Reviews of program experiences that implemented such integrated immunization activities suggest that integration can be challenging and highlight the need for a thoughtful consideration of the feasibility of joint intervention; careful, context-specific planning and implementation; strong community-based leadership; and timely and reliable monitoring strategies [9,48]. Analyses of the geographic overlap of populations in need of improved vaccination services and other interventions—such as those presented in this study—could serve as valuable additional input into this decision-making and planning process. Moreover, the heterogeneous patterns of overlap between countries and indicators illustrated by this study reinforce the need for context-specific decision-making about the integration of service delivery and integration plans that are tailored to the needs of each country and community.

This study is subject to several important limitations. First, this analysis focuses on district-level, population overlaps between the distribution of no-DTP children and other health services. This type of analysis helps to define geographic areas that might benefit from joint prioritization of immunization and other service delivery. This approach, however, does not examine other dimensions of overlap that may be important to understand when evaluating the potential benefits of integrated service delivery. These results should be paired with local expertise, as well as individual-level analyses such as those recently published [12], which can provide a more nuanced understanding of the associations between no-DTP status, lack of access to other health services, and other important non-geographic factors, such as poverty and race/ethnicity. Second, geospatial modeled estimates are often generated from survey data, which can vary in representativeness, temporal availability, and accuracy across indicators and between countries, and are subject to important forms of bias (including recall bias). Survey data representativeness may vary due to limitations of the available population estimates to inform sampling designs in some countries. In cases where populations at high risk for being zero-dose—for instance, those living in urban poor areas or migrant populations—are not adequately represented in the survey data, the resulting geospatial estimates will reflect these underlying biases. Third, these analyses rely on gridded population estimates from the WorldPop project [36] to convert between the prevalence of each indicator and counts of individuals at risk. In settings where no recent census data are available or migration is common, however, inaccurate population estimates could substantially bias prioritization decisions. To support accurate prioritization and planning, reliable target population estimates are critical. Last, we note that the classifications for the indicators presented here may not translate directly with the unmet needs. For example, coverage of ITNs on its own does not account for the endemicity of malaria. This limitation emphasizes the need for a framework such as that proposed here to be considered alongside a broad range of additional factors, context, and local expertise. For additional limitations, please see the Supplemental Material (Supplemental Methods).

As this paper has highlighted, contextual knowledge is crucial for the effective use of any analyses to be used in decision-making. That contextual information can be highly localized and unique to each situation. We also note that the work in this paper is presented here without that contextual input of those most affected by under-immunization. While we have attempted to present many different analytical facets to address a range of possible use cases, we nevertheless acknowledge this critical component still missing from these analyses. Therefore, we invite feedback from global, regional, national and local experts in vaccine delivery and health service delivery as to how this work may be improved, modified and/or tailored to best support the efforts to reach zero-dose children and provide essential health services.

5. Conclusions

As the global immunization community works to fulfill the ambitious goals of IA2030, new strategies to reach zero-dose children and communities will be needed. Integrating immunization with other essential health services, as part of robust primary health care systems, has the potential to improve efficiency and achieve greater equity in health outcomes, particularly for communities that are most at risk. The potential benefits of integration—and the ideal strategies to plan and implement these efforts—are likely to vary from country to country. Spatial analyses of the overlap between gaps in immunization services and other key health indicators can help to define the potential for joint geographic targeting of integrated service delivery to help ensure a future where all people have equitable access to lifesaving vaccines.

Supplementary Materials: The following supporting information can be downloaded at: https://www.mdpi.com/article/10.3390/vaccines11040802/s1, Supplemental Methods; Table S1: Ten countries with highest no-DTP counts in 2019 and indicator data availability details; Table S2: Surveys included in DTP modeling; Table S3: Surveys excluded from DTP modeling; Table S4: GATHER Compliance checklist; Table S5: Geospatial covariates used in modeling; Figures S1–S23: Country-specific AUC step plots; Figures S24–S46: Country-specific, all quartile overlap; Figure S47–S69: Country-specific, highest quartile overlap; Figures S70–S73: Multi-indicator overlap of country-specific highest quartiles; Figures S74–S77: Multinational all quartile overlap by prevalence; Figures S78–S81: Multinational highest quartile overlap by prevalence; Figures S82–S85: Multinational all quartile overlap by counts; Figures S86–S89: Multinational highest quartile overlap by counts. References [49–52] are cited in the Supplemental Methods.

Author Contributions: E.H. and J.F.M. conceptualized the project. E.H., S.R. and J.Q.N. participated in data curation, and E.H. conducted the formal analysis and investigation. E.H. and J.F.M. developed the methodology. E.H. contributed to software development. J.F.M. supervised the project. J.F.M. provided the validation of the results. E.H. created visualizations. E.H. and J.F.M. wrote the original draft, and S.R., O.N., J.Q.N. and N.F. were involved in the critical review, commentary, and revision during the writing process. E.H., S.R., J.Q.N. and J.F.M. had full access to and verified the underlying data used to generate the estimates presented in this article. All other authors had access to and reviewed the estimates as part of the research evaluation process, which included additional formal stages of review. The corresponding author had final responsibility for the decision to submit for publication. All authors have read and agreed to the published version of the manuscript.

Funding: This work was supported by grants from the Bill & Melinda Gates Foundation (OPP1152504 and INV-037425) and Gavi (MEL 11507 5 22).

Institutional Review Board Statement: Not applicable.

Informed Consent Statement: Not applicable.

Data Availability Statement: The findings of this study are supported by data available in public online repositories and data publicly available upon request of the data provider. Details of data sources and availability are publicly available in the Global Health Data Exchange (https://ghdx.healthdata.org/record/ihme-data/dtp-vaccines-zerodose-overlap). All computer code is available online and can be found at (https://github.com/ihmeuw/vaccines-zerodose-overlap).

Acknowledgments: We acknowledge, with gratitude, the time, expertise, and effort of the survey teams who gathered the data used to inform these modeled estimates, as well as all the participants in these surveys.

Conflicts of Interest: IHME is primarily funded by the Bill and Melinda Gates Foundation (BMGF). J.F.M., E.H., O.N., J.Q.N. and S.R. additionally report receiving funding from BMGF and Gavi. NF has received funding from Gates Ventures since June 2020, for work around childhood vaccination and vaccine delivery in low- and middle-income countries.

References

1. WHO. Essential Programme on Immunization. Available online: https://www.who.int/teams/immunization-vaccines-and-biologicals/essential-programme-on-immunization (accessed on 2 February 2023).
2. Toor, J.; Echeverria-Londono, S.; Li, X.; Abbas, K.; Carter, E.D.; Clapham, H.E.; Clark, A.; De Villiers, M.J.; Eilertson, K.; Ferrari, M.; et al. Lives Saved with Vaccination for 10 Pathogens across 112 Countries in a Pre-COVID-19 World. *ELife* **2021**, *10*, e67635. [CrossRef]
3. Galles, N.C.; Liu, P.Y.; Updike, R.L.; Fullman, N.; Nguyen, J.; Rolfe, S.; Sbarra, A.N.; Schipp, M.F.; Marks, A.; Abady, G.G.; et al. Measuring Routine Childhood Vaccination Coverage in 204 Countries and Territories, 1980–2019: A Systematic Analysis for the Global Burden of Disease Study 2020, Release 1. *Lancet* **2021**, *398*, 503–521. [CrossRef]
4. WHO & UNICEF. WHO/UNICEF Estimates of National Immunization Coverage. Available online: https://www.who.int/teams/immunization-vaccines-and-biologicals/immunization-analysis-and-insights/global-monitoring/immunization-coverage/who-unicef-estimates-of-national-immunization-coverage (accessed on 2 February 2023).
5. Causey, K.; Fullman, N.; Sorensen, R.J.D.; Galles, N.C.; Zheng, P.; Aravkin, A.; Danovaro-Holliday, M.C.; Martinez-Piedra, R.; Sodha, S.V.; Velandia-González, M.P.; et al. Estimating Global and Regional Disruptions to Routine Childhood Vaccine Coverage during the COVID-19 Pandemic in 2020: A Modelling Study. *Lancet* **2021**, *398*, 522–534. [CrossRef] [PubMed]
6. WHO. COVID-19 Pandemic Fuels Largest Continued Backslide in Vaccinations in Three Decades. Available online: https://www.who.int/news/item/15-07-2022-covid-19-pandemic-fuels-largest-continued-backslide-in-vaccinations-in-three-decades (accessed on 2 February 2023).
7. WHO. Immunization Agenda 2030: A Global Strategy to Leave No One Behind. Available online: http://www.who.int/immunization/immunization_agenda_2030/en/ (accessed on 2 February 2023).
8. Joint SDG Fund Sustainable Development Goals. Available online: https://jointsdgfund.org/sustainable-development-goals/goal-3-good-health-and-well-being (accessed on 2 February 2023).
9. Wallace, A.S.; Ryman, T.K.; Privor-Dumm, L.; Morgan, C.; Fields, R.; Garcia, C.; Sodha, S.V.; Lindstrand, A.; Nic Lochlainn, L.M. Leaving No One behind: Defining and Implementing an Integrated Life Course Approach to Vaccination across the next Decade as Part of the Immunization Agenda 2030. *Vaccine* **2022**, S0264410X22014529. [CrossRef]
10. WHO. Implementing the Immunization Agenda. 2023. Available online: https://www.who.int/publications/m/item/implementing-the-immunization-agenda-2030 (accessed on 2 February 2023).

11. Cata-Preta, B.O.; Santos, T.M.; Mengistu, T.; Hogan, D.R.; Barros, A.J.D.; Victora, C.G. Zero-Dose Children and the Immunisation Cascade: Understanding Immunisation Pathways in Low and Middle-Income Countries. *Vaccine* **2021**, *39*, 4564–4570. [CrossRef]
12. Wendt, A.; Santos, T.M.; Cata-Preta, B.O.; Arroyave, L.; Hogan, D.R.; Mengistu, T.; Barros, A.J.D.; Victora, C.G. Exposure of Zero-Dose Children to Multiple Deprivation: Analyses of Data from 80 Low- and Middle-Income Countries. *Vaccines* **2022**, *10*, 1568. [CrossRef]
13. Wigley, A.; Lorin, J.; Hogan, D.; Utazi, C.E.; Hagedorn, B.; Dansereau, E.; Tatem, A.J.; Tejedor-Garavito, N. Estimates of the Number and Distribution of Zero-Dose and under-Immunised Children across Remote-Rural, Urban, and Conflict-Affected Settings in Low and Middle-Income Countries. *PLoS Glob. Public Health* **2022**, *2*, e0001126. [CrossRef]
14. Santos, T.M.; Cata-Preta, B.O.; Mengistu, T.; Victora, C.G.; Hogan, D.R.; Barros, A.J.D. Assessing the Overlap between Immunisation and Other Essential Health Interventions in 92 Low- and Middle-Income Countries Using Household Surveys: Opportunities for Expanding Immunisation and Primary Health Care. *eClinicalMedicine* **2021**, *42*, 101196. [CrossRef] [PubMed]
15. Johri, M.; Rajpal, S.; Subramanian, S.V. Progress in Reaching Unvaccinated (Zero-Dose) Children in India, 1992–2016: A Multilevel, Geospatial Analysis of Repeated Cross-Sectional Surveys. *Lancet Glob. Health* **2021**, *9*, e1697–e1706. [CrossRef]
16. Restrepo-Méndez, M.C.; Barros, A.J.D.; Wong, K.L.M.; Johnson, H.L.; Pariyo, G.; Wehrmeister, F.C.; Victora, C.G. Missed Opportunities in Full Immunization Coverage: Findings from Low- and Lower-Middle-Income Countries. *Glob. Health Action* **2016**, *9*, 30963. [CrossRef] [PubMed]
17. Mosser, J.F.; Gagne-Maynard, W.; Rao, P.C.; Osgood-Zimmerman, A.; Fullman, N.; Graetz, N.; Burstein, R.; Updike, R.L.; Liu, P.Y.; Ray, S.E. Mapping Diphtheria-Pertussis-Tetanus Vaccine Coverage in Africa, 2000–2016: A Spatial and Temporal Modelling Study. *Lancet* **2019**, *393*, 1843–1855. [PubMed]
18. Sbarra, A.N.; Rolfe, S.; Nguyen, J.Q.; Earl, L.; Galles, N.C.; Marks, A.; Abbas, K.M.; Abbasi-Kangevari, M.; Abbastabar, H.; Abd-Allah, F.; et al. Mapping Routine Measles Vaccination in Low- and Middle-Income Countries. *Nature* **2021**, *589*, 415–419. [CrossRef]
19. Takahashi, S.; Metcalf, C.J.E.; Ferrari, M.J.; Tatem, A.J.; Lessler, J. The Geography of Measles Vaccination in the African Great Lakes Region. *Nat. Commun.* **2017**, *8*, 15585. [CrossRef]
20. Utazi, C.E.; Aheto, J.M.K.; Wigley, A.; Tejedor-Garavito, N.; Bonnie, A.; Nnanatu, C.C.; Wagai, J.; Williams, C.; Setayesh, H.; Tatem, A.J.; et al. Mapping the Distribution of Zero-Dose Children to Assess the Performance of Vaccine Delivery Strategies and Their Relationships with Measles Incidence in Nigeria. *Vaccine* **2023**, *41*, 170–181. [CrossRef]
21. Utazi, C.E.; Aheto, J.M.K.; Chan, H.M.T.; Tatem, A.J.; Sahu, S.K. Conditional Probability and Ratio-Based Approaches for Mapping the Coverage of Multi-Dose Vaccines. *Stat. Med.* **2022**, *41*, 5662–5678. [CrossRef]
22. Burgert-Brucker, C.R.; Dontamsetti, T.; Gething, P.W. The DHS Program's Modeled Surfaces Spatial Datasets. *Stud. Fam. Plan.* **2018**, *49*, 87–92. [CrossRef]
23. Dimitrova, A.; Carrasco-Escobar, G.; Richardson, R.; Benmarhnia, T. Essential Childhood Immunization in 43 Low- and Middle-Income Countries: Analysis of Spatial Trends and Socioeconomic Inequalities in Vaccine Coverage. *PLoS Med.* **2023**, *20*, e1004166. [CrossRef]
24. Burstein, R.; Henry, N.J.; Collison, M.L.; Marczak, L.B.; Sligar, A.; Watson, S.; Marquez, N.; Abbasalizad-Farhangi, M.; Abbasi, M.; Abd-Allah, F.; et al. Mapping 123 Million Neonatal, Infant and Child Deaths between 2000 and 2017. *Nature* **2019**, *574*, 353–358. [CrossRef] [PubMed]
25. Kinyoki, D.K.; Osgood-Zimmerman, A.E.; Pickering, B.V.; Schaeffer, L.E.; Marczak, L.B.; Lazzar-Atwood, A.; Collison, M.L.; Henry, N.J.; Abebe, Z.; Adamu, A.A.; et al. Mapping Child Growth Failure across Low- and Middle-Income Countries. *Nature* **2020**, *577*, 231–234. [CrossRef]
26. Haeuser, E.; Serfes, A.L.; Cork, M.A.; Yang, M.; Abbastabar, H.; Abhilash, E.S.; Adabi, M.; Adebayo, O.M.; Adekanmbi, V.; Adeyinka, D.A.; et al. Mapping Age- and Sex-Specific HIV Prevalence in Adults in Sub-Saharan Africa, 2000–2018. *BMC Med.* **2022**, *20*, 488. [CrossRef]
27. Deshpande, A.; Miller-Petrie, M.K.; Lindstedt, P.A.; Baumann, M.M.; Johnson, K.B.; Blacker, B.F.; Abbastabar, H.; Abd-Allah, F.; Abdelalim, A.; Abdollahpour, I.; et al. Mapping Geographical Inequalities in Access to Drinking Water and Sanitation Facilities in Low-Income and Middle-Income Countries, 2000–2017. *Lancet Glob. Health* **2020**, *8*, e1162–e1185. [CrossRef]
28. Graetz, N.; Friedman, J.; Osgood-Zimmerman, A.; Burstein, R.; Biehl, M.H.; Shields, C.; Mosser, J.F.; Casey, D.C.; Deshpande, A.; Earl, L.; et al. Mapping Local Variation in Educational Attainment across Africa. *Nature* **2018**, *555*, 48–53. [CrossRef] [PubMed]
29. Carrasco-Escobar, G.; Manrique, E.; Tello-Lizarraga, K.; Miranda, J.J. Travel Time to Health Facilities as a Marker of Geographical Accessibility Across Heterogeneous Land Coverage in Peru. *Front. Public Health* **2020**, *8*, 498. [CrossRef]
30. Chamberlain, H.R.; Lazar, A.N.; Tatem, A.J. High-Resolution Estimates of Social Distancing Feasibility, Mapped for Urban Areas in Sub-Saharan Africa. *Sci. Data* **2022**, *9*, 711. [CrossRef] [PubMed]
31. Bertozzi-Villa, A.; Bever, C.A.; Koenker, H.; Weiss, D.J.; Vargas-Ruiz, C.; Nandi, A.K.; Gibson, H.S.; Harris, J.; Battle, K.E.; Rumisha, S.F.; et al. Maps and Metrics of Insecticide-Treated Net Access, Use, and Nets-per-Capita in Africa from 2000–2020. *Nat. Commun.* **2021**, *12*, 3589. [CrossRef] [PubMed]
32. Unwin, H.J.T.; Mwandigha, L.; Winskill, P.; Ghani, A.C.; Hogan, A.B. Analysis of the Potential for a Malaria Vaccine to Reduce Gaps in Malaria Intervention Coverage. *Malar. J.* **2021**, *20*, 438. [CrossRef]
33. World Health Organization. Health Equity Assessment Toolkit. Available online: https://www.who.int/data/health-equity/assessment_toolkit (accessed on 12 February 2023).

34. Global Health Data Exchange. GHDx. Available online: http://ghdx.healthdata.org/ (accessed on 16 June 2020).
35. WorldPop. WorldPop Dataset. Available online: https://hub.worldpop.org/ (accessed on 20 March 2020).
36. Tatem, A.J. WorldPop, Open Data for Spatial Demography. Available online: https://www.nature.com/articles/sdata20174 (accessed on 17 January 2018).
37. Global Administrative Areas. GADM Maps and Data. v.3.6. Available online: https://gadm.org/ (accessed on 4 December 2018).
38. Wiens, K.E.; Lindstedt, P.A.; Blacker, B.F.; Johnson, K.B.; Baumann, M.M.; Schaeffer, L.E.; Abbastabar, H.; Abd-Allah, F.; Abdelalim, A.; Abdollahpour, I.; et al. Mapping Geographical Inequalities in Oral Rehydration Therapy Coverage in Low-Income and Middle-Income Countries, 2000–2017. *Lancet Glob. Health* **2020**, *8*, e1038–e1060. [CrossRef]
39. Cromwell, E.A.; Schmidt, C.A.; Kwong, K.T.; Pigott, D.M.; Mupfasoni, D.; Biswas, G.; Shirude, S.; Hill, E.; Donkers, K.M.; Abdoli, A.; et al. The Global Distribution of Lymphatic Filariasis, 2000–2018: A Geospatial Analysis. *Lancet Glob. Health* **2020**, *8*, e1186–e1194. [CrossRef]
40. Wallace, A.; Dietz, V.; Cairns, K.L. Integration of Immunization Services with Other Health Interventions in the Developing World: What Works and Why? Systematic Literature Review. *Trop. Med. Int. Health* **2009**, *14*, 11–19. [CrossRef]
41. World Health Organization; United Nations Children's Fund (UNICEF). *Ending Preventable Child Deaths from Pneumonia and Diarrhoea by 2025: The Integrated Global Action Plan for Pneumonia and Diarrhoea (GAPPD)*; World Health Organization: Geneva, Switzerland, 2013; ISBN 978-92-4-150523-9.
42. Olofin, I.; McDonald, C.M.; Ezzati, M.; Flaxman, S.; Black, R.E.; Fawzi, W.W.; Caulfield, L.E.; Danaei, G.; Membership for the Nutrition Impact Model Study (anthropometry cohort pooling). Associations of Suboptimal Growth with All-Cause and Cause-Specific Mortality in Children under Five Years: A Pooled Analysis of Ten Prospective Studies. *PLoS ONE* **2013**, *8*, e64636. [CrossRef]
43. Prendergast, A.J. Malnutrition and Vaccination in Developing Countries. *Phil. Trans. R. Soc. B* **2015**, *370*, 20140141. [CrossRef] [PubMed]
44. Mejía-Guevara, I.; Zuo, W.; Bendavid, E.; Li, N.; Tuljapurkar, S. Age Distribution, Trends, and Forecasts of under-5 Mortality in 31 Sub-Saharan African Countries: A Modeling Study. *PLoS Med.* **2019**, *16*, e1002757. [CrossRef]
45. World Health Organization. *GVIS: Global Immunization Vision and Strategy 2006–2015*; World Health Organization: Geneva, Switzerland, 2005.
46. World Health Organization. *Global Vaccine Action Plan 2011–2020*; World Health Organization: Geneva, Switzerland, 2013.
47. World Health Organization. *Working Together: An Integration Resource Guide for Immunization Services throughout the Life Course*; World Health Organization: Geneva, Switzerland, 2018; ISBN 978-92-4-151473-6.
48. Partapuri, T.; Steinglass, R.; Sequeira, J. Integrated Delivery of Health Services During Outreach Visits: A Literature Review of Program Experience Through a Routine Immunization Lens. *J. Infect. Dis.* **2012**, *205*, S20–S27. [CrossRef]
49. Stevens, G.A.; Alkema, L.; Black, R.E.; Boerma, J.T.; Collins, G.S.; Ezzati, M.; Grove, J.T.; Hogan, D.R.; Hogan, M.C.; Horton, R.; et al. Guidelines for Accurate and Transparent Health Estimates Reporting: The GATHER Statement. *The Lancet* **2016**, *388*, e19–e23. [CrossRef] [PubMed]
50. Faraway, J.J. *Linear Models with R*; Chapman & Hall/CRC Press: Boca Raton, FL, USA, 2004.
51. R Core Team R. A Language and Environment for Statistical Computing. 2022. Available online: https://www.utstat.toronto.edu/~brunner/books/LinearModelsWithR.pdf (accessed on 2 February 2023).
52. Rue, H.; Martino, S.; Chopin, N. Approximate Bayesian Inference for Latent Gaussian Models by Using Integrated Nested Laplace Approximations. *J. R. Stat. Soc. Ser. B (Stat. Methodol.)* **2009**, *71*, 319–392. [CrossRef]

vaccines MDPI

Article

Sociodemographic Factors Associated with COVID-19 Vaccination among People in Guatemalan Municipalities

Rewa Choudhary [1,*], Emily Carter [2], Jose Monzon [3], Allison Stewart [3], Jennifer Slotnick [4], Leslie L. Samayoa Jerez [5], David S. Rodriguez Araujo [6], Emily Zielinski-Gutierrez [3] and Parminder S. Suchdev [3]

1 Epidemic Intelligence Service, Centers for Disease Control and Prevention, Atlanta, GA 30329, USA
2 Division of Global Health Protection, Centers for Disease Control and Prevention, Atlanta, GA 30329, USA
3 Centers for Disease Control and Prevention Central America Regional Office, Guatemala City 01015, Guatemala
4 U.S. Agency for International Development (USAID), Guatemala City 01016, Guatemala
5 Ministerio Salud Publica y Asistencia Social, Guatemala City 01011, Guatemala
6 Council of Ministers of Health of Central America, San Salvador, El Salvador
* Correspondence: nwa5@cdc.gov

Abstract: The Republic of Guatemala's reported COVID-19 vaccination coverage is among the lowest in the Americas and there are limited studies describing the disparities in vaccine uptake within the country. We performed a cross-sectional ecological analysis using multi-level modeling to identify sociodemographic characteristics that were associated with low COVID-19 vaccination coverage among Guatemalan municipalities as of 30 November 2022. Municipalities with a higher proportion of people experiencing poverty ($\beta = -0.25$, 95% CI: -0.43–-0.07) had lower vaccination coverage. Municipalities with a higher proportion of people who had received at least a primary education ($\beta = 0.74$, 95% CI: 0.38–1.08), children ($\beta = 1.07$, 95% CI: 0.36–1.77), people aged 60 years and older ($\beta = 2.94$, 95% CI: 1.70–4.12), and testing for SARS-CoV-2 infection ($\beta = 0.25$, 95% CI: 0.14–0.36) had higher vaccination coverage. In the simplified multivariable model, these factors explained 59.4% of the variation in COVID-19 vaccination coverage. Poverty remained significantly associated with low COVID-19 vaccination coverage in two subanalyses restricting the data to the time period of the highest national COVID-19-related death rate and to COVID-19 vaccination coverage only among those aged 60 years or older. Poverty is a key factor associated with low COVID-19 vaccination and focusing public health interventions in municipalities most affected by poverty may help address COVID-19 vaccination and health disparities in Guatemala.

Keywords: COVID-19 vaccination; Guatemala; equity

Citation: Choudhary, R.; Carter, E.; Monzon, J.; Stewart, A.; Slotnick, J.; Samayoa Jerez, L.L.; Rodriguez Araujo, D.S.; Zielinski-Gutierrez, E.; Suchdev, P.S. Sociodemographic Factors Associated with COVID-19 Vaccination among People in Guatemalan Municipalities. *Vaccines* **2023**, *11*, 745. https://doi.org/10.3390/vaccines11040745

Academic Editors: Ahmad Reza Hosseinpoor, M. Carolina Danovaro, Devaki Nambiar, Aaron Wallace and Hope Johnson

Received: 6 March 2023
Revised: 22 March 2023
Accepted: 25 March 2023
Published: 28 March 2023

1. Introduction

Guatemala has the largest population among Central American countries (over 17 million) and is bordered by Mexico, Belize, Honduras, and El Salvador [1]. While considered an upper-middle-income country due to a GDP of $4603 per capita in 2020 [1], Guatemala has marked inequalities, with wealth held in a small sector of the population, low access to basic services for much of the population, and an overall lack of investment in the public sector [1–3].

Guatemala has the lowest COVID-19 vaccination coverage in Central America and is among the lowest compared with its regional neighbors in South America [4,5]. As of November 2022, there have been over one million SARS-CoV-2 cases and nearly 20,000 COVID-19-related deaths reported in Guatemala [6,7]. Within Guatemala, it was estimated that COVID-19-related mortality has been higher in people aged 60–69 years and in frontline healthcare workers [8]. As part of the National Vaccination Plan Against COVID-19, frontline healthcare workers were prioritized for vaccines when they initially became available in March 2021 [8,9]. In later phases, people aged 50 years and older and those with underlying medical conditions were prioritized [8,9]. Vaccines became available free of charge to the general public in May 2021 [8,9]. Vaccines were obtained through donations, via the COVID-19 Vaccines Global Access (COVAX) mechanism for which Guatemala was a "self-pay" country, and one bilateral purchase of the Sputnik vaccine [9]. To date, there are four COVID-19 vaccines available to Guatemalans and all of them are two-dose primary series courses (Pfizer/BioNTech, Oxford/AstraZeneca, Moderna, and Sputnik V) [10]. As of 30 November 2022, 19,960,793 COVID-19 vaccines had been administered, with 49.4% of the total population having received at least one dose, and approximately seven million people, or 40.0% of the total population, having completed a primary COVID-19 vaccination series with two doses [4,6,7,10]. Of those who had completed a primary vaccination series, 42.8% had received Moderna, 23.0% received Oxford/AstraZeneca, 18.4% received Sputnik V, and 15.9% had received Pfizer/BioNTech vaccines [11]. In addition, about four million people, or 24.0% of the population, had received one or two booster doses by 30 November 2022 [12].

The inequity in the global distribution of COVID-19 vaccines with preferential access for countries with higher per capita incomes and gross domestic products has been well-documented [13–15]. However, there are limited studies describing COVID-19 vaccination disparities within low- and middle-income countries, and many focus on vaccination intent. Studies that have explored sociodemographic factors associated with COVID-19 vaccination coverage have primarily focused on the United States. One survey conducted among U.S. adults found that participants with lower incomes, lower educational attainments, those without health insurance, who were non-Hispanic Black, and who lived outside of metropolitan areas had the lowest reported COVID-19 vaccination coverage and intent to get vaccinated [16]. Two other analyses showed that vaccination coverage was lower in rural compared with urban U.S. counties [17], and lower in counties with a higher percentage of people with incomes below the poverty threshold, experiencing unemployment, and not graduating from high school [18].

Several reasons have been posited for the low COVID-19 vaccination coverage in Guatemala. The country faces multiple challenges in its healthcare and public health system such as inadequate financing of the health sector, disparities in access to public health services in rural areas, and a shortage of healthcare workers [19,20]. COVID-19 vaccination coverage has been highest in the capital, Guatemala City, while rural areas with higher concentrations of Indigenous people have had lower vaccination coverage [5,21]. In the 2018 census, the Maya comprised 41.7% of the total population, and the Xinca were 1.8% of the total population [22]. The disproportionate burden of COVID-19 on Indigenous people and those of low socioeconomic status has been studied regionally, for instance, in Colombia [23]. A 2021 UNESCO report on COVID-19 vaccination in Latin America and the Caribbean noted that in communities with higher "unemployment or informal employment, or where ethnic groups live, there is a higher prevalence of COVID-19 and a higher risk of mortality" [24]. Moreover, there is evidence of vaccine hesitancy among people with lower levels of institutional trust, those living in rural areas, and those experiencing economic insecurity [25–27]. Early vaccination outreach in Guatemala was often conducted in Spanish using mainstream media instead of through local organizations, and using local Indigenous languages, according to a Pan American Health Organization report [5]. As part of the Ministry of Public Health and Social Assistance (MSPAS) *Strategy to Strengthen the COVID-19 Vaccination Plan in Rural Areas*, vaccination activities have more recently incorporated community leader guidance and local media campaigns [28].

Given the limited studies describing COVID-19 vaccination coverage disparities within Guatemala, we performed an ecological analysis to understand the association between sociodemographic factors and primary vaccination coverage among the 340 Guatemalan municipalities. Identifying factors associated with low vaccination could inform strategies to improve COVID-19 vaccine coverage and other public health interventions in Guatemala.

2. Materials and Methods

We performed a cross-sectional analysis of aggregated COVID-19 vaccination coverage data in Guatemala from 13 February 2020 to 30 November 2022. As the lowest level of data availability was at the municipal level, we conducted an ecological analysis of factors associated with primary COVID-19 vaccine series' coverage by municipality.

Sociodemographic data variables at the municipal level were obtained through the 2018 Guatemala Population and Housing Census (Table 1) [22]. Municipalities are organized into 22 departments, and some variables only available at the departmental level were obtained through the 2014–2015 Demographic and Health Survey [29]. We chose sociodemographic variables *a priori* that could be proxies for healthcare access, poverty, and related variables that we hypothesized to be related to vaccination uptake [30–32]. We elected to use the general poverty indicator (percentage of each municipality population experiencing poverty) developed by Figueroa Chávez and colleagues and shared with our team [33]. Figueroa Chávez and colleagues developed the general poverty indicator by using the associations between sociodemographic variables in the 2018 Census and the poverty measure in the 2014 National Survey of Living Conditions [34] to estimate poverty at the municipality level [35]. According to their findings, the general poverty indicator ranged from 10.56% in the Jocotenango municipality in Sacatepéquez, to 94.59% in the Senahú municipality in Alta Verapaz [35]. COVID-19 vaccination data differentiated by municipality, department, and age were available at the MSPAS of Guatemala surveillance websites from 25 February 2021 to 30 November 2022 [11,12]. SARS-CoV-2 testing data (either antigen or polymerase chain reaction tests) and death data were also available through MSPAS from 13 February 2020 to 30 November 2022 [11]. A completed primary COVID-19 vaccination course was considered to be two doses of any of the four nationally available vaccines among people aged six years and older, consistent with current national guidelines [11]. The data used in this study were all de-identified, aggregated, and, with the exception of the general poverty indicator, publicly available.

Table 1. Data elements used in the analysis.

Variable	Source
Total municipality population	2018 Guatemala Population and Housing Census
Female sex population in the municipality	2018 Guatemala Population and Housing Census
Population aged 0–17 years in municipality	2018 Guatemala Population and Housing Census
Population aged 18–59 years in municipality	2018 Guatemala Population and Housing Census
Population aged 60 years or older in municipality	2018 Guatemala Population and Housing Census
Ethnicity identification in the municipality	2018 Guatemala Population and Housing Census
Population in a municipality having received at least primary school education	2018 Guatemala Population and Housing Census
Population in municipality with household in a rural location	2018 Guatemala Population and Housing Census
Population in municipality experiencing poverty	Figueroa Chavez et al., 2020 [30]
Department-level childhood mortality rate (deaths per 1000 livebirths) among children aged under five years	2014–2015 Demographic and Health Survey
Percentage of women aged 15–49 years in department who reported having problems accessing health services when ill due to distance to a health establishment	2014–2015 Demographic and Health Survey
Percent of children aged 12–23 months in the department who have received the third Pentavalent vaccine dose	2014–2015 Demographic and Health Survey
Department Gini coefficient (%)	2014–2015 Demographic and Health Survey
SARS-CoV-2 vaccination status among the municipality population aged six years or older (incomplete, complete, one booster dose, two booster doses)	Ministry of Public Health and Social Assistance (MSPAS) of Guatemala, 2021–2022
Municipality population aged 60 years or older with completed SARS-CoV-2 primary vaccination course	Ministry of Public Health and Social Assistance (MSPAS) of Guatemala, 2021–2022
SARS-CoV-2 tests reported per municipal population.	Ministry of Public Health and Social Assistance (MSPAS) of Guatemala, 2020–2022
Deaths due to COVID-19 among the municipality population	Ministry of Public Health and Social Assistance (MSPAS) of Guatemala, 2020–2022

Municipal-level independent variables included in the model were the percentage of each municipality population reported to be of Mayan ethnicity, living in a rural residence, of the female sex, having attained primary school or higher educational level, experiencing poverty, aged 0–17 years or ≥60 years, and having died due to COVID-19 (Table 1). The reported number of SARS-CoV-2 tests by municipality was an additional independent variable. Independent variables at the departmental level included the under-five childhood mortality rate, the percentage of women aged 15–49 years who reported problems accessing health services when ill due to distance to a health establishment, the percentage of children aged 12–23 months who had received a third dose of Pentavalent vaccine (a combination vaccine against diphtheria, tetanus, pertussis, hepatitis B, and *Haemophilus influenzae* type b), and the Gini coefficient indicating income inequality. The dependent variable was the percent coverage of each municipality population with a complete primary COVID-19 vaccination course. Proportions of municipalities with completed COVID-19 vaccination and SARS-CoV-2 tests exceeding 100.0% (as total population estimates were from 2018) were capped at 99.0%. Given that the proportion of the population that died from COVID-19 by municipality was relatively small, the variable was scaled by 100 in the model to achieve a similar order of magnitude to the other variables.

Two subanalyses were also performed to assess whether the demographic associations with vaccination in the overall model were consistent among the subgroups. In the first, the dependent variable was limited to the population aged 60 years or older who had completed COVID-19 vaccination. We chose this subgroup given the initial national focus on vaccinating older adults. In the second subanalysis, the SARS-CoV-2 cases and COVID-19 vaccination data were confined to the period of the highest national COVID-19-related death rate, from 13 February 2020 to 1 October 2021 [6]. All count variables (derived from the census and the MSPAS) were converted to percentages to account for differences in municipal total populations. Data on deaths due to COVID-19 were missing for four municipalities (San Juan Tecuaco, Santa Rosa; Concepción, Sololá; Santa Catarina Palopó, Sololá; Río Blanco, San Marcos) and were removed from the multivariable models.

We calculated descriptive statistics for sociodemographic characteristics among municipalities and departments. We used Pearson correlation coefficients and variance inflation factors to assess potential collinearity within our model. The poverty indicator used in our analysis was developed using some of the variables included in our model, however, these common variables were not heavily weighted in the poverty index [33,35]. As this was the most robust measure of poverty by municipality despite potential collinearity, we performed a sensitivity analysis of the model without the poverty indicator and found similar results and chose to retain this variable (Supplementary Table S1). We identified municipalities with high Indigenous populations, rurality, and poverty who achieved a COVID-19 vaccination coverage of at least 70%, according to World Health Organization (WHO) guidelines [36]. We assessed relationships between municipal- and departmental-level factors and COVID-19 vaccination using multi-level modeling, allowing for random department-level intercepts to account for differences between departments. The model results were robust to different specifications of the underlying error distribution. A multi-level linear regression model was selected to maximize both model fit and interpretability. All variables were included in the full multivariable model, and those variables with associations significant at $p < 0.05$ were included in the simplified multivariable model. We used a normal approximation of a 1000 replicate parametric bootstrap to generate our 95% confidence intervals and present both the marginal R^2 (representing the proportion of the variance explained by the model-fixed effects) and conditional R^2 (representing the proportion of the variance explained by both the fixed and random effects) for each model. All analyses were performed using R Statistical Software (v.4.2.2; Vienna, Austria) [37]. We hypothesized, based on our literature review, that COVID-19 vaccination would be negatively associated with higher poverty, rurality, and Indigenous population.

3. Results

3.1. Demographic Data

Among the 340 municipalities, as of 30 November 2022, 7.05 million persons had completed a primary COVID-19 vaccine course. The median proportion of vaccination coverage among people aged at least six years in the municipalities was 42.3% (interquartile range, IQR, 31.8–53.8%) (Table 2). The median proportion of the female sex among municipalities was 51.3% (IQR 50.6–52.2%). The median proportion of the population aged 60 years or older among all municipalities was 7.8% (IQR 6.9–9.3%), and the median proportion of those identifying as Maya was 30.0% (IQR 2.9–91.4%). Four out of 151 majority Maya municipalities, San José Chacayá, Santa Catarina Barahona, Chimaltenango, and San Lorenzo, had at least 70% of their populations who had completed COVID-19 vaccination, and this relationship was inversely correlated ($\rho = -0.299$, $p < 0.001$) (Figure 1A). Guatemala, Mixco, Jocotenango, and San Lucas Sacatepéquez municipalities had the highest proportion of their populations (≥40%) who had received at least a primary school education. The median proportion of rural residence among all municipalities was 64.8% (IQR 37.1–82.7%), with an inverse correlation ($\rho = -0.417$, $p < 0.001$) with COVID-19 vaccination coverage (Figure 1B). The median proportion of people experiencing poverty among the municipalities was 60.8% (IQR 43.8–75.8%), with an inverse correlation with COVID-19 vaccination ($\rho = -0.634$, $p < 0.001$) (Figure 1C). Overall, the municipalities with the highest COVID-19 vaccination coverage were Guatemala, San José, and San José del Golfo. By November 2022, 23 municipalities had completed primary series vaccination in at least 70% of their populations (Figure 2). Additional summarizing demographic data among the municipalities are shown in Table 2.

3.2. Factors Associated with COVID-19 Vaccination

In the bivariate analysis of all COVID-19 vaccination data as of 30 November 2022, significant factors ($\alpha = 0.05$) negatively associated with primary COVID-19 vaccination course coverage by municipality, adjusting for departmental level differences, included the proportion of the municipality identifying as Mayan ($\beta = -0.15$, 95% CI: −0.21–−0.10), the proportion of the municipality living in a rural residence ($\beta = -0.19$, 95% CI: −0.25–−0.13), the proportion of the municipality experiencing poverty ($\beta = -0.54$, 95% CI: −0.63–−0.46), the proportion of the municipality in the 0–17 years age group ($\beta = -1.81$, 95% CI: −2.16–−1.47), departmental-level under-five childhood mortality rate ($\beta = -0.09$, 95% CI: −0.46–0.27), the proportion of those in the department reporting difficulty accessing healthcare due to distance from a health facility ($\beta = -0.82$, 95% CI: −1.12–−0.53), and the department's Gini coefficient ($\beta = -0.62$, 95% CI: −1.20–−0.08) (Table 3).

Factors positively associated with primary COVID-19 vaccination series coverage by municipality, adjusting for departmental level differences, included the proportion of the municipality with at least a primary school education ($\beta = 1.40$, 95% CI: 1.18–1.62), the proportion of female sex in the municipality ($\beta = 2.53$, 95% CI: 1.02–4.03), proportion of the municipality in the 60 years and older age group ($\beta = 4.54$, 95% CI: 3.57–5.49), proportion of the municipality tested for SARS-CoV-2 infection ($\beta = 0.52$, 95% CI: 0.43–0.61), reported deaths due to COVID-19 in the municipality ($\beta = 1.17$, 95% CI: 0.94–1.41), and proportion of 12–23 months old children in the department who had received the third Pentavalent vaccine ($\beta = 0.65$, 95% CI: 0.20–1.11).

After adjusting for all covariates and departmental effects in the full model, the proportions of the municipal population who (1) had received at least a primary school education, (2) were experiencing poverty, (3) were below the age of 18 years, (4) were aged 60 years and above, and (5) tested for SARS-CoV-2 remained significantly associated with complete vaccination coverage (Table 3, Section "Full multivariable model"). In the simplified multivariable model (Table 3, Section "Simplified multivariable model"), when adjusting for covariates and departmental level differences, a 10% higher proportion of people experiencing poverty within a municipality was associated with 2.5% lower COVID-19 vaccination coverage (95% CI: −4.33–−0.70). Conversely, a 10% increase in the proportion of the municipality having received at least a primary school education was associated with 7.4% higher COVID-19 vaccination coverage (95% CI: 3.83–10.75); a 10% increase in the proportion of the municipality aged <18 years was associated with 10.7% higher COVID-19 vaccination coverage (95% CI: 3.55–17.67); a 10% increase in the proportion of the municipality in the 60 years and older age group was associated with 29.4% higher COVID-19 vaccination coverage (95% CI: 17.00–41.21); and a 10% higher proportion of the municipality tested for SARS-CoV-2 infection was associated with a 2.5% higher COVID-19 vaccination coverage (95% CI: 1.37–3.55). Overall, the marginal R^2 value was 0.496, and the conditional R^2 value accounting for the covariates and departmental-level differences was 0.594.

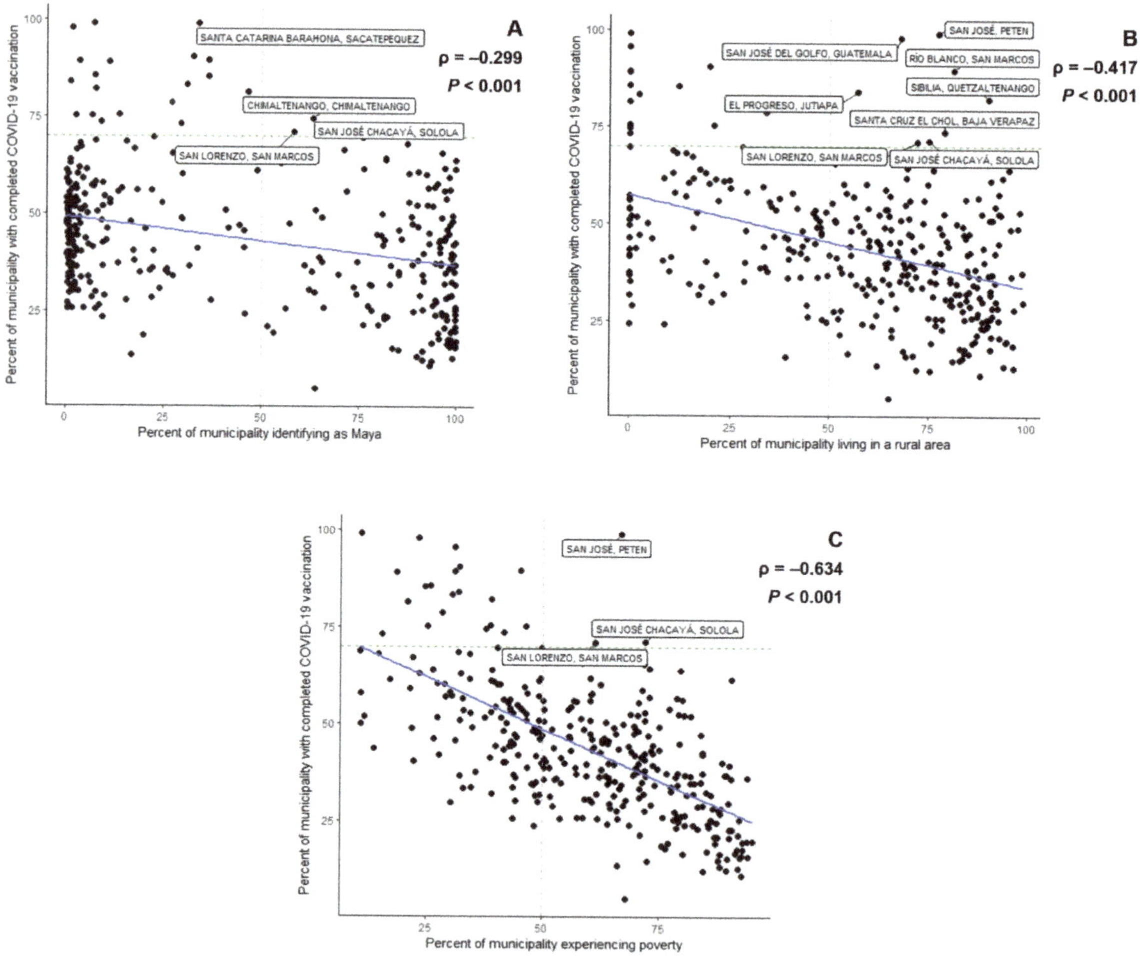

Figure 1. Guatemalan municipalities by percent of primary COVID-19 vaccination series coverage versus (**A**) percent of municipality population of Mayan identity, (**B**) percent of municipality population living in a rural area, and (**C**) percent of municipality population experiencing poverty. Labeled municipalities are those with >70% completed COVID-19 vaccination (green dashed line) and >50% of the Mayan population (**A**), rural residence (**B**), or people experiencing poverty (**C**) (gray dashed line).

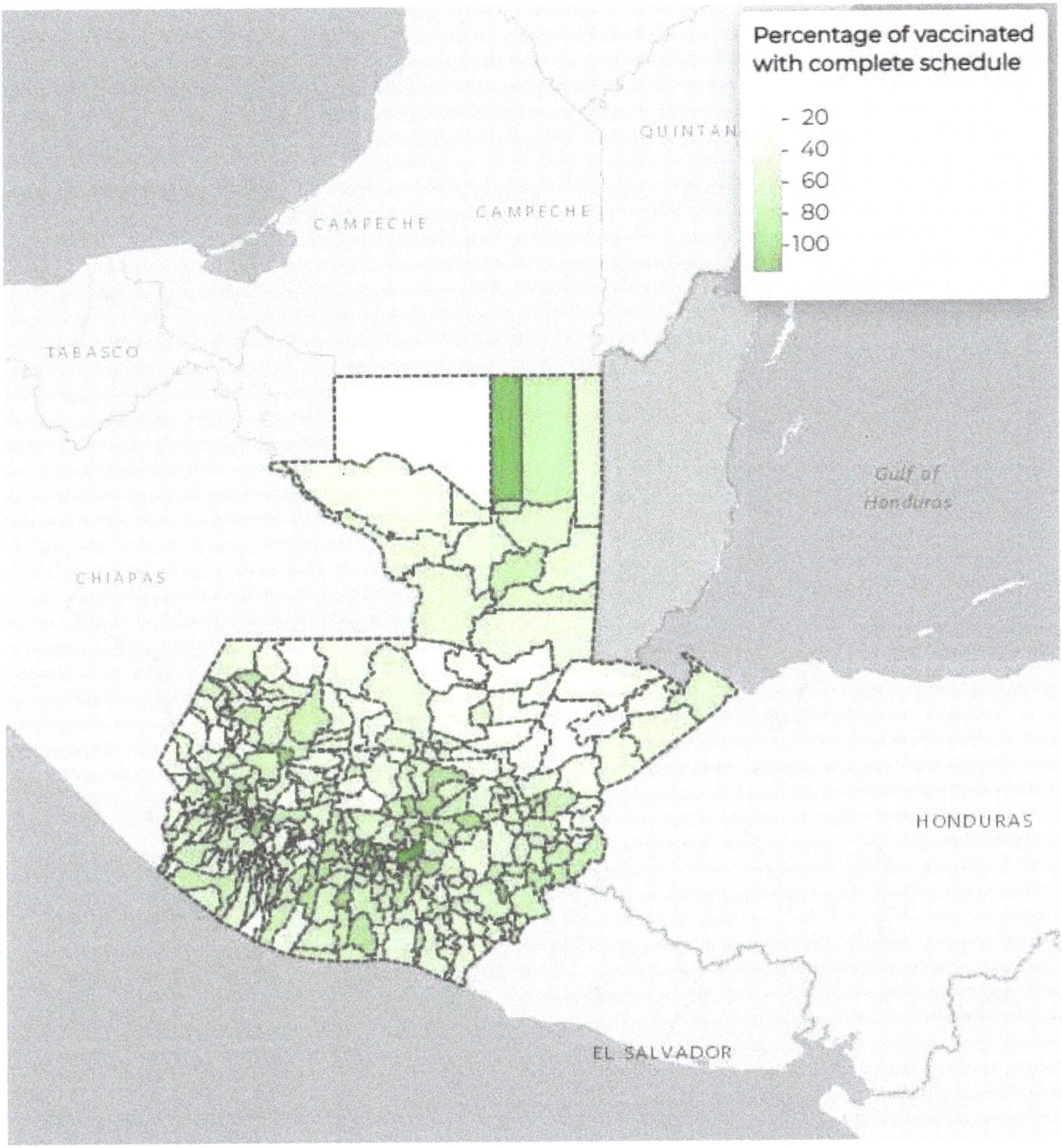

Figure 2. Primary COVID-19 vaccination series coverage by municipality in Guatemala. Image adapted from Guatemala Ministry of Health and Social Assistance, 25 February 2021 to 30 November 2022 [11].

Table 2. Demographic characteristics among the 340 municipalities and 22 departments in Guatemala. Data source: Guatemala Population and Housing Census 2018, 2014–2015 Demographic and Health Survey, and Guatemala Ministry of Health and Social Assistance. The poverty variable is a model estimate from Figueroa Chávez et al. (2020) [33,35]. SARS-CoV-2 cases and vaccination data are from 13 February 2020 to 30 November 2022, except where indicated.

Municipality Characteristic	N Median (IQR)	% [a] Median (IQR)
Population	28,156.5 (15,730.8–51,426.0)	-
Female sex	14,580.0 (8067.3–27,052.3)	51.3 (50.6–52.2)
Age group (years)		
0–17	11,599.5 (6227.3–21,980.8)	40.8 (37.4–45.3)
18–59	14,131.0 (7891.3–25,263.5)	51.1 (48.0–53.4)
≥60	2226.0 (1321.0–3797.8)	7.8 (6.9–9.3)
Ethnicity		
Maya	7129.0 (1008.8–25,847.5)	30.0 (2.9–91.4)
Garifuna	25.0 (13.0–50.8)	0.1 (0.1–0.1)
Xinka	4.0 (1.0–16.0)	0.0 (0.0–0.1)
Latino(a)	11,362.5 (2463.0–26,008.5)	63.7 (8.2–93.5)
Educational level primary school and above	18,065.0 (10,058.5–32,712.8)	74.4 (68.5–78.9)
Household rural location	13,458.5 (6260.5–28,052.5)	64.8 (37.1–82.7)
People experiencing poverty	16,086.0 (7909.0–30,343.5)	60.8 (43.8–75.8)
SARS-CoV-2 vaccination status		
Vaccine eligible population (≥6 years)	27,156.0 (15,180.3–50,978.5)	-
Incomplete	13,853.5 (7890.8–23,373.3)	53.0 (43.0–66.6)
Complete	10,633.5 (6286.3–18,466.8)	42.3 (31.8–53.8)
One booster dose	4813.0 (2887.5–8097.5)	18.8 (13.1–27.0)
Two booster doses	385.5 (183.8–952.0)	1.7 (0.9–3.0)
MSPAS [b] SARS-CoV-2 indicators		
Confirmed cases	917.5 (442.0–1899.8)	3.0 (1.7–5.4)
Tests reported	5248.5 (2798.0–10,824.5)	19.4 (10.7–28.6)
Deaths due to COVID-19	20.0 (10.0–38.0)	0.07 (0.0–0.1)
People aged 60 or more years with complete vaccination	1173.5 (733.8–2071.0)	53.0 (41.5–66.9)
Measures as of 1 October 2021		
Complete vaccination	3160.5 (1918.0–5897.8)	13.1 (8.5–19.6)
Tests reported	2129.0 (966.5–4492.8)	7.9 (4.5–12.4)
Deaths due to COVID-19	16.5 (8.0–30.8)	5.6 (3.2–9.5)
Departmental Characteristic		**% Median (IQR)**
Under-5 childhood mortality rate (deaths per 1000 live births)		37.0 (31.0–42.5)
Difficult access to healthcare facilities due to distance		38.6 (33.8–46.9)
12–23 months old children receiving third Pentavalent vaccine		86.9 (82.0–90.4)
Gini coefficient		30.0 (30.0–40.0)

[a] Proportion derived by dividing by total population as provided by respective data source. [b] Ministry of Public Health and Social Assistance.

3.3. Factors Associated with COVID-19 Vaccination among People Aged 60 Years or Older

Nationally, 61.9% of those aged 60 years or older had completed COVID-19 vaccination by 30 November 2022 [12]. In the analysis of this subgroup, significant factors ($\alpha = 0.05$) in the bivariate model negatively associated with COVID-19 vaccination, adjusting for departmental level differences, were similar to the overall analysis and included the proportion of the municipality identifying as Mayan, the proportion living in a rural residence, and the proportion experiencing poverty, but did not include the departmental-level under-five childhood mortality rate and the department's Gini coefficient (Table 4). Factors positively associated in the bivariate model were the same as in the overall analysis.

After adjusting for all covariates and departmental effects in the full model, the proportions of the municipal population (1) living in a rural residence, (2) having received at least a primary school education, (3) experiencing poverty, (4) of female sex and (5) tested for SARS-CoV-2 remained significantly associated with complete vaccination coverage (Table 4, Section "Full multivariable model"). In the simplified multivariable model (Table 4, Section "Simplified multivariable model"), when adjusting for covariates and departmental level differences, a 10% higher proportion of people experiencing poverty within a municipality was associated with 2.0% lower complete COVID-19 vaccination coverage (95% CI: −3.79–−0.28). A 10% increase in the proportion of the municipality living in a rural residence was associated with a 0.9% higher COVID-19 vaccination coverage (95% CI: 0.27–1.59); having received at least a primary school education was associated with 9.8% higher COVID-19 vaccination coverage (95% CI: 5.66–13.72); a 10% increase in the proportion of the municipality of female sex was associated with 20.6% higher COVID-19 vaccination coverage (95% CI: 6.39–34.51); and a 10% higher proportion of the municipality tested for SARS-CoV-2 infection was associated with a 3.1% higher COVID-19 vaccination coverage (95% CI: 1.90–4.37). The marginal R^2 value was 0.487, and the conditional R^2 value accounting for the covariates and departmental-level differences was 0.600.

3.4. Factors Associated with COVID-19 Vaccination up to 1 October 2021

As of 1 October 2021, immediately after the peak of COVID-19-related deaths in Guatemala, 2.58 million persons (15.1% of the total population) had completed a primary COVID-19 vaccine course [11]. In the bivariate analysis of all COVID-19 vaccination data up to 1 October 2021, significant factors negatively associated with COVID-19 vaccination coverage by municipality ($\alpha = 0.05$), adjusting for departmental level differences, were similar to the overall analysis and included the proportion of the municipality identifying as Mayan, the proportion living in a rural residence, and proportion experiencing poverty, but did not include the departmental-level under-five childhood mortality rate and the department's Gini coefficient (Table 5). Factors positively associated in the bivariate model were the same as in the overall analysis.

After adjusting for all covariates and departmental effects in the full model, the proportion of the municipal population (1) having received at least a primary school education, (2) experiencing poverty, (3) aged 60 and above, and (4) tested for SARS-CoV-2 remained significantly associated with complete vaccination coverage (Table 5, Section "Full multivariable model"). In the simplified multivariable model (Table 5, Section "Simplified multivariable model"), when adjusting for covariates and departmental level differences, a 10% higher proportion of people experiencing poverty within a municipality was associated with 1.1% lower COVID-19 vaccination coverage (95% CI: −1.90–−0.39); a 10% increase in the proportion of the municipality having received at least a primary school education was associated with 1.6% higher COVID-19 vaccination coverage (95% CI: −0.12–3.28); a 10% increase in the proportion of the municipality in the 60 years and older age group was associated with 13.9% higher COVID-19 vaccination coverage (95% CI: 8.93–18.73); and a 10% higher proportion of the municipality tested for SARS-CoV-2 infection was associated with a 2.6% higher COVID-19 vaccination coverage (95% CI: 1.46–3.80) (conditional $R^2 = 0.615$).

Table 3. Association between sociodemographic factors (by municipalities and departments) and two-dose vaccination coverage (%) by municipalities in Guatemala (N = 336). SARS-CoV-2 case and vaccination data are from 13 February 2020 to 30 November 2022.

	Bivariate Model					Full Multivariable Model					Simplified Multivariable Model				
	Coefficient	95% Confidence Interval		Marginal R^2	Conditional R^2	Coefficient	95% Confidence Interval		Marginal R^2	Conditional R^2	Coefficient	95% Confidence Interval		Marginal R^2	Conditional R^2
Null multi-level model	43.766	39.645	47.949	0.000	0.239										
Municipal level variables															
% Mayan	−0.151	−0.206	−0.095	0.120	0.342	0.048	−0.008	0.105			-	-	-		
% Rural residence	−0.188	−0.251	−0.127	0.111	0.246	0.005	−0.061	0.068			-	-	-		
% Educational level primary school or above	1.400	1.184	1.616	0.400	0.451	0.894	0.534	1.259			0.736	0.383	1.075		
% Experiencing poverty	−0.542	−0.625	−0.460	0.405	0.462	−0.216	−0.409	−0.026			−0.249	−0.433	−0.070		
% Female sex	2.527	1.022	4.026	0.036	0.281	1.239	−0.210	2.662			-	-	-		
% in 0–17 age group	−1.813	−2.158	−1.470	0.296	0.388	0.999	0.296	1.714	0.523	0.581	1.065	0.355	1.767	0.496	0.594
% in 60 or older age group	4.538	3.566	5.485	0.218	0.412	2.552	1.299	3.862			2.935	1.700	4.121		
% tested for SARS-CoV-2	0.521	0.431	0.613	0.314	0.460	0.215	0.085	0.344			0.246	0.137	0.355		
% died due to COVID-19	1.171	0.939	1.406	0.249	0.406	0.162	-0.148	0.463			-	-	-		
Departmental level variables															
Under-5 childhood mortality rate	−0.087	−0.461	0.268	0.003	0.249	0.199	−0.035	0.424			-	-	-		
% reporting difficulty accessing healthcare facilities due to distance	−0.822	−1.121	−0.532	0.176	0.249	−0.053	−0.447	0.338			-	-	-		
% 12–23 month olds receiving third Pentavalent vaccine	0.653	0.201	1.106	0.073	0.244	0.111	−0.273	0.496			-	-	-		
Gini coefficient	−0.619	−1.195	−0.084	0.052	0.245	−0.145	−0.594	0.298			-	-	-		

Table 4. Association between sociodemographic factors (by municipalities and departments) and two-dose vaccination coverage (%) among patients aged 60 years or older by municipalities in Guatemala (N = 336). SARS-CoV-2 case and vaccination data are from 13 February 2020 to 30 November 2022.

	Bivariate Model					Full Multivariable Model					Simplified Multivariable Model				
	Coefficient	95% Confidence Interval		Marginal R^2	Conditional R^2	Coefficient	95% Confidence Interval		Marginal R^2	Conditional R^2	Coefficient	95% Confidence Interval		Marginal R^2	Conditional R^2
Null multi-level model	55.119	50.395	59.914	0.000	0.246										
Municipal level variables															
% Mayan	−0.205	−0.268	−0.143	0.162	0.415	−0.016	−0.080	0.050			-	-	-		
% Rural residence	−0.181	−0.253	−0.112	0.079	0.241	0.097	0.027	0.165			0.094	0.027	0.159		
% Educational level primary school or above	1.649	1.394	1.903	0.409	0.513	0.965	0.558	1.377			0.978	0.566	1.372		
% Experiencing poverty	−0.638	−0.736	−0.542	0.411	0.526	−0.206	−0.392	−0.025			−0.201	−0.379	−0.028		
% Female sex	2.370	0.662	4.073	0.025	0.269	1.887	0.250	3.504	0.477	0.615	2.057	0.639	3.451	0.487	0.600
% tested for SARS-CoV-2	0.595	0.492	0.699	0.310	0.484	0.301	0.151	0.451			0.314	0.190	0.437		
% died due to COVID-19	1.271	1.003	1.543	0.213	0.441	0.037	−0.318	0.385			-	-	-		
Departmental level variables															
Under-5 childhood mortality rate	−0.141	−0.568	0.263	0.006	0.256	0.241	−0.129	0.597			-	-	-		
% reporting difficulty accessing healthcare facilities due to distance	−0.824	−1.215	−0.445	0.138	0.251	0.265	−0.355	0.881			-	-	-		
% 12–23 month olds receiving third Pentavalent vaccine	0.641	0.099	1.181	0.055	0.252	0.147	−0.449	0.743			-	-	-		
Gini coefficient	−0.817	−1.447	−0.232	0.070	0.247	−0.475	−1.174	0.209			-	-	-		

Table 5. Association between sociodemographic factors (by municipalities and departments) and two-dose vaccination coverage (%) by municipalities in Guatemala (N = 336). SARS-CoV-2 case and vaccination data are from 13 February 2020 to 1 October 2021.

	Bivariate Model					Full Multivariable Model					Simplified Multivariable Model				
	Coefficient	95% Confidence Interval		Marginal R^2	Conditional R^2	Coefficient	95% Confidence Interval		Marginal R^2	Conditional R^2	Coefficient	95% Confidence Interval		Marginal R^2	Conditional R^2
Null multi-level model	15.205	13.290	17.150	0.000	0.183										
Municipal level variables															
% Mayan	−0.091	−0.118	−0.063	0.166	0.307	0.023	−0.005	0.051			-	-	-		
% Rural residence	−0.106	−0.138	−0.074	0.130	0.223	0.001	−0.032	0.032			-	-	-		
% Educational level primary school or above	0.715	0.601	0.829	0.384	0.438	0.230	0.049	0.413			0.161	−0.012	0.328		
% Experiencing poverty	−0.308	−0.350	−0.266	0.467	0.521	−0.174	−0.271	−0.079			−0.113	−0.190	−0.039		
% Female sex	1.039	0.246	1.829	0.023	0.225	−0.022	−0.752	0.695			-	-	-		
% in 0–17 age group	−1.094	−1.259	−0.931	0.395	0.441	0.332	−0.020	0.691	0.550	0.615	-	-	-	0.546	0.615
% in 60 or older age group	2.832	2.351	3.301	0.315	0.450	1.679	1.053	2.335			1.393	0.893	1.873		
% tested for SARS-CoV-2	0.621	0.521	0.722	0.358	0.455	0.203	0.063	0.341			0.262	0.146	0.380		
% died due to COVID-19	0.784	0.646	0.923	0.304	0.397	0.140	-0.048	0.323			-	-	-		
Departmental level variables															
Under-5 childhood mortality rate	−0.056	−0.230	0.108	0.005	0.193	0.073	−0.051	0.192			-	-	-		
% reporting difficulty accessing healthcare facilities due to distance	−0.376	−0.518	−0.239	0.140	0.194	−0.011	−0.220	0.197			-	-	-		
% 12–23 month olds receiving third Pentavalent vaccine	0.290	0.080	0.501	0.056	0.180	−0.015	−0.218	0.188			-	-	-		
Gini coefficient	−0.137	−0.427	0.132	0.010	0.190	0.106	−0.132	0.339			-	-	-		

4. Discussion

In this cross-sectional analysis of COVID-19 vaccination coverage among Guatemalan municipalities, we provide population-level information on sociodemographic and health system variables associated with vaccination. In the adjusted multi-level model evaluating vaccination data as of 30 November 2022, municipalities with higher proportions of people experiencing poverty had lower COVID-19 vaccination coverage. Municipalities with higher proportions of people who had received at least a primary school education, children, people aged 60 years or older, and testing for SARS-CoV-2 infection had higher COVID-19 vaccination coverage. In our subanalyses, the timing of the country's response to the pandemic did not appear to notably affect the results, as factors associated with vaccination coverage in the overall model were similar to the point at which Guatemala had just passed its highest daily death rate. Additionally, poverty, educational level, and prevalence of testing for SARS-CoV-2 infection remained significant factors associated with COVID-19 vaccination coverage among Guatemalans aged ≥60 years.

Our findings are generally consistent with those from previous studies. Prior studies have largely focused on factors related to the intent to vaccinate rather than the completion of COVID-19 vaccination. A 2022 global, population-based analysis noted that participants identifying as female, in older age groups, with a higher level of education, and with health insurance reported being more willing to get vaccinated [32]. In a study of Latin American and Caribbean countries, those with a university education, residence in an urban area, and a higher perceived likelihood of contracting COVID-19 had higher intentions to be vaccinated [31]. With regards to age, our model showed that municipalities with more children and people aged 60 years or older had higher vaccine coverage when adjusting for other covariates and variations at the departmental level. This is expected given that older populations were prioritized under national vaccination planning given their elevated risk of severe COVID-19 [8]. The role of children is less clear, especially as vaccines for children under 12 years of age only became available in 2022, and there are no vaccines for children under six years of age at the time of analysis [38]. Possibly, concern over the well-being of children motivated parents' vaccination, or that when vaccines were available for children, other family members were also vaccinated. The role of children in the community could be an area of further investigation.

It is also expected that municipalities with more SARS-CoV-2 testing had a higher proportion of the population that was vaccinated for COVID-19 as these municipalities may have more access to health facilities or services. The MSPAS provided free testing to people with symptoms or to those who were COVID-19 contacts, however, these services were generally offered at health facilities that were not always accessible to rural populations [9,21,39]. It is possible that the presence of more testing resources could positively influence individuals to receive COVID-19 vaccinations. This would support public health interventions, such as making SARS-CoV-2 testing more accessible in rural areas through mobile health units. In our model, higher proportions of deaths due to COVID-19 in the municipalities were not significantly associated with increased vaccination. While Guatemala has reported less excess mortality compared with other countries within the region [40], the excess mortality was found to be 46% higher compared with confirmed COVID-19 death counts, according to a study by Martinez-Folgar and colleagues [41], indicating that mortality and case estimates are likely underestimated, which may have affected our analysis. Moreover, their study showed that most deaths appeared to occur at home, further highlighting barriers to healthcare access that are likely reflected in low COVID-19 vaccination coverage and possibly higher mortality.

In unadjusted models, we observed significant associations between lower COVID-19 vaccination coverage and Indigenous identity, rural residence, poverty, and self-reported difficulty accessing healthcare. In the adjusted model, of these sociodemographic variables, only the proportion of the municipality experiencing poverty remained negatively associated with vaccination coverage. It is possible that poverty partially explains the observed associations between COVID-19 vaccination and other sociodemographic variables, such as Indigenous identity, rurality, and healthcare access. We found a few municipalities with high rurality and Indigenous populations that reached at least 70% vaccination coverage. There were only three municipalities with 50% or more of their population experiencing poverty that reached 70% vaccination coverage. Poverty remained significantly associated with low vaccination coverage when the analysis was restricted to the time that COVID-19 deaths peaked, or to coverage among those aged 60 years or older. Even as the risk of mortality due to COVID-19 has been shown to be higher among those in the lowest socioeconomic strata [23], there is evidence that economic insecurity was associated with fear of adverse effects from the vaccine in Latin America [27]. Additionally, the monetary and opportunity costs of accessing vaccination sites, missing work, arranging childcare, etc., have been described as potential barriers to vaccine access [5,21]. Therefore, while Indigenous and rural communities are at a higher risk for low vaccine access, it may be particularly effective to use poverty indices when designing community-wide vaccination interventions in Guatemalan municipalities, and to focus on interventions such as transportation, childcare, and alternative hours of service that can overcome cost-related barriers. Further, research to better understand the structural determinants of poverty, including class, gender, and race, can help guide future interventions [42]. Additional research on the monetary and opportunity costs of accessing vaccination within Guatemala may be needed. Lastly, outreach specifically to areas with lower access to primary school education and vaccination programming that accommodates potential literacy issues may be considered.

There are limitations to this study which should be considered. Our analysis was conducted at the municipal level as we did not have access to community estimates or individual-level data that could possibly provide more complex explanations of low vaccination coverage among certain sociodemographic groups. Our conclusions at the population level may not be applicable to specific sociodemographic groups within municipalities. Secondly, factors such as poverty, Indigenous identity, and rurality are complex and interrelated, and it is difficult to assess their relationship to vaccination and healthcare access in isolation. The proxies we used for healthcare access, such as testing for SARS-CoV-2 infections and vaccination program reach, such as childhood Pentavalent vaccination coverage, may not capture the intricacies of the political, economic, and historical reasons for low COVID-19 vaccination coverage. Additionally, our analysis may differ depending on alternative definitions of vaccination coverage, such as partial vaccination with one dose or coverage with booster doses. Lastly, as we relied on data from the most recent national census, some of our findings may not reflect the population during the COVID-19 pandemic.

5. Conclusions

Through our multi-level modeling approach, we were able to identify sociodemographic factors associated with COVID-19 vaccination at the municipality level. Our findings show more granularly where COVID-19 vaccination is lagging in Guatemala and which municipalities could benefit from more focused vaccination activities. Municipalities with populations experiencing higher poverty had lower vaccination coverage, and municipalities with higher proportions of primary education completion, children, people aged 60 years and older, and more testing for SARS-CoV-2 infection had higher vaccination coverage. COVID-19 vaccine delivery and public health outreach may be focused on communities experiencing more poverty. While there has historically been a difficulty with healthcare delivery to communities experiencing poverty, interventions based on poverty indices may help mitigate the effects of the COVID-19 pandemic on such communities and ultimately improve health equity.

Supplementary Materials: The following supporting information can be downloaded at: https://www.mdpi.com/article/10.3390/vaccines11040745/s1, Table S1: Association between sociodemographic factors (by municipalities and departments) and two-dose vaccination coverage (%) by municipalities in Guatemala (N = 336). SARS-CoV-2 case and vaccination data are from 13 February 2020 to 1 October 2021.

Author Contributions: Conceptualization, R.C., E.C., J.M., J.S., L.L.S.J., D.S.R.A., E.Z.-G. and P.S.S.; methodology, R.C., E.C., J.M., E.Z.-G. and P.S.S.; software, R.C. and E.C.; validation, R.C., E.C., J.M., E.Z.-G. and P.S.S.; formal analysis, R.C., E.C., J.M., E.Z.-G. and P.S.S.; resources, R.C., E.C., J.M., A.S., E.Z.-G. and P.S.S.; data curation, R.C.; writing—original draft preparation, R.C.; writing—review and editing, R.C., E.C., J.M., A.S., J.S., L.L.S.J., D.S.R.A., E.Z.-G. and P.S.S.; visualization, R.C. and E.C.; supervision, E.Z.-G. and P.S.S. All authors have read and agreed to the published version of the manuscript.

Funding: This research received no external funding.

Institutional Review Board Statement: This activity was reviewed by a Centers for Disease Control and Prevention (CDC) Human Subjects Representative and was consistently conducted with applicable federal law and CDC policy [see e.g., 45 C.F.R. part 46; 21 C.F.R. part 56; 42 U.S.C. §241(d), 5 U.S.C. §552a, 44 U.S.C. §3501 et seq]. The findings and conclusions in this report are those of the authors and do not necessarily represent the official position of the CDC.

Informed Consent Statement: Not applicable.

Data Availability Statement: Publicly available datasets were analyzed in this study. These data can be found here: Guatemala Population and Housing Census 2018 https://www.censopoblacion.gt/ (accessed on 5 December 2022); Guatemala Demographic and Health Survey https://dhsprogram.com/publications/publication-fr318-dhs-final-reports.cfm (accessed on 5 December 2022).; Ministry of Public Health and Social Assistance (MSPAS) of Guatemala https://tablerocovid.mspas.gob.gt/tablerocovid/ (accessed on 4 December 2022) and https://gtmvigilanciacovid.shinyapps.io/Coberturas_Tablero/ (accessed on 4 December 2022). Restrictions apply to the availability of the poverty indicator data. Data were obtained from Paolo Marsicovetere and are available from the author.

Acknowledgments: The authors thank Karin Slowing, Oscar Chavez, and Paolo Marsicovetere of the Laboratorio de Datos Guatemala for their assistance with data sources, including the general poverty indicator, for this investigation. We thank Sofia Ortiz Neidhart for assistance with project conceptualization.

Conflicts of Interest: The authors declare no conflict of interest.

References

1. The World Bank. The World Bank in Guatemala. 2022. Available online: https://www.worldbank.org/en/country/guatemala/overview (accessed on 11 January 2023).
2. Pan American Health Organization. *Health in the Americas 2012 Edition*; Pan American Health Organization: Guatemala City, Guatemala, 2012.
3. United States Agency for International Development. Prosperity in Guatemala. Available online: https://www.usaid.gov/guatemala/prosperity (accessed on 6 February 2023).
4. Mathieu, E.; Ritchie, H.; Rodés-Guirao, L.; Appel, C.; Giattino, C.; Hasell, J.; Macdonald, B.; Dattani, S.; Beltekian, D.; Ortiz-Ospina, E.; et al. Coronavirus Pandemic (COVID-19). 2020. Available online: https://ourworldindata.org/coronavirus (accessed on 6 December 2022).
5. Taylor, L. Guatemala's COVID vaccine roll-out failed: Here's what researchers know. *Nature* **2022**. [CrossRef] [PubMed]
6. World Health Organization. WHO Health Emergency Dashboard. Available online: https://covid19.who.int/region/amro/country/gt (accessed on 4 December 2022).
7. Johns Hopkins University. Coronavirus Resource Center. 2022. Available online: https://coronavirus.jhu.edu/region/guatemala (accessed on 4 December 2022).
8. Republic of Guatemala Ministry of Health Public and Social Assistance (MSPAS). National Vaccination Plan against COVID-19. 2021. Available online: https://oiss.org/wp-content/uploads/2021/02/Plan-Nacional-de-Vacunacion-contra-la-COVID-19.pdf (accessed on 4 December 2022).
9. COVID-19 Observatory in Latin America and the Caribbean. Economic and Social Impact. 2022. Available online: https://statistics.cepal.org/forms/covid-countrysheet/index.html?country=GTM (accessed on 4 December 2022).
10. COVID-19 Vaccine Tracker. 4 Vaccines Approved for Use in Guatemala. 2022. Available online: https://covid19.trackvaccines.org/country/guatemala/ (accessed on 4 December 2022).
11. Gobierno de Guatemala Ministerio de Salud Publica y Asistencia Social. COVID-19 Situation in Guatemala. 2022. Available online: https://tablerocovid.mspas.gob.gt/tablerocovid/ (accessed on 5 December 2022).
12. Gobierno de Guatemala Ministerio de Salud Publica y Asistencia Social. COVID-19 Vaccination in Guatemala (Tablero). 2022. Available online: https://gtmvigilanciacovid.shinyapps.io/Coberturas_Tablero/ (accessed on 5 December 2022).

13. Sobral, M.F.F.; Bezerra de Oliveira, B.R.; Gomes da Penha Sobral, A.I.; Monteiro Marinho, M.L.; Duarte, G.B.; de Souza Melo, A. SARS-CoV-2 Vaccines: What Indicators are Associated with the Worldwide Distribution of the First Doses. *Inquiry* **2021**, *58*, 469580211060184. [CrossRef] [PubMed]
14. Etienne, C.F. COVID-19 has revealed a pandemic of inequality. *Nat. Med.* **2022**, *28*, 17. [CrossRef] [PubMed]
15. Gozzi, N.; Chinazzi, M.; Dean, N.E.; Longini, I.M.; Halloran, M.E.; Perra, N.; Vespignani, A. Estimating the impact of COVID-19 vaccine allocation inequities: A modeling study. *medRxiv* **2022**. [CrossRef]
16. Baack, B.N.; Abad, N.; Yankey, D.; Kahn, K.E.; Razzaghi, H.; Brookmeyer, K.; Kolis, J.; Wilhelm, E.; Nguyen, K.H.; Singleton, J.A. COVID-19 Vaccination Coverage and Intent among Adults Aged 18–39 Years—United States, March–May 2021. *MMWR Morb. Mortal. Wkly. Rep.* **2021**, *70*, 928–933. [CrossRef] [PubMed]
17. Murthy, B.P.; Sterrett, N.; Weller, D.; Zell, E.; Reynolds, L.; Toblin, R.L.; Murthy, N.; Kriss, J.; Rose, C.; Cadwell, B.; et al. Disparities in COVID-19 Vaccination Coverage between Urban and Rural Counties—United States, December 14, 2020–April 10, 2021. *MMWR Morb. Mortal. Wkly. Rep.* **2021**, *70*, 759–764. [CrossRef]
18. Hughes, M.M.; Wang, A.; Grossman, M.K.; Pun, E.; Whiteman, A.; Deng, L.; Hallisey, E.; Sharpe, J.D.; Ussery, E.N.; Stokley, S.; et al. County-Level COVID-19 Vaccination Coverage and Social Vulnerability—United States, December 14, 2020–March 1, 2021. *MMWR Morb. Mortal. Wkly. Rep.* **2021**, *70*, 431–436. [CrossRef]
19. Avila, C.; Bright, R.; Gutierrez, J.; Hoadley, K.; Manuel, C.; Romero, N.; Rodriguez, M.P. *Guatemala Health System Assessment, August 2015*; Health Finance & Governance Project, Abt Associates Inc.: Bethesda, MD, USA, 2015.
20. Lou-Meda, R.; Méndez, S.; Calgua, E.; Orozco, M.; Hall, B.J.; Fahsen, N.; Taicher, B.M.; Doty, J.P.; Colindres, J.G.; Menegazzo, C.S.; et al. Developing a national patient safety plan in Guatemala. *Rev. Panam. Salud Pública* **2019**, *43*, e64. [CrossRef]
21. Laboratorio de Datos GT. *COVID-19 Vaccination and Vulnerable Populations: Inequality and Institutional Barriers (MSPAS) of Access to Vaccination*; Laboratorio de Datos GT: Guatemala City, Guatemala, 2022.
22. National Institute of Statistics (Guatemala); United Nations Population Fund (UNFPA). Guatemala Population and Housing Census 2018. 2018. Available online: https://www.censopoblacion.gt/ (accessed on 5 December 2022).
23. Cifuentes, M.P.; Rodriguez-Villamizar, L.A.; Rojas-Botero, M.L.; Alvarez-Moreno, C.A.; Fernández-Niño, J.A. Socioeconomic inequalities associated with mortality for COVID-19 in Colombia: A cohort nationwide study. *J. Epidemiol. Community Health* **2021**, *75*, 610–615. [CrossRef]
24. United Nations Educational, Scientific and Cultural Organization (UNESCO). *COVID-19 and Vaccination in Latin America and the Caribbean*; United Nations Educational, Scientific and Cultural Organization (UNESCO): Paris, France, 2021.
25. Pires, C. Global Predictors of COVID-19 Vaccine Hesitancy: A Systematic Review. *Vaccines* **2022**, *10*, 1349. [CrossRef]
26. Morales-García, W.C.; Huancahuire-Vega, S.; Saintila, J.; Morales-García, M.; Fernández-Molocho, L.; Ruiz Mamani, P.G. Predictors of Intention to Vaccinate against COVID-19 in a Peruvian Sample. *J. Prim. Care Community Health* **2022**, *13*, 21501319221092254. [CrossRef] [PubMed]
27. Urrunaga-Pastor, D.; Bendezu-Quispe, G.; Herrera Añazco, P.; Uyen-Cateriano, A.; Toro-Huamanchumo, C.; Rodriguez-Morales, A.; Hernandez, A.V.; Benites-Zapata, V.A. Cross-sectional analysis of COVID-19 vaccine intention, perceptions and hesitancy across Latin America and the Caribbean. *Travel Med. Infect. Dis.* **2021**, *41*, 102059. [CrossRef] [PubMed]
28. Health Policy Plus. Guatemala's Tailored, Rural Vaccination Plan Strengthens COVID-19 Vaccine Coverage. 2021. Available online: http://www.healthpolicyplus.com/GuateRuralVacc.cfm (accessed on 26 January 2023).
29. Ministerio de Salud Pública y Asistencia Social—MSPAS/Guatemala; Instituto Nacional de Estadística—INE/Guatemala; Secretaría de Planificación y Programación del la Presidencia—Segeplán/Guatemala; ICF International. *Encuesta Nacional de salud Materno Infantil 2014–2015: Informe Final*; Ministerio de Salud Pública y Asistencia Social (MSPAS): Guatemala City, Guatemala; Instituto Nacional de Estadística (INE): Guatemala City, Guatemala; Secretaría de Planificación y Programación de la Presidencia (Segeplán): Guatemala City, Guatemala; ICF International: Rockville, MD, USA, 2017.
30. Caycho-Rodríguez, T.; Tomás, J.M.; Carbajal-León, C.; Vilca, L.W.; Reyes-Bossio, M.; Intimayta-Escalante, C.; Vivanco-Vidal, A.; Saroli-Araníbar, D.; Esteban, R.F.C.; White, M. Sociodemographic and Psychological Predictors of Intention to Receive a COVID-19 Vaccine in Elderly Peruvians. *Trends Psychol.* **2022**, *30*, 206–223. [CrossRef]
31. Caycho-Rodríguez, T.; Valencia, P.D.; Vilca, L.W.; Carbajal-León, C.; Vivanco-Vidal, A.; Saroli-Araníbar, D.; Reyes-Bossio, M.; White, M.; Rojas-Jara, C.; Polanco-Carrasco, R.; et al. Prevalence and Predictors of Intention to be Vaccinated against COVID-19 in Thirteen Latin American and Caribbean Countries. *Trends Psychol.* **2022**, 1–25. [CrossRef]
32. Huang, J.; Chan, S.C.; Ko, S.; Wang, H.H.X.; Yuan, J.; Xu, W.; Zheng, Z.J.; Xue, H.; Zhang, L.; Jiang, J.Y.; et al. Factors Associated with Vaccination Intention against the COVID-19 Pandemic: A Global Population-Based Study. *Vaccines* **2022**, *10*, 1539. [CrossRef] [PubMed]
33. Choudhary, R.; Centers for Disease Control and Prevention, Atlanta, GA, USA; Marsicovetere, P.; University of the Valley of Guatemala, Guatemala City, Guatemala. Personal communication, 2022.
34. Instituto Nacional de Estadística—INE/Guatemala. *Encuesta Nacional de Condiciones de Vida 2014*; Instituto Nacional de Estadística (INE): Guatemala City, Guatemala, 2016.
35. Figueroa Chávez, W.; Peñate, M.; Marsicovetere, P. Estimación de Pobreza a Nivel Municipal en Guatemala Mediante la Utilización de Machine Learning. 2020. Available online: https://www.researchgate.net/publication/343678849_Estimacion_de_pobreza_a_nivel_municipal_en_Guatemala_mediante_la_utilizacion_de_machine_learning (accessed on 5 December 2022).

36. World Health Organization. Achieving 70% COVID-19 Immunization Coverage by Mid-2022. 2021. Available online: https://www.who.int/news/item/23-12-2021-achieving-70-covid-19-immunization-coverage-by-mid-2022#:~:text=%5B4%5D%20These%20targets%20were%20then,population%20coverage%20by%20mid%2D2022 (accessed on 6 February 2023).
37. R Core Team. R: A Language and Environment for Statistical Computing. 2021. Available online: https://www.R-project.org/ (accessed on 18 December 2022).
38. Infobae. Guatemala Starts Vaccination against COVID-19 for Children Aged 6 to 11. 2022. Available online: https://www.infobae.com/en/2022/03/14/guatemala-starts-vaccination-against-covid-19-for-children-aged-6-to-11/ (accessed on 23 January 2023).
39. Gobierno de Guatemala Ministerio de Salud Publica y Asistencia Social. MSPAS Habilita Pruebas COVID-19 en dos Puestos de Vacunación. 2022. Available online: https://prensa.gob.gt/comunicado/mspas-habilita-pruebas-covid-19-en-dos-puestos-de-vacunacion (accessed on 6 February 2023).
40. Lima, E.E.C.; Vilela, E.A.; Peralta, A.; Rocha, M.; Queiroz, B.L.; Gonzaga, M.R.; Piscoya-Díaz, M.; Martinez-Folgar, K.; García-Guerrero, V.M.; Freire, F.H.M.A. Investigating regional excess mortality during 2020 COVID-19 pandemic in selected Latin American countries. *Genus* **2021**, *77*, 30. [CrossRef] [PubMed]
41. Martinez-Folgar, K.; Alburez-Gutierrez, D.; Paniagua-Avila, A.; Ramirez-Zea, M.; Bilal, U. Excess Mortality during the COVID-19 Pandemic in Guatemala. *Am. J. Public Health* **2021**, *111*, 1839–1846. [CrossRef] [PubMed]
42. Akanbi, O.A. Structural and Institutional Determinants of Poverty in Sub-Saharan African Countries. *J. Hum. Dev. Capab.* **2015**, *16*, 122–141. [CrossRef]

vaccines

Article

"Zero Dose" Children in the Democratic Republic of the Congo: How Many and Who Are They?

Daniel Katuashi Ishoso [1,2,*], M. Carolina Danovaro-Holliday [3], Aimé Mwana-Wabene Cikomola [4], Christophe Luhata Lungayo [4], Jean-Crispin Mukendi [4], Dieudonné Mwamba [5], Christian Ngandu [5], Eric Mafuta [2], Paul Samson Lusamba Dikassa [2], Aimée Lulebo [2], Deo Manirakiza [6], Franck-Fortune Mboussou [7], Moise Désiré Yapi [1], Gaga Fidele Ngabo [1], Richard Bahizire Riziki [1,8], Cedric Mwanga [1], John Otomba [1] and Marcellin Mengouo Nimpa [1]

1 World Health Organization (WHO) Country Office, Kinshasa, Democratic Republic of the Congo
2 Kinshasa School of Public Health, University of Kinshasa, Kinshasa, Democratic Republic of the Congo
3 Immunization, Analytics and Insights (IAI), Department of Immunization, Vaccines and Biologicals (IVB), World Health Organization (WHO), 1202 Geneva, Switzerland
4 Expanded Program of Immunization, Kinshasa, Democratic Republic of the Congo
5 National Institute of Public Health, Kinshasa, Democratic Republic of the Congo
6 United Nations Children's Fund (UNICEF) Country Office, Kinshasa, Democratic Republic of the Congo
7 World Health Organization African Regional Office, Brazzaville, Democratic Republic of the Congo
8 Higher Institute of Medical Techniques of Nyangezi, Public Health Section, Sud-Kivu, Democratic Republic of the Congo
* Correspondence: dishosok@gmail.com; Tel.: +243-821605955

Citation: Ishoso, D.K.; Danovaro-Holliday, M.C.; Cikomola, A.M.-W.; Lungayo, C.L.; Mukendi, J.-C.; Mwamba, D.; Ngandu, C.; Mafuta, E.; Lusamba Dikassa, P.S.; Lulebo, A.; et al. "Zero Dose" Children in the Democratic Republic of the Congo: How Many and Who Are They? *Vaccines* **2023**, *11*, 900. https://doi.org/10.3390/vaccines11050900

Academic Editor: Pedro Plans-Rubió

Received: 1 March 2023
Revised: 24 March 2023
Accepted: 31 March 2023
Published: 26 April 2023

Abstract: (1) Background: The Democratic Republic of the Congo (DRC) is one of the countries with the highest number of never vaccinated or "zero-dose" (ZD) children in the world. This study was conducted to examine the proportion of ZD children and associated factors in the DRC. (2) Methods: Child and household data from a provincial-level vaccination coverage survey conducted between November 2021–February 2021 and 2022 were used. ZD was defined as a child aged 12 to 23 months who had not received any dose of pentavalent (diphtheria-tetanus-pertussis-*Haemophilus influenzae* type b (Hib)-Hepatitis B) vaccine (by card or recall). The proportion of ZD children was calculated and associated factors were explored using logistic regression, taking into account the complex sampling approach. (3) Results: The study included 51,054 children. The proportion of ZD children was 19.1% (95%CI: 19.0–19.2%); ZD ranged from 62.4% in Tshopo to 2.4% in Haut Lomami. After adjustment, being ZD was associated with low level of maternal education and having a young mother/guardian (aged $\leq$ 19 years); religious affiliation (willful failure to disclose religious affiliation as the highest associated factor compared to being Catholic, followed by Muslims, revival/independent church, Kimbanguist, Protestant); proxies for wealth such as not having a telephone or a radio; having to pay for a vaccination card or for another immunization-related service; not being able to name any vaccine-preventable disease. A child's lack of civil registration was also associated with being ZD. (4) Conclusions: In 2021, one in five children aged 12–23 months in DRC had never been vaccinated. The factors associated with being a ZD child suggest inequalities in vaccination that must be further explored to better target appropriate interventions.

Keywords: Democratic Republic of the Congo; immunization; vaccination coverage; zero-dose; inequity; determinants; non-vaccination

1. Introduction

Routine childhood immunization is one of the most important advances in global health and development [1]. Global routine childhood vaccination programs provided protection to 86% of children in 2019, before the COVID-19 pandemic hit, greatly reducing the effects of diseases such as polio, measles, and several others on children, helping them grow up healthy. Vaccination is considered one of the most cost-effective ways to promote global well-being [2] and even development.

Despite all the proven benefits, vaccination coverage has remained low in some settings, and this was worsened through the pandemic. In 2021, for example, nearly 25 million children remained undervaccinated, 6 million more than in 2019 and the highest number since 2009 [2]. In addition, the number of "children zero dose", defined as those who did not receive any dose of a diphtheria-pertussis-tetanus vaccine as proxy for lack of access to vaccination services [3], increased from 13.6 million in 2019 to 18.2 million in 2021 [2,3]. Many of these children live in countries affected by conflict, in urban slums, or in remote areas that are hard to reach [2,3], but characterizing them in each country remains important. Gavi, the Vaccine Alliance, through its action plan, has expressed the goal of reducing the ZD children by 25% by 2025 and more than 50% by 2030 [4].

The Democratic Republic of the Congo (DRC), located in the heart of Africa, had an estimated population of 98.3 million in 2016 according to the results of the count organized by the health zones [5]. About 70% of this population lives in rural areas and 30% in urban areas [5]. This population is young, 48% are less than 15 years old, 18.9% are less than 5 years old and about 4% are less than one-year-old [5]. The health system comprises three levels (central, intermediate, and peripheral), and vaccination activities are an integral part of the minimum package of activities of health facilities [5]. The DRC has made significant efforts to improve immunization through the implementation of the Mashako Plan, which is an emergency plan to strengthen the expanded immunization program aimed at reviving routine immunization activities to avoid epidemic outbreaks of certain vaccine-preventable diseases (VPDs) by increasing immunization coverage [5]. Yet, vaccination coverage remains way below the 90% global target according to national surveys and WHO/UNICEF estimates [2]. The DRC is one of the countries in Africa, and the world, with the highest number of ZD children, which results in repeated outbreaks of vaccine-preventable diseases such as vaccine-derived polio, measles, and yellow fever [2,6].

The present study was conducted to examine the proportion of ZD children in each of the 26 provinces of DRC in 2021, as well as the factors associated with being ZD, using data from a provincial-level survey. This information will help better characterize this population and serve as a benchmark to evaluate progress.

2. Materials and Methods

2.1. Study Design

This study is an analytical cross-sectional study aimed at estimating the proportion of ZD children in the DRC and associated factors. It used data from a vaccination coverage survey in 511 of the 519 health zones of the 26 provinces of the DRC conducted between December 2021 and February 2022. Seven health zones were excluded due to insecurity linked to the presence of active armed groups or of poachers.

2.2. Sampling

Sampling was representative at the provincial level, and all 26 provinces of the DRC were surveyed. Multistage sampling was use in each province. First stage: simple random sampling of 5 health areas within each health zone. Second stage: simple random sampling of 30% of avenues/villages within each selected health area. Third stage: systematic random sampling of 34 households with at least one eligible child within each selected avenue/village. Scheme 1 summarizes the sampling approach down to the number of children surveyed.

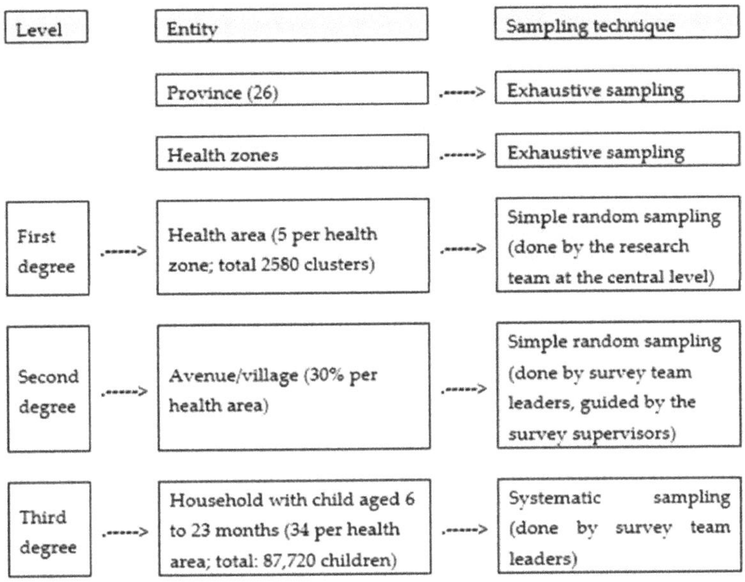

Scheme 1. Sampling procedure by level, 2021–2022 Vaccination Coverage Survey, DRC.

In accordance with the objectives, this survey consisted of 3 distinct statistical units: the child aged 12 to 23 months (though, to estimate other indicators, children aged 6–11 months were also included) living in the household, the head of household sheltering a child aged 12 to 23 months, and the mother/guardian of the child aged 12 to 23 months living in the household. Response rate at the household level was 99.7%.

2.3. Data Collection

As mentioned earlier, this is a secondary analysis for data collected from a nation-wide, provincial-level survey that collected data through interview, observation, and document review. The interview was conducted with heads of household, mothers/caregivers of children aged 6 to 23 months, and nurses from health centers or their assistants. The observation and document review were of vaccination cards and health facility registries (for children for whom a card was not seen at home) in order to transcribe vaccination dates into the data collection tool.

All data collected for the survey was encoded on an android tablet by trained study staff using the SurveyCTO application [7]. All data, including GPS coordinates, was transmitted from the surveyors' tablets to a secure virtual server after data quality checks were conducted by the field supervisor. Vaccination status was ascertained, by hierarchical order, by the observation of data on the vaccination card or records kept at home, the registers at the health care facilities where available, or the use of recall or verbal history if documented vaccination history was not available.

2.4. Variables

The outcome of interest was not having received any dose of the pentavalent vaccine. The explanatory variables used were: household urban/rural location; wealth quintiles calculated from household proxies for socio-economic status using Principal Component Analysis (PCA); presence of a telephone or a radio set as a possible means of communication in the household; maternal/caregiver characteristics including relationship with the child, age, marital status, educational level, occupation, religion, the number of children in the household; gender of the child; birth registration of the child with the civil authority; potential financial barriers from the household such as having to pay for a vaccination card or for another immunization-related service; and caregiver knowledge of vaccine-preventable diseases.

2.5. Data Analysis

We performed weighted descriptive analyses of household characteristics in the study sample with categorical variables reported as frequencies and percentages and continuous variables summarized using means and standard deviations or medians and inter-quartile ranges, depending on normality of the distribution.

The extrapolation of ZD children in the general population was made based on the target number of the DRC surviving infants estimated at 4,037,161 for 2021.

We conducted a bivariate analysis between ZD and factors using the Rao-Scott chi-square test, as it is adequate for multistage sampling, to compare the proportions according to the socio-demographic, economic, communicational characteristics, and those related to the system when the expected minimum was ≥5. Then, a multivariable logistic regression model was fitted. The automatic selection of variables using the forward type was used with an entry probability of 0.05. We considered it acceptable after verification of the area under the receiver operating characteristic curve (ROC area = 0.6640). We used the Archer–Lemeshow test to assess the goodness-of-fit of the logistic regression model, as the data was data collected using a complex survey design that involved clustering. Measures of association between each variable and ZD were reported as Adjusted Odd Ratio (AOR) along with their 95% Confidence Intervals (95% CI). Before gauging the final model, we checked the collinearity effect among the variables. The final model only included the variables whose effects remained significant after adjustment.

All analyses were conducted using Stata version 17 (StataCorp, College Station, TX, USA). To account for the complex sampling design, the svy command and the weighting taking into account the multistage design were used.

2.6. Ethical Considerations

The Kinshasa School of Public Health Ethical committee approved the vaccination coverage survey before data collection (approval number: ESP/CE/175/2021). Authorization was also provided by health and politico-administrative authorities. Before starting the interview, oral informed consent was obtained from the study participants. The research team provided the respondent with information about the nature of the study, its objectives, the risks and benefits incurred, the freedom to participate or not without any prejudice, the confidentiality, and the contact details of the person in charge of the study for subsequent contact if necessary. Confidentiality was respected by anonymizing the dataset.

3. Results

3.1. Description of the Sample

3.1.1. Characteristics of Mothers/Caregivers of 12–23 Month Old Children and Gender of the Child

Table 1 describes the characteristics of the sample of 51,054 children aged 12–23 months. Mothers/caregivers had a median age of 27 years (interquartile range (IQR) = 22–33) with the youngest at 13 and the oldest at 81 (a non-mother caregiver), were mostly married (52.5%) or in a free union (38.1%), had completed primary (38.0%) or secondary education (45.5%), were professionally occupied (68.8%, with 42.4% being farmers/breeders), had religious beliefs (98.5%), and had other children under their care (99.9%). Over half of the children 12–23 months were male (54%), and almost all (93.9%) mothers/caregivers cited at least one vaccine-preventable disease (VPD).

Table 1. Socio-demographic, economic, communicational, and system-related characteristics, 2021–2022 Vaccination Coverage Survey, DRC.

Socio-Demographic Characteristics of the Mother/Guardian of the Child and Gender

Variable	n	Weighted %
Relationship between respondent and child		
Child's mother	48,838	95.8
Other caregiver	2216	4.2
Total	51,054	100.0
Age		
Median: 27 years		
IQR: 22–33 years		
Range: 13–81 years		
≤19 years	3643	7.0
20 to 29 years	26,718	52.6
30 to 39 years	17,351	34.2
40 to 49 years	2903	5.4
≥50 years	429	0.8
Total	51,054	100.0
Current marital status		
Married	25,066	52.5
Free union	21,199	38.1
Separated	1082	1.9
Single	3004	6.1
Divorced	225	0.4
Widow	478	0.9
Total	51,054	100.0
Educational level		
No level	7156	12.7
Primary	20,851	38
Secondary	21,493	45.5
Superior	1342	3.3
Do not know	40	0.1
No response	172	0.4
Total	51,054	100.0
At least one vaccine-preventable disease cited by the respondent		
Yes	47,674	93.9
No	3380	6.1
Total	51,054	100.0

Variable	n	Weighted %
Occupation		
No occupation	15,034	32.2
Teacher	1687	3.4
Official	673	1.5
Farmer/Breeder	24,722	42.4
Fisherman	277	0.5
Trader	4806	11.6
Worker	564	1.3
Others	2081	4.7
Pupil/Student	1210	2.5
Total	51,054	100.0
Number of other children		
0	17	0.1
1	49,589	97.2
2	1347	2.5
3	101	0.2
Total	51,054	100.0
Religion		
No religion	826	1.5
Catholic	14,964	28.9
Protestant	13,711	25
Kimbanguist	1460	2.7
Muslim	773	1.7
Revival Church	17,063	35.5
Other religion	2158	4.5
Do not know	23	0.1
Failure to disclose RA	76	0.1
Total	51,054	100.0
Gender of the child		
Male	27,493	54
Female	23,561	46
Total	51,054	100.0

Household Socio-Economic, Communicational, and System-Related Characteristics

Variable	n	Weighted %
Household wealth quintile		
Lowest	21,955	40.7
Second	24,500	49.0
Middle	3949	8.9
Fourth	630	1.3
Highest	20	0.1
Total	51,054	100.0
Household location environment		
Rural	41,041	73.2
Urban	10,013	26.8
Total	51,054	100.0
Registration of birth with the civil authority		
Yes	12,863	29.4
No	37,598	69.4
Do not know	593	1.2
Total	51,054	100.0
Having to pay for the vaccination card		
Yes	16,174	39.8
No	27,697	59.7
Do not know	250	0.5
Total	44,121	100.0
Having to pay for another immunization-related service		
Yes	7712	21.2
No	36,066	78.1
Do not know	343	0.7
Total	44,121	100.0
Telephone use		
Yes	29,845	64.8
No	21,209	35.2
Total	51,054	100.0
Radio		
Yes	25,883	54.2
No	25,171	45.8
Total	51,054	100.0

n = number of subjects; % = percentage; IQR = interquartile range; Min = smallest observed value; Max = largest observed value; RA = religious affiliation.

3.1.2. Household Socio-Economic, Communicational, and System-Related Characteristics

In terms of household socio-economic, communicational, and system-related characteristics, the majority (89.7%) were in the bottom two wealth quintiles, living in rural areas, with unregistered children (69.4%). Over half had a home radio and telephone. Even though most had not paid money either for the vaccination card or for a vaccination-related service, 39.8% did report having to pay for a card and 21.2% reported having to pay some other immunization-related fee (Table 1).

3.2. Proportion of ZD Children 12–23 Months in DRC

The percentage of ZD children aged 12–23 months was 19.1% (95% CI: 19.0–19.2%), which would correspond to a target population of between 767,061 and 775,135 surviving infants in the DRC. This proportion varied importantly between provinces in the DRC. The provinces with prevalence of ZD above the national mean included: Tshopo, Maniema, Sankuru, Mongala, Bas Uele, Tshuapa, Maindombe, Kasai Oriental, Sud Ubangi, Kasai, Haut Uele, and Nord Ubangi (Figure 1).

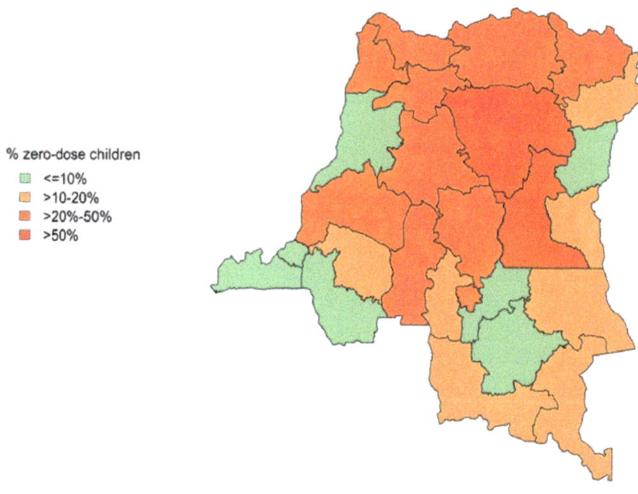

Province	Weighted % zero-dose
Tshopo	62.4% (62.1-62.7%)
Maniema	57.7% (57.4-58.1%)
Sankuru	49.2% (48.9-49.6%)
Mongala	48.1% (47.8-48.4%)
Bas Uele	47.6% (47.2-48.1%)
Tshuapa	44.1% (43.7-44.4%)
Maindombe	41.8% (41.5-42.2%)
Kasai Oriental	29.2% (29.0-29.4%)
Sud Ubangi	24.6% (24.4-24.9%)
Kasai	24.6% (24.4-24.8%)
Haut Uele	22.3% (22.0-22.6%)
Nord Ubangi	21.7% (21.4-22.0%)
Tanganyika	19.0% (18.8-19.3%)
Haut Katanga	18.5% (18.3-18.6%)
Lualaba	18.3% (18.0-18.5%)
Sud Kivu	15.2% (15.0-15.3%)
Kasai Central	12.6% (12.5-12.8%)
Ituri	12.6% (12.5-12.8%)
Kwilu	10.3% (10.1-10.4%)
Lomami	9.8% (9.6-9.9%)
Equateur	8.4% (8.2-8.6%
Kwango	7.8% (7.7-8.0%)
Kongo Central	5.8% (5.6-5.9%)
Nord Kivu	4.0% (3.9-4.1%)
Kinshasa	3.0% (2.9-3.1%)
Haut Lomami	2.4% (2.3-2.5%)
Total	**19.1%**

Figure 1. Proportion of ZD children aged 12–23 months by province in DRC, 2021–2022 Vaccination Coverage Survey.

3.3. Factors Associated with Zero-Dose Vaccine in Children Aged 12 to 23 Months in the DRC

After adjusting for independent variables, being zero-dose was significantly associated with the age of the mother or guardian being less than or equal to 19 years (AOR = 1.23 (95% CI 1.06 to 1.44)); maternal education (lack of education AOR = 3.46 (95% CI 1.99 to 5.99), primary AOR = 3.14 (95% CI 1.81 to 5.42), and secondary level AOR = 3.87 (95% CI 2.22 to 6.75) compared to the level of higher or university education); religious affiliation (willful failure to disclose religious affiliation AOR = 4.22 (95% CI 1.63 to 10.94), Muslim AOR = 1.71 (95% CI 1.25 to 2.33), revival/independent Church AOR = 1.35 (95% CI 1.22 to 1.50), Kimbanguist AOR = 1.31 (95% CI 1.03 to 1.66), and Protestant AOR = 1.12 (95% CI 1.01 to 1.25) compared to the Catholic); proxies for wealth such as not having a telephone to use AOR = 1.59 (95% CI 1.45 to 1.75) or a radio AOR = 1.48 (95% CI 1.34 to 1.63); and lack of civil registration AOR =2.04 (95% CI 1.81 to 2.24). Parents who reported having to pay for a vaccination card or for another immunization-related service were more likely to have a ZD child AOR =2.02 (95% CI 1.81 to 2.24) and AOR =3.22 (95% CI 2.57 to 4.03), respectively.

Finally, not being able to name any vaccine-preventable disease (VPD) was also associated with being ZD, AOR = 3.37 (95% CI 2.94 to 3.87). Summary of these findings are in Table 2.

Table 2. Bivariate and multivariate analysis of the association "zero-dose" and socio-demographic, economic, communication, and system-related characteristics, 2021–2022 Vaccination Coverage Survey, DRC.

Variables		Bivariate		Multivariate	
	Weighted % Zero-Doses	**OR (95% CI)**	***p*-Value**	**AOR (95% CI)**	***p*-Value**
Age groups					
20 to 29 years	18.9	1.00		1.00	
30 to 39 years	17.9	0.94 (0.89 to 0.99)	0.034	1.01 (0.93 to 1.11)	0.760
40 to 49 years	21.6	1.19 (1.07 to 1.32)	0.002	0.97 (0.81 to 1.15)	0.680
≥50 years	29.3	1.79 (1.38 to 2.31)	<0.001	1.14 (0.74 to 1.75)	0.561
≤19 years	24.0	1.36 (1.24 to 1.49)	<0.001	1.23 (1.06 to 1.44)	0.007
Relationship between respondent and child					
Child's mother	18.8	1.00			
Other caregiver	27.8	1.67 (1.49 to 1.87)	<0.001		
Current marital status					
Married	18.1	1.00			
Free union	19.4	1.09 (1.03 to 1.15)	0.002		
separated	28.2	1.77 (1.51 to 2.08)	<0.001		
Single	20.8	1.19 (1.07 to 1.32)	0.002		
Divorced	34.4	2.37 (1.70 to 3.32)	<0.001		
Widow	28.8	1.83 (1.46 to 2.29)	<0.001		
Educational level					
Superior	4.6	1.00		1.00	
No level	22.8	6.18 (4.64 to 8.23)	<0.001	3.46 (1.99 to 5.99)	<0.001
Primary	14.6	3.59 (2.69 to 4.79)	<0.001	3.14 (1.81 to 5.42)	<0.001
Secondary	28.0	8.14 (6.09 to 10.89)	<0.001	3.87 (2.22 to 6.75)	<0.001
Occupation					
No occupation	17.5	1.00			
Teacher	13.0	0.71 (0.60 to 0.83)	<0.001		
Official	9.7	0.51 (0.38 to 0.67)	<0.001		
Farmer/Breeder	22.7	1.38 (1.30 to 1.47)	<0.001		
Fisherman	32.4	2.25 (1.66 to 3.05)	<0.001		
Trader	13.7	0.75 (0.67 to 0.83)	<0.001		
Worker	17.0	0.96 (0.75 to 1.24)	0.777		
Others	19.1	1.11 (0.98 to 1.27)	0.103		
Pupil/Student	18.4	1.06 (0.89 to 1.27)	0.507		
Religion					
Catholic	15.1	1.00		1.00	
No religion	30.2	2.44 (2.02 to 2.95)	<0.001	1.12 (080 to 1.56)	0.510
Protestant	19.7	1.39 (1.29 to 1.49)	<0.001	1.12 (1.01 to 1.25)	0.031
Kimbanguist	20.7	1.47 (1.27 to 1.71)	<0.001	1.31 (1.03 to 1.66)	0.026
Muslim	30.4	2.46 (2.05 to 2.96)	<0.001	1.71 (1.25 to 2.33)	0.001
Revival/Ind. Church	20.5	1.45 (1.36 to 1.55)	<0.001	1.35 (1.22 to 1.50)	<0.001
Other religion	21.9	1.58 (1.39 to 1.80)	<0.001	1.13 (0.91 to 1.39)	0.267
Do not know	14.8	0.98 (0.36 to 2.70)	0.972	0.85 (0.23 to 3.12)	0.804
Failure to disclose RA	52.0	6.12 (3.45 to 10.85)	<0.001	4.22 (1.63 to 10.94)	<0.001
Household wealth quintile					
Lowest	26.3	9.44 (1.23 to 72.29)	0.031		
Second	15.6	4.88 (0.64 to 37.50)	0.127		
Middle	8.1	2.34 (0.30 to 18.02)	0.415		
Fourth	6.6	1.86 (0.25 to 14.76)	0.557		
Highest	3.7	1.00			
Household location environment					
Urban	12.7	1.00			
Rural	21.5	1.89 (1.76 to 2.04)	<0.001		
Child's gender					
Male	19.4	1.00			
Female	18.9	0.97 (0.92 to 1.02)	0.241		
Registration of birth with the civil authority					
Yes	6.2	1.00		1.00	
No	24.5	4.91 (4.50 to 5.35)	<0.001	2.04 (1.81 to 2.29)	<0.001
Do not know	28.9	6.17 (4.83 to 7.86)	<0.001	2.36 (1.65 to 3.36)	<0.001

Table 2. *Cont.*

Variables	Bivariate			Multivariate	
	Weighted % Zero-Doses	OR (95% CI)	*p*-Value	AOR (95% CI)	*p*-Value
Having to pay for the vaccination card					
Yes	3.8	1.00		1.00	
No	11.0	3.10 (2.81 to 3.42)	<0.001	2.02 (1.81 to 2.24)	<0.001
Do not know	38.0	15.44 (11.29 to 21.12)	<0.001	5.14 (3.46 to 7.65)	<0.001
Having to pay for another immunization-related service					
Yes	1.8	1.00		1.00	
No	9.8	5.81 (4.76 to 7.10)	<0.001	3.22 (2.57 to 4.03)	<0.001
Do not know	28.9	21.75 (15.58 to 30.37)	<0.001	5.80 (3.82 to 8.82)	<0.001
Telephone use					
Yes	13.8	1.00		1.00	
No	28.9	2.54 (2.41 to 2.67)	<0.001	1.59 (1.45 to 1.75)	<0.001
Radio					
Yes	13.2	1.00		1.00	
No	26.2	2.33 (2.21 to 2.45)	<0.001	1.48 (1.34 to 1.63)	<0.001
At least one vaccine-preventable disease cited by the respondent					
Yes	16.7	1.0		1.00	
No	56.4	6.44 (5.90 to 7.03)	<0.001	3.37 (2.94 to 3.87)	<0.001

With n = number of subjects in the sample; OR = Odd Ratio; AOR = Adjusted Odd Ratio; 95% CI = 95% Confidence Interval; RA = religious affiliation.

4. Discussion

The results from this survey showed 19.1% ZD, representing between 767,061 and 775,135 ZD children in the DRC. This result is similar to the proportion estimated by WHO and UNICEF relating to the national vaccination coverage estimates of 19% for the DRC in 2021 [6]. The fact that almost 1 in 5 children aged 12 to 23 months was ZD in the DRC in 2021 is high in comparison to other low- and low-middle-income countries including those in Africa [2]. There was an increase in the prevalence of zero-dose children in sub-Saharan Africa from 6.8% in 2010 to 14% during the COVID-19 pandemic year of 2021 [2].

Our study found that zero-dose children were significantly associated with several factors. Zero-dose children were positively associated with young mothers, which is similar to findings from several studies. The older the mother gets, the less she may hesitate and the fewer barriers she may face to have the child vaccinated [8–11]. Our study also found that uneducated mothers and those who had only primary or secondary education were more likely to have a ZD child compared to those with higher or university education. Maternal education has been associated with vaccination in most settings [12–24]. This may be affected by changes affected by education in attitudes, traditions, and beliefs, and even increased autonomy and control over household resources that would improve health-care seeking [12–20]. Zero-dose status was also associated with religious affiliation in the DRC, with those not reporting an affiliation having the highest odds of having an unvaccinated child. A pooled cross-sectional study of individual and national data obtained from Demographic and Health Surveys of 33 sub-Saharan African countries found that the children of Muslims were significantly more likely to be zero-dose than children of Christians (25.2% versus 12.3%) [25]. However, Costa et al., in an analysis of 66 low and middle income countries with standardized national surveys since 2010, found that the relationship between religion and vaccination was not consistent across the world [26]. The latter suggests that various cultural and community-level factors may modulate the relationship between religious affiliation and immunization. Working with religious leaders may be an appropriate solution.

Zero-dose children are significantly related to proxies for wealth such as not having a telephone to use or a radio. These two elements are currently important channels through which messages can pass to reach a large part of the population. This significant link somehow reflects the existence of a dissemination of messages likely to encourage parents to have their children vaccinated. However, information and communication are a major challenge in the viability of an initiative. Its success or failure depends on communication and information [27]. Vaccination services, which are the subject of so much controversy, cannot do without communication. Communicating to convince cannot be improvised either at the risk of reaping the opposite effects of what is expected. It is, therefore, worthwhile to rely on the socio-cultural realities of the populations in order to develop appropriate communication strategies, including those adapted to these two channels, to better explain the advantages of vaccination. In the DRC, ZD children were also significantly linked to the lack of civil registration. This result opens a window of action to linking immunization and birth registration, as has been discussed by many in recent years [28,29]. Another finding that is of significance is the high proportion of people reporting having to pay for a vaccination card or another immunization-related fee, as this is a potentially modifiable factor. This study suggests an inhibiting role of fees on child vaccination, and this has been reported as an important barrier elsewhere. This undoubtedly goes against the official free vaccination policy of the DRC, which is aimed at breaking down the financial barrier to give the population maximum access to vaccination services; several studies support that making vaccination free plays a most fundamental role in improving immunization coverage [30,31].

Finally, not being able to name any VPD was also associated with being zero-dose. This association has also been found in several studies conducted in sub-Saharan Africa, particularly in Ethiopia, Burkina-Faso, or Nigeria, including systematic reviews. The lower the level of knowledge, the less likely the caregiver is to vaccinate the child. Working on improving maternal and community knowledge about vaccination, about the diseases that are targeted for protection, the consequences of not vaccinating the child, the vaccination schedule, and on awareness of vaccination campaigns can help improve vaccination [8,17,21,24,32].

The literature suggests that to reduce inequalities in immunization, targeted and pro-equity interventions should be explicitly developed. Such interventions need to be multicomponent to mainly facilitate access through the proper offer of services and community-based mobilization, outreach, and education, adapted to the language and health literacy of the population [33]. Using the results of the 2021–2022 Vaccination Coverage Survey, along with periodic monitoring of process indicators, each province, and health zone, in the DRC is tailoring its immunization delivery strategy. The survey and this analysis were conducted in the context of the Mashako Plan [5]. Alongside other system-strengthening actions, the Mashako Plan is a multipartner and multicomponent initiative that is addressing access and inequalities through simple and targeted interventions developed in collaboration with many stakeholders. The Plan started targeting 9 provinces and has now been extended to all but two of the provinces. It took lessons from previous experiences, including work to improve coverage in Kinshasa [34]. The focus is to favor access to vaccination by strengthening local-level data use and accountability for better micro-planning, outreach, and reduction of vaccine stock-outs, supportive supervision and outreach monitoring, as well as demand generation through community engagement [5].

Limitations

This study reflects one point in time, and it does not provide longitudinal data. It relies on survey data that can be affected by selection and information biases. The sampling frame was derived from 1984 census data that is known to be inaccurate. To tackle this issue, a household listing exercise was conducted in all selected clusters. Only 7 of 519 health zones were excluded due to insecurity and non-response was 0.3%, with 86920 HHs participating out of 87166 selected HHs. Yet, communities not included in the sampling frame may have been left out and such communities may also be less likely to be reached with vaccines. Vaccination history obtained from cards or facility records may have errors, as records can be incomplete or difficult to read or interpret [35,36]. Additionally, the proportion of vaccination status ascertained by recall was 30%, which can lead to recall bias; although, stating that a child was not vaccinated might be more accurate than indicating which vaccines or how many doses a child has received [37]. Similarly, the ascertainment of factors that relate to vaccination might also suffer from desirability or other biases that are difficult to quantify. Finally, while we assessed factors that were related to being ZD, our study did not go into root cause analysis of the actual reasons for not being vaccinated, or even the factors related to the provision of vaccination services that may affect vaccination.

5. Conclusions

Zero-dose is frequent and contributes to the serious health problems in the Democratic Republic of the Congo, with some provinces having over half of their children unvaccinated. Important geographic, demographic, and socio-economic inequalities were observed and quantified. Several factors were associated with not being vaccinated; yet, only better understanding of the underlying causes of ZD will help to inform strategic and operational decisions and to tailor interventions aiming at reducing the ZD burden. Inequalities in immunization should continue to be monitored to assess progress.

Author Contributions: Conceptualization, D.K.I., M.M.N., M.C.D.-H., E.M., P.S.L.D. and A.L.; methodology, D.K.I., M.M.N., E.M., P.S.L.D. and A.L.; formal analysis, D.K.I. and M.M.N.; investigation, E.M., P.S.L.D. and A.L.; writing—original draft preparation, D.K.I., M.M.N. and M.C.D.-H.; writing—review and editing, D.K.I., M.M.N., M.C.D.-H., E.M., P.S.L.D., A.L., J.-C.M., M.D.Y., C.M., G.F.N., R.B.R., F.-F.M., A.M.-W.C., C.L.L., D.M. (Dieudonné Mwamba), C.N., D.M. (Deo Manirakiza) and J.O. All authors have read and agreed to the published version of the manuscript.

Funding: The survey that generated the data used in this study was funded by the United Nations Children Emergency Funds (UNICEF) after mobilizing a significant funding from GAVI. The funders had no role in study design, data collection and analysis, decision to publish, or preparation of the manuscript.

Institutional Review Board Statement: The study protocol was approved by the institutional review board of the Kinshasa School of Public Health Ethical committee (n° ESP/CE/175/2021). This study was conducted in accordance with the Helsinki Declaration II. Authorization was also provided by health and politico-administrative authorities.

Informed Consent Statement: Verbal informed consent was obtained from all subjects involved in the study. The research team provided the respondent with information about the nature of the study, its objectives, the risks and benefits incurred, and the freedom to participate or not without any prejudice.

Data Availability Statement: The data presented in this study are available on request from the WHO-DRC office at the email address "nimpamengouom@who.int". The data are not publicly available due to the sensitivity of certain information from health facilities.

Acknowledgments: We are very thankful to the team of research nurses and physicians for their involvement in the collection of data used in this study. We are also very grateful for the direction of the Kinshasa School of Public Health for their flexibility in collaboration during the survey and to Dale RHODA for advice on the statistical methods used.

Conflicts of Interest: The authors declare no conflict of interest. The funders had no role in the design of the study; in the collection, analyses, or interpretation of data; in the writing of the manuscript; or in the decision to publish the results.

References

1. Greenwood, B. The contribution of vaccination to global health: Past, present and future. *Philos. Trans. R. Soc. Lond. B Biol. Sci.* **2014**, *369*, 20130433. [CrossRef] [PubMed]
2. WHO. *Global Immunization Coverage 2021 [Internet]*; WHO: Geneva, Switzerland, 2021; (WHO Estimates of National Immunization Coverage (Data as of July 2022)). Available online: https://www.who.int/news-room/fact-sheets/detail/immunization-coverage (accessed on 10 November 2022).

3. Wigley, A.; Lorin, J.; Hogan, D.; Utazi, C.E.; Hagedorn, B.; Dansereau, E.; Tatem, A.J.; Tejedor-Garavito, N. Estimates of the number and distribution of zero-dose and under-immunised children across remote-rural, urban, and conflict-affected settings in low and middle-income countries. *PLoS Glob. Public Health* **2022**, *2*, e0001126. [CrossRef] [PubMed]
4. Gavi, the Vaccine Alliance. The Zero-Dose Child: Explained. Vaccines Work, 26 April 2021. Available online: https://www.gavi.org/vaccineswork/zero-dose-child-explained (accessed on 12 November 2022).
5. Ministère de la Santé Publique de RDC. *Plan D'urgence Pour la Relance de la Vaccination de Routine Dit «Plan Marshall sur la Vaccination de Routine» (Plan MASHAKO). Programme Elargi de Vaccination*; Ministère de la Santé Publique de RDC: Kinshasa, Democratic Republic of the Congo, July 2018.
6. WHO/UNICEF. *Estimates of National Immunization Coverage 2021 [Internet]*; WHO/UNICEF: Geneva, Switzerland. Available online: https://www.who.int/teams/immunization-vaccines-and-biologicals/immunization-analysis-and-insights/global-monitoring/immunization-coverage/who-unicef-estimates-of-national-immunization-coverage (accessed on 12 November 2022).
7. Dobiliti, Inc., USA. Available online: https://www.surveycto.com/ (accessed on 12 November 2022).
8. Abebe, A.M.; Mengistu, T.; Mekuria, A.D. Measles case, immunization coverage and its determinant factors among 12–23 month children, in Bassona Worena Woreda, Amhara Region, Ethiopia, 2018. *BMC Res. Notes* **2019**, *12*, 71. [CrossRef]
9. Negussie, A.; Kassahun, W.; Assegid, S.; Hagan, A.K. Factors associated with incomplete childhood immunization in Arbegona district, southern Ethiopia: A case—Control study. *BMC Public Health* **2015**, *16*, 27. [CrossRef] [PubMed]
10. Mohamud, A.N.; Feleke, A.; Worku, W.; Kifle, M.; Sharma, H.R. Immunization coverage of 12–23 months old children and associated factors in Jigjiga District, Somali National Regional State, Ethiopia. *BMC Public Health* **2014**, *14*, 865. [CrossRef] [PubMed]
11. Zewdie, A.; Letebo, M.; Mekonnen, T. Reasons for defaulting from childhood immunization program: A qualitative study from Hadiya zone, Southern Ethiopia. *BMC Public Health* **2016**, *16*, 1240. [CrossRef]
12. Mekonnen, Z.A.; Gelaye, K.A.; Were, M.C.; Tilahun, B. Timely completion of vaccination and its determinants among children in northwest, Ethiopia: A multilevel analysis. *BMC Public Health* **2020**, *20*, 908. [CrossRef]
13. Girmay, A.; Dadi, A.F. Full Immunization Coverage and Associated Factors among Children Aged 12–23 Months in a Hard-to-Reach Areas of Ethiopia. *Int. J. Pediatr.* **2019**, *2019*, 1924941. [CrossRef]
14. Kinfe, Y.; Gebre, H.; Bekele, A. Factors associated with full immunization of children 12–23 months of age in Ethiopia: A multilevel analysis using 2016 Ethiopia Demographic and Health Survey. *PLoS ONE* **2019**, *14*, e0225639. [CrossRef]
15. Tamirat, K.S.; Sisay, M.M. Full immunization coverage and its associated factors among children aged 12–23 months in Ethiopia: Further analysis from the 2016 Ethiopia demographic and health survey. *BMC Public Health* **2019**, *19*, 1019. [CrossRef]
16. Kagoné, M.; Yé, M.; Nébié, E.; Sie, A.; Schoeps, A.; Becher, H.; Muller, O.; Fisker, A.B. Vaccination coverage and factors associated with adherence to the vaccination schedule in young children of a rural area in Burkina Faso. *Glob. Health Action* **2017**, *10*, 1399749. [CrossRef]
17. Kiptoo, E.; Esilaba, M.; Kobia, G.; Ngure, R. Factors Influencing Low Immunization Coverage Among Children Between 12–23 Months in East Pokot, Baringo Country, Kenya. *Int. J. Vaccines Vaccin.* **2015**, *1*, 00012. [CrossRef]
18. Gidado, S.; Nguku, P.; Biya, O.; Waziri, N.E.; Mohammed, A.; Nsubuga, P.; Akpan, H.; Oyemakinde, A.; Nasidi, A.; Suleman, I.; et al. Determinants of routine immunization coverage in Bungudu, Zamfara State, Northern Nigeria, May 2010. *Pan Afr. Med. J.* **2014**, *18*, 9. [CrossRef]
19. Adedokun, S.T.; Uthman, O.A.; Adekanmbi, V.T.; Wiysonge, C.S. Incomplete childhood immunization in Nigeria: A multilevel analysis of individual and contextual factors. *BMC Public Health* **2017**, *17*, 236. [CrossRef]
20. Duru, C.B.; Iwu, A.C.; Uwakwe, K.A.; Diwe, K.C.; Merenu, I.A.; Emerole, C.A.; Adaeze, C.A.; Onyekuru, C.U.; Ihunnia, O. Assessment of Immunization Status, Coverage and Determinants among under 5-Year-Old Children in Owerri, Imo State, Nigeria. *Open Access Libr. J.* **2016**, *3*, e2753. [CrossRef]
21. Legesse, E.; Dechasa, W. An assessment of child immunization coverage and its determinants in Sinana District, Southeast Ethiopia. *BMC Pediatr.* **2015**, *15*, 31. [CrossRef]
22. Tadesse, H.; Deribew, A.; Woldie, M. Predictors of defaulting from completion of child immunization in south Ethiopia, May 2008—A case control study. *BMC Public Health* **2009**, *9*, 150. [CrossRef]
23. Johri, M.; Rajpal, S.; Subramanian, S.V. Progress in reaching unvaccinated (zero-dose) children in India, 1992–2016: A multilevel, geospatial analysis of repeated cross-sectional surveys. *Lancet Glob. Health* **2021**, *9*, e1697–e1706. [CrossRef]
24. Toirambe, S.E.; Camara, T.; Khalis, M.; Serhier, Z.; Darkaoui, N.; Hassouni, K.; Belouali, R.; Jallal, M. Facteurs prédictifs de la non-complétude vaccinale chez des enfants migrants de moins de 5 ans, Maroc. *St. Publique* **2021**, *33*, 435–443. [CrossRef]
25. Ozigbu, C.E.; Olatosi, B.; Li, Z.; Hardin, J.W.; Hair, N.L. Correlates of Zero-Dose Vaccination Status among Children Aged 12–59 Months in Sub-Saharan Africa: A Multilevel Analysis of Individual and Contextual Factors. *Vaccines* **2022**, *10*, 1052. [CrossRef]
26. Santos, T.M.; Cata-Preta, B.O.; Wendt, A.; Arroyave, L.; Hogan, D.R.; Mengistu, T.; Barros, A.J.D.; Victora, C.G. Religious Affiliation as a Driver of Immunization Coverage: Analyses of Zero-Dose Vaccine Prevalence in 66 Low- and Middle-Income Countries. *Front. Public Health* **2022**, *10*, 977512. [CrossRef] [PubMed]
27. Balle, F. Les Médias. In *Que Sais-Je?* PUF: Paris, France, 2006.

28. Corrêa, G.; Verstraete, P.; Soundardjee, R.; Shankar, M.; Paterson, C.; Hampton, L.; Jackson, D.; Muniz, M.; Mwamba, R.; Wenz, K.; et al. Immunization programmes and notifications of vital events. *Bull. World Health Organ.* **2019**, *97*, 306–308. [CrossRef] [PubMed]
29. Pan American Health Organization (PAHO). Immunization and Birth Registration. *Immun. Newsl.* **2012**, *34*, 1–2. Available online: www.paho.org/immunization/newsletter (accessed on 20 November 2022).
30. Jiang, X.; Shang, X.; Lin, J.; Zhao, Y.; Wang, W.; Qiu, Y. Impacts of free vaccination policy and associated factors on influenza vaccination behavior of the elderly in China: A quasi-experimental study. *Vaccine* **2021**, *39*, 846–852. [CrossRef] [PubMed]
31. Fang, R.; Ma, Y.; Wu, J.; Lv, M.; Tian, L.; Xie, Z. Free influenza vaccination coverage and its influencing factors about cognition among elderly population in Beijing. *Chin. Gen. Pract.* **2013**, *17*, 1403–1406. [CrossRef]
32. Crocker-Buque, T.; Mindra, G.; Duncan, R.; Mounier-Jack, S. Immunization, urbanization and slums—A systematic review of factors and interventions. *BMC Public Health* **2017**, *17*, 556. [CrossRef]
33. Machado, A.A.; Edwards, S.A.; Mueller, M.; Saini, V. Effective interventions to increase routine childhood immunization coverage in low socioeconomic status communities in developed countries: A systematic review and critical appraisal of peer-reviewed literature. *Vaccine* **2021**, *39*, 2938–2964. [CrossRef]
34. JSI Inc. Attendre les Enfants non Vaccinés: Leçons Tirées de L'assistance Technique de JSI au Gouvernement de RDC Pour L'amélioration de L'accès aux Services de Vaccination de Routine et Pour une Meilleure Utilisation de ces Services. 2020. Available online: https://publications.jsi.com/JSIInternet/Inc/Common/_download_pub.cfm?id=23343&lid=6 (accessed on 20 November 2022).
35. Kaboré, L.; Méda, C.Z.; Sawadogo, F.; Bengue, M.M.; Kaboré, W.M.; Essoh, A.T.; Gervaix, A.; Galetto-Lacour, A.; Médah, I.; Betsem, E. Quality and reliability of vaccination documentation in the routine childhood immunization program in Burkina Faso: Results from a cross-sectional survey. *Vaccine* **2020**, *38*, 2808–2815. [CrossRef]
36. Mansour, Z.; Brandt, L.; Said, R.; Fahmy, K.; Riedner, G.; Danovaro-Holliday, M.C. Home-based records' quality and validity of caregivers' recall of children's vaccination in Lebanon. *Vaccine* **2019**, *37*, 4177–4183. [CrossRef]
37. Dansereau, E.; Brown, D.; Stashko, L.; Danovaro-Holliday, M.C. A systematic review of the agreement of recall, home-based records, facility records, BCG scar, and serology for ascertaining vaccination status in low and middle-income countries. *Gates Open Res.* **2020**, *3*, 923. [CrossRef]

vaccines

MDPI

Article

Low Vaccine Coverage and Factors Associated with Incomplete Childhood Immunization in Racial/Ethnic Minorities and Rural Groups, Central Brazil

Juliana de Oliveira Roque e Lima [1], Valéria Pagotto [1], Bárbara Souza Rocha [1], Paulo Sérgio Scalize [2], Rafael Alves Guimarães [1,3], Márcio Dias de Lima [4], Leandro Nascimento da Silva [5], Michele Dias da Silva Oliveira [1], Winny Éveny Alves Moura [1], Sheila Araújo Teles [1], Claci Fátima Weirich Rosso [1] and Karlla Antonieta Amorim Caetano [1,*]

1 Faculty of Nursing, Federal University of Goiás, Goiânia 74605-080, GO, Brazil
2 School of Civil and Environmental Engineering, Federal University of Goiás, Goiânia 74605-220, GO, Brazil
3 Institute of Tropical Pathology and Public Health, Federal University of Goiás, Goiânia 74605-050, GO, Brazil
4 Federal Institute of Education, Science, and Technology of Goiás, Goiânia 74055-110, GO, Brazil
5 Municipal Health Department, Goiânia 74884-092, GO, Brazil
* Correspondence: karlla@ufg.br

Abstract: Discrimination and limited access to healthcare services in remote areas can affect vaccination coverage. Therefore, this study aimed to estimate vaccination coverage for children living in quilombola communities and rural settlements in the central region of Brazil during their first year of life and to analyze the factors associated with incomplete vaccination. An analytical cross-sectional study was conducted on children born between 2015 and 2017. The percentage of children who received all vaccines recommended by the National Immunization Program in Brazil by 11 months and 29 days was used to calculate immunization coverage. Children who received the following vaccines were considered as having a complete basic vaccination schedule: one dose of BCG; three doses of Hepatitis B, of Diphtheria-Tetanus-Pertussis (DPT), of *Haemophilus influenzae* type b (Hib), and of Poliovirus (Polio); two doses of Rotavirus, of 10-valent pneumococcal (PCV10), and of Serogroup C meningococcal conjugate (MenC); and one dose of Yellow Fever (YF). Measles-mumps-rubella (MMR) and other doses recommended at or after 12 months were not included. Consolidated logistic regression was used to identify factors associated with incomplete vaccination coverage. Overall vaccination coverage was 52.8% (95% CI: 45.5–59.9%) and ranged from 70.4% for the Yellow Fever vaccine to 78.3% for the Rotavirus vaccine, with no significant differences between the quilombola and settler groups. Notably, the likelihood of incomplete general vaccination coverage was higher among children who did not receive a visit from a healthcare professional. Urgent strategies are required to achieve and ensure health equity for this unique and traditionally distinct group with low vaccination coverage.

Keywords: vaccination coverage; rural population; immunization schedules

Citation: de Oliveira Roque e Lima, J.; Pagotto, V.; Rocha, B.S.; Scalize, P.S.; Guimarães, R.A.; de Lima, M.D.; da Silva, L.N.; da Silva Oliveira, M.D.; Moura, W.É.A.; Teles, S.A.; et al. Low Vaccine Coverage and Factors Associated with Incomplete Childhood Immunization in Racial/Ethnic Minorities and Rural Groups, Central Brazil. *Vaccines* **2023**, *11*, 838. https://doi.org/10.3390/vaccines11040838

Academic Editors: Ahmad Reza Hosseinpoor, M. Carolina Danovaro, Devaki Nambiar, Aaron Wallace and Hope Johnson

Received: 31 January 2023
Revised: 21 March 2023
Accepted: 23 March 2023
Published: 13 April 2023

1. Introduction

The World Health Organization (WHO) has addressed immunization inequity, and global efforts to promote vaccine access are encouraged [1]. In 2021, 25 million children worldwide (19%) did not receive basic vaccines, such one or more doses of the Diphtheria-Tetanus-Pertussis vaccine (DTP). This number of undervaccinated children has increased by 5.9 million since 2019. Countries such as Angola, Brazil, the Democratic Republic of Congo, Ethiopia, India, Indonesia, Myanmar, Nigeria, Pakistan, and the Philippines comprise 60% of these children [2].

In Brazil, the National Immunization Program (NIP) was established in 1973, and it is considered an international benchmark due to its scope and performance, offering most WHO-recommended vaccines free of charge [3,4]. However, the country still faces challenges in achieving the expected worldwide vaccine coverage [5].

Incomplete childhood vaccination may be associated with demographic, socioeconomic, and policy-related factors [6]. Additionally, gender inequalities, ethnic discrimination, and limited access to health services in remote areas may also affect vaccination coverage [7].

In rural Brazil, significant inequalities are observed regarding urban environments and diverse races, peoples, and cultures. Settlers are rural groups that rely on family agricultural production, demanding agrarian reform [8]. Quilombolas are ethnic groups distributed throughout Brazil, residing in rural or urban areas, predominantly black, with their own historical ties [9]. Settlers and traditional quilombola communities stand out in this scenario, characterized by cultural isolation, popular struggles of resistance, and deprioritization. Little is known about their living and health conditions [10].

To date, there are no data on vaccination coverage for children residing in settlements and quilombola areas in Brazil. Therefore, situational diagnoses regarding access and factors associated with vaccination in vulnerable areas of the country are critical. These data can guide the development of more effective actions, informing decision-making in public policies and promoting universal access to health services.

This study aims to estimate vaccination coverage for the complete basic schedule during the first year (Table 1) and analyze the factors associated with incomplete vaccination in settled and quilombola children in the state of Goiás, Brazil, in response to the gaps in vaccination for children in rural Brazil.

2. Materials and Methods

2.1. Study Design

A cross-sectional retrospective cohort analytical study was conducted in 36 municipalities in the state of Goiás. This investigation is part of the "Sanitation and Environmental Health in Rural and Traditional Communities of Goiás-SanRural Project" matrix project. The SanRural Project aims to promote knowledge about sanitation conditions and the environmental health of settled and traditional communities, such as riverside communities and remnants of quilombos.

2.2. Context

The State of Goiás is located in the Center-West Region of Brazil and comprises 246 municipalities distributed in five mesoregions (Centro Goiano, East Goiano, Northwest Goiano, North Goiano, and South Goiano). Goiás is the most populous state in the Midwest region and has the ninth-largest economy in the country. Agriculture is the main economic activity in the state and one of the main factors responsible for the rapid process of agro-industrialization in Goiás. The state of Goiás has an estimated population of 6 million people, with approximately 10% residing in rural areas [11]. According to the IBGE, 117 quilombola communities existed in the state of Goiás in 2019 [12]. In 2017, 309 settlements were registered in Goiás [13].

2.3. Participants

The study's target population was children born from January 2015 to December 2017, living in settled communities or traditional communities of quilombola descendants in the state of Goiás. Children reported by the head of the household as not living in the home were excluded from the study.

2.4. Sampling

Sampling for the SanRural Project was carried out in multiple stages. Initially, municipalities with one or more certified and recognized quilombola community in the state of Goiás were included, and information was checked in the official sources of accreditation [14]. Therefore, of the municipalities in Goiás (n = 246), 45 (18.3%) met this criterion and were included in the study. In addition, in these 45 municipalities, all communities of recognized settlements were included [15]. Thus, this study included all quilombola communities and settlements in the selected municipalities, representing 44 quilombola communities and 62 settlements, totaling 106 communities. Municipalities and communities were selected based on community certification criteria.

Next, the SanRural Project encompassed the following sampling units: (i) families and (ii) individuals. Families were selected by systematic random sampling. In each community, the first individual was selected by simple random sampling, and for every two households (k = 2), one family was interviewed until reaching the sample size. The sample calculation parameters for the SanRural Project study were considered, so the estimates of proportions of the leading indicators were obtained with 95% Confidence Intervals, a maximum margin of error per community of 10%, and a margin of error for the totality of communities of the same type of 2%. After selecting the family, vaccination card information was collected from all individuals in the household, including the children. Thus, all eligible children from the selected family were included in the study. Since the family was selected by systematic random sampling, we considered this sampling unit as the primary sampling unit (PSU) and the individuals as the secondary sampling unit (SSU).

In this study, we used data only from children born from January 2015 to December 2017. Information from children in 36 municipalities (80% of the SanRural Project municipalities), 44 settled communities (71% of the total SanRural Project settlements), and 37 quilombola communities (84.1% of the total quilombola communities in the SanRural Project) were included. Thus, data from 81 communities were analyzed, including information from 227 children (94 from settlements and 133 from quilombola communities).

Figure 1 shows the distribution map of communities and municipalities according to the mesoregions of the state of Goiás.

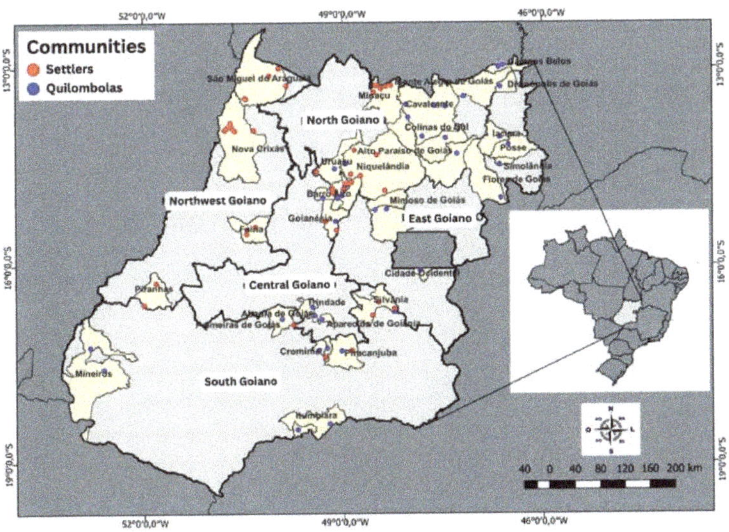

Figure 1. Distribution of communities and municipalities according to the mesoregions of the state of Goiás. Note: Map made using ArcGIS, version 3.24.3.

A field team collected data from February 2018 to September 2019, conducting interviews on portable computers. The person responsible for the family, aged over 18, was asked to answer the research questions in each residence.

The electronic instrument for data collection contained questions about the family's socioeconomic status, housing conditions, and the health characteristics of household residents. In addition, at the time of the interviews, the vaccination cards of all household residents were photographed.

The study included a total of 227 children distributed across settler communities (n = 94) and quilombola communities (n = 133). For children who did not present their vaccination cards during the interview (n = 80), vaccination data were obtained from the Information System of the National Immunization Program (SI-PNI) in Brazil. Of the investigated children (n = 227), 23 had no vaccination records and were considered unvaccinated [16].

2.5. Variables

The construction of variables related to vaccination was based on definitions supported by Brazil's National Immunization Program recommendations and the World Health Organization [4,17].

Vaccines recommended and distributed free of charge by the Brazilian government for children under one year: BCG (single dose), Hepatitis B (4 doses), Rotavirus (2 doses), pentavalent DTP/Hib/Hepatitis B (3 doses), Polio (3 doses), PCV10 (2 doses), MenC (2 doses), and YF (single dose), offering protection against more than 11 diseases [17].

Doses: We considered the recommended doses according to the national child vaccination schedule for the first year, without considering the interval between doses. For multiple-dose vaccines, the record of the last dose was considered [17].

Complete basic vaccination schedule: Defined as the doses of vaccines recommended for the first year established by the basic vaccination schedule in force and applied up to 11 months and 29 days, including one dose of BCG vaccine (Bacillus Calmette-Guérin), the last dose of Hepatitis B vaccine, the last dose of Diphtheria-Tetanus-Pertussis vaccine (DTP), the last dose of Hemophilus influenzae type b vaccine (Hib), the last dose of Poliovirus vaccine (Polio), the last dose of 10-valent pneumococcal vaccine, the last dose of Rotavirus vaccine, the last dose of Serogroup C meningococcal conjugate vaccine, and one dose of Yellow Fever vaccine [17].

Incomplete basic vaccination schedule: Not receiving at least one of the doses described in the complete basic vaccination schedule.

Table 1 presents the changes made to the National Vaccination Calendars of the National Immunization Program in Brazil of the vaccines recommended for the first year between 2015 and 2017.

Table 1. Changes made to the National Vaccination Calendars of the National Immunization Program in Brazil of vaccines recommended for the first year between 2015 and 2017.

Vaccines	Schedule	Years		
		2015	Second Semester/2016	2017
BCG	1 dose	-	-	-
DTP	2, 4, and 6 months			
Hib	2, 4, and 6 months			
Rotavirus	2 and 4 months	-	-	-
YF	9 months	-	-	-
Hepatitis B	At birth, 2, 4, and 6 months	-	-	-
MenC	3 and 5 months, booster 15 months	-	3 and 5 months, booster 12 months	-
Polio	2 and 4 months (IPV), 6 months (OPV)	-	2, 4, and 6 months (IPV)	-
PCV10	2, 4, and 6 months, booster 12 months	-	2 and 4 months, booster 12 months	-

BCG: Bacillus Calmette-Guérin vaccine; DTP: Diphtheria-Tetanus-Pertussis vaccine; Hib: *Haemophilus influenzae* type b vaccine; Polio: Poliovirus vaccine (inactivated Polio vaccine (IPV))/oral Polio vaccine (OPV)); PCV10: 10-valent pneumococcal vaccine; MenC: Serogroup C meningococcal conjugate vaccine; YF: Yellow Fever vaccine. Source: Ordinances and technical reports of the National Immunization Program [18–22]. Note: In this study, the recommended vaccine doses up to 11 months and 29 days were included; therefore, the first dose of the measles-mumps-rubella (MMR) vaccine and the booster of the PCV10 vaccine were not considered.

General vaccine coverage: Vaccination coverage (VC) was calculated according to the applied doses and was defined as the percentage of children with a complete basic vaccination schedule, namely:

$$\text{VC} = \frac{\text{number of children with vaccination records and complete basic vaccination schedule}}{\text{total number of children with vaccination records}} \times 100$$

The dependent variable in this study was incomplete general vaccination coverage related to the vaccination situation (yes or no) according to the applied doses described in the basic vaccination schedule, evaluated at 11 months and 29 days.

The independent variables included the sex of the child (male or female), the type of community (settlement or quilombola), housing zone (rural or urban/periurban), mesoregion of Goiás (Central Goiano, East Goiano, Northwest Goiano, North Goiano, or South Goiano), mother's age ($\leq$28 or $\geq$29 years), number of people in the house ($\leq$5 or $\geq$6), internet access (yes or no), income ($\leq$USD 277.91 or $\geq$ USD 277.92), health professional visit in the last year (yes or no), and community healthcare unit availability (yes or no). Quantitative variables, such as the mother's age, number of people in the house, and income, were categorized based on their mean (less than or equal to the mean versus greater than or equal to the mean).

2.6. Statistical Analysis

The data collected during the interview, information about the vaccines recorded on the vaccination card, and the vaccine data obtained from the *SI-PNI* were exported to statistical analysis software (IBM SPSS®, version 24 and StataCorp. 2021. Stata Statistical Software: Release 17. College Station, TX, USA: StataCorp LLC.).

All analyses were performed using the complex sample design. Stata's "survey" package was used. The selected families were included as PSU, and the type of community (settlement/quilombola communities) was used as a stratum. Individual selection sample weights were included for each child [23], considering the selection probability according to their community, sex, and age group.

A descriptive analysis of the participants' characteristics was carried out initially, followed by Pearson's chi-square test corrected for design to assess differences in characteristics between children from settlements and communities. Estimates of the coverage of the complete immunization schedule by type of vaccine and type of community were then calculated, along with 95% Confidence Intervals (95%CI). Next, bivariate and multiple analyses were performed using binary logistic regression to identify the factors associated with incomplete general vaccination coverage. In the bivariate analysis, the dependent variable was associated with each of the independent variables analyzed. Next, the variables that presented a p-value < 0.25 were included in the multiple logistic regression model, single input method. The magnitude of the multiple analysis effect was presented as Adjusted Odds Ratios (AOR) and 95%CI. Variables with p-values < 0.05 were considered significantly associated with the outcome.

2.7. Ethical Aspects

The SanRural Project was approved by the Research Ethics Committee of the Federal University of Goiás (CAAE number 2.886.174/2018). All participants signed the Terms of Free and Informed Consent applied to the family by signature or fingerprint of the interviewee.

3. Results

In the investigated communities, there were 227 children born between 2015 and 2017, with 94 (41.4%) from settlements and 133 (58.6%) from quilombola communities.

Population Characteristics:

Table 2 shows the characteristics of the participants by type of community. Of the total children included in the study (n = 227), 56.7% were male and 43.3% were female. Regarding the children's mothers, 63.2% were aged 28 or younger. Concerning the children's families, 66.4% had five people or fewer, 53.0% had access to the internet, and 61.5% had a gross income of less than or equal to USD 277.91. Furthermore, most children lived in quilombola communities (n = 133; 58.6%), rural areas (n = 172; 75.8%), and municipalities located in the North Goiano region (n = 77; 36.8%). As for the characteristics of access to health services for the children's families, it was identified that, in the last year, 59.9% received a visit from a health professional and 66.2% of the communities where the children lived did not have a public health unit.

Table 2. Sociodemographic characteristics according to the type of community of 227 settled and quilombola children in the state of Goiás, 2015–2017.

Variables	Total	Settlers	Quilombolas	χ^2 *	p-Value
	n = 227	n = 94	n = 133		
Sex, n (%)					
Male	126 (56.7)	52 (54.0)	74 (57.9)	0.254	0.615
Female	101 (43.3)	42 (46.0)	59 (42.1)		
Housing zone, n(%)					
Urban/Periurban	55 (24.2)	0 (0.0)	55 (44.8)	44.272	<0.001
Rural	172 (75.8)	94 (100.0)	78 (55.2)		
Mesoregion, n (%)					
Central Goiano	47 (21.0)	19 (18.8)	28 (21.9)	20.719	<0.001
East Goiano	32 (14.0)	0 (0.0)	32 (20.0)		
Northwest Goiano	36 (12.9)	36 (42.6)	0 (0.0)		
North Goiano	77 (36.8)	27 (28.5)	50 (40.5)		
South Goiano	35 (15.3)	12 (10.1)	23 (17.6)		
Mother's age (years), n (%)					
≤28 years	141 (63.2)	62 (65.6)	79 (62.2)	0.202	0.654
≥29 years	86 (36.8)	32 (34.4)	54 (37.8)		
Number of people in the house, n (%)					
≤5 people	158 (66.4)	77 (79.6)	81 (60.7)	5.742	0.017
≥6 people	69 (33.6)	17 (20.4)	52 (39.3)		
Has internet, n (%)					
Yes	120 (53.0)	41 (42.5)	79 (57.6)	3.659	0.057
No	107 (47.0)	53 (57.5)	54 (42.4)		
Income (USD) **, n (%)					
≤277.91	138 (61.5)	54 (56.5)	84 (63.7)	0.837	0.361
≥277.92	89 (38.5)	40 (43.5)	49 (36.3)		
Health professional visits in the last year, n (%)					
Yes	137 (59.9)	59 (58.0)	78 (61.0)	0.113	0.737
No	90 (40.1)	35 (42.0)	55 (39.3)		
Community public health unit, n (%)					
Yes	63 (33.8)	6 (6.8)	57 (45.5)	34.719	<0.001
No	164 (66.2)	88 (93.2)	76 (54.5)		

Notes: Mother's age (years)—mean 27.9, standard deviation 6.5; number of people in the house—mean 4.9, standard deviation 1.6; income (USD)—mean 277.91, standard deviation 226.2. * Pearson's chi-square test corrected for study design. ** Per month.

After a global evaluation of the variables, a statistical difference was observed between the communities ($p < 0.05$) concerning the following characteristics: area of residence, mesoregion, number of people in the home, access to the internet, and the existence of a public health unit in the community ($p = 0.000$).

3.1. Vaccination Coverage

Table 3 presents the vaccination coverage of the basic vaccination schedule for the first year evaluated at 11 months and 29 days. The overall vaccination coverage at 11 months and 29 days was 52.8% (95% CI: 45.5–59.9%). By community, the general vaccination coverage for the first year was 63.6% (95% CI: 51.7–74.1%) for settler communities and 48.0% (95% CI: 39.3–56.9%) for quilombola communities. The vaccine coverage by the investigated vaccine ranged from 70.4% for the Yellow Fever vaccine to 78.3% for the Rotavirus vaccine.

Table 3. Complete vaccination coverage and vaccine coverage, according to doses in the first year, evaluated at 12 months in settler and quilombola children in the state of Goiás, 2015–2017.

Vaccines	Complete Vaccine Schedule								
	General (n = 227)			Settler (n = 94)			Quilombola (n = 133)		
	n	%	95%CI	n	%	95%CI	n	%	95%CI
BCG	176	75.9	69.1–81.5	78	82.0	71.1–89.4	98	73.2	64.5–80.4
Hepatitis B	167	72.4	65.1–78.7	69	75.1	63.7–81.3	98	71.2	61.9–79.1
DTP	171	74.3	67.1–80.4	70	75.6	64.2–84.3	101	73.8	64.5–81.3
Hib	167	72.4	65.1–78.7	69	75.1	63.7–83.9	98	71.2	61.9–79.1
Polio	171	75.8	68.9–81.6	70	75.8	64.6–84.6	101	75.7	66.8–82.9
PCV10	184	77.9	71.0–83.5	75	81.4	71.1–88.6	109	76.3	67.3–83.5
Rotavirus	177	78.3	71.6–83.7	72	79.0	68.5–86.7	105	78.0	69.3–84.7
MenC	179	78.0	71.0–83.5	75	81.4	71.1–88.6	104	76.3	67.3–83.5
YF	161	70.4	63.1–76.8	65	72.9	61.8–81.7	96	69.3	60.0–77.4
General vaccine coverage	121	52.8	45.5–59.9	54	63.6	51.7–74.1	67	48.0	39.3–56.9

BCG: Bacillus Calmette-Guérin vaccine; DTP: Diphtheria-Tetanus-Pertussis vaccine; Hib: *Haemophilus influenzae* type b vaccine; Polio: Poliovirus vaccine; PCV10: 10-valent pneumococcal vaccine; MenC: Serogroup C meningococcal conjugate vaccine; YF: Yellow Fever vaccine.

3.2. Factors Associated with Incomplete General Immunization Coverage

The binary logistic regression model was adjusted for the child's sex, type of community, housing zone, mesoregion, number of people in the house, and health professional visits in the last year. These variables had a p-value of less than 0.25 in the bivariate analysis. Based on the multiple analysis, it was observed that the odds of an incomplete vaccination schedule were higher in children who had not received a visit from a health professional in the last year (AOR: 1.96; 95%CI: 1.03–3.73) compared to those who had received such visits (Table 4).

Table 4. Factors associated with incomplete general vaccination coverage for the first year. Goiás, Brazil, 2015–2017.

Variables	Bivariate Analysis					Multiple Analysis *	
	Vaccine Schedule (n = 227)						
	Total (n = 227)	Incomplete (n = 106)	Complete (n = 121)	p-Value	OR (95%CI)	p-Value	AOR (95%CI)
Sex							
Male	126	66 (52.3%)	60 (47.7%)		1.00		1.00
Female	101	40 (40.6%)	61 (59.4%)	0.119	0.62 (0.34–1.13)	0.273	0.78 (0.37–1.4)
Community type							
Settler	94	40 (36.4%)	54 (63.6%)		1.00		1.00
Quilombola	133	66 (52.0%)	67 (48.0%)	0.040	1.89 (1.03–3.48)	0.882	1.08 (0.40–2.89)
Housing zone							
Rural	172	75 (40.3%)	97 (59.7%)		1.00		1.00
Urban/periurban	55	31 (62.6%)	24 (37.4%)	0.008	2.48 (1.28–4.80)	0.092	2.28 (0.87–5.92)

Table 4. *Cont.*

Variables	Bivariate Analysis					Multiple Analysis *	
	Vaccine Schedule (*n* = 227)						
	Total (*n* = 227)	Incomplete (*n* = 106)	Complete (*n* = 121)	*p*-Value	OR (95%CI)	*p*-Value	AOR (95%CI)
Mesoregion							
Central Goiano	47	28 (61.2%)	19 (38.8%)		1.00		1.00
East Goiano	32	10 (33.9%)	22 (66.1%)	0.027	0.32 (0.12–0.88)	0.122	0.43 (0.15–1.26)
Northwest Goiano	36	13 (30.1%)	23 (69.9%)	0.014	0.27 (0.09–0.76)	0.132	0.40 (0.12–1.32)
North Goiano	77	38 (49.1%)	39 (50.9%)	0.241	0.61 (0.27–1.39)	0.726	0.84 (0.32–2.24)
South Goiano	35	17 (50.4%)	18 (49.6%)	0.371	0.64 (0.25–1.69)	0.370	0.63 (0.23–1.74)
Mother's age (years)							
≤28	141	73 (51.2%)	68 (48.8%)		1.00		1.00
≥29	86	33 (40.4%)	53 (59.6%)	0.156	0.65 (0.35–1.18)	0.101	0.58 (0.30–1.11)
Number of people in the house							
≤5	158	68 (43.4%)	90 (56.6%)		1.00		1.00
≥6	69	38 (54.8%)	31 (45.2%)	0.148	1.58 (0.84–2.93)	0.092	1.82 (0.90–3.65)
Has internet							
Yes	120	56 (46.8%)	64 (53.2%)		1.00		
No	107	50 (47.8%)	57 (52.2%)	0.889	1.04 (0.58–1.87)		
Income (USD)							
≤277.91	138	68 (47.8%)	70 (52.2%)		1.00		
≥277.92	89	38 (46.3%)	51 (53.7%)	0.847	0.94 (0.51–1.73)		
Health professional visit in the last year							
Yes	137	52 (40.8%)	84 (59.2%)		1.00		1.00
No	90	54 (56.9%)	37 (43.1%)	0.035	1.91 (1.05–3.49)	0.039	1.96 (1.03–3.73)
Is a community healthcare unit available?							
Yes	63	29 (50.8%)	34 (49.2%)		1.00		
No	164	77 (45.5%)	87 (54.5%)	0.505	0.80 (0.43–1.52)		

Note: Incomplete and complete vaccination coverage is presented as *n* (%), where *n* is the number of observations in the sample and % is the percentage weighted by the complex sampling design. AOR: Adjusted Odds Ratio; 95.0%CI: 95% Confidence Interval; OR: Odds Ratio. * Binary logistic regression model adjusted for child's gender, type of community, housing zone, mesoregion, number of people in the house, and health professional visit in the last year.

4. Discussion

In Brazil, information on the health and vaccination status of racial/ethnic minorities and rural groups is still scarce [10,24,25]. Therefore, this study presents the first information regarding vaccination coverage for children in rural settlements and quilombola communities in Goiás.

The present study showed a predominance of children from low-income families. However, investigations on these populations also suggest a predominance of disadvantaged groups with characteristics that make them individually, socially, and programmatically vulnerable [24,26,27].

This study identified low overall vaccination coverage, a relevant indicator of this population's precarious living and health conditions. While the World Health Organization encourages all countries to achieve global immunization coverage greater than or equal to 90% for vaccines regulated by the country [28], the present study showed an overall vaccination coverage of 52.8% (95%CI: 45.5–59.9%). It is essential to highlight that no statistical differences were observed between general vaccination coverage stratified by the investigated community (settlers and quilombolas).

In Brazil, investigations in urban municipalities also showed higher vaccination coverage in children compared to the present study's general vaccination coverage [29]. Indeed, the last immunization coverage survey in urban areas was carried out in the country in 2007 and evaluated immunization coverage for vaccines recommended in the first year, including a dose of the MMR vaccine. A total of 17,149 children from 26 Brazilian state capitals and the Federal District were investigated and had complete vaccination coverage of 81.0% (95%CI: 80.4–81.6%) at 18 months [29], which is about 1.5 times greater than the general vaccination coverage of the present study.

Garcia et al. [30] conducted a study in a medium-sized municipality in the Southeast Region of Brazil and analyzed the vaccination coverage of the complete schedule at 12 months in children born in 2015. The result was a coverage of 77.1% (95%CI: 72.6–81.0%). Similar data were also identified in a study in the southern region of Brazil, which showed vaccination coverage for the complete basic vaccination schedule (one dose of BCG, one dose of SCR, three doses of Polio, and three doses of pentavalent) among children born in 2015 to be 77.2% (95% CI: 75.8–78.4%) [31].

At the international level, wide variations in general immunization coverage have been observed in different regions worldwide. In African countries, immunization coverage for recommended vaccines during the first year was estimated at 29.7% in Ethiopia and 67.6% in Senegal [32,33]. In India, among children aged 12 to 36 months residing in rural areas of 26 states, complete immunization coverage, i.e., one dose of the BCG vaccine, three doses of the DTP vaccine, and one dose of the measles vaccine, was 53.2% (95% CI: 52.7–53.7%) [34].

In developed countries such as the United States and China, recent investigations have revealed specific differences in vaccine coverage. For example, a national survey conducted in the United States in 2017 found that vaccination coverage for children aged 19 to 35 months living in rural areas was 66.8% (95% CI: 63.6–69.9%) for the complete schedule of vaccines (acellular DTP, Polio, SCR, Hib, Hepatitis B, varicella, and pneumococcal) [35]. In China, data from 2016 showed that 94.0% (95%CI: 91.4–95.9%) of children aged 24 to 35 months living in rural areas were fully vaccinated with scheduled vaccines for the first year (BCG, Hepatitis B, Polio, DTPa, and measles and rubella (MR)) [36].

These inequalities in vaccination coverage can be explained by the diversity of vaccines recommended in each country's vaccination schedules, making vaccination programs and schemes more complex [5]. In addition, of course, these economic, social, and health discrepancies exist worldwide. It is important to remember that, as of 2016, underdeveloped countries such as Senegal, Ethiopia, and India began to receive financial resources from Gavi, The Vaccine Alliance, to introduce and increase vaccine access for thousands of children [37].

When evaluating vaccination coverage for each vaccine, none reached the recommended minimum coverage of 90%. While the Yellow Fever vaccine had the lowest coverage of 70.4%, the Rotavirus vaccine had the highest coverage of 78.3%. This result may be related to the immunization program's recommended age for these vaccines. In Brazil, the Rotavirus vaccine is recommended earlier, at 2 and 4 months, while the Yellow Fever vaccine is recommended at 9 months [17]. Studies have shown greater adherence to vaccination in the first months, as vaccination dates correspond to the child's routine consultation, which happens monthly in the first six months [38,39].

In the present study, vaccination coverage was associated with the health services offered to the investigated population. Families that did not receive a home visit from a health professional in the last year had odds of having incompletely vaccinated children that were 1.96 times higher than those who received a visit from a healthcare worker.

Brazil's national primary care policy is crucial in discussing these data since the results are linked to the Family Health Strategy, which significantly reorganized Primary Health Care in the Unified Health System. In Brazil, one of the primary objectives of the Family Health Strategy Program (FHS-ESF) is to provide comprehensive, accessible, and continuous care with resolvability and good quality at public health units and homes through a multidisciplinary team [40,41]. In the present study, home visits seem to contribute to increased vaccination coverage of the investigated children. Furthermore, this interactive healthcare technology identifies susceptible groups in a differentiated and equitable way, promoting health education actions [42].

Although public policies in Brazil have positively impacted vaccination coverage in this study, the results show a low vaccination coverage panorama for children from racial/ethnic minorities and rural groups. Therefore, health services must be rethought for difficult-to-access groups with unique cultural characteristics. We believe it is necessary to understand the reasons for vaccine hesitancy in these groups and that creating bonds and security should be the first step towards effective health actions.

Finally, it is necessary to consider some limitations of this investigation. The SanRural Project is a household survey to investigate the health and sanitation situation of the rural and traditional populations in the state of Goiás. Therefore, other determinants to assess the factors associated with vaccine incompleteness were not investigated. Although participant compliance was high, the response rate was not measured. More studies are encouraged to address this knowledge gap in these vulnerable groups. Another limitation was the absence of some vaccination cards during data collection. However, to increase the veracity of the analysis of information on vaccination coverage, all means of searching for vaccine data were accessed from public agencies in Brazil. Another relevant point was the long period of data collection, but it is important to highlight the great difficulty that exists in accessing these groups, as they live in rural regions with difficult geographic mobility. Only quilombola communities recognized by responsible bodies in Brazil participated in this study, which restricted the participation of other communities that are in the certification process. However, we believe that the characteristics of the communities not included are similar to those that were studied, as both are located in the same geographic region, share the same public health policies, and have the same challenges inherent to the traditional population of Brazil.

Author Contributions: Conceptualization, J.d.O.R.e.L. and K.A.A.C.; methodology, J.d.O.R.e.L., K.A.A.C., R.A.G. and S.A.T.; software, K.A.A.C., R.A.G. and M.D.d.L.; validation, K.A.A.C. and S.A.T.; formal analysis, J.d.O.R.e.L., K.A.A.C. and R.A.G.; investigation, J.d.O.R.e.L., K.A.A.C., L.N.d.S. and V.P.; resources, P.S.S. and B.S.R.; data curation, J.d.O.R.e.L., K.A.A.C., P.S.S. and V.P.; writing—original draft preparation, J.d.O.R.e.L., K.A.A.C., C.F.W.R. and M.D.d.L.; writing—review and editing, J.d.O.R.e.L., K.A.A.C., W.É.A.M. and M.D.d.S.O.; visualization, J.d.O.R.e.L. and K.A.A.C.; supervision, K.A.A.C. and C.F.W.R.; project administration, J.d.O.R.e.L., K.A.A.C., P.S.S. and B.S.R.; funding acquisition, P.S.S. and B.S.R. All authors have read and agreed to the published version of the manuscript.

Funding: This research was funded by the National Health Foundation/Fundação Nacional da Saúde (FUNASA), through the project "Sanitation and Environmental Health in Rural and Traditional Communities of Goiás", SanRural. Grant number, Term of Decentralized Execution (TED) 05/2017.

Institutional Review Board Statement: The study was conducted in accordance with the Declaration of Helsinki and approved by Ethics Committee of The Federal University of Goiás (CAAE nº 2.886.174/2018).

Informed Consent Statement: Informed consent was obtained from all subjects involved in the study. Written informed consent has been obtained from the participants to publish this paper.

Data Availability Statement: The datasets used and/or analyzed during the current study are available from the corresponding author upon reasonable request.

Acknowledgments: We thank the study participants, patterns, and the executing team for their commitment and the funding agency for providing the means to carry out this work.

Conflicts of Interest: The authors declare no conflict of interest. The funders had no role in the design of the study; in the collection, analyses, or interpretation of data; in the writing of the manuscript; or in the decision to publish the results.

References

1. World Health Organization. *Immunization Agenda 2030: A Global Strategy to Leave no one Behind*; World Health Organization: Geneva, Switzerland, 2020; pp. 1–29.
2. World Health Organization. Immunization Coverage. 2020. Available online: https://www.who.int/news-room/fact-sheets/detail/immunization-coverage (accessed on 2 December 2022).
3. Ministério da Saúde. *Programa Nacional de Imunizações (PNI): 40 Anos*; Ministério da Saúde, Secretaria de Vigilância em Saúde, Departamento de Vigilância Epidemiológica, Biblioteca Virtual em Saúde: Brasília, Brazil, 2013. Available online: https://bvsms.saude.gov.br/bvs/publicacoes/programa_nacional_imunizacoes_pni40.pdf (accessed on 2 December 2022).

4. World Health Organization. *Table 1: Summary of WHO Position Papers-Recommendations for Routine Immunization*; World Health Organization: Geneva, Switzerland, 2020; pp. 1–11.
5. Domingues, C.M.A.S.; Maranhão, A.G.K.; Teixeira, A.M.; Fantinato, F.F.S.; Domingues, R.A.S. 46 anos do Programa Nacional de Imunizações: Uma história repleta de conquistas e desafios a serem superados. *Cad. Saude Publica* **2020**, *36*, 1–17. [CrossRef]
6. Tauil, M.C.; Sato, A.P.S.; Waldman, E.A. Factors associated with incomplete or delayed vaccination across countries: A systematic review. *Vaccine* **2016**, *34*, 2635–2643. [CrossRef] [PubMed]
7. Chopra, M.; Bhutta, Z.; Blanc, D.C.; Checchi, F.; Gupta, A.; Lemango, E.T.; Levine, O.S.; Lyimo, D.; Nandy, R.; O'brien, K.L.; et al. Addressing the persistent inequities in immunization coverage. *Bull. World Health Organ.* **2020**, *98*, 146–148. [CrossRef]
8. Figueiredo, G.C.; Pinto, J.M. Acampamento e assentamento: Participação, experiência e vivência em dois momentos da luta pela terra. *Psicol Soc.* **2014**, *26*, 562–571. [CrossRef]
9. Vieira, F.; Trotta, M.; Carlet, F. Sob o rufar dos ng'oma: O judiciário em disputa pelos quilombolas. *Rev. Direito Práxis* **2017**, *8*, 556–591. [CrossRef]
10. Cairo, S.M.; Teixeira, C.S.; Da Silva, T.O.; Da Silva, E.K.; Martins, P.C.; Bezerra, V.M.; De Medeiros, D.S. Overweight in Rural Quilombola and Non-quilombola Adolescents From the Northeast of Brazil. *Front. Nutr.* **2021**, *7*, 593929. [CrossRef]
11. Instituto Brasileiro de Geografia e Estatística (IBGE). *Dados do censo demográfico entre 1940 a 2010. Ministério da Economia*; IBGE: Rio de Janeiro, Brazil, 2011.
12. Instituto Brasileiro de Geografia e Estatística (IBGE). *Base de Informações Geográficas e Estatísticas sobre os Indígenas e Quilombolas para Enfrentamento da COVID-19*; IBGE: Rio de Janeiro, Brazil, 2020.
13. Instituto Nacional de Colonização e Reforma Agrária (INCRA). *Painel de Assentamentos-SR04*; Inst Nac Colon e Reforma Agrária: Brasília, Brazil, 2017. Available online: http://painel.incra.gov.br/sistemas/index.php (accessed on 6 August 2020).
14. Instituto Brasileiro de Geografia e Estatística (IBGE). *Pesquisa de Informações Básicas Municipais–Munic*; IBGE: Rio de Janeiro, Brazil, 2013.
15. Instituto Nacional de Colonização e Reforma Agrária (INCRA). Available online: http://www.incra.gov.br/pt/ (accessed on 10 February 2020).
16. Moraes, J.C.; Ribeiro, M.C.S.A. Desigualdades sociais e cobertura vacinal: Uso de inquéritos domiciliares. *Rev. Bras. Epidemiol.* **2008**, *11*, 113–124. [CrossRef]
17. Ministério da Saúde. *Anexo V–Instrução Normativa Referente ao Calendário Nacional de Vacinação 2020*; Ministério da Saúde, Secretaria de Vigilância em Saúde, Departamento de Vigilância Epidemiológica, Coordenação Geral do Programa Nacional de Imunizações: Brasília, Brazil, 2020. Available online: https://saude.es.gov.br/Media/sesa/Calend%C3%A1rio%20de%20Vacina%C3%A7%C3%A3o/INSTRUCAO%20NORMATIVA%202020.pdf (accessed on 6 August 2020).
18. Ministério da Saúde. *Manual de Normas e Procedimentos para Vacinação*; Ministério da Saúde, Secretaria de Vigilância em Saúde, Departamento de Vigilância epidemiológica, Coordenação-geral do Programa de Imunizações: Brasília, Brazil, 2014. Available online: https://bvsms.saude.gov.br/bvs/publicacoes/manual_procedimentos_vacinacao.pdf (accessed on 6 August 2020).
19. Ministério da Saúde. *Informe Técnico da Introdução da Vacina Pentavalente: Vacina Adsorvida Difteria, Tétano, Pertussis, Hepatite B (Recombinante) e Haemophilus Influenzae Tipo b (Conjugada)*; Ministério da Saúde, Secretaria de Vigilância em Saúde, Departamento de Vigilância Epidemiológica, Coordenação Geral do Programa Nacional de Imunizações: Brasília, Brazil, 2012. Available online: https://www.saude.go.gov.br/images/imagens_migradas/upload/arquivos/2012-06/informe-tecnico-vacina-pentavalente.pdf (accessed on 6 August 2020).
20. Ministério da Saúde. *Informe Técnico da Vacina Pneumocócica 10-Valente (Conjugada)*; Ministério da Saúde: Brasília, Brazil, 2010. Available online: http://epidemiologia.alfenas.mg.gov.br/download/informe_t%C3%A9cnico_pneumo_.pdf (accessed on 6 August 2020).
21. Ministério da Saúde. *Portaria no 1.498, de 19 de julho de 2013. Redefine o Calendário Nacional de Vacinação, o Calendário Nacional de Vacinação dos Povos Indígenas e as Campanhas Nacionais de Vacinação, no âmbito do Programa Nacional de Imunizações (PNI), em todo o território*; Diário Oficial da União: Brasília, Brazil, 2013. Available online: https://bvsms.saude.gov.br/bvs/saudelegis/gm/2013/prt1498_19_07_2013.html (accessed on 6 August 2020).
22. Ministério da Saúde. *Portaria no 1.533, de 18 de agosto de 2016. Redefine o Calendário Nacional de Vacinação, o Calendário Nacional de Vacinação dos Povos Indígenas e as Campanhas Nacionais de Vacinação, no âmbito do Programa Nacional de Imunizações (PNI)*; Diário Oficial da União: Brasília, Brazil, 2016. Available online: https://bvsms.saude.gov.br/bvs/saudelegis/gm/2016/prt1533_18_08_2016.html (accessed on 6 August 2020).
23. Vasconcellos, M.T.L.D.; Silva, P.L.D.N.; Szwarcwald, C.L. Sampling design for the world health survey in Brazil. *Cad. Saúde Pública* **2005**, *21*, S89–S99. [CrossRef]
24. Caetano, K.A.; Bergamaschi, F.P.; Carneiro, M.A.; Pinheiro, R.S.; Araújo, L.A.; Matos, M.A.; Teles, S.A. Hepatotropic viruses (hepatitis A, B, C, D and E) in a rural Brazilian population: Prevalence, genotypes, risk factors and vaccination. *Trans. R. Soc. Trop. Med. Hyg.* **2020**, *114*, 91–98. [CrossRef] [PubMed]
25. Motta-Castro, A.R.C.; Gomes, S.A.; Yoshida, C.F.T.; Miguel, J.C.; Teles, S.A.; Martins, R.M.B. Compliance with and response to hepatitis B vaccination in remaining quilombo communities in Central Brazil. *Cad. Saude Publica* **2009**, *25*, 738–742. [CrossRef]
26. Arruda, N.M.; Maia, A.G.; Alves, L.C. Desigualdade no acesso à saúde entre as áreas urbanas e rurais do Brasil: Uma decomposição de fatores entre 1998 a 2008. *Cad. Saude Publica.* **2018**, *34*, 1–14. [CrossRef]
27. Sowe, A.; Johansson, K. Disentangling the rural-urban immunization coverage disparity in The Gambia: A Fairlie decomposition. *Vaccine* **2019**, *37*, 3088–3096. [CrossRef]

28. World Health Organization. *Immunization Agenda 2030*; World Health Organization: Geneva, Switzerland, 2021.
29. De Moraes, J.C.; de Luna, E.A.; Barbosa, H.; Guibu, I.A.; Ribeiro, M.C.S.A.; Veras, M.A.M.; Rujula, M.J.P.; de Mello, M.L.R.; Simões, O.; de Castro, P.C.; et al. *Inquérito de cobertura vacinal nas áreas urbanas das capitais Brasil-Cobertura vacinal 2007*; Centro de Estudos Augusto Leopoldo Ayrosa Galvão: São Paulo, Brazil, 2007.
30. Garcia, É.M.; Palombo, C.N.T.; Waldman, E.A.; Sato, A.P.S. Factors associated with the completeness of the vaccination schedule of children at 12 and 24 months of Age in a Brazilian medium-size municipality. *J. Pediatr. Nurs.* **2021**, *60*, e46–e53. [CrossRef] [PubMed]
31. Buffarini, R.; Barros, F.C.; Silveira, M.F. Vaccine coverage within the first year of life and associated factors with incomplete immunization in a Brazilian birth cohort. *Arch. Public Health* **2020**, *78*, 21. [CrossRef] [PubMed]
32. Geweniger, A.; Abbas, K.M. Childhood vaccination coverage and equity impact in Ethiopia by socioeconomic, geographic, maternal, and child characteristics. *Vaccine* **2020**, *38*, 3627–3638. [CrossRef] [PubMed]
33. Sarker, A.R.; Akram, R.; Ali, N.; Chowdhury, Z.I.; Sultana, M. Coverage and determinants of full immunization: Vaccination coverage among senegalese children. *Medicina* **2019**, *55*, 480. [CrossRef]
34. Shrivastwa, N.; Wagner, A.L.; Boulton, M.L. Analysis of state-specific differences in childhood vaccination coverage in rural India. *Vaccines* **2019**, *7*, 24. [CrossRef]
35. Hill, H.A.; Elam-Evans, L.D.; Yankey, D.; Singleton, J.A.; Kang, Y. Vaccination Coverage Among Children Aged 19-35 Months-United States, 2017. *Morb. Mortal Wkly Rep.* **2018**, *67*, 1123–1128. [CrossRef]
36. Hu, Y.; Wang, Y.; Chen, Y.; Liang, H. Analyzing the urban-rural vaccination coverage disparity through a fair decomposition in Zhejiang Province, China. *Int. J. Environ. Res. Public Health* **2019**, *16*, 4575. [CrossRef]
37. GAVI. *The 2016–2020 Investment Opportunity*; The Vaccine Alliance: Gavi, Spain, 2015; Volume 23.
38. Veras, A.A.C.A.; Lima, E.J.F.; Caminha, M.D.F.C.; Silva, S.L.; Castro, A.A.M.; Bernardo, A.L.B.; Batista Filho, M. Vaccine uptake and associated factors in an irregular urban settlement in northeastern Brazil: A cross-sectional study. *BMC Public Health* **2020**, *20*, 1152. [CrossRef]
39. Silva, F.D.S.; Barbosa, Y.C.; Batalha, M.A.; Ribeiro, M.R.C.; Simões, V.M.F.; Branco, M.D.R.F.C.; Silva, A.A.M.D. Incompletude vacinal infantil de vacinas novas e antigas e fatores associados: Coorte de nascimento BRISA, São Luís, Maranhão, Nordeste do Brasil. *Cad. Saúde Pública* **2018**, *34*, 1–21. [CrossRef] [PubMed]
40. Ministério da Saúde. *Saúde da Família: Uma Estratégia para a Reorientação do Modelo Assistencial*; Ministério da Saúde, Secretaria de Assistência à Saúde, Coordenação de Saúde da Comunidade: Brasília, Brazil, 1997.
41. Ministério da Saúde. *Política Nacional de Atenção Básica*; Ministério da Saúde, Secretaria de Atenção à Saúde, Departamento de Atenção Básica: Brasília, Brazil, 2012.
42. Nunes, C.A.; Aquino, R.; Medina, M.G.; Vilasbôas, A.L.Q.; Pinto Júnior, E.P.; Luz, L.A.D. Visitas domiciliares no Brasil: Características da atividade basilar dos Agentes Comunitários de Saúde. *Saúde Em Debate* **2018**, *42*, 127–144. [CrossRef]

vaccines

Article

Immunization Gender Inequity in Pakistan: An Analysis of 6.2 Million Children Born from 2019 to 2022 and Enrolled in the Sindh Electronic Immunization Registry

Danya Arif Siddiqi [1,*], Sundus Iftikhar [2], Muhammad Siddique [2], Mariam Mehmood [2], Vijay Kumar Dharma [2], Mubarak Taighoon Shah [1], Hamidreza Setayesh [3] and Subhash Chandir [1,2]

[1] IRD Global, Singapore 049145, Singapore
[2] IRD Pakistan, Karachi 75190, Pakistan
[3] Gavi, The Vaccine Alliance, 1218 Geneva, Switzerland
* Correspondence: danya.arif@ird.global

Abstract: Gender-based inequities in immunization impede the universal coverage of childhood vaccines. Leveraging data from the Government of Sindh's Electronic Immunization Registry (SEIR), we estimated inequalities in immunization for males and females from the 2019–2022 birth cohorts in Pakistan. We computed male-to-female (M:F) and gender inequality ratios (GIR) Tfor enrollment, vaccine coverage, and timeliness. We also explored the inequities by maternal literacy, geographic location, mode of vaccination delivery, and gender of vaccinators. Between 1 January 2019, and 31 December 2022, 6,235,305 children were enrolled in the SEIR, 52.2% males and 47.8% females. We observed a median M:F ratio of 1.03 at enrollment and at Penta-1, Penta-3, and Measles-1 vaccinations, indicating more males were enrolled in the immunization system than females. Once enrolled, a median GIR of 1.00 indicated similar coverage for females and males over time; however, females experienced a delay in their vaccination timeliness. Low maternal education; residing in remote-rural, rural, and slum regions; and receiving vaccines at fixed sites, as compared to outreach, were associated with fewer females being vaccinated, as compared to males. Our findings suggeste the need to tailor and implement gender-sensitive policies and strategies for improving equity in immunization, especially in vulnerable geographies with persistently high inequalities.

Keywords: gender inequity; routine immunization; male-to-female ratio; female vaccination; timeliness of immunization

Citation: Siddiqi, D.A.; Iftikhar, S.; Siddique, M.; Mehmood, M.; Dharma, V.K.; Shah, M.T.; Setayesh, H.; Chandir, S. Immunization Gender Inequity in Pakistan: An Analysis of 6.2 Million Children Born from 2019 to 2022 and Enrolled in the Sindh Electronic Immunization Registry. *Vaccines* **2023**, *11*, 685. https://doi.org/10.3390/vaccines11030685

Academic Editors: Ahmad Reza Hosseinpoor, M. Carolina Danovaro, Devaki Nambiar, Aaron Wallace and Hope Johnson

Received: 15 February 2023
Revised: 13 March 2023
Accepted: 14 March 2023
Published: 17 March 2023

1. Introduction

Vaccination is considered one of the most successful and cost-effective interventions in public health, with a potential return on investment of up to USD 16 per dollar spent [1]. However, many countries, particularly low- and middle-income countries (LMICs), struggle to equitably vaccinate all children, leading to persistent immunization inequities across multiple socio-demographic dimensions, with gender-based inequities being a prominent factor [2]. Although there are apparently no significant differences in coverage rates between males and females at the global level, several country-specific studies have provided contrary evidence [3]. Studies have shown there were significant biases in immunization coverage rates that disadvantaged females in South and Southeast Asia, with Pakistan reporting a 7.8 percentage-point difference between males and females in terms of complete immunization; Cambodia reporting a difference of 4.9 percentage points; Nepal, a difference of 4.3 percentage points; and India, with the largest gap of 13.4 percentage points [4]. In addition to varying inequities at the country level, substantial differences also exist within countries, highlighting an interplay of complex socio-cultural, economic, and geographic factors that leave females at a disadvantage when accessing immunization services.

Pakistan is among the countries where gender inequity in immunizations is a growing concern. As per the Global Gender Gap Index Report 2022 [5], the country ranked 143 out of a total of 146 countries for health and survival, highlighting the adverse position of females relative to males, with inequities manifesting in areas such as healthcare and immunizations. The Pakistan Demographic and Health Survey (2017–18) [6] showed there was a significant difference in coverage rates between females and males, with females being less likely to receive all basic vaccinations, as compared to males (63% vs. 68%), eventually contributing to higher morbidity and mortality among females over the long term. Although concerted efforts in recent decades have resulted in improved immunization coverage rates in the country overall [7], the trend of differential coverage rates among females and males remains, underscoring the gaps in equitable coverage. This is partly due to the lack of gender-sensitive immunization strategies, which are difficult to design in the face of the unavailability of gender-disaggregated data at the micro-level. This has led to a lack of evidence regarding the true estimates and the extent of immunization inequities in the regions where females are most likely to fall behind males. Additionally, there is insufficient information regarding the risk factors associated with unequal coverage rates, and understanding of the demand- and supply-side barriers that consistently prevent females from accessing immunizations.

Major global immunization initiatives, including the Immunization Agenda 2030 and the Gavi 5.0 strategy, were designed around the themes of "Leave No One Behind" and "endeavor to reach the furthest behind first" [8], highlighting the need for identifying, understanding, and addressing the gender-related barriers to immunizations. It is critically important for governments and other stakeholders to estimate the true extent of female-based gender inequities in immunization outcomes at a micro-geographic level and delineate the contributing factors. It is also vital to identify the supply-side barriers that can adversely impact immunization uptake by females. This crucial information is important for immunization systems to implement targeted approaches for reaching missed female children, ensuring their immunization completion as per the WHO-recommended immunization schedule, and promoting gender-based equity in immunizations.

We leveraged the individual child-level data from the Government of Sindh's Electronic Immunization Registry (SEIR) to uncover a detailed picture of the gender inequities in childhood immunizations. We estimated the male-to-female ratios for coverage and timeliness at the micro-geographic level by districts and union councils (UCs; smallest geographic administrative unit) in Sindh Province, Pakistan. Additionally, we also examined the gender inequality ratios for the above as an additional measure. We examined how maternal literacy levels, geographic area (urban, rural, remote-rural, and slum areas), and supply-side factors (gender of vaccinators and modality of immunization service delivery) affect gender inequities in immunization.

2. Methods

2.1. Population

As per the population estimates for 2022, Sindh Province has an annual birth cohort of 1.9 million [9], and a total population of 53.8 million people, with a population density of 381.1 people/sq. km [10]. The province comprises 6 divisions, which are further divided into 30 districts with 1130 UCs [11]. The median population of the UCs is 46,401 (range: 8371–574,2572). The urban and rural median populations of the UCs are 59,293 (range: 8371–574,257) and 37,936 (range: 13,000–95,886), respectively. The poverty index of the province is 0.28 (district range: 0.02–0.50) [12]. The literacy rate for the province is 58% (male = 68%; female = 47%; urban = 73%; rural = 39%) [13]. The annual target population (0–23-month-old children) for the Expanded Programme on Immunization (EPI) was 1.9 million in 2022. Immunizations in Sindh are administered predominantly through public services supplemented by private clinics [14]. Traditionally, approximately 60% of all provincial immunizations were provided through fixed immunization centers, whereas the rest were delivered through routine outreach sessions [15]. However, after the COVID-19 pandemic, this proportion has reversed, with almost 60% of the immunizations now being provided through outreach [16]. Routine outreach comprises immunization sessions held at a site other than the immunization center, from which vaccinators can go out and return the same day, whereas enhanced outreach is defined as a series of immunization outreach sessions covering a geographic area outside the radius of routine activities [17].

2.2. Data Source

We used geospatial-enabled immunization records from the SEIR (also known as Zindagi Mehfooz *(Safe Life)* Electronic Immunization Registry; ZM-EIR). SEIR is an Android-based application that allows vaccinators to enroll and track children's immunization records. The SEIR captures routinely collected data, including the child's demographic details (child's name, father's name, caregiver national identity card number (optional), and contact information) and immunization details (vaccination status, dates, and modality). Additionally, the SEIR also captures the health facility and vaccinator details and the geolocation of each vaccination. Each child's record is tracked through a unique identifier assigned to the child at the time of enrollment in the SEIR. Performance management of the data of vaccinators, including attendance and compliance of usage of the system, is also captured.

The SEIR was scaled up in October 2017 across 28 districts of Sindh and was later rolled out to the remaining 2 districts, Khairpur and Dadu (where primary health care is delivered through a public–private partnership) on 24 February 2020 and 29 June 2020, respectively. Currently, the SEIR is being used across all 30 districts of Sindh, by 3565 vaccinators (including 15.0% female vaccinators) working at 1785 public and 373 private immunization clinics. As of 31 December 2022, the SEIR enrolled >7.7 million children and >2.6 million females and recorded >90 million immunization events. The SEIR enrolled 108.34%, 96.49%, 97.26%, and 95.34% of the EPI estimated annual birth cohorts of 2019, 2020, 2021, and 2022, respectively (1,340,207; 1,638,386; 1,642,773; and 1,682,569, respectively), in the districts where it was operational.

2.3. Study Design and Procedure

We analyzed the child-level longitudinal immunization records in the SEIR from 1 January 2019 to 31 December 2022, for all 30 districts of Sindh. Data from District Khairpur and District Dadu were not shown for children who had received their vaccinations in 2019, as the SEIR was launched in these districts in 2020. We extracted data related to the demographic profile (gender, age, and maternal literacy level), immunization history (vaccines, date of administration, and geo-coordinates of vaccine administration site); modality of immunization service delivery (fixed, routine outreach, or enhanced outreach), and geographical location of household (district, UC, urban vs. rural area, rural vs. remote-rural area and slums vs. non-slums) of children from the 2019–2022 birth cohorts enrolled in the SEIR. Out of 1130 UCs in the province, 464 were classified as urban, and 666 as rural. Within the rural UCs, 88 were classified as remote-rural UCs, and within the urban UCs, 89 were classified as slum areas. An slum area was defined as a contiguous settlement where the inhabitants are characterized as having inadequate housing and basic services. Slum UCs were defined as having >75% population living in poverty. The slum area analysis was limited to EPI-identified slums in the eight districts of Karachi and Hyderabad [18]. All slum UCs in Karachi and Hyderabad were in urban areas. Remote-rural UCs were classified according to the Government of Sindh's School Education and Literacy Department classification of hard-area UCs that were located in remote coastal, desert, or mountainous areas [19]. Remote-rural UCs were mostly concentrated in the eastern and western peripheries of the province; urban UCs were found within the cities of Karachi and Hyderabad; and the rest of the remaining UCs in the province were predominantly rural (Supplementary, Figure S1). In addition to the geo-location data, we also extracted the gender profile of vaccinators who used the SEIR across the province.

2.4. Vaccination Schedule

Pakistan's routine immunization schedule included the following vaccines: BCG (Bacille Calmette-Guérin) and oral polio vaccine (OPV) vaccine at birth; 3 doses of pentavalent (DPT, HepB, Hib) vaccine; 3 doses of pneumococcal conjugate vaccine (PCV) and 3 doses of OPV at 6, 10, and/or 14 weeks of age; 2 doses of rotavirus vaccines at 6 and 10 weeks of age; 2 doses of inactivated polio vaccine (IPV) at 14 weeks and 9 months of age; and 2 doses of measles–rubella vaccine and typhoid conjugate vaccine (TCV) at 9 and 15 months of age. TCV, second dose of IPV, and rubella vaccine were added to the EPI schedule on 1 January 2020, 3 May 2021, and 15 November 2021, respectively [20].

2.5. Ethics

This analysis was deemed to be exempt by the Institutional Review Board of Interactive Research and Development under 45 CFR 46.101(b). The IRB was registered with the U.S. Department of Health and Human Services Office for Human Research Protections with registration number IRB 404 00005148.

2.6. Outcome

The primary outcome was the male-to-female ratios (M:F) at enrollment and by antigens among children from the 2019, 2020, 2021, and 2022 birth cohorts enrolled in the SEIR. The M:F ratio was the number of vaccinated males relative to females. Enrollment was defined as the first encounter of the child with the SEIR. We calculated the M:F ratios at the district and UC levels. We adjusted the M:F ratios using the sex ratios at birth (1.055) in Pakistan [21]. We computed the M:F ratios for the up-to-date vaccination coverage for Pentavalent-1, Pentavalent-3, and Measles-1 at 6, 9, 12, 18, and 24 months. Up-to-date coverage was defined as the proportion of 0–24 months children who received vaccinations by the specified months of age. In order to examine timely coverages, we also calculated the up-to-date coverage of Penta-1 at 10 weeks, Penta-3 at 18 weeks, and Measles-1 at 10 months to account for the timeliness criteria used by EPI-Sindh (an additional 4 weeks' time duration beyond the age at which each vaccine is due, as per the WHO-specified EPI schedule). Furthermore, we compared the M:F ratios by maternal literacy level, geographic residential location of the child (urban vs. rural, rural vs. remote-rural and slums vs. non-slums), modality of vaccination (fixed center, outreach, and enhanced outreach), and the sex ratio of vaccinators in the province. As a secondary outcome, we also calculated the Gender Inequality Ratio (GIR) for all the above analyses, where the gender inequality ratio was defined as the proportion of vaccinated males among those who were due for vaccination, relative to the proportion of vaccinated females who were due for vaccination.

2.7. Statistical Analysis

We reported the median and interquartile range (IQR) of the UCs for the M:F ratios, along with the ranges at the UC level. UCs with no children vaccinated for any particular vaccine were excluded from the analysis for that particular vaccine only. A male-to-female ratio of 0.00 indicated that there were no males or females vaccinated in the particular UC. This was due to the reduced population sizes when we examined our indicators across the sub-categories (maternal literacy and geographic location of vaccination) within a UC.

For our secondary outcome, we computed the GIR by dividing the proportion of males who were due and received vaccinations by the proportion of females who were due and received vaccinations. A GIR of 1.00 implied no differential in coverage rates between females and males, whereas a GIR of above 1.00 indicated inequalities (with higher coverage rates for males relative to females). We performed statistical analyses with Stata, release 17 (StataCorp, College Station, TX, USA). We used digital maps to review the immunization coverage by the district and UC using QGIS (3.16.7-Hannover).

3. Results

Between 1 January 2019, to 31 December 2022, a total of 6,235,305 children were enrolled in the SEIR from the 2019 (23.29%), 2020 (25.35%), 2021 (25.62%), and 2022 (25.73%) birth cohorts. The proportion of males enrolled in the SEIR, as compared to females, was consistently higher across all birth cohorts (2019: 52.11%, 2020: 52.14%; 2021: 52.30%; 2022: 52.25%) (data not shown).

Across districts, we found a distinctive pattern in districts Kashmore, Ghotki, Jacobabad, and Tharparkar, having the highest adjusted median M:F ratios at enrollment: (Kashmore: 1.11 (IQR: 1.04–1.25); Ghotki: 1.11 (IQR: 1.04–1.16); Jacobabad: 1.07 (IQR: 1.00–1.13), and Tharparkar: 1.12 (IQR: 1.02–1.18)) (Table 1). The findings were similar for Penta-1, Penta-3, and Measles-1 vaccinations. A consistent trend, therefore, emerged, showing females falling behind males consistently in these districts from enrollment into the SEIR until their Measles-1 vaccination. At the UC-level, a high median M:F ratio emerged for selected UCs in District Thatta, where thrice the number of males were vaccinated, as compared to females.

When examining the GIR, we observed that once children were enrolled in the SEIR, coverage rates for vaccines were similar for females and males, as shown by the UC-level median GIR for Penta-1 (median: 1.00, IQR: 1.00–1.01), Penta-3 (median: 1.00, IQR: 0.99–1.01), and Measles-1 (median: 1.00, IQR: 0.99–1.01) (Supplementary Table S1).

Tracking the M:F ratios for vaccines over the 4 years showed high inequities in the number of females vaccinated, as compared to males, in 2019 for Penta-3 (1.14, range: 0.24–8.00) and Measles-1 (1.14, range: 0.14–5.00), which declined to 1.10 (Penta-3 range: 0.49–5.00; Measles-1 range: 0.25–2.07) in 2020 and remained at the same level for the following 2 years. The M:F ratios for Penta-1 remained roughly the same between 2019 and 2022, showing no major progress was made in reducing these disparities over the last 4 years (Supplementary Figure S2). The GIR reflected a similar picture of slightly higher inequalities in coverage among the enrolled children in 2019. Thereafter, coverage rates became more balanced between females and males (GIR: 1.00) for all the vaccines in 2020–2022 (Supplementary Figure S3). At the UC level, we found that 11.6% (131/1129) of the UCs showed a M:F > 1.10 for Penta-1 consistently over the four years. This proportion was 10.7% (121/1129) for Penta-3 and 8.9% (101/1129) for Measles-1, reflecting certain geographic pockets had persistently higher numbers of males being vaccinated, as compared to females, year-on-year (Supplementary Table S3). A closer geographic examination revealed that these UCs were spread throughout the province, as opposed to being located in clusters (Supplementary Figure S4).

The up-to-date coverages at specific age intervals for Penta-1, Penta-3, and Measles-1 showed more males were vaccinated, as compared to females, at each age (M:F $\geq$ 1.10) (Figure 1).

Among the enrolled children, 1 out of every 2 UCs in the province had females falling behind males on timely vaccinations of Penta-1, Penta-3, and Measles-1, as denoted by GIRs > 1.00. Notably, 60.7% (685/1129), 57.4% (648/1129), and 54.5% (615/1128) of UCs had GIRs > 1.00 for up-to-date coverage of Penta-1 at 10 weeks, Penta-3 at 18 weeks, and Measles-1 at 10 months. This proportion continued to decline across ages, demonstrating a narrowing of the inequity gap at the UC level as children aged (Figure 2).

Table 1. District-wise adjusted male-to-female ratios of 0–23-month-old children in 2019–2022 birth cohorts enrolled in SEIR and vaccinated, by district (n = 6,235,305) (1 January 2019–31 December 2022).

					At Vaccination									
Enrollment/ Vaccination District	# of UCs	Enrollment	Median (IQR)	UC Range	Penta-1	Median (IQR)	UC Range	Penta-3	Median (IQR)	UC Range	Measles-1	Median (IQR)	UC Range
Badin	46	1.05	1.02 (0.98–1.11)	0.89–1.55	1.05	1.03 (0.98–1.11)	0.89–1.55	1.06	1.02 (0.99–1.12)	0.90–1.57	1.06	1.03 (0.97–1.11)	0.90–1.64
Dadu	52	1.04	1.02 (0.96–1.09)	0.80–1.20	1.04	1.02 (0.98–1.09)	0.82–1.19	1.04	1.03 (0.99–1.09)	0.83–1.21	1.04	1.04 (0.99–1.09)	0.82–1.22
Ghotki	40	1.1	1.11 (1.04–1.16)	0.90–1.42	1.1	1.10 (1.04–1.15)	0.90–1.40	1.1	1.09 (1.04–1.16)	0.93–1.39	1.09	1.10 (1.04–1.14)	0.93–1.33
Hyderabad	54	1	1.02 (0.96–1.05)	0.69–1.26	1	1.01 (0.95–1.05)	0.73–1.28	0.99	1.01 (0.95–1.04)	0.69–1.35	1	1.01 (0.94–1.05)	0.68–1.31
Jacobabad	40	1.07	1.07 (1.00–1.13)	0.89–1.41	1.07	1.06 (1.01–1.13)	0.86–1.40	1.08	1.07 (1.01–1.17)	0.89–1.35	1.08	1.07 (1.01–1.17)	0.91–1.28
Jamshoro	28	1.04	1.02 (0.97–1.13)	0.85–2.26	1.04	1.02 (0.97–1.10)	0.86–2.03	1.04	1.01 (0.96–1.10)	0.83–1.78	1.04	1.03 (0.97–1.10)	0.85–1.77
Kambar	40	1	1.02 (0.95–1.05)	0.71–1.20	1	1.02 (0.96–1.06)	0.79–1.22	1	1.01 (0.98–1.05)	0.77–1.22	0.99	1.00 (0.97–1.04)	0.75–1.19
Karachi Central	51	0.99	0.98 (0.93–1.03)	0.63–1.33	0.99	0.98 (0.94–1.02)	0.63–1.28	0.99	0.98 (0.95–1.03)	0.59–1.19	0.99	0.99 (0.95–1.03)	0.60–1.19
Karachi East	28	0.98	0.99 (0.94–1.02)	0.85–1.08	0.99	1.00 (0.96–1.03)	0.85–1.10	0.98	0.98 (0.96–1.01)	0.84–1.09	0.98	0.99 (0.94–1.03)	0.90–1.12
Karachi South	26	0.99	0.99 (0.97–1.03)	0.91–1.11	1	1.01 (0.98–1.04)	0.91–1.20	1	1.01 (0.98–1.04)	0.89–1.09	1.01	1.02 (0.97–1.05)	0.90–1.15
Karachi West	22	0.98	0.97 (0.95–1.03)	0.88–1.06	0.98	0.97 (0.96–1.02)	0.89–1.07	0.97	0.98 (0.95–1.03)	0.87–1.06	0.97	0.96 (0.95–1.03)	0.86–1.04
Kashmore	37	1.15	1.11 (1.04–1.25)	0.92–1.56	1.14	1.12 (1.06–1.22)	0.95–1.46	1.13	1.12 (1.04–1.21)	0.91–1.35	1.12	1.11 (1.05–1.22)	0.90–1.36
Kemari	21	0.98	0.98 (0.96–1.01)	0.83–1.17	0.99	0.98 (0.96–1.02)	0.85–1.13	0.98	0.99 (0.96–1.03)	0.86–1.10	0.99	1.00 (0.96–1.03)	0.85–1.09
Khairpur	76	1.06	1.03 (1.00–1.11)	0.83–1.41	1.06	1.04 (1.00–1.12)	0.86–1.36	1.07	1.05 (1.00–1.12)	0.88–1.41	1.07	1.04 (0.99–1.12)	0.88–1.38
Korangi	30	1.01	1.02 (0.98–1.04)	0.86–1.29	1.01	1.02 (0.99–1.04)	0.89–1.24	1	1.01 (0.99–1.02)	0.90–1.18	1	1.00 (0.98–1.03)	0.89–1.17
Larkana	46	1.04	1.03 (0.97–1.07)	0.89–1.58	1.04	1.03 (0.98–1.08)	0.90–1.49	1.05	1.04 (1.01–1.09)	0.90–1.46	1.05	1.03 (0.98–1.11)	0.91–1.45
Malir	19	0.99	1.00 (0.97–1.02)	0.94–1.03	1	1.00 (0.98–1.02)	0.94–1.05	1	1.00 (0.97–1.02)	0.95–1.05	1	1.01 (0.99–1.02)	0.85–1.04
Matiari	18	1.1	1.06 (1.01–1.10)	0.95–1.53	1.1	1.05 (1.02–1.11)	0.94–1.51	1.1	1.05 (1.03–1.11)	0.94–1.58	1.08	1.04 (1.02–1.11)	0.93–1.51
Mirpurkhas	41	1.03	1.02 (0.98–1.06)	0.93–1.27	1.03	1.03 (0.97–1.07)	0.93–1.25	1.03	1.02 (0.99–1.07)	0.90–1.31	1.02	1.01 (0.98–1.06)	0.91–1.29
Naushero Feroz	51	1.04	1.05 (0.97–1.11)	0.89–1.22	1.05	1.05 (0.97–1.10)	0.92–1.21	1.05	1.05 (0.98–1.09)	0.93–1.23	1.04	1.01 (0.99–1.08)	0.92–1.23
Sanghar	55	1.09	1.08 (1.00–1.15)	0.82–1.37	1.09	1.08 (1.00–1.14)	0.87–1.38	1.08	1.06 (1.02–1.15)	0.95–1.32	1.08	1.08 (1.01–1.15)	0.94–1.28
Shaheed Benazirabad	51	1.05	1.06 (1.01–1.10)	0.92–1.24	1.04	1.06 (1.01–1.10)	0.93–1.23	1.04	1.04 (1.01–1.09)	0.93–1.21	1.04	1.04 (1.00–1.11)	0.92–1.22
Shikarpur	49	1.02	1.02 (0.97–1.07)	0.88–1.22	1.02	1.01 (0.98–1.07)	0.89–1.21	1.01	1.01 (0.97–1.06)	0.86–1.20	1.01	1.00 (0.97–1.05)	0.89–1.21
Sujawal	25	1.05	1.06 (0.97–1.09)	0.89–1.33	1.05	1.06 (0.98–1.09)	0.89–1.30	1.04	1.04 (0.98–1.09)	0.89–1.29	1.04	1.03 (0.98–1.09)	0.89–1.26
Sukkur	46	1.08	1.05 (1.02–1.11)	0.71–1.82	1.07	1.05 (1.03–1.13)	0.76–1.63	1.07	1.07 (1.01–1.11)	0.80–1.47	1.07	1.07 (1.01–1.11)	0.84–1.47
Tando Allahyar	20	1.06	1.05 (1.00–1.10)	0.93–1.23	1.06	1.03 (1.01–1.09)	0.96–1.21	1.05	1.05 (1.01–1.09)	0.95–1.19	1.05	1.05 (1.02–1.09)	0.95–1.14
Tando Muhammad Khan	17	1.02	1.03 (0.97–1.10)	0.72–1.40	1.02	1.02 (0.98–1.11)	0.73–1.41	1.03	1.02 (1.00–1.09)	0.71–1.40	1.03	1.04 (0.99–1.10)	0.69–1.36
Tharparkar	44	1.11	1.12 (1.02–1.18)	0.85–1.69	1.11	1.11 (1.03–1.17)	0.85–1.68	1.11	1.13 (1.02–1.17)	0.85–1.65	1.11	1.12 (1.03–1.19)	0.86–1.55
Thatta	30	1.09	1.07 (1.02–1.12)	0.75–3.00	1.09	1.06 (1.02–1.11)	0.76–2.85	1.09	1.07 (1.02–1.12)	0.75–2.82	1.08	1.06 (1.02–1.11)	0.71–2.73
Umerkot	27	1.05	1.06 (1.01–1.11)	0.90–1.21	1.05	1.05 (1.00–1.10)	0.91–1.18	1.05	1.05 (0.98–1.09)	0.92–1.20	1.03	1.03 (0.98–1.05)	0.92–1.14
Total	1130	1.04	1.03 (0.98–1.10)	0.63–3.00	1.04	1.04 (0.98–1.10)	0.63–2.85	1.04	1.03 (0.99–1.09)	0.59–2.82	1.04	1.03 (0.98–1.09)	0.60–2.73

#: number.

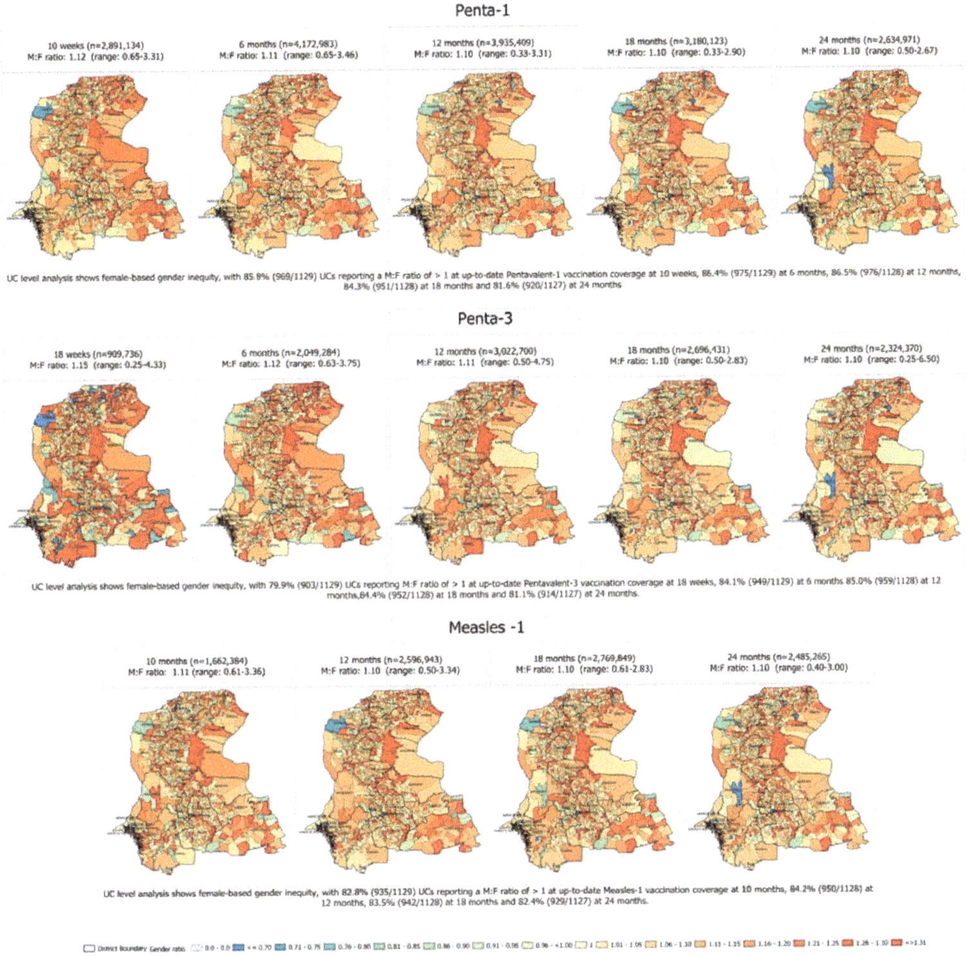

Figure 1. Male-to-female ratios of up-to-date vaccination coverage of Pentavalent-1 at 10 weeks and 6, 12, 18, and 24 months; Pentavalent-3 at 18 weeks and 6, 12, 18, and 24 months; and Measles-1 at 10, 6, 12, 18, and 24 months, in 0–23-month-old children in 2019–2022 birth cohorts enrolled in SEIR (1 January 2019–31 December 2022).

By observing the inequities in enrollment and the number of vaccinated males and females across maternal literacy levels, we found higher inequities among children with mothers who had only primary education (1–5 years of education), as compared to mothers with higher education levels and those who were not educated at all (Table 2). This was evident for Penta-1 (median M:F ratio: 1.09 (IQR: 0.92–1.3)), Penta-3 (median: 1.10 (IQR: 0.91–1.33)), and Measles-1 (median: 1.10 (IQR: 0.93–1.33)). With increasing education levels, the inequities were reduced, as shown by the median M:F ratio declining to 1.00. However, when examining the inequities at the UC level, individual UCs had high inequities in enrollment and the number of vaccinated males vs. females (M:F ratio between 7.00–10.00), even when mothers had high literacy levels (≥11 years of education).

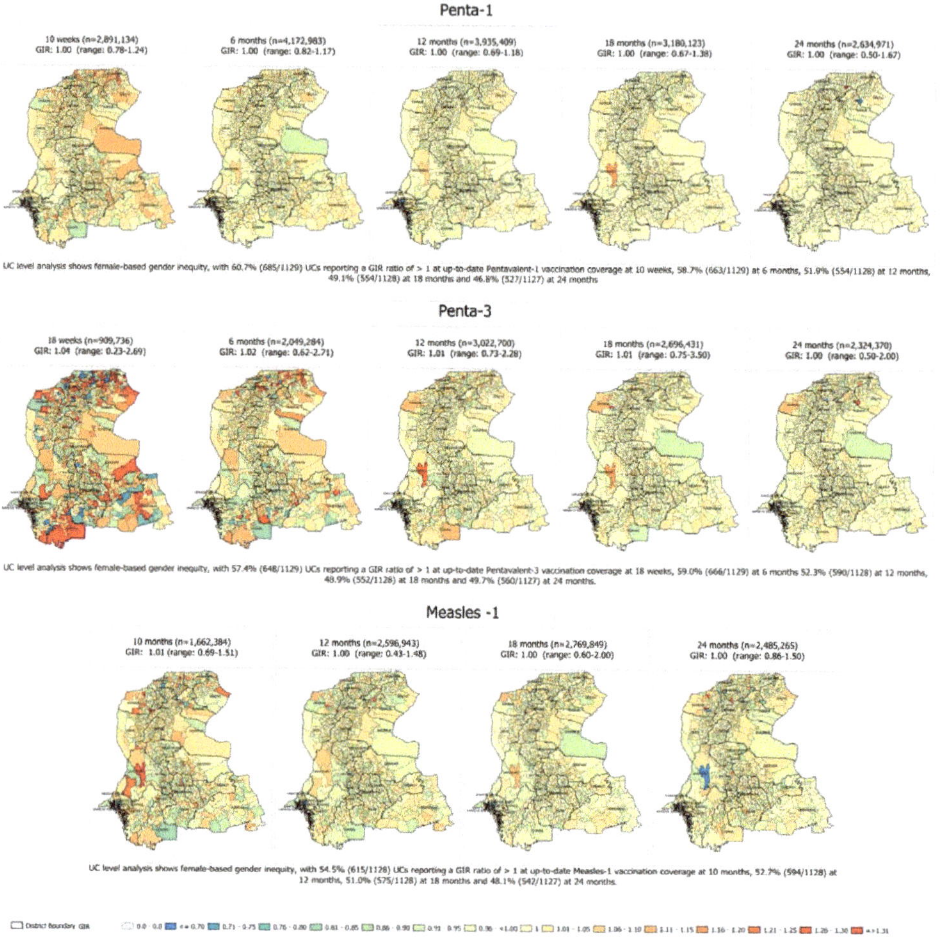

Figure 2. Gender inequality ratio (GIR) at up-to-date vaccination coverage of Pentavalent-1 at 10 weeks and 6, 12, 18, and 24 months; Pentavalent-3 at 18 weeks and 6, 12, 18, and 24 months; and Measles-1 at 10, 6, 12, 18, and 24 months, in 0–23-month-old children in 2019–2022 birth cohorts enrolled in SEIR (1 January 2019–31 December 2022).

Rural UCs had higher median M:F ratios, as compared to urban UCs, for Penta-1 (median M:F ratio 1.11 vs. 1.06), Penta-3 (M:F ratio: 1.11 vs. 1.06), and Measles-1 vaccinations (M:F ratio: 1.10 vs. 1.07). The UC-level ranges, however, demonstrated that there were selected UCs with as many as five times more males being vaccinated than females for Measles-1, even in urban areas. Within the rural UCs, the remote-rural UCs reflected worse equity outcomes, with median M:F ratios as high as 1.14 for Penta-1. The slum UCs had the worst median M:F ratios for Penta-1 (1.07 (IQR: 1.03–1.11)), Penta-3 (1.07 (IQR: 1.03–1.12)), and Measles-1 (1.07 (IQR: 1.03–1.12)), as compared to non-slum UCs (Penta-1: 1.05 (IQR: 1.01–1.09), Penta-3: 1.05 (IQR: 1.02–1.09), and Measles-1 1.06 (IQR: 1.01–1.09).

Table 2. Male-to-Female ratios of 0–23-month-old children in 2019–2022 birth cohorts enrolled in SEIR in Sindh Province, Pakistan, by maternal literacy levels, geographic profile, vaccination modality, and vaccinator sex ratio at enrollment for Pentavalent-1, Pentavalent-3 and Measles-1 vaccines (n = 6,235,305) (1 January 2019–31 December 2022).

	Enrollment			Pentavalent-1			Pentavalent-3			Measles-1		
	M:F Ratio	**Median (IQR)**	**UC Range**	**M:F Ratio**	**Median (IQR)**	**UC Range**	**M:F Ratio**	**Median (IQR)**	**UC Range**	**M:F Ratio**	**Median (IQR)**	**UC Range**
Mother's education (years)												
0	1.09	1.06 (0.93–1.21)	0.00–5.00	1.09	1.04 (0.82–1.33)	0.00–11.00	1.09	1.05 (0.86–1.38)	0.00–9.00	1.08	1.04 (0.85–1.35)	0.00–7.00
1–5	1.11	1.04 (0.84–1.24)	0.00–8.00	1.11	1.09 (0.92–1.30)	0.00–7.00	1.11	1.10 (0.91–1.33)	0.00–9.00	1.11	1.10 (0.93–1.33)	0.00–5.00
6–8	1.12	1.00 (0.67–1.35)	0.00–8.00	1.12	1.00 (0.50–1.33)	0.00–7.00	1.12	1.00 (0.50–1.38)	0.00–7.00	1.12	1.00 (0.50–1.33)	0.00–11.00
9–10	1.09	1.00 (0.54–1.27)	0.00–7.00	1.09	1.00 (0.50–1.37)	0.00–9.00	1.10	1.00 (0.50–1.42)	0.00–9.00	1.10	1.00 (0.50–1.47)	0.00–10.00
≥11	1.07	1.00 (0.50–1.33)	0.00–10.00	1.07	1.00 (0.33–1.33)	0.00–11.00	1.07	1.00 (0.50–1.25)	0.00–6.00	1.07	1.00 (0.25–1.33)	0.00–7.00
Geographic location												
Rural	1.12	1.11 (1.06–1.17)	0.00–2.38	1.12	1.11 (1.06–1.17)	0.50–2.14	1.12	1.11 (1.06–1.18)	0.50–1.80	1.12	1.10 (1.05–1.17)	0.00–2.17
Urban	1.07	1.07 (1.02–1.11)	0.00–2.37	1.07	1.06 (1.02–1.11)	0.50–2.50	1.07	1.06 (1.02–1.11)	0.00–2.61	1.07	1.07 (1.02–1.12)	0.44–5.00
Remote-rural	1.15	1.14 (1.08–1.21)	0.71–2.07	1.15	1.14 (1.07–1.21)	0.69–1.77	1.15	1.13 (1.07–1.22)	0.94–1.74	1.15	1.13 (1.08–1.22)	0.80–1.75
Rural	1.12	1.10 (1.05–1.17)	0.00–2.38	1.12	1.10 (1.06–1.16)	0.50–2.14	1.12	1.11 (1.06–1.17)	0.50–1.80	1.11	1.10 (1.05–1.17)	0.00–2.17
Slums	1.08	1.07 (1.03–1.11)	0.00–2.37	1.08	1.07 (1.03–1.11)	0.50–2.50	1.08	1.07 (1.03–1.12)	0.00–2.61	1.08	1.07 (1.03–1.12)	0.44–5.00
Non-slums	1.05	1.05 (1.02–1.08)	0.83–1.76	1.05	1.05 (1.01–1.09)	0.81–1.70	1.05	1.05 (1.02–1.09)	0.82–1.56	1.05	1.06 (1.01–1.09)	0.90–2.38
Vaccination modality												
Fixed	1.09	1.03–1.17	0.00–8.00	1.09	1.09 (1.03–1.18)	0.00–4.18	1.09	1.09 (1.02–1.19)	0.00–3.50	1.09	1.09 (1.01–1.19)	0.00–6.00
Outreach	1.09	1.01–1.17	0.54–3.25	1.09	1.08 (1.01–1.16)	0.00–3.51	1.10	1.09 (1.02–1.17)	0.00–3.51	1.10	1.08 (1.02–1.16)	0.00–3.67
EOA	1.09	1.00–1.17	0.00–3.08	1.08	1.07 (0.99–1.17)	0.00–5.00	1.09	1.07 (1.00–1.17)	0.00–6.00	1.09	1.07 (1.00–1.16)	0.00–5.00
Vaccinators' sex												
No female vaccinator	1.11	1.00 (1.00–1.20)	0.80–3.00	1.11	1.20 (1.00–1.20)	0.80–3.00	1.11	1.00 (1.00–1.20)	0.80–2.80	1.11	1.00 (1.00–1.20)	0.80–2.80
M:F ratio ≥ 2	1.08	1.00 (1.00–1.20)	0.80–1.60	1.08	1.00 (1.00–1.20)	1.00–1.60	1.07	1.00 (1.00–1.20)	0.80–1.40	1.08	1.00 (1.00–1.20)	1.00–1.40
1 < M:F ratio < 2	1.07	1.00 (1.00–1.20)	0.80–1.20	1.07	1.00 (1.00–1.20)	1.00–1.20	1.06	1.00 (1.00–1.00)	1.00–1.20	1.06	1.00 (1.00–1.00)	1.00–1.20
M:F ratio = 1	1.06	1.00 (1.00–1.00)	0.60–1.80	1.05	1.00 (1.00–1.00)	0.60–1.60	1.05	1.00 (1.00–1.00)	0.60–1.60	1.05	1.00 (1.00–1.00)	0.60–1.60
M:F ratio < 1	1.03	1.00 (1.00–1.00)	1.00–1.20	1.04	1.00 (1.00–1.00)	1.00–1.20	1.04	1.00 (1.00–1.00)	1.00–1.20	1.04	1.00 (1.00–1.00)	1.00–1.20
No vaccinator	1.16	1.20 (1.20–1.20)	1.20–1.20	1.25	1.20 (1.20–1.20)	1.20–1.20	1.01	1.00 (1.00–1.00)	1.00–1.00	1.21	1.20 (1.20–1.20)	1.20–1.20

Based on M:F ratios by mode of vaccination, we found marginally higher inequities in the number of males vaccinated, as compared to females, among vaccinations conducted at fixed immunization centers, as compared to immunizations by routine outreach (Penta-1: 1.09 vs. 1.08; Measles-1: 1.09 vs. 1.08)). Lower median M:F ratios were found for immunizations administered by EOAs, (Penta-1: 1.07; Penta-3: 1.07; and Measles-1: 1.07), showing more equity between the number of females and males vaccinated during the intensive periods of EOAs conducted in the province.

Slight variations in M:F ratios were also observed when investigating inequities across UCs with varying numbers of female and male vaccinators. No differences between the number of males and females vaccinated (across any antigen) were observed when examining the median M:F ratios. However, we observed slightly increased inequities at the UC level in areas where there were no female vaccinators (UC range: 0.80–3.00 for Penta-1 and 0.80–2.80 for Penta-3 and Measles-1). We noted that even in areas where there were more female than male vaccinators (selected UCs in Karachi Division, Supplementary Figure S5), there were UCs that still had fewer females vaccinated than males (UC range: 1.00–1.20).

Conducting the above analysis according to the GIR did not reveal substantial inequalities in coverage rates between males and females (median GIR of UCs ranged between 0.99–1.03). Selected UCs demonstrated high inequalities. Nevertheless, a clear correlational pattern between inequality in coverage and maternal literacy, geographic location, modality of vaccination, and sex ratio of vaccinators, was not always obvious (Supplementary Table S2).

4. Discussion

We found that for every 100 females, 103 males were enrolled and vaccinated in the SEIR over the last 4 years. However, the sub-national analysis at the UC level shows the difference increased to 300 males being vaccinated for every 100 females in specific UCs. Merely observing the aggregate levels for evidence of gender differentials masked these nuanced yet more pronounced inequities. Moreover, recent reports by Gavi [22] and WHO [23] asserted that subnational variations in immunization coverage were 'one of the tractable but unfinished challenges of immunization inequity globally.' Differences at the micro-geographic level reflected subtle and persistent forms of gender bias and discrimination that continue to affect health outcomes for females over the long term. When comparing the male-to-female ratios and gender inequality ratios, we observed a larger number of males than females made contact with the immunization system (even after adjusting for the male-to-female baseline population). However, once they had been enrolled (in the SEIR), the vaccine coverage rates were similar for both females and males, although females still fell behind males in receiving timely vaccinations.

Our findings have important implications for the zero-dose children that have yet to make contact with the health system. Since more males than females have been enrolled in the immunization system, this reflects substantial inequities, indicating more females than males are left behind and being added to the higher proportion of zero-dose children. There is a need for rethinking and emphasizing the narrative of 'zero-dose females', and ensuring the use of gender-disaggregated data and gender-sensitive strategies in order to reach the missing children. We also observed that gender inequities continue to persist over time. The analysis of individual UCs suggested there were certain pockets and regions spread throughout the province where females continuously fell behind males on their vaccinations, year-on-year. Targeted, intensified efforts directed to hotspots showing high inequities could be a potential measure to break the pattern of persistent inequities.

Although parity in coverage rates among females and males enrolled in the SEIR was a positive finding, we observed equality was not uniformly reflected across all age groups. Females were more likely to be delayed in their vaccinations than males. While reflecting well on the overall view of equality, it was imperative to note that as females were delayed on their vaccination, they remained susceptible to vaccine-preventable diseases (VPDs) for longer periods, leading to a higher risk of morbidity and mortality over time. Delayed vaccination for females could have a considerable impact on child survival rates overall, a pertinent implication for Pakistan, where infant and child mortality rates are some of the highest globally. A study from Bangladesh showed children receiving BCG within the first 6 months of life had a lower risk of diseases than those vaccinated later [24]. Similar results were also reported for the delayed administration of the diphtheria–tetanus and pertussis vaccines [25].

Our findings of higher inequities in the number of vaccinated females and males in rural areas, as compared to urban areas, and slums, as compared to non-slums [26,27], have been repeatedly emphasized in existing literature [28,29]. We went a step further to demonstrate that within the rural areas, the category of remote-rural and hard-to-reach areas fared even worse, with M:F ratios as high as 1.14. Several underlying factors have been cited to explain the inequities, the most prominent being the deep-rooted socio-cultural practice of "son preference", which is inherently common in Pakistan [30] and other South Asian countries [29,31]. Persistent patriarchal practices favor sons over daughters due to factors such as carrying forward the family lineage, providing old-age support, financial support, and practices pertaining to dowries. The phenomenon of son preference has been closely associated with several adverse practices, including gender-selective abortions, female infanticide, and neglect of the health and education of females. In rural and remote-rural regions, not only are these practices more deeply entrenched, but when coupled with multiple other deprivations, including poverty, lack of affordable transportation, and long distances to healthcare services, they lead to discriminatory attitudes by caregivers in favor of males. This was underscored in our findings with higher inequities in the number of females and males vaccinated at fixed immunization centers. Immunizations administered during both routine and enhanced outreach tended to be more equitable for females, reflecting that caregivers were not inherently opposed to vaccination, but when faced with the logistical and financial challenges of taking children to vaccination centers, they were more likely to favor males over females.

Within remote-rural settings, several additional dynamics are at play that adversely impacted equitable immunization, such as the higher marginal cost of reaching remote children, retention and motivation of personnel, geographic remoteness, and limited socio-political power among communities [32]. The factors were further undercut by gender issues where, in the event of male vaccinators, mothers and female caregivers faced even greater societal restrictions when accompanying children for immunization. Our findings showed that not only did this have an adverse impact on vaccination rates overall, but the lack of female vaccinators disproportionately and adversely affected vaccination outcomes for females, as compared to males. The absence of gender-sensitive policies for immunization was highlighted in our study (none of the 87 remote-rural UCs in Sindh Province had a single female vaccinator (Supplementary Table S4) and mentioned elsewhere including no segregated waiting rooms at immunization facilities for female caregivers and a shortage of female vaccinators in urban impoverished areas, which was a "discouraging factor" for the attendance of females and children at health facilities [26]. Our results showed that the districts of Ghotki, Jacobabad, and Kashmore had high prevalence rates of inequities for females at enrollment and for subsequent antigens. These districts are located within the northern belt of the province, which remains deeply rooted in conservative tribal culture with a high prevalence of other discriminatory practices against females, including domestic violence and forced child marriages [33]. Gender equity in immunizations is not an isolated concept but deeply intertwined with females' empowerment, agency, and autonomy. Increasing females access to education is a proven mechanism to break the perpetual cycle of discrimination. Within the context of immunizations, our findings were in line with others that showed higher maternal education [34,35] led to reduced vaccination inequities for females. However, our study showed that, even with very high levels of maternal education (>11 years), there remained UCs that had extreme inequalities (M:F ratio: 11.0). Upon closer geographic examination, we observed 4 of such UCs were clustered fairly close together, suggesting there could be other prevalent socio-cultural or logistical challenges causing inequities that even higher maternal education levels were unable to overcome.

Vaccine hesitancy is one particular challenge that merits further investigation within the context of gender inequities in immunization. One study has articulated the reasons for vaccine hesitancy in Pakistan as a triad of religious traditions, misconceptions, and political factors. [36]. Vaccine hesitancy may contribute to gender inequities in immunization by perpetuating cultural norms and beliefs that prioritize males over females and fuel misinformation and misconceptions about vaccines that disproportionately affect females, limiting access to health services and decision-making power for females.

Addressing gender inequities in immunization requires multilevel, complementary approaches. Feasible policy measures include the inclusion of more female vaccinators in the health workforce. Due to sociocultural and gender norms in underserved communities of LMICs such as Pakistan, only female frontline health workers have unrestricted access to households, are able to interact with mothers and provide health education, and deliver vaccines to children. More female vaccinators could, therefore, promote building trust concerning vaccines and encourage immunization uptake among vulnerable communities. To enhance the female position in the immunization decision-making process for their children, we must focus on overall education for females, specifically in health literacy. A previous study revealed that females who were health literate, regardless of their educational level, were more likely to vaccinate their children, in both rural and urban settings [37]. Additionally, female groups in local settings and communities can be initiated or leveraged as a platform for counseling focused on health literacy. These groups could be complemented with programs to involve fathers, including facilitating regular sessions with females and males to foster collaborative parenting and decision-making. A gender-centric approach to the overall health system should be strengthened by measures such as separate waiting areas for females in immunization clinics and the introduction of female-only transport to immunization centers, which could increase immunization rates among females.

Our study had a few limitations. The adjusted M:F ratios reported in the analyses represented a best-guess given the lack of reliable sex ratios in birth data at district and UC levels. Although 1.055 represented an aggregate number for the country, this masked the heterogeneity and inequities in M:F ratios across districts and union councils. Additionally, studies have shown that sex ratios at birth varied by levels of maternal education [38–40], ethnicity, the birth order of the child, as well as the economic and cultural heterogeneities [41]. Therefore, adjustments using aggregate M:F ratios at birth could mask the true extent of prevailing inequities at the sub-national level. Moreover, the M:F ratios calculated for maternal literacy, geographic location, and mode of vaccination delivery were not adjusted for the underlying proportion of males and females in the population due to the unavailability of baseline population proportions for these categories. Nonetheless, we speculated that even if these were to be adjusted, the high M:F ratios (up to 5.00 at the UC level) still reflected substantial inequities between females and males. To validate our estimates of M:F ratios further, we correlated them with the gender-wise proportions in the Multiple Indicators Cluster Survey (MICs). However, since the sample size in the MICs was small when compared against our analysis categories, no meaningful, statistically significant correlations were found between the gender proportions in our analysis and MICs. Additionally, only 58% of the remote-rural UCs in the province, as per our source, were matched with the UC database in SEIR due to different names and a variation in UC categorization used by the health and education departments. Lastly, we acknowledge that a long-term horizon of four years to observe inequity trends did not account for various factors that typically change over time (district-level government staff including supervisors and vaccinators, external shocks such as COVID-19, and unprecedented flooding), and these may have confounded the impact of the gender-based inequities over the last four years. However, by also focusing on regions that have persistently demonstrated worse immunization outcomes for females, we showed the deep-seated inequities that continue to persist despite external changes over time.

5. Conclusions

Our study demonstrated evidence of the gender-based inequities in Sindh Province, Pakistan, over the last four years, with a higher number of males than females being enrolled and immunized. Once enrolled, the coverage rates of females and males were similar, although females tended to be delayed in receiving their vaccinations, as compared to males. We also observed geographical pockets where females continued to fall behind males, year-on-year, reflecting the persistent nature of the inequalities. Our findings have important implications for the inequities among zero-dose children who are more likely to be females. We also demonstrated that certain factors such as maternal literacy, place of residence, and supply-side factors (mode of vaccination delivery, gender of vaccinators), were both a cause and consequence of gender-based inequities. Socio-cultural factors are inextricably linked to characteristics that lead to poor immunization outcomes for females. A deeper qualitative investigation at the sub-national level is needed to uncover the complex dynamics that impact equities in coverage, so that tailored and targeted strategies can be implemented to ensure females and males have the same opportunities to access and benefit from life-saving immunizations.

Supplementary Materials: The following supporting information can be downloaded at: https://www.mdpi.com/article/10.3390/vaccines11030685/s1, Figure S1: Location of Urban, Rural, and Remote-Rural UCs in Sindh Province, Pakistan (n = 1130); Figure S2: Annual male-to-female ratios among children (>6 weeks) who received Penta-1, Penta-3, and Measles-1 vaccinations in 2019–2022 birth cohorts enrolled in SEIR (1 January 2019–31 December 2022); Figure S3: Annual gender inequality ratios (GIR) among children (>6 weeks) who received Penta-1, Penta-3, and Measles-1 vaccinations in 2019–2022 birth cohorts enrolled in SEIR (1 January 2019–31 December 2022); Figure S4: Geographical distribution of UCs showing annual male-to-female ratios of >1.10 among children (>6 weeks) who received Penta-1, Penta-3, and Measles-1 vaccinations in 2019–2022 birth cohorts enrolled in SEIR (1 January 2019–31 December 2022); Figure S5: Location of UCs with differing sex ratios of vaccinators in Sindh Province, Pakistan (n = 3354); Table S1: Gender inequality ratios of 0–23-month-old children in 2019–2022 birth cohorts in SEIR at enrollment and vaccination coverage in Sindh Province, Pakistan, by district (n = 6,235,305) (1 January 2019–31 December 2022); Table S2: Gender inequality ratios of 0–23-month-old children in 2019–2022 birth cohorts in SEIR at enrollment and by antigens by maternal literacy levels, geographic location, vaccinators sex ratio, and modality of immunization delivery (n = 6,235,305) (1 January 2019–31 December 2022); Table S3: Number of UCs showing persistent gender inequities in vaccination (M:F > 1.05) from 2019–2022 (n = 1129);Table S4: Categorization of remote-rural, rural, and urban UCs by sex ratio of vaccinators (n = 1130).

Author Contributions: Conceptualization, D.A.S., H.S. and S.C.; Data curation, S.I. and M.S.; Formal analysis, S.I., M.S. and M.M.; Funding acquisition, D.A.S. and S.C.; Methodology, D.A.S., H.S. and S.C.; Project administration, V.K.D. and M.T.S.; Resources, V.K.D. and M.S.; Supervision, S.C.; Visualization, D.A.S., S.I., M.S., H.S. and S.C.; Writing—original draft, D.A.S. and M.M.; Writing—review & editing, H.S. and S.C. All authors have read and agreed to the published version of the manuscript.

Funding: This work was supported by grants from GiveWell and Gavi, the Vaccine Alliance, to support the Government of Sindh for implementing SEIR. The funders had no role in study design, data collection, data interpretation, or report writing.

Institutional Review Board Statement: This analysis was deemed to be exempt by the Institutional Review Board of Interactive Research and Development under 45 CFR 46.101(b) (study number: IRD_IRB_2020_04_018). The IRB was registered with the U.S. Department of Health and Human Services Office for Human Research Protections with registration number IRB 404 00005148.

Informed Consent Statement: Not applicable.

Data Availability Statement: Data may be obtained from a third party and are not publicly available. The data used for this analysis from Sindh Electronic Immunization Registry (SEIR; also known as Zindagi Mehfooz program) can be requested from the Government of Sindh's Expanded Programme on Immunization (EPI).

Acknowledgments: We thank Rozina Feroz Ali for supporting the literature review for the manuscript. We are grateful to the EPI-Sindh and the frontline health workers who vaccinate children and maintain the SEIR, and their supervisors and support staff.

Conflicts of Interest: The authors declare that they have no known competing financial interest or personal relationships that could have influenced the work reported in this paper.

References

1. UNICEF, Regional Office for South Asia (ROSA). *Immunization and Gender: A Practical Guide to Integrate a Gender Lens into Immunization Programmes*; UNICEF, 2019; p. 35.
2. Feikin, D.R.; Flannery, B.; Hamel, M.J.; Stack, M.; Hansen, P.M. Vaccines for children in low-and middle-income countries. *Reprod. Matern. Newborn Child Health Dis. Control. Priorities* **2006**, *2*, 187–205. [CrossRef]
3. The Vaccine Alliance Gavi. Immunisation and the Sustainable Development Goals. September 2019. Available online: https://www.gavi.org/sites/default/files/document/2019/Immunisation%20and%20the%20SDGs%20%281%29.pdf (accessed on 12 December 2022).
4. Gwatkin, D.R.; Devishwar-Bahl, G. *Immunization Coverage Inequalities: An Overview of Socioeconomic and Gender Differentials in Developing Countries*; World Bank: Washington DC, USA, 2001.
5. Schwab, K.; Samans, R.; Zahidi, S.; Leopold, T.A.; Ratcheva, V.; Hausmann, R.; Tyson, L.D. *The Global Gender Gap Report 2022*; World Economic Forum: Geneva, Switzerland, 2022.
6. NIPS and ICF, Pakistan. *Pakistan Demographic and Health Survey 2017-18*; NIPS/Pakistan and ICF: Islamabad, Pakistan, 2019.
7. Butt, M.; Mohammed, R.; Butt, E.; Butt, S.; Xiang, J. Why have immunization efforts in Pakistan failed to achieve global standards of vaccination uptake and infectious disease control? *Risk Manag. Healthc. Policy* **2020**, *13*, 111. [CrossRef] [PubMed]
8. Wallace, A.S.; Ryman, T.K.; Privor-Dumm, L.; Morgan, C.; Fields, R.; Garcia, C.; Sodha, S.V.; Lindstrand, A.; Lochlainn, L.N. Leaving no one behind: Defining and implementing an integrated life course approach to vaccination across the next decade as part of the immunization Agenda 2030. *Vaccine* **2022**, in press. [CrossRef] [PubMed]
9. Pakistan Bureau of Statistics (PBS). Final Results (Census-2017). 2017. Available online: https://www.pbs.gov.pk/content/final-results-census-2017 (accessed on 20 December 2022).
10. EPI. *Annual Targets*; Office of the Project Director, Expanded Programme on Immunization: Karachi, Pakistan, 2022.
11. EPI Sindh. Mid-term review for National Immunization Support Project (NISP). In Proceedings of the Technical Workshop, Pakistan, 3–5 February 2020.
12. Oxford Poverty and Human Development Initiative (OPHI). *Multidimensional Poverty in Pakistan 2016 Report*; University of Oxford, Ed.; Planning Commission of Pakistan, Ministry of Planning, Development and Reform: Islamabad, Pakistan, 2016.
13. Ministry of Finance. *Pakistan Economic Survey, 2020–2021*; Finance Division, Government of Pakistan: Islamabad, Pakistan, 2021.
14. Mangrio, N.K.; Alam, M.M.; Shaikh, B.T. Is Expanded Programme on Immunization doing enough? Viewpoint of health workers and managers in Sindh, Pakistan. *J. Pak. Med. Assoc.* **2008**, *58*, 64. [PubMed]
15. Chandir, S.; Siddiqi, D.A.; Dharma, V.K.; Shah, M.T.; Turab, A.; Khan, M.I.; Habib, A.; Khan, A.J. Zindagi Mehfooz (safe life) digital immunization registry: Leveraging low-cost technology to improve immunization coverage and timeliness in Pakistan. *Iproceedings* **2018**, *4*, e11770. [CrossRef]
16. Sindh Electronic Immunization Registry (SEIR). Zindagi Mehfooz (Safe Life). In *Analysis*; Sindh Electronic Immunization Registry (SEIR): Sindh, Pakistan, 2023.
17. Mehmood, M.; Setayesh, H.; Siddiqi, D.A.; Siddique, M.; Iftikhar, S.; Soundardjee, R.; Dharma, V.K.; Bhurgri, A.K.; Stuckey, E.M.; Sultan, M.A.; et al. Prevalence, geographical distribution and factors associated with pentavalent vaccine zero dose status among children in Sindh, Pakistan: Analysis of data from the 2017 and 2018 birth cohorts enrolled in the provincial electronic immunisation registry. *BMJ Open* **2022**, *12*, e058985. [CrossRef] [PubMed]
18. Civil Society Human and Institutional Development Programme CHIP. Profiling of Slums in Hyderabad and Karachi. 2020. Available online: https://chip-pk.org/researches/ (accessed on 17 January 2023).
19. Government of Sindh, School Education and Literacy Department. *Notification*; School Education and Literacy Department: Karachi, Pakistan, 2021.
20. Khawar, H. Vaccination Drive. *Dawn*, 11 November 2021.
21. The World Bank. Sex Ratio at Birth (Male Births per Female Births)-Pakistan. 2022. Available online: https://data.worldbank.org/indicator/SP.POP.BRTH.MF (accessed on 17 January 2023).
22. Gavi Full Country Evaluations Team. *Gavi Full Country Evaluations: 2016 Dissemination Report–Bangladesh*; IHME: Seattle, WA, USA, 2017.
23. World Health Organization. *Explorations of Inequality: Childhood Immunization*; World Health Organization: Geneva, Switzerland, 2018.
24. Breiman, R.F.; Streatfield, P.K.; Phelan, M.; Shifa, N.; Rashid, M.; Yunus, M. Effect of infant immunisation on childhood mortality in rural Bangladesh: Analysis of health and demographic surveillance data. *Lancet* **2004**, *364*, 2204–2211. [CrossRef] [PubMed]
25. Briand, V.; Bonmarin, I.; Lévy-Bruhl, D. Study of the risk factors for severe childhood pertussis based on hospital surveillance data. *Vaccine* **2007**, *25*, 7224–7232. [CrossRef]

26. Ahmed, K.A.; Grundy, J.; Hashmat, L.; Ahmed, I.; Farrukh, S.; Bersonda, D.; Shah, M.A.; Yunus, S.; Banskota, H.K. An analysis of the gender and social determinants of health in urban poor areas of the most populated cities of Pakistan. *Int. J. Equity Health* **2022**, *21*, 52. [CrossRef]
27. Crocker-Buque, T.; Mindra, G.; Duncan, R.; Mounier-Jack, S. Immunization, urbanization and slums–a systematic review of factors and interventions. *BMC Public Health* **2017**, *17*, 556. [CrossRef]
28. Rheingans, R.; Anderson IV, J.D.; Bagamian, K.H.; Laytner, L.A.; Pecenka, C.J.; Gilani, S.S.A.; Ahmed, M. Effects of geographic and economic heterogeneity on the burden of rotavirus diarrhea and the impact and cost-effectiveness of vaccination in Pakistan. *Vaccine* **2018**, *36*, 7780–7789. [CrossRef] [PubMed]
29. Singh, P.K. Trends in child immunization across geographical regions in India: Focus on urban-rural and gender differentials. *PLoS ONE* **2013**, *8*, e73102. [CrossRef] [PubMed]
30. Ali, T.S.; Krantz, G.; Gul, R.; Asad, N.; Johansson, E.; Mogren, I. Gender roles and their influence on life prospects for women in urban Karachi, Pak0istan: A qualitative study. *Glob. Health Action* **2011**, *4*, 7448. [CrossRef] [PubMed]
31. Hossain, M.E. Influence of the preference for sons on fertility in Bangladesh. *SN Soc. Sci.* **2022**, *2*, 94. [CrossRef]
32. Levine, O. Tackling Inequities in Immunization Outcomes in Remote Rural Contexts. 2019. Available online: https://www.comminit.com/unicef/content/tackling-inequities-immunization-outcomes-remote-rural-contexts (accessed on 25 January 2023).
33. Amar, P. Big voices, smaller cities: In a first, women in northern Sindh march for rights. *GEO*, 7 March 2020.
34. Wendt, A.; Santos, T.M.; Cata-Preta, B.O.; Costa, J.C.; Mengistu, T.; Hogan, D.R.; Victora, C.G.; Barros, A.J. Children of more empowered women are less likely to be left without vaccination in low-and middle-income countries: A global analysis of 50 DHS surveys. *J. Glob. Health* **2022**, *12*, 04022. [CrossRef] [PubMed]
35. Thorpe, S.; VanderEnde, K.; Peters, C.; Bardin, L.; Yount, K.M. The influence of women's empowerment on child immunization coverage in low, lower-middle, and upper-middle income countries: A systematic review of the literature. *Matern. Child Health J.* **2016**, *20*, 172–186. [CrossRef]
36. Abbasi, F.H.; Shaikh, A.A.; Mehraj, J.; Raza, S.M.; Rasool, S.; Bullo, U.F.; Mehraj, S.; Phul, Z.A.; Sahitia, S.; Zardari, A.A.; et al. Vaccine Hesitancy and Perceptions of the Community about Polio in High-Risk Areas of Karachi, Sindh, Pakistan. *Vaccines* **2023**, *11*, 70. [CrossRef]
37. Feletto, M.; Sharkey, A. The influence of gender on immunisation: Using an ecological framework to examine intersecting inequities and pathways to change. *BMJ Glob. Health* **2019**, *4*, e001711. [CrossRef]
38. Abrevaya, J. Are there missing girls in the United States? Evidence from birth data. *Am. Econ. J. Appl. Econ.* **2009**, *1*, 1–34. [CrossRef]
39. Bhat, P.N.M.; Zavier, A.J.F. Factors influencing the use of prenatal diagnostic techniques and the sex ratio at birth in India. *Econ. Political Wkly.* **2007**, *42*, 2292–2303.
40. Jha, P.; Kumar, R.; Vasa, P.; Dhingra, N.; Thiruchelvam, D.; Moineddin, R. Low female-to-male sex ratio of children born in India: National survey of 1.1 million households. *Lancet* **2006**, *367*, 211–218. [PubMed]
41. Emily Rauscher, Haoming Song; Learning to Value Girls: Balanced Infant Sex Ratios at Higher Parental Education in the United States, 1969–2018. *Demography* **2022**, *59*, 1143–1171. [CrossRef] [PubMed]

vaccines

Article

Tetanus and Diphtheria Seroprotection among Children Younger Than 15 Years in Nigeria, 2018: Who Are the Unprotected Children?

Rania A. Tohme [1,*,†], Heather M. Scobie [1,†], Oyeladun Okunromade [2], Temitope Olaleye [3], Faisal Shuaib [4], Tunde Jegede [2], Ridwan Yahaya [2], Ndodo Nnaemeka [2], Bola Lawal [2], Abiodun Egwuenu [2], Nishanth Parameswaran [5], Gretchen Cooley [5], Qian An [1], Melissa Coughlin [6], Bassey B. Okposen [4], Ifedayo Adetifa [2], Omotayo Bolu [1] and Chikwe Ihekweazu [2]

1 Global Immunization Division, Centers for Disease Control and Prevention, Atlanta, GA 30329, USA
2 Nigeria Center for Disease Control, Abuja 900211, Nigeria
3 Institute of Human Virology, FCT, Abuja 900211, Nigeria
4 National Primary Healthcare Development Agency, Area 11, Garki, Abuja 900247, Nigeria
5 Division of Parasitic Diseases and Malaria, Centers for Disease Control and Prevention, Atlanta, GA 30329, USA
6 Division of Viral Diseases, Centers for Disease Control and Prevention, Atlanta, GA 30329, USA
* Correspondence: rtohme@cdc.gov
† These authors contributed equally to this work.

Abstract: Serological surveys provide an objective biological measure of population immunity, and tetanus serological surveys can also assess vaccination coverage. We undertook a national assessment of immunity to tetanus and diphtheria among Nigerian children aged <15 years using stored specimens collected during the 2018 Nigeria HIV/AIDS Indicator and Impact Survey, a national cross-sectional household-based survey. We used a validated multiplex bead assay to test for tetanus and diphtheria toxoid-antibodies. In total, 31,456 specimens were tested. Overall, 70.9% and 84.3% of children aged <15 years had at least minimal seroprotection (≥0.01 IU/mL) against tetanus and diphtheria, respectively. Seroprotection was lowest in the north west and north east zones. Factors associated with increased tetanus seroprotection included living in the southern geopolitical zones, urban residence, and higher wealth quintiles ($p < 0.001$). Full seroprotection (≥0.1 IU/mL) was the same for tetanus (42.2%) and diphtheria (41.7%), while long-term seroprotection (≥1 IU/mL) was 15.1% for tetanus and 6.0% for diphtheria. Full- and long-term seroprotection were higher in boys compared to girls ($p < 0.001$). Achieving high infant vaccination coverage by targeting specific geographic areas and socio-economic groups and introducing tetanus and diphtheria booster doses in childhood and adolescence are needed to achieve lifelong protection against tetanus and diphtheria and prevent maternal and neonatal tetanus.

Keywords: seroprevalence; tetanus; diphtheria; Nigeria; serology; vaccine preventable diseases

Citation: Tohme, R.A.; Scobie, H.M.; Okunromade, O.; Olaleye, T.; Shuaib, F.; Jegede, T.; Yahaya, R.; Nnaemeka, N.; Lawal, B.; Egwuenu, A.; et al. Tetanus and Diphtheria Seroprotection among Children Younger Than 15 Years in Nigeria, 2018: Who Are the Unprotected Children? *Vaccines* **2023**, *11*, 663. https://doi.org/10.3390/vaccines11030663

Academic Editor: Davide Gori

Received: 16 February 2023
Revised: 9 March 2023
Accepted: 13 March 2023
Published: 15 March 2023

1. Introduction

Historically, vaccination coverage surveys have been used to assess the performance of immunization programs and identify areas at risk for vaccine-preventable diseases (VPDs). However, data have shown that VPD coverage surveys have limitations due to poor documentation of immunization history and parental recall bias [1]. In settings with weak surveillance or unreliable vaccination coverage, serological surveillance can potentially play an important role for appropriately directing interventions to improve population immunity [2,3]. Serological surveys are increasingly being used to guide immunization policy and strategy from support of vaccine introduction, evidence generation for optimizing timing of booster doses, to the verification of disease elimination [2–14]. In the case of tetanus, serological surveys can also assess routine vaccination coverage as tetanus infection does not lead to development of protective antibodies [14]. Tetanus serosurveys can identify areas or subgroups yet to be reached with routine immunization and also assess duration of vaccine-induced immunity to inform introduction of tetanus (and diphtheria) booster doses [14]. Depending on the disease, serum antibody levels can be maintained for years following a person's vaccination or exposure to a pathogen, like the one that causes diphtheria; therefore, specimens collected during cross-sectional surveys contain an immense amount of information about current and past pathogen exposure and levels of immunity [4].

High tetanus burden in Nigeria has been documented [15], with the tetanus case fatality ratio (CFR) estimated at 43% [16]. In addition, high diphtheria burden and recurring diphtheria outbreaks with high CFR have been documented in Nigeria, including a recent outbreak in 2023 [17–19]. In 2011, over 60% of diphtheria cases occurred among children younger than 10 years of age and over 95% were unvaccinated [17]. Nigeria's immunization schedule includes three doses of diphtheria-tetanus-pertussis (DTP) containing vaccine at 6, 10, and 14 weeks of age. However, diphtheria and tetanus immunity wane over time and by school age (5–6 years old), many children are susceptible to infection. For this reason, in addition to the three primary DTP (DTP3) doses given before the age of one year, WHO recommends three booster doses of tetanus- and diphtheria-containing vaccines be provided to children and adolescents at the ages of 12–23 months, 4–7 years and 9–15 years to provide protection across the life-course [20,21].

Data on tetanus and diphtheria immunity among children in Nigeria are needed to evaluate susceptibility to VPDs and for use in program improvement to prevent tetanus cases and diphtheria epidemics. We conducted a national serological assessment to estimate immunity to tetanus and diphtheria among Nigerian children born during 2004–2018 (aged <15 years old at the time of the survey in 2018) and by subpopulation (age, sex, zone, state, urban/rural, and wealth quintile) to identify immunity gaps and specific populations that might need targeted interventions to improve vaccination coverage.

2. Materials and Methods

2.1. Study Population and Sampling

The target population included children younger than 15 years of age and residing in Nigeria. We used stored specimens collected during the 2018 Nigeria HIV/AIDS Indicator and Impact Survey (NAIIS) (https://www.naiis.ng/ (accessed on 15 January 2023). NAIIS was a national cross-sectional, household-based survey with a multi-stage cluster sampling design. In the first stage, clusters (enumeration areas) were selected using projected census data. Within each selected enumeration area, households were chosen through systematic sampling. Children less than 15 years of age were sampled in every 4th household (28,220 households sampled for inclusion of children aged 0–14 years). The eligibility criteria for children included having resided in the selected household or spent the night in that household before the survey; parents or guardians willing to provide written informed consent/permission in English, Hausa, Yoruba, or Igbo; and for children aged 10–14 years, the child is able and willing to provide written assent in English, Hausa, Yoruba, or Igbo. Further information on NAIIS methodology is available [22].

Assuming the most conservative estimate of 50% seroprevalence for tetanus and diphtheria with a 95% confidence interval, a design effect of 2, and a 5% non-response rate (e.g., not enough specimen), a sample size of 810 children per state (270 children each in age groups 0–4 years, 5–9 years and 10–14 years) would produce a precision of +/−9% for state- and age-level estimates. In total, 30,000 children would be needed from all 36 states and Abuja Federal Capital Territory (FCT) (10,000 specimens per age group). NAIIS collected specimens from 32,480 children ages 0–14 years, of which 32,337 (99%) assented for storage and future testing of specimens and were included in this study.

2.2. Laboratory Methods and Testing

From each participant, we used 6 mm sections punched from dried blood spots collected on Whatman filter paper corresponding to 5 μL of serum to test for tetanus and diphtheria IgG on a multiplex bead assay platform. An additional 6 mm section was used in 10% of the samples to repeat testing for quality control.

2.2.1. Antigens and Couplings

Tetanus toxoid was purchased from Massachusetts Biological Laboratories (Boston, MA, USA) and diphtheria toxoid was purchased from List Biological Laboratories (Campbell, CA, USA). Antigens were coupled to MagPlex microspheres (Luminex Corp, Austin, TX, USA), as described previously [5,23], using antigen concentrations of 12.5 μg/12.5 × 10^6 microspheres for tetanus toxoid and 60 μg/12.5 × 10^6 microspheres for diphtheria toxoid.

2.2.2. Sample Preparation and Bead Assay

Samples were diluted to a final serum concentration of 1:400 in Buffer B (PBS pH 7.2 plus 0.5% casein, 0.8% PVP, 0.5% PVA, 0.3% Tween 20, 0.02% sodium azide and 3 μg/mL of Escherichia coli lysate containing GST). All incubation steps were performed at room temperature in 50 μL reaction volumes protected from light while shaking at 600 rpm. Incubation steps were followed by three washes with 200 μL PBS pH 7.2 containing 0.05% Tween 20 (PBST) using a handheld magnet. Diluted samples were incubated with 625 microspheres/antigen/well for 90 min, followed by 45 min incubation with secondary antibodies at a concentration of 50 ng/well for anti-human IgG and 40 ng/well for anti-IgG4 (Southern Biotech, Birmingham, AL, USA). Incubations with 250 ng/well streptavidin-R phycoerythrin (Invitrogen, Waltham, MA, USA) and assay buffer alone were carried out, as previously described [5]. Beads were resuspended in 100 μL PBS pH 7.2 and stored overnight at 4 °C prior to reading on MAGPIX (Luminex Corporation, Austin, TX, USA).

2.2.3. Quality Control and Assurance

Data were output as median fluorescence intensity (MFI). To control for background reactivity, each assay included 2 blank wells containing Buffer B only. Samples were run in singlicate. Each plate also contained 1 negative serum control and 2 positive serum controls run in duplicate, as well as a positive pool serum control that was serially diluted to make an 8-point curve to cover the linear range of MFI for most antigens. Samples and controls were analyzed with the average of the plate background subtracted (MFI-BG). As a measure of assay-to-assay variation, the average reactivities of the antigens with the controls was used to create criteria for accepting or rejecting plate data.

2.2.4. Cutoffs and Interpolation

WHO international standards TE-3 and 10/262 were used to convert MFI-BG for tetanus and diphtheria, respectively, to IU/mL. Dilutions of each standard were run on separate plates over the course of the study at approximately one-month intervals, with a total of seven individual runs averaged to create a single curve per antigen for all samples. Curve fitting and interpolation were performed in GraphPad Prism v.9 using 5PL non-linear regression. Conversion of values to IU/mL was conducted in SAS.

Tetanus and diphtheria antibody seroprotection were defined using the standard cut-off of 0.01 IU/mL, which corresponds to the minimum level of antibody required for protection against tetanus and diphtheria [20,21,24]. Tetanus IgG testing on MBA has been previously validated against the reference standard double antigen ELISA IgG with a sensitivity of 99% and specificity of 92% at the ≥0.01 IU/mL cutoff [5]. Diphtheria IgG testing on MBA was validated against the Vero cell neutralization assay IgG with a sensitivity of 95% and specificity of 83% at the ≥0.01 IU/mL cutoff for minimal protection [23]. Increasing antibody concentrations against tetanus are associated with decreased risk of infection and increased duration of protection [25], and tetanus antibody concentrations ≥1 IU/mL are typically associated with long-term protection [6,25]. Tetanus and diphtheria antibody seroprotection were further categorized as IgG < 0.01 IU/mL (lack of protection), 0.01–<0.1 IU/mL (minimal protection), 0.10–<1 IU/mL (full protection), and ≥1 IU/mL (long-term protection) [5,6,23–26].

2.3. Statistical Analyses

Statistical analyses followed the WHO tetanus serosurvey guidance published in 2018 [14]. Estimates of tetanus and diphtheria seroprotection (at ≥0.01, ≥0.1 and ≥1.0 IU/mL antibody levels) and Wilson 95% confidence intervals were calculated using sample weights and a Taylor series linearization method to account for survey design. To assess risk factors, seroprotection was calculated by sociodemographic characteristics (age, sex, zone, state, urban/rural, and wealth quintile) and associations were assessed using Rao-Scott chi-square tests. A p-value of <0.05 was considered statistically significant. To assess waning immunity and the need for tetanus–diphtheria booster dose introduction, estimates of the proportions of children by age and different antibody level categories for tetanus and diphtheria (<0.01, 0.01 to 0.099, 0.1 to 0.99, and ≥1.0 IU/mL) were calculated; geometric mean antibody levels and 95% confidence intervals (95%CI) were also calculated accounting for the survey design. We assessed the contribution of routine immunization, waning immunity, and natural exposure (for diphtheria) by assessing percentage of children seroprotected (≥0.01 IU/mL) against diphtheria (including through natural infection) but not against tetanus (<0.01 IU/mL) by age group (4–11 months, 12–23 months, 24–35 months, 36–47 months, and 48–59 months; 0–4, 5–9 and 10–14 years). All statistical analyses were conducted using SAS v9.4 (SAS Institute, Inc., Cary, NC, USA).

Finally, we triangulated data on the proportion of children with minimal and full seroprotection to tetanus by age with vaccination coverage to assess comparability between serosurvey results and vaccination coverage results in those age groups given that tetanus immunity can only be achieved by vaccination. For this purpose, we used DTP3 coverage among children 12–23 months of age reported from three data sources that covered the birth cohorts included in this survey (born during 2004–2018): (1) WHO/UNICEF estimates of national immunization coverage (WUENIC); (2) country-reported official estimates for DTP3 coverage for each birth cohort [27]; and (3) when available for the birth cohorts included in this survey, we also used vaccination coverage survey estimates of DTP3 coverage among children 12–23 months from Demographic and Health Surveys (DHS) (for 2018, 2013, and 2008) [28] and Multiple Indicator Cluster Surveys (MICS) (for 2016, 2011, and 2007) [29].

3. Results

3.1. General Demographics of Study Population

Of the 32,337 available specimens from children aged 0–14 years, 31,456 (97%) specimens yielded results for tetanus and diphtheria immunity. A slightly higher percentage of 5–9-year-olds (39.5%) compared to younger (30.2%) and older (30.3%) age groups, and an almost equal proportion of males (51.0%) and females (49.0%) were tested. The highest proportion of participants tested was in the north west geopolitical zone (27.9%) compared to almost equal proportions in other zones (range: 12.7–16.0%). Rural areas accounted for a higher proportion of specimens tested (58.6%) than urban areas (41.4%) (Table 1).

Table 1. Demographic characteristics of children tested for tetanus and diphtheria, Nigeria, 2018.

	Number (N = 31,456)	Percentage
Age group		
0–4	9487	30.2
5–9	12,435	39.5
10–14	9534	30.3
Sex		
Female	15,425	49.0
Male	16,031	51.0
Geopolitical zone		
North central	4634	14.7
North east	5045	16.0
North west	8784	27.9
South south	4387	13.9
South east	4000	12.7
South west	4606	14.6
Location		
Urban	13,008	41.4
Rural	18,448	58.6

3.2. *Tetanus and Diphtheria Seroprotection*

Overall, 70.9% (95% confidence interval (CI): 69.9–72.0%) of children aged <15 years had at least minimal seroprotection (≥0.01 IU/mL) against tetanus and 84.3% (95%CI: 83.6–85.0%) had at least minimal seroprotection (≥0.01 IU/mL) against diphtheria (Table 2). Full seroprotection (≥0.1 IU/mL) was 42.2% (95% CI: 41.2–43.3%) for tetanus and 41.7% (95% CI: 40.9–42.5%) for diphtheria; long-term seroprotection (≥1.0 IU/mL) was 15.1% (95% CI: 14.5–15.7%) for tetanus and 6.0% (95% CI: 5.7–6.4%) for diphtheria (Tables 2 and S1).

The proportion of children aged <15 years with seroprotection against tetanus and diphtheria increased with age ($p < 0.001$). While minimal tetanus seroprotection was not different between male and female children, full- and long-term tetanus and diphtheria seroprotection were higher in male compared to female children (Tables 2 and S1). Tetanus and diphtheria minimal, full, and long-term seroprotection levels were lowest in the north west and north east geopolitical zones, while the south east and south south geopolitical zones had the highest tetanus and diphtheria seroprotection levels (Tables 2 and S1).

Tetanus and diphtheria seroprotection varied significantly by state and age group (Figure 1). The proportion of children with minimal tetanus seroprotection among children aged 0–4 years was at least 90% in Enugu, Ebonyi, Cross-river, and Edo states in the south east and south south zones. While most of the states in the north east and north west geopolitical zones had very low seroprotection against tetanus, three states, Adamawa, Taraba, and Yobe, had higher minimal tetanus seroprotection (>70%) among children aged 0–4 years in these zones. Only three states, FCT Abuja, Edo, and Ebonyi, had >70% of children aged 0–4 years with full tetanus seroprotection; however, seven states had >70% full tetanus seroprotection among children aged 10–14 years (Figure 1b). It is noticeable that tetanus seroprotection was higher among children aged 10–14 years compared with children aged 5–9 years in some states in the north west and north east geopolitical zones despite the lack of childhood Td booster doses in the national immunization program. The proportion of children with diphtheria seroprotection increased with age across the majority of the states (Figure 1c,d). While Sokoto, Zamfara, and Jigawa in the north west zone had less than 50% of children aged 10–14 years who had minimal seroprotection against tetanus, those states had greater than 90% of children with minimal diphtheria seroprotection (Figure 1a,c).

Table 2. Tetanus and diphtheria seroprotection among children aged <15 years, Nigeria, 2018.

		Tetanus ≥ 0.01 IU/mL			Tetanus ≥ 0.1 IU/mL			Diphtheria ≥ 0.01 IU/mL			Diphtheria ≥ 0.1 IU/mL		
	N	n	Percentage (95% CI)	*p*-Value	n	Percentage (95% CI)	*p*-Value	n	Percentage (95% CI)	*p* Value	n	Percentage (95% CI)	*p* Value
Overall	31,456	22,727	70.9 (69.9–72.0)	-	13,698	42.2 (41.2–43.3)	-	26,702	84.3 (83.6–85.0)	-	13,200	41.7 (40.9–42.5)	-
Age group (years)													
0–4	9487	6663	68.4 (66.9–70.0)	<0.0001	4579	46.4 (44.8–48.0)	<0.0001	7484	77.2 (75.8–78.6)	<0.0001	3472	35.0 (33.7–36.3)	<0.0001
5–9	12,435	8793	68.5 (67.1–69.8)		4863	37.0 (35.8–38.3)		10,425	82.5 (81.5–83.4)		4920	38.4 (37.3–39.6)	
10–14	9534	7271	75.4 (74.2–76.6)		4256	43.8 (42.4–45.2)		8793	92.1 (91.3–92.8)		4808	50.5 (49.2–51.7)	
Sex													
Female	15,425	11,147	70.9 (69.7–72.1)	0.9231	6473	40.6 (39.4–41.8)	<0.0001	12,920	83.0 (82.1–83.9)	<0.0001	5943	38.0 (37.1–39.0)	<0.0001
Male	16,031	11,580	71.0 (69.8–72.1)		7225	43.8 (42.6–45.0)		13,782	85.6 (84.7–86.3)		7257	45.2 (44.1–46.2)	
Zone													
North central	4634	3718	79.8 (77.3–82.1)	<0.0001	2463	53.5 (50.6–56.3)	<0.0001	4116	89.2 (87.9–90.4)	<0.0001	2134	46.7 (44.6–48.8)	<0.0001
North east	5045	3359	65.8 (63.2–68.2)		1920	37.3 (34.9–39.9)		4139	83.0 (81.5–84.5)		1984	40.6 (38.6–42.6)	
North west	8784	4608	52.8 (50.5–55.1)		2326	26.6 (24.6–28.7)		6870	77.1 (75.5–78.6)		3593	40.3 (38.6–42.0)	
South south	4387	3648	83.1 (81.2–84.8)		2176	49.2 (47.0–51.5)		3999	91.6 (90.7–92.5)		1951	45.2 (43.3- 47.2)	
South east	4000	3716	93.0 (91.8–94.0)		2707	68.0 (65.8–70.1)		3640	91.3 (90.2–92.2)		1810	45.6 (43.8–47.5)	
South west	4606	3678	79.6 (77.9–81.3)		2106	45.7 (43.7–47.7)		3938	85.5 (84.2–86.7)		1728	36.6 (34.8–38.4)	
Location													
Urban	13,008	9894	74.4 (72.7–76.1)	<0.0001	6247	46.1 (44.5–47.9)	<0.0001	10,893	83.0 (81.8–84.1)	0.0026	5034	38.4 (37.2–39.6)	<0.0001
Rural	18,448	12,833	68.2 (66.7–69.6)		7451	39.1 (37.7–40.6)		15,809	85.4 (84.4–86.3)		8166	44.3 (43.2–45.5)	

CI: confidence interval.

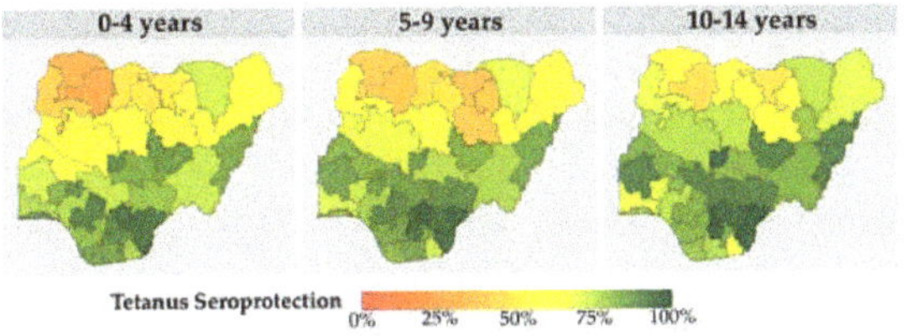

(**a**) Minimal tetanus seroprotection (≥0.01 IU/mL) by age group and state

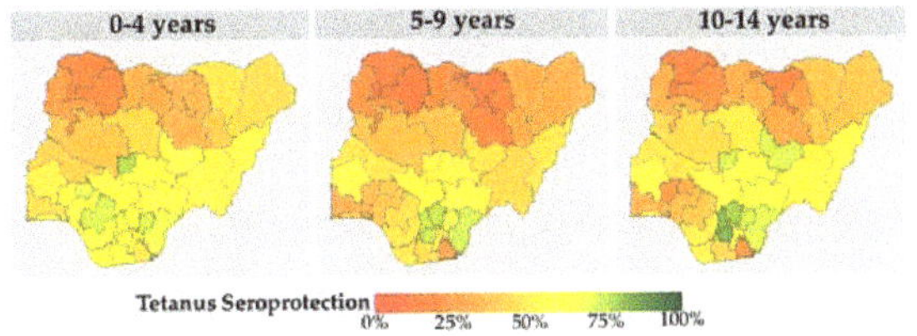

(**b**) Full tetanus seroprotection (≥0.1 IU/mL) by age group and state

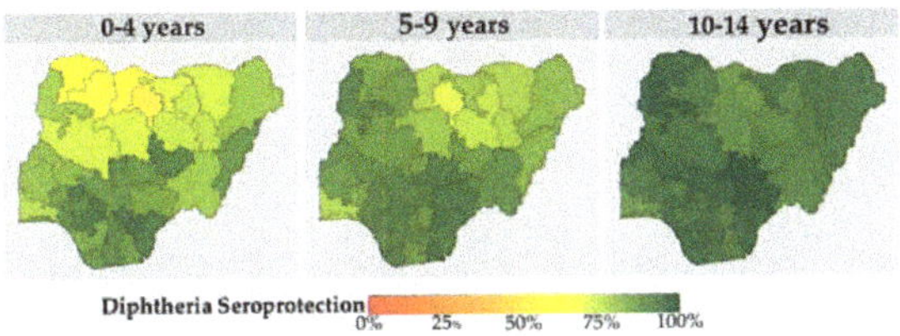

(**c**) Minimal diphtheria seroprotection (≥0.01 IU/mL) by age group and state

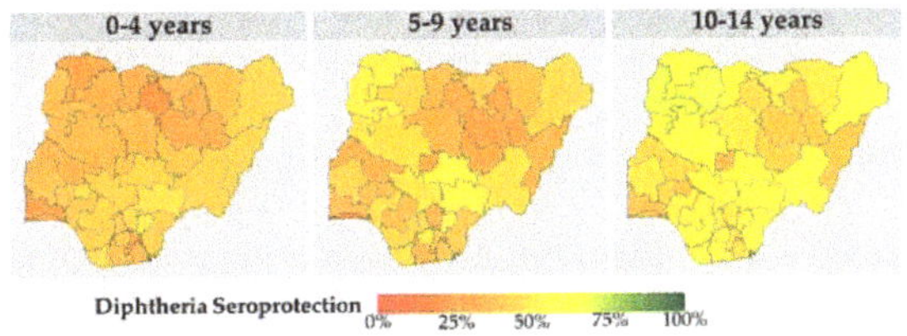

(**d**) Full diphtheria seroprotection (≥0.1 IU/mL) by age group and state

Figure 1. Tetanus and diphtheria minimal and full seroprotection among children aged <15 years by age group and state, Nigeria, 2018 (**a**–**d**).

The proportion of children <15 years with minimal or full tetanus seroprotection was higher in urban compared to rural areas (Table 2) and was statistically significantly different in all geopolitical zones ($p < 0.05$) except in the north east zone (Figure 2a). The largest discrepancy between urban and rural areas with regard to proportion of children seroprotected against tetanus was in the south west zone (Figure 2a). In comparison, the proportion of children <15 years with minimal or full diphtheria seroprotection was higher in rural compared to urban areas ($p < 0.05$) (Table 2). However, no significant difference was observed in the proportion of children who were seroprotected against diphtheria between rural and urban areas by geopolitical zone except for the south south and south west zones, where the proportion seroprotected was higher in rural areas ($p < 0.05$) (Figure 2b).

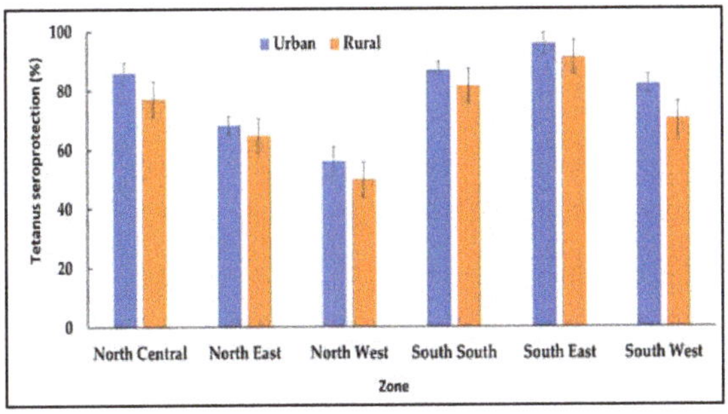

(**a**) Tetanus seroprotection among children aged <15 years by zone and location

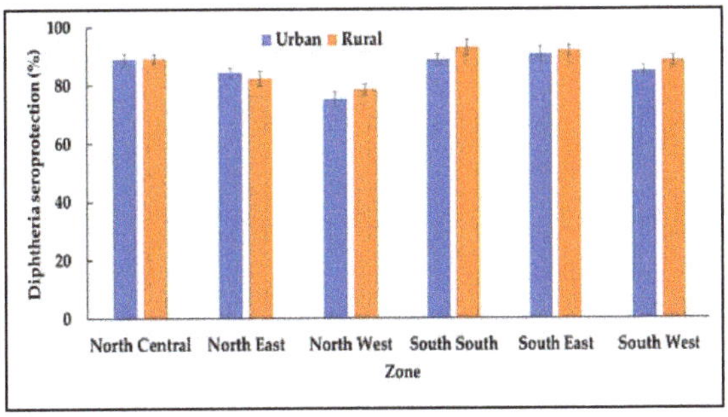

(**b**) Diphtheria seroprotection among children aged <15 years by zone and location

Figure 2. Tetanus and diphtheria minimal seroprotection (≥0.01 IU/mL) among children aged <15 years by zone and location, Nigeria, 2018 (**a**,**b**).

The proportion of children <15 years who had minimal seroprotection against tetanus was higher in more wealthy quintiles, a pattern that was significant across all geopolitical zones (Figure 3a). In comparison, the proportion of children <15 years who had minimal seroprotection against diphtheria did not show a specific trend by wealth quintile. A significant difference in the proportion of children <15 years with minimal diphtheria seroprotection was observed by wealth quintile in the north central and south south geopolitical zones ($p < 0.01$) (Figure 3b).

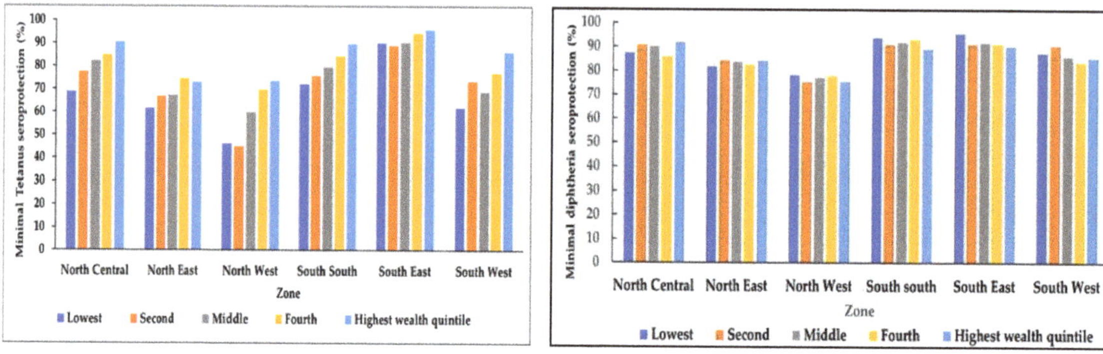

(**a**) Tetanus seroprotection by zone and wealth quintile

(**b**) Diphtheria seroprotection by zone and wealth quintile

Figure 3. Tetanus and diphtheria at least minimal seroprotection (≥0.01 IU/mL) among children aged <15 years by zone and wealth quintile, Nigeria, 2018 (**a**,**b**).

Among children aged <5 years, the proportion of children with minimal seroprotection for tetanus and diphtheria was 77.7% for children aged 4–11 months, 72.5% for 12–23 months, 66.2% for 24–35 months, 59.4% for 36–47 months, and 55.2% for 48–59 months, while the proportions of those children without seroprotection to both tetanus and diphtheria were 12.4%, 17.9%, 20.8%, 19.6%, and 19.0%, respectively. The proportion of children who had minimal seroprotection against diphtheria but not against tetanus increased with age from 5.8% among children aged 4–11 months, to 6.6% for 12–23 months, 9.4% for 24–35 months, 16.3% for 36–47 months, and 20.2% for 48–59 months. Overall, 13.2% of children aged 0–4 years, 20.7% of children aged 5–9 years, and 21.6% of children 10–14 years had minimal seroprotection to diphtheria but no seroprotection to tetanus.

By one-year age cohort, the proportion of children who were seroprotected against tetanus was lowest in children aged 2–10 years old, and waning immunity to tetanus was observed starting at the age of 3 years based on the drop in geometric mean antibody level (Figure 4a). The proportion of children with long-term tetanus seroprotection was highest in children aged younger than 1 year followed by 11–14 year-olds which corresponded to a similar trend in geometric mean antibody levels (Figure 4a). In comparison, geometric mean antibody levels and the proportions of children seroprotected against diphtheria were lowest among children aged 2–5 years but increased gradually among children aged 6–14 years (Figure 4b).

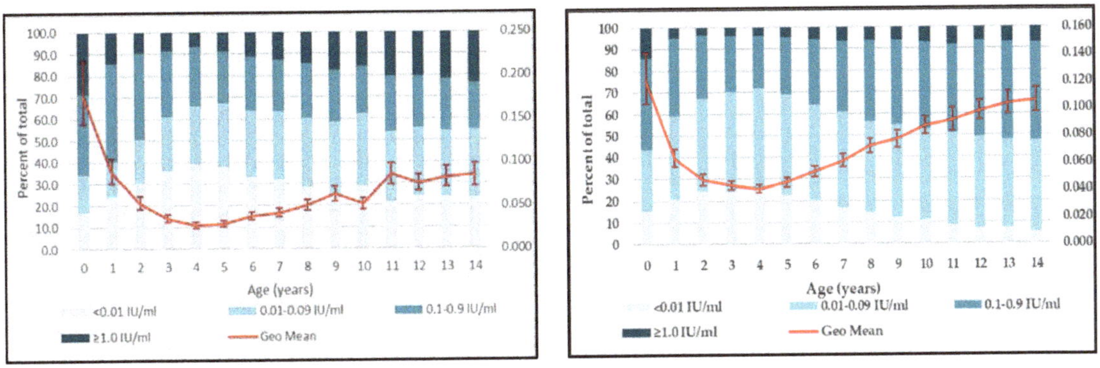

(**a**) Tetanus seroprotection levels and geometric mean antibody level by age

(**b**) Diphtheria seroprotection levels and geometric mean antibody level by age

Figure 4. Tetanus and diphtheria seroprotection levels and geometric mean antibody level by age, Nigeria, 2018 (**a**,**b**).

3.3. Triangulation of Tetanus Seroprotection and Vaccination Coverage

The proportions of children with minimal tetanus seroprotection (≥0.01 IU/mL) were higher than annual estimates of DTP3 coverage from WHO/UNICEF estimates of national vaccination coverage (WUENIC) and vaccination coverage surveys (DHS/MICS) in all age cohorts but lower than official country-reported DTP3 coverage among children aged 4, 5 and 8 years (Figure 5). When available, estimates of DTP3 coverage from DHS or MICS surveys correlated better with the proportion of children who had full seroprotection against tetanus compared with minimal seroprotection.

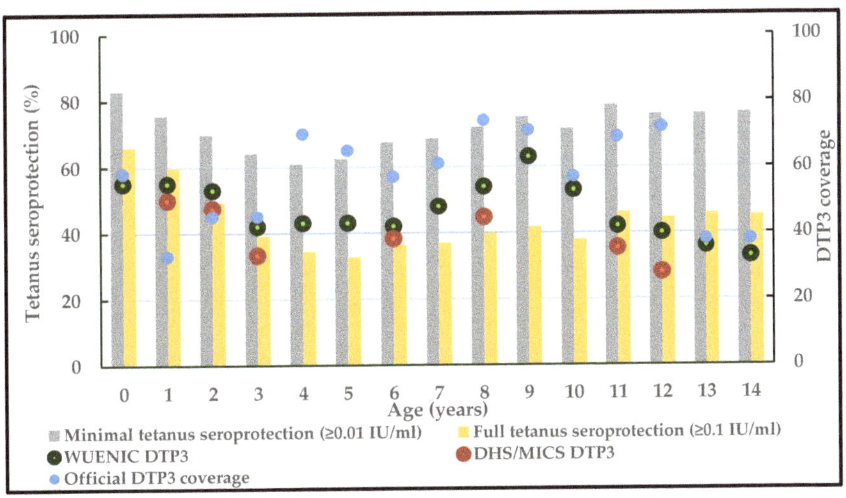

Figure 5. Triangulation of tetanus seroprotection and DTP3 vaccination coverage among children aged <15 years, Nigeria, 2018. WUENIC: WHO/UNICEF estimates of national immunization coverage; DTP3: 3 doses of diphtheria-tetanus-pertussis vaccine; DHS: Demographic and Health Survey; MICS: Multiple Indicator Cluster Survey.

4. Discussion

This serological assessment using specimens previously collected in 2018 from over 30,000 children aged less than 15 years provided the first estimates of tetanus and diphtheria seroprotection among children in Nigeria. Overall, both tetanus and diphtheria seroprotection were below the recommended vaccination coverage levels of at least 80% for tetanus [25] and 90% for diphtheria [26] to prevent infections in the population, especially among younger age groups. Full and long-term seroprotection against tetanus and diphtheria were low across all age groups and geographies. The survey also identified demographic and socio-economic factors that were associated with decreased seroprotection to tetanus and diphtheria. Tetanus seroprotection varied significantly by age, sex, geopolitical zone, state, urban/rural, and wealth quintile. Diphtheria seroprotection varied mainly by age, sex, geopolitical zone, and state.

Comparisons of tetanus seroprotection by age showed that children aged 2–5 years had the highest proportions of children who lacked tetanus seroprotection and the lowest geometric mean antibody levels; this finding correlates with studies reporting decreases in tetanus seroprotection starting at the age of 2 years [25]. Similarly, diphtheria seroprotection and geometric mean antibody levels were lowest in children who were 2–6 years old. When comparing tetanus and diphtheria seroprotection by age group and state, we observed that proportions of children with diphtheria seroprotection among older age groups were highest in the areas that had the lowest tetanus seroprotection (Figure 1), which highlighted the important contribution of natural infection to diphtheria seroprotection in children ages five years and older. For example, Kano State had one of the lowest minimal seroprotection levels against tetanus (49%) and diphtheria (52%) among children aged <4 years, reflecting low routine immunization coverage, yet diphtheria immunity reached 87% in children aged 10–14 years. Similar observations were noted in Borno and other northern states, likely reflecting the frequent occurrence of diphtheria outbreaks mainly in Northern Nigeria [17,18]. The most recent outbreak in Kano during 2022–2023 caused over 25 deaths, mostly among children [19]. Hence, in addition to improving DTP3 vaccination coverage, Nigeria needs to consider introducing the WHO-recommended booster doses for tetanus and diphtheria at the ages of 12–23 months, 4–7 years, and 9–15 years to ensure long-term protection across the life-course and prevent recurring diphtheria outbreaks, as well as sustain maternal and neonatal tetanus elimination [20,21].

Given that tetanus seroprotection is an indirect measure of DTP3 vaccination coverage especially in younger age groups, tetanus seroprotection levels highlighted areas and populations requiring urgent attention to improve vaccination coverage. Girls had significantly lower levels of full and long-term seroprotection to tetanus and diphtheria compared to boys, indicating the need to ensure that girls are reached with immunization services and are adequately protected against VPDs. Gender-based inequity in access to vaccination services and protection from VPDs has been noted in multiple countries with associations in some cases with maternal education [11,30]. In Nigeria, higher maternal education was associated with higher childhood vaccination coverage based on analysis of the 2018 DHS [31] and with higher utilization of essential maternal and child health services based on analysis of five national household surveys [32].

Geographic variations in tetanus and diphtheria seroprotection highlighted zones and states that require remediation to decrease the number of children susceptible to VPDs. The north west and north east geopolitical zones had the lowest proportions of tetanus and diphtheria seroprotection indicating the need for catch-up vaccination as well as strengthening infant immunization coverage. However, heterogeneity in seroprotection among children aged 0–4 years was also observed between states within the same geopolitical zone reflecting variation in routine immunization coverage. For example, Adamawa state in the north east had >80% minimal seroprotection against tetanus and diphtheria among children aged 0–4 years, indicating better routine immunization performance relative to the north east zone, which had <70% tetanus seroprotection overall. Similarly, inequities in seroprotection against tetanus were also observed in states located in the south south and south east geopolitical zones which were better performing overall than other geopolitical zones. Therefore, serosurvey results highlighted subnational geographies that would benefit from intensive support to improve vaccination coverage and remediations efforts to prevent diphtheria outbreaks. Our findings were similar to a mapping of areas at risk for measles in Nigeria, which indicated that susceptibility to multiple VPDs tended to cluster in similar states and geopolitical zones [33]. Inequities in seroprotection against tetanus were noted in rural versus urban areas and lower versus higher wealth quintiles. These factors have been shown to be associated with tetanus seroprotection, vaccination coverage or access to maternal and child health services in Nigeria and other countries [11,30–32,34,35].

Triangulating different data sources enabled further interpretation of serosurvey findings. When comparing seroprevalence and vaccination coverage data, DTP3 coverage underestimated seroprotection to tetanus across children of all ages. Immunity can result from a partial series of a multidose vaccine (i.e., DTP2) [14]. Vaccination coverage surveys are also at risk of information and recall bias, and both card documentation and recall have been found to underestimate actual vaccination coverage [9]. The limitations of measuring vaccination coverage based on card or recall have been noted in other tetanus serosurveys [5,7,10,11]. We observed increased tetanus seroprotection among children aged 10–14 years compared with those aged 5–9 and 0–4 years, unlike the gradual decrease in tetanus seroprotection with age documented in other countries related to waning immunity and not providing childhood booster doses against tetanus and diphtheria [8,11,12]. The increased tetanus seroprotection in children aged 10–14 years and the gradual increase in geometric mean antibodies starting at the age of 6 years in Nigeria is most likely a result of the multiple meningitis vaccination campaigns targeting ages 1–29 years in states at high-risk for meningitis in Northern Nigeria during 2011–2014 [36,37]. These campaigns used the meningococcal A conjugate vaccine (MACV) which is conjugated to tetanus toxoid [38] and has been shown to boost tetanus immunity in other countries in the African meningitis belt [39,40]. A tetanus serosurvey conducted in Mali before and after the MACV campaigns showed increase in geometric mean concentrations and tetanus immunity among people aged 1–29 years from 57% to 88% [39]. In addition, clinical studies on MACV showed robust tetanus serologic response in people aged 1–29 years after MACV vaccination [40]. Therefore, the four rounds of MACV campaigns in 17 states in northern Nigeria might have helped boost tetanus immunity and contribute to the higher proportion of minimal, full, and long-term tetanus seroprotection in older children compared to younger age groups.

This serologic assessment used existing stored specimens from NAIIS, which was designed and implemented to make the survey as representative as possible. However, any deviations from protocol implementation may limit generalizability of the findings to the Nigerian population. For example, 72 (1.8%) enumeration areas out of a total of 4035 selected for NAIIS were unable to be visited because of security challenges and one area was not visited due to flooding, potentially limiting representativeness of survey estimates in these areas. The response rate for blood collection in children aged 0–9 years (68.5%) was lower than in children aged 10–14 years (92.3%), and while the distribution of children whose parents refused use of specimens for other tests was similar across gender, age, zone and cluster compared to those who were tested for tetanus and diphtheria, more of these children were in Lagos (15.6%) and Kano (11.0%) [22]. However, the survey included a large sample size which allowed for precise estimates of seroprotection down to the state level, and the overall population distribution of the NAIIS survey was similar to the population of Nigeria [41]. Finally, while the serosurvey results represent a specific time point (2018), results are still relevant in 2023 as vaccination coverage in Nigeria has not changed significantly compared to 2018. DTP3 coverage estimates were 56% during 2019–2021 compared to 55% in 2018 based on WUENIC estimates [27] and 57% in the MICS 2021 compared to 50% in the 2018 DHS [28,42]. These vaccination coverage estimates were still below the seroprotective levels needed to prevent infections. Hence, results in this serosurvey are still relevant to inform public health interventions and policy. In the future, it would be beneficial if testing for vaccine-preventable diseases could be integrated in parallel with other disease-specific testing in large population-based surveys, such as NAIIS, instead of waiting until completion of testing for other diseases to be able to access the specimens. This would enable timely availability of data showing granular differences in seroprotection in specific demographic and socio-economic groups and would help inform immediate targeted public health actions to address inequities in immunization.

5. Conclusions

This study provided the first estimates of tetanus and diphtheria seroprotection in Nigeria. The findings highlighted the need to target specific geographic areas and to consider gender and socio-economic equity in improving access and demand for vaccinations, as well as the need to introduce tetanus and diphtheria containing booster doses at 12–23 months, 4–7 years, and 9–15 years of age to address waning immunity and prevent tetanus cases and diphtheria outbreaks. The survey results also highlighted the benefit of supplementing vaccination coverage data with seroprevalence data and other data sources to provide a better assessment of the vaccination program and to help identify immunity gaps.

Supplementary Materials: The following supporting information can be downloaded at: https://www.mdpi.com/article/10.3390/vaccines11030663/s1, Table S1: Long term tetanus and diphtheria seroprotection among children aged <15 years, Nigeria 2018.

Author Contributions: All authors meet the four criteria for authorship in the ICMJE Recommendations. Conceptualization, R.A.T. and H.M.S.; Formal analysis, H.M.S., T.O., T.J., R.Y., N.N., B.L., A.E., N.P., G.C., Q.A. and M.C.; Funding acquisition, R.A.T., H.M.S. and O.B.; Methodology, R.A.T., H.M.S., G.C. and Q.A.; Supervision, R.A.T., F.S., O.B., I.A. and C.I.; Validation, N.P., G.C. and M.C.; Writing—original draft, R.A.T.; Writing—review and editing, H.M.S., O.O., T.O., F.S., T.J., R.Y., N.N., B.L., A.E., N.P., G.C., Q.A., M.C., O.B., B.B.O., I.A. and C.I. All authors have read and agreed to the published version of the manuscript.

Funding: This research was funded by the U.S. Centers for Disease Control and Prevention.

Institutional Review Board Statement: The study was conducted in accordance with the Declaration of Helsinki, and approved by the National Health Research Ethics Committee of Nigeria (NHREC) (protocol code NHREC/01/01/2007, date of approval: 27 August 2019) and the Human Subjects Review Board at the US Centers for Disease Control and Prevention where it was determined to be non-research as the study involved testing previously collected de-identified specimens.

Informed Consent Statement: Written informed consent to use specimens to test for diseases other than HIV was obtained from all subjects involved in the study.

Data Availability Statement: Data are unavailable due to privacy consideration as datasets include global positioning system coordinates which might enable identification of location of study subjects. Only restricted individuals had access to the datasets for analyses purposes only.

Acknowledgments: Erasogie Evbuomwan, Nigeria Center for Disease Control; Oluwaseun Akinmulero, Mudiaga Esiekpe Kayode, Institute of Human Virology, Abuja, Nigeria; Gavin Grant, Stacie Greby, Ryan Wiegand, Barbara Marston, Diana Martin, Mahesh Swaminathan, Ibrahim Dalhatu, Matthias Alagi, McPaul Okoye, Centers for Disease Control and Prevention; and the NAIIS project team and respondents.

Conflicts of Interest: The authors declare no conflict of interest.

References

1. MacNeil, A.; Lee, C.W.; Dietz, V. Issues and considerations in the use of serologic biomarkers for classifying vaccination history in household surveys. *Vaccine* **2014**, *32*, 4893–4900. [CrossRef]
2. Cutts, F.T.; Hanson, M. Seroepidemiology: An underused tool for designing and monitoring vaccination programmes in low- and middle-income countries. *Trop. Med. Int. Health* **2016**, *21*, 1086–1098. [CrossRef]
3. E Metcalf, C.J.; Farrar, J.; Cutts, F.T.; Basta, N.E.; Graham, A.L.; Lessler, J.; Ferguson, N.M.; Burke, D.S.; Grenfell, B.T. Use of serological surveys to generate key insights into the changing global landscape of infectious disease. *Lancet* **2016**, *388*, 728–730. [CrossRef] [PubMed]
4. Arnold, B.F.; Scobie, H.M.; Priest, J.W.; Lammie, P.J. Integrated serologic surveillance of population immunity and disease transmission. *Emerg. Infect. Dis.* **2018**, *24*, 1188–1194. [CrossRef] [PubMed]

5. Scobie, H.M.; Mao, B.; Buth, S.; Wannemuehler, K.A.; Sørensen, C.; Kannarath, C.; Jenks, M.H.; Moss, D.M.; Priest, J.W.; Soeung, S.C.; et al. Tetanus Immunity among Women Aged 15 to 39 Years in Cambodia: A National Population-Based Serosurvey, 2012. *Clin. Vaccine Immunol.* **2016**, *23*, 546–554. [CrossRef] [PubMed]
6. Wagner, K.S.; White, J.M.; Andrews, N.J.; Borrow, R.; Stanford, E.; Newton, E.; Pebody, R.G. Immunity to tetanus and diphtheria in the UK in 2009. *Vaccine* **2012**, *30*, 7111–7117. [PubMed]
7. Deming, M.S.; Roungo, J.B.; Kristiansen, M.; Heron, I.; Yango, A.; Guenengafo, A.; Ndamobissi, R. Tetanus toxoid coverage as an indicator of serological protection against neonatal tetanus. *Bull. World. Health Organ.* **2002**, *80*, 696–703.
8. Scobie, H.M.; Patel, M.; Martin, D.; Mkocha, H.; Njenga, S.M.; Odiere, M.R.; Pelletreau, S.; Priest, J.W.; Thompson, R.; Won, K.Y.; et al. Tetanus Immunity Gaps in Children 5–14 Years and Men ≥15 Years of Age Revealed by Integrated Disease Serosurveillance in Kenya, Tanzania, and Mozambique. *Am. J. Trop. Med. Hyg.* **2017**, *96*, 415–420. [CrossRef]
9. Travassos, M.A.; Beyene, B.; Adam, Z.; Campbell, J.D.; Mulholland, N.; Diarra, S.S.; Kassa, T.; Oot, L.; Sequeira, J.; Reymann, M.; et al. Immunization Coverage Surveys and Linked Biomarker Serosurveys in Three Regions in Ethiopia. *PLoS ONE* **2016**, *11*, e0149970. [CrossRef]
10. Minta, A.A.; Andre-Alboth, J.; Childs, L.; Nace, D.; Rey-Benito, G.; Boncy, J.; Adrien, P.; Francois, J.; Charles, N.P.J.; Blot, V.; et al. Seroprevalence of measles, rubella, tetanus, and diphtheria antibodies among children in Haiti, 2017. *Am. J. Trop. Med. Hyg.* **2020**, *103*, 1717–1725. [CrossRef]
11. Cheng, A.; Ghanem-Uzqueda, A.; Hoff, N.A.; Ashbaugh, H.; Doshi, R.H.; Mukadi, P.; Budd, R.; Higgins, S.G.; Randall, C.; Gerber, S.; et al. Tetanus seroprotection among children in the democratic republic of the Congo, 2013–2014. *PLoS ONE* **2022**, *17*, e0268703. [CrossRef] [PubMed]
12. Heron, I.; Hey, A.S.; Kurtzhals, J.A.L.; Okong'o-Odera, E.A.; Kjeldsen, K. Immunity to Tetanus and Diphtheria in.Rural Africa. *Am. J. Trop. Med. Hyg.* **1997**, *56*, 576–579.
13. Campbell, J.D.; Pasetti, M.F.; Oot, L.; Adam, Z.; Tefera, M.; Beyane, B.; Mulholland, N.; Steinglass, R.; Krey, R.; Chen, W.H.; et al. Linked vaccination coverage surveys plus serosurveys among Ethiopian toddlers undertaken three years apart to compare coverage and serologic evidence of protection in districts implementing the RED-QI approach. *Vaccine* **2021**, *39*, 5802–5813. [CrossRef] [PubMed]
14. World Health Organization. Vaccine Preventable Diseases Surveillance Standards: Annex 2 Tetanus Serosurveys. Available online: https://www.who.int/publications/m/item/vaccine-preventable-diseases-surveillance-standards-annex2 (accessed on 25 January 2023).
15. Dalal, S.; Samuelson, J.; Reed, J.; Yakubu, A.; Ncube, B.; Baggaley, R. Tetanus disease and deaths in men reveal need for vaccination. *Bull. World Health Organ.* **2016**, *94*, 613–621. [CrossRef] [PubMed]
16. Woldeamanuel, Y.W.; Andemeskel, A.T.; Kyei, K.; Woldeamanuel, M.W.; Woldeamanuel, W. Case fatality of adult tetanus in Africa: Systematic review and meta-analysis. *J. Neurol. Sci.* **2016**, *368*, 292–299. [CrossRef] [PubMed]
17. Besa, N.C.; Coldiron, M.E.; Bakri, A.; Raji, A.; Nsuami, M.J.; Rousseau, C.; Hurtado, N.; Porten, K. Diphtheria outbreak with high mortality in northeastern Nigeria. *Epidemiol. Infect.* **2014**, *142*, 797–802. [CrossRef]
18. Sadoh, A.E.; Oladokun, R.E. Re-emergence of diphtheria and pertussis: Implications for Nigeria. *Vaccine* **2012**, *30*, 7221–7228. [CrossRef] [PubMed]
19. The Guardian Nigeria. NCDC Confirm 123 Diphtheria Cases, 38 Deaths in 4 States. Available online: https://guardian.ng/news/ncdc-confirms-123-diphtheria-cases-38-deaths-in-4-states/ (accessed on 26 January 2023).
20. World Health Organization. Tetanus vaccines: WHO position paper–February 2017. *Wkly. Epidemiol. Rec.* **2017**, *92*, 53–76.
21. World Health Organization. Diphtheria vaccines: WHO position paper–August 2017. *Wkly. Epidemiol. Rec.* **2017**, *92*, 417–436.
22. Federal Ministry of Health, Nigeria. Nigeria HIV/AIDS Indicator and Impact Survey (NAIIS) 2018: Technical Report. Abuja, Nigeria. October 2019. Available online: https://www.naiis.ng/resource/NAIIS-Report-2018.pdf (accessed on 1 February 2023).
23. Scobie, H.M.; Khetsuriani, N.; Efstratiou, A.; Priest, J.W. Validation of a diphtheria toxoid multiplex bead assay for serosurveys. *Diagn. Microbiol. Infect. Dis.* **2021**, *100*, 115371. [CrossRef]
24. Plotkin, S.O.W.; Offit, P.; Edwards, K.M. *Plotkin's Vaccines*, 7th ed.; Elsevier: Philadelphia, PA, USA, 2018.
25. World Health Organization (Ed.) *The Immunological Basis for Immunization Series: Module 3: Tetanus Update 2018*; World Health Organization: Geneva, Switzerland, 2018.
26. World Health Organization (Ed.) *The Immunological Basis for Immunization Series: Module 2: Diphtheria Update 2009*; World Health Organization: Geneva, Switzerland, 2009.
27. World Health Organization. Immunization Dashboard. *Diphtheria Tetanus Toxoid and Pertussis (DTP)3 Vaccination Coverage: Nigeria.* Available online: https://immunizationdata.who.int/pages/coverage/DTP.html?CODE=NGA&ANTIGEN=DTPCV3&YEAR= (accessed on 1 February 2023).
28. Demographic Health Surveys: Nigeria. Available online: https://dhsprogram.com/search/index.cfm?_srchd=1&bydoctype=publication&bypubtype=5%2C21%2C26%2C30%2C39%2C100&bycountry=30 (accessed on 1 February 2023).
29. Multiple Indicator Cluster Surveys: Nigeria. Available online: https://mics.unicef.org/surveys (accessed on 1 February 2023).
30. Glatman-Freedman, A.; Nichols, K.A. The effect of social determinants on immunization programs. *Hum. Vaccin. Immunother.* **2012**, *8*, 293–301. [CrossRef] [PubMed]
31. Aheto, J.M.K.; Pannell, O.; Dotse-Gborgbortsi, W.; Trimner, M.K.; Tatem, A.J.; Rhoda, D.A.; Cutts, F.T.; Utazi, C.E. Multilevel analysis of predictors of multiple indicators of childhood vaccination in Nigeria. *PLoS ONE* **2022**, *17*, e0269066. [CrossRef]

32. Kawakatsu, Y.; Adolph, C.; Mosser, J.F.; Baffoe, P.; Cheshi, F.; Aiga, H.; Watkins, D.; Sherr, K.H. Factors consistently associated with utilization of essential maternal and child health services in Nigeria: Analysis of the five Nigerian national household surveys (2003–2018). *BMJ Open* **2022**, *12*, e061747. [CrossRef] [PubMed]
33. Utazi, C.E.; Aheto, J.M.; Wigley, A.; Tejedor-Garavito, N.; Bonnie, A.; Nnanatu, C.C.; Wagai, J.; Williams, C.; Setayesh, H.; Tatem, A.J.; et al. Mapping the distribution of zero-dose children to assess the performance of vaccine delivery strategies and their relationships with measles incidence in Nigeria. *Vaccine* **2023**, *41*, 170–181. [CrossRef]
34. Malande, O.O.; Munube, D.; Afaayo, R.N.; Annet, K.; Bodo, B.; Bakainaga, A.; Ayebare, E.; Njunwamukama, S.; Mworozi, E.A.; Musyoki, A.M. Barriers to effective uptake and provision of immunization in a rural district in Uganda. *PLoS ONE* **2019**, *14*, e0212270. [CrossRef] [PubMed]
35. Vasudevan, L.; Baumgartner, J.N.; Moses, S.; Ngadaya, E.; Mfinanga, S.G.; Ostermann, J. Parental concerns and uptake of childhood vaccines in rural Tanzania—A mixed methods study. *BMC Public Health* **2020**, *20*, 1573. [CrossRef]
36. Bwaka, A.; Bita, A.; Lingani, C.; Fernandez, K.; Durupt, A.; Mwenda, J.M.; Mihigo, R.; Djingarey, M.H.; Ronveaux, O.; Prezios, M.P. Status of the rollout of the meningococcal serogroup A conjugate vaccine in African Meningitis belt countries in 2018. *J. Infect. Dis.* **2019**, *220*, S140–S147. [CrossRef] [PubMed]
37. World Health Organization. Epidemic meningitis control in countries of the African meningitis belt, 2017. *Wkly. Epidemiol. Rec.* **2018**, *14*, 173–184.
38. Meningitis Vaccine Project. Available online: https://www.meningvax.org/developingconjugatevaccine.html (accessed on 1 February 2023).
39. Basta, N.E.; Borrow, R.; Berthe, A.; Onwuchekwa, U.; Dembele, A.T.; Almond, R.; Frankland, S.; Patel, S.; Wood, D.; Nascimento, M.; et al. Higher Tetanus Toxoid Immunity 2 Years After PsA-TT Introduction in Mali. *Clin. Infect. Dis.* **2015**, *61*, S578–S585. [CrossRef]
40. Borrow, R.; Tang, Y.; Yakubu, A.; Kulkami, P.S.; LaForce, F.M. MenAfriVac as an antitetanus vaccine. *Clin. Infect. Dis.* **2015**, *61*, S570–S577. [CrossRef]
41. National Bureau of Statistics. Demographic Statistics Bulletin: 2017. Available online: https://www.nigerianstat.gov.ng/download/775 (accessed on 1 February 2023).
42. National Bureau of Statistics (NBS) and United Nations Children's Fund (UNICEF). *Multiple Indicator Cluster Survey 2021, Survey Findings Report*; National Bureau of Statistics and United Nations Children's Fund: Abuja, Nigeria, 2022.

vaccines

MDPI

Article

Disparities in Coverage of Adult Immunization among Older Adults in India

Damini Singh †, Abhinav Sinha †, Srikanta Kanungo * and Sanghamitra Pati

ICMR—Regional Medical Research Centre, Bhubaneswar 751023, India
* Correspondence: srikantak109@gmail.com
† These authors contributed equally to this work.

Abstract: A lack of a universal adult immunization scheme in India poses a challenge to achieve universal health coverage. Healthcare disparity is one of the biggest challenges in low- and middle-income countries such as India. We aimed to estimate the disparities in coverage of various adult vaccines among older adults in India using nationally representative data. An observational analysis among 31,464 participants aged ≥60 years from the Longitudinal Ageing Study in India, 2017–2018, was conducted. Vaccination coverage across wealth quintiles and selected non-communicable diseases were reported as frequencies and weighted proportions along with their 95% confidence intervals as a measure of uncertainty. The highest coverage was of the diphtheria and tetanus vaccine (2.75%) followed by typhoid (1.84%), hepatitis B (1.82%), influenza (1.59%), and pneumococcal (0.74%). The most affluent groups had a higher coverage of all vaccines. Participants having high cholesterol, psychiatric conditions, and cancer had the highest coverage of all vaccines. Overall, a very low coverage of all vaccines was observed. The coverage was influenced by social determinants of health, depicting a disparity in accessing immunization. Hence, at-risk groups such as the deprived and multimorbid patients need to be covered under the ambit of free immunization to achieve universal health coverage.

Keywords: vaccines; adult immunization; disparities; VPDs; India; pneumococcal; influenza; hepatitis B; typhoid; diphtheria and tetanus; multimorbidity

Citation: Singh, D.; Sinha, A.; Kanungo, S.; Pati, S. Disparities in Coverage of Adult Immunization among Older Adults in India. *Vaccines* **2022**, *10*, 2124. https://doi.org/10.3390/vaccines10122124

Academic Editors: Ahmad Reza Hosseinpoor, M. Carolina Danovaro, Devaki Nambiar, Aaron Wallace and Hope Johnson

Received: 26 November 2022
Accepted: 6 December 2022
Published: 12 December 2022

1. Introduction

Immunization has been considered one of the most cost-effective public health interventions worldwide [1]. Its efficacy and transparency have already been marked for eradicating smallpox globally. The launch of the Expanded Program of Immunization (EPI) by the World Health Organization (WHO) has configured the Universal Immunisation Program (UIP) which aims at achieving coverage of vaccines for all neonates, children, and pregnant women [1]. However, some vaccine-preventable diseases (VPDs) may equally affect the adult population. Moreover, owing to the current demographic transition in low- and middle-income countries (LMICs) such as India, the adult population is on the rise [1]. An increase in the adult population highlights the urgent need for their immunization to achieve universal health coverage (UHC). Adult immunization has become a major concern, especially in LMICs such as India where this group is more susceptible to acquiring diseases during outbreaks or various other conditions associated with non-communicable diseases (NCDs) [1,2]. Additionally, waning immunity and age-related factors (including immunosenescence) also highlight the need for adult vaccination [2,3].

The measles and rubella (MR) vaccine and consideration of the human papillomavirus (HPV) for potential inclusion in the UIP under the ambit of public vaccination efforts have brought the transition of childhood vaccination programs towards adolescents. Vaccines such as tetanus toxoid (TT) vaccines for pregnant ladies and Japanese encephalitis (JE) vaccines for adults residing in endemic districts are also provided free of cost by the government. Moreover, TT and JE have the highest coverage among adult vaccines [1]. However, other adult vaccines such as influenza, pneumococcal, hepatitis B, typhoid, and diphtheria and tetanus vaccines are also available but are often underutilized. Still, adult vaccination remains a challenge, especially amongst deprived groups [2,4]. Additionally, various groups such as adults with multimorbidity (simultaneous occurrence of two or more chronic conditions in an individual without considering index disease) are at a higher risk of contracting VPDs and may immediately need vaccination [2,3].

Adult immunization is one of the keys to empowering a life course initiative for health care services. The sustainability of vaccines depends on availability and affordability. However, India does not have a clear mandate for providing universal adult vaccination which makes these vaccines underused. This becomes grave with the under-recognition of outbreaks and a deficiency of data on the real burden of VPDs among adults [1,5]. Further, this points toward an urgent need to generate evidence on the present adult vaccination coverage in India. This would help in planning future policies for transitioning conventional childhood and recent adolescent immunization towards adults to avert mortality and morbidity in this age group. Additionally, there is a dearth of literature on adult immunization coverage in India. The available studies represent either a city or some particular region with no national-level data. Hence, this study was conducted to estimate the coverage of the influenza vaccine, pneumococcal vaccine, hepatitis B vaccine, typhoid vaccine, and diphtheria and tetanus (DT) vaccine among adults in India using nationally representative data.

2. Methods

An observational analysis based on the first wave of the Longitudinal Ageing Study in India (LASI), 2017–2019, was conducted. The LASI is a community-based study proposed to be conducted every two years among the aging population aged ≥60 years and above and their spouses, irrespective of age. The LASI is a multi-partner undertaking by the Harvard School of Public Health (HSPH), the International Institute of Population Sciences (IIPS), and the University of Southern California. The LASI utilizes a multistage stratified area probability cluster sampling design to achieve the ultimate sampling unit. A response rate of 87.3% was registered by the first wave of the study. Face-to-face interviews were conducted among 31,464 participants aged ≥60 years which formed the ultimate sample for our study. The detailed methods related to the LASI survey can be found on their website [6].

2.1. Outcome Variables

The individual survey schedule of the LASI asked "have you ever received any immunizations for adults, such as the influenza vaccine, pneumococcal vaccine, hepatitis B vaccine, or typhoid vaccine?". Multiple answers were allowed for the above question. If the response was "yes" for a particular vaccine, then we considered an individual to be vaccinated for that particular vaccine such as influenza vaccine, pneumococcal vaccine, hepatitis B vaccine, or typhoid vaccine which formed the main outcomes of interest for our study.

2.2. Independent Variables

We took into account the following socio-economic and demographic factors: age (in years), sex, residence, caste, education, occupation, marital status, MPCE quintile, and health insurance. Answers to the age-based question "how old were you on your last birthday?" were categorized into three groups, namely 60–69 years, 70–79 years, and >80 years. Sex was recorded based on observation as male or female. The residence of the respondents was divided as urban or rural. Caste was classified into four groups, namely scheduled caste, scheduled tribe, other backward class, and others (includes: no caste/tribe and none of these) based on two questions "what is your caste or tribe?" followed by "Do you belong to a scheduled caste, a scheduled tribe, other backward class, or none of these?". Education of the respondents was assessed through the question "have you ever attended school?" with responses yes or no corresponding with formal education and no formal education, respectively. The current occupation status of the respondent grouped as currently employed or currently unemployed was based on the responses to "have you ever worked for at least 3 months during your lifetime?". Marital status was classified based on "what is your current marital status?" with responses grouped as with partners (currently married or live-in relationship) or without partners (widowed, divorced, separated, deserted, or never married). The economic status was based on the monthly per capita expenditure (MPCE) grouped into quintiles ranging from the most deprived to the most affluent class. The health insurance coverage among participants was assessed through "are you covered by health insurance?" with responses as yes or no. Based on an extensive literature search, ten self-reported most common NCDs such as hypertension, diabetes, cancer, chronic lung disease, chronic heart disease, stroke, arthritis, psychiatric problems, and high cholesterol were taken into account based on one of the questions: "has any health professional ever diagnosed you with the following chronic conditions or diseases?". Multimorbidity was defined as having two or more chronic conditions out of the above-mentioned chronic conditions.

2.3. Statistical Analysis

We employed STATA version 16.0 (Stata Corp™, College Station, TX, USA) for the analysis. Descriptive statistics included mean and standard deviation along with range, frequencies, and percentages to assess the respondents' background characteristics and estimate the coverage of vaccines. Vaccination coverage across various socio-demographic attributes and selected NCDs was reported. A multi-variable logistic regression model assessed the association between various levels of uptake for adult vaccines and wealth quintiles adjusted for other socio-demographic characteristics. A weighted analysis was conducted to compensate for complex survey designs. We reported a 95% confidence interval (CI) for all weighted proportions as a measure of uncertainty.

2.4. Ethics Statement

The LASI received ethical endorsement from the Indian Council of Medical Research (ICMR), New Delhi, and the International Institute for Population Sciences (IIPS), Mumbai. Entrants were given a prospectus containing the information on the aims and objectives of the survey, confidentiality of their personal information, and safety of health assessment. Written consent forms were subjugated at household and individual levels. The LASI employed informed written consent forms. This study is based on anonymous secondary data from the LASI; hence, no ethical concerns arise.

3. Results

This study was based on 31,464 participants aged $\geq$60 years with a mean age of 68.87 $\pm$ 7.51 years. Almost half of the participants (58.51%) were 60–69 years of age (Table 1). We observed a female predilection (52.55%) in the study population. Around 70.55 of the respondents lived in rural areas. We found that 43.48% of the participants had formal education and 74.06% of respondents were currently employed. We observed that 18.24% of the participants had health insurance coverage.

The overall coverage of the diphtheria and tetanus vaccine (2.75% (95% CI: 2.75–3.12)) was highest, followed by the typhoid vaccine (1.84% (95% CI: 1.69–1.99)), hepatitis B vaccine (1.82% (95% CI: 1.67–1.97)), influenza vaccine (1.59% (95% CI: 1.45–1.73)), and pneumococcal vaccine (0.74% (95% CI: 0.65–0.84)). Further, it was observed that the participants from the most affluent group had a higher coverage of adult vaccinations compared to any other group. Diphtheria and tetanus vaccines were mostly (4.21%) taken by the most affluent group. The pneumococcal vaccine had the minimum coverage among the most deprived group, i.e., only 0.16% (Table 2).

Table 1. Characteristics of the study population.

Characteristics	Weighted n (%)
Age in years (n = 31,464)	
60–69	18,410, (58.51)
70–79	9501, (30.20)
>80	3553 (11.29)
Sex (n = 31,464)	
Male	14,931, (47.45)
Female	16,533, (52.55)
Residence (n = 31,464)	
Rural	22,196, (70.55)
Urban	9268, (29.45)
Caste (n = 31,198)	
Scheduled caste	5926, (18.99)
Scheduled tribe	2546, (8.16)
Other backward class	14,175, (45.44)
Others	8551, (27.41)
Education (n = 31,464)	
Formal Education	13,681, (43.48)
No formal education	17,783, (56.52)
Occupation (n = 31,460)	
Currently Employed	23,151, (74.06)
Currently Unemployed	8309, (26.41)
Marital Status (n = 31,464)	
Without partner	11,928, (37.91)
With partner	19,536, (62.09)
MPCE Quintile (n = 31,464)	
Most deprived	6829, (21.70)
2	6832, (21.71)
3	6590, (20.95)
4	6038, (19.19)
Most affluent	5175, (16.45)
Health insurance (N = 31,162)	
Yes	5685, (18.24)
No	25,477, (81.76)

Table 2. Coverage of various adult vaccines across wealth quintiles among older adults in India.

Wealth Quintiles	Influenza Vaccine n, % (95% CI)	Pneumococcal Vaccine n, % (95% CI)	Hepatitis B n, % (95% CI)	Typhoid n, % (95% CI)	Diphtheria and Tetanus n, % (95% CI)
Most deprived	57, 0.84, (0.64–1.08)	11, 0.16, (0.08–0.28)	37, 0.55, (0.38–0.75)	56, 0.82, (0.62–1.07)	95, 1.40, (1.13–1.71)
2	78, 1.16, (0.91–1.43)	34, 0.51, (0.35–0.70)	101, 1.49, (1.21–1.81)	103, 1.52, (1.24–1.84)	190, 2.81, (2.42–3.22)
3	90, 1.41, (1.13–1.72)	40, 0.63, (0.44–0.85)	102, 1.60, (1.30–1.93)	124, 1.93, (1.61–2.30)	190, 2.97, (2.56–3.41)
4	94, 1.58, (1.27–1.93)	59, 0.99, (0.75–1.27)	138, 2.32, (1.95–2.73)	118, 1.98, (1.64–2.37)	220, 3.70, (3.23–4.20)
Most affluent	172, 3.37, (2.88–3.89)	85, 1.68, (1.33–2.05)	185, 3.63, (3.12–4.17)	170, 3.33, (2.85–3.85)	215, 4.21, (3.67–4.79)

The adjusted multi-variable model revealed that the most affluent group had a higher chance of getting vaccinated for influenza (AOR: 3.32 (95% CI: 2.52–4.39)), pneumococcal

(AOR: 5.53 (3.41–8.99)), hepatitis B (AOR: 5.24 (95% CI: 3.99–6.87)), typhoid (AOR: 3.53 (95% CI: 2.65–4.70)), and diphtheria and tetanus (AOR: 3.60 (95% CI: 2.96–4.39)) than the most deprived group (Table 3).

Table 3. Association between uptake of various adult vaccines and wealth quintiles among older adults in India.

Wealth Quintiles	Influenza Vaccine AOR (95% CI)	Pneumococcal Vaccine AOR (95% CI)	Hepatitis B AOR (95% CI)	Typhoid AOR (95% CI)	Diphtheria and Tetanus AOR (95% CI)
Most deprived			Ref		
2	1.25 (90.98–1.71)	1.99 (1.16–3.41)	1.86 (1.37–2.52)	1.90 (1.40–2.59)	1.59 (1.28–1.98)
3	1.64 (1.21–2.21)	2.88 (1.73–4.80)	2.18 (1.62–2.93)	2.24 (1.66–3.02)	2.01 (1.63–2.47)
4	2.26 (1.69–3.02)	3.61 (2.18–5.95)	3.38 (2.55–4.48)	2.41 (1.79–3.25)	2.67 (2.18–3.27)
Most affluent	3.32 (2.52–4.39)	5.53 (3.41–8.99)	5.24 (3.99–6.87)	3.53 (2.65–4.70)	3.60 (2.96–4.39)

Adjusted for age, sex, residence, caste, occupation, and health insurance.

It was found that respondents with psychiatric problems (5.28%) followed by high cholesterol (3.69%), multimorbidity (2.59%), and stroke (2.46%) had taken influenza vaccines more than participants having other selected chronic conditions. Pneumococcal vaccination coverage was observed to be higher among respondents having high cholesterol (2.56%) followed by psychiatric problems (2.29%) and cancer (2.20%). The coverage for the hepatitis B vaccine was found to be higher in respondents with high cholesterol (5.53%) followed by cancer (5.51%) and psychiatric problems (5.06%). Typhoid vaccination coverage was found to be higher in respondents having high cholesterol (4.59%) followed by psychiatric problems (5%) and cancer (4.46%). Respondents with high cholesterol (10.05%) followed by psychiatric problems (6.86%) and cancer (6.84%) had higher coverage of diphtheria and tetanus vaccines (Table 4).

Table 4. Coverage of adult vaccines across selected non-communicable diseases among adults in India.

Non-Communicable Disease	Influenza Vaccine n, % (95% CI)	Pneumococcal Vaccine n, % (95% CI)	Hepatitis B Vaccine n, % (95% CI)	Typhoid Vaccine n, % (95% CI)	Diphtheria and Tetanus n, % (95% CI)
Hypertension	334, 2.28 (2.04–2.53)	139, 0.95 (0.79–1.11)	360, 2.46 (2.21–2.72)	403, 2.75 (2.50–3.03)	545, 3.72 (3.42–4.04)
Diabetes	145, 2.16 (1.82–2.54)	60, 0.90 (0.68- 1.15)	162, 2.41 (2.06–2.81)	138, 2.06 (1.73–2.42)	221, 3.29 (2.87–3.75)
Cancer	5, 1.37 (0.49–3.50)	7, 2.20 (0.85–4.32)	18, 5.51 (3.26–8.48)	15, 4.46 (2.56–7.38)	23, 6.84 (4.47–10.27)
Chronic lung disease	86, 2.31 (1.85–2.85)	40, 1.09 (0.77–1.46)	68, 1.83 (1.42–2.32)	90, 2.43 (1.95–2.97)	131, 3.54 (2.96–4.17)
Chronic heart disease	51, 2.41 (1.79–3.14)	32, 1.53 (1.03–2.11)	53, 2.50 (1.87–3.24)	52, 2.47 (1.83–3.19)	76, 3.60 (2.82–4.45)

Table 4. *Cont.*

Non-Communicable Disease	Influenza Vaccine n, % (95% CI)	Pneumococcal Vaccine n, % (95% CI)	Hepatitis B Vaccine n, % (95% CI)	Typhoid Vaccine n, % (95% CI)	Diphtheria and Tetanus n, % (95% CI)
Stroke	27, 2.46 (1.59–3.49)	14, 1.29 (0.68–2.09)	28, 2.52 (1.67–3.59)	32, 2.84 (1.96–4.01)	51, 4.59 (3.41–5.95)
Arthritis	207, 2.37 (2.05–2.70)	78, 0.89 (0.70–1.10)	234, 2.68 (2.34–3.03)	253, 2.89 (2.54–3.26)	289, 3.29 (2.93–3.69)
Psychiatric problem	64, 5.28 (4.09–6.69)	28, 2.29 (1.54–3.32)	61, 5.06 (3.87–6.42)	60, 5.00 (3.79–6.32)	83, 6.86 (5.49–8.42)
High cholesterol	44, 3.69 (2.65–4.85)	31, 2.56 (1.74–3.62)	67, 5.53 (4.32–6.98)	55, 4.59 (3.45–5.88)	121, 10.05 (8.37–11.84)
Multimorbidity	193, 2.59 (2.24–2.97)	94, 1.26 (1.01–1.54)	211, 2.83 (2.46–3.23)	212, 2.85 (2.47–3.24)	318, 4.26 (3.82–4.75)

4. Discussion

The overall coverage of adult vaccination was considerably low among the participants belonging to deprived groups. The highest coverage was of the DT vaccine followed by those of typhoid, hepatitis B, influenza, and pneumococcal. Participants having high cholesterol, psychiatric conditions, and cancer had the highest coverage for all vaccines.

We observed that the DT vaccine had the highest coverage followed by typhoid, hepatitis B, influenza, and pneumococcal vaccines. A recent facility-based study conducted at an adult vaccination center in Jodhpur observed that tetanus toxoid, anti-rabies, and yellow fever vaccines had the highest coverage [1]. However, the coverage of the hepatitis B vaccine (8%), followed by the pneumococcal vaccine (7%) and typhoid vaccine (3%) was reported higher than the findings of our study [1]. Interestingly, the coverage of the influenza vaccine (1%) was found to be lower compared to the present study. Notably, there is a dearth of literature on adult vaccination in India which makes comparing our findings with similar studies difficult. A 2018 US report on adult vaccination surveillance observed the coverage of the influenza vaccine to be around 46.1%, hepatitis B around 30%, and pneumococcal around 23.3%, which is significantly lower than the coverage of adult immunization in India [7]. The major reason for this could be the disparity in accessing vaccines in India, as adult vaccination is not covered in the routine universal immunization schedule.

The increase in antibiotic-resistant bacterial strains such as *S. pneumonia* [8] due to over-the-counter drugs has led to a rise in pneumococcal infections which may also invade the bloodstream, causing meningitis. Older adults are particularly at a higher risk of becoming severely ill and dying; hence, they must be vaccinated [8,9]. This could be the probable reason for the higher coverage of the pneumococcal vaccine among participants aged ≥61 years. Influenza caused by the influenza virus affects individuals of all ages but it has the highest risk of complications among older adults [8]. However, the effectiveness of the influenza vaccine is lower among older adults [10,11]. The WHO advises for an annual influenza immunization for older adults [8,12]. Our findings are consistent with the WHO's recommendations for vaccinating older adults; however, the coverage is considerably low which may pose a challenge for UHC [8]. Pneumococcal and influenza vaccines are indicated among diabetes patients since they have irregularities in immune function, leading to a rise in morbidity and mortality from infection [11,13]. Further, diabetics have a higher chance of complications from influenza and pneumococcal infections leading to hospitalization and death [11]. Diabetics have an appropriate humoral immune response to immunization [11]. Nonetheless, previous studies have reported that the influenza vaccine has reduced hospital admission during epidemics, whereas the pneumococcal vaccine has been effective in reducing bacteremic infections [11]. Our findings show a very low coverage of both of these vaccines among diabetics which is a grave concern.

Typhoid fever continues to be an endemic disease in Southeast Asia with a substantial number of cases among teenagers and young adults [14]. Poor sanitation facilities, especially among deprived groups, is a major cause of typhoid [14,15]. However, we observed that deprived strata had a lower coverage of the typhoid vaccine which may lead to an increased case burden in this group. Additionally, both acute and chronic infections of hepatitis B cause disproportionately higher mortality and morbidity in LMICs, where it is a significant public health issue [16]. Evidence suggests catch-up immunization for younger adults is beneficial above costs [17]. Hence, for adults in India, catch-up immunization must be planned for those who were not vaccinated in their childhood. This should specifically be for the adults who are at a higher risk of infection such as drug abusers and individuals with liver diseases. Similar to the hepatitis B vaccine, the coverage of the DT vaccine during childhood is high but previous studies have reported unsatisfactory antibody levels among adults [18]. This highlights a need for adult DT vaccination [19]. It is to be noted that we found a low coverage of all vaccines which might lead to a high disease burden among adults.

We observed a variation in the coverage of various adult vaccines across wealth indexes. Participants belonging to the most affluent groups had the highest coverage of all vaccines. Our findings are consistent with the reports from other LMICs such as China, where a study observed that people living with a finance-reimbursed vaccination policy had a higher vaccination rate [20]. Moreover, a study conducted in Pakistan observed that the majority of the participants were not receiving adult vaccines due to lack of awareness [21]. A probable reason for this could be their ability to pay. Since we do not have a universal program for adult vaccination in India, individuals need to pay to receive the vaccines. However, the disparities across deprived and affluent groups may lead to a low coverage of vaccines which needs to be equitably dealt with. These findings are relevant with the conceptual framework of the Commission on Social Determinants of Health (CSDH) [22,23]. Additionally, our findings are consistent with the findings of a systematic review which investigated the role of social determinants and seasonal influenza vaccination in adults aged 65 years and above and found that age, gender, education, ethnicity, etc. influenced immunization [22]. Here, it is worth noting that older adults in India might need information, education, and communication (IEC) to take up vaccination as, conventionally, it is thought to be for children. Lack of awareness can be a major barrier in increasing immunization coverage which needs to be strengthened.

4.1. Implications for Policy and Practice

The National Technical Advisory Group on Immunization in India (NTAGI) does not provide a clear mandate on adult vaccination in India. However, their recommendations can shape the future course of adult immunization in India. Similar to COVID-19 vaccination, a phase-wise coverage based on the assessment of risk factors is required for all adult vaccines in India. Additionally, the provision of subsidized vaccines can also help in achieving higher immunization coverage. Along with the at-risk groups, women and economically deprived groups also need to be focused on. People living in hard-to-reach areas and tribal groups also are vulnerable to VPDs; hence, they require support for vaccination. The Ayushman Bharat scheme should establish adult vaccination in the bundle of services for the deprived class. Systematic mechanisms to vaccinate individuals with chronic conditions and multimorbidity is required. For equitable and egalitarian access, the availability of vaccines should be at the nearest healthcare centers. Furthermore, IEC and behavioral change communication (BCC) are required for beneficiaries to understand the need for vaccines. Adult immunization should be included in mainstream medical education and training curricula. Future studies on operational feasibility and enablers and barriers to adult immunization need to be explored.

4.2. Strengths and Limitations

This study used nationally representative data to investigate adult immunization coverage in India. To the best of our knowledge, this is the first study on nationwide adult immunization coverage. However, our study is limited by self-reported vaccination status which is susceptible to recall bias.

5. Conclusions

We observed a very low coverage of all vaccines among adults. Furthermore, the coverage was higher in affluent groups, depicting a disparity in accessing immunization. However, universal vaccination may not be feasible in India due to the huge population of at-risk groups and disadvantaged sections of society such as deprived strata and women, who need to be covered under the ambit of free immunization, which can help in achieving universal health coverage.

Author Contributions: Conceptualization, formal analysis, methodology, writing—original draft preparation, D.S.; conceptualization, formal analysis, methodology, writing—original draft preparation, A.S.; methodology, writing—review and editing, S.K.; methodology, writing—review and editing, S.P. All authors have read and agreed to the published version of the manuscript.

Funding: No funds were received to conduct the present research.

Institutional Review Board Statement: The present study utilizes de-identified data from a secondary source. The data have been archived in the public repository of the LASI held at IIPS. The access to the data requires registration which is granted specifically for legitimate research purposes. The LASI received mandatory ethical approval from the Indian Council of Medical Research and the Institutional Review Board (IRB) held at IIPS, Mumbai. Data from the LASI are archived in a public repository; therefore, there is no need for additional ethical approval to conduct the present study. All methods were carried out in accordance with the relevant guidelines and regulations.

Informed Consent Statement: At the unit level, individuals were supplied with a catalogue containing the information on the purpose of the survey, confidentiality, and safety of health assessment. Written consent forms were administered at household and individual levels, in accordance with the Human Subject Protection. However, we used secondary anonymous data obtained from public source for the present study.

Data Availability Statement: The dataset analyzed during the current study is available in the LASI data repository held at ICT, IIPS https://iipsindia.ac.in/content/lasi-wave-I (accessed on 10 December 2022). Requests to access the data should be made to datacenter@ipsindia.ac.in.

Acknowledgments: The authors are grateful to the Longitudinal Ageing Study in India (LASI) for assembling and publishing accurate, nationally representative data on a range of health biomarkers and healthcare utilization indicators for the population in the age range of 45 years and older. The authors are also grateful to the LASI's project partners: the International Institute for Population Sciences (IIPS), Harvard, the T. H. Chan School of Public Health (HSPH), and the University of Southern California (USC).

Conflicts of Interest: The authors declare that they have no competing interests.

References

1. Lahariya, C.; Bhardwaj, P. Adult vaccination in India: Status and the way forward. *Hum. Vaccines Immunother.* **2020**, *16*, 1508–1510. [CrossRef] [PubMed]
2. Dash, R.; Agrawal, A.; Nagvekar, V.; Lele, J.; Di Pasquale, A.; Kolhapure, S.; Parikh, R. Towards adult vaccination in India: A narrative literature review. *Hum. Vaccines Immunother.* **2020**, *16*, 991–1001. [CrossRef] [PubMed]
3. Vora, A.; Di Pasquale, A.; Kolhapure, S.; Agrawal, A.; Agrawal, S. The need for vaccination in adults with chronic (non-communicable) diseases in India–lessons from around the world. *Hum. Vaccines Immunother.* **2022**, *18*, 2052544. [CrossRef] [PubMed]
4. De Gomensoro, E.; Del Giudice, G.; Doherty, T.M. Challenges in adult vaccination. *Ann. Med.* **2018**, *50*, 181–192. [CrossRef] [PubMed]
5. Mehta, B.; Chawla, S.; Kumar Dharma, V.; Jindal, H.; Bhatt, B. Adult immunization: The need to address. *Hum. Vaccines Immunother.* **2014**, *10*, 306–309. [CrossRef] [PubMed]

6. International Institute for Population Sciences (IIPS). *Longitudinal Aging Study in India (LASI)*; IIPS: Mumbai, India, 2020.
7. Lu, P.J.; Hung, M.C.; Srivastav, A.; Grohskopf, L.A.; Kobayashi, M.; Harris, A.M.; Dooling, K.L.; Markowitz, L.E.; Rodriguez-Lainz, A.; Williams, W.W. Surveillance of vaccination coverage among adult populations—United States, 2018. *MMWR Surveill. Summ.* **2021**, *70*, 1–26. [CrossRef] [PubMed]
8. Verma, R.; Khanna, P.; Chawla, S. Vaccines for the elderly need to be introduced into the immunization program in India. *Hum. Vaccines Immunother.* **2014**, *10*, 2468–2470. [CrossRef] [PubMed]
9. Chen, Y.; Gu, W.; He, B.; Gao, H.; Sun, P.; Li, Q.; Chen, E.; Miao, Z. Impact of a community-based health education intervention on awareness of influenza, pneumonia, and vaccination intention in chronic patients. *Hum. Vaccines Immunother.* **2022**, *18*, 1–8. [CrossRef]
10. Maggi, S. Vaccination and healthy aging. *Expert Rev. Vaccines* **2010**, *9* (Suppl. S3), 3–6. [CrossRef]
11. American Diabetes Association. Immunization and the prevention of influenza and pneumococcal disease in people with diabetes. *Diabetes Care* **2003**, *26* (Suppl. S1), s126–s128. [CrossRef]
12. Aguado, M.T.; Barratt, J.; Beard, J.R.; Blomberg, B.B.; Chen, W.H.; Hickling, J.; Hyde, T.B.; Jit, M.; Jones, R.; Poland, G.A.; et al. Report on WHO meeting on immunization in older adults: Geneva, Switzerland, 22–23 March 2017. *Vaccine* **2018**, *36*, 921–931. [CrossRef] [PubMed]
13. Alzahrani, Z.; Bashrahil, B.; Alzahrani, M.S.; Alghamdi, N.; Nooh, M.; Alsolami, H.; Alghamdi, A.F.; Alabbasi, A.A.; Khan, M.A.; Alzahrani, A.M. Trends In Hepatitis, B. Influenza, And Pneumococcal Vaccination In Diabetic Patients. *Res. Sq.* **2022**. *Preprint*. [CrossRef]
14. Isahak, I. Adult immunization-a neglected issue in Southeast Asia. *Southeast Asian J. Trop. Med. Public Health* **2000**, *31*, 173–184.
15. Poulos, C.; Bahl, R.; Whittington, D.; Bhan, M.K.; Clemens, J.D.; Acosta, C.J. A cost-benefit analysis of typhoid fever immunization programmes in an Indian urban slum community. *J. Health Popul. Nutr.* **2004**, *22*, 311–321. [PubMed]
16. Wright, C.M.; Boudarène, L.; Ha, N.T.; Wu, O.; Hawkins, N. A systematic review of hepatitis B screening economic evaluations in low-and middle-income countries. *BMC Public Health* **2018**, *18*, 373. [CrossRef]
17. Ota, M.O.; de Moraes, J.C.; Vojtek, I.; Constenla, D.; Doherty, T.M.; Cintra, O.; Kirigia, J.M. Unveiling the contributions of immunization for progressing towards Universal Health Coverage. *Hum. Vaccines Immunother.* **2022**, *18*, 2036048. [CrossRef]
18. Böttiger, M.; Gustavsson, O.; Svensson, Å. Immunity to tetanus, diphtheria and poliomyelitis in the adult population of Sweden in 1991. *Int. J. Epidemiol.* **1998**, *27*, 916–925. [CrossRef]
19. Hasselhorn, H.M.; Nübling, M.; Tiller, F.W.; Hofmann, F. Factors influencing immunity against diphtheria in adults. *Vaccine* **1998**, *16*, 70–75. [CrossRef]
20. Fan, J.; Cong, S.; Wang, N.; Bao, H.; Wang, B.; Feng, Y.; Lv, X.; Zhang, Y.; Zha, Z.; Yu, L.; et al. Influenza vaccination rate and its association with chronic diseases in China: Results of a national cross-sectional study. *Vaccine* **2020**, *38*, 2503–2511. [CrossRef]
21. Zaki, S.; Usman, A.; Tariq, S.; Shah, S.; Azam, I.; Qidwai, W.; Nanji, K. Frequency and factors associated with adult immunization in patients visiting family medicine clinics at a Tertiary Care Hospital, Karachi. *Cureus* **2018**, *10*, e2083. [CrossRef]
22. Nagata, J.M.; Hernández-Ramos, I.; Kurup, A.S.; Albrecht, D.; Vivas-Torrealba, C.; Franco-Paredes, C. Social determinants of health and seasonal influenza vaccination in adults $\geq$ 65 years: A systematic review of qualitative and quantitative data. *BMC Public Health* **2013**, *13*, 388. [CrossRef] [PubMed]
23. Solar, O.; Irwin, A. *A Conceptual Framework for Action on the Social Determinants of Health*; WHO Document Production Services; WHO: Geneva, Switzerland, 2010.

vaccines

MDPI

Review

Within-Country Inequality in COVID-19 Vaccination Coverage: A Scoping Review of Academic Literature

Nicole Bergen [1], Nicole E. Johns [1], Diana Chang Blanc [2] and Ahmad Reza Hosseinpoor [1,*]

1 Department of Data and Analytics, World Health Organization, 20 Avenue Appia, 1211 Geneva, Switzerland
2 Department of Immunization, Vaccines and Biologicals, World Health Organization, 20 Avenue Appia, 1211 Geneva, Switzerland
* Correspondence: hosseinpoora@who.int; Tel.: +41-22-791-3205

Abstract: Since December 2020, COVID-19 vaccines have become increasingly available to populations around the globe. A growing body of research has characterised inequalities in COVID-19 vaccination coverage. This scoping review aims to locate, select and assess research articles that report on within-country inequalities in COVID-19 vaccination coverage, and to provide a preliminary overview of inequality trends for selected dimensions of inequality. We applied a systematic search strategy across electronic databases with no language or date restrictions. Our inclusion criteria specified research articles or reports that analysed inequality in COVID-19 vaccination coverage according to one or more socioeconomic, demographic or geographic dimension of inequality. We developed a data extraction template to compile findings. The scoping review was carried out using the PRISMA-ScR checklist. A total of 167 articles met our inclusion criteria, of which half (n = 83) were conducted in the United States. Articles focused on vaccine initiation, full vaccination and/or receipt of booster. Diverse dimensions of inequality were explored, most frequently relating to age (n = 127 articles), race/ethnicity (n = 117 articles) and sex/gender (n = 103 articles). Preliminary assessments of inequality trends showed higher coverage among older population groups, with mixed findings for sex/gender. Global research efforts should be expanded across settings to understand patterns of inequality and strengthen equity in vaccine policies, planning and implementation.

Keywords: COVID-19; dimension of inequality; disparity; health equity; immunisation; inequality; research; scoping review; vaccination

Citation: Bergen, N.; Johns, N.E.; Chang Blanc, D.; Hosseinpoor, A.R. Within-Country Inequality in COVID-19 Vaccination Coverage: A Scoping Review of Academic Literature. *Vaccines* **2023**, *11*, 517. https://doi.org/10.3390/vaccines11030517

Academic Editor: Pedro Plans-Rubió

Received: 3 February 2023
Revised: 17 February 2023
Accepted: 20 February 2023
Published: 23 February 2023

1. Introduction

The COVID-19 pandemic has brought substantial attention to matters of health inequality, which is defined as a difference in a measurable aspect of health across socially relevant population subgroups [1]. Health inequalities have been evident in COVID-19 exposure risks, outcomes, responses and impacts and, since the mass rollout of COVID-19 vaccination beginning in December 2020, COVID-19 vaccination coverage [2,3]. In this paper, we review the current state of research about inequalities in COVID-19 vaccination coverage.

The development of vaccines against COVID-19 was a major breakthrough in the scientific world and a turning point for controlling the progression of the pandemic [4,5]. Initially, limited global vaccine supplies meant that vaccination implementation plans prioritised certain population groups. Guidance issued by the World Health Organization (WHO) recommended prioritisation of older adults, health workers and immunocompromised persons [6]. As vaccine supplies have become more widely available, however, the inadequate uptake of vaccines by some populations has limited their potential for impact. As of January 2023, nearly 70% of the global population has received at least one dose of a COVID-19 vaccine, although only one-quarter of people in low-income countries have this level of coverage [7]. Inequalities in COVID-19 vaccination coverage are also evident within countries, as certain population subgroups remain systematically disadvantaged; that is, unvaccinated or under-vaccinated. For instance, there were early indications of racial inequity just weeks after vaccine distribution began in the United States, as available data suggested lower vaccination among Black and Hispanic people alongside higher shares of cases and deaths [8]. More recently, data from 14 million adults across 90 countries suggested pervasive education-related inequalities in self-reported receipt of a COVID-19 vaccine in nearly every country, with higher vaccination among the more educated [9].

Distinct factors contribute to COVID-19 vaccination inequalities between countries versus inequalities within countries [10,11]. In this review, we focus on a growing body of research dedicated to exploring within-country inequalities in COVID-19 vaccination coverage. Broadly, the body of research addresses how coverage varies according to dimensions of inequality (i.e., criteria that define population subgroups, such as age, economic status, education level, place of residence, sex or subnational region) that are relevant within a specified population and context. Research efforts to characterise these inequalities offer important insights into situations that may be inequitable (unfair, unjust and/or avoidable through reasonable means [1]). Namely, assessments of inequalities in vaccination coverage can provide evidence about which population subgroups had access to and received the vaccine, and which did not. This evidence can inform how national policies and programmes may be targeted to reach disadvantaged groups and, when repeated over time, monitoring inequalities can support enhanced accountability for upholding and advancing health equity [12].

The present review considers research pertaining to COVID-19 vaccination coverage—the actual receipt or non-receipt of a vaccine. We pose the question: what is the current status of research on within-country inequalities in COVID-19 vaccination coverage? COVID-19 vaccination coverage is defined based on the receipt or non-receipt of a COVID-19 vaccine and/or booster dose. The primary objective of the paper is to describe how within-country inequalities in COVID-19 vaccination coverage have been researched and characterised in the academic literature. Specifically, we seek to understand the settings, populations, vaccination indicators, dimensions of inequality and reporting practices featured in this body of research. A secondary objective is to provide a preliminary narrative overview of the trends in inequalities reported for dimensions of inequality that are most frequently addressed by this body of literature. Our findings will be useful to identify and justify areas for further study on this topic, including the design of more detailed systematic literature reviews and meta-analyses.

2. Methods

To address the research question, we conducted a scoping review. Scoping reviews are appropriate "to determine the scope or coverage of a body of literature on a given topic and give clear indication of the volume of literature and studies available as well as an overview (broad or detailed) of its focus" [13]. Further, scoping reviews are useful for assessing an emerging body of evidence to determine specific avenues for further study, for example, through more focused systematic reviews and meta-analyses [13]. Drawing from guidance in the JBI Manual for Evidence Synthesis [14], we developed a protocol for this scoping review, which was refined throughout the process of the review (Supplementary Materials S1). No major deviations from the protocol were introduced. In preparing this manuscript, we followed the Preferred Reporting Items for Systematic reviews and Meta-Analyses extension for Scoping Reviews (PRISMA-ScR) checklist [15].

2.1. Eligibility Criteria

Our focus was on the state of research on inequalities in COVID-19 vaccination, as characterised in the academic literature. Therefore, research articles and reports with primary or secondary data were considered for inclusion, as well as peer-reviewed preprints, brief reports and short research communications. Opinion pieces such as comments, letters and editorials, were excluded along with publications of a journalistic and/or less-academic nature (e.g., news stories, biographies and interviews). Relevant publications pertained to human populations. No language restrictions were applied. For inclusion in the review, the full text of the article needed to be available.

Articles were considered for inclusion if the objective pertained to reporting inequalities in COVID-19 vaccination coverage by one or more dimension of inequality. For the purpose of this review, we considered a broad conceptualisation of COVID-19 vaccination (Table 1). Articles were considered for inclusion if the COVID-19 vaccination coverage indicator was defined based on the receipt or non-receipt of any one or more COVID-19 vaccine and/or booster. To be considered for inclusion, dimensions of inequality could encompass any or multiple socioeconomic, demographic or geographic factors; publications that focused on reporting vaccination coverage according to medical factors were excluded. Our scoping review is focused on within-country inequality; therefore, dimensions of inequality could be measured at the individual, household, community or small-area level. Articles that primarily reported between-country inequality were excluded.

Table 1. Criteria to determine relevance of COVID-19 vaccination coverage indicator for a scoping review about inequalities in COVID-19 vaccination coverage.

Inclusion Criteria	Exclusion Criteria
• Indicator captures receipt or non-receipt of COVID-19 vaccine and/or booster dose • May specify any number of vaccine or booster doses • May be self-reported, reported by a proxy (such as a parent) or obtained through administrative source or health records	• Indicator captures: ○ intention to vaccinate ○ attitudes about vaccination ○ vaccine availability, accessibility or eligibility ○ access to vaccination sites ○ vaccine readiness ○ vaccine decision-making factors ○ participation in vaccination trials ○ strategies for increasing vaccination uptake ○ predictive modelling of vaccination uptake ○ perceptions about vaccination uptake

2.2. Search Strategy and Screening Process

A systematic search was conducted on 27 October 2022 in PubMed, Scopus and Web of Science. Additional potential sources were obtained through handsearching reference lists. No language, article type or date restrictions were applied to the search (though due to the nature of the research question, eligible articles were published after the rollout of COVID-19 vaccines, which began in late 2020). The electronic search strategy consisted of three domains related to 'inequality' AND 'COVID-19' AND 'vaccines' search terms, incorporating medical subject heading (MeSH) indexed terms, keywords, topic terms and terms used in the title or abstract (Supplementary Materials S2). In the case of PubMed, additional searches were conducted using MeSH terms related to 'COVID-19 vaccines'.

The results from the literature search were imported to Covidence software for removal of duplicates, title and abstract screening, full text review and data extraction. Title and abstract screening was done by one reviewer, followed by full text review conducted in duplicate by two reviewers. Any discrepancies were resolved through discussion and in consultation with a third reviewer, as needed. For studies excluded during the full text review, the first reason for exclusion was recorded, according to the following ordered list:

1. Wrong article type;
2. Does not pertain to humans;
3. Study objective not relevant;
4. Does not meet criteria for COVID-19 vaccination coverage;

5. Does not meet criteria for dimension of inequality;
6. Only reports on between-country inequality;
7. Full text not available;
8. Insufficient information to assess eligibility.

If the full text of the article was not available online, we requested it from the corresponding authors. Likewise, if we did not have sufficient information to assess the eligibility of the study, we made multiple attempts for clarification from corresponding authors.

2.3. Data Extraction and Analysis

Data extraction was performed using the Covidence Extraction 2 tool, based on a custom data extraction template. The template covered general information about the article and where it was published; characteristics of the study setting, population, study objective and design; characteristics of the COVID-19 vaccination indicator; characteristics of the dimensions of inequality; analysis methods; results; and conclusions. After reviewing 10% of studies in tandem to ensure consistency in the interpretation and application of the template, data extraction was performed by one of two reviewers. The reviewers reached consensus on any questions or points of ambiguity that arose with input from a third reviewer.

Using the data extraction outputs, descriptive data analysis was undertaken to assess and tabulate study characteristics. In describing the frequency of dimensions of inequality and inequality trends, we used the PROGRESS-Plus framework as a starting point for grouping dimensions of inequality pertaining to common themes. PROGRESS factors include place of residence, race/ethnicity/culture/language, occupation, gender/sex, religion, education, socioeconomic status and social capital [16]. We also identified the following categories, some of which align with the factors described in the "Plus" component of the above framework: age; disability status; family size or composition; health insurance; housing type or characteristic; marital status; migration status; sexual orientation; subnational region or area; and vulnerability, deprivation or poverty index.

As an extension of our analysis, we assessed the preliminary trends in the findings related to dimensions of inequality that appeared most often in the assessed articles. To this end, we coded and compiled reported findings for age; race, ethnicity, cultural group, language and nationality or country of birth; and sex or gender. For age and sex or gender, where the criteria for measuring the dimension were largely comparable across most studies (as years or male/female, respectively), we coded the main findings according to the directionality of the inequality. For race, ethnicity, cultural group, language and nationality or country of birth, where the criteria for measuring the dimension were heterogeneous, we coded whether inequality related to this dimension was reported as meaningful or not meaningful. Our coding of results as meaningful or not meaningful was based on the conclusions reported in the original studies. Most, but not all, studies defined this as statistically significant in comparisons at $p < 0.05$; however, the nature of statistical comparisons differed by paper and not all papers reported statistical significance.

3. Results

3.1. Selection of Sources

Our search identified 7784 items (after removing duplicates) that were considered for inclusion. After screening titles and abstracts, 315 were retained for full-text review. A total of 148 items were excluded at the full-text review stage because the study objective was not relevant, the criteria for COVID-19 vaccination coverage was not met, the article type did not meet the inclusion criteria, the criteria for dimension of inequality was not met, the article only reported between-country inequality or there was insufficient information to assess eligibility. In total, 167 articles were included from which data were extracted (Figure 1).

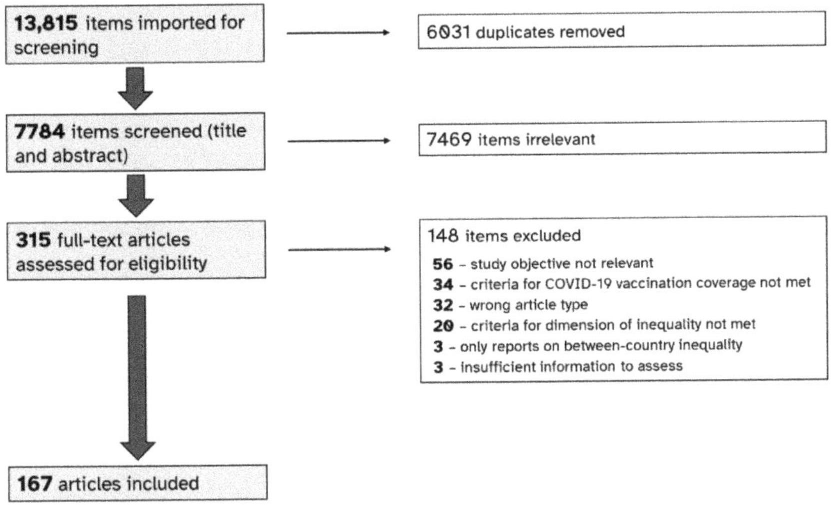

Figure 1. PRISMA flow diagram depicting stages of selecting sources for a scoping review about inequalities in COVID-19 vaccination coverage.

The included articles were published in 2021 (43 articles) or 2022 (124 articles), across a total of 82 academic journals (Supplementary Materials S3). Journals represented by five or more included articles were: *Vaccines* (18 articles); *Morbidity and Mortality Weekly Report* (15 articles); *Vaccine* (11 articles); *International Journal of Environmental Research and Public Health* and *PLoS One* (7 articles each); and *BMJ Open* (5 articles). The articles were of variable lengths and scope/depth of analysis, context and discussion. To provide an indication of the type of articles included, we categorised them as full research papers (around six pages or longer, with greater analytical scope and contextual detail) or short research papers (around five pages or less with more limited analytical and contextual detail). The article type designated by the journal also informed the categorisation. Most included articles were designated as full research papers (119 articles, including 1 review), with the remaining designated as short research papers (48 articles).

3.2. Study Characteristics

3.2.1. Setting and Study Populations

Most articles contained data from a single country setting (161 out of 167 articles), representing a total of 38 countries. Eighty-three of the single country studies were conducted in the United States of America, followed by studies in the United Kingdom (13 articles), Israel (7 articles),Canada (6 articles) and Hong Kong (5 articles). Six articles included data from multiple countries (representing a total of 18 countries). In total, the number of unique countries represented across all studies was 47. According to the current World Bank classifications [17], 26 of the 47 countries are high-income countries (55%), 11 are upper-middle-income countries (23%), 6 are lower-middle-income countries (13%), and 3 are low-income countries (6%); the remaining 1, Palestine, is not classified (Table 2).

While many studies drew from a national population, others pertained to one or more subnational administrative areas or specified institutions (such as hospitals, universities and prisons). Noting that some articles included more than one of the populations listed below, study populations included general public/adults (88 articles); health care workers (21 articles); older adults (14 articles); pregnant or postpartum women (12 articles); children/adolescents (10 articles); military personnel/veterans (7 articles); university students and staff (5 articles). A smaller number of articles focused on the following populations: people defined based on migratory status (3 articles); incarcerated people (2 articles); LGBTQ+

people (2 articles); people who inject drugs (1 article); EMTs and paramedics (1 article); teachers/staff at schools (1 article); and nursing home residents and staff (1 article).

Table 2. Countries represented by one or more study included in a scoping review about inequalities in COVID-19 vaccination coverage.

Country Income Group Classification	Countries
High income	Australia (2 articles); Canada (6 articles); Czech Republic (1 article); France (2 articles); Germany (1 article); Greece (2 articles); Hong Kong (5 articles); Hungary (2 articles); Israel (7 articles); Italy (2 articles); Japan [a] (2 articles); Kuwait [a] (1 article); Latvia (1 article); Netherlands (1 article); New Zealand (1 article); Norway [a] (1 article); Qatar [a] (1 article); Romania (1 article); Saudi Arabia [a] (3 articles); Singapore (2 articles); Slovakia [a] (1 article); Spain (1 article); Sweden [a] (4 articles); United Arab Emirates [a] (2 articles); United Kingdom [a] (15 articles); United States of America [a] (86 articles)
Upper-middle income	Belarus (1 article); Brazil (2 articles); China (3 articles); Guatemala [a] (1 article); Iraq [a] (1 article); Jordan [a] (1 article); Kazakhstan [a] (1 article); Mexico [a] (3 articles); Peru (1 article); Serbia (1 article); Thailand (1 article)
Lower-middle income	Bangladesh (1 article); Egypt (1 article); India [a] (3 articles); Indonesia (1 article); Lebanon [a] (1 article); Pakistan (1 article)
Low income	Ethiopia (1 article); Guinea (1 article); Malawi (2 articles)
Not classified	Palestine [a] (3 articles)

[a] Country included in at least one multi-country study or review article.

3.2.2. COVID-19 Vaccination Coverage

As per our inclusion criteria, all 167 included studies defined COVID-19 vaccination coverage based on the receipt or non-receipt of any one or more COVID-19 vaccine and/or booster. Many articles focused on vaccine initiation, that is, receipt or non-receipt of at least one dose of vaccine (97 articles). In 29 articles, COVID-19 vaccination coverage was defined as 'fully vaccinated' according to the specifications of the study setting, and in 4 articles, the focus was on receipt or non-receipt of a COVID-19 vaccine booster. A total of 33 articles looked at multiple COVID-19 indicators that met our inclusion criteria, and the remaining 4 articles did not clearly state the number of vaccine doses or boosters used to define the receipt or non-receipt of a COVID-19 vaccination.

Information about COVID-19 vaccination coverage was sourced from surveys (84 articles), and administrative or surveillance records, including health records (84 articles), noting that one article used data from both of these types of sources. In some cases, administrative or surveillance data were linked to census data to derive denominator values. COVID-19 vaccination coverage was commonly measured at the level of the individual (138 articles), although some articles presented data aggregated at the small-area level (such as county, municipality, zip-code area, province/state or census area) (27 articles), or by institution (such as nursing home or school) (2 articles).

3.2.3. Dimensions of Inequality

Articles assessed inequalities in COVID-19 vaccination coverage according to diverse socioeconomic, demographic and/or geographic dimensions of inequality (Table 3). In 157 out of 167 articles, inequality in vaccine coverage was reported for at least two dimensions of inequality. The most common dimension of inequality applied was age (127 articles), followed by dimensions of inequality related to race, ethnicity, cultural group, language and nationality or country of birth (117 articles). Inequalities according to sex or gender were reported in 103 articles and 81 articles reported data disaggregated by occupation- or employment-related factors. Other dimensions of inequality that were featured in 10 or more articles include education (76 articles); subnational region or area (68 articles); economic status (68 articles); place of residence (39 articles); vulnerability, deprivation or poverty index (38 articles); marital status (30 articles); family size or composition (27 articles); health insurance (27 articles); and disability status (10 articles). Religion (8 articles), housing type or characteristic (7 articles), migration status (5 articles), social capital (3 articles) and sexual orientation (3 articles) were included less often. Articles relied on different criteria to define and measure dimensions of inequality, with variation depending on the context of the study.

Table 3. Dimensions of inequality featured in sources for a scoping review about inequalities in COVID-19 vaccination coverage, including corresponding number of articles, percentage of total number of articles (n = 167) and examples of measurement criteria.

Dimension of Inequality	Number of Articles (% of Total) [a]	Illustrative Examples of Measurement Criteria [b]
Age	127 (76%)	years; parental age; above or below median age of population
Race, ethnicity, cultural group, language, nationality or country of birth	117 (70%)	White, Black, Hispanic, Asian or Other (applicable to studies based in the United States); language at home; national or foreigner
Sex or gender	103 (62%)	male or female; transgender or non-binary (yes/no)
Occupation- or employment-related factor	81 (49%)	employed or unemployed; employment in healthcare industry (yes/no); essential worker, non-essential worker, or non-working status; public or private sector employee; military ranking; profession
Education level	76 (46%)	years of schooling; highest level of schooling completed; highest qualification
Subnational region or area	68 (41%)	state/province; region; municipality; census tract; county; health zone
Economic status	68 (41%)	household income; above or below defined poverty line; self-perceived financial status; level of difficulty covering household expenses
Place of residence	39 (23%)	urban or rural; metro or non-metro; urban, rural or camp; population size of zip code
Vulnerability, deprivation or poverty index	38 (23%)	Social Vulnerability Index (applicable to studies based in the United States); Index of Multiple Deprivation (applicable to studies based in the United Kingdom); Human Development Index; Multi-Dimensional Poverty Index
Marital status	30 (18%)	single, married, cohabitating, divorced, widowed; living with partner (yes/no)
Family size or composition	27 (16%)	number of children; household size; elderly living with family (yes/no); children living in household (yes/no); living alone (yes/no)
Health insurance	27 (16%)	insured or uninsured status; private or public health insurance type
Disability status	10 (6%)	self-reported living with a disability (yes/no); extent of daily activity limitation
Religion	8 (5%)	religious affiliation (e.g., Christian, Buddhist, Hindu, Jewish, Muslim, Sikh, other, none)
Housing type or characteristic	7 (4%)	homeless (yes/no); house owned, private rented, social rented, other; type of housing: mobile, detached house, attached house, multiunit apartment, etc.

Table 3. *Cont.*

Dimension of Inequality	Number of Articles (% of Total) [a]	Illustrative Examples of Measurement Criteria [b]
Migration status	5 (3%)	citizen, landed immigrant, refugee, temporary/other; migration history (yes/no)
Social capital	3 (2%)	trust in others; civic participation; social capital index
Sexual orientation	3 (2%)	bisexual, gay/lesbian, heterosexual
Other: food security, incarceration status, income inequality, car ownership, computer ownership, school type	1–2 each	

[a] The scoping review included a total of 167 articles; most articles featured more than one dimension of inequality.
[b] Note that this is not an exhaustive list of all approaches to measuring the dimensions of inequality.

Information about dimensions of inequality was sourced from surveys (93 articles) and administrative or surveillance data, including health records (79 articles) and censuses (20 articles) (note that 24 articles relied on more than one type of data source). In most articles, dimensions of inequality were measured at the same level as the corresponding COVID-19 vaccination indicator (149 articles). In some articles, various dimensions of inequality measurements included both individual and small-area levels (15 articles). Three articles measured the dimension of inequality at the small-area level and the COVID-19 vaccination indicator at the individual level.

3.2.4. Reporting Practices

In general, articles presented disaggregated data and association or regression measures when reporting inequality findings (108 articles). Thirty-three articles included disaggregated estimates only, while 16 articles reported association or regression measures only. Sixteen articles included difference, ratio, slope index of inequality and/or relative index of inequality summary measures.

About a third of articles (54 out of 167) reported multiple disaggregation; that is, they presented data about vaccination coverage broken down by two or more dimensions of inequality simultaneously. For example, several articles explored sex- or age-related inequalities across different urban–rural classifications [18–21].

3.3. *Study Findings: Preliminary Trends for Selected Dimensions of Inequality*

3.3.1. Age

Of the 127 articles that reported COVID-19 vaccination coverage by age, the majority (89 articles, or 70%) found higher vaccination among older groups. The age ranges and categorisation (groupings) of these 89 articles were diverse: while many study populations included those aged 18 years and older, some were limited to other age groupings. For example, a study in England reported higher rates of being unvaccinated in younger individuals of study populations aged 50 years or older [22]. Similarly, vaccination with one or more doses of a COVID-19 vaccine was higher among those aged over 75 years compared to those 65–74 years in Connecticut, United States [23], and higher among those 75 or older compared to those 60–74 years in Sweden [24]. A study by Khatatbeh et al. (2022) in the Eastern Mediterranean Region, looked at COVID-19 vaccination in children aged 12 or younger versus those aged 12–17; it also explored the association between parental age and receipt of a COVID-19 vaccine in their child(ren). In both cases—child age and parental age—older ages were predictive of the child being vaccinated [25]. Studies in other settings, including Indonesia [26] and the United States [27,28] also reported positive associations between age and COVID-19 vaccination coverage within child/adolescent populations.

In contrast, the opposite pattern—higher vaccination among younger groups—was reported in 8 articles (6%). These articles focused on adult populations across different settings, including health care workers in China [29] and Egypt [30]; university students or staff in the United States [31,32]; active military personnel in Israel [33]; pregnant or post-partum women in the United States [34]; and general adult populations in Singapore [35] and the United States [36].

Nineteen of the articles that reported on age-related inequality (15%) found no/minimal inequality and 9 articles (7%) demonstrated other patterns (such as higher vaccination coverage in a mid-range age group) or mixed patterns (such as different age-related patterns for different population groups, or for different COVID-19 vaccination indicators). Two articles (2%) did not report age-related findings in the main text of the article.

3.3.2. Race, Ethnicity, Cultural Group, Language, Nationality or Country of Birth

Overall, 117 articles reported on COVID-19 vaccination coverage by race, ethnicity, cultural group, language, nationality and/or country of birth. Nearly all of these articles (101 articles, or 86%) reported meaningful inequality according to this dimension of inequality, while 18 articles (15%) reported no meaningful inequality (noting that 3 articles included in the above counts reported both meaningful and non-meaningful findings for different variables in this category). One article (1%) did not report the findings for this dimension in the main text of the article.

Most of the studies conducted in the United States included a dimension of inequality related to race, ethnicity, cultural group, language, nationality and/or country of birth (73 out of 83, or 88%), and in 88% of these studies (64 out of 73), authors reported meaningful inequality by at least one of these dimensions. Although standardised racial/ethnic diversity categories used in the United States Census are applied in many studies, it is difficult to assess trends in the findings due to different study designs and comparison groups. We observed, however, that Asian and/or White subgroups were often among the most advantaged with regards to COVID-19 vaccination coverage. For instance, in a study of race/ethnicity inequalities in the United States, subgroups identifying as Asian or White had higher booster uptake than Black and Hispanic populations in all of the states for which there were data (24 states plus Washington, D.C.) [37]. Di Rago et al. (2022), assessing COVID vaccination rates across eight American cities over a three-week period, found increasing gaps in vaccination between White or Asian and Black or Hispanic communities [38].

3.3.3. Sex or Gender

A total of 103 articles reported on COVID-19 vaccination coverage by sex or gender, of which 45 articles (44%) found no or minimal difference between subgroups. In 31 articles (30%), COVID-19 vaccination was higher among males; in 25 articles (24%), vaccination was higher among females. Two articles (2%) reported different patterns of sex-related inequality across age groupings [39] or by disability status [40].

Two studies, both focusing on LGBT or LGBTQ+ adults in the United States, considered sex and gender as separate variables in their analysis. Low et al. (2022) reported no differences based on sex assigned at birth (categorised as female, male and intersex) or gender identity (categorised as cisgender and transgender/nonbinary/other gender minority) [41]. McNaghten et al. (2022) reported higher vaccination among females than males, but no difference based on gender identity (dichotomously categorised as transgender/nonbinary or not) [42].

4. Discussion

In this scoping review, we assessed the current state of research pertaining to within-country inequalities in COVID-19 vaccination coverage. Our findings show that this body of research covers a diversity of populations and settings, suggesting a wide interest in assessing and understanding the patterns of vaccination coverage inequality across populations. The geographical representation of study settings within this literature favoured high-income countries in North America and Europe—for example, half of articles were conducted in the United States, with only five articles based on populations in the African continent. High-income countries accounted for more than half of the countries represented in this body of literature, whereas low-income countries accounted for less than 10%. This finding was not surprising, as populations in high-income countries tended to have earlier access to vaccines than lower-income countries, and thus implemented vaccine programmes sooner; moreover, timelines, access and incentives for publishing in academic journals may differ between settings. Nevertheless, more research on inequalities in COVID-19 vaccination coverage is warranted in lower-income countries, particularly as vaccines become more widely available in these settings.

We found that demographic factors, including age, race/ethnicity/cultural group/ language/nationality/country of birth and sex/gender, were the most commonly reported dimensions of inequality in vaccine coverage rates in this body of literature. Indeed, early into the COVID-19 pandemic, the scientific community made strong calls to enhance the collection and reporting of data disaggregated by these factors [43–46]. In the cases of age and sex/gender, the application of similar measurement criteria (years and male/female, respectively) allowed us to comment on the general trends in the directionality of inequality reported in these articles. Our preliminary assessment of this literature suggested that vaccination coverage tended to be higher among (relatively) older population groups, across many age ranges. This is in line with WHO guidance [6], suggesting the implementation of vaccine rollout strategies that initially prioritised older age groups. With regards to findings on sex/gender-related inequality, a substantial proportion of articles that reported on this dimension concluded that there were no meaningful differences. Of those articles that did report a difference, the directionality was variable, with vaccination coverage more often reported to be higher in males than in females. It was not feasible to do even preliminary comparisons of findings for the race/ethnicity/cultural group/language/nationality/country of birth dimension of inequality, as the measurement of this dimension is context specific (i.e., not standardised across settings). There were, however, common approaches applied within particular country settings, which could be explored through more narrowly-focused systematic reviews and/or meta-analyses. Indeed, more rigorous meta-analyses, including quality assessments, are warranted to delve into vaccination coverage inequalities by demographic factors.

Among the other dimensions of inequality highlighted in our scoping review were those related to socioeconomic factors (most frequently occupation/employment, education level, economic status and vulnerability, deprivation or poverty indices) and those related to geographical factors (most frequently subnational region/area and place of residence). Characterising patterns of socioeconomic inequality offers deeper understanding into the motivations and barriers experienced by population groups, while geographic patterns of inequality may have immediate and practical implications for program delivery and resource allocation [47]. Other dimensions of inequality, such as sexual orientation, social capital, and migration status, received less attention in the research, although some of these articles provide initial indications that these may be meaningful avenues for future study. For instance, the three articles that reported inequality in COVID-19 vaccination coverage related to a measure of social capital all reported higher vaccination among groups with greater social capital [20,48,49].

The application of multiple disaggregation in one-third of studies permitted exploration of the intersection of different dimensions of inequality. Multiple disaggregation can begin to lend insight into more nuanced patterns of inequality, for example, suggesting how multiple vulnerabilities may put certain groups at heightened risk for lower vaccination coverage [50]. Multiple disaggregation should be incorporated, to the extent possible, in future inequality analyses in this topic [51].

We reported variability in how dimensions of inequality were measured, reflecting diverse study populations, settings and research aims. In some cases, standardised criteria were applied within a country (such as race/ethnicity categories in the United States), enhancing comparability across these studies. For most dimensions of inequality, however, the lack of standardised criteria for measuring dimensions of inequality limits the extent to which direct comparisons of inequality can be made across studies and across settings.

Our scoping review extends on a previous review by Bayati et al. (2022), which had a broader aim of assessing both between-country and within-country factors associated with COVID-19 vaccine distribution [11]. The portion of the review focused on within-country factors included 19 studies, and concluded that "age, race, ethnic, household income, residency in the deprived areas, employment, poverty, location (urban/rural) and gender were most often mentioned in the literature". Our scoping review, encompassing 167 studies, highlights additional dimensions of inequality that have been explored in the literature, including education level, indices of vulnerability, deprivation or poverty, marital status and family characteristics. Additionally, it provides a more detailed overview of the study settings, data sources, reporting practices and preliminary findings.

The findings of this scoping review are broadly in line with previous reviews exploring inequalities in COVID-19 vaccination intentions and attitudes [52,53]. For instance, the directionality of the age- and sex/gender-related inequality that we reported corresponds with those reported in a meta-analysis on inequalities in COVID-19 vaccination intention, which included 28 nationally representative populations across 13 countries. It reported female sex, younger age and belonging to an ethnic minority group to be consistently associated with lower intention to vaccinate, highlighting "an urgent need to address social inequalities in vaccine hesitancy and promote widespread uptake of vaccines as they become available" [52]. Similarly, a meta-analysis including 63 surveys and more than 30 countries concluded that age, gender and education level were among the factors most often associated with willingness or hesitancy to be vaccinated [53]. We note, however, an important distinction between the body of research pertaining to vaccination coverage from research on vaccination intentions and attitudes. Attitudes towards vaccines have been found to shift over time [9], and do not directly translate into behaviours. A study of vaccination uptake during the 2009 influenza (H1N1) pandemic, for example, found that only a small percentage of those reporting a positive intention to vaccinate followed through on receiving the vaccine after two months [54].

Limitations and Further Considerations

Our findings and their interpretations are subject to a number of limitations and considerations. We acknowledge that there is a bias in this body of literature towards settings where vaccines have been rolled out, studied and reported. Settings that lack reliable data collection about COVID-19 vaccinations are less likely to be represented in published academic literature, and therefore less likely to be included in this scoping review.

Across studies, approaches to defining COVID-19 vaccination coverage were not standardised. For the purpose of our scoping review, we adopted a broad definition for the COVID-19 vaccination coverage indicator and included studies reporting on receipt (or non-receipt) of a single dose, multiple doses and/or booster doses. Nearly one in five of the articles included in our review reported on more than one vaccination coverage indicator that met our inclusion criteria. The application of common definitions for COVID-19 vaccination coverage would facilitate greater cross-study comparability and more nuanced analyses.

We relied on the PROGRESS-Plus framework as a starting point to guide how we grouped and labelled dimensions of inequality. Alternate frameworks may have yielded different conclusions about the most frequently reported dimensions of inequality. We did not report political factors as relevant dimensions of inequality, although we noted that 13 of the 167 articles reported on inequalities based on political views or voting patterns. Of these studies, 11 were conducted in the United States, all of which found lower vaccination among Republican voters and/or higher vaccination among Democrat voters.

Our exploration of inequality trends for selected dimensions of inequality in this scoping review was premised on findings that may be of variable quality. Approaches and thresholds to determine the 'meaningfulness' of inequality were different across studies. More rigorous meta-analyses incorporating quality assessments are required as an extension of our initial findings.

As per the design of our scoping review, we did not account for how countries may have prioritised different populations during phased vaccine rollouts. Initially, COVID-19 vaccine doses were in limited supply and inequality during the early stages of their distribution was inevitable (though COVID-19 vaccination coverage equity remains an end goal for most countries) [10]. Many of the included articles, however, did take this into account in their study design. We did not focus on the reasons underlying vaccination status, such as whether population subgroups remained unvaccinated by choice (low acceptance of the vaccine) or their circumstance (low access to the vaccine). Explorations of the drivers of inequality were outside the scope of this review. We did not differentiate between studies conducted in general populations versus studies that evaluated a specific campaign or programme, which may have been targeted towards certain populations.

5. Conclusions

In this scoping review, we assessed 167 research articles to provide an overview of how within-country COVID-19 vaccination coverage inequality has been studied. Our findings demonstrate that most research to date has been conducted in higher income countries, underscoring the need for expanded research in other contexts to gain a fuller understanding of patterns of inequalities across populations and settings. While we characterised research on diverse dimensions of inequality, those most frequently studied were related to demographic factors. The trends that we reported for inequalities by age, race/ethnicity/cultural group/language/nationality/country of birth, and sex/gender dimensions of inequality were intended to be preliminary and exploratory. More detailed analyses across these and other dimensions of inequality are warranted, including dedicated systematic reviews and meta-analyses to draw more reliable and specific conclusions. Research in this topic area can be further strengthened by adopting standardised COVID-19 vaccination indicators, which would promote greater cross-study comparability.

As COVID-19 vaccination programmes, including the administration of booster doses, continue to expand globally, ongoing efforts are needed to grow this body of research and capture the evolution of inequalities in vaccination coverage, both globally and locally within countries. The characterisation of inequalities related to multiple, diverse dimensions of inequality (encompassing both context-specific and universally applicable dimensions) stands to offer relevant lessons and insights for strengthening equity in vaccine policies, planning and implementation.

Supplementary Materials: The following supporting information can be downloaded at: https://www.mdpi.com/article/10.3390/vaccines11030517/s1, S1: Scoping review protocol. This document contains the protocol that was followed in conducting the scop-ing review. It indicates where modifications and clarifications were made to the initial protocol; S2: Search terms. This document contains the terms used to conduct systematic searches within PubMed, Scopus and Web of Science; S3: Study sources. This document contains information about the journals where sourced articles were published. Table S1: Number of articles included in a scoping review about inequalities in COVID-19 vaccination coverage, by journals where pub-lished. Refs. [13,14,52] are cited in Supplementary Materials.

Author Contributions: Conceptualisation, N.B. and A.R.H.; study selection and data extraction—N.B. and N.E.J. with guidance from A.R.H.; writing—original draft, N.B.; writing—review and editing, N.B., N.E.J., D.C.B. and A.R.H. All authors have read and agreed to the published version of the manuscript.

Funding: This research was funded by Gavi, the Vaccine Alliance.

Institutional Review Board Statement: Not applicable.

Informed Consent Statement: Not applicable.

Data Availability Statement: A list of the articles included in the review is available upon request from the authors.

Conflicts of Interest: The authors declare no conflict of interest. The funders had no role in the design of the study; in the collection, analyses, or interpretation of data; in the writing of the manuscript; or in the decision to publish the results.

References

1. Arcaya, M.C.; Arcaya, A.L.; Subramanian, S.V. Inequalities in Health: Definitions, Concepts, and Theories. *Glob. Health Action* **2015**, *8*, 27106. [CrossRef] [PubMed]
2. High-Level Committee on Programmes Inequalities Task Team. *COVID-19, Inequalities and Building Back Better: Policy Brief by the HLCP Inequalities Task Team*; United Nations: New York, NY, USA, 2020.
3. Burström, B.; Tao, W. Social Determinants of Health and Inequalities in COVID-19. *Eur. J. Public Health* **2020**, *30*, 617–618. [CrossRef] [PubMed]
4. Watson, O.J.; Barnsley, G.; Toor, J.; Hogan, A.B.; Winskill, P.; Ghani, A.C. Global Impact of the First Year of COVID-19 Vaccination: A Mathematical Modelling Study. *Lancet Infect. Dis.* **2022**, *22*, 1293–1302. [CrossRef] [PubMed]
5. Kumari, M.; Lu, R.-M.; Li, M.-C.; Huang, J.-L.; Hsu, F.-F.; Ko, S.-H.; Ke, F.-Y.; Su, S.-C.; Liang, K.-H.; Yuan, J.P.-Y.; et al. A Critical Overview of Current Progress for COVID-19: Development of Vaccines, Antiviral Drugs, and Therapeutic Antibodies. *J. Biomed. Sci.* **2022**, *29*, 68. [CrossRef]
6. World Health Organization. *WHO SAGE Roadmap for Prioritizing Uses of COVID-19 Vaccines*; World Health Organization: Geneva, Switzerland, 2022.
7. Mathieu, E.; Ritchie, H.; Ortiz-Ospina, E.; Roser, M.; Hasell, J.; Appel, C.; Giattino, C.; Rodés-Guirao, L. A Global Database of COVID-19 Vaccinations. *Nat. Hum. Behav.* **2021**, *5*, 947–953. [CrossRef]
8. Ndugga, N.; Pham, O.; Hill, L.; Artiga, S.; Mengistu, S. *Early State Vaccination Data Raise Warning Flags for Racial Equity*; Kaiser Family Foundation: Oakland, CA, USA, 2021.
9. Bergen, N.; Kirkby, K.; Fuertes, C.V.; Schlotheuber, A.; Menning, L.; Mac Feely, S.; O'Brien, K.; Hosseinpoor, A.R. Global State of Education-Related Inequality in COVID-19 Vaccine Coverage, Structural Barriers, Vaccine Hesitancy, and Vaccine Refusal: Findings from the Global COVID-19 Trends and Impact Survey. *Lancet Glob. Health* **2023**, *11*, e207–e217. [CrossRef]
10. Bolcato, M.; Rodriguez, D.; Feola, A.; Di Mizio, G.; Bonsignore, A.; Ciliberti, R.; Tettamanti, C.; Trabucco Aurilio, M.; Aprile, A. COVID-19 Pandemic and Equal Access to Vaccines. *Vaccines* **2021**, *9*, 538. [CrossRef]
11. Bayati, M.; Noroozi, R.; Ghanbari-Jahromi, M.; Jalali, F.S. Inequality in the Distribution of COVID-19 Vaccine: A Systematic Review. *Int. J. Equity Health* **2022**, *21*, 122. [CrossRef]
12. World Health Organization. *Handbook on Health Inequality Monitoring: With a Special Focus on Low-and Middle-Income Countries*; World Health Organization: Geneva, Switzerland, 2013; ISBN 92-4-154863-0.
13. Munn, Z.; Peters, M.D.J.; Stern, C.; Tufanaru, C.; McArthur, A.; Aromataris, E. Systematic Review or Scoping Review? Guidance for Authors When Choosing between a Systematic or Scoping Review Approach. *BMC Med. Res. Methodol.* **2018**, *18*, 143. [CrossRef]
14. Peters, M.D.J.; Godfrey, C.; McInerney, P.; Munn, Z.; Tricco, A.C.; Khalil, H. Chapter 11—Scoping Reviews. In *JBI Manual for Evidence Synthesis*; Aromataris, E., Munn, Z., Eds.; JBI: North Adelaide, Australia, 2020.
15. Tricco, A.C.; Lillie, E.; Zarin, W.; O'Brien, K.K.; Colquhoun, H.; Levac, D.; Moher, D.; Peters, M.D.J.; Horsley, T.; Weeks, L.; et al. PRISMA Extension for Scoping Reviews (PRISMA-ScR): Checklist and Explanation. *Ann. Intern. Med.* **2018**, *169*, 467–473. [CrossRef]
16. The Cochrane Collaboration. PROGRESS-Plus. Available online: https://methods.cochrane.org/equity/projects/evidence-equity/progress-plus (accessed on 12 January 2023).
17. The World Bank Group. World Bank Country and Lending Groups. Available online: https://datahelpdesk.worldbank.org/knowledgebase/articles/906519-world-bank-country-and-lending-groups (accessed on 31 January 2023).
18. Barry, V.; Dasgupta, S.; Weller, D.L.; Kriss, J.L.; Cadwell, B.L.; Rose, C.; Pingali, C.; Musial, T.; Sharpe, J.D.; Flores, S.A.; et al. Patterns in COVID-19 Vaccination Coverage, by Social Vulnerability and Urbanicity—United States, December 14, 2020–May 1, 2021. *MMWR Morb. Mortal. Wkly. Rep.* **2021**, *70*, 818–824. [CrossRef] [PubMed]
19. Murthy, B.P.; Sterrett, N.; Weller, D.; Zell, E.; Reynolds, L.; Toblin, R.L.; Murthy, N.; Kriss, J.; Rose, C.; Cadwell, B.; et al. Disparities in COVID-19 Vaccination Coverage Between Urban and Rural Counties—United States, December 14, 2020–April 10, 2021. *MMWR Morb. Mortal. Wkly. Rep.* **2021**, *70*, 759–764. [CrossRef] [PubMed]
20. Qiao, S.; Li, Z.; Zhang, J.; Sun, X.; Garrett, C.; Li, X. Social Capital, Urbanization Level, and COVID-19 Vaccination Uptake in the United States: A National Level Analysis. *Vaccines* **2022**, *10*, 625. [CrossRef] [PubMed]
21. Saelee, R.; Zell, E.; Murthy, B.P.; Castro-Roman, P.; Fast, H.; Meng, L.; Shaw, L.; Gibbs-Scharf, L.; Chorba, T.; Harris, L.Q.; et al. Disparities in COVID-19 Vaccination Coverage Between Urban and Rural Counties—United States, December 14, 2020–January 31, 2022. *MMWR Morb. Mortal. Wkly. Rep.* **2022**, *71*, 335–340. [CrossRef] [PubMed]

22. Tessier, E.; Rai, Y.; Clarke, E.; Lakhani, A.; Tsang, C.; Makwana, A.; Heard, H.; Rickeard, T.; Lakhani, S.; Roy, P.; et al. Characteristics Associated with COVID-19 Vaccine Uptake among Adults Aged 50 Years and above in England (8 December 2020–17 May 2021): A Population-Level Observational Study. *BMJ Open* **2022**, *12*, e055278. [CrossRef] [PubMed]
23. Wang, H.; Xu, R.; Qu, S.; Schwartz, M.; Adams, A.; Chen, X. Health Inequities in COVID-19 Vaccination among the Elderly: Case of Connecticut. *J. Infect. Public Health* **2021**, *14*, 1563–1565. [CrossRef] [PubMed]
24. Spetz, M.; Lundberg, L.; Nwaru, C.; Li, H.; Santosa, A.; Leach, S.; Gisslén, M.; Hammar, N.; Rosvall, M.; Nyberg, F. The Social Patterning of Covid-19 Vaccine Uptake in Older Adults: A Register-Based Cross-Sectional Study in Sweden. *Lancet Reg. Health Eur.* **2022**, *15*, 100331. [CrossRef]
25. Khatatbeh, M.; Albalas, S.; Khatatbeh, H.; Momani, W.; Melhem, O.; Al Omari, O.; Tarhini, Z.; A'aqoulah, A.; Al-Jubouri, M.; Nashwan, A.J.; et al. Children's Rates of COVID-19 Vaccination as Reported by Parents, Vaccine Hesitancy, and Determinants of COVID-19 Vaccine Uptake among Children: A Multi-Country Study from the Eastern Mediterranean Region. *BMC Public Health* **2022**, *22*, 1375. [CrossRef]
26. Efendi, D.; Rifani, S.R.; Milanti, A.; Efendi, F.; Wong, C.L.; Rustina, Y.; Wanda, D.; Sari, D.; Fabanjo, I.J.; De Fretes, E.D.; et al. The Role of Knowledge, Attitude, Confidence, and Sociodemographic Factors in COVID-19 Vaccination Adherence among Adolescents in Indonesia: A Nationwide Survey. *Vaccines* **2022**, *10*, 1489. [CrossRef]
27. Gray, A.; Fisher, C.B. Determinants of COVID-19 Vaccine Uptake in Adolescents 12–17 Years Old: Examining Pediatric Vaccine Hesitancy among Racially Diverse Parents in the United States. *Front. Public Health* **2022**, *10*, 844310. [CrossRef]
28. Murthy, N.C.; Zell, E.; Fast, H.E.; Murthy, B.P.; Meng, L.; Saelee, R.; Vogt, T.; Chatham-Stephens, K.; Ottis, C.; Shaw, L.; et al. Disparities in First Dose COVID-19 Vaccination Coverage among Children 5–11 Years of Age, United States. *Emerg. Infect. Dis.* **2022**, *28*, 986–989. [CrossRef]
29. Yan, Y.-Y.; Wang, H.-T.; Fan, T.-Y.; Sun, X.-J.; Du, Z.-H.; Sun, X.-M. Vaccination Coverage among COVID-19 Prevention and Control Management Teams at Primary Healthcare Facilities in China and Their Attitudes towards COVID-19 Vaccine: A Cross-Sectional Online Survey. *BMJ Open* **2022**, *12*, e056345. [CrossRef] [PubMed]
30. Elkhayat, M.R.; Hashem, M.K.; Helal, A.T.; Shaaban, O.M.; Ibrahim, A.K.; Meshref, T.S.; Elkhayat, H.; Moustafa, M.; Mohammed, M.N.A.; Ezzeldin, A.M.; et al. Determinants of Obtaining COVID-19 Vaccination among Health Care Workers with Access to Free COVID-19 Vaccination: A Cross-Sectional Study. *Vaccines* **2022**, *10*, 39. [CrossRef]
31. Nicolo, M.; Kawaguchi, E.S.; Ghanem-Uzqueda, A.; Kim, A.E.; Soto, D.; Deva, S.; Shanker, K.; Rogers, C.; Lee, R.; Casagrande, Y.; et al. Characteristics Associated with COVID-19 Vaccination Status among Staff and Faculty of a Large, Diverse University in Los Angeles: The Trojan Pandemic Response Initiative. *Prev. Med. Rep.* **2022**, *27*, 101802. [CrossRef] [PubMed]
32. Nguyen, K.H.; Irvine, S.; Epstein, R.; Allen, J.D.; Corlin, L. Prior COVID-19 Infection, Mental Health, Food and Financial Insecurity, and Association with COVID-19 Vaccination Coverage and Intent among College-Aged Young Adults, US, 2021. *Prev. Chronic Dis.* **2021**, *18*, 210260. [CrossRef]
33. Shapiro, G.; Bez, M.; Talmy, T.; Shakargy, J.D.; Furer, A.; Karp, E.; Segal, D. SARS-CoV-2 Vaccine Acceptance Disparity among Israeli Defense Forces Personnel. *Mil. Med.* **2022**, *187*, 279. [CrossRef]
34. Jones, A.; Wallis, D. Using the Health Belief Model to Identify Predictors of COVID-19 Vaccine Acceptance among a Sample of Pregnant Women in the U.S.: A Cross-Sectional Survey. *Vaccines* **2022**, *10*, 842. [CrossRef]
35. Cheng, J.Y.J.; Loong, S.S.E.; Ho, C.E.S.M.; Ng, K.J.; Ng, M.M.Q.; Chee, R.C.H.; Chin, T.X.L.; Fong, F.J.Y.; Goh, S.L.G.; Venkatesh, K.N.S.; et al. Knowledge, Attitudes, and Practices of COVID-19 Vaccination among Adults in Singapore: A Cross-Sectional Study. *Am. J. Trop. Med. Hyg.* **2022**, *107*, 540–550. [CrossRef] [PubMed]
36. Kriss, J.L.; Hung, M.-C.; Srivastav, A.; Black, C.L.; Lindley, M.C.; Lee, J.T.; Koppaka, R.; Tsai, Y.; Lu, P.-J.; Yankey, D.; et al. COVID-19 Vaccination Coverage, by Race and Ethnicity—National Immunization Survey Adult COVID Module, United States, December 2020–November 2021. *MMWR Morb. Mortal. Wkly. Rep.* **2022**, *71*, 757–763. [CrossRef]
37. Baker, L.; Phillips, B.; Faherty, L.J.; Ringel, J.S.; Kranz, A.M. Racial and Ethnic Disparities in COVID-19 Booster Uptake: Study Examines Racial and Ethnic Disparities in the Uptake of COVID-19 Booster Shots. *Health Aff.* **2022**, *41*, 1202–1207. [CrossRef]
38. DiRago, N.V.; Li, M.; Tom, T.; Schupmann, W.; Carrillo, Y.; Carey, C.M.; Gaddis, S.M. COVID-19 Vaccine Rollouts and the Reproduction of Urban Spatial Inequality: Disparities Within Large US Cities in March and April 2021 by Racial/Ethnic and Socioeconomic Composition. *J. Urban Health* **2022**, *99*, 191–207. [CrossRef]
39. Diesel, J.; Sterrett, N.; Dasgupta, S.; Kriss, J.L.; Barry, V.; Vanden Esschert, K.; Whiteman, A.; Cadwell, B.L.; Weller, D.; Qualters, J.R.; et al. COVID-19 Vaccination Coverage among Adults—United States, December 14, 2020–May 22, 2021. *MMWR Morb. Mortal. Wkly. Rep.* **2021**, *70*, 922–927. [CrossRef] [PubMed]
40. Ryerson, A.B.; Rice, C.E.; Hung, M.-C.; Patel, S.A.; Weeks, J.D.; Kriss, J.L.; Peacock, G.; Lu, P.-J.; Asif, A.F.; Jackson, H.L.; et al. Disparities in COVID-19 Vaccination Status, Intent, and Perceived Access for Noninstitutionalized Adults, by Disability Status—National Immunization Survey Adult COVID Module, United States, May 30–June 26, 2021. *MMWR Morb. Mortal. Wkly. Rep.* **2021**, *70*, 1365–1371. [CrossRef] [PubMed]
41. Low, A.; Wright, C.; Platt, J.; Chang, C.; Mantell, J.E.; Romero, E.; Hoos, D.; Mannheimer, S.; Greenleaf, A.; Castor, D.; et al. COVID-19 Vaccine Uptake and Factors Associated with Being Unvaccinated among Lesbian, Gay, Bisexual, Transgender, Queer, and Other Sexual Identities (LGBTQ+) New Yorkers. *Open Forum Infect. Dis.* **2022**, *9*, ofac260. [CrossRef] [PubMed]

42. McNaghten, A.D.; Brewer, N.T.; Hung, M.-C.; Lu, P.-J.; Daskalakis, D.; Abad, N.; Kriss, J.; Black, C.; Wilhelm, E.; Lee, J.T.; et al. COVID-19 Vaccination Coverage and Vaccine Confidence by Sexual Orientation and Gender Identity—United States, August 29–October 30, 2021. *Morb. Mortal. Wkly. Rep.* **2022**, *71*, 171–176. [CrossRef]
43. Heidari, S.; Ahumada, C.; Kurbanova, Z. Towards the Real-Time Inclusion of Sex- and Age-Disaggregated Data in Pandemic Responses. *BMJ Glob. Health* **2020**, *5*, e003848. [CrossRef]
44. Yaya, S.; Yeboah, H.; Charles, C.H.; Otu, A.; Labonte, R. Ethnic and Racial Disparities in COVID-19-Related Deaths: Counting the Trees, Hiding the Forest. *BMJ Glob. Health* **2020**, *5*, e002913. [CrossRef]
45. Kocher, K.; Delot-Vilain, A.; Spencer, D.; LoTempio, J.; Délot, E.C. Paucity and Disparity of Publicly Available Sex-Disaggregated Data for the COVID-19 Epidemic Hamper Evidence-Based Decision-Making. *Arch. Sex Behav.* **2021**, *50*, 407–426. [CrossRef]
46. Pareek, M.; Bangash, M.N.; Pareek, N.; Pan, D.; Sze, S.; Minhas, J.S.; Hanif, W.; Khunti, K. Ethnicity and COVID-19: An Urgent Public Health Research Priority. *Lancet* **2020**, *395*, 1421–1422. [CrossRef]
47. Hosseinpoor, A.R.; Bergen, N. Area-Based Units of Analysis for Strengthening Health Inequality Monitoring. *Bull. World Health Organ.* **2016**, *94*, 856–858. [CrossRef]
48. Dolman, A.J.; Fraser, T.; Panagopoulos, C.; Aldrich, D.P.; Kim, D. Opposing Views: Associations of Political Polarization, Political Party Affiliation, and Social Trust with COVID-19 Vaccination Intent and Receipt. *J. Public Health* **2022**, fdab401. [CrossRef]
49. Machida, M.; Kikuchi, H.; Kojima, T.; Nakamura, I.; Saito, R.; Nakaya, T.; Hanibuchi, T.; Takamiya, T.; Odagiri, Y.; Fukushima, N.; et al. Individual-Level Social Capital and COVID-19 Vaccine Hesitancy in Japan: A Cross-Sectional Study. *Hum. Vaccines Immunother.* **2022**, *18*, 2086773. [CrossRef]
50. World Health Organization. *Explorations of Inequality: Childhood Immunization*; World Health Organization: Geneva, Switzerland, 2018.
51. World Health Organization. *Inequality Monitoring in Immunization: A Step-by-Step Manual*; World Health Organization: Geneva, Switzerland, 2019.
52. Robinson, E.; Jones, A.; Lesser, I.; Daly, M. International Estimates of Intended Uptake and Refusal of COVID-19 Vaccines: A Rapid Systematic Review and Meta-Analysis of Large Nationally Representative Samples. *Vaccine* **2021**, *39*, 2024–2034. [CrossRef] [PubMed]
53. Nehal, K.R.; Steendam, L.M.; Campos Ponce, M.; van der Hoeven, M.; Smit, G.S.A. Worldwide Vaccination Willingness for COVID-19: A Systematic Review and Meta-Analysis. *Vaccines* **2021**, *9*, 1071. [CrossRef] [PubMed]
54. Liao, Q.; Cowling, B.J.; Lam, W.W.T.; Fielding, R. Factors Affecting Intention to Receive and Self-Reported Receipt of 2009 Pandemic (H1N1) Vaccine in Hong Kong: A Longitudinal Study. *PLoS ONE* **2011**, *6*, e17713. [CrossRef] [PubMed]

vaccines

MDPI

Article

Uncovering the Drivers of Childhood Immunization Inequality with Caregivers, Community Members and Health System Stakeholders: Results from a Human-Centered Design Study in DRC, Mozambique and Nigeria

Jessica C. Shearer [1,*], Olivia Nava [2], Wendy Prosser [3], Saira Nawaz [1], Salva Mulongo [4], Thérèse Mambu [5], Eric Mafuta [5], Khatia Munguambe [6], Betuel Sigauque [7], Yakubu Joel Cherima [8], Olawale Durosinmi-Etti [8], Obehi Okojie [9], Idris Suleman Hadejia [10], Femi Oyewole [11], Dessie Ayalew Mekonnen [3], Natasha Kanagat [3], Carol Hooks [12], Rebecca Fields [3], Vanessa Richart [3] and Grace Chee [3]

1 PATH USA, Seattle, WA 98102, USA
2 Independent Consultant, Oakland, CA 94608, USA
3 JSI Research and Training Institute USA, Arlington, VA 22202, USA
4 PATH DRC, Kinshasa 7525, Democratic Republic of the Congo
5 Kinshasa School of Public Health, University of Kinshasa, Kinshasa 11, Democratic Republic of the Congo
6 Community Health Department, Eduardo Mondlane University, Maputo 1102, Mozambique
7 JSI Research and Training Institute Mozambique, Maputo, Mozambique
8 JSI Research and Training Institute Nigeria, Abuja, Nigeria
9 Department of Community Health, University of Benin, Benin City 300271, Nigeria
10 Department of Community Medicine, Ahmadu Bello University, Zaria 810107, Nigeria
11 Consultant Public Health Physician, Lagos, Nigeria
12 Manoff Group, Washington, DC 20008, USA
* Correspondence: jshearer@path.org

Citation: Shearer, J.C.; Nava, O.; Prosser, W.; Nawaz, S.; Mulongo, S.; Mambu, T.; Mafuta, E.; Munguambe, K.; Sigauque, B.; Cherima, Y.J.; et al. Uncovering the Drivers of Childhood Immunization Inequality with Caregivers, Community Members and Health System Stakeholders: Results from a Human-Centered Design Study in DRC, Mozambique and Nigeria. *Vaccines* **2023**, *11*, 689. https://doi.org/10.3390/vaccines11030689

Academic Editor: Pedro Plans-Rubió

Received: 25 January 2023
Revised: 17 February 2023
Accepted: 27 February 2023
Published: 17 March 2023

Abstract: Background: The importance of immunization for child survival underscores the need to eliminate immunization inequalities. Few existing studies of inequalities use approaches that view the challenges and potential solutions from the perspective of caregivers. This study aimed to identify barriers and context-appropriate solutions by engaging deeply with caregivers, community members, health workers, and other health system actors through participatory action research, intersectionality, and human-centered design lenses. Methods: This study was conducted in the Demographic Republic of Congo, Mozambique and Nigeria. Rapid qualitative research was followed by co-creation workshops with study participants to identify solutions. We analyzed the data using the UNICEF Journey to Health and Immunization Framework. Results: Caregivers of zero-dose and under-immunized children faced multiple intersecting and interacting barriers related to gender, poverty, geographic access, and service experience. Immunization programs were not aligned with needs of the most vulnerable due to the sub-optimal implementation of pro-equity strategies, such as outreach vaccination. Caregivers and communities identified feasible solutions through co-creation workshops and this approach should be used whenever possible to inform local planning. Conclusions: Policymakers and managers can integrate HCD and intersectionality mindsets into existing planning and assessment processes, and focus on overcoming root causes of sub-optimal implementation.

Keywords: health inequalities; immunization; equity; inequality; human-centered design; vaccination services; zero-dose children; community

1. Introduction

Immunization is widely recognized as one of the most important public health interventions for reducing childhood morbidity and mortality [1]. Enormous efforts led to a significant increase in global coverage of the third dose of diphtheria–tetanus–pertussis

(DTP3) vaccine over the past two decades, reaching its highest point at 86% in 2019, although this fell to 83% in 2020 due to the COVID-19 pandemic, and 81% in 2021 [2]. Immunization services miss millions of children each year, including those who are not fully vaccinated and those considered zero-dose, defined as not having received the first dose of a DTP-containing vaccine. It is estimated that 16 million children were zero-dose in 2020 and 18 million were zero-dose in 2021. These children are at risk of illness or death, and are likely to live in circumstances that further exacerbate this risk [2].

Research exists on the drivers of immunization inequality [3–10], yet most of the existing research focuses either on individual attributes or health system drivers, without analysis of the social and structural processes that produce inequalities [11]. Recent attention to the role of gender in immunization (in)equity is overdue [8,12] but too often, gender is explored alone, without consideration of how it intersects and interacts with other social, institutional, and structural dimensions of inequality, including social determinants of health. Novel research approaches are needed to reconceptualize immunization inequality—and potential solutions to overcoming it—from caregivers' lived perspectives.

This study seeks a way forward to engage and support individuals, caregivers, families, communities, and the health system to co-produce immunization equity. We apply paradigms and approaches from a human-centered design (HCD) and intersectionality [11,13], to reconceptualize the barriers, facilitators, and root causes of no immunization and under-immunization from the perspective of caregivers of infants and young children. When applied to health, intersectionality is the theory that individuals' lives are shaped by multiple social, institutional, and structural axes, that work together and interact to produce advantages or disadvantages [11,13]. Through this lens, we shift towards understanding each caregivers' experience as unique to their situation and the role that all social forces play in empowering or disempowering them. HCD has been used in global health programs to better understand the needs and context of end-users, and to co-create context-appropriate solutions [14], which this study sought to do. In all steps of the study's design and implementation, we sought to increase empathy for caregivers, an important step towards equity and justice.

1.1. Country Contexts

1.1.1. Democratic Republic of the Congo

The DRC remains among the most vulnerable countries in the world for the spread of vaccine-preventable diseases, as evidenced by the most recent outbreaks in measles, polio and yellow fever. DRC is home to poor infrastructure and difficult access, as well as remote missed communities, mobile and conflict-affected populations, and weak health systems, all leading to a high proportion of zero-dose and under-immunized children, and substantial within-country inequalities. In 2021, the WHO and UNICEF estimated that more than 700,000 children in the DRC were zero-dose [2]. Causes of no immunization and under-immunization include frequent vaccine stockouts, weak funding and governance, limited and demotivated human resources, poor service experience [15], and access difficulties. Analyses of the 2013 Demographic and Health Survey (DHS) survey data indicate a DTP3 coverage gap of more than 20-percent points between the lowest and highest wealth quintiles, and between rural and urban residents [6].

1.1.2. Mozambique

Mozambique has a history of political commitment to vaccination and primary health care; however the WUENIC estimate of DTP3 coverage dropped from 88% in 2019, to 79% in 2020, to 61% in 2021, in large part due to vaccine stockouts. Equity analyses of the 2015 DHS data show that while the wealth gap has narrowed since 1997, there remains a 20-percent point difference between the lowest and highest wealth quintiles. Children of educated mothers and mothers living in urban settings have DTP3 coverage approximately 15 percentage points higher than uneducated mothers or those living in rural areas [6]. Mozambique also has substantial within-country geographic inequalities, with a DTP3 ranging from 74.6% in Nampula, to 97.5% in Maputo Province in the 2015 DHS survey [16]. Evidence suggests that the general public and caregivers of young children, in particular, have positive attitudes toward child vaccination [17]. However, long travel distances, frequent stockouts, the perception of adverse outcomes from administering multiple vaccines at the same time and fear of being mistreated by healthcare providers contribute to low vaccine coverage and wide geographic inequalities [17–19].

1.1.3. Nigeria

In 2021, Nigeria had one of the highest numbers of zero-dose children (2.2 million) in the world [2], a challenge that was exacerbated by COVID-19. Equity analyses of 2013 and 2018 DHS data demonstrate stark inequalities based on wealth (over 70 percentage points), maternal education (50 percentage points), and place of residence (nearly 40 percentage points). Nigeria is one of the few countries where, nationally, more boys are vaccinated than girls [6]. Geographic inequality is significant between Nigeria's states, and within them, the majority of zero-dose and under-immunized children are living in the northern states. Qualitative research of barriers to vaccination has highlighted mistrust of the government and vaccines, lack of awareness, fear of adverse events following immunization, shortage of health workers, long waiting times, and long travel times [20]. COVID-19 has also exacerbated some of these barriers and recent research on the reasons behind the slow uptake of COVID-19 vaccinations point to many of the same determinants [21].

2. Materials and Methods

2.1. Study Design

Each country implemented a qualitative study to identify the barriers and facilitators of vaccination faced by caregivers of zero-dose and under-immunized children, and to identify context-tailored solutions from the perspective of caregivers and other stakeholders. This study was implemented as part of the USAID-funded MOMENTUM Routine Immunization Transformation and Equity project, and a major objective of this study was to inform the design of locally tailored solutions to include in the project's activity workplans. We drew from participatory action research, intersectionality, and human-centered design (HCD) approaches to design a study that would ensure the engagement and collaboration of stakeholders at all levels. A key innovation was the inclusion of community-based co-creation workshops, which sought to validate initial study findings, build empathy for caregivers among other stakeholders, and use HCD tools to identify potential interventions to overcome barriers. Our approach aligns with draft guidance from UNICEF on integrating HCD into sub-national immunization coverage and equity assessments [22].

2.1.1. Analytical Framework

The research team drew on three similar analytical frameworks to inform research questions and data collection tools: the UNICEF Journey to Health and Immunization framework [22]; the WHO Behavioural and Social Drivers framework [23]; and the Determinants of childhood vaccine coverage model [5,24]. These frameworks all explain vaccine uptake as a function of three main factors: behavioral drivers such as knowledge, awareness and beliefs, attitudes, and social norms; the practical and access issues caregivers face, including geographic and financial access; and characteristics of the health system, such as service convenience, quality, and experience of care. We used the UNICEF framework to guide analysis as it most closely represents empathy for a caregiver and concepts of HCD and intersectionality, by situating them in the center of an ecosystem [25] and explicitly recognizing the influence of multiple levels (Figure 1). This framework also captures issues faced by health personnel.

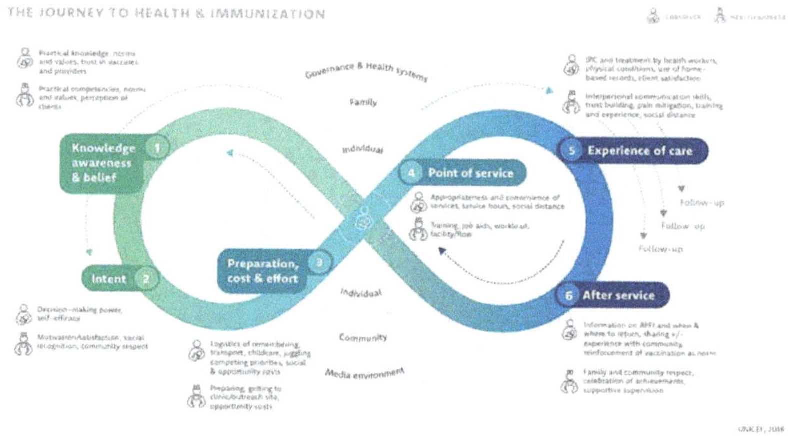

Figure 1. The UNICEF Journey to Health and Immunization framework. UNICEF, Demand for health services field guide: a human-centered approach. New York: UNICEF, 2018.

These models and our pilot phase forced us to clarify the meaning of 'caregiver' in our study countries. In the DRC, Mozambique, and Nigeria, we observed that mothers, or occasionally other adult female family members, had the socially prescribed role to get a child vaccinated, and so we use the term 'caregiver' in this paper with an understanding that the data primarily reflects the experiences of mothers. We acknowledge that caregivers could be men, including fathers, but these findings specifically reflect the gendered realities of the female caregivers we interacted with.

2.1.2. Study Setting and Sampling Criteria

The study was implemented in the DRC (May–June 2021), Mozambique (July–August 2021), and Nigeria (October 2022) by research teams comprising qualitative researchers and project staff with expertise in immunization. The selection of study states/provinces, districts, health facilities, and communities was done stepwise with health system managers at each level. As a qualitative study, we did not use sample size calculations, but did aim to interview enough respondents to achieve theoretical saturation on our research questions. The first sub-national unit, states or provinces, were selected with the project funder and national immunization managers, to ensure that this project's eventual interventions were implemented in provinces in need of an immunization technical partner. Within those states/provinces, we used survey or administrative data to rank districts by their proportion of un- and under-vaccinated children. Among those districts with the highest proportion of un- and under-vaccinated children, we purposefully selected districts that were accessible to our study team during the study period (all countries), represented a mix of both urban and rural districts (DRC), and were free from security concerns (Nigeria). The number of districts selected in each country depended on available financial and human resources to implement the study, resulting in seven districts (health zones) in the DRC, six in Mozambique, and three in Nigeria. Within the selected districts, we worked with district-level managers to select health facilities that represented typical cases of that district, and then selected one community linked to each facility with high proportions of zero-dose or missed communities. We worked with community leaders and CHWs to identify mothers of zero-dose and under-vaccinated children in selected communities.

2.2. Data Collection and Analysis, including Co-Creation Workshops

2.2.1. Data Collection

The research team and additionally trained data collectors collected data for this study through semi-structured and open-ended in-depth interviews (IDIs), focus group discussions (FGDs; Nigeria only), and co-creation workshops. In Nigeria, FGDs were used instead of interviews at the community level, with caregivers and community members separately, to optimize time and resources. Interview and FGD guides reflected the analytical frameworks, and we adapted during implementation based on emerging insights. The teams also collected health facility data for common indicators of facility readiness and performance, as found in existing health facility surveys and immunization-specific supportive supervision checklists. While these quantitative data were later used to inform our project's intervention design, we did not include them in the analysis presented at co-creation workshops due to the rapid implementation timelines (1–2 weeks for data collection, analysis, and co-creation) of these qualitative studies; thus, we do not report them here.

2.2.2. Data Analysis and Synthesis

The research teams took notes during interviews and FGDs and wrote memos summarizing the key findings of each interview. Teams met daily in-person or online to discuss new data, emerging themes, and questions to probe further on. Upon completion of data collection in a study area, the teams rapidly sorted the data, key insights, and emerging themes into text-based tables, categorized according to the domains of the analytical frameworks. This step helped to identify key barriers and facilitators to vaccination in that community. Through this process, the research team selected three key issues to explore further during the local co-creation workshops, with the goals of strengthening participants' empathy for caregivers by highlighting the challenges they face, and identifying common barriers that had the potential to be resolved through local solutions. The research team developed 'personas'—short stories centered around a caregivers' experiences based on the synthesized data—to illustrate each selected challenge at the co-creation workshop, while ensuring the confidentiality of the research participants. Following all data collection and workshops, country research teams synthesized all analyzed data into reports which informed the development of the project's activity workplan.

2.2.3. Co-Creation Workshops

Immediately following data collection, the research teams facilitated workshops with study participants and other relevant stakeholders at the district level. These co-creation workshops aimed to validate emerging findings from the data collection phase, strengthen feelings of empathy for caregivers, and identify locally relevant interventions to overcome identified barriers. The research team first summarized findings and facilitated discussion, and then implemented HCD tools adapted by the project to achieve the empathy and solution-identification objectives: the mothers' vaccination ecosystem; solution briefs; and a solutioning activity (Table 1). All study participants were invited and workshops were attended by 20–30 individuals, including caregivers. Experienced facilitators were attentive to the possibly negative consequences of mixing multiple levels of social power, and took care to ensure the respect for and confidentiality of the caregiver attendees. Caregivers' confidentiality was protected by the use of persona tools to share fictionalized findings based on the synthesis of experiences across all interviewees (Table 2). Community-level co-creation workshops were followed by district-level and then state/provincial and/or national workshops, to share insights and solutions from the level below, validate findings at each level, and assess motivation and priority for community-developed solutions across the other levels. Research teams generated additional insights on stakeholder motivations, preferences, and needs by observing the group discussions and taking notes.

Table 1. HCD tools used during co-creation workshops.

HCD Tool	Brief Description	Purpose
Mothers' Vaccination Ecosystem	Visual bullet eye diagram to represent a mother (or female caregiver) and her baby, and the barriers she faces at each ecosystem level: family, community, health system. Used as a discussion and group-work tool.	• To generate empathy for mothers by illustrating the many intersecting barriers they face. • To encourage responsibility and collective action by other stakeholders by seeing and discussing barriers faced by mothers, and generate ideas to reduce barriers mothers face.
Solution Brief	The solution brief is a persona tool that draws data from synthesized findings from in-depth interviews and focus group discussions. Drawing from the data, the tool includes a persona (a fictionalized representation of an individual; see Table 2), assumptions about the root causes of immunization barriers, and problem or opportunity statements for specific user personas, which could include caregivers, health workers, or others. The end of the brief outlines a specific problem, or solution framing in the form of a question to address; this is the beginning point of the solutioning activity.	• To generate empathy for specific users (e.g., healthcare workers, caregivers, community health workers). • To simplify the complex system of barriers to immunization by seeing the barriers from the perspective of a specific user.
Solutioning Activity	This solutioning activity tool is a collaborative problem-solving exercise for small group breakout teams. Each team receives a solution brief detailing the user persona and their challenges, as well as a specific problem for the group to address, based on the user's perspective. As a group often including users who share this challenge, the team works through a set of prompts from brainstorming, to using a rubric to decide which ideas to build out, to finally building out two solutions for the user's problem.	• To generate multiple-solution ideas to a specific immunization barrier in a short period of time. • To build the relationship between community and health system by working toward shared solutions. • Triangulate data collected from in-depth interviews and focus groups.

Table 2. Select caregiver personas used during co-creation workshops, based on study findings.

Study Theme	Problem Statements from Solution Briefs/Personas
Theme 1: Caregiver facing multiple intersecting and interacting barriers based on her context	• When mother was able to get to the health center, she was not provided vaccines because she did not have a vaccination card. • Mother did not have money for a card (although these should be free, she was told she would need to pay for one). • Mother was insulted by a nurse for having a baby outside of the health center, but she had no way to get to the health center for her birth, as it was 35 km away.
Theme 2: Immunization services not aligned with a caregivers' needs	• Mother has missed vaccinations due to lack of time (she was busy with household chores). • She makes decisions about her child's health on her own, but has the support/advice of her husband, and he is the one who takes them to the health facility. • Mother received advice on child health from her aunt. • Mother heard about the mobile brigade through the religious leader. • Mother regrets the fact that the mobile vaccination services sometimes postpone, and when this happens mothers are not informed in advance; she had already gone to the scheduled place and date in vain. • Unlike the other mothers, she preferred the mobile vaccination services to be in the morning, so she can dedicate the rest of the day to her errands.

2.2.4. Cross-Country Synthesis

The research team reviewed country finding reports and manually re-coded data and findings according to the UNICEF framework and through the lens of intersectionality and power dynamics at the individual, institutional, and structural levels [13]. The team discussed key findings to better understand barriers and facilitators faced by caregivers and how they differed by context. This led to the identification of three mid-level themes which the team considered to be of broad importance and actionable, and emphasized the empathy mindset for caregivers and communities.

Ethical approval was granted from the Kinshasa School of Public Health (DRC), the University Eduardo Mondlane (Mozambique), and the Edo and Jigawa State Health and Research Ethics Committee (Nigeria). Consent to participate was obtained by investigators trained in ethical procedures and prior to any observation or engagement. Team members read the consent form to participants in the local language and provided time to ask questions and clarify concerns. The team obtained written or verbal consent (in some situations) after answering the participants' questions and before beginning the activity or observation. As described in the consent form provided to the participants, all participants could request to withdraw from participation at any time.

3. Results

Table 3 summarizes the number of study participants by country and level of the health system. The section below presents synthesized findings from across the three countries, according to three emergent mid-level themes.

Table 3. Study participants.

		Number of Participants by Type and Country		
Health System Level	**Participant Type**	**DRC (Kasaï (Ndjoko Punda, Kalonda Ouest); Kasaï Oriental (Nzaba, Cilundu); Lualaba (Dilala, Kazenze))**	**Mozambique (Zambezia (Gurue, Ile, Molumbo) Nampula (Murrupula, Erati, Mossuril))**	**Nigeria (Edo (Ikpoba Okha) and Jigawa (Buji))**
Community	Caregivers	24	20	18 (FGDs)
	Community leaders and activists; community health workers and volunteers; traditional birth attendants	12	25	10 (FGDs)
Health facility	Facility-level healthcare worker; vaccinators; nurse managers	12	10	8
District/health zone	District/zonal EPI manager, community engagement focal point, monitoring and evaluation focal point, financial officer, health Education officer	6	11	14
Province	Provincial logistics focal point, EPI manager, MEL, finance officer, community engagement/health education focal point	6	6	16
	TOTAL	60	72	66

FGD: focus group discussion; EPI: Expanded Program on Immunization; MEL: Monitoring, Evaluation, and Learning.

3.1. Social and Structural Factors Intersect to Produce Inequitable Power Relationships and Limit Health System Actors' Empathy for Caregivers

Across all the countries, most of the caregivers interviewed expressed the desire for their child to be vaccinated, and most were aware of the general benefits of vaccines. However, gender, social factors, and structural inequalities intersected and interacted to produce a variety of barriers for caregivers (Table 4). The type and magnitude of these barriers differed by a caregivers' social status, wealth, place of residence, and economic role—which in turn varied by country and region—and often played out as power dynamics that produced inequitable access to and quality of immunization services. Most caregivers reported some difficulty juggling their gender-prescribed tasks related to childcare and domestic work with getting a child vaccinated. These difficulties were more common among caregivers who faced other financial or time-related resource barriers, whether because of poverty or because the child's father worked or lived away from the home. Gender inequality was sometimes apparent in the caregivers' lack of agency to make a decision about whether to vaccinate her child. While most caregivers said they were able to make a decision themselves about vaccination, we also heard cases where caregivers noted they were not the key decision-makers, and this pertained more often to caregivers of zero-dose children. Decision-making divergence worked in both directions: sometimes women followed their male partners' preference to not get vaccinated, and sometimes they followed his preference to get vaccinated. When decision-making agency intersected with wealth and women relied on their male partners for financial support to access vaccination, it often resulted in the child not getting vaccinated. When husbands assisted with practical aspects, such as childcare or transport, which was reported by some respondents, caregivers were more likely to seek vaccination. Gender dynamics were also presented in conversations related to adverse events following immunization (AEFI). Many caregivers reported that they feared AEFI, such as fever or fussiness, as an uncomfortable infant disrupted the household dynamic, and this fear increased if their husband had complained.

Table 4. Examples of findings through the intersectionality lens.

Intersection	Resulting Interaction	Impact on Vaccination Outcomes, Particularly Zero-Dose Children
Gender × wealth	Caregivers with fewer resources were less able to overcome gender barriers related to their paid or unpaid work and opportunity costs of going to the health facility.	These caregivers were more likely to have zero-dose children than other caregivers.
Gender × geographic access	Caregivers felt unsafe traveling to distant health facilities, up to 2 days in Mozambique, and did not have resources for other forms of transport.	Many caregivers of zero-dose children cited this barrier, and these also comprise missed communities.
Wealth × service experience	Caregivers of low socioeconomic status faced more disrespectful care.	Typically resulted in under-vaccination, where caregivers who were treated poorly did not return for additional vaccines.
Wealth × governance × financing	Caregivers who could not afford fees for services or cards could not access vaccination services. These fees were often charged as a substitute for formal income.	Many caregivers of zero-dose children cited this barrier.
Wealth × geographic access × financing	Caregivers in the most remote and poorest communities were least likely to be reached by outreach vaccination services.	Many caregivers of zero-dose children cited this barrier.

Equity-limiting power dynamics also existed within the health system, where health workers wielded power from relative privilege over clients, and experienced disempowerment from managers and institutions that did not value them. This created a vicious cycle of negative power relations between health workers and clients. We observed that caregivers of low socioeconomic status experienced more disrespectful care from health workers (all countries) and were most likely to be blamed for not vaccinating their children (DRC). These particular caregivers expressed feelings of shame for being inappropriately dressed (DRC, Mozambique). In the DRC and Mozambique, caregivers of zero-dose children felt a sense of shame or exclusion that prevented them from accessing services, and caregivers who experienced blame or disrespect at the vaccination facility were the least likely to return. Caregivers in the DRC and Nigeria reported having to pay illicit fees for vaccine services or cards, and transport costs, which resulted in some caregivers being unable to afford services. In the DRC these illicit fees were the consequence of health workers being unpaid; in Nigeria they were explained as necessary to run an underfunded system. Many caregivers reported being unable to overcome at least one cost-related barrier, whether the service fees, costs of transportation to reach the facility, or opportunity costs of leaving paid or unpaid work. In Nigeria, financial and non-financial incentives were given by partners to caregivers, to cover the opportunity cost and transport costs. In the DRC many respondents reported that they had appreciated receiving nutritional and other non-cash incentives in the past, and had lost trust in the health system when those incentives were ended. Cost barriers were most challenging for caregivers of zero-dose children and intersected with gender and other access barriers to limit vaccination (see Table 2 for caregiver personas used during the co-creation workshops to illustrate these intersections).

Negative beliefs or misinformation about vaccination or vaccines were rarely the sole barrier to vaccination, although they did exist and interact with other barriers in a caregivers' overall influencing environment, particularly for the caregivers of zero-dose children.

Interviews highlighted the critical role of religious leaders in influencing decisions—either towards or away from vaccines—in all countries. Our data suggest a lesser influence of CHWs or community health volunteers, often because they themselves did not have sufficient information on immunization services to counteract misinformation or provide practical information. In all communities, they faced retention and motivation challenges due to limited financing for community health, weakening their potential as a trusted link to the health system.

3.2. *Insufficient Accountability, Governance, and Financing Respectively Contribute to Sub-Optimal Person-Centredness*

At an institutional level, our findings indicated that the health systems faced multiple design and implementation constraints to fully delivering pro-equity or people-centered immunization and PHC services. Strategies to improve equity by aligning service design and delivery to the needs and preferences of those at greatest risk of access barriers—such as vaccination in communities (e.g., outreach or mobile vaccination services), expanded clinic hours, and community mobilization activities—existed in policy and facilities' operational plans and budgets, but were sub-optimally implemented. The lack of person-centeredness was most acute for caregivers and communities that were geographically inaccessible, socially excluded, or faced financial access barriers. For example, many caregivers decided not to seek vaccination services because of the long, difficult, or unsafe walks to health centers, as well as long wait-times once there, and this was exacerbated among low-income women and those who were socially isolated. Planned outreach vaccination sessions are meant to overcome these barriers, but a theme across all three countries was dissatisfaction with the low frequency of these services or not knowing when they would occur. When community-based or outreach services were implemented, they were implemented in communities close to the health facility, as health workers faced their own challenges—financial or logistical—in reaching remote communities.

Respondents in all countries described insufficient or poorly planned and managed immunization and PHC budgets, which led to insufficient operational funds to implement these strategies. Triangulation of data across multiple levels of the health system identified the root causes of weak governance and accountability, insufficient and fragmented financial resources, and weak leadership and management capability. Poor resource generation, allocation, and management, thus, most affected communities that already faced access barriers to immunization services. In Mozambique and Nigeria, national policies supporting integrated health services were sub-optimally implemented due to insufficient and fragmented finances stemming from weak governance. In all countries there was a recognition that certain remote or migrant communities were missed entirely with health and social services, and that no mechanism existed to identify these communities and link them to services.

Current or previous experience with vaccine stockouts weakened caregivers' trust in vaccination services. Many zero-dose children in the DRC were unvaccinated due to an ongoing shortage of BCG vaccines; the likelihood of a caregiver returning again after a missed opportunity for vaccination depended on the intersection of other barriers. Sub-optimal health worker motivation and performance was an important barrier to vaccination in all countries, ranging from absenteeism that led to missed opportunities for vaccination, to disrespectful care, to poor clinical quality of care. Caregiver reports of service quality varied across interviewees, but we noted that mothers of under-vaccinated children were likely to report poor service experience as a reason for not returning for additional doses. This included perceptions that sub-optimal clinical quality resulted in common side effects, such as swelling or sores at the vaccination site. As noted above, health workers themselves experienced institutional inequality and disempowerment. Despite these conditions, and as noted elsewhere, many health workers and other health system staff noted their commitment and intrinsic motivation to their roles [26].

3.3. *Local Solutions Address Power Imbalances*

Local co-creation workshops succeeded in reconceptualizing the problem of no immunization and under-immunization among participants, by presenting challenges from caregivers' or healthcare workers' perspectives. The exercise challenged each participant to empathize with caregivers and healthcare workers by better understanding the barriers they face in getting children vaccinated. By facilitating group discussions with caregivers and health workers, it allowed all community and health system participants in the workshop to work together to identify how they were responsible in supporting caregivers to overcome barriers. It was a new experience for all participants to be brought into a workshop where district, health facility, community leaders, and caregivers were invited as equals. In the DRC and Mozambique, district and provincial stakeholders expressed that the workshops were enlightening, and their perspectives changed about mothers related to the barriers they face and their agency in overcoming them.

Community-level participants from all countries expressed excitement at how they could support caregivers in getting their children to the health center. Solutions that emerged from the workshop included forming walking groups of caregivers to travel together to health facilities (Mozambique), husbands helping with transport (Mozambique) or childcare (Nigeria), and championship by community and religious leaders, who themselves are supported with training and information (DRC and Mozambique). These solutions suggest that participants were motivated by feelings of social cohesion. All co-creation workshops also proposed better implementation of existing solutions, such as outreach vaccination. Health system participants often uncovered new knowledge about financing challenges between levels of the health system that inhibited their ability to better support healthcare workers in adhering to their facility's immunization goals or implement outreach activities. Multiple solutions reflected ideas of people-centered care and improved service experience, such as joint planning for outreach services across health programs to better reach remote communities, integrated delivery of all child health services at facilities, reducing waiting times, and expanded service hours.

4. Discussion

The drivers of vaccination, identified through this study, are consistent with other studies, but we provide a new way of reconceptualizing them through HCD and intersectional lenses. Viewed through a caregivers' perspective, each individual has a unique set of social, institutional, and structural circumstances that intersect and interact to constrain or enable her options and outcomes. As Crenshaw argued when she proposed the intersectionality theory [27], it is limiting to group caregivers into binary categories, such as race or gender or to attribute a single characteristic—such as religion, education, or wealth—to explain immunization inequalities. A complete understanding of the drivers of inequality requires analyzing the joint influence of multiple factors related to the individual, as well as the health system and greater structural context. Our study used qualitative interviews guided by an HCD mindset to identify the lived experiences, challenges, and needs of caregivers of un- and under-vaccinated children. Presentation of their stories in community-level workshops built empathy and enabled co-design of locally relevant solutions that addressed the needs and preferences of caregivers. Some of the solutions were novel to the researchers, such as community walking groups, but many were in fact the improved implementation of existing strategies, such as outreach vaccination. As a project with the goal of overcoming entrenched obstacles to immunization equity, the resulting solutions guided our choice of activities and their design, with a focus on strengthening the local capacity for gender integration, strengthening community partnerships, and addressing root causes of sub-optimal service experience.

Our empirical data demonstrated the lack of person-centeredness or alignment of immunization programs with client needs, particularly for caregivers and communities facing multiple intersecting vulnerabilities.

Despite the many pro-equity strategies that exist and are budgeted and planned for [28], very few were actually implemented due to financial resource constraints at the operational level stemming from weak accountability and governance. We note that strategies to reach zero-dose children likely cost more, and that at the operational level, vaccinating individuals and communities at a higher risk of morbidity and mortality should be prioritized [29]. With the increased global investment in pro-equity strategies to reach zero-dose children and missed communities, we note the importance of also strengthening accountability for implementation and stronger health system governance and management.

Another root cause of the lack of people-centeredness stems from the way in which power structures are entrenched in health systems. On an interpersonal level, this can result in inconvenient or disrespectful services, but on an institutional level, results in weak accountability and insufficient resources to improve access, quality and experience. We saw evidence that stakeholders at operational and community levels were interested in and committed to taking actions to support caregivers to access vaccination, ensure the implementation of outreach vaccination services, and improve the overall convenience of services. Will they succeed? We believe this is the level where efforts to reorient PHC around user needs can have the most traction, although tangible pathways towards improved empathy and person-centeredness exist also at planning, policy and funding levels. Policies and programs can invest in or encourage approaches that are gender responsive, people-centered, integrate HCD and intersectional lenses, and explicitly address institutional and structural root causes. For example, tools for operational planning, such as integrated microplans, can be revised to ensure identification of the barriers and needs of the hardest-to-reach, and can engage caregivers and communities in the identification of solutions. Technical partners, such as our project, can catalyze the engagement of non-traditional partners to fill resource gaps needed to implement pro-equity strategies (e.g., local businesses) and ensure accurate sharing of information from trusted voices (e.g., religious leaders). Policymakers and external funders can support efforts to integrate the delivery of all PHC services for improved efficiency and client satisfaction, address human resource motivation, and improve management skills.

4.1. Comparison with Other Research

This study identified similar determinants of vaccine inequality as has been observed across other qualitative and quantitative research on drivers of immunization coverage and equity, including access, cost, health systems readiness, gender-related barriers, vaccine supply, fear of side effects, community engagement, lack of knowledge, and provider absenteeism [3–5,10]. Our study contributes to this literature by identifying the relationships among these barriers and how those interactions contribute to no vaccination or under-vaccination. As noted in the recent systematic review of vaccination barriers by Kaufman [7], less than half of all global studies report barriers across all determinants of vaccination, but our study was designed to holistically and comprehensively explore barriers from the perspective of caregivers. A handful of published studies use HCD approaches to study vaccination barriers and solutions, including ones from Mozambique [19], India [30], and the Philippines [31]. The Mozambique study identified similar patterns of barriers to vaccination, including the role of gender barriers and power imbalances with health workers. Cross-national quantitative analyses of household survey data show that immunization inequalities are associated with household wealth and maternal education [6], and that the prevalence of zero-dose children is associated with gender inequality [8], birth order, birth weight, maternal education, maternal occupation, household wealth, and the number of antenatal care visits [9].

4.2. Limitations

Our study had some limitations related to the design and implementation. The intentional selection of study units with high proportions of zero-dose children means that our findings are not necessarily representative of the countries, or even states/provinces within the countries, and these findings should not be interpreted to represent the most common or typical barriers to vaccination, but rather the barriers faced by those most excluded from access to quality immunization services. Because we sought to tailor the study design for the context of each country, comparing or synthesizing the findings across countries should be treated with caution. We did not originally design the study with the intersectionality lens in mind, and as such, we missed the opportunity to explore specific intersections and interactions during data collection. We were able to identify and interview caregivers of zero-dose children in most study settings, but not the Edo province in Nigeria. Similarly, the study was not implemented in regions with refugees, displacement, or conflict-affected populations, which we know face many barriers to vaccination. We designed the study to be implemented rapidly to inform timely program design, but the short duration of the data collection period limited the number of respondents interviewed in each community, which may mean the findings are biased. In Nigeria, we used FGDs instead of in-depth interviews with caregivers and community members to optimize the limited time available, but FGDs may have consequences on the type of information shared, particularly for sensitive information. Similarly, because we prioritized the ability to validate most findings in co-creation workshops immediately following data collection, we did not have time to analyze quantitative data during the rapid study period.

5. Conclusions

This qualitative study presents drivers of immunization inequality from the perspectives of caregivers, who face multiple, often compounding, barriers related to social, institutional, and structural dynamics. Applying HCD and intersectional approaches highlights the little agency caregivers face in their journeys to vaccinate their children, and how vaccination and PHC services are not designed with their needs in mind. We found that caregivers who face the greatest number of barriers to accessing and receiving quality immunization services tend to face a double burden of living in communities where outreach vaccination strategies are unimplemented due to weak governance and accountability. Based on our experiences, implementing this study and our observation that it was feasible to build empathy and co-design solutions with caregivers, communities, and health system actors, we recommend the integration of HCD and intersectionality approaches and tools in immunization research and programs. Immunization and PHC professionals at all levels can take simple steps to integrate HCD and intersectionality into their planning, management, and implementation processes, such as:

- As part of routine coverage and equity analyses that many countries undertake [32], select qualitative methods that engage directly with caregivers and communities and work with them to identify locally relevant solutions.
- Revise existing planning processes (e.g., annual planning processes, funding applications) and tools (e.g., microplanning tools, supervision checklists) to provide guidance or requirements related to gender integration, engaging communities, and addressing root causes of sub-optimal implementation.
- Invest in strengthening skills and culture related to gender, intersectionality, and HCD among immunization stakeholders to ensure strategies, activities, and interventions address the needs of the most vulnerable caregivers and families.
- Encourage donors, such as Gavi, to target investments towards interventions that are gender-responsive or transformative, towards activities that are designed to reach caregivers and communities furthest from health justice, and towards supporting larger health systems and governance reforms that improve the availability, quality, and convenience of people-centered PHC approaches.
- Encourage and fund research and evaluation of the effectiveness and equity consequences of existing and new interventions to reach zero-dose children and missed communities [28], and on how to overcome entrenched obstacles related to their implementation.

We found that the power of local knowledge must be leveraged as a catalyst for all of these steps.

Author Contributions: Authors contributed in the following manners: Conceptualization, J.C.S., O.N., W.P., S.N., S.M., K.M., Y.J.C., D.A.M., N.K., C.H., R.F. and V.R.; Methodology, J.C.S., O.N., S.N., K.M., B.S., Y.J.C., O.D.-E., O.O., I.S.H., F.O., D.A.M., N.K., C.H., R.F., V.R. and G.C.; Validation, J.C.S., O.N., W.P., S.N., S.M., Y.J.C. and N.K.; Formal Analysis, J.C.S., O.N., S.N., S.M., T.M., K.M., O.O. and I.S.H.; Investigation, O.N., S.M., T.M., E.M., K.M., O.O., I.S.H. and F.O.; Resources, J.C.S., O.N., S.N., D.A.M., N.K. and C.H.; Data Curation, T.M., E.M., K.M., O.O. and I.S.H.; Writing—Original Draft Preparation, J.C.S., O.N., W.P., S.N., T.M., E.M., K.M. and D.A.M.; Writing—Review & Editing, J.C.S., O.N., W.P., S.N., B.S., Y.J.C., O.O., I.S.H., D.A.M., N.K., R.F., V.R. and G.C.; Visualization, J.C.S., O.N.; Supervision, J.C.S., O.N., W.P., S.N., S.M., B.S., Y.J.C. and V.R.; Project Administration, S.M., B.S., Y.J.C., V.R. and G.C.; Funding Acquisition, V.R. and G.C. All authors have read and agreed to the published version of the manuscript.

Funding: MOMENTUM Routine Immunization Transformation and Equity and this research was funded by the U.S. Agency for International Development (USAID) as part of the MOMENTUM suite of awards, and implemented by the JSI Research & Training Institute, Inc. with partners PATH, Accenture Development Partnerships, Results for Development, CORE Group, and The Manoff Group under USAID cooperative agreement #7200AA20CA00017. For more information about MOMENTUM, visit www.usaidmomentum.org (accessed on 15 January 2023). The contents of this journal article are the sole responsibility of the JSI Research & Training Institute, Inc., and do not necessarily reflect the views of USAID or the United States Government.

Institutional Review Board Statement: The study was conducted according to the guidelines of the Declaration of Helsinki, and approved by the Institutional Review Board (or Ethics Committee) of Kinshasa School of Public Health (DRC), Eduardo Mondlane University (Mozambique), the Edo and Jigawa State Health and Research Ethics Committee (Nigeria), and the JSI Research and Training Institute.

Informed Consent Statement: Informed consent was obtained from all subjects involved in the study.

Data Availability Statement: The data presented in this study are available on request from the corresponding author. The data are not publicly available due to privacy concerns of the respondents.

Acknowledgments: We would like to thank the following who contributed extensively to research design or implementation: in DRC, Godefroid Mpanya, Constant Kingongo, Eugene Mankiya, Fedy Mukendi, Joel Bompongo, Andre Tonda, Moza Diakiese, Nick'son Sonabo, Rachel Kukia and Anna Acquistapace; in Mozambique, Vasco Muchanga, Valerio Govo, Estevão Manhice, Raquel Carrilho, Melanie Picolo, Agostinho Mauire and Santos Sipaneque; in Nigeria, Otaniyenuwa Eloghosa Obarisiagbon, Amos Paul Bassi, Jagun Moriam Olaide, Chioma Victoria Ugochukwu, Sa'adatu U. Ibrahim Ringim, Ahmed Mohammed Naiya and Olutobi Daniel Adeogo. We are grateful for the support and engagement of national and provincial EPI programs in the three countries, with special thanks to Bassey Okposen and Faisal Shuaib (National Primary Health Care Development Agency, Nigeria). Other technical contributors include Kris Ansin, Benjamin Picillo, Sheetal Sharma, Emma Stewart, and Andi Sutter. We are appreciative of the management support from Katie Wallner, Suyane Viana, Fatou Ceesay and Siessourby-Eileen Soma. Finally, this study would not have been possible without the trust and engagement of mothers, family members, community leaders, community health workers and volunteers, health workers, and health system managers.

Conflicts of Interest: The authors declare no conflict of interest.

References

1. Bloom, D.E.; Canning, D.; Weston, M. The value of vaccination. *World Econ. Henley Thames* **2005**, *6*, 15.
2. World Health Organization; UNICEF. Progress and Challenges with Achieving Universal Immunization Coverage: 2021 WHO/UNICEF Estimates of National Immunization Coverage (WUENIC) 2022. Available online: https://cdn.who.int/media/docs/default-source/immunization/wuenic-progress-and-challenges-15-july-2022.pdf?sfvrsn=b5eb9141_7&download=true (accessed on 28 February 2023).
3. Rainey, J.J.; Watkins, M.; Ryman, T.K.; Sandhu, P.; Bo, A.; Banerjee, K. Reasons related to non-vaccination and under-vaccination of children in low and middle income countries: Findings from a systematic review of the published literature, 1999–2009. *Vaccine* **2011**, *29*, 8215–8221. [CrossRef] [PubMed]

4. LaFond, A.K.; Kanagat, N.; Sequeira, J.S.; Steinglass, R.; Fields, R.; Mookherji, S. Drivers of Routine Immunization System Performance at the District Level: Study Findings from Three Countries. *Health Policy Plan.* **2012**, *30*, 298–308. [CrossRef] [PubMed]
5. Phillips, D.E.; Dieleman, J.L.; Lim, S.S.; Shearer, J. Determinants of effective vaccine coverage in low and middle-income countries: A systematic review and interpretive synthesis. *BMC Health Serv. Res.* **2017**, *17*, 681. [CrossRef] [PubMed]
6. World Health Organization. *State of Inequality: Childhood Immunization*; World Health Organization: Geneva, Switzerland, 2017.
7. Kaufman, J.; Tuckerman, J.; Bonner, C.; Durrheim, D.N.; Costa, D.; Trevena, L.; Thomas, S.; Danchin, M. Parent-level barriers to uptake of childhood vaccination: A global overview of systematic reviews. *BMJ Glob. Health* **2021**, *6*, e006860. [CrossRef] [PubMed]
8. Johns, N.E.; Kirkby, K.; Goodman, T.S.; Heidari, S.; Munro, J.; Shendale, S.; Hosseinpoor, A.R. Subnational Gender Inequality and Childhood Immunization: An Ecological Analysis of the Subnational Gender Development Index and DTP Coverage Outcomes across 57 Countries. *Vaccines* **2022**, *10*, 1951. [CrossRef]
9. Ozigbu, C.E.; Olatosi, B.; Li, Z.; Hardin, J.W.; Hair, N.L. Correlates of Zero-Dose Vaccination Status among Children Aged 12–59 Months in Sub-Saharan Africa: A Multilevel Analysis of Individual and Contextual Factors. *Vaccines* **2022**, *10*, 1052. [CrossRef]
10. Périères, L.; Séror, V.; Boyer, S.; Sokhna, C.; Peretti-Watel, P. Reasons given for non-vaccination and under-vaccination of children and adolescents in sub-Saharan Africa: A systematic review. *Hum. Vaccines Immunother.* **2022**, *18*, 2076524. [CrossRef]
11. Gkiouleka, A.; Huijts, T.; Beckfield, J.; Bambra, C. Understanding the micro and macro politics of health: Inequalities, intersectionality & institutions-A research agenda. *Soc. Sci. Med.* **2018**, *200*, 92–98. [CrossRef]
12. Why Gender Matters: Immunization Agenda 2030. Available online: https://www.who.int/publications-detail-redirect/9789240033948 (accessed on 15 January 2023).
13. López, N.; Gadsden, V.L. *Health Inequities, Social Determinants, and Intersectionality*; National Academy of Medicine: Washington, DC, USA, 2016.
14. LaFond, A.; Cherney, M. A theory of change for guiding the integration of human-centered design into global health programming. *Glob. Health Sci. Pract.* **2021**, *9*, S209–S216. [CrossRef]
15. Kayembe-Ntumba, H.-C.; Vangola, F.; Ansobi, P.; Kapour, G.; Bokabo, E.; Mandja, B.-A.; Bompangue, D. Vaccination dropout rates among children aged 12-23 months in Democratic Republic of the Congo: A cross-sectional study. *Arch. Public Health* **2022**, *80*, 18. [CrossRef]
16. Ministério da Saúde, Instituto Nacional de Estatística. Inquérito de Indicadores de Imunização, Malária e HIV/SIDA Em Moçambique-IMASIDA, 2015–2018. Available online: http://dhsprogram.com/pubs/pdf/AIS12/AIS12.pdf (accessed on 28 February 2023).
17. Jani, J.V.; De Schacht, C.; Jani, I.V.; Bjune, G. Risk factors for incomplete vaccination and missed opportunity for immunization in rural Mozambique. *BMC Public Health* **2008**, *8*, 161. [CrossRef]
18. Shemwell, S.A.; Peratikos, M.B.; Gonzalez-Calvo, L.; Renom-Llonch, M.; Boon, A.; Martinho, S.; Cherry, C.B.; Green, A.F.; Moon, T.D. Determinants of full vaccination status in children aged 12–23 months in Gurùé and Milange districts, Mozambique: Results of a population-based cross-sectional survey. *Int. Health* **2017**, *9*, 234–242. [CrossRef]
19. Powelson, J.; Magadzire, B.P.; Draiva, A.; Denno, D.; Ibraimo, A.; Benate, B.B.L.; Jahar, L.C.; Marrune, Z.; Chilundo, B.; Chinai, J.E.; et al. Determinants of immunisation dropout among children under the age of 2 in Zambézia province, Mozambique: A community-based participatory research study using Photovoice. *BMJ Open* **2022**, *12*, e057245. [CrossRef]
20. Akwataghibe, N.N.; Ogunsola, E.A.; Broerse, J.E.; Popoola, O.A.; Agbo, A.I.; Dieleman, M.A. Exploring factors influencing immunization utilization in Nigeria—A mixed methods study. *Front. Public Health* **2019**, *7*, 392. [CrossRef]
21. Uzochukwu, I.C.; Eleje, G.U.; Nwankwo, C.H.; Chukwuma, G.O.; Uzuke, C.A.; Uzochukwu, C.E.; Mathias, B.A.; Okunna, C.S.; Asomugha, L.A.; Esimone, C.O. COVID-19 vaccine hesitancy among staff and students in a Nigerian tertiary educational institution. *Ther. Adv. Infect. Dis.* **2021**, *8*, 20499361211054924. [CrossRef]
22. UNICEF. *Embedding a Human Centered Design Approach into Sub-National Coverage and Equity Assessments (v3)*; UNICEF: New York, NY, USA, 2020.
23. World Health Organization. Understanding the behavioural and social drivers of vaccine uptake WHO position paper-May 2022. *Wkly. Epidemiol. Rec.* **2022**, *97*, 209–224.
24. Phillips, D.E.; Dieleman, J.L.; Shearer, J.C.; Lim, S.S. Childhood vaccines in Uganda and Zambia: Determinants and barriers to vaccine coverage. *Vaccine* **2018**, *36*, 4236–4244. [CrossRef]
25. Sallis, J.F.; Owen, N.; Fisher, E. Ecological models of health behavior. *Health Behav. Theory Res. Pract.* **2015**, *5*, 43–64.
26. Muthuri, R.N.D.K.; Senkubuge, F.; Hongoro, C. Determinants of Motivation among Healthcare Workers in the East African Community between 2009–2019: A Systematic Review. *Healthcare* **2020**, *8*, 164. [CrossRef]
27. Crenshaw, K. Demarginalizing the intersection of race and sex: A Black feminist critique of antidiscrimination doctrine, feminist theory, and antiracist politics [1989]. In *Feminist Legal Theories*; Routledge: Oxford, UK, 2018; pp. 57–80.
28. Dadari, I.; Higgins-Steele, A.; Sharkey, A.; Charlet, D.; Shahabuddin, A.; Nandy, R.; Jackson, D. Pro-equity immunization and health systems strengthening strategies in select Gavi-supported countries. *Vaccine* **2021**, *39*, 2434–2444. [CrossRef] [PubMed]
29. MOMENTUM Routine Immunization Transformation and Equity. Addressing Insufficient Operational Funding to Reach Zero-Dose Children and Missed Communities. 2022. Available online: https://usaidmomentum.org/wp-content/uploads/2022/11/Financing-Brief-Final508.pdf (accessed on 28 February 2023).

30. Holroyd, T.A.; Yan, S.D.; Srivastava, V.; Srivastava, A.; Wahl, B.; Morgan, C.; Kumar, S.; Yadav, A.K.; Jennings, M.C. Designing a Pro-Equity HPV Vaccine Delivery Program for Girls Who Have Dropped Out of School: Community Perspectives From Uttar Pradesh, India. *Health Promot. Pract.* **2021**, *23*, 1039–1049. [CrossRef] [PubMed]
31. Reñosa, M.D.; Wachinger, J.; Bärnighausen, K.; Aligato, M.F.; Landicho-Guevarra, J.; Endoma, V.; Landicho, J.; Bravo, T.A.; Demonteverde, M.P.; Guevarra, J.R.; et al. How can human-centered design build a story-based video intervention that addresses vaccine hesitancy and bolsters vaccine confidence in the Philippines? A mixedmethod protocol for project SALUBONG. *BMJ Open* **2021**, *11*, e046814. [CrossRef] [PubMed]
32. UNICEF. *Guidance Note–Coverage and Equity Assessments for Immunization Programs*; UNICEF: New York, NY, USA, 2019.

vaccines

Article

Determinants of Equity in Coverage of Measles-Containing Vaccines in Wales, UK, during the Elimination Era

Malorie Perry [1,2,*], Simon Cottrell [1], Michael B. Gravenor [2] and Lucy Griffiths [2]

1 Vaccine Preventable Disease Programme and Communicable Disease Surveillance Centre, Public Health Wales, 2 Capital Quarter, Tyndall Street, Cardiff CF10 4BZ, UK
2 Population Data Science, Health Data Research UK, Swansea University Medical School, Swansea SA2 8PP, UK
* Correspondence: malorie.perry@wales.nhs.uk

Abstract: In the context of the WHO's measles and rubella elimination targets and European Immunization Agenda 2030, this large cross-sectional study aimed to identify inequalities in measles vaccination coverage in Wales, UK. The vaccination status of individuals aged 2 to 25 years of age, alive and resident in Wales as of 31 August 2021, was ascertained through linkage of the National Community Child Health Database and primary care data. A series of predictor variables were derived from five national datasets and all analysis was carried out in the Secure Anonymised Information Linkage Databank at Swansea University. In these 648,895 individuals, coverage of the first dose of measles-containing vaccine (due at 12–13 months of age) was 97.1%, and coverage of the second dose (due at 3 years and 4 months) in 4 to 25-year-olds was 93.8%. In multivariable analysis, excluding 0.7% with known refusal, the strongest association with being unvaccinated was birth order (families with six or more children) and being born outside of the UK. Living in a deprived area, being eligible for free school meals, a lower level of maternal education, and having a recorded language other than English or Welsh were also associated with lower coverage. Some of these factors may also be associated with refusal. This knowledge can be used to target future interventions and prioritise areas for catch up in a time of limited resource.

Keywords: vaccination; immunisation; socioeconomic factors; measles; MMR; measles, mumps and rubella vaccine

Citation: Perry, M.; Cottrell, S.; Gravenor, M.B.; Griffiths, L. Determinants of Equity in Coverage of Measles-Containing Vaccines in Wales, UK, during the Elimination Era. *Vaccines* **2023**, *11*, 680. https://doi.org/10.3390/vaccines11030680

Academic Editors: Ahmad Reza Hosseinpoor, M. Carolina Danovaro, Devaki Nambiar, Aaron Wallace and Hope Johnson

Received: 11 February 2023
Revised: 12 March 2023
Accepted: 15 March 2023
Published: 17 March 2023

1. Introduction

The 2012 WHO Global Measles and Rubella Strategic Plan outlined the aim to achieve elimination of measles and rubella in at least five of the six WHO regions by the end of 2020 [1]. In 2018, the UK lost its measles elimination status, and since 2020 endemic transmission remains re-established [2]. Although there has not been a confirmed case of rubella in Wales (one of the four nations of the UK) since 2010, there have been regular and sometimes large outbreaks of measles [3–5]. A milestone achievement in the 2012 strategy was to ensure countries have at least a 95% uptake of two routine doses of measles- and rubella-containing vaccine by 2020. In line with these aims, the Wales Measles Elimination Task Group Action Plan 2019–2021 specifically highlighted the importance of increasing measles, mumps and rubella (MMR) vaccination coverage in young people [6].

Public Health Wales has produced COVER (Coverage of Vaccination Evaluated Rapidly) reports for over 30 years [7]. These reports present uptake of all routine childhood immunisations up to 16 years of age. These figures are fed back to vaccination providers to guide service improvements and requirements for catch-up. Data for these reports come from the National Community Child Health Database (NCCHD), which is a population register of all children in Wales registered with the National Health Service (NHS). Primary care doctors and nurses, school nurses and immunisation teams administering vaccines send completed vaccination forms to their health board child health office, detailing vaccinations that have been given. This information is then entered into the health board child health database, with the records extracted on a monthly basis and combined to form the NCCHD. The first dose of MMR is due at 12–13 months of age with a second routine dose at 3 years and 4 months, before school entry. Vaccination status checks are encouraged at routine primary care appointments, on entry to primary and secondary school, and alongside administration of teenage immunisations.

Routine reporting in Wales has shown that national coverage of one dose of MMR reported at two years of age has ranged between 86% and 98% over the last 20 years, whilst coverage of two doses at five years of age has varied between 71% and 94% [7]. Currently coverage is generally high; however, coverage in teenagers is lower and varies by region. Coverage in those aged older than 16 years is not routinely reported due to archiving of NCCHD data around this age. At an ecological level, there is lower vaccine uptake in more deprived areas compared to less deprived areas across all age groups [8]. Equitable access and coverage of vaccinations has been highlighted in the WHO European Immunization Agenda 2030 [9]. Socioeconomic factors are often associated with vaccination coverage for routine childhood immunisations. In developed countries, areas experiencing poverty, families that have a lower income, parents with a lower level of education and those experiencing unemployment are generally associated with lower vaccine uptake [10,11]. In contrast, higher education status [12] and higher income [13] have also been shown to be associated with lower uptake of vaccines in some populations. The association between poverty and low vaccine coverage is also seen in many low and middle income countries [14]. Vaccination coverage also appears to be lower in children resident in large or single parent households [11,15,16]. Demographic factors such as ethnicity, age of mother, country of birth, religion and gender have also been shown to be predictors of vaccination status [14,17–20].

Large ecological studies looking at routine childhood immunisations are still rare, and specific reasons for low uptake in Wales have not been previously explored. In this study we used data linkage of national datasets to identify factors associated with lower coverage of measles-containing vaccine, with the aim that this knowledge can be used to investigate what the barriers are for uptake of vaccination, develop interventions and prioritise areas for catch-up in a time of limited resources.

2. Materials and Methods

Analyses were completed within the Secure Anonymised Information Linkage (SAIL) Databank held at Swansea University [21]. A cohort of individuals aged 2 to 25 years of age, alive and resident in Wales as of 31 August 2021, was created using the Welsh Demographic Service Dataset. Individuals who do not have a record in the NCCHD or were registered to a GP that does not submit data to SAIL were excluded. Approximately 80% of GP practices in Wales submit data to SAIL [22].

Measles vaccination status was assigned using an extract from the NCCHD, supplemented by Read coded vaccination status data from primary care GPs. MMR, measles and rubella (MR) and single antigen measles vaccination were all considered valid vaccinations in this analysis. In line with UK guidance, the first dose of vaccine had to have been given at 12 months of age or later with the second dose given at least one month after the first at 15 months of age or later [23].

A series of independent variables were identified to test for association with vaccination coverage. Gender, age as of 31 August 2021, month of birth, mothers' age at birth, health board of residence, and age first moved to Wales were taken from the Welsh Demographic Service Dataset. Urban/rural classification and deprivation quintile of residence were derived as described previously [24]. Broad ethnic group was derived from the Office for National Statistics 2011 census, with information taken from the Education Wales Schools and Pupils Dataset or primary care GP record, if census data were unavailable. Total number of primary care visits in the 1 September 2020 to 31 August 2021 year and age first registered with a primary care GP in Wales were calculated using data from primary care GPs, and flags were derived for learning disability, diagnosed sight loss and hearing loss based on published primary care Read code sets [25,26]. Mothers' unique identifier, birth order, maternal smoker flag and premature status (born before 37 weeks' gestation) were taken from the NCCHD. A flag for ever being eligible for free school meals, attendance at a special school or ever being excluded from school was taken from the Education Wales Schools and Pupils Dataset. Information on mothers' highest qualification was taken from the 2011 census. Religion was as recorded in census data, otherwise as recorded in data from primary care GPs. Where there were contradicting values, the most recent record was kept. Mothers' religion was used as default; otherwise, where this was missing, the child's recorded religion was used. Country of birth (COB) was derived from the Office for National Statistics Annual District Birth Extract. If a child was born in Wales they appear in this data; otherwise, this information was taken from the 2011 census or data from primary care GPs. Where a child's COB was unknown, mother's COB was used. Mother and child's recorded language was taken from census data, and where this was unavailable, language data from primary care GPs was used. If this information was not recorded in either dataset but they were born in Wales it was assumed English/Welsh was a primary language. A Charlson Comorbidity Index score was created using data from primary care GPs based on published Read code sets [27]. Previous vaccinations (three doses of pertussis-containing vaccine, one of pneumococcal vaccine and two of rotavirus vaccine) as outlined in the UK schedule were derived using the same methods used for measles-containing vaccine.

The odds of being vaccinated with one and two doses of measles-containing vaccine were calculated, with independent variables considered significant at the 0.05 level. In a multivariable analysis of those aged 4 to 25 years, records with missing information were dropped. The maternal smoker flag was dropped due to a high proportion of missing data. Mothers' recorded language and age first moved to Wales were excluded from the multivariable model due to co-linearity with child's recorded language and age first registered with a Wales GP, respectively. The final model was constructed stepwise in order of strength of association as indicated by the univariable analysis; variables which did not improve the Akaike Information Criterion score were dropped.

Unvaccinated individuals with a vaccine refusal Read code (68NY., 68NB., 68NP., 68NR., 68Nb., 68Na., 8I3x., 68N6., 68NM.) on their GP record were excluded from the equality analysis and described separately.

3. Results

3.1. Coverage of Measles-Containing Vaccine in the Study Population

There were 795,734 individuals aged 2 to 25 years of age, alive and resident in Wales as of 31 August 2021. Of these, 35,254 did not have a record in the NCCHD and a further 111,585 were not registered with a GP who submits data to the SAIL Databank. Using NCCHD data only, coverage of one dose of measles-containing vaccine in these 648,895 remaining individuals was 96.2% and coverage of two doses in those aged 4 to 25 years of age was 92.0%. After reconciling with GP data, coverage increased to 97.1% for one dose and 93.8% for two doses (Figure 1). Of those who were vaccinated, 1620 had received measles-containing vaccines other than MMR for their first dose and 2781 had received measles-containing vaccines other than MMR for their second dose. The majority of non-MMR measles vaccines were given to those aged 15 to 21 years (with the highest proportion received by 20-year-olds, 1.3%). The proportion of all measles vaccines received that were non-MMR was under 0.5% in all other age groups.

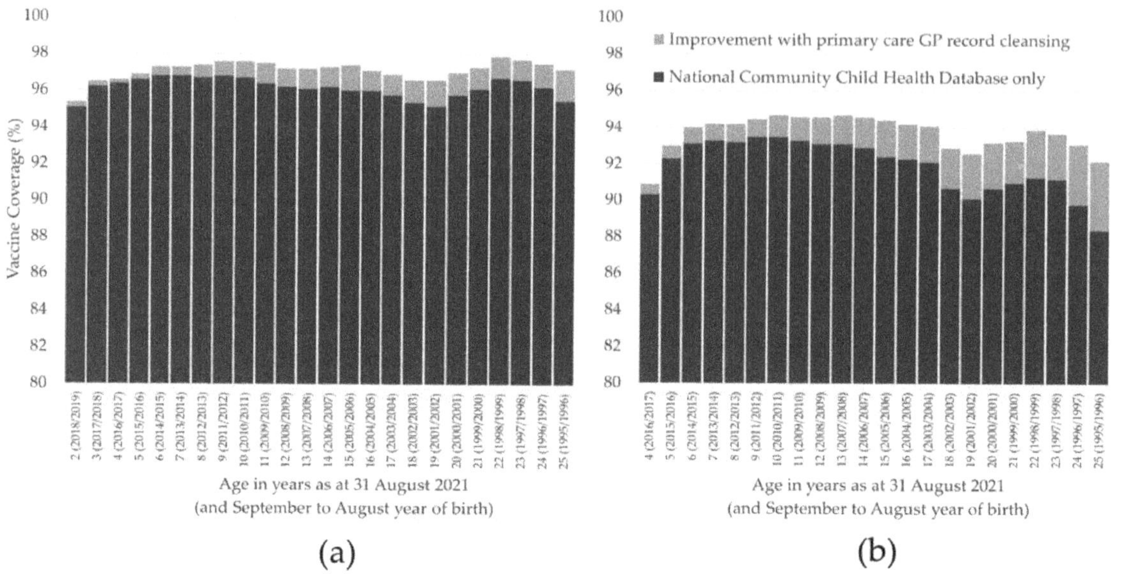

Figure 1. Coverage of one (**a**) and two (**b**) doses of measles-containing vaccine in those aged 2 to 25 years of age, alive and resident in Wales as of 31 August 2021. The improvement in coverage from reconciling the National Community Child Health Database and primary care GP data is also shown.

3.2. Determinants of Measles Vaccination Coverage

After exclusion of 4688 individuals with vaccine refusal codes, there were 644,207 individuals aged 2 to 25 years in the equity study population. In a univariable analyses, month of birth was the only variable that was not significantly associated with vaccination uptake of either dose. Having had previous vaccinations was strongly associated with having had at least one dose of measles-containing vaccine; OR 177.45 (95% CI 162.99–193.60) for pneumococcal vaccine, OR 100.25 (95% CI 96.52–104.14) for three doses of pertussis vaccine and OR 27.60 (95% CI 25.82–29.50) for two doses of rotavirus vaccine.

Age first registered with a primary care GP in Wales was most strongly associated with vaccine coverage, with those first registering at secondary school age (12 to 16 years of age) least likely to be recorded as vaccinated, compared to those born in Wales. Those born outside of the UK were less likely to be vaccinated, OR 0.07 (95% CI 0.06–0.07) for one dose. For groups with at least 100 persons, coverage of one dose was under 80% in those born in Romania, Bulgaria, Syria, Lithuania, Turkey, Slovakia, Czech Republic, Nigeria, Zimbabwe, Iraq, South Africa and Asia (not otherwise specified). Coverage was also higher in those who had English or Welsh recorded as a language, OR 8.45 (95% CI 7.88–9.06) for one dose. For groups with at least 100 persons, coverage of one dose was under 80% in those recorded as speaking Bulgarian, Romanian, Lithuanian, Russian, Hungarian, Slovak, Italian and Spanish. There was also association with ethnicity and coverage, with those who were in a combined Black, Asian, Mixed or other ethnic group having lower coverage than those in the combined White ethnic group. In the univariable analysis those with a recorded religion of Buddhism, Islam, Pagan or other religions were less likely to be vaccinated than those who stated they had no religion.

Females were more likely to be vaccinated than males, OR 1.09 (95% CI 1.05–1.12) for one dose. Mothers who were older (36 years and over) and younger (under 17) when giving birth were less likely to have children who were vaccinated, as well as those born in to families with more children (OR 0.16 95% CI 0.14–0.18 if sixth or greater compared to first born). There was variation by health board and deprivation quintile of residence, with vaccination less likely in more deprived areas. Coverage was also lower in urban areas, compared to rural areas, OR 0.74 (95% CI 0.71–0.77) for one dose. Those who have ever been eligible for free school meals were less likely to be vaccinated, OR 0.86 (95% CI 0.82–0.89) as well as those who were born to mothers who smoked during pregnancy (OR 0.76 95% CI 0.69–0.84) and mothers who had no qualifications compared to those with at least GCSE qualifications. People were less likely to be vaccinated with two doses if they had a school exclusion record (OR 0.76 95% CI 0.72–0.80), although this association was not seen with one dose. This association was stronger for those with a permanent exclusion record compared to a temporary exclusion record.

There was no association with vaccination and premature birth for dose one but coverage of two doses was significantly lower, OR 0.92 (95% CI 0.87–0.97). Those who consulted with their GP at least once between 1 September 2020 and 31 August 2021 were more likely to be vaccinated, and coverage was significantly higher in those with recorded comorbidities. Those with chronic pulmonary disease, renal disease and uncomplicated diabetes were significantly more likely to be vaccinated, and those with liver disease, peptic ulcer and rheumatic disease were significantly less likely to be vaccinated. Coverage of at least one dose in those with hearing loss or sight loss was higher than the rest of the study population; coverage of two doses in those with sight loss was not significantly different. Coverage of two doses in those with a learning disability was lower than the general population, OR 0.62 (95% CI 0.55–0.71), although there was no difference for one dose. Those who attend, or have attended, a special school had lower coverage of one and two doses.

The univariable analyses including the full cohort can be found in Supplementary Table S1.

The variables included in the final model are presented in Table 1. The cohort was restricted to those aged 4 to 25 years without missing information across all variables, producing a study population of 419,405. This restricted cohort had higher vaccine coverage overall, and led to some notably different estimates in the univariable analyses. Although having a comorbidity score of one was associated with higher vaccination coverage compared to those with no comorbidities, those with a score of three or more were less likely to be vaccinated in the restricted cohort. Also, younger mothers (aged under 17) in the restricted cohort were more likely to have vaccinated children compared to the univariable analysis in the full cohort, which showed they were less likely.

In the multivariable analysis, after controlling for other factors, the strongest association with vaccination uptake was birth order (OR 0.21 95% CI 0.17–0.26 for one dose if sixth or greater compared to first born) and being born outside of the UK (OR 0.21 95% CI 0.18–0.25 for one dose). Living in a more deprived area of residence was still associated with lower coverage but the association was not as strong. The association with recorded language, free school meal eligibility and mothers' highest qualification was also slightly reduced. Having a comorbidity score of 3 or more was no longer significant. However, the biggest difference was seen in ethnicity, where those in the combined Asian ethnic group were more likely to be vaccinated with at least one and two doses after controlling for other factors (OR 1.58 (95% CI 1.27–1.97) for at least one dose), and those in the combined Black ethnic group were no longer significantly less likely to be vaccinated. Differences were also seen in those who had recorded religion of Islam, who were more likely to be vaccinated with one and two doses after controlling for other factors (OR 1.45 (95% CI 1.13–1.87) for at least one dose).

Table 1. Uptake of one or two doses of measles-containing vaccine in those aged 4 to 25 years alive and resident in Wales as of 31 August 2021, without a vaccine refusal code, by individual characteristics. Odds Ratios and 95% Confidence Intervals are also presented. Analysis restricted to those with complete information across all variables.

Characteristic	Category	One Dose of Measles-Containing Vaccine (4–25 Year Olds)					Two Doses of Measles-Containing Vaccine (4–25 Year Olds)				
		Vaccinated (n)	Population (n)	Uptake (%)	OR (95% CI)	aOR (95% CI)	Vaccinated (n)	Population (n)	Uptake (%)	OR (95% CI)	aOR (95% CI)
Gender	Male	213,518	215,626	99.0	Baseline	Baseline	208,567	215,626	96.7	Baseline	Baseline
	Female	202,068	203,779	99.2	1.17 (1.09–1.24)	1.11 (1.03–1.18)	197,973	203,779	97.2	1.15 (1.11–1.20)	1.11 (1.07–1.15)
Age cohort	Primary school (4–11)	132,916	133,857	99.3	Baseline	Baseline	130,258	133,857	97.3	Baseline	Baseline
	Secondary school (12–16)	109,335	110,028	99.4	1.12 (1.01–1.23)	1.38 (1.24–1.52)	107,809	110,028	98.0	1.34 (1.27–1.42)	1.60 (1.51–1.69)
	College (17–18)	40,779	41,175	99.0	0.73 (0.65–0.82)	0.90 (0.80–1.02)	39,946	41,175	97.0	0.90 (0.84–0.96)	1.08 (1.01–1.16)
	University (19–21)	54,384	55,079	98.7	0.55 (0.50–0.61)	0.70 (0.63–0.78)	52,902	55,079	96.0	0.67 (0.64–0.71)	0.83 (0.78–0.88)
	Young adults (22–25)	78,172	79,266	98.6	0.51 (0.46–0.55)	0.66 (0.60–0.73)	75,625	79,266	95.4	0.57 (0.55–0.60)	0.73 (0.69–0.77)
Health board of residence	HB1	81,805	82,299	99.4	Baseline	Baseline	80,763	82,299	98.1	Baseline	Baseline
	HB2	57,912	58,599	98.8	0.51 (0.45–0.57)	0.51 (0.45–0.57)	56,282	58,599	96.0	0.46 (0.43–0.49)	0.46 (0.43–0.49)
	HB3	43,403	44,002	98.6	0.44 (0.39–0.49)	0.44 (0.39–0.49)	42,355	44,002	96.3	0.49 (0.46–0.52)	0.47 (0.44–0.50)
	HB4	6801	6902	98.5	0.41 (0.33–0.51)	0.38 (0.31–0.48)	6636	6902	96.1	0.47 (0.42–0.54)	0.45 (0.39–0.51)
	HB5	76,485	77,197	99.1	0.65 (0.58–0.73)	0.62 (0.55–0.69)	74,573	77,197	96.6	0.54 (0.51–0.58)	0.54 (0.51–0.58)
	HB6	79,422	80,048	99.2	0.77 (0.68–0.86)	0.76 (0.68–0.86)	77,768	80,048	97.2	0.65 (0.61–0.69)	0.66 (0.62–0.71)
	HB7	69,758	70,358	99.1	0.70 (0.62–0.79)	0.80 (0.71–0.91)	68,163	70,358	96.9	0.59 (0.55–0.63)	0.64 (0.60–0.68)
Deprivation quintile of residence	Most deprived	97,159	98,266	98.9	Baseline	Baseline	94,183	98,266	95.8	Baseline	Baseline
	2	87,377	88,209	99.1	1.20 (1.09–1.31)	1.06 (0.97–1.17)	85,432	88,209	96.9	1.33 (1.27–1.40)	1.15 (1.09–1.21)
	3	75,674	76,343	99.1	1.29 (1.17–1.42)	1.10 (1.00–1.23)	74,185	76,343	97.2	1.49 (1.41–1.57)	1.16 (1.10–1.23)
	4	72,632	73,239	99.2	1.36 (1.23–1.51)	1.11 (0.99–1.23)	71,339	73,239	97.4	1.63 (1.54–1.72)	1.18 (1.11–1.26)
	Least deprived	82,744	83,348	99.3	1.56 (1.41–1.73)	1.13 (1.01–1.26)	81,401	83,348	97.7	1.81 (1.72–1.91)	1.22 (1.15–1.30)
Ethnic group	White	392,908	396,329	99.1	Baseline	Baseline	384,621	396,329	97.0	Baseline	Baseline
	Other	1817	1868	97.3	0.31 (0.24–0.42)	1.08 (0.77–1.54)	1745	1868	**93.4**	0.43 (0.36–0.52)	1.08 (0.86–1.36)
	Asian	9762	9900	98.6	0.62 (0.52–0.73)	1.58 (1.27–1.97)	9473	9900	95.7	0.68 (0.61–0.75)	1.31 (1.14–1.50)
	Mixed	9201	9338	98.5	0.58 (0.49–0.70)	0.76 (0.64–0.92)	8920	9338	95.5	0.65 (0.59–0.72)	0.78 (0.71–0.87)
	Black	1898	1970	96.3	0.23 (0.18–0.29)	0.99 (0.75–1.33)	1781	1970	**90.4**	0.29 (0.25–0.33)	0.92 (0.77–1.11)
Comorbidity score	0	328,434	331,538	99.1	Baseline	Baseline	32,1268	331,538	96.9	Baseline	Baseline
	1	79,664	80,288	99.2	1.21 (1.11–1.32)	1.17 (1.07–1.28)	77,985	80,288	97.1	1.08 (1.03–1.13)	1.10 (1.05–1.16)
	2	5353	5404	99.1	0.99 (0.76–1.33)	1.03 (0.78–1.39)	5209	5404	96.4	0.85 (0.74–0.99)	0.95 (0.82–1.10)
	3+	2135	2175	98.2	0.50 (0.37–0.70)	0.58 (0.42–0.81)	2078	2175	95.5	0.68 (0.56–0.85)	0.87 (0.71–1.09)
Age first registered with primary care GP in Wales	At birth	358,121	360,620	99.3	Baseline	Baseline	351,458	360,620	97.5	Baseline	Baseline
	Young child (2–3)	33,881	34,335	98.7	0.52 (0.47–0.58)	0.70 (0.63–0.78)	32,798	34,335	95.5	0.56 (0.53–0.59)	0.69 (0.65–0.73)
	Primary school (4–11)	11,535	12,120	95.2	0.14 (0.13–0.15)	0.31 (0.27–0.35)	10,663	12,120	**88.0**	0.19 (0.18–0.20)	0.36 (0.33–0.39)
	Secondary school (12–16)	1609	1761	**91.4**	0.07 (0.06–0.09)	0.16 (0.13–0.20)	1472	1761	**83.6**	0.13 (0.12–0.15)	0.25 (0.22–0.29)
	College (17–18)	672	691	97.3	0.25 (0.16–0.40)	0.37 (0.24–0.61)	645	691	**93.3**	0.37 (0.27–0.50)	0.53 (0.39–0.73)
	University (19–21)	5266	5330	98.8	0.57 (0.45–0.74)	0.70 (0.54–0.91)	5133	5330	96.3	0.68 (0.59–0.79)	0.78 (0.68–0.91)
	Young adult (22–25)	4502	4548	99.0	0.68 (0.52–0.93)	0.84 (0.63–1.15)	4371	4548	96.1	0.64 (0.55–0.75)	0.77 (0.66–0.90)

Table 1. *Cont.*

Characteristic	Category	One Dose of Measles-Containing Vaccine (4–25 Year Olds)					Two Doses of Measles-Containing Vaccine (4–25 Year Olds)				
		Vaccinated (n)	Population (n)	Uptake (%)	OR (95% CI)	aOR (95% CI)	Vaccinated (n)	Population (n)	Uptake (%)	OR (95% CI)	aOR (95% CI)
Mother's age at delivery	Under 17	2987	3002	99.5	1.69 (1.05–2.95)	1.91 (1.18–3.37)	2905	3002	96.8	0.90 (0.74–1.11)	0.97 (0.79–1.20)
	17–18	14,508	14,610	99.3	1.21 (0.99–1.49)	1.30 (1.05–1.62)	14,143	14,610	96.8	0.91 (0.83–1.01)	0.92 (0.83–1.02)
	19–20	26,875	27,051	99.3	1.30 (1.11–1.53)	1.33 (1.13–1.58)	26,293	27,051	97.2	1.04 (0.97–1.13)	1.03 (0.95–1.13)
	21–25	95,435	96,284	99.1	0.95 (0.87–1.05)	1.02 (0.93–1.12)	93,125	96,284	96.7	0.89 (0.85–0.93)	0.92 (0.88–0.97)
	26–30	125,482	126,548	99.2	Baseline	Baseline	122,849	126,548	97.1	Baseline	Baseline
	31–35	102,444	103,414	99.1	0.90 (0.82–0.98)	0.88 (0.80–0.96)	100,419	103,414	97.1	1.01 (0.96–1.06)	0.99 (0.94–1.04)
	36–40	41,039	41,555	98.8	0.68 (0.61–0.75)	0.70 (0.63–0.78)	40,176	41,555	96.7	0.88 (0.82–0.93)	0.91 (0.85–0.97)
	Over 40	6816	6941	98.2	0.46 (0.39–0.56)	0.60 (0.49–0.73)	6630	6941	95.5	0.64 (0.57–0.72)	0.79 (0.70–0.90)
Birth order	First born	160,101	160,931	99.5	Baseline	Baseline	157,847	160,931	98.1	Baseline	Baseline
	Second born	182,014	183,880	99.0	0.51 (0.47–0.55)	0.74 (0.68–0.81)	177,856	183,880	96.7	0.58 (0.55–0.60)	0.70 (0.66–0.73)
	Third born	48,304	48,845	98.9	0.46 (0.42–0.52)	0.54 (0.49–0.61)	46,895	48,845	96.0	0.47 (0.44–0.50)	0.50 (0.47–0.53)
	Forth born	16,425	16,726	98.2	0.28 (0.25–0.32)	0.37 (0.32–0.43)	15,713	16,726	**93.9**	0.30 (0.28–0.33)	0.35 (0.33–0.38)
	Fifth born	5506	5658	97.3	0.19 (0.16–0.22)	0.27 (0.23–0.33)	5209	5658	**92.1**	0.23 (0.20–0.25)	0.29 (0.26–0.32)
	Sixth or more	3236	3365	96.2	0.13 (0.11–0.16)	0.21 (0.17–0.26)	3020	3365	**89.7**	0.17 (0.15–0.19)	0.23 (0.20–0.26)
Total primary care GP visits 1 September 2020 to 31 August 2021	None	38,114	38,843	98.1	Baseline	Baseline	36,931	38,843	95.1	Baseline	Baseline
	1–2	114,209	115,168	99.2	2.28 (2.07–2.51)	2.18 (1.97–2.41)	111,863	115,168	97.1	1.75 (1.65–1.86)	1.72 (1.62–1.83)
	3–4	72,737	73,290	99.2	2.52 (2.25–2.81)	2.53 (2.25–2.84)	71,298	73,290	97.3	1.85 (1.74–1.98)	1.92 (1.80–2.05)
	5–9	90,044	90,745	99.2	2.46 (2.21–2.73)	2.52 (2.26–2.81)	88,290	90,745	97.3	1.86 (1.75–1.98)	1.98 (1.86–2.11)
	10–14	40,422	40,743	99.2	2.41 (2.11–2.75)	2.64 (2.30–3.04)	39,565	40,743	97.1	1.74 (1.62–1.87)	1.97 (1.82–2.13)
	15–19	23,819	23,992	99.3	2.63 (2.24–3.12)	3.06 (2.57–3.65)	23,298	23,992	97.1	1.74 (1.59–1.90)	2.09 (1.91–2.30)
	20–24	13,989	14,122	99.1	2.01 (1.68–2.43)	2.43 (2.01–2.97)	13,632	14,122	96.5	1.44 (1.30–1.60)	1.82 (1.64–2.03)
	25–49	19,737	19,952	98.9	1.76 (1.51–2.05)	2.31 (1.96–2.74)	19,222	19,952	96.3	1.36 (1.25–1.49)	1.88 (1.71–2.07)
	50+	2515	2550	98.6	1.37 (0.99–1.97)	2.12 (1.51–3.09)	2441	2550	95.7	1.16 (0.96–1.42)	1.90 (1.55–2.35)
Recorded language English or Welsh	No	5525	5863	**94.2**	Baseline	Baseline	5170	5863	**88.2**	Baseline	Baseline
	Yes	410,061	413,542	99.2	7.21 (6.41–8.07)	1.71 (1.44–2.03)	401,370	413,542	97.1	4.42 (4.07–4.79)	1.33 (1.18–1.49)
Ever eligible for free school meals	No	296,942	299,262	99.2	Baseline	Baseline	291,750	299,262	97.5	Baseline	Baseline
	Yes	118,644	120,143	98.8	0.62 (0.58–0.66)	0.73 (0.68–0.79)	114,790	120,143	95.5	0.55 (0.53–0.57)	0.73 (0.70–0.76)
Ever attended a special school	No	410,837	414,573	99.1	Baseline	Baseline	402,105	414,573	97.0	Baseline	Baseline
	Yes	4749	4832	98.3	0.52 (0.42–0.65)	0.67 (0.53–0.85)	4435	4832	91.8	0.35 (0.31–0.38)	0.43 (0.39–0.48)
Mother's highest qualification	None	59,223	60,034	98.6	Baseline	Baseline	57,107	60,034	95.1	Baseline	Baseline
	A-levels	63,435	63,907	99.3	1.84 (1.64–2.06)	1.12 (0.99–1.27)	62,375	63,907	97.6	2.09 (1.96–2.22)	1.25 (1.17–1.34)
	GCSE/O-Level high grades	85,168	85,779	99.3	1.91 (1.72–2.12)	1.25 (1.12–1.40)	83,527	85,779	97.4	1.90 (1.80–2.01)	1.25 (1.17–1.32)
	GCSE/O-Level any grades	74,792	75,459	99.1	1.54 (1.39–1.70)	1.10 (0.99–1.22)	72,997	75,459	96.7	1.52 (1.44–1.61)	1.11 (1.04–1.17)
	Degree	120,598	121,585	99.2	1.67 (1.52–1.84)	1.10 (0.98–1.23)	118,564	121,585	97.5	2.01 (1.91–2.12)	1.18 (1.11–1.26)
	Apprenticeship	2965	2999	98.9	1.19 (0.86–1.72)	0.83 (0.59–1.20)	2910	2999	97.0	1.68 (1.36–2.09)	1.12 (0.91–1.40)
	Other	9405	9642	97.5	0.54 (0.47–0.63)	0.97 (0.82–1.16)	9060	9642	**94.0**	0.80 (0.73–0.88)	1.06 (0.95–1.17)

Table 1. *Cont.*

Characteristic	Category	One Dose of Measles-Containing Vaccine (4–25 Year Olds)					Two Doses of Measles-Containing Vaccine (4–25 Year Olds)				
		Vaccinated (n)	**Population (n)**	**Uptake (%)**	**OR (95% CI)**	**aOR (95% CI)**	**Vaccinated (n)**	**Population (n)**	**Uptake (%)**	**OR (95% CI)**	**aOR (95% CI)**
Recorded religion	No religion	187,177	188,816	99.1	Baseline	Baseline	18,2806	188,816	96.8	Baseline	Baseline
	Christianity	214,191	216,089	99.1	0.99 (0.92–1.06)	1.11 (1.03–1.19)	209,973	216,089	97.2	1.13 (1.09–1.17)	1.09 (1.05–1.13)
	Buddhism	1093	1146	95.4	0.18 (0.14–0.24)	0.40 (0.29–0.56)	1044	1146	**91.1**	0.34 (0.28–0.42)	0.56 (0.45–0.71)
	Islam	9219	9342	98.7	0.66 (0.55–0.79)	1.45 (1.13–1.87)	8961	9342	95.9	0.77 (0.70–0.86)	1.42 (1.23–1.66)
	Other religions	2344	2412	97.2	0.30 (0.24–0.39)	0.38 (0.30–0.50)	2251	2412	**93.3**	0.46 (0.39–0.54)	0.51 (0.43–0.60)
	Paganism	*	*	*	0.22 (0.15–0.32)	0.32 (0.22–0.48)	729	797	**91.5**	0.35 (0.28–0.46)	0.43 (0.33–0.56)
	Hinduism	*	*	*	1.00 (0.51–2.33)	1.70 (0.83–4.08)	776	803	96.6	0.94 (0.66–1.42)	1.34 (0.90–2.07)
UK Born	Yes	410,890	414,182	99.2	Baseline	Baseline	40,2474	414,182	97.2	Baseline	Baseline
	No	4696	5223	**89.9**	0.07 (0.06–0.08)	0.21 (0.18–0.25)	4066	5223	**77.8**	0.10 (0.10–0.11)	0.23 (0.21–0.26)

* Data suppressed to comply with statistical disclosure policy; Groups with uptake under 95% are indicated with bold text.

3.3. Individuals Refusing Measles Vaccination

A total of 4688 individuals aged 2 to 25 years had a vaccine refusal code on their GP record (0.7% of the full study population). Of these, 1814 had received one dose of measles-containing vaccine but not two. The proportion of recorded refusals were highest in those aged 2 and 3 years (over 1.0%).

In a univariable analysis comparing individuals who had received one dose of measles-containing vaccine, with those who had a vaccine refusal code; those resident in urban areas were more likely to be vaccinated than have a refusal code compared to those resident in rural areas (OR 1.51 95% CI 1.40–1.63). Additionally, those with a recorded language of English or Welsh were more likely to be vaccinated (OR 1.53 95% CI 1.27–1.81), as well as those in less deprived areas compared to more deprived areas (OR 1.19 95% CI 1.06–1.35). Children born to mothers who were over 30 years of age were less likely to be vaccinated than have a refusal code, compared to those aged 26–30 years (OR 0.54 95% CI 0.46–0.62 for mothers aged over 40), as well as those with more siblings (OR 0.31 95% CI 0.24–0.40 if sixth or greater compared to first born) and those eligible for free school meals (OR 0.83 95% CI 0.76–0.91). Having a recorded religion of Buddhism (OR 0.27 95% CI 0.17–0.44) or Paganism (OR suppressed due to small numbers) was associated with being less likely to be vaccinated than have a refusal code, compared to those with no religion, whereas having a recorded religion of Christian was associated with being more likely to be vaccinated (OR 1.22 95% CI 1.11–1.34). Those in the combined Asian ethnic group were more likely to be vaccinated compared to those in the combined White ethnic group (OR 2.21 95% CI 1.57–3.24), whereas those in the combined Black ethnic group (OR 0.65 95% CI 0.45–0.98) or combined Mixed ethnic group (OR 0.70 95% CI 0.57–0.87) were less likely to be vaccinated than have a refusal code.

4. Discussion

Measles vaccination uptake in this cohort of children and young adults in Wales is reassuringly high, with coverage of one dose over 95% in all NHS-registered children aged 2 to 25 years. However, potential remains for outbreaks of measles where unvaccinated individuals are clustered. All routine childhood vaccinations in Wales should be recorded in the child health system until 16 years of age to manage appointment call and re-call and enable accurate reporting. However, we have seen that administrative records are not always correct, and reconciling multiple data systems may help improve accuracy. Despite high coverage, minor improvements in some age groups may be the difference between reaching the 95% coverage target or not. Although the oldest individuals in this analysis would have been scheduled for vaccination in the latter years of the decline in MMR uptake seen following the Wakefield scandal, coverage appears high. However, the young adults who were young children at the time of the negative publicity might explain some of the significantly reduced odds of vaccination in those aged 19 years and older. This analysis may also exclude a number of individuals who are not registered with the NHS, and therefore not included in the datasets used to produce these figures.

MMR coverage is frequently reported as a measure of the proportion of the population protected from measles infection. These analyses have identified that over 4000 single (or duel MR) antigen measles doses had been received by those in the study cohort. However, the receipt of non-MMR vaccines has decreased in younger age groups. Some of these records may be miscoded and validation of the type of vaccination received would be necessary to have accurate records of which viruses individuals are protected against.

A small proportion of the study population (0.7%) had a GP Read code indicating measles vaccine refusal. A higher proportion of those in younger age groups had a refusal code, which could be an indication of a recent increase in vaccine hesitancy. However, this trend could also be due to improvement in coding over time. Although this study tries to focus on factors associated with low coverage in those who have not actively refused vaccination, there is suggestion of variation in refusal by different characteristics, some of which, such as residing in rural areas, appear to be associated with refusal but not other reasons for being unvaccinated. Monitoring refusals would be beneficial to highlight any concerns or mistrust as early as possible [28]. The USA has seen a recent increase in exemptions for MMR vaccine due to religious, philosophical or personal reasons, which may be contributing to a resurgence in cases [29].

Excluding those with known refusal, we have seen that inequitable coverage is particularly prevalent in households with more children and for those born outside of the UK. Living in a deprived area, being eligible for free school meals, lower level of maternal education, and having a recorded language other than English or Welsh were also associated with lower coverage. These factors are similar to those mentioned in previously published literature [10,12,15,30]. Lower coverage persists in deprived urban areas, and factors relating to deprivation are complex and hard to separate out.

Evidence from this study is useful to develop tailored interventions; for example, community health care visits [31], which in this case could be prioritised for large households with multiple unvaccinated children, or joint scheduling for siblings that require catch-up. Having had previous vaccines meant there was a higher chance of having had measles-containing vaccine, suggesting it may be efficient for catch-up campaigns to target more than one vaccine programme. Improving accessibility of resources and using tailored public health messaging may reduce inequities [32]. In addition, using the WHO Tailoring Immunisation Programmes approach can help us understand specific barriers in communities identified as having lower coverage [33,34].

A recent review has suggested migrants are half as likely to be vaccinated compared to non-migrants [35]. Challenges specifically relating to migrants who have transited through a number of countries, and refugees, include lack of information on vaccination status at arrival, fear of registration with medical authorities and lack of coordination between public health authorities of neighbouring countries [36]. It is likely that recording of immunisations in those who were on vaccination schedules different to the UK is difficult and parents often do not have evidence of their child's previous vaccinations, which makes entering dates into the system, and scheduling further doses, challenging. UK guidance indicates restarting a vaccine course if vaccination history is uncertain [37]. Tailoring immunisation services to ensure there are no language barriers when carrying out vaccination status checks and ensuring flexible systems for recording immunisations from overseas could be beneficial. Low vaccination coverage in Eastern European communities has been linked to measles outbreaks in the UK, with language, literacy and trust of health care providers identified as potential barriers [38]. Building trusting relationships with minority groups such as Gypsies, Travellers and Roma may also improve utilisation of health care services including uptake of vaccination [39].

There are limitations to this study. Some individuals will not be registered with NHS health services, and those who do not have a NCCHD record were excluded, which will affect those who first resided in Wales after 16 years of age. Additionally, some vaccinations recorded in primary care GP data, but not on the NCCHD record, for older ages may be due to catch-up immunisations given more recently. There is the possibility of 'ghost records' for those who have moved away and not notified the system. The multivariable analysis was restricted to those without missing information, which disproportionately affected some groups. This analysis would exclude those families who moved to Wales since 2011 when the census took place, as variables such as mothers' highest education level were derived from census data only. The higher vaccine coverage and reduction in effects that were seen in the multivariable analysis may therefore be due to this restricted cohort only including those who have been settled in Wales for a longer time period. It is challenging to draw conclusions around those factors, which showed different associations in the univariable analyses when using the full and restricted study population, including comorbidities and mothers' age. Additionally, some data may not reflect the current status of an individual as it may be out of date. This includes information taken from the 2011 census and information on language, as even if a language other than English or Welsh is recorded, a person could be bilingual or have sufficient understanding of English or Welsh to access services and make an informed decision around vaccination. However, this analysis is still a useful indicator to highlight areas at risk of outbreaks and where coverage could be improved. This is a large population study that has been able to provide new evidence on a number of characteristics associated with measles vaccination coverage in Wales.

Reducing inequalities in vaccination coverage remains key for preventing measles outbreaks and reaching the WHO measles elimination targets [1]. Disruption to routine vaccine schedules during the COVID-19 pandemic may have exacerbated the inequalities reported here, making the need for catch-up activities even more pressing [40]. Reported measles cases in Europe decreased from mid-2020 [41], but now that travel restrictions have been fully lifted, the likelihood of a resurgence in cases is high and identifying/reducing inequalities in vaccine coverage should remain a priority.

Supplementary Materials: The following supporting information can be downloaded at: https://www.mdpi.com/article/10.3390/vaccines11030680/s1, Table S1: Uptake of one or two doses of measles-containing vaccine in those aged 4 to 25 years alive and resident in Wales as of 31 August 2021, without a vaccine refusal code, by individual characteristics. Univariable Odds Ratios and 95% Confidence Intervals are also presented. Groups with uptake under 95% are indicated with bold text. Analysis is presented for the whole study cohort.

Author Contributions: Conceptualization, M.P., S.C., M.B.G. and L.G.; methodology, M.P.; formal analysis, M.P.; data curation, M.P.; writing—original draft preparation, M.P.; writing—review and editing, M.P., S.C., M.B.G. and L.G.; visualization, M.P.; supervision, S.C., M.B.G. and L.G.; project administration, M.P. and S.C. All authors have read and agreed to the published version of the manuscript.

Funding: This research received no external funding.

Institutional Review Board Statement: Not applicable.

Informed Consent Statement: Not applicable.

Data Availability Statement: The data used in this study is available from the SAIL Databank at Swansea University, Swansea, UK, which is part of the national e-health records research infrastructure for Wales. All proposals to use SAIL data are subject to review by an independent Information Governance Review Panel (IGRP). Before any data can be accessed, approval must be given by the IGRP. The IGRP gives careful consideration to each project to ensure proper and appropriate use of SAIL data. When access has been approved, it is gained through a privacy-protecting safe haven and remote access system referred to as the SAIL Gateway. SAIL has established an application process to be followed by anyone who would like to access data via SAIL at: https://saildatabank.com/data/apply-to-work-with-the-data/ (accessed on 16 March 2023).

Acknowledgments: This work was led by M.P. as part of her PhD at Swansea University. The authors acknowledge members of the SAIL Databank who have made the data available for use in this project as well as all the immunisation teams across Wales who facilitate the recording and data quality of the vaccination data in the Wales Children and Young Persons Integrated System.

Conflicts of Interest: The authors declare no conflict of interest.

References

1. World Health Organization. Global Measles and Rubella Strategic Plan 2012-2020, World Health Organization: Switzerland, 2012. Available online: https://www.who.int/publications/i/item/9789241503396 (accessed on 6 February 2023).
2. UK Health Security Agency. Guidance: UK Measles and Rubella Elimination Indicators and Status. UK Health Security Agency, 2022. Available online: https://www.gov.uk/government/publications/measles-and-rubella-elimination-uk/uk-measles-and-rubella-elimination (accessed on 6 February 2023).
3. Currie, J.; Davies, L.; McCarthy, J.; Perry, M.; Moore, C.; Cottrell, S.; Bowley, M.; Williams, C.; Shankar, A.G.; Stiff, R. Measles outbreak linked to European B3 outbreaks, Wales, United Kingdom, 2017. *Euro Surveill.* **2017**, *22*, 17–00673. [CrossRef] [PubMed]

4. le Polain de Waroux, O.; Saliba, V.; Cottrell, S.; Young, N.; Perry, M.; Bukasa, A.; Ramsay, M.; Brown, K.; Amirthalingam, G. Summer music and arts festivals as hot spots for measles transmission: Experience from England and Wales, June to October 2016. *Euro Surveill.* **2016**, *21*, 30390. [CrossRef] [PubMed]
5. UK Health Security Agency. Confirmed Cases of Measles in England and Wales by Region and Age: 2012 to 2021. UK Health Security Agency, 2022. Available online: https://www.gov.uk/government/publications/measles-confirmed-cases/confirmed-cases-of-measles-in-england-and-wales-by-region-and-age-2012-to-2014 (accessed on 6 February 2023).
6. Public Health Wales. Wales Measles and Rubella Elimination Task Group Action Plan 2019–2021, Public Health Wales: Cardiff, 2019. Available online: https://phw.nhs.wales/topics/measles/wales-measles-and-rubella-elimination-task-group-action-plan-2019-2021/ (accessed on 6 February 2023).
7. COVER–National Childhood Immunisation Uptake Data. Public Health Wales, 2022. Available online: https://phw.nhs.wales/topics/immunisation-and-vaccines/cover-national-childhood-immunisation-uptake-data/ (accessed on 6 February 2023).
8. Public Health Wales. *Inequalities in Uptake of Routine Childhood Immunisations in Wales 2021–2022*; Public Health Wales: Cardiff, Wales, 2022; Available online: https://phw.nhs.wales/topics/immunisation-and-vaccines/cover-national-childhood-immunisation-uptake-data/cover-inequalities-reports/inequalities-in-uptake-of-routine-childhood-immunisations-in-wales-2021-22/ (accessed on 6 February 2023).
9. World Health Organization Regional Office for Europe. European Immunization Agenda 2030, World Health Organization: Copenhagen, 2021. Available online: https://www.who.int/europe/initiatives/the-european-immunization-agenda-2030 (accessed on 6 February 2023).
10. Bocquier, A.; Ward, J.; Raude, J.; Peretti-Watel, P.; Verger, P. Socioeconomic differences in childhood vaccination in developed countries: A systematic review of quantitative studies. *Expert Rev. Vaccines* **2017**, *16*, 1107–1118. [CrossRef] [PubMed]
11. Gilbert, N.L.; Gilmour, H.; Wilson, S.E.; Cantin, L. Determinants of non-vaccination and incomplete vaccination in Canadian toddlers. *Hum. Vaccin. Immunother.* **2017**, *13*, 1–7. [CrossRef] [PubMed]
12. Pearce, A.; Law, C.; Elliman, D.; Cole, T.J.; Bedford, H.; Millennium Cohort Study Child Health Group. Factors associated with uptake of measles, mumps, and rubella vaccine (MMR) and use of single antigen vaccines in a contemporary UK cohort: Prospective cohort study. *BMJ.* **2008**, *336*, 754–757. [CrossRef]
13. Foty, R.G.; Guttmann, A.; Kwong, J.C.; Maaten, S.; Manuel, D.; Stieb, D.M.; Dell, S.D. Predictors of universal influenza vaccination uptake in grades 1 and 2 Toronto school children: Effective vaccination strategies should not end with at risk children. *Vaccine* **2010**, *28*, 6518–6522. [CrossRef]
14. Ahmed Ali, H.; Hartner, A.M.; Echeverria-Londono, S.; Roth, J.; Li, X.; Abbas, K.; Portnoy, A.; Vynnycky, E.; Woodruff, K.; Ferguson, N.M.; et al. Vaccine equity in low and middle income countries: A systematic review and meta-analysis. *Int. J. Equity Health* **2022**, *21*, 82. [CrossRef]
15. Pearce, A.; Marshall, H.; Bedford, H.; Lynch, J. Barriers to childhood immunisation: Findings from the Longitudinal Study of Australian Children. *Vaccine* **2015**, *33*, 3377–3383. [CrossRef]
16. Stronegger, W.J.; Freid, W. A hierarchical analysis of social determinants of measles vaccination coverage in Austrian schoolchildren. *Eur. J. Public Health* **2010**, *20*, 354–359. [CrossRef]
17. Tiley, K.S.; White, J.M.; Andrews, N.; Tessier, E.; Edelstein, M. Equity of the Meningitis B vaccination programme in England, 2016-2018. *Vaccine* **2022**, *40*, 6125–6132. [CrossRef]
18. Arat, A.; Moore, H.C.; Goldfeld, S.; Östberg, V.; Sheppeard, V.; Gidding, H.F. Childhood vaccination coverage in Australia: An equity perspective. *BMC Public Health* **2021**, *21*, 1337. [CrossRef]
19. Doherty, E.; Walsh, B.; O'Neill, C. Decomposing socioeconomic inequality in child vaccination: Results from Ireland. *Vaccine* **2014**, *32*, 3438–3444. [CrossRef] [PubMed]
20. Tessier, E.; Warburton, F.; Tsang, C.; Rafeeq, S.; Boddington, N.; Sinnathamby, M.; Pebody, R. Population-level factors predicting variation in influenza vaccine uptake among adults and young children in England, 2015/16 and 2016/17. *Vaccine* **2018**, *36*, 3231–3238. [CrossRef] [PubMed]
21. Jones, K.H.; Ford, D.V.; Thompson, S.; Lyons, R.A. A Profile of the SAIL Databank on the UK Secure Research Platform. *Int. J. Popul. Data Sci.* **2019**, *4*, 1134. [CrossRef]
22. Thayer, D.; Rees, A.; Kennedy, J.; Collins, H.; Harris, D.; Halcox, J.; Ruschetti, L.; Noyce, R.; Brooks, C. Measuring follow-up time in routinely-collected health datasets: Challenges and solutions. *PLoS ONE* **2020**, *15*, e0228545. [CrossRef] [PubMed]
23. UK Health Security Agency. *Measles: The Green Book, Chapter 21*; UK Health Security Agency: London, UK, 2019. Available online: https://www.gov.uk/government/publications/measles-the-green-book-chapter-21 (accessed on 6 February 2023).
24. Perry, M.; Akbari, A.; Cottrell, S.; Gravenor, M.B.; Roberts, R.; Lyons, R.A.; Bedston, S.; Torabi, F.; Griffiths, L. Inequalities in coverage of COVID-19 vaccination: A population register based cross-sectional study in Wales, UK. *Vaccine* **2021**, *39*, 6256–6261. [CrossRef]
25. CPRD @ Cambridge–Codes Lists (GOLD). University of Cambridge, 2018. Available online: https://www.phpc.cam.ac.uk/pcu/research/research-groups/crmh/cprd_cam/codelists/v11/ (accessed on 6 February 2023).
26. Open Code Lists, Wider Learning Disability. Available online: https://www.opencodelists.org/codelist/primis-covid19-vacc-uptake/learndis/v.1.5.3/ (accessed on 6 February 2023).
27. Metcalfe, D.; Masters, J.; Delmestri, A.; Judge, A.; Perry, D.; Zogg, C.; Gabbe, B.; Costa, M. Coding algorithms for defining Charlson and Elixhauser co-morbidities in Read-coded databases. *BMC Med. Res. Methodol.* **2019**, *19*, 115. [CrossRef] [PubMed]

28. Wilder-Smith, A.B.; Qureshi, K. Resurgence of Measles in Europe: A Systematic Review on Parental Attitudes and Beliefs of Measles Vaccine. *J. Epidemiol Glob. Health* **2020**, *10*, 46–58. [CrossRef]
29. Nimblett-Clarke, A. The role of vaccine exemptions in the resurgence of measles. *JAAPA*. **2021**, *34*, 36–40. [CrossRef]
30. Pearce, A.; Mindlin, M.; Cortina-Borja, M.; Bedford, H. Characteristics of 5-year-olds who catch-up with MMR: Findings from the UK Millennium Cohort Study. *BMJ Open* **2013**, *3*, e003152. [CrossRef]
31. Wightman, P.; McCue, K.; Sabo, S.; Annorbah, R.; Jiménez, D.; Pilling, V.; Butler, M.; Celaya, M.F.; Rumann, S. Community health worker intervention improves early childhood vaccination rates: Results from a propensity-score matching evaluation. *BMC Public Health* **2022**, *22*, 1854. [CrossRef] [PubMed]
32. Sangster, A.V.; Barratt, J.M. Towards Ending Immunization Inequity. *Vaccines* **2021**, *9*, 1378. [CrossRef] [PubMed]
33. World Health Organization Regional Office for Europe. *TIP–Tailoring Immunization Programmes*; World Health Organization: Copenhagen, Denmark, 2019; Available online: https://apps.who.int/iris/bitstream/handle/10665/329448/9789289054492-eng.pdf?sequence=1&isAllowed=y (accessed on 6 February 2023).
34. Jama, A.; Appelqvist, E.; Kulane, A.; Karregård, S.; Rubin, J.; Nejat, S.; Habersaat, K.B.; Jackson, C.; Butler, R.; Lindstrand, A.; et al. Design and implementation of tailored intervention to increase vaccine acceptance in a Somali community in Stockholm, Sweden–based on the Tailoring Immunization Programmes approach. *Public Health Pract* **2022**, *4*, 100305. [CrossRef] [PubMed]
35. Rojas-Venegas, M.; Cano-Ibáñez, N.; Khan, K.S. Vaccination coverage among migrants: A systematic review and meta-analysis. *Semergen* **2022**, *48*, 96–105. [CrossRef] [PubMed]
36. Mipatrini, D.; Stefanelli, P.; Severoni, S.; Rezza, G. Vaccinations in migrants and refugees: A challenge for European health systems. A systematic review of current scientific evidence. *Pathog. Glob. Health.* **2017**, *111*, 59–68. [CrossRef]
37. UK Health Security Agency. *Vaccination of Individuals with Uncertain Or Incomplete Immunisation Status*; UK Health Security Agency: London, UK, 2022. Available online: https://www.gov.uk/government/publications/vaccination-of-individuals-with-uncertain-or-incomplete-immunisation-status (accessed on 6 February 2023).
38. Bell, S.; Saliba, V.; Ramsay, M.; Mounier-Jack, S. What have we learnt from measles outbreaks in 3 English cities? A qualitative exploration of factors influencing vaccination uptake in Romanian and Roma Romanian communities. *BMC Public Health* **2020**, *20*, 381. [CrossRef]
39. Jackson, C.; Bedford, H.; Cheater, F.M.; Condon, L.; Emslie, C.; Ireland, L.; Kemsley, P.; Kerr, S.; Lewis, H.J.; Mytton, H.; et al. Needles, Jabs and Jags: A qualitative exploration of barriers and facilitators to child and adult immunisation uptake among Gypsies, Travellers and Roma. *BMC Public Health* **2017**, *17*, 254. [CrossRef]
40. World Health Organization. *COVID-19 Pandemic Leads to Major Backsliding On Childhood Vaccinations, New WHO, UNICEF Data Shows*; World Health Organization: Geneva, Switzerland, 2021; Available online: https://www.who.int/news/item/15-07-2021-covid-19-pandemic-leads-to-major-backsliding-on-childhood-vaccinations-new-who-unicef-data-shows (accessed on 6 February 2023).
41. European Centre for Disease Control. *Monthly Measles And Rubella Monitoring*; ECDC: Stockholm, Sweden, 2022. Available online: https://www.ecdc.europa.eu/en/measles/surveillance-and-disease-data/monthly-measles-rubella-monitoring-reports (accessed on 6 February 2023).

vaccines

MDPI

Article

The Hidden Impact of the COVID-19 Pandemic on Routine Childhood Immunization Coverage in Cameroon

Yauba Saidu [1,2,*], Pietro Di Mattei [3], Sangwe Clovis Nchinjoh [1,4], Nnang Nadege Edwige [1], Bernard Nsah [1], Nkwain Jude Muteh [3], Shalom Tchokfe Ndoula [5], Rakiya Abdullahi [6], Chen Stein Zamir [4], Andreas Ateke Njoh [5,7], Amani Adidja [8], Sidy Ndiaye [9], Owens Wiwa [1], Emanuele Montomoli [2,10,11] and Sue Ann Costa Clemens [2,12]

1 Clinton Health Access Initiative Inc., Yaounde P.O. Box 2664, Cameroon
2 Institute for Global Health, University of Siena, 53100 Siena, Italy
3 Gavi, The Vaccine Alliance, 1202 Geneva, Switzerland
4 Faculty of Medicine, The Hebrew University-Hadassah Braun School of Public Health and Community Medicine, Jerusalem 91120, Israel
5 Expanded Program on Immunization, Cameroon Ministry of Public Health, Yaounde P.O. Box 2084, Cameroon
6 Global Vaccine Team, Clinton Health Access Initiative Inc., Boston, MA 02127, USA
7 School of Global Health and Bioethics, Euclid University, Bangui BP 157, Central African Republic
8 Faculty of Medicine and Biomedical Sciences, University of Yaoundé 1, Yaounde B.P. 337, Cameroon
9 Regional Office for Africa, World Health Organization, Brazzaville P.O. Box 06, Congo
10 Department Molecular Medicine, University of Siena, Via Aldo Moro 3, 53100 Siena, Italy
11 VisMederi srl, Via Ferrini 53, 53035 Siena, Italy
12 Department of Pediatrics, University of Oxford, Oxford OX1 2JD, UK
* Correspondence: ysaidu@clintonhealthaccess.org; Tel.: +237-650828451

Abstract: Background: The third round of the global pulse survey demonstrated that the abrupt and rapid progression of the COVID-19 pandemic significantly disrupted childhood immunization in many countries. Although Cameroon has reported over 120,000 COVID-19 cases, the reported national childhood vaccination coverage during the pandemic seems to have increased compared to that during the pre-COVID-19 period. Indeed, the first dose of the diphtheria, tetanus, and pertussis-containing vaccine (DTP-1) coverage increased from 85.4% in 2019 to 87.7% in 2020, and DTP-3 coverage increased from 79.5% in 2019 to 81.2% in 2020. The paucity of literature on the impact of COVID-19 on childhood vaccination in COVID-19 hotspot regions poses a challenge in developing a context-specific immunization recovery plan, hence the need to conduct this study. **Methodology**: We conducted a cross-sectional study using 2019 (pre-pandemic period) and 2020 (pandemic period) district childhood immunization data from the DHIS-2 database, weighted using completeness for each data entry against regional data completeness in 2020. Based on COVID-19 incidence, two hotspot regions were selected, with all districts (56/56) included in the final analysis. The Chi-square test was used to compare DTP-1 and DTP-3 coverage during the pre-pandemic and pandemic periods. **Results**: In the two hotspot regions, 8247 children missed DTP-1, and 12,896 children did not receive DTP-3 vaccines in the pandemic period compared to the results from the pre-pandemic period. Indeed, there was a significant drop in DTP-1 and DTP-3 coverage of 0.8% ($p = 0.0002$) and 3.1% ($p = 0.0003$), respectively, in the Littoral Region. Moreover, the Centre Region reported a 5.7% ($p < 0.0001$) and 7.6% ($p < 0.0001$) drop in DTP-1 and DTP-3 coverage, respectively. Most districts in the hotspot regions reported a decline in childhood immunization access (62.5%) and utilization (71.4%). Indeed, in the Littoral Region, 46% (11/24) and 58% (14/24) of districts experienced decreased vaccination access and utilization, respectively. Meanwhile, 75% (24/32) and 81% (26/32) of districts in the Centre Region experienced a drop in vaccination access and utilization, respectively. **Conclusion**: This study reported a situation where the national immunization indicators mask the impact of COVID-19 on childhood immunization in heavily hit regions. Therefore, this study presents valuable information for ensuring continuous vaccination service delivery during public health emergencies. The findings could also contribute to developing an immunization recovery plan and informing policy on future pandemic preparedness and response.

Keywords: COVID-19 impact; childhood vaccination; Cameroon

Citation: Saidu, Y.; Di Mattei, P.; Nchinjoh, S.C.; Edwige, N.N.; Nsah, B.; Muteh, N.J.; Ndoula, S.T.; Abdullahi, R.; Zamir, C.S.; Njoh, A.A.; et al. The Hidden Impact of the COVID-19 Pandemic on Routine Childhood Immunization Coverage in Cameroon. *Vaccines* **2023**, *11*, 645. https://doi.org/10.3390/vaccines11030645

Academic Editors: Ahmad Reza Hosseinpoor, M. Carolina Danovaro, Devaki Nambiar, Aaron Wallace and Hope Johnson

Received: 7 January 2023
Revised: 16 February 2023
Accepted: 27 February 2023
Published: 14 March 2023

1. Background

Complex emergencies and natural disasters are associated with outbreaks of infectious diseases due to disruptions in health service delivery, including vaccination and nutrition [1]. Although there is limited literature on the impact of pandemics on essential health service delivery, the COVID-19 pandemic forced countries to observe social isolation, physical distancing, lockdowns, curfews, and quarantines. This may have posed a population health risk similar to the case of complex emergencies and natural disasters. Since 2019, the SARS-CoV-2 virus has rapidly spread from China, infecting over 650 million people, with 6.6 million deaths recorded globally as of 22 December 2022 [2].

The abrupt and rapid progression of the COVID-19 pandemic has caused significant disruptions in essential health service delivery in many countries, reversing past efforts to improve health indicators [3–5]. Indeed, according to the third round of the global pulse survey on the continuity of essential health services during the COVID-19 pandemic, over 90% of countries reported a serious continuous disruption in the delivery of essential health services [6]. Moreover, 53% of countries reported persistent disruptions in primary health care, with about 40% experiencing increased backlogs during the second half of 2021 [6]. These disruptions are mainly due to decreased care seeking in 25% of countries, but also unintended disruptions resulting from the lack of healthcare resources and intentional service delivery modifications in one-third of surveyed countries [6]. Moreover, a systemic review suggested a significant decline in vaccination coverage due to COVID-19, leading to a four-fold increase in polio cases in polio-endemic countries [7]. According to the authors, factors contributing to the observed decline include: fear of being exposed to the virus at healthcare facilities, restriction on city-wide movements, a shortage of workers, and diversion of resources from child health to address the pandemic, among others [7].

Cameroon, with an estimated population size of 27 million in 2022, has recorded over 120,000 COVID-19 cases and about 2000 COVID-19-related deaths, yet the reported national childhood routine vaccination coverage seems to have improved compared to the pre-COVID-19 period [2]. For instance, the first dose of the diphtheria, tetanus, pertussis-containing vaccine (DTP-1) coverage increased by almost 2 percentage points (pp), rising from 85.4% in 2019 to 87.7% in 2020. Similarly, the third dose of DTP-containing vaccine (DPT-3) increased from 79.5% in 2019 to 81.2% in 2020. The observed increase in coverage suggests an increased access to, and utilization of, vaccination services during the COVID-19 pandemic [8]. This observation runs contrary to what has been reported by previous studies, which all showed serious disruptions in regards to other essential health system indicators. These authors reported serious disruptions in blood donation services, utilization of radiology units, geriatric consultations, pediatric hospitalization, and HIV service utilization, among others [9–15]. Another cross-sectional study assessed the impact of COVID-19 on immunization services in a single hospital setting in Cameroon—posing a problem for result generalizability [16]. In the current study we aimed to contribute by filling the existing knowledge gap concerning the impact of COVID-19 on routine childhood immunizations in Cameroon, which might be critical in ensuring continuous vaccination service delivery during public health emergencies. In addition, findings from this study will provide salient recommendations that could contribute to developing the COVID-19 recovery plan and informing policy on future pandemic preparedness and response.

2. Methodology

2.1. Study Design and Setting

This cross-sectional study compared childhood routine immunization access and utilization in the pre-pandemic period (2019) to the pandemic period (2020). The study considered aggregated secondary district-level data on routine childhood immunization from the District Health Information System (DHIS)-2. All districts found in the top two COVID-19 hotspot regions were considered for analysis.

2.2. Key Operational Definitions

In this study, childhood routine immunization access was measured using diphtheria, pertussis, tetanus first dose (DTP-1) vaccination coverage as an indicator, while routine immunization utilization was based on DTP-3 vaccination coverage, DTP-1 and DTP-3 were used as indicators to align with the Cameroon ministry of public health's definitions for vaccination access and utilization; thus allowing for result dissemination and use by policy makers. Moreover, we defined COVID-19 hotspot regions as those with the highest number of cumulative COVID-19 cases as of July 2022.

2.3. Sampling and Data Collection

Based on administrative data, the Littoral Region, with 32,995 COVID-19 cases representing 28.27% of national cumulative cases, and the Centre Region, with 36,506 COVID-19 cases representing 31.28% of national cumulative cases, were considered COVID-19 hotspot regions, and were included in the study. The secondary data on annual district DTP-1 and DTP-3 coverages in all districts in the two hotspot regions were extracted from DHIS-2 and prepared for analysis. A total of 56 of 189 health districts (29.6%) in Cameroon were included in the study, notably 24 from the Littoral Region and 32 from the Centre Region.

2.4. Data Management and Analysis

The data were exported as a Microsoft Excel 2013 worksheet into R Statistical Software (v4.1.2; R Core Team 2021) for statistical analysis. District vaccination coverage was weighted using completeness of the data entry according to regional data completeness in 2020. Data on regional and district data entry completeness reported in the DHIS-2 database (in percentages) was downloaded and cleaned, and the formulas below were used to calculate the adjusted vaccine coverages.

$$Adjusted\ DTP-1\ coverage = \frac{Regional\ data\ completeness}{District\ data\ completeness} \times DTP-1\ coverage \quad (1)$$

$$Adjusted\ DTP-3\ coverage = \frac{Regional\ data\ completeness}{District\ data\ completeness} \times DTP-3\ coverage \quad (2)$$

Using the Chi-square test, we compared the adjusted DTP-1 and DTP-3 coverages in 2019 (pre-pandemic) and 2020 (pandemic). The 2020 data were considered the observed outcome, and the 2019 data reflected the expected outcome in the analysis. A p-value < 0.05 was considered statistically significant.

2.5. Ethical Considerations

This study did not involve any individual-level data, so ethical clearance was not required.

3. Results

This study included annual DTP-1 and DTP-3 vaccination coverages from all districts in the COVID-19 hotspot regions, representing one-third of districts (56/189) in Cameroon. Based on the DHIS-2 data quality assessment tool, data completeness in the pre-pandemic period was 96% and 100% in the Littoral and Centre regions, respectively. In addition, in the pandemic period, data exhibited 91% and 94% completeness in the Littoral and Centre regions, respectively.

Basing on these assumptions, our results unveiled a significant drop in vaccination coverage of 3.3% and 5.4% in DTP-1 and DTP-3 coverages, respectively. As a result, 8247 children missed DTP-1, and 12,896 children did not receive DTP-3 vaccines in the pandemic period compared to the results for pre-pandemic period in the two hotspot regions. This is contrary to the trend in national data, as shown in Figures 1 and 2. Additionally, most districts reported a decline in childhood immunization access (62.5%) and utilization (71.4%), ranging from a drop of 0.1% to 43.7% in vaccination coverage.

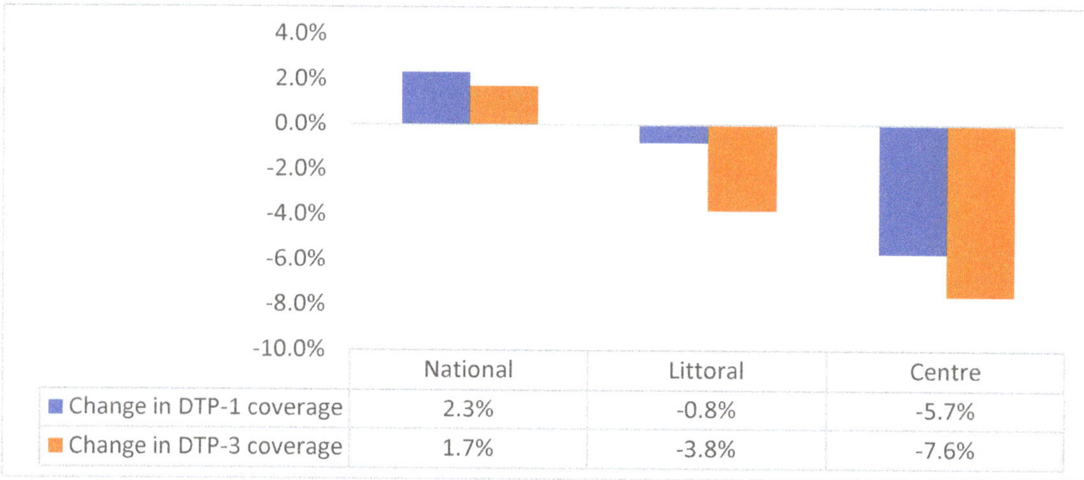

Figure 1. Change in DTP-1 and DTP-3 coverage in hotspot regions during the pandemic.

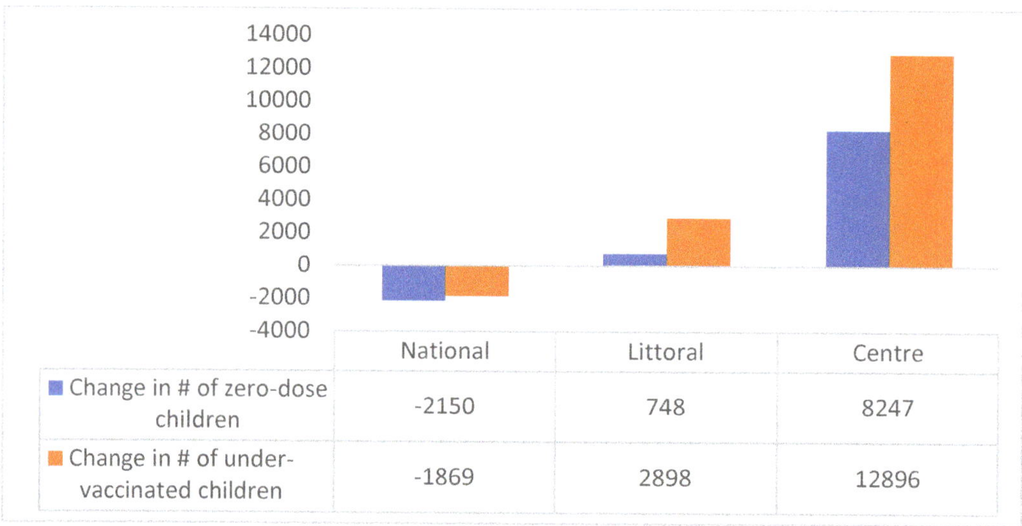

Figure 2. Number of children who missed vaccination in hotspot regions and contrasting national gain in children vaccinated during the pandemic.

As presented in Tables 1 and 2, in the Littoral Region, 46% (11/24) of districts experienced a decreased vaccination access, which ranged from 2.6% to 29.4%. Moreover, 58% (14/24) of districts experienced decreased vaccine utilization, which ranged from 0.1% to 28.3%. The adjusted drop in vaccination coverage in the Littoral Region was 0.8% ($p = 0.0002$) and 3.1% ($p = 0.0003$) for DTP-1 and DTP-3 vaccination coverages, respectively. This implies that about 748 children missed DTP-1 vaccines, and 2898 children the Littoral Region did not receive DTP-3 vaccines during the pandemic compared to the pre-pandemic period.

Table 1. DTP-1 coverage variations in the pre-pandemic and pandemic period in the Littoral Region.

District	2019 Weight	2019 Coverage	Adjusted 2019 Coverage	2020 Weight	2020 Coverage	Adjusted 2020 Coverage	Variation *	Adjusted Variation *
Abo	0.98	131.3	128.2	1.12	107.8	120.7	−23.5 *	−7.5 *
Bangue	1.08	88.2	95.0	1.06	91.4	97.3	3.2	2.3
Boko	0.93	49.1	45.8	0.91	47.3	43.2	−1.8 *	−2.6 *
Bonassama	1.02	96	97.5	1.00	101.6	101.5	5.6	4.0
Cite Des Palmiers	1.18	101.3	119.6	1.13	81.6	92.2	−19.7 *	−27.3 *
Deido	0.91	95.7	87.1	0.88	65.3	57.7	−30.4 *	−29.4 *
Dibombari	0.97	101.7	98.5	0.92	135.6	124.9	33.9	26.4
Edea	1.04	76	79.1	1.12	82.5	92.8	6.5	13.7
Japoma	1.16	72.6	84.2	1.14	85.8	97.5	13.2	13.3
Logbaba	1.26	89.8	112.7	1.41	84.5	119.4	−5.3 *	6.7
Loum	0.98	119.5	117.2	0.98	116.5	113.6	−3 *	−3.6 *
Manjo	1.15	86.9	99.8	1.12	74.5	83.4	−12.4 *	−16.5 *
Manoka	2.43	15.4	37.4	1.04	23.8	24.8	8.4	−12.6 *
Mbanga	1.11	72.4	80.2	1.15	63.4	73.1	−9 *	−7.0 *
Melong	0.97	100.4	97.8	1.10	88.8	97.8	−11.6 *	0.0
Ndom	1.07	45.1	48.1	1.39	43.4	60.5	−1.7 *	12.4
New Bell	0.97	70.8	68.4	0.99	94.8	93.9	24	25.5
Ngambe	1.09	51.6	56.4	0.91	65.2	59.3	13.6	3.0
Njombe Penja	1.42	89	126.2	1.13	95.1	107.1	6.1	−19.0 *
Nkondjock	0.99	101.9	101.1	0.95	103.8	98.2	1.9	−2.9 *
vvNkongsamba	0.99	106.6	105.3	1.07	99.9	107.0	−6.7 *	1.6
Nylon	0.91	94.3	86.2	0.93	96.9	90.4	2.6	4.2
Pouma	1.09	100.3	109.6	1.46	80.3	116.9	−20 *	7.3
Yabassi	1.27	76.7	97.6	1.32	65.3	86.4	−11.4 *	−11.2 *

* The negative sign (−) shows a drop in coverage after the pandemic compared to before, while a positive sign (+) indicates an increase in coverage.

Table 2. DTP-3 coverage variations in the pre-pandemic and pandemic period in the Littoral Region.

District	2019 Weight	2019 Coverage	Adjusted 2019 Coverage	2020 Weight	2020 Coverage	Adjusted 2020 Coverage	Variation *	Adjusted Variation *
Abo	0.98	122.4	119.5	1.12	108.9	121.9	−13.5 *	2.4
Bangue	1.08	89.3	96.2	1.06	90.4	96.2	1.1	0.0
Boko	0.93	52.3	48.8	0.91	49.6	45.3	−2.7 *	−3.4 *
Bonassama	1.02	92.7	94.1	1.00	96.3	96.2	3.6	2.0
Cite Des Palmiers	1.18	99.8	117.8	1.13	80.1	90.5	−19.7 *	−27.2 *
Deido	0.91	88.6	80.6	0.88	59.2	52.3	−29.4 *	−28.3 *
Dibombari	0.97	94.7	91.7	0.92	133.5	123.0	38.8	31.3
Edea	1.04	72.9	75.9	1.12	71.4	80.3	−1.5 *	4.4
Japoma	1.16	70.8	82.1	1.14	77.1	87.6	6.3	5.5
Logbaba	1.26	82.4	103.4	1.41	71.3	100.8	−11.1 *	−2.7 *
Loum	0.98	109.4	107.3	0.98	109.1	106.4	−0.3 *	−0.9 *
Manjo	1.15	89.2	102.5	1.12	75.9	85.0	−13.3 *	−17.5 *
Manoka	2.43	8.4	20.4	1.04	8.3	8.6	−0.1 *	−11.8 *
Mbanga	1.11	81.6	90.3	1.15	59.5	68.6	−22.1 *	−21.7 *
Melong	0.97	97.4	94.9	1.10	79.9	88.0	−17.5 *	−6.9 *
Ndom	1.07	44.6	47.5	1.39	34	47.4	−10.6 *	−0.1 *
New Bell	0.97	64.5	62.3	0.99	83.8	83.0	19.3	20.7
Ngambe	1.09	48.7	53.2	0.91	60	54.6	11.3	1.4
Njombe Penja	1.42	80	113.4	1.13	94.2	106.1	14.2	−7.3 *
Nkondjock	0.99	106.4	105.6	0.95	101.8	96.3	−4.6 *	−9.3 *

Table 2. *Cont.*

District	2019 Weight	2019 Coverage	Adjusted 2019 Coverage	2020 Weight	2020 Coverage	Adjusted 2020 Coverage	Variation *	Adjusted Variation *
Nkongsamba	0.99	95.8	94.7	1.07	90.7	97.1	−5.1 *	2.4
Nylon	0.91	90.1	82.4	0.93	94.1	87.8	4	5.4
Pouma	1.09	97.7	106.7	1.46	72.3	105.3	−25.4 *	−1.5 *
Yabassi	1.27	77.9	99.1	1.32	65.6	86.8	−12.3 *	−12.4 *

* The negative sign (−) shows a drop in coverage after the pandemic compared to before, while a positive sign (+) indicates an increase in coverage.

Meanwhile, as shown in Tables 3 and 4, the Centre Region experienced a 5.7% ($p < 0.0001$) drop in DTP-1 and a 7.6% ($p < 0.0001$) drop in DTP-3 coverage, with about 7498 children missing DTP-1 and 9998 others missing DTP-3 during the pandemic compared to the pre-pandemic period. This decrease in DTP-1 vaccination coverage was reported in 75% (24/32) of districts, ranging from a 2.1% to a 31.6% drop in coverage. Likewise, 81% (26/32) of districts showed a decreased DTP-3 vaccination coverage in the pandemic period, with a 2.5% to a 43.7% drop in coverage.

Table 3. DTP-1 coverage variations in the pre-pandemic and pandemic period in the Centre Region.

District	2019 Weight	2019 Coverage	Adjusted 2019 Coverage	2020 Weight	2020 Coverage	Adjusted 2020 Coverage	Variation *	Adjusted Variation *
Akonolinga	0.94	97.8	92.2	0.93	81.1	75.8	−16.7 *	−16.4 *
Awae	0.94	100.9	94.8	0.94	67.3	63.3	−33.6 *	−31.6 *
Ayos	0.95	88.2	83.5	1.05	69.9	73.4	−18.3 *	−10.1 *
Bafia	0.94	95.3	89.3	0.95	87.5	82.9	−7.8 *	−6.4 *
Biyem Assi	0.97	164.2	158.6	0.94	157.7	148.4	−6.5 *	−10.2 *
Cite Verte	1.04	89.1	92.3	1.34	82	110.0	−7.1 *	17.6
Djoungolo	0.89	93.4	83.4	0.92	86.3	79.3	−7.1 *	−4.1 *
Ebebda	0.80	99.7	79.4	0.81	79.8	64.3	−19.9 *	−15.1 *
Efoulan	0.96	86	82.6	1.04	84.3	87.9	−1.7 *	5.4
Elig Mfomo	0.94	102.5	96.4	0.94	99	93.1	−3.5 *	−3.3 *
Eseka	0.91	82.7	75.0	0.91	59.2	53.7	−23.5 *	−21.3 *
Esse	0.88	100.7	88.4	0.90	83.8	75.6	−16.9 *	−12.8 *
Evodoula	0.94	112.2	105.5	0.95	75.1	71.2	−37.1 *	−34.3 *
Mbalmayo	0.98	82.5	81.0	0.93	87.6	81.7	5.1	0.7
Mbandjock	1.00	111.9	111.9	0.95	105.3	99.6	−6.6 *	−12.3 *
Mbankomo	0.88	131.1	115.4	1.06	107.3	114.1	−23.8 *	−1.3 *
Mfou	0.97	128.8	124.3	1.17	142.2	166.5	13.4	42.2
Monatele	0.94	81.3	76.4	1.03	72.2	74.3	−9.1 *	−2.1 *
Mvog-Ada	0.97	160	154.9	1.01	151.1	152.4	−8.9 *	−2.5 *
Nanga Eboko	0.94	89.8	84.4	0.97	68	65.9	−21.8 *	−18.5 *
Ndikinimeki	0.95	75.1	71.0	0.94	68.7	64.6	−6.4 *	−6.4 *
Ngog Mapubi	0.94	85.5	80.1	0.94	91.8	86.3	6.3	6.2
Ngoumou	0.94	96.5	90.7	0.94	86	80.8	−10.5 *	−9.9 *
Nkolbisson	0.92	81.8	75.1	0.92	92.4	85.2	10.6	10.1
Nkolndongo	0.92	88.7	81.4	0.94	82.6	77.6	−6.1 *	−3.8 *
Ntui	0.94	97.5	91.2	0.95	84.9	80.4	−12.6 *	−10.8 *
Obala	0.94	105.7	99.7	0.98	76.8	75.4	−28.9 *	−24.2 *
Odza	0.94	85.9	80.3	0.93	88	82.0	2.1	1.6
Okola	0.96	125.4	120.2	1.07	96.7	103.4	−28.7 *	−16.7 *
Sa'a	0.95	95.6	90.5	0.94	91.5	85.8	−4.1 *	−4.7 *
Soa	0.94	124.4	116.9	0.97	154.6	149.8	30.2	32.9
Yoko	1.03	83.2	85.3	0.94	69	64.9	−14.2 *	−20.4 *

* The negative sign (−) shows a drop in coverage after the pandemic compared to before, while a positive sign (+) indicates an increase in coverage.

Table 4. DTP-3 coverage variations in the pre-pandemic and pandemic period in the Centre Region.

District	2019 Weight	2019 Coverage	Adjusted 2019 Coverage	2020 Weight	2020 Coverage	Adjusted 2020 coverage	Variation *	Adjusted Variation *
Akonolinga	0.94	99.8	94.1	0.93	83.7	78.2	−16.1 *	−15.9 *
Awae	0.94	94.2	88.5	0.94	47.7	44.8	−46.5 *	−43.7 *
Ayos	0.95	67.9	64.3	1.05	53.3	56.0	−14.6 *	−8.3 *
Bafia	0.94	88.3	82.8	0.95	77.6	73.5	−10.7 *	−9.2 *
Biyem Assi	0.97	161.6	156.1	0.94	151.5	142.6	−10.1 *	−13.6 *
Cite Verte	1.04	82.6	85.6	1.34	72.5	97.2	−10.1 *	11.6
Djoungolo	0.89	87.9	78.5	0.92	79.7	73.2	−8.2 *	−5.2 *
Ebebda	0.80	89	70.8	0.81	75.1	60.5	−13.9 *	−10.3 *
Efoulan	0.96	89.6	86.0	1.04	85.5	89.2	−4.1 *	3.2
Elig Mfomo	0.94	91.3	85.8	0.94	82.7	77.7	−8.6 *	−8.1 *
Eseka	0.91	84.7	76.8	0.91	55.9	50.7	−28.8 *	−26.1 *
Esse	0.88	90.9	79.8	0.90	71.7	64.7	−19.2 *	−15.1 *
Evodoula	0.94	98	92.1	0.95	76.5	72.5	−21.5 *	−19.6 *
Mbalmayo	0.98	71.4	70.1	0.93	76.3	71.2	4.9	1.0
Mbandjock	1.00	85.1	85.1	0.95	86.9	82.2	1.8	−2.9 *
Mbankomo	0.88	115.6	101.7	1.06	89.2	94.9	−26.4 *	−6.9 *
Mfou	0.97	118	113.9	1.17	126.3	147.8	8.3	34.0
Monatele	0.94	75.5	71.0	1.03	61.4	63.2	−14.1 *	−7.8 *
Mvog-Ada	0.97	155.5	150.5	1.01	139.7	140.9	−15.8 *	−9.6 *
Nanga Eboko	0.94	73.4	69.0	0.97	57.6	55.8	−15.8 *	−13.2 *
Ndikinimeki	0.95	73.1	69.1	0.94	64.7	60.8	−8.4 *	−8.3 *
Ngog Mapubi	0.94	83.2	78.0	0.94	84.5	79.4	1.3	1.5
Ngoumou	0.94	92.3	86.8	0.94	79.2	74.4	−13.1 *	−12.3 *
Nkolbisson	0.92	76.9	70.6	0.92	86.1	79.3	9.2	8.8
Nkolndongo	0.92	80.7	74.1	0.94	72.7	68.3	−8 *	−5.7 *
Ntui	0.94	84.5	79.0	0.95	67.7	64.1	−16.8 *	−14.9 *
Obala	0.94	101.8	96.0	0.98	71	69.7	−30.8 *	−26.2 *
Odza	0.94	85	79.5	0.93	82.7	77.0	−2.3 *	−2.5 *
Okola	0.96	113.6	108.9	1.07	88.7	94.9	−24.9 *	−14.0 *
Sa'a	0.95	87.8	83.1	0.94	84.4	79.1	−3.4 *	−4.0 *
Soa	0.94	125.3	117.8	0.97	146.2	141.7	20.9	23.9 *
Yoko	1.03	65.5	67.1	0.94	47.3	44.5	−18.2 *	−22.7 *

* The negative sign (−) shows a drop in coverage after the pandemic compared to before, while a positive sign (+) indicates an increase in coverage.

4. Discussion

Analyzing data from the two COVID-19 hotspot regions in Cameroon revealed a significant drop in DTP-1 coverage of 3.3% and in DTP-3 coverage of 5.4%. This drop resulted into 8247 and 12,896 children missing out on their DTP-1 and DPT-3 vaccines, respectively, in the pandemic period compared to the pre-pandemic period. Moreover, the DTP series vaccination dropout rate increased from 7.5% to 9.3% in the Centre Region and from 3.7 to 6.0 in the Littoral Region. Our findings run contrary to national administrative data, which suggested improved childhood vaccination access and utilization during the pandemic period. Improvement at the national level is understandable, because vaccination has mainly been driven by the organization of periodic intensification of routine immunization (PIRIs) in many districts of some regions, particularly those in the Southwest and Northwest regions [17]. Moreover, several vaccination campaigns were organized in other regions in response to VPD epidemics, coupled with the introduction of a second dose of measle and rubella vaccine [18,19]. This may have had a significant impact on the coverage of other antigens, increasing national vaccination coverage.

Despite this improvement in national coverage, which was purely driven by the PIRIs, our findings clearly align with those reported by the third round of the global pulse survey on the impact of COVID-19 on immunization services [6]. The survey revealed that 70% (64/91) of participating countries reported disruptions in routine immunization services, with 18% (16/91) experiencing severe disruptions between February and August 2020 [20]. Moreover, a study conducted in a tertiary hospital in Cameroon revealed a decreased demand for childhood immunization services during the COVID-19 pandemic, with a significant drop in the coverage of DTP-containing vaccines [16]. Other studies reported a similar decline in immunization indicators during the pandemic [21,22].

The significant drop in vaccination coverage in our study can be explained by the advent of a novel pandemic that encountered an unprepared and weak health system, hence the grave challenges in meeting the demands of pandemic control. This led to task shifting in favor of the pandemic, creating an unintended negative impact on essential health services, such as routine immunization. Additionally, sub-optimal training of clinicians regarding routine patient care, including vaccination amid the pandemic, created, the fear of contracting COVID-19 when offering health services [9]. This fear was worsened by inadequate personal protective equipment and standards of operation to keep the disease in check in a clinical setting [9]. Delays in COVID-19 confirmatory diagnosis due to limited test kits and diagnostics targeted every patient presenting in a clinical setting with upper or lower respiratory tract symptoms as a suspected case, leading to poor care, even for patients presenting with other ailments [9]. This complexity and uncertainty associated with contracting the COVID-19 infection may have created a spillover effect of COVID-19 stigma and hesitancy toward other routine essential health care services, including immunization services.

Although districts recorded varying degrees of change in vaccination access and the utilization of tracer indicators between the pre-pandemic and pandemic period, more than two-thirds of them reported a drop in DTP-1 (62.5%) and DTP-3 coverages (71.4%). Up to a 31.6% and a 43.7% drop in DTP-1 and DTP-3 coverage, respectively, was reported in some districts. This finding lends support to the results of a cross-sectional study in Senegal that showed a significant decrease in immunization uptake at the health facility level [23]. This further emphasizes the need for a real-time assessment tool to be used at the different tiers of vaccination service delivery, including health facilities. This is important because aggregated data at higher administrative levels may mask prevailing low performance at lower operational levels. The role of such a tool in data-driven decision making at all levels is invaluable.

The region most heavily hit by the COVID-19 pandemic (the Center Region) recorded a higher drop in vaccination access and utilization in the pandemic period, with more districts reporting a drop in vaccination indicators compared to the results from the Littoral Region. The drop ranged from 5.7% ($p < 0.0001$) to 0.8% ($p = 0.0002$) in the Centre and Littoral regions, respectively. There was also a significant drop in the utilization of immunization services in both regions, and estimates stood at 7.6% ($p < 0.0001$) and 3.1% ($p = 0.0003$) in the Center and Littoral regions, respectively. In a country such as Cameroon, with limited health resources, this piece of information may be helpful to prioritize regions and districts with higher decline in RI indicators, as this may guide the development of a post-COVID-19 recovery plan to reverse the impact of the pandemic on key RI indicators. This finding can also be employed in informing policy on future pandemic management.

Despite the potential usefulness and application of our findings, there are certain limitations that must be acknowledged. These limitations are essentially linked to data completeness on the DHIS-2 platform, which was the main source of data for our study. Based on the DHIS-2 data quality assessment tool, data completeness in the pre-pandemic period was 96% and 100% in the Littoral and Centre regions, respectively; however, during the pandemic period, data completeness was at 91% and 94% in the Littoral and Centre regions, respectively. In this study, we adjusted this limitation by weighting the data against regional data completeness. The data weighting may have introduced bias in some districts by disproportionately increasing or decreasing vaccination coverage.

Based on our findings, we will first recommend a further survey in a sample of these districts to identify factors associated with the decline in vaccination coverage during the pandemic. Second, we recommend the development and validation of a digital tool that can support the early detection of the impact of a pandemic on RI variables at all health system tiers. These two recommendations may be valuable in developing tailored strategies to detect and reverse-inverse trends of the pandemic on RI performance.

5. Conclusions

This study presented a practical scenario in Cameroon, where national data masked the impact of the COVID-19 pandemic on childhood immunization in COVID-19 hotspot regions. Indeed, the study revealed a remarkable decrease in vaccination access and utilization in the two COVID-19 hotspot regions, with an increase in DTP-series dropout rate during the pandemic compared to the pre-pandemic period. Therefore, there is a resounding need to develop and implement recovery and catch-up immunization strategies to mitigate the impact of the pandemic on routine childhood immunization in these regions. To ensure the continuity of childhood routine immunization in future pandemics, there is need to set up a system that will drive the early detection of the impact of the pandemic on immunization services. Moreover, a digital tool that would evaluate the impact of the pandemic at all operational levels in real-time will be of great value. This will help unveil the pandemic's true impact and support data-driven decision making. Additionally, the study findings can be leveraged to inform policies on sustaining immunization services during future pandemics in Cameroon.

Author Contributions: Conceptualization, Y.S., P.D.M., S.C.N., E.M. and S.A.C.C.; data curation, Y.S. and S.C.N.; formal analysis, Y.S. and S.C.N.; funding acquisition, Y.S. and P.D.M.; investigation, Y.S.; methodology, Y.S., P.D.M., S.C.N., E.M. and S.A.C.C.; project administration, Y.S.; supervision, P.D.M., C.S.Z., E.M. and S.A.C.C.; validation, Y.S.; writing—original draft, Y.S. and S.C.N.; writing—review and editing, Y.S., P.D.M., S.C.N., N.N.E., B.N., S.T.N., R.A., C.S.Z., A.A.N., A.A., N.J.M., O.W., S.N. and E.M. All authors have read and agreed to the published version of the manuscript.

Funding: This research received no external funding.

Informed Consent Statement: This study did not involve individual-level data, so ethical clearance was not required.

Data Availability Statement: Data from the corresponding author of this research is available upon reasonable request. However, the Cameroon DHIS-2 databased was used as the data source.

Acknowledgments: This study was nested in a project that was funded by Gavi, the Vaccine Alliance. We are grateful to this institution for its generous financial support to Clinton Health Access Initiative, Inc., for the realization of this and other similar projects. It is important to highlight that while acknowledging the support of these institution, the institutions had not role in deciding whether or not to publish these data. As a result, the content of the paper is purely the responsibly of the authors. We would also like to thank the staff of Cameroon's Expanded Program on Immunization for sharing field observations that inspired this study.

Conflicts of Interest: The authors declare no conflict of interest.

References

1. Culver, A.; Rochat, R.; Cookson, S.T. Public health implications of complex emergencies and natural disasters. *Confl. Health* **2017**, *11*, 32. [CrossRef] [PubMed]
2. WHO. Coronavirus (COVID-19) Dashboard with Vaccination Data. 2021. Available online: https://covid19.who.int/table (accessed on 25 August 2022).
3. Mansour, Z.; Arab, J.; Said, R.; Rady, A.; Hamadeh, R.; Gerbaka, B.; Bizri, A.R. Impact of COVID-19 pandemic on the utilization of routine immunization services in Lebanon. *PLoS ONE* **2021**, *16*, e0246951. [CrossRef] [PubMed]
4. Chandir, S.; Siddiqi, D.A.; Mehmood, M.; Setayesh, H.; Siddique, M.; Mirza, A.; Soundardjee, R.; Dharma, V.K.; Shah, M.T.; Abdullah, S.; et al. Impact of COVID-19 pandemic response on uptake of routine immunizations in Sindh, Pakistan: An analysis of provincial electronic immunization registry data. *Vaccine* **2020**, *38*, 7146–7155. [CrossRef] [PubMed]
5. Desta, A.A.; Woldearegay, T.W.; Gebremeskel, E.; Alemayehu, M.; Getachew, T.; Gebregzabiher, G.; Ghebremedhin, K.D.; Zgita, D.N.; Aregawi, A.B.; Redae, G. Impacts of COVID-19 on essential health services in Tigray, Northern Ethiopia: A pre-post study. *PLoS ONE* **2021**, *16*, e0256330. [CrossRef] [PubMed]

6. Third Round of the Global Pulse Survey on Continuity of Essential Health Services during the COVID-19 Pandemic. 2021. Available online: https://www.who.int/publications-detail-redirect/WHO-2019-nCoV-EHS_continuity-survey-2022.1 (accessed on 25 August 2022).
7. Lassi, Z.S.; Naseem, R.; Salam, R.A.; Siddiqui, F.; Das, J.K. The Impact of the COVID-19 Pandemic on Immunization Campaigns and Programs: A Systematic Review. *Int. J. Environ. Res. Public Health* **2021**, *18*, 988. [CrossRef] [PubMed]
8. WHO. Immunization Data Portal. Available online: https://immunizationdata.who.int/pages/profiles/cmr.html (accessed on 27 August 2022).
9. Ngeh, E.N.; Kuaban, C. COVID-19: Challenges and the impact on care in clinical settings in Cameroon. *Pan. Afr. Med. J.* **2020**, *35* (Suppl. 2), 122. [CrossRef]
10. Chelo, D.; Nkwelle, I.M.; Nguefack, F.; Awa, H.D.M.; Enyama, D.; Nguefack, S.; Njinkui, D.N.; Nengom, J.T.; Nguefack-Tsague, G.; Ndombo, P.O.K. Decrease in hospitalizations and increase in deaths during the COVID-19 epidemic in a pediatric Hospital, Yaounde-Cameroon and prediction for the coming months. *Fetal Pediatr. Pathol.* **2021**, *40*, 18–31. [CrossRef] [PubMed]
11. Chiabi, A.; Forgwei, M.N.; Bissong, M.; Niba, L.; Abah, J.N.; Nsame, D. Trends in Pediatric Hospitalizations and Mortality during the COVID-19 Pandemic in an Urban Setting in Cameroon. *J. Trop. Pediatr.* **2022**, *68*, fmac026. [CrossRef] [PubMed]
12. Essomba, M.J.N.; Nzana, V.; Noubiap, J.J.; Zingui-Ottou, M.; Ciaffi, L.; Sobngwi, E.; Ashuntantang, G. The follow-up and well-being of geriatric outpatients during COVID-19 pandemic in Cameroon: Insights from the Yaounde Central Hospital. *Gerontol. Geriatr. Med.* **2020**, *6*, 2333721420959242. [CrossRef] [PubMed]
13. Tagny, C.T.; Lendem, I.; Sack, F.N.; Balogog, P.N.; Ninmou, C.; Dongmo, A.; Ndoumba, A.; Tante, E.; Ateba, N.; Ndemanou, M. Trends in blood donations, blood donors' knowledge, practices and expectations during the COVID-19 pandemic in Cameroon. *Vox Sang.* **2021**, *116*, 637–644. [CrossRef] [PubMed]
14. Onana, Y.; Tambe, J.; Aminou, M.; Mvondo, S.M.; Ndongo, F.A.; Amougou, J.C.M.; Amvene, J.M.; Guena, M.N.; Onana, H.; Moifo, B. Impact of the COVID-19 Pandemic on Patient Attendance and Trends in the Use of Medical Imaging Modalities in a Referral Hospital in the City of Douala, Cameroon. *Open J. Med. Imaging* **2022**, *12*, 16–24. [CrossRef]
15. Mewoabi, S.; Clement, A.J. The Impact of COVID-19 Pandemic and Gender-Based Violence on Uptake of HIV Services in Touboro District Hospital, Cameroon. *TIJPH* **2021**, *10*, 296–306. [CrossRef]
16. Chelo, D.; Nguefack, F.; Enyama, D.; Nansseu, R.; Tefoueyet, G.F.; Awa, H.M.; Nkwelle, I.M.; Nguefack-Tsague, G.; Ndenbe, P.; Ndombo, P.K. Impact and projections of the COVID-19 epidemic on attendance and routine vaccinations at a pediatric referral hospital in Cameroon. *Arch Pédiatrie* **2021**, *28*, 441–450. [CrossRef] [PubMed]
17. Njoh, A.A.; Saidu, Y.; Bachir, H.B.; Ndoula, S.T.; Mboke, E.; Nembot, R.; Tambasho, A.C.; Abizou, M.B.; Seungue, J.; Mbanga, C. The Contribution of Periodic Intensification of Routine Immunization to Vaccination Coverage and Disease Surveillance in the South West Region of Cameroon amid Sociopolitical Crisis and COVID-19 Outbreak in 2020. Available online: https://assets.researchsquare.com/files/rs-961555/v1/ab4a9460-ed3f-4c1f-8c3b-d66850f25a87.pdf?c=1634741437 (accessed on 3 January 2023).
18. Kindzeka, M.E.; Cameroon Launches Vaccination Campaign to Contain Measles Outbreak. VOA. Available online: https://www.voanews.com/a/africa_cameroon-launches-vaccination-campaign-contain-measles-outbreak/6180570.html (accessed on 3 January 2023).
19. Cameroon: Measles/Rubella—Govt Launches Vast Vaccination Campaign. Cameroon Tribune. 4 December 2019. Available online: https://allafrica.com/stories/201912040285.html (accessed on 3 January 2023).
20. Pulse Survey on Continuity of Essential Health Services during the COVID-19 Pandemic: Interim Report, 27 August 2020. Available online: https://www.who.int/publications-detail-redirect/WHO-2019-nCoV-EHS_continuity-survey-2020.1 (accessed on 27 October 2022).
21. Bramer, C.A.; Kimmins, L.M.; Swanson, R.; Kuo, J.; Vranesich, P.; Jacques-Carroll, L.A.; Shen, A.K. Decline in Child Vaccination Coverage During the COVID-19 Pandemic—Michigan Care Improvement Registry, May 2016–2020. *MMWR Morb. Mortal Wkly. Rep.* **2020**, *69*, 630–631. [CrossRef] [PubMed]
22. McDonald, H.I.; Tessier, E.; White, J.M.; Woodruff, M.; Knowles, C.; Bates, C.; Parry, J.; Walker, J.L.; Scott, J.A.; Smeeth, L.; et al. Early impact of the coronavirus disease (COVID-19) pandemic and physical distancing measures on routine childhood vaccinations in England, January to April 2020. *Euro Surveill. Bull. Eur. Sur. Mal. Transm. Eur. Commun. Dis. Bull.* **2020**, *25*, 2000848. [CrossRef] [PubMed]
23. Impact of COVID19 on Routine Immunization: A Cross-Sectional Study in Senegal. Available online: https://www.scirp.org/journal/paperinformation.aspx?paperid=106540 (accessed on 27 October 2022).

vaccines

MDPI

Article

Challenges Addressing Inequalities in Measles Vaccine Coverage in Zambia through a Measles–Rubella Supplementary Immunization Activity during the COVID-19 Pandemic

Yangyupei Yang [1], Natalya Kostandova [2], Francis Dien Mwansa [3], Chola Nakazwe [4], Harriet Namukoko [4], Constance Sakala [3], Patricia Bobo [3], Penelope Kalesha Masumbu [5], Bertha Nachinga [4], David Ngula [3], Andrea C. Carcelen [1], Christine Prosperi [1], Amy K. Winter [6], William J. Moss [1,2,7] and Simon Mutembo [1,*]

1 Department of International Health, International Vaccine Access Center, Johns Hopkins Bloomberg School of Public Health, Baltimore, MD 21231, USA
2 Department of Epidemiology, Johns Hopkins Bloomberg School of Public Health, Baltimore, MD 21231, USA
3 Ministry of Health, Government of the Republic of Zambia, Lusaka 10101, Zambia
4 Zambia Statistics Agency, Lusaka 10101, Zambia
5 Zambia Country Office, World Health Organization, Lusaka 10101, Zambia
6 Department of Epidemiology, University of Georgia, Athens, GA 30602, USA
7 W Harry Feinstone Department of Molecular Microbiology and Immunology, Johns Hopkins Bloomberg School of Public Health, Baltimore, MD 21231, USA
* Correspondence: smutemb1@jhmi.edu

Citation: Yang, Y.; Kostandova, N.; Mwansa, F.D.; Nakazwe, C.; Namukoko, H.; Sakala, C.; Bobo, P.; Masumbu, P.K.; Nachinga, B.; Ngula, D.; et al. Challenges Addressing Inequalities in Measles Vaccine Coverage in Zambia through a Measles–Rubella Supplementary Immunization Activity during the COVID-19 Pandemic. *Vaccines* **2023**, *11*, 608. https://doi.org/10.3390/vaccines11030608

Academic Editor: Vincenzo Baldo

Received: 14 February 2023
Revised: 2 March 2023
Accepted: 5 March 2023
Published: 7 March 2023

Abstract: Background: Measles–rubella supplementary immunization activities (MR-SIAs) are conducted to address inequalities in coverage and fill population immunity gaps when routine immunization services fail to reach all children with two doses of a measles-containing vaccine (MCV). We used data from a post-campaign coverage survey in Zambia to measure the proportion of measles zero-dose and under-immunized children who were reached by the 2020 MR-SIA and identified reasons associated with persistent inequalities following the MR-SIA. Methods: Children between 9 and 59 months were enrolled in a nationally representative, cross-sectional, multistage stratified cluster survey in October 2021 to estimate vaccination coverage during the November 2020 MR-SIA. Vaccination status was determined by immunization card or through caregivers' recall. MR-SIA coverage and the proportion of measles zero-dose and under-immunized children reached by MR-SIA were estimated. Log-binomial models were used to assess risk factors for missing the MR-SIA dose. Results: Overall, 4640 children were enrolled in the nationwide coverage survey. Only 68.6% (95% CI: 66.7%, 70.6%) received MCV during the MR-SIA. The MR-SIA provided MCV1 to 4.2% (95% CI: 0.9%, 4.6%) and MCV2 to 6.3% (95% CI: 5.6%, 7.1%) of enrolled children, but 58.1% (95% CI: 59.8%, 62.8%) of children receiving the MR-SIA dose had received at least two prior MCV doses. Furthermore, 27.8% of measles zero-dose children were vaccinated through the MR-SIA. The MR-SIA reduced the proportion of measles zero-dose children from 15.1% (95% CI: 13.6%, 16.7%) to 10.9% (95% CI: 9.7%, 12.3%). Zero-dose and under-immunized children were more likely to miss MR-SIA doses (prevalence ratio (PR): 2.81; 95% CI: 1.80, 4.41 and 2.22; 95% CI: 1.21 and 4.07) compared to fully vaccinated children. Conclusions: The MR-SIA reached more under-immunized children with MCV2 than measles zero-dose children with MCV1. However, improvement is needed to reach the remaining measles zero-dose children after SIA. One possible solution to address the inequalities in vaccination is to transition from nationwide non-selective SIAs to more targeted and selective strategies.

Keywords: zero-dose; under-immunization; measles; rubella; vaccination; supplementary immunization activity; campaign; children; inequality

1. Introduction

Measles and rubella remain important causes of morbidity and mortality. In 2021, there were an estimated 9.5 million measles cases and 128,000 measles deaths globally [1].

Rubella results in an estimated 100,000 annual deaths globally due to congenital rubella syndrome [2]. Both viruses are endemic in sub-Saharan Africa, and the elimination targets for all member states in the World Health Organization (WHO) Africa region are far from being reached [3].

Zambia has made significant progress in increasing coverage with measles-containing vaccines (MCVs) over the past two decades and attained high routine vaccination coverage of 93% with the first dose of MCV (MCV1) in 2019. However, routine vaccination coverage with the second dose of MCV (MCV2) has lagged behind at approximately 66% [4]. Following widespread disruptions to immunization services because of the COVID-19 pandemic, there are concerns that children who missed their routine and campaign vaccination doses could form clusters of susceptible populations that drive measles outbreaks [5–8]. To fill these population immunity gaps that arise when routine immunization services fail to reach all children with two doses of MCV, the Zambian Ministry of Health has conducted a nationwide non-selective measles–rubella supplementary immunization activity (MR-SIA) every four years since 2003 to avoid accumulation of a cohort of measles-susceptible children. The most recent MR-SIA was conducted in November 2020 during the COVID-19 pandemic, targeting children between the ages of 9 and 59 months [9].

After the MR-SIA, a nationwide, population-level post-campaign coverage survey (PCCS) was conducted in October 2021 as required by Gavi [10]. A PCCS should typically be conducted within three months of SIA completion to measure MR-SIA coverage, defined as the proportion of children in the target age group who received an MR vaccine dose during the SIA. The PCCS for the 2020 MR-SIA was delayed and conducted almost a year after the SIA due to the COVID-19 pandemic. For a PCCS to measure progress towards the goals of the Immunization Agenda 2030, a global strategy "to leave no one behind", it is critical to estimate MR-SIA coverage among subpopulations who had not previously received MCV from routine services (referred to as measles zero-dose children) and subpopulations of those eligible for MCV2 who had not received MCV2 before the MR-SIA (measles under-immunized children) [11,12]. We used national, cross-sectional data from the PCCS to understand how MR-SIA can address vaccination inequalities by estimating routine and SIA MCV coverages, as well as the proportion of measles zero-dose and under-immunized children reached by the MR-SIA, and identified reasons associated with missing the MR-SIA. Our study will help program managers and researchers understand vaccination inequalities that are overlooked when implementing SIA and when measuring the impact of SIAs using the PCCS.

2. Methods

2.1. Study Design and Population

Using data from a nationwide, cross-sectional survey conducted in Zambia, we estimated the proportion of measles zero-dose and under-immunized children who were vaccinated during the 2020 MR-SIA. The PCCS was conducted in October 2021 following a non-selective, nationwide MR-SIA in November 2020. The survey enrolled children between the ages of 9 and 59 months at the time of the November 2020 SIA. Therefore, all children born between December 2015 and the end of February 2020 residing in the selected households were eligible for the survey.

2.2. Sampling Strategy

Sample selection was based on a two-stage stratified cluster sample design. In total, 110 and 162 enumeration areas (EAs) were selected within urban and rural strata, respectively, with probability proportional to size. Before selection, EAs were sorted by province, district, constituency, ward, rural/urban status, census supervisory area, and standard enumeration area to assure implicit representation.

In the second stage, an updated listing of the households in the selected EAs was generated to ensure that key information in the selected EAs was updated, as well as the accuracy of the number of residential households and households with at least one child aged 9 to 59 months at the time of the SIA. From each EA, 20 households with eligible children were selected using systematic random sampling, and data were collected on all children in the household who met the eligibility criteria. In EAs with 20 or fewer households with eligible children, all households with eligible children were eligible for enrolment (see Supplementary Methods for more detail).

2.3. Data Collection

Prior to the interview, informed consent was obtained from the parents or legal guardians. After obtaining parental permission, survey staff collected sociodemographic characteristics and vaccination history from the parents or caregivers of the child using a standardized, tablet-based questionnaire. Receipt of routine and campaign MCV doses was collected by first asking caregivers to recall the child's vaccination history; then, this was verified by reviewing the under-5 immunization card or any documents (i.e., journals, piece of paper with vaccination notes) where vaccinations were recorded. Standardized questions previously used in demographic and health surveys were asked to collect information on routine and campaign doses of MCV, routine diphtheria–tetanus–pertussis (DTP) vaccine, and routine Bacille Calmette-Guérin (BCG) vaccine.

2.4. Statistical Analysis

The weighted study outcomes were, (1) the percentage of children who received the MR vaccine during the SIA, (2) the percentage of measles zero-dose children who received the MR vaccine during the SIA, and (3) MCV1 and MCV2 coverage before and after the SIA. In addition, the impact of the MR-SIA was estimated by calculating the increase in MCV1 and MCV2 coverage after the SIA. For children whose vaccination cards or records were available, we assessed routine vaccination status before the SIA to estimate the proportion of Gavi-defined zero-dose, under-immunized and fully vaccinated children [13]. Gavi defined "zero-dose children" as children who have not received the first dose of the DTP vaccine. "Under-immunized" children were defined as those who missed a third dose of the DTP vaccine. Together, zero-dose and under-immunized children formed missed communities. To assess MCV coverage, we defined "measles zero-dose" children as children who did not receive MCV1. Unvaccinated was defined as children whose parents or caregivers could not recall their children's vaccination status. Sensitivity analyses were conducted by (1) treating these children as vaccinated and (2) restricting the analysis to children whose vaccination status was card-confirmed.

Log-binomial regression analysis was performed to assess factors associated with missing MR-SIA vaccination. Participant characteristics for enrolled children (sex, setting, age, and DTP vaccination status) and household characteristics (relationship of head of household with enrolled children, maternal education level, maternal COVID-19 vaccination status, and travel time) were included in the univariable analysis to identify social determinants associated with missing MR-SIA vaccination. The prevalence ratio (PR) and the corresponding 95% confidence intervals (95% CI) were calculated. Age-adjusted log-binomial regression was used to address heterogeneity between age categories. Forward and backward stepwise selection methods were used to select the best-fit model. The final multivariable model included variables with a p-value < 0.05 from age-adjusted univariable analyses and variables that were of public health importance. Log-likelihood and Akaike's information criteria (AIC) were used to determine the goodness of fit, and the model with the lowest AIC was selected as the best-fit model. All statistical analyses were performed in R version 4.1.3, and the model was run using the survey package to account for sampling weights [14,15]. Figures were generated using the ggplot2 package [16].

3. Results

3.1. Characteristics of Survey Respondents

Overall, 5440 households with at least one child younger than 15 years of age at the time of the SIA were selected. Respondents from 5155 (95%) households were available during the survey period. Of the available households, only 4641 (90%) were eligible for the survey after excluding 514 households that had no child between the ages 9 and 59 months. Of these households, only 51 (1%) respondents refused to participate in the survey. After applying the exclusion and inclusion criteria, data were collected on 4640 eligible children during the MR-SIA (Figure 1). After weighting, 49.8% (95% CI: 48.1%, 51.3%) of the children were male, and 59.2% (95% CI: 57.6%, 60.7%) lived in rural areas. About two-fifths (40.5%, 95% CI: 37.6%, 43.1%) did not have vaccination cards or other documents that showed their vaccination status. Overall, 88.2% (95% CI: 87.2%, 89.2%) were fully vaccinated with all recommended DTP doses for their age (Table 1). A proportion of mothers had a primary school education (41.0%, 95% CI: 39.5%, 42.6%), and only 7.7% (95% CI: 6.8%, 8.6%) had an education level higher than secondary school. More than three-quarters of adults (79.1%; 95% CI: 78.2%, 80.0%) who lived in the selected households were not vaccinated against SARS-CoV-2 at the time of PCCS. Only 24.9% (95% CI: 23.5%, 26.3%) of the parents or guardians traveled fewer than 15 min to get to the nearest health facility, regardless of the mode of transport.

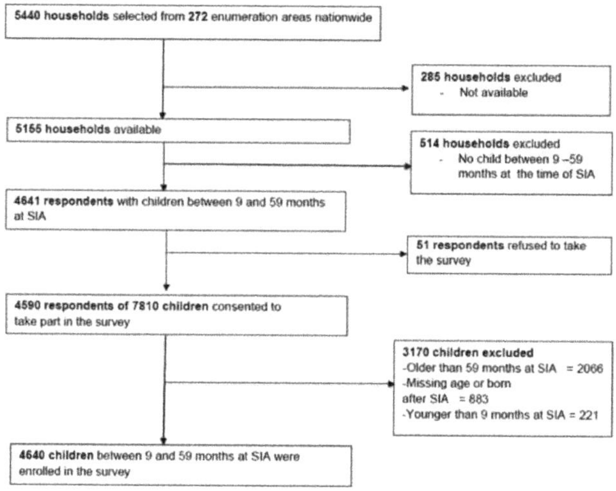

Figure 1. Study flow diagram.

Table 1. Participants and household characteristics.

Characteristics	Unweighted N (%)	Weighted % (95% CI)
Total	4640	
Gender		
Male	2310 (49.8)	49.8 (48.2, 51.3)
Female	2330 (50.2)	50.2 (48.7, 51.8)
Setting		
Rural	2876 (62.0)	59.2 (57.6, 60.7)
Urban	1764 (38.0)	40.8 (39.3, 42.4)
Province		
Central	447 (9.6)	10.3 (9.4, 11.3)
Copperbelt	631 (13.6)	14.1 (13.0, 15.2)
Eastern	601 (13.0)	11.8 (10.7, 12.8)
Luapula	379 (8.2)	7.7 (6.9, 8.6)
Lusaka	816 (17.6)	17.7 (16.6, 18.9)
Muchinga	281 (6.1)	6.1 (5.4, 6.9)

Table 1. *Cont.*

Characteristics	Unweighted N (%)	Weighted % (95% CI)
Northern	387 (8.3)	8.8 (8.0, 9.7)
North-Western	292 (6.3)	5.6 (4.9, 6.3)
Southern	510 (11.0)	12.0 (10.9, 13.1)
Western	296 (6.4)	6.0 (5.4, 6.7)
Age at SIA		
9–17 months	710 (15.3)	15.4 (14.3, 16.6)
18–59 months	3930 (84.7)	84.6 (83.4, 85.7)
Availability of vaccination card		
Card available and verified	2626 (56.6)	56.6 (55.1, 58.2)
Card not available but another document verified with vaccination status	136 (2.9)	2.9 (2.4, 3.4)
Reported card available but could not provide a document with vaccination status	405 (8.8)	8.8 (7.6, 10.0)
No card and no other document	1473 (31.7)	31.7 (30.0, 33.1)
DTP vaccination status (both card and recall) [1]		
Fully vaccinated for DTP	4076 (87.8)	88.2 (87.2, 89.2)
Under-immunized for DTP	45 (1.0)	1.0 (0.7, 1.4)
Zero-dose for DTP	97 (2.1)	2.2 (1.7, 2.6)
Unknown	424 (9.1)	8.7 (7.9, 9.6)
Head of the household		
Biological parent	3435 (74.0)	74.3 (73.0, 75.6)
Other	1205 (26.0)	25.7 (24.4, 27.1)
Maternal education level		
No education	471 (10.2)	9.6 (8.7, 10.5)
Primary	1959 (42.2)	41.0 (39.5, 42.6)
Secondary	1373 (29.6)	30.3 (28.9, 31.8)
Higher	312 (6.7)	7.7 (6.8, 8.6)
Unknown	525 (11.3)	11.4 (10.4, 12.4)
COVID-19 vaccination status of the adults in the household [2] (N = 9780)		
Fully vaccinated	1610 (16.5)	17.0 (16.1, 17.8)
Partially vaccinated	354 (3.6)	4.0 (3.5, 4.4)
Not vaccinated	7816 (79.9)	79.1 (78.2, 80.0)
Time to health facility for routine vaccinations		
Less than 15 min	1115 (24.0)	24.9 (23.5,26.3)
15–30 min	1188 (25.6)	25.7 (24.3, 27.0)
31 min–1 h	1204 (26.0)	26.0 (24.6, 27.4)
More than 1 h	1040 (22.4)	21.6 (20.4, 23.0)
Unknown	93 (2.0)	1.2 (0.9, 1.6)

[1] Gavi zero-dose children are those who have not received any routine vaccines. For operational purposes, Gavi defined "zero-dose children" as children who have not received the first dose of a diphtheria–tetanus–pertussis-containing vaccine (DPT1) as a proxy measure. "Under-immunized" was defined as children missing a third dose of a diphtheria–tetanus–pertussis-containing vaccine (DPT3). [2] The COVID-19 vaccination status of all the adults living in the same household as the enrolled child. Fully vaccinated: one dose of Johnson & Johnson or two doses of AstraZeneca vaccine.

3.2. *SIA Coverage and Added Value in Addressing Inequalities*

Based on verbal recall and card-confirmed weighted results, 84.9% (95% CI: 81.8%, 88.0%) of children received at least one dose of routine MCV before the 2020 MR-SIA (Figure 2, Table S1). Routine MCV1 coverage before the SIA for children between the ages of 9 and 17 months was 83.9% (95% CI: 76.3%, 91.6%) and 85.7% (95% CI: 81.7%, 86.6%)

for those 18 months and older (Table S2). When treating children with unknown MCV vaccination status as vaccinated, the percentage of children who received at least one MCV dose increased from 84.9% to 90.6% (Table S3).

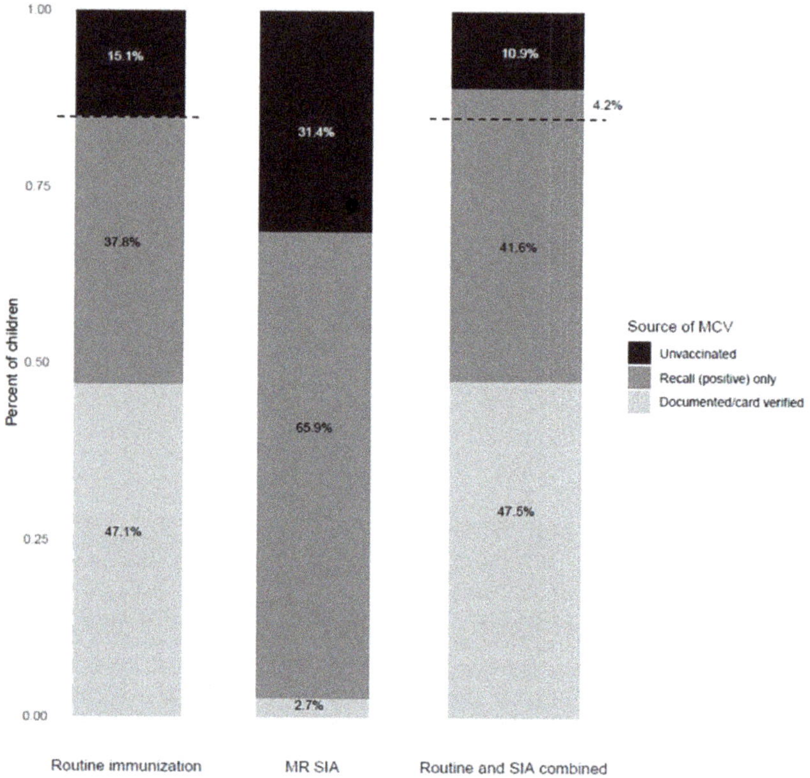

Figure 2. Measles and rubella vaccination coverage (at least one dose) among children between the ages of 9 and 59 months. The dashed line and percentage indicate the change in percentage of unvaccinated children before and after the MR-SIA.

Overall, 68.6% (95% CI: 66.7%, 70.6%) of children eligible for the 2020 MR-SIA received MCV during the SIA. Only 2.7% of these eligible children had documented evidence of receiving the MR-SIA dose, and the rest were identified by caregiver recall. When routine and SIA MCV coverage was combined, coverage of at least one dose of MCV increased by 4.2%, from 84.9% (95% CI: 81.8%, 88.0%) to 89.1% (95% CI: 86.0%, 92.2%), as assessed by card and verbal recall. Before the MR-SIA, 15.1% (95% CI: 13.6%, 16.8%) of children were measles zero-dose. Of these measles zero-dose children, 27.8% were vaccinated during the SIA when unknown vaccination status was categorized as unvaccinated. This implies that the MR-SIA reduced the proportion of measles zero-dose children from 15.1% (95% CI: 13.6%, 16.7%) to 10.9% (95% CI: 9.7% to 12.3%) (Figure 2, Table S1). Although the study was not powered for comparisons between provinces, Central Province had the lowest SIA coverage and Eastern and Copperbelt Provinces had the highest SIA coverage (Figure 3A). Western Province had a higher proportion of measles zero-dose children who remained unvaccinated after the SIA (18.9%, 95% CI: 12.8%, 22.5%) (Figure 3B). Prior to the SIA, 59 (8.3%) measles zero-dose children were also DTP zero-dose. After the SIA, 55 (95%) of those children remained zero-dose for both MCV and DTP.

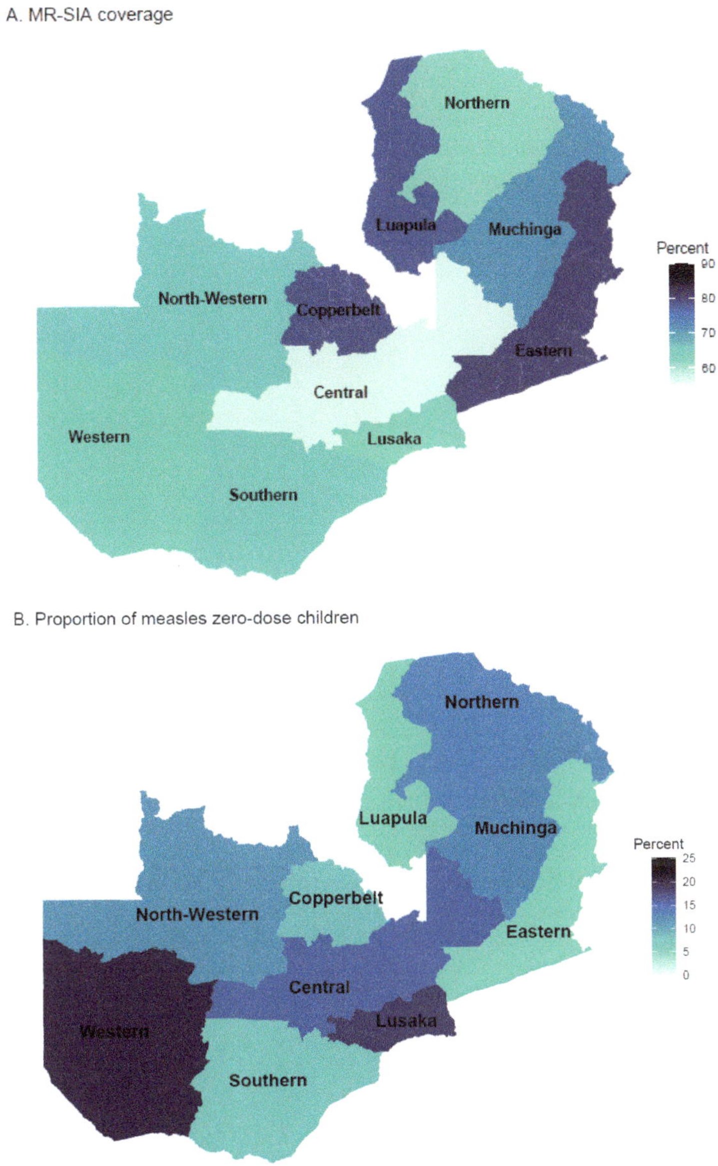

Figure 3. Provincial-level MR-SIA coverage and the proportion of measles zero-dose children.

During the SIA, 6.3% (95% CI: 5.6%, 7.1%) of enrolled children received MCV2, and 58.1% (95% CI: 59.8%, 62.8%) received a third or further MCV dose (Figure 4, Table S4). The sensitivity analysis restricted to children who had a vaccination card or other documentation of vaccines (N = 2762) showed that 1.5% (95% CI: 1.0%, 2.0%) of the children received MCV1 through the SIA, 2.7% (95% CI: 2.1%, 3.4%) of children received MCV2, and 3.6% (95% CI: 2.9%, 4.4%) remained measles zero-dose after the SIA (Table S5).

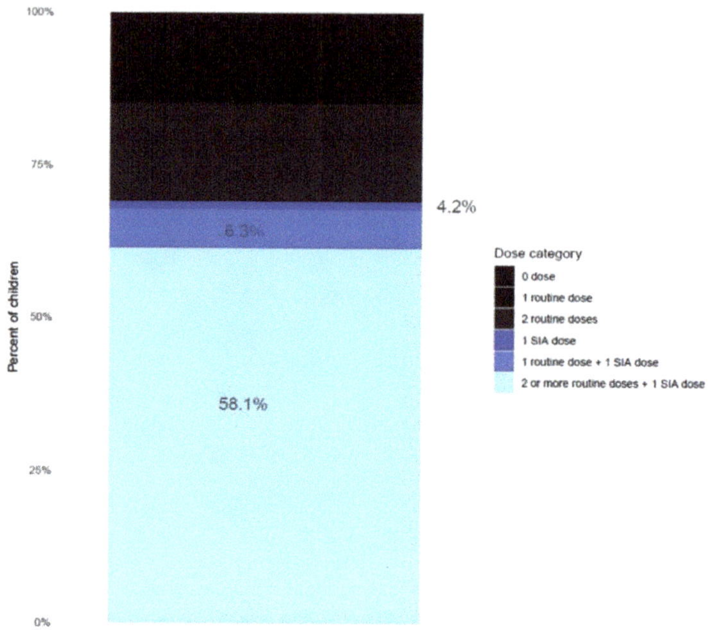

Figure 4. Receipt of measles and rubella vaccine among children 9–59 months post SIA, including documented or recalled evidence of vaccination. 0 dose: children who had a documented record or recalled not having received any MCV doses though routine immunization or SIA; 1 routine dose: children who had a documented record or recalled having received MCV1 through routine immunization; 2 routine doses: children who had a documented record or recalled having received MCV1 and MCV2 through routine immunization; 1 SIA dose: children who had a documented record or recalled not having received any MCV through routine immunization and a had documented record or recalled having received MCV1 through SIA; 1 routine dose + 1 SIA dose: children who had a documented record or recalled having received MCV1 through routine immunization and had a documented record or recalled having received MCV2 through SIA; 2 or more routine doses + 1 SIA dose: children who had a documented record or recalled having received MCV1 and MCV2 and/or additional MCVs through routine immunization and recalled having received an additional MCV through SIA.

3.3. Persistent Inequalities after the SIA

Among children eligible for the 2020 MR-SIA, 1454 (31%) were missed by the 2020 MR-SIA (Table 2). Compared to fully vaccinated children using the Gavi definition, zero-dose children were 2.8 times more likely to miss the SIA dose (PR:2.8; 95% CI: 1.8, 4.4), and under-immunized children were 2.2 times more likely to miss the SIA dose (PR:2.2; 95% CI: 1.2, 4.1) after adjusting for age, sex, maternal education level, and travel time to health facilities (Table 2). Children in urban areas were 39% more likely to miss the SIA dose than those in rural areas (PR: 1.39; 95% CI: 1.18, 1.63). Children whose mothers had primary and secondary education were less likely to miss the SIA vaccination than children whose mothers had no formal education (PR: 0.73; 95% CI: 0.58 and 0.92, and PR 0.60; 95% CI: 0.47 and 0.77, respectively) (Table 2). Increased travel time to the nearest health center increased the likelihood of children missing the SIA dose. With children living less than 15 min away from the health center as the reference group, children who lived 30 to 60 min away from a health center were 51% more likely to miss the SIA dose (PR: 1.51; 95% CI: 1.23, 1.84), while those who lived more than 1 h from the health center were 70% more likely (PR: 1.70, 95% CI: 1.37, 2.11) to miss the MR vaccination during SIA (Table 2).

Table 2. Risk factors associated with self-reported missing of campaign MR dose.

Characteristic	Children Included in the Survey, N (%)	Children Who Missed the Campaign Measles Dose, n (%)	Unadjusted Univariable Log-Binomial Regression			Age-Adjusted Univariable Log-Binomial Regression			Multivariable Log-Binomial Regression		
			PR [1]	95% CI [2]	*p*-Value	PR	95% CI	*p*-Value	PR	95% CI	*p*-Value
Total	4640	1454									
Age					0.83			—			0.5
Age 9–17 months	710 (15.3)	230 (15.8)	—	—		—	—		—	—	
Age 18–59 months	3930 (84.7)	1224 (84.2)	0.98	0.81, 1.18		—	—		0.93	0.77, 1.13	
Sex					0.45			0.4			0.4
Male	2330 (50.2)	723 (49.7)	—	—		—	—		—	—	
Female	2310 (49.8)	731 (50.3)	1.05	0.92, 1.21		1.05	0.92, 1.21		1.06	0.92, 1.22	
Setting					0.36			0.4			<0.001
Rural	2876 (62.0)	883 (60.7)	—	—		—	—		—	—	
Urban	1764 (38.0)	571 (39.3)	1.07	0.93, 1.22		1.07	0.93, 1.22		1.39	1.18, 1.63	
DTP vaccination status					<0.001			<0.001			<0.001
Fully vaccinated	4076 (87.8)	1212 (83.4)	—	—		—	—		—	—	
Under-immunized	45 (1.0)	22 (1.5)	2.31	1.24, 4.29		2.30	1.24, 4.28		2.22	1.21, 4.07	
Zero-dose	97 (2.1)	59 (4.2)	3.79	2.45, 5.87		3.80	2.45, 5.88		2.81	1.80, 4.41	
Unknown	424 (9.1)	161 (10.9)	1.61	1.27, 2.04		1.61	1.27, 2.04		1.44	1.12, 1.84	
Maternal education level					<0.001			<0.001			<0.001
No formal education	471 (10.2)	195 (13.4)	—	—		—	—		—	—	
Primary education	1959 (42.2)	604 (41.6)	0.73	0.58, 0.92		0.73	0.58, 0.92		0.73	0.58, 0.92	
Secondary education	1373 (29.6)	387 (26.6)	0.61	0.48, 0.78		0.61	0.48, 0.78		0.60	0.47, 0.77	
Higher education	312 (6.7)	92 (6.3)	0.67	0.48, 0.94		0.67	0.48, 0.93		0.66	0.46, 0.95	
Unknown	525 (11.3)	176 (12.1)	0.97	0.73, 1.29		0.97	0.73, 1.29		0.91	0.68, 1.22	
Time to health facility for routine vaccinations					<0.001			<0.001			<0.001
<15 min	1115 (24.0)	291 (20.0)	—	—		—	—		—	—	
15–30 min	1188 (25.6)	339 (23.3)	1.15	0.94, 1.40		1.15	0.94, 1.40		1.17	0.96, 1.43	
31 min to 1 h	1204 (26.0)	411 (28.3)	1.44	1.19, 1.75		1.44	1.19, 1.75		1.51	1.23, 1.84	
>1 h	1040 (22.4)	381 (26.2)	1.61	1.32, 1.97		1.61	1.32, 1.97		1.70	1.37, 2.11	
Unknown	93 (2.0)	32 (2.2)	2.17	0.60, 7.88		2.15	0.59, 7.80		1.64	0.44, 6.06	
Mother's COVID vaccination status					0.028			0.027			
Not vaccinated	3265 (70.4)	1015 (69.8)	—	—		—	—				
Partially vaccinated	127 (2.7)	37 (2.6)	1.08	0.70, 1.65		1.08	0.70, 1.65				
Fully vaccinated	689 (14.9)	198 (13.6)	0.94	0.77, 1.14		0.94	0.77, 1.14				
Unknown	559 (12.0)	204 (14.0)	1.61	0.77, 3.40		1.60	0.76, 3.36				
Head of the household					0.072			0.072			
Biological parent	3435 (74.0)	1051 (72.3)	—	—		—	—				
Other	1205 (26.0)	403 (27.8)	1.15	0.99, 1.34		1.15	0.99, 1.34				

[1] PR: prevalence ratio. [2] 95% CI: 95% confidence interval.

4. Discussion

Prior to the November 2020 SIA in Zambia, 84.9% of children aged 9 to 59 months had received at least one dose of MCV. However, during the 2020 MR-SIA, only 68.6% of children in this age group received a campaign MR vaccine dose. Among the 709 measles zero-dose children, only 27.8% were vaccinated during the MR-SIA. Overall, the MR-SIA increased MCV1 coverage from 84.9% to 89.1%. An additional 6.3% of enrolled children in the PCCS received MCV2, and 58.1% received a third dose. Living in an urban area and longer travel time to a health center were associated with missing the MR-SIA vaccine dose. Zero-dose children and children whose mothers had lower education levels were less likely to be vaccinated during the SIA.

Previous MR-SIAs in Zambia reported coverages higher than 95% [17]. Although the 2020 MR-SIA used strategies similar to previous SIAs, coverage was lower for two likely reasons. First, the 2020 MR-SIA was implemented at the time when all COVID-19 control measures were instituted, including stopping all public gatherings, and when the COVID-19 vaccine was just beginning to be rolled out. During this period, a decline and delay in vaccinations were observed in many parts of the world [18]. Secondly, a Child Health Week (CHW) that included MR vaccination was conducted 5 months prior to the MR-SIA [9]. Many children may have received the MR vaccine during the CHW and therefore were not brought to the MR-SIA. Because of the general decline in the coverage of the SIA as compared to previous SIAs, the Ministry of Health must intensify routine immunization activities such as school vaccination activities and periodic intensified routine immunizations to reach children who were missed by the SIA.

According to our analysis, 27.8% of measles zero-dose children were vaccinated during the MR-SIA. This number is higher than was estimated in 11 other countries on the African continent based on an analysis of Demographic and Health Survey (DHS) data. Specifically, Portnoy et al. estimated that the proportion of measles zero-dose children vaccinated by a measles SIA ranged from 3% in Lesotho to 20% in Burkina Faso in 2003 [19]. Although PCCS and DHS do not have the same sampling frames, given that both datasets are meant to be nationally representative, this comparison may be possible and shows that Zambia's MR-SIA does comparably well in reaching measles zero-dose children. However, further work is needed for MR-SIAs to reach more measles zero-dose children and address the inequity of routine vaccination. Ideally, SIAs do not perpetuate the inequities in routine vaccination such that SIA doses are independent of routine administered doses. This means that an SIA dose is equally as likely to reach measles zero-dose children as measles-vaccinated children; in this analysis, we expected 84.9% MR-SIA coverage among all children, regardless of previous vaccination status. An even more ambitious goal is that the SIA effectively reverse inequities in routine vaccination such that SIAs reach a larger proportion of unvaccinated children than that of all targeted children; in this analysis, we expected the proportion of measles zero-dose children reached by the MR-SIA to be greater than 84.9%. When planning SIAs, the Ministry of Health must consider utilizing and triangulating administrative coverage and local survey data to identify missed communities and develop SIA microplans that target such communities with intensive vaccination activities.

Although the MR-SIA did not vaccinate a large proportion of measles zero-dose children, it did particularly well in reaching under-immunized children who were eligible for MCV2 but had only received MCV1 at the time of the SIA. Achieving high MR-SIA coverage in the under-immunized subpopulation is a good result for the Zambia expanded program on immunization because routine coverage for MCV2 has lagged (66%) compared to routine MCV1, which is normally above 90% [4]. We postulate that the large difference in coverage between zero-dose and under-immunized subpopulations was observed because these subpopulations have different vulnerabilities and therefore require different approaches to be reached. When developing SIAs, these subpopulations must be considered carefully, and microplans must be developed according to their needs. Approximately 58% of children vaccinated during the SIA already had two MCV doses before the SIA, indicating unnecessary doses, resulting in excess costs, given that these children were fully vaccinated against measles prior to the SIA [20]. However, evidence of vaccination was based on parental recall for a considerable proportion of children; therefore, reaching these children may have provided a missing dose to children who were misclassified as vaccinated. We recommend that the vaccination card be updated to explicitly provide a section for SIA doses and dates when the SIA doses are administered.

The regression analysis showed that zero-dose children were less likely to be reached by the SIA than fully vaccinated children. In most cases, PCCSs do not report coverage among zero-dose and under-immunized children. Children who lived further from a health center or lived in an urban area were less likely to receive the MR-SIA dose. Previous studies reported increasing distance and travel time as impediments to routine vaccination [21]. Long distance to vaccination sites also affects coverage of SIAs, especially among missed communities. Our analysis confirms findings from a study conducted during the 2020 Zambia MR-SIA, which demonstrated a lower vaccination coverage among measles zero-dose children as the distance to the nearest vaccination site increased [22]. Differences in vaccination coverage between urban and rural areas have been reported previously [23]. Most countries have higher coverage in urban areas because of easy access to primary health facilities, as well as less travel time and cost [23]. Although routine MCV administrative coverage in Zambia is generally higher in urban areas than in rural areas, poor urban communities in high-population-density areas may have large numbers of unvaccinated children [24]. Not reaching zero-dose children in high-population-density urban areas may result in clusters of susceptible children that can sustain measles outbreaks. Other studies have shown that adjusting for other social-determinant factors diluted the urban–rural differential, suggesting it is not the driving factor but correlated with more proximal determinants [23]. Routine and SIA planning must deliberately address factors driving rural–urban vaccination inequalities to reach missed communities.

This study has several limitations. Inferences about the impact of the 2020 MR-SIA on reaching measles zero-dose and under-immunized children may have been constrained by recall bias. Firstly, the time between the SIA and PCCS was longer than the recommended 3 months [10]. This may have resulted in misclassification of vaccination status because caregivers may have forgotten the details of events that happened 10 months ago. Secondly, although card retention was high, SIA doses were rarely documented and could only be measured by caregivers' recall. To address the potential impact of recall bias, we performed sensitivity analyses by restricting the analysis to only children with vaccination cards (Table S5).

5. Conclusions

We have shown the MR-SIA's strengths and limitations in addressing inequalities in immunization through reaching and failing to reach measles zero-dose and under-immunized children. The SIA reached more under-immunized children in a context in which MCV2 coverage is low. However, the SIA only reached a small proportion of measles zero-dose children. To reduce vaccination inequalities for missed communities, further work is needed for both MR-SIA and routine immunization programs in Zambia to reach more measles zero-dose children and address the inequity of routine vaccination. When developing SIAs, the vulnerability of zero-dose and under-immunized subpopulations must be considered carefully, and microplans must be developed according to their needs. One possible solution is to transition from nationwide non-selective SIAs to more targeted and selective strategies.

Supplementary Materials: The following supporting information can be downloaded at: https://www.mdpi.com/article/10.3390/vaccines11030608/s1, Table S1: Measles and rubella vaccination coverage (at least one dose) among children between 9 months to 59 months; Table S2: Measles and rubella vaccination coverage (at least one dose) among children between 9 months to 59 months, stratified by 9–17 months and 18–59 months; Table S3: Measles and rubella vaccination coverage (at least one dose) among children between 9 months to 59 months, treating unknown as vaccinated;

Table S4: Unweighted and weighted estimates of the number of routine and SIA MR doses that each child 9–59 months had received; Table S5: Receipt of MR vaccine among children 9–59 months post-SIA by strategy, including only documented vaccination; Table S6: Details of survey design. Table S7: Sample allocation within provinces.

Author Contributions: Conceptualization, Y.Y., F.D.M., P.B., P.K.M. and S.M.; Formal analysis, Y.Y., N.K., B.N., A.C.C. and S.M.; Funding acquisition, F.D.M. and S.M.; Investigation, P.B.; Methodology, Y.Y., F.D.M., H.N., C.S., P.K.M., D.N. and S.M.; Project administration, F.D.M. and C.N.; Software, N.K. and B.N.; Supervision, W.J.M. and S.M.; Visualization, Y.Y.; Writing—original draft, Y.Y., N.K., F.D.M., C.P., A.K.W., W.J.M. and S.M.; Writing—review and editing, Y.Y., N.K., F.D.M., C.N., H.N., C.S., P.B., P.K.M., B.N., D.N., A.C.C., C.P., A.K.W. and S.M. All authors have read and agreed to the published version of the manuscript.

Funding: The 2020 MR and PCCS were funded by World Health Organization, JHPIEGO Zambia country office, Macha Research Trust, and the Gavi the Vaccine Alliance through the Ministry of Health, Zambia. S.M. and Y.Y. were supported by the Grand Challenges Explorations initiative (grant number INV-016016).

Institutional Review Board Statement: The PCCS protocol was reviewed and approved by the ERES Converge Institutional Review Board, and permission was obtained from the Zambia National Health Research Authority.

Informed Consent Statement: Not applicable.

Data Availability Statement: The study protocol and dataset can be made available upon request to the corresponding author (smutemb1@jhmi.edu). Data were obtained from Zambia Ministry of Health and the Zambia National Health Research Authority under data-sharing agreements and can only be shared with permission from the Ministry of Health.

Acknowledgments: This work was only possible through the contributions of many other individuals and organizations. We thank the Ministry of Health personnel that was involved in the implementation of the SIA and the data collectors who conducted the PCCS. We thank the Zambia Ministry of Health for providing guidance on the objectives. Finally, we are greatly indebted to the World Health Organization, JHPIEGO Zambia country office, Macha Research Trust and Gavi the Vaccine Alliance, who provided the funding for the implementation of the MR-SIA and the PCCS.

Conflicts of Interest: Y.Y. reports funding from Pfizer in the past year unrelated to the submitted work. All other authors have no conflict of interest to declare. The funders had no role in the design of the study; in the collection, analyses, or interpretation of data; in the writing of the manuscript; or in the decision to publish the results.

References

1. Minta, A.A.; Ferrari, M.; Antoni, S.; Portnoy, A.; Sbarra, A.; Lambert, B.; Hauryski, S.; Hatcher, C.; Nedelec, Y.; Datta, D.; et al. Progress Toward Regional Measles Elimination—Worldwide, 2000–2021. *Morb. Mortal. Wkly. Rep.* **2022**, *71*, 1489–1495. [CrossRef] [PubMed]
2. World Health Organization. Rubella vaccines: WHO position paper—July 2020. *Wkly. Epidemiol. Rec.* **2020**, *27*, 306–324.
3. Wariri, O.; Nkereuwem, E.; Erondu, N.A.; Edem, B.; Nkereuwem, O.O.; Idoko, O.T.; Agogo, E.; Enegela, J.E.; Sesay, T.; Conde, I.S.; et al. A scorecard of progress towards measles elimination in 15 west African countries, 2001–2019: A retrospective, multicountry analysis of national immunisation coverage and surveillance data. *Lancet Glob. Health* **2021**, *9*, e280–e290. [CrossRef]
4. World Health Organization. Immunization Zambia 2022 Country Profile. Available online: https://www.who.int/publications/m/item/immunization-zmb-2022-country-profile (accessed on 5 January 2023).
5. Shet, A.; Carr, K.; Danovaro-Holliday, M.C.; Sodha, S.V.; Prosperi, C.; Wunderlich, J.; Wonodi, C.; Reynolds, H.W.; Mirza, I.; Gacic-Dobo, M.; et al. Impact of the SARS-CoV-2 pandemic on routine immunisation services: Evidence of disruption and recovery from 170 countries and territories. *Lancet Glob. Health* **2022**, *10*, e186–e194. [CrossRef] [PubMed]
6. Ho, L.L.; Gurung, S.; Mirza, I.; Nicolas, H.D.; Steulet, C.; Burman, A.L.; Danovaro-Holliday, C.; Sodha, S.; Kretsinger, K. Impact of the SARS-CoV-2 pandemic on vaccine-preventable disease campaigns. *Int. J. Infect. Dis.* **2022**, *119*, 201–209. [CrossRef] [PubMed]
7. Durrheim, D.N.; Andrus, J.K.; Tabassum, S.; Bashour, H.; Githanga, D.; Pfaff, G. A dangerous measles future looms beyond the COVID-19 pandemic. *Nat. Med.* **2021**, *27*, 360–361. [CrossRef] [PubMed]
8. Causey, K.; Fullman, N.; Sorensen, R.J.D.; Galles, N.C.; Zheng, P.; Aravkin, A.; Danovaro-Holliday, M.C.; Martinez-Piedra, R.; Sodha, S.V.; Velandia-González, M.P.; et al. Estimating global and regional disruptions to routine childhood vaccine coverage during the COVID-19 pandemic in 2020: A modelling study. *Lancet* **2021**, *398*, 522–534. [CrossRef] [PubMed]

9. Ministry of Health Zambia. *Post Coverage Measles-Rubella Campaign Evaluation Survey*; Ministry of Health Zambia: Lusaka, Zambia, 2021.
10. World Health Organization. *World Health Organization Vaccination Coverage Cluster Surveys: Reference Manual*; World Health Organization: Geneva, Switzerland, 2018.
11. McKee, A.; Ferrari, M.J.; Shea, K. Correlation between measles vaccine doses: Implications for the maintenance of elimination. *Epidemiol. Infect.* **2018**, *146*, 468–475. [CrossRef] [PubMed]
12. Cutts, F.; Dansereau, E.; Ferrari, M.; Hanson, M.; McCarthy, K.; Metcalf, C.; Takahashi, S.; Tatem, A.; Thakkar, N.; Truelove, S.; et al. Using models to shape measles control and elimination strategies in low- and middle-income countries: A review of recent applications. *Vaccine* **2020**, *38*, 979–992. [CrossRef] [PubMed]
13. Gavi. Gavi Phase 5 Strategy (2021–2025). Available online: https://www.gavi.org/our-alliance/strategy/phase-5-2021-2025 (accessed on 5 January 2023).
14. R Core Team. *R: A Language and Environment for Statistical Computing*; R Foundation for Statistical Computing: Vienna, Austria, 2019; Available online: https://www.R-project.org/ (accessed on 5 January 2023).
15. Lumley, T. Analysis of Complex Survey Samples. *J. Stat. Softw.* **2004**, *9*, 1–19. [CrossRef]
16. Wickham, H. *Ggplot2: Elegant Graphics for Data Analysis*; Springer: Berlin/Heidelberg, Germany, 2016.
17. Hayford, K.; Mutembo, S.; Carcelen, A.; Matakala, H.K.; Munachoonga, P.; Winter, A.; Wanyiri, J.W.; Searle, K.; Mwansa, F.D.; Mwiche, A.; et al. Measles and rubella serosurvey identifies rubella immunity gap in young adults of childbearing age in Zambia: The added value of nesting a serological survey within a post-campaign coverage evaluation survey. *Vaccine* **2019**, *37*, 2387–2393. [CrossRef] [PubMed]
18. SeyedAlinaghi, S.; Karimi, A.; Mojdeganlou, H.; Alilou, S.; Mirghaderi, S.P.; Noori, T.; Shamsabadi, A.; Dadras, O.; Vahedi, F.; Mohammadi, P.; et al. Impact ofCOVID-19 pandemic on routine vaccination coverage of children and adolescents: A systematic review. *Health Sci. Rep.* **2022**, *5*, e00516. [CrossRef]
19. Portnoy, A.; Jit, M.; Helleringer, S.; Verguet, S. Impact of measles supplementary immunization activities on reaching children missed by routine programs. *Vaccine* **2017**, *36*, 170–178. [CrossRef] [PubMed]
20. Hagedorn, B.L.; Dabbagh, A.; McCarthy, K.A. The cost saving opportunity of introducing a card review into measles-containing vaccination campaigns. *Vaccine* **2019**, *37*, 6093–6101. [CrossRef] [PubMed]
21. Abdulraheem, I.S.; Onajole, A.T.; Jimoh, A.A.G.; Oladipo, A.R. Reasons for incomplete vaccination and factors for missed opportunities among rural Nigerian children. *J. Public Health Epidemiol.* **2011**, *3*, 194–203.
22. Arambepola, R.; Yang, Y.; Hutchinson, K.; Mwansa, F.D.; Doherty, J.A.; Bwalya, F.; Ndubani, P.; Musukwa, G.; Moss, W.J.; Wesolowski, A.; et al. Using geospatial models to map zero-dose children: Factors associated with zero-dose vaccination status before and after a mass measles and rubella vaccination campaign in Southern province, Zambia. *BMJ Glob. Health* **2021**, *6*, e007479. [CrossRef] [PubMed]
23. Ali, H.A.; Hartner, A.M.; Echeverria-Londono, S.; Roth, J.; Li, X.; Abbas, K.; Portnoy, A.; Vynnycky, E.; Woodruff, K.; Ferguson, N.; et al. Vaccine equity in low and middle income countries: A systematic review and meta-analysis. *Int. J. Equity Health* **2022**, *21*, 82. [CrossRef] [PubMed]
24. Weiss, W.M.; Winch, P.J.; Burnham, G. Factors Associated with Missed Vaccination during Mass Immunization Campaigns. *J. Health Popul. Nutr.* **2009**, *27*, 358–367. [CrossRef] [PubMed]

vaccines

MDPI

Article

Factors Associated with Zero-Dose Childhood Vaccination Status in a Remote Fishing Community in Cameroon: A Cross-Sectional Analytical Study

Sangwe Clovis Nchinjoh [1,2,*], Yauba Saidu [1,3], Valirie Ndip Agbor [1,4], Clarence Mvalo Mbanga [1], Nkwain Jude Muteh [5], Andreas Ateke Njoh [6,7], Shalom Tchofke Ndoula [6], Bernard Nsah [1], Nnang Nadege Edwige [1], Sveta Roberman [2,8] and Chen Stein Zamir [2]

1 Clinton Health Access Initiative Inc., Yaounde P.O. Box 2664, Cameroon
2 Faculty of Medicine, The Hebrew University-Hadassah Braun School of Public Health and Community Medicine, Jerusalem 91120, Israel
3 Institute for Global Health, University of Siena, 53100 Siena, Italy
4 Nuffield Department of Population Health, University of Oxford, Oxford OX1 2JD, UK
5 Gavi, The Vaccine Alliance, 1202 Geneva, Switzerland
6 Expanded Program on Immunization, Cameroon Ministry of Public Health, Yaoundé P.O. Box 2084, Cameroon
7 School of Global Health and Bioethics, Euclid University, Bangui BP 157, Central African Republic
8 The Gordon Academic College of Education, Haifa 3570503, Israel
* Correspondence: sangweclovis@gmail.com; Tel.: +237-678-687-939

Citation: Nchinjoh, S.C.; Saidu, Y.; Agbor, V.N.; Mbanga, C.M.; Jude Muteh, N.; Njoh, A.A.; Ndoula, S.T.; Nsah, B.; Edwige, N.N.; Roberman, S.; et al. Factors Associated with Zero-Dose Childhood Vaccination Status in a Remote Fishing Community in Cameroon: A Cross-Sectional Analytical Study. *Vaccines* **2022**, *10*, 2052. https://doi.org/10.3390/vaccines10122052

Academic Editor: Pedro Plans-Rubió

Received: 20 October 2022
Accepted: 25 November 2022
Published: 30 November 2022

Abstract: Background: Cameroon's suboptimal access to childhood vaccinations poses a significant challenge to achieving the Immunization Agenda 2030 goal—ranking among the top 15 countries with a high proportion of zero-dose (unvaccinated) children worldwide. There are clusters of zero-dose children in pockets of communities that traditionally miss essential healthcare services, including vaccination. The Manoka Health District (MHD) is home to such settlements with consistently low vaccination coverages (DPT-HepB-Hib-1: 19.8% in 2021) and frequent outbreaks of vaccine-preventable diseases (VPD). Therefore, the absence of literature on zero-dose children in this context was a clarion call to characterize zero-dose children in fragile settings to inform policy and intervention design. **Methodology**: This cross-sectional analytical study involved 278 children, 0–24 months of age, selected from a 2020 door-to-door survey conducted in the two most populous health areas in an archipelago rural district, MHD (Cap-Cameroon and Toube). We used R Statistical Software (v4.1.2; R Core Team 2021) to run a multivariable logistic regression to determine zero-dose associated factors. **Results**: The survey revealed a zero-dose proportion of 91.7% (255) in MHD. Children who were delivered in health facilities were less likely to be zero-dose than those born at home (AOR: 0.07, 95% CI: 0.02–0.30, $p = 0.0003$). Compared to children born of Christian mothers, children born to minority non-Christian mothers had higher odds of being zero-dose (AOR: 6.55, 95% CI: 1.04–41.25, $p = 0.0453$). Children born to fathers who are immigrants were more likely to be zero-dose children than Cameroonians (AOR: 2.60, 95% CI = 0.65–10.35, $p = 0.0016$). Younger children were likely to be unvaccinated compared to older peers (AOR: 0.90, 95% CI: 0.82–1.00, $p = 0.0401$). **Conclusions**: In the spirit of "leaving no child behind," the study highlights the need to develop context-specific approaches that consider minority religious groups, immigrants, and younger children, including newborns, often missed during vaccination campaigns and outreaches

Keywords: zero-dose; childhood vaccination; Cameroon

1. Background

In the past half century, morbidity and mortality due to vaccine-preventable diseases (VPD) have reduced tremendously in children [1]. This is primarily because of the substantial progress in vaccination coverage worldwide since the creation of the Expanded

Program on Immunization (EPI) in 1974 [2]. In addition to the eradication of smallpox, the recent certification of the African Region as wild poliovirus-free, making it the fifth of six World Health Organization (WHO) regions, is another excellent example of the impact of effective vaccination [3]. Despite successes in global immunization, an estimated 21.8 million infants worldwide are still not being reached by routine immunization services [4]. Among the 19.7 million children worldwide who did not complete the three-dose of Diphtheria, Tetanus, and Pertussis-containing vaccine (DTP) series in 2019, 13.8 million (70%) were zero-dose children [2]. This number has witnessed a steep rise following the abrupt and rapid progression of the COVID-19 pandemic, which has significantly disrupted essential health service delivery in many countries, reversing past efforts to improve health indicators, including childhood immunization [5–7]. In 2021, about 25 million infants did not receive basic vaccines (the highest number since 2009), and the number of completely unvaccinated children (the so-called zero-dose children) increased by 5 million since the onset of the COVID-19 pandemic in 2019 [8].

Although many low- and medium-income countries (LMIC) have seen a steady increase in national-level vaccination coverage, many did not reach the 90% target for 2020 established by the World Health Organization (WHO) [9]. In fact, an estimated 20% of children in the African region are under-vaccinated despite the mammoth benefits of vaccination [10]. As a result, about three million children die annually of infectious diseases in this region, most of which are preventable by vaccination [10,11]. This is mainly due to suboptimal vaccination coverage in hard-to-reach subpopulations [12]. Therefore, achieving universal coverage with all recommended vaccines will require tailored, context-specific strategies to reach communities with substantial proportions of zero-dose and under-vaccinated children, particularly those in remote rural, poor semi-urban, conflict, and fragile settings [13].

In Cameroon, the EPI is responsible for childhood immunization, which is free for children under two years of age as shown in Table 1 below [14]. A household Demographic Health Survey (DHS) conducted in 2018 reported an immunization coverage (both from declaration and proofs of vaccination) of 86.7%, 71.5%, and 65.3% for Bacilli Calmette-Guérin (BCG), DTP-3, and measles-containing vaccines (MCV), respectively, with a zero-dose proportion of 9.7% [14]. The significantly low immunization coverage most likely explains the increase in reported cases of VPDs in Cameroon [15,16]. To reach global coverage goals with vaccines recommended across the life course, hard-to-reach and hard-to-vaccinate populations must be at the center of vaccination interventions [17]. The Manoka Health District (MHD) in the Littoral Region of Cameroon is one of such hard-to-reach districts with low vaccination coverage and several poorly documented outbreaks of VPDs. In 2021, the estimated DTP-1 vaccination coverage in MHD from the District Health Information Software 2 (DHIS2) was 19.8%, which is far below the 90% mark adopted by the Cameroon Ministry of Public Health (MoPH) during the World Health Assembly in 2012 [18].

Several studies in Cameroon have attempted to describe factors associated with incomplete vaccination and low vaccination coverage [14,17,19–21]. These factors include non-utilization of antenatal care services, younger mothers, being the ≥3rd born child in the family, lack of access to vaccination information, and longer distances from vaccinating facilities [17,22]. However, these studies are primarily hospital-based, conducted in urban settings, and did not characterize unvaccinated children living in pockets of communities that traditionally miss primary healthcare services, including immunization—the so-called missed communities. Therefore, this study aimed to close the knowledge gap on factors associated with zero-dose vaccination status among children 0–2 years of age in a missed community in Cameroon. These findings can be leveraged to inform policy and to design tailored programs to reduce the zero-dose proportion in the MHD and similar settings.

Table 1. Cameroon EPI Calendar.

Contacts	Age	Antigenes *
1st contact	At birth	BCG, OPV 0
2nd contact	Six weeks	Penta 1 (DPT-1 + Hep B1 + HIB1), OPV-1, Pneumo 13-1, Rota-1
3rd contact	Ten weeks	Penta 2 (DPT-2 + Hep B2 + HIB2), OPV-2, Pneumo 13-2, Rota-2
4th contact	14 weeks	Penta 3 (DPT-3 + Hep B3 + HIB3), OPV-3, Pneumo 13-3, IPV
5th contact	Nine months	MR1, yellow fever vaccine
6th contact	15 months	MR2

* BCG = Bacillus Calmette-Guerin, Penta = Pentavalent vaccine, DPT = Diphtheria, Pertussis, and Tetanus vaccine, Hep B1 = Hepatitis B vaccine, HIB = *Haemophilus influenzae* vaccine, OPV = Oral Polio vaccine, Pneumo 13 = Pneumococal 13 valent conjugate vaccine, IPV = Injectable polio vaccine.

2. Methodology

2.1. Study Design and Setting

The study design was a cross-sectional analytical study. It was conducted in MHD, in the Littoral Region of Cameroon, over 20 km from Douala city. It is an enclaved archipelago district with about 19,943 persons distributed unequally across 47 islets. Most of the inhabitants are peasant fishermen who live in temporal houses with large family sizes of 5–12 persons. The men spend most of their time at sea fishing, while the women spend time at home with the children—their principal activities being fish 'smoking' and household chores. The island's population comprises native Cameroonians and people from other countries (like Nigeria and Mali) who migrated for fishing. Immigrants make up over 70% of the total population. Most of these immigrants lack a residence permit that grants them legal status to live in Cameroon, limiting the freedom to travel to other towns/cities for essential commodities and services, including health services. Therefore, they depend on local boat couriers to purchase goods from out-of-town, and roadside drug vendors, dispensaries, and traditional healers for their health care. A single health facility serves the entire district. Pregnant women mostly deliver at home in the hands of traditional birth attendants and relatives, resulting in a considerable proportion of unregistered live births. Consequently, children in this district are generally missed by routine vaccination and other primary health care services.

2.2. Data Collection and Sampling

This study was based on secondary data collected in 2020 by the Clinton Health Access Initiative (CHAI) in partnership with Gavi, the vaccine alliance, and the Cameroon EPI. During this period, they conducted a door-to-door survey in MHD to identify zero-dose and under-immunized children. The field team employed convenience sampling to select health areas (administrative level 4) in MHD for the survey based on population size. Trained community health workers (CHWs) used convenience sampling to administer structured survey tools to caregivers based on their availability in the two most populous health areas (Cap-Cameroon and Toube)—the combined population constitutes over a third of the entire population of the MHD. Data captured were primarily vaccination status and relevant socio-demographic factors, such as the parent's level of education, religion, educational level, sex, age, and place of delivery.

The vaccination status of children was based on caregivers' recall because it was realized that most children were only vaccinated during Supplementary Immunization Activities (SIA) and vaccination campaigns—in the past five years, vaccination cards were only issued during routine immunization. The team, therefore, decided to rely on caregiver recall to avoid losing valuable data due to the exclusion of children without vaccination cards and birth certificates. Moreover, data collectors corroborated caregivers' information on children's vaccination status with a checklist containing the timing of SIA and vaccination campaigns conducted in MHD in the past five years to minimize bias. All children under two years of age surveyed in the zero-dose identification project in MHD were considered for the study. However, children whose caregivers were unable to recall whether they were vaccinated were excluded.

2.3. Key Operational Definitions

Where vaccination cards or birth certificates were unavailable, the study relied on caregivers' recall to attribute the vaccination status of children. The outcome of interest was zero-dose vaccination status. Zero-dose children were those who had never received any recommended vaccine antigen for their age based on the Cameroon EPI calendar. Completely vaccinated children included those who had received all vaccines recommended for their age. Incompletely vaccinated children were those who had received at least one dose of any of the recommended vaccines but had not completed vaccines that were appropriate for their age. Finally, at least single-dose (ASD) vaccinated children were those who had received at least one dose of any vaccine. Therefore, ASD encompassed both incomplete and completely vaccinated children.

2.4. Data Management and Analysis

The zero-dose project dataset on children born between 31/11/2018 and 30/08/2020 was exported as a Microsoft Excel 2013 worksheet into R Statistical Software (v4.1.2; R Core Team 2021) for statistical analysis. Categorical variables (sex, birth site, vaccination status, availability of birth certificate, health area (administrative level 4), child's birth order, marital status, parents' educational level, occupation, religion, and nationality) were summarized in percentages. Collinearity was evaluated for predictor variables before including them in the final regression model. Missing data points were included in the analysis. Univariate analysis was used to determine associations between individual explanatory variables and the zero-dose vaccination status of children. The factors independently associated with zero-dose vaccination status and explanatory variables with $p < 0.2$ in univariate analysis were included in the multivariate logistic regression with zero-dose status as an outcome. The adjusted odd ratios (AOR) with corresponding 95% Confidence Intervals (CI) were then calculated. The decision to use explanatory variables with $p < 0.2$ in the univariate analysis as factors in the multivariate model was to maximize the chance of capturing variables that might have an effect on the association or explain some of the variances in the outcome, even though they were not significantly associated with it. To verify the robustness of our results, they were compared to those obtained from a multivariable model that includes all potential explanatory variables as factors.

2.5. Ethical Considerations

CHAI had obtained ethical clearance from the Cameroon National Ethics Committee before data collection. Authorization from appropriate CHAI Cameroon administrative authorities was obtained to gain access to the zero-dose project dataset. Furthermore, the data was used solely for this study and not shared with any third party.

3. Results

During the zero-dose identification, head counting of children under two was conducted in all households (100%) in the two most populous islets (Cap-Cameroon and Toube)—284 children under two years of age were identified. However, six children were excluded from the analysis because their parents were unavailable during the survey, and the available relatives could not provide information about their vaccination status.

The mean age of children included in the study was 11.6 months (SD = $\pm$6.7), with male children overrepresented (53.2%). A considerable proportion of the children (92.8%) were born at home with the aid of traditional birth attendants. As such, most of them had no proof of dates of birth (birth certificates), 93.5%, making information on child age heavily reliant on the caregiver's recall. Children had immigrant mothers for the most part (87.1%) and were mainly from the Cap-Cameroon health area (57.6%).

Of the 278 children retained for the final analysis, 8.3% were ASD children (1.8% completely vaccinated and 6.5% incompletely vaccinated), while 91.7% were zero-dose cases. ASD cases were mainly vaccinated during a national vaccination campaign (78.3%), with BCG being the most utilized antigen (73.9%). The details of the socio-demographic characteristics of all the children surveyed, the distribution of zero-dose children by socio-demographic factors, and the chi-square test results are outlined in Table 2 below. Table 3 highlights the vaccination profile of the surveyed children. This univariate analysis revealed that the child's age, birth site, owning a birth certificate, and nationality of both parents are significantly associated with zero-dose vaccination status. There was no significant difference in the distribution of zero-dose children among the variables of the other socio-demographic factors. However, the birth order, mother's age, mother's religion, and mother's educational level were included in the multivariate analysis based on $p < 0.2$ to increase the chance of capturing variables that might be associated with the zero-dose vaccination status.

Table 2. Distribution of zero-dose vaccination status by socio-demographic factors.

Characteristic	N = 278	Zero-Dose (%)	*p*-Value
Sex			
Male	148 (53.2%)	137 (92.6%)	0.7453
Female	129 (46.4%)	118 (91.5%)	
Health Area			
Cap-Cameroon	160 (57.6%)	145 (90.1%)	0.5781
Toube	118 (42.4%)	110 (93.2%)	
Birth Site			
Home	258 (92.8%)	244 (94.6%)	0.0000
Health facility	20 (7.2%)	11 (55%)	
Birth Certificate			
Yes	18 (6.5%)	13 (72.2%)	0.0077
No	260 (93.5%)	242 (93.1%)	
Father's nationality			
Cameroonian	46 (16.5%)	33 (71.7%)	0.0000
Immigrants	211 (75.9%)	202 (95.7%)	
Father's Profession			
Fishing	220 (79.1%)	202 (91.8%)	0.8702
Others	38 (13.7%)	34 (89.4%)	
Father's Religion			
Christian	241 (86.7%)	221 (91.7%)	0.7748
Others	14 (5.0%)	12 (85.7%)	
Father's Educational level			
Not Educated	182 (65.5%)	166 (91.2%)	0.8450
Primary Education	46 (16.5%)	43 (93.5%)	
Secondary Education	30 (10.8%)	27 (90%)	
Mother's nationality			
Cameroonian	35 (12.6%)	25 (71.4%)	0.0000
Immigrant	242 (87.1%)	229 (94.6%)	
Mother's Profession			
Housewife	167 (60.1%)	155 (92.8%)	0.5431
Others	110 (39.6%)	99 (90%)	
Mother's Religion			
Christian	256 (92.1%)	237 (92.6%)	0.0623
Non-Christians	15 (5.4%)	13 (86.7%)	

Table 2. *Cont.*

Characteristic	N = 278	Zero-Dose (%)	*p*-Value
Mother's Educational level			
None	104 (37.4%)	98 (94.2%)	0.1589
Primary Education	135 (48.6%)	124 (91.9%)	
Secondary Education	38 (13.7%)	32 (84.2%)	
Marital Status of Mother			
Married	242 (87.1%)	222 (91.7%)	1
Others	33 (11.9%)	30 (90.9%)	

Table 3. Vaccination status of the children surveyed.

Characteristic	Frequency (%)
Vaccination Status (N = 278)	
Complete	5 (1.8)
Incomplete	18 (6.5)
Zero-dose	255 (91.7)
Vaccination site for ASD (N = 23)	
Manoka District Hospital	17 (73.9)
Other Districts	5 (21.7)
Vaccination strategy for ASD (N = 23)	
Vaccination campaigns	18 (78.3)
Routine vaccination in a health facility	4 (17.4)
Antigen received by ASD (N = 23)	
BCG	17 (73.9)
OPV 0	13 (56.5)
OPV 1	5 (21.7)
OPV 2	4 (17.4)
OPV 3	3 (13)
IPV	3 (13)
Penta 1, PCV 1	4 (17.4)
Penta 2, PCV 2	4 (17)
Penta 3, PCV 3	3 (13)
Rota 1	4 (17.4)
Rota 2	2 (8.7)
Measles/yellow fever	0 (0.0)
Reason for non-vaccination among zero-dose children (N = 255)	
No health facility	234 (91.7)
No transportation means	10 (3.9)
No reason	11 (4.3)

Factors Associated with Zero-Dose Vaccination Status

Table 4 highlights multivariable logistic regression results to determine factors independently associated with being a zero-dose child. Factors associated with zero-dose vaccination status are younger children, children born at home, children born of immigrant fathers, and of non-Christian mothers. As seen from the Table, the odds of being a zero-dose child decrease with the child's age and birth in a health facility, but increase among children born to immigrant fathers or non-Christian mothers. Children delivered in health facilities are less likely to be zero-dose than those born at home (AOR: 0.07, 95% CI: 0.02–0.30, $p = 0.0003$). Similarly, compared to a Christian mother, children born to minority non-Christian mothers have higher odds of being zero-dose (AOR: 6.55, 95% CI: 1.04–41.25, $p = 0.0453$). Children born to fathers who are non-nationals are likelier to be zero-dose children than Cameroonians (AOR: 2.60, 95% CI = 0.65–10.35, $p = 0.0016$). Also, younger children are likely to be unvaccinated compared to older peers (AOR: 0.90, 95% CI: 0.82–1.00, $p = 0.0401$).

Table 4. Factors associated with zero-does status.

	Univariate Logistic Analysis				Multivariate Logistic Analysis	
	N	Zero-Dose (%)	COR (95%CI)	p Value	AOR (95% CI)	p Value
Age of child (months)	-	-	0.91 (0.84–0.97)	0.0074	0.90 (0.82–1.00)	0.0401
Child's birth order	-	-	1.27 (1.01–1.60)	0.0426	1.33 (0.97–1.81)	0.0753
Birth site						
Home	258	94.6	1		1	
Health facility	20	55	0.07 (0.02–0.20)	0.0000	0.07 (0.02–0.30)	0.0003
Birth Certificate						
No	18	72.2	1		1	
Yes	260	93.1	0.19 (0.06–0.60)	0.0046	0.76 (0.15–3.85)	0.7354
Mother's educational level						
Not Educated	104	94.2	1		1	
Primary Education	135	91.9	0.69 (0.25–1.93)	0.4802	0.76 (0.19–2.93)	0.6903
Secondary Education	38	84.2	0.33 (0.01–1.08)	0.0675	0.53 (0.09–2.96)	0.4692
Mother's Religion						
Christian	256	96.2	1		1	
Non-Christians	15	86.7	0.26 (0.08–0.88)	0.0299	6.55 (1.04–41.25)	0.0453
Mother's Nationality						
Cameroonian	35	71.4	1		1	
Immigrants	242	94.6	7.05 (2.80–17.72)	0	2.60 (0.65–10.35)	0.1760
Father's Nationality						
Cameroonian	46	71.7	1		1	
Immigrants	211	95.7	8.84 (3.50–22.32)	0	8.92 (2.29–34.65)	0.0016
Mother's Age	–	–	1.01 (0.95–1.07)	0.7362	1.00 (0.92–1.09)	0.9794

4. Discussion

This research reveals a zero-dose proportion of 91.7% (255/278), almost ten times the Cameroon national zero-dose proportion of 9.7% reported in 2020 [23]. This low vaccination coverage contributing to the low national EPI coverage could be explained partly by factors peculiar to its hard-to-reach characteristics. These factors include the absence of health facilities in the study health areas, distance from the lone health facility, multiple poorly accessible communities (islets), and frequent diurnal flooding, making access an uphill task. Our findings are consistent with a publication by Ozawa et al. in 2019 on the characteristics of hard-to-reach communities—based on an extensive literature review from 2000 to 2018 [24]. In our study, the primary service delivery approach employed in vaccinating children was mass vaccination campaigns—78.3% of vaccinated children were vaccinated through this approach. This highlights the importance of Supplementary Immunization Activities (SIA) and vaccination campaigns in improving vaccination coverage in hard-to-vaccinate communities, similar to the role of SIA in preventing measles outbreaks during the COVID-19 pandemic in Kenya [25].

Based on the multivariable logistic regression analysis, the log odds of being a zero-dose child decreased with the child's age and being born in a health facility. However, children born to immigrant fathers and non-Christian mothers had higher odds of being zero-dose children than those born to Cameroonian fathers and Christian mothers, respectively. Younger children are likely to be unvaccinated compared to their older peers

(AOR: 0.90, 95% CI: 0.82–1.00, p = 0.0401). This can be explained by the fact that this population depends solely on outreach and mobile strategies for vaccination and most often have to wait for a national vaccination campaign or an interventional vaccination program during an epidemic to receive routine vaccines. By reviewing demographic and health surveys in sub-Saharan Africa, Mutua et al. showed that on-time vaccination was relatively low in sub-Saharan Africa and varied depending on different factors, including place of residence [1]. This implies younger children are likely to miss their vaccines and only get them at an older age. This is also consistent with a study by Stein-Zamir et al. in Israel, which showed that age-specific vaccine delays would lead to fewer vaccination cases at younger ages compared to older children [26]. A study in 2018 showed the impact of a mobile vaccination strategy in hard-to-reach communities, with children of older ages having higher vaccination coverages than those of younger age groups, similar to the findings in this study [27]. It is, therefore, of significant value to design tailored approaches that permit routine vaccination of children from birth to ensure all children benefit from vaccine protection throughout childhood.

Children born in health facilities were less likely to be unvaccinated than those delivered at home (AOR: 0.07, 95% CI: 0.02–0.30, p = 0.0003). Since women deliver at home, they miss the vaccines given to the child at birth, including vaccination-related counseling and scheduling, which can explain this finding. Also, 93.5% of children in this study did not have birth certificates, which presents a challenge in determining a child's age, posing a problem in terms of logistics, routine vaccination micro-planning, and the vaccination activity itself, as it relies on the ages of the children. This is consistent with other studies, though they did not focus on zero-dose cases, but were more interested in incomplete and complete vaccination cases [24,28–30]. In missed communities, a context-specific approach, such as setting up micro-health facilities or collaborating with traditional birth attendants to identify, track and vaccinate children from birth, will significantly improve immunization coverage and the fight against VPDs.

Children born to immigrant fathers were likely to be zero-dose children compared to children whose fathers were native Cameroonians (AOR: 2.60, 95% CI = 0.65–10.35, p = 0.0016). Most immigrants do not have a residence permit and as such, they cannot easily access essential health services outside their current residence. As a result, they tend to depend on traditional healers, birth attendants, roadside drug vendors, and unregistered private dispensaries for their healthcare needs. As such, even if parents are willing to vaccinate their children, they would have no choice but to wait for an outreach vaccination program since they cannot travel to get vaccines outside of this setting. A systemic review of studies in sub-Saharan Africa and the European region revealed migration as a factor associated with low vaccination coverage [31,32]. Also, comparatively lower vaccination coverage was found among immigrants in India compared to the locals because of the high prevalence of home births, lack of awareness of the location of health facilities, mobility, and fear of vaccine side effects [33].

In the same line, this study reveals that children born to minority non-Christian mothers are likelier to be zero-dose children than those born by Christian mothers (AOR: 6.55, 95% CI: 1.04–41.25, p = 0.0453). The non-Christian communities in MHD represent a minority population, with only 5.4% of mothers belonging to this population as opposed to their Christian counterparts, 93.8%. To leave no child unvaccinated, the finding in this study further emphasizes the need to identify minority communities; employ human-centered design and tools, such as the WHO framework of behavioral and social drivers (BeSD), to have in-depth knowledge on supply and demand barriers specific to minority populations; and develop context-specific strategies.

Unlike most studies, birth order was not significantly associated with zero-dose vaccination status, AOR, 1.33, 95% CI: 0.97–1.81, p = 0.0753 [28,34,35]. For instance, a nested case-control study conducted on a cohort of 110,902 Israeli children under the age of 5 revealed that birth order progression is inversely associated with vaccine utilization [36]. The critical explanation is that previous parental vaccination service delivery experiences with their firstborns tend to shape parents' new attitudes towards vaccination [36]. Birth order was probably insignificant in this study because vaccination coverage was too low in these health areas to significantly impact subsequent parental attitudes toward vaccination.

5. Conclusions

This study establishes an association between being a zero-dose child and home-based births, being the younger child, being born to immigrant fathers, and minority non-Christian mothers. Therefore, the study highlights the need to develop context-specific approaches to vaccinating children in hard-to-reach communities to close health equity gaps. This can be achieved by paying more attention to minority groups, immigrants, and younger children, including newborns, who are often missed during vaccination campaigns. The study findings also reemphasize the value of SIA in such a missed community.

5.1. Limitations

A major flaw in this study is the possibility of non-differential misclassification of the vaccination status of children since more than 90% of children did not have birth certificates, and their ages were estimated based on their parents' recall. Although this may have affected the proportion of incomplete and complete vaccination cases, it did not affect the multivariable logistic regression findings because the outcome variable was solely based on whether the child had ever received any vaccine antigen on the Cameroon EPI calendar (zero-dose vaccination status). Also, we minimized bias stemming from the caregiver's recall by corroborating the children's vaccination status with a checklist of timing of SIA and national vaccination campaigns in the past five years.

The certainty of the evidence is limited by the small sample size of specific populations, such as non-Christian mothers and fathers, and the number of health facility-based births. Apart from the limited statistical power of this study, the cross-sectional study design conducted using secondary data posed a challenge of generalizability. However, the findings are aligned with many similar studies in other countries.

Convenience sampling was employed which, may have compromised the generalizability of this study. However, the sampling approach took into consideration the most populous islets in MHD with high zero-dose proportion. The population dynamics and social activities of these communities make availability a major issue—this is the reason why convenience sampling was a great fit so as not to lose valuable data.

5.2. Recommendation

A qualitative study to establish in-depth reasons for zero-dose and under-vaccinated children will further close the knowledge gap on missed communities in Cameroon.

Author Contributions: Conceptualization, S.C.N.; methodology, S.C.N.; data curation, S.C.N.; formal analysis; writing—original draft preparation, S.C.N.; writing—review and editing, Y.S., V.N.A., C.M.M., N.J.M., A.A.N., S.T.N., B.N., N.N.E. and C.S.Z.; supervision, Y.S., S.R. and C.S.Z. All authors have read and agreed to the published version of the manuscript.

Funding: This research received no external funding. The primary data collection was funded by Gavi through CHAI. These institutions had no role in the preparation and submission of this manuscript.

Institutional Review Board Statement: This study was conducted in compliance with the Helsinki Declaration and all applicable national laws and institutional rules and has been approved by the author's institutional review board. Ethical approval was granted by the Cameroon National Ethics Committee for Human Health Research with the reference 2019/07/1174/CE/CNERSH/SP on the 12 of July 2019.

Informed Consent Statement: Informed consent was obtained from all subjects involved in the study.

Data Availability Statement: Data used for this research are available from the corresponding author upon reasonable request.

Acknowledgments: Our gratitude to Clinton Health Access Initiative, Cameroon, for granting us access to this data and to Gavi the vaccine alliance, for providing the funds for the primary survey. Also, we would like to acknowledge the staff and IMPH research committee at the Hebrew University and Hadassah Braun School of Public Health and Community Medicine, Jerusalem, Israel.

Conflicts of Interest: The authors declare no conflict of interest.

References

1. Mutua, M.K.; Mohamed, S.F.; Porth, J.M.; Faye, C.M. Inequities in On-Time Childhood Vaccination: Evidence From Sub-Saharan Africa. *Am. J. Prev. Med.* **2020**, *60*, S11–S23. [CrossRef] [PubMed]
2. Chard, A.N.; Gacic-Dobo, M.; Diallo, M.S.; Sodha, S.V.; Wallace, A.S. Routine Vaccination Coverage—Worldwide, 2019. *Morb. Mortal. Rep.* **2000**, *69*, 1706–1710. [CrossRef] [PubMed]
3. World Polio Day 2020. 2020. Available online: https://www.cdc.gov/globalhealth/immunization/wpd/index.html (accessed on 4 July 2021).
4. Global Vaccine Action Plan. Available online: https://www.who.int/teams/immunization-vaccines-and-biologicals/strategies/global-vaccine-action-plan (accessed on 25 December 2020).
5. Mansour, Z.; Arab, J.; Said, R.; Rady, A.; Hamadeh, R.; Gerbaka, B.; Bizri, A.R. Impact of COVID-19 pandemic on the utilization of routine immunization services in Lebanon. *PLoS ONE* **2021**, *16*, e0246951. [CrossRef] [PubMed]
6. Chandir, S.; Siddiqi, D.A.; Mehmood, M.; Setayesh, H.; Siddique, M.; Mirza, A.; Soundardjee, R.; Dharma, V.K.; Shah, M.T.; Abdullah, S.; et al. Impact of COVID-19 pandemic response on uptake of routine immunizations in Sindh, Pakistan: An analysis of provincial electronic immunization registry. *Vaccine* **2020**, *38*, 7146–7155. [CrossRef] [PubMed]
7. Desta, A.A.; Woldearegay, T.W.; Gebremeskel, E.; Alemayehu, M.; Getachew, T.; Gebregzabiher, G.; Ghebremedhin, K.D.; Zgita, D.N.; Aregawi, A.B.; Redae, G. Impacts of COVID-19 on essential health services in Tigray, Northern Ethiopia: A pre-post study. *PLoS ONE* **2021**, *16*, e0256330. [CrossRef]
8. WHO. Immunization Coverage. 2021. Available online: https://www.who.int/news-room/fact-sheets/detail/immunization-coverage (accessed on 10 November 2021).
9. World Health Organization, Regional Office for Africa. Regional Strategic Plan for Immunization, 2014–2020. 2015. Available online: http://apps.who.int/iris/bitstream/10665/204373/1/9789290232780.pdf (accessed on 26 December 2020).
10. In 5 Children in Africa Do not Have Access to Life-Saving Vaccines. WHO | Regional Office for Africa. Available online: https://www.afro.who.int/news/1-5-children-africa-do-not-have-access-life-saving-vaccines (accessed on 26 December 2020).
11. Liu, L.; Oza, S.; Hogan, D.; Perin, J.; Rudan, I.; Lawn, J.E.; Cousens, S.; Mathers, C.; Black, R.E. Global, regional, and national causes of child mortality in 2000–13, with projections to inform post-2015 priorities: An updated systematic analysis. *Lancet* **2015**, *385*, 430–440. [CrossRef]
12. Restrepo-Méndez, M.C.; Barros, A.; Wong, K.; Johnson, H.L.; Pariyo, G.; França, G.V.; Wehrmeister, F.C.; Victora, C. Inequalities in full immunization coverage: Trends in low- and middle-income countries. *Bull. World Health Organ.* **2016**, *94*, 794–805. [CrossRef]
13. Chopra, M.; Bhutta, Z.; Blanc, D.C.; Checchi, F.; Gupta, A.; Lemango, E.T.; Levine, O.S.; Lyimo, D.; Nandy, R.; O'Brien, K.L.; et al. Addressing the persistent inequities in immunization coverage. *Bull. World Health Organ.* **2019**, *98*, 146–148. [CrossRef]
14. Ateudjieu, J.; Yakum, M.N.; Goura, A.P.; Tembei, A.M.; Ingrid, D.K.; Landry, B.B.; Kenfack, B.; Amada, L.; Tadzong, I.; Bissek, A.C. EPI immunization coverage, timeliness and dropout rate among children in a West Cameroon health district: A cross sectional study. *BMC Public Health* **2020**, *20*, 1–11. [CrossRef]
15. ENQUÊTE DÉMOGRAPHIQUE ET DE SANTÉ ET À INDICATEURS MULTIPLES [cited 2021 Apr 24]. Available online: https://dhsprogram.com/pubs/pdf/FR260/FR260.pdf (accessed on 26 December 2020).
16. Parpia, A.S.; Skrip, L.A.; Nsoesie, E.O.; Ngwa, M.C.; Abah, A.S.A.; Galvani, A.P.; Ndeffo-Mbah, M.L. Spatio-temporal dynamics of measles outbreaks in Cameroon. *Ann. Epidemiol.* **2020**, *42*, 64–72.e3. [CrossRef]
17. Russo, G.; Miglietta, A.; Pezzotti, P.; Biguioh, R.M.; Mayaka, G.B.; Sobze, M.S.; Stefanelli, P.; Vullo, V.; Rezza, G. Vaccine coverage and determinants of incomplete vaccination in children aged 12-23 months in Dschang, West Region, Cameroon: A cross-sectional survey during a polio outbreak. *BMC Public Health* **2015**, *15*, 630. [CrossRef]
18. Centers for Disease Control and Prevention (CDC). Global routine vaccination coverage–2012. *MMWR Morb. Mortal. Wkly. Rep.* **2013**, *62*, 858–861.
19. Ebile Akoh, W.; Ateudjieu, J.; Nouetchognou, J.S.; Yakum, M.N.; Djouma Nembot, F.; Nafack Sonkeng, S.; Saah Fopa, M.; Watcho, P. The expanded program on immunization service delivery in the Dschang health district, west region of Cameroon: A cross sectional survey. *BMC Public Health* **2016**, *16*, 801. [CrossRef]
20. Chiabi, A.; Nguefack, F.D.; Njapndounke, F.; Kobela, M.; Kenfack, K.; Nguefack, S.; Ma, E.; Nguefack-Tsague, G.; Angwafo, F., III. Vaccination of Infants Aged 0 to 11 Months at the Yaounde Gynaeco-Obstetric and Pediatric Hospital in Cameroon: How Complete and How Timely? In *BMC Pediatr*. Available online: https://www.ncbi.nlm.nih.gov/pmc/articles/PMC5735527/ (accessed on 26 December 2020).
21. Pouth, S.F.B.B.; Kazambu, D.; Delissaint, D.; Kobela, M. Couverture vaccinale et facteurs associés à la non complétude vaccinale des enfants de 12 à 23 mois du district de santé de Djoungolo-Cameroun en 2012. *Pan. Afr. Med. J.* Available online: https://www.panafrican-med-journal.com/content/article/17/91/full/ (accessed on 26 December 2020).

22. Ewang, B.F.; Eyong, M.E.; Cumber, S.N.; Nkfusai, C.N.; Yankam, B.M.; Anye, C.S.; Achu, J.R.; Suh, B.M.; Nkeng, M.N.; Nzoyom, R.B.; et al. Vaccination Coverage Under the Expanded Program on Immunization in South West Cameroon. *Int. J. Matern. Child Health AIDS (IJMA)* **2020**, *9*, 242–251. [CrossRef]
23. Institut National de la Statistique, (INS), Yaoundé, Cameroun. ENQUÊTE DÉMOGRAPHIQUE ET DE SANTÉ 2018. 2020. Available online: https://www.dhsprogram.com/pubs/pdf/FR360/FR360.pdf (accessed on 26 December 2020).
24. Ozawa, S.; Yemeke, T.T.; Evans, D.R.; Pallas, S.; Wallace, A.S.; Lee, B.Y. Defining hard-to-reach populations for vaccination. *Vaccine* **2019**, *37*, 5525–5534. [CrossRef]
25. Mburu, C.N.; Ojal, J.; Chebet, R.; Akech, D.; Karia, B.; Tuju, J.; Sigilai, A.; Abbas, K.; Jit, M.; Funk, S.; et al. The importance of supplementary immunisation activities to prevent measles outbreaks during the COVID-19 pandemic in Kenya. *BMC Med.* **2021**, *19*, 1–10. [CrossRef]
26. Stein-Zamir, C.; Israeli, A. Age-appropriate versus up-to-date coverage of routine childhood vaccinations among young children in Israel. *Hum. Vaccines Immunother.* **2017**, *13*, 2102–2110. [CrossRef]
27. Bawa, S.; Shuaib, F.; Saidu, M.; Ningi, A.; Abdullahi, S.; Abba, B.; Idowu, A.; Alkasim, J.; Hammanyero, K.; Warigon, C.; et al. Conduct of vaccination in hard-to-reach areas to address potential polio reservoir areas, 2014–2015. *BMC Public Health* **2018**, *18*, 1312. [CrossRef]
28. Girmay, A.; Dadi, A.F. Full Immunization Coverage and Associated Factors among Children Aged 12-23 Months in a Hard-to-Reach Areas of Ethiopia. *Int. J. Pediatr.* **2019**, *2019*, 1–8. [CrossRef]
29. Tesema, G.A.; Tessema, Z.T.; Tamirat, K.S.; Teshale, A.B. Complete basic childhood vaccination and associated factors among children aged 12–23 months in East Africa: A multilevel analysis of recent demographic and health surveys. *BMC Public Health* **2020**, *20*, 1–14. [CrossRef]
30. Aalemi, A.K.; Shahpar, K.; Mubarak, M.Y. Factors influencing vaccination coverage among children age 12–23 months in Afghanistan: Analysis of the 2015 Demographic and Health Survey. *PLoS ONE* **2020**, *15*, e0236955. [CrossRef] [PubMed]
31. Bangura, J.B.; Xiao, S.; Qiu, D.; Ouyang, F.; Chen, L. Barriers to childhood immunization in sub-Saharan Africa: A systematic review. *BMC Public Health* **2020**, *20*, 1–15. [CrossRef] [PubMed]
32. Ekezie, W.; Awwad, S.; Krauchenberg, A.; Karara, N.; Dembiński, Ł.; Grossman, Z.; del Torso, S.; Dornbusch, H.J.; Neves, A.; Copley, S.; et al. Access to Vaccination among Disadvantaged, Isolated and Difficult-to-Reach Communities in the WHO European Region: A Systematic Review. *Vaccines* **2022**, *10*, 1038. [CrossRef] [PubMed]
33. Kusuma, Y.; Kaushal, S.; Sundari, A.; Babu, B. Access to childhood immunisation services and its determinants among recent and settled migrants in Delhi, India. *Public Health* **2018**, *158*, 135–143. [CrossRef]
34. Schaffer, S.J.; Szilagyi, P.G. Immunization status and birth order. *Arch Pediatr Adolesc Med.* **1995**, *149*, 792–797. [CrossRef]
35. Zenbaba, D.; Sahiledengle, B.; Debela, M.B.; Tufa, T.; Teferu, Z.; Lette, A.; Gezahegn, H.; Solomon, D.; Tekalegn, Y. Determinants of Incomplete Vaccination Among Children Aged 12 to 23 Months in Gindhir District, Southeastern Ethiopia: Unmatched Case–Control Study. *Risk Manag. Health Policy* **2021**, *14*, 1669–1679. [CrossRef]
36. Gavrielov-Yusim, N.; Battat, E.; Neumann, L.; Friger, M.; Balicer, R.D. Birth order and private voluntary immunization—A study of 110,902 children. *Vaccine* **2012**, *30*, 442–447. [CrossRef]

vaccines

MDPI

Article

Advancing Immunization Coverage and Equity: A Structured Synthesis of Pro-Equity Strategies in 61 Gavi-Supported Countries

Vesela Ivanova [1], A. S. M. Shahabuddin [2,*], Alyssa Sharkey [3] and Mira Johri [4,5]

1 Public Health Agency of Canada, Ottawa, ON K1A 0K9, Canada
2 Primary Health Care and Health Systems Strengthening (PHC-HSS) Unit, MNCAH Programme, UNICEF Headquarters, New York, NY 10017, USA
3 School of Public and International Affairs, Princeton University, Princeton, NJ 08544, USA
4 Centre de Recherche du Centre Hospitalier de l'Université de Montréal (CRCHUM), Montréal, QC H2X 0A9, Canada
5 Départment de Gestion, d'Évaluation, et de Politique de Santé, École de Santé Publique (ESPUM), Université de Montréal, Montréal, QC H3N 1X9, Canada
* Correspondence: ashahabuddin@unicef.org

Abstract: Background: Global immunization inequities persist, reflected in the 25 million underimmunized and 18 million zero-dose children in 2021. To identify country approaches to reach underimmunized and zero-dose children, we undertook a structured synthesis of pro-equity strategies across 61 countries receiving programmatic support from Gavi, the Vaccine Alliance. Methods: We extracted data from 174 Country Joint Appraisals and Multi-Stakeholder Dialogue reports (2016–2020). We identified strategies via a targeted keyword search, informed by a determinants of immunization coverage framework. Strategies were synthesized into themes consolidated from UNICEF's Journey to Health and Immunization (JTHI) and the Global Routine Immunization Strategies and Practices (GRISP) frameworks. Results: We found 607 unique strategies across 61 countries and 24 themes. Strategies to improve care at the point of service (44%); to improve knowledge, awareness and beliefs (25%); and to address preparation, cost and effort barriers (13%) were common. Fewer strategies targeted experience of care (8%), intent, (7%) and after-service (3%). We also identified strategies addressing gender-related barriers to immunization and targeting specific types of communities. Conclusions: We summarize the range of pro-equity immunization strategies employed in Gavi-supported countries and interpret them thematically. Findings are incorporated into a searchable database which can be used to inform equity-driven immunization programs, policies and decision-making which target underimmunized and zero-dose communities.

Keywords: immunization; children; equity; gender; rural; remote; conflict; urban; poor

Citation: Ivanova, V.; Shahabuddin, A.S.M.; Sharkey, A.; Johri, M. Advancing Immunization Coverage and Equity: A Structured Synthesis of Pro-Equity Strategies in 61 Gavi-Supported Countries. *Vaccines* **2023**, *11*, 191. https://doi.org/10.3390/vaccines11010191

Academic Editor: Pedro Plans-Rubió

Received: 19 December 2022
Revised: 11 January 2023
Accepted: 11 January 2023
Published: 16 January 2023

1. Introduction

Despite tremendous immunization progress in recent decades, global inequities persist, reflected in the 25 million underimmunized and 18 million zero-dose children in 2021 [1]. Zero-dose children are defined by the Immunisation Agenda 2030 consortium (IA2030) as those that lack access to or are never reached by routine immunization services, measured by the lack of the first dose of diphtheria-tetanus-pertussis containing vaccine (DTP1) [2]. Health inequities are significant drivers of the gaps in immunization coverage and challenges in reaching the most under-served communities in low- and middle-income countries (LMICs) [3,4]. It is estimated that half of zero-dose children reside in three key geographic contexts: urban poor areas, remote communities and conflict-affected settings [5]. Moreover, gender-related barriers to immunization create additional challenges, with indicators such as maternal education and age being significant determinants of immunization coverage [3,4,6,7].

To improve immunization coverage and equity, the World Health Organization has launched the Immunization Agenda 2030 (IA2030), with the goal of "leaving no one behind", including a core objective to extend immunization services to reach zero-dose and underimmunized children and communities [8]. Aligned with IA2030, Gavi has launched its 5.0 Strategy with the goal of reducing the number of zero-dose children by 25% by 2025 and by 50% by 2030 [9,10]. Through several funding streams, Gavi supports immunization programs in more than 70 LMICs [11]. Gavi also supports UNICEF to conduct implementation research to improve policies and programs, identify implementation bottlenecks and promote equity in immunization delivery [12].

To understand how countries are currently addressing these gaps and where there is scope for improvement, we undertook a mapping and structured synthesis of pro-equity strategies for immunization across 61 low-income countries receiving programmatic support from Gavi, expanding on a more targeted mapping exercise by Dadari and colleagues [13]. The synthesis aimed to identify current practices and promising opportunities to reach zero-dose and underimmunized children in LMICs and to inform the creation of a searchable database to enable countries to identify potential solutions to immunization challenges and support country-level programmatic planning.

2. Materials and Methods

Strategy mapping followed a two-phased approach. Phase I (2019) led by Dadari and colleagues focused on 13 Gavi-supported countries (Afghanistan, Central African Republic, Chad Republic, Democratic Republic of Congo, Ethiopia, India, Kenya, Kyrgyzstan, Madagascar, Myanmar, Nigeria, Pakistan, Uganda) [13]. Phase II (expanded mapping in 2021) considered data from 48 additional Gavi-supported countries. A list of countries selected for both phases is available in Appendix A.

2.1. *Methods for the Initial Mapping by Dadari et al.*

The extraction of pro-equity strategies was guided by the development of a conceptual framework by UNICEF researchers, including the determinants of immunization coverage, key thematic areas and associated keywords. Methods for the first phase are described in detail in previous published work by Dadari et al. [13].

2.2. *Methods for the Expanded Mapping*

The expanded mapping sought to include data from 48 additional Gavi-supported countries, as well as incorporate more recent data from phase I countries, when available. We also aimed to interpret data by applying additional equity filters, considering gender-related barriers to immunization and inequities in immunization for target populations (urban poor, remote rural, conflict). Lastly, we sought to organize strategies thematically and identify opportunities to make findings accessible to countries, development partners and other interested parties

2.2.1. Data Source Selection

The mapping considered Gavi Annual Country Joint Appraisals (JA) reports between 2016 and 2019, aligning with the Gavi 5.0 strategy timeline. JA reports describe country-level implementation progress and the performance of Gavi funding support [14]. Countries were selected based on eligibility for Gavi support in 2020. In view of the COVID-19 pandemic in 2020, countries did not submit JA reports. Instead, countries conducted "Multi-Stakeholder Dialogues" (MSD), which aim to convene relevant stakeholders to discuss country-level barriers to immunization and align future objectives and actions. MSD reports summarizing key findings from these sessions were included as data points for that year. JAs and MSDs were obtained from the Gavi website and the Gavi Secretariat.

A total of 126 JAs (n = 106) and MSDs (n = 20) from 48 additional countries were selected for the data extraction. Up to three most recent data points were chosen for each country, when available. Additionally, given that Syria only became eligible for Gavi support in 2019 and there were no JAs or MSDs available, a report on Syria's National Immunization Strategy was obtained as an alternative data source.

2.2.2. Data Extraction and Synthesis

Strategies were identified via a targeted keyword search, informed by the phase I conceptual framework. The data extraction method was initially calibrated by manually extracting strategies from randomly selected JAs used in phase I. After careful review of the initial mapping and JA reports, additional keywords were generated for the thematic areas to improve the identification of strategies and increase the scope of the extraction.

Data extraction was facilitated by the "text retrieval" feature of the freely available qualitative analysis software QDA Miner Lite to accommodate a large dataset and increase the reliability of results. For efficiency and convenience, keywords were searched across all JA and MSD reports simultaneously. Paragraphs where keywords appeared were analyzed for their relevance and presence of strategies corresponding to the thematic areas. An Excel extraction matrix, including countries, thematic areas and keywords, was populated with strategies.

Data extraction was performed by the first author, with supplemental cross-check for 10% of the data by a second reviewer. Independently obtained results between both reviewers were compared at multiple occasions. Differences in data extraction and strategy capture were discussed among reviewers and co-authors until a consensus was reached and appropriate adjustments or calibrations were made. Additionally, all keywords were translated in French to enable data extraction from reports available only in French. The final set of keywords used for extraction can be found in Appendix B.

Data from phase I and II were collated, yielding a total of 607 unique strategies, extracted from 174 reports and 61 countries. The thematic synthesis of pro-equity strategies was informed by the analysis led by Dadari and colleagues in Phase I, UNICEF's Journey to Health and Immunization (JTHI) framework, and the Global Routine Immunization Strategies and Practices (GRISP) framework [13,15,16]. The JTHI framework is a tool used to identify the factors influencing different points of the immunization service delivery, including before, during, and after immunization. The framework also offers an opportunity for a more targeted identification of barriers and solutions. Table 1 outlines key dimensions related to each step of the JTHI framework.

Table 1. Key caregiver and health worker dimensions of the JTHI framework [15].

JTHI Step	Caregiver	Health Worker
1: Knowledge, Awareness and Beliefs	Practical knowledge, norms and values, trust in vaccines and providers	Practical competencies, norms and values, perception of clients
2: Intent	Decision-making power, self-efficacy	Motivation/satisfaction, social recognition, community respect
3: Preparation, Cost and Effort	Logistics of remembering, transport, childcare, juggling competing priorities, social and opportunity costs	Preparing getting to clinic/outreach site, opportunity costs
4: Point of Service	Appropriateness and convenience of services, service hours, social distance	Training, job aids, workload, facility/flow
5: Experience of Care	IPC and treatment by health workers, physical conditions, use of home-based records, client satisfaction	Interpersonal communication skills, trust building, pain mitigation, training and experience, social distance
6: After-Service	Information on AEFI and when and where to return, sharing +/− experience with community, reinforcement of vaccination as norm	Family and community respect, celebration of achievements, supportive supervision

The thematic synthesis of strategies was also informed by the Global Routine Immunization Strategies and Practices (GRISP) framework [16]. The GRISP comprehensive framework of strategies and practices for routine immunization introduces key areas of action to strengthen immunization systems and improve coverage. The framework also describes a systemic approach to address barriers by tackling four categories of actions: maximizing reach, managing the program, mobilizing people and monitoring progress [16]. Among these actions, GRISP highlights nine transformative investments, aimed to guide governments to transform immunization programs and achieve better outcomes [16].

We thematically synthesized the collated pro-equity strategies, building on the themes identified in phase I, JTHI steps and GRISP dimensions. When relevant, GRISP approaches were included in the themes. Examples of GRISP themes include the integration of immunization with other routine services, strategies to address vaccine hesitancy and misinformation and practices to build the capacity of healthcare workers. Given that some strategies were found to be relevant to more than one theme and JTHI step, we opted to include them in all relevant dimensions and themes, leading to a total of $n = 740$ data points used for the analysis. To support knowledge use, a learning tool and searchable database of strategies was created by UNICEF. The tool allows filtering of results by country, JTHI steps, health system element, relevance to key populations and the application of a gender lens [17].

3. Results

The number of unique strategies reported by each country ranged from a minimum of one strategy (Cambodia, Mongolia, Philippines, DPR Korea, Syria) to a maximum of twenty-seven strategies (Nigeria) (see Figure 1).

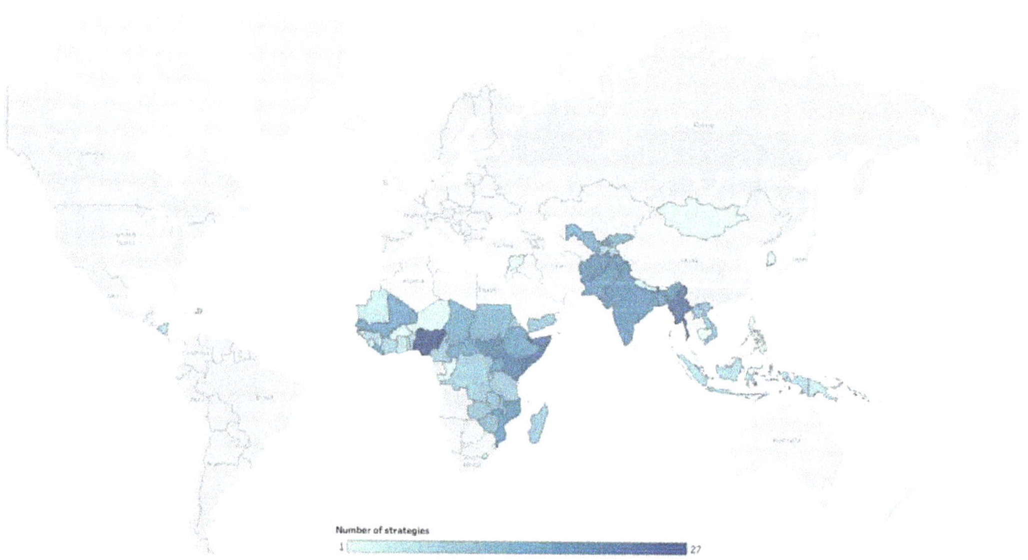

Figure 1. Number of strategies per country.

3.1. Strategies Addressing JTHI Steps

Strategies targeting JTHI step 4 (Point of Service, $n = 328$ [44%]), step 1 (Knowledge, Awareness and Beliefs, $n = 181$ [25%]) and step 3 (Preparation, Cost and Effort, $n = 98$ [13%]) were the most common. Countries less frequently reported strategies targeting step 5 (Experience of Care, $n = 58$ [8%]), step 2 (Intent, $n = 54$ [7%]) and step 6 (After-Service, $n = 20$ [3%]). Figure 2 illustrates the number and relative proportion of strategies by JTHI step and determinants of immunization coverage.

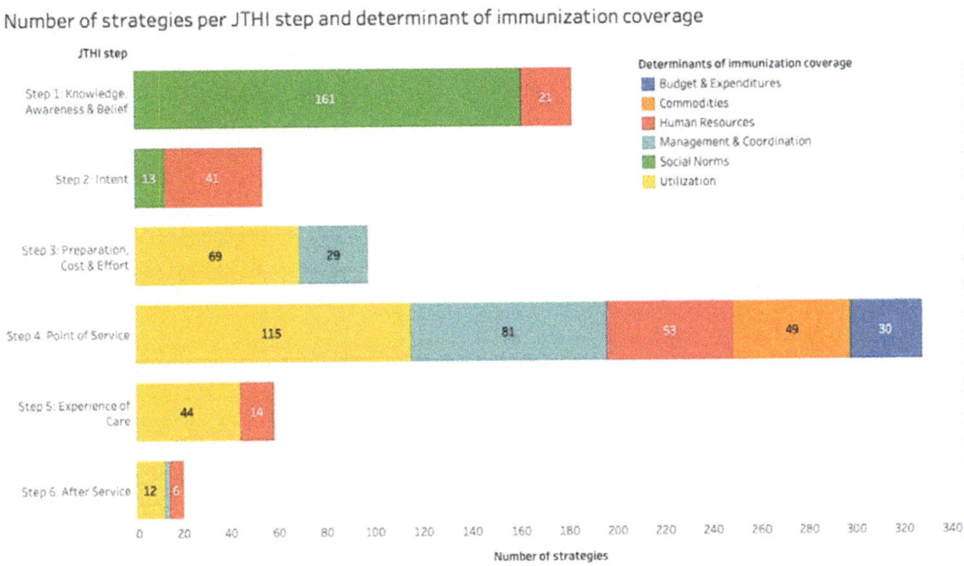

Figure 2. Relative proportion of strategies per JTHI step and determinant of immunization coverage.

Moreover, nested within each step and determinant of immunization coverage, we consolidated strategies into 24 themes (see Figure 3).

Figure 3. Number of strategies per JTHI step, determinant of immunization coverage and theme.

Pro-equity strategies relevant to JTHI step 4 (Point of Service) targeted a variety of determinants and themes, including Utilization (n = 115 [16%]), Management and Coordination (n = 81 [11%]), Human Resources (n = 53 [7%]), Commodities (n = 49 [6%])

and Budget and Expenditures (n = 30 [4%]). The most common theme identified at this step was: tailoring the location of service delivery (n = 81 [11%]), which is related to factors influencing the utilization of services by clients. For example, in Guinea, immunization supplies and equipment were installed in private, religious and armed forces infrastructures in order to expand the supply of vaccination services for populations that are harder to reach in urban areas.

Further, strategies relevant to step 1 (Knowledge, Awareness and Beliefs) targeted the determinants Social Norms (n = 161 [22%]) and Human Resources (n = 21 [3%]). The themes most commonly identified at this step were: engaging local leaders to address misinformation and raise awareness (n = 84 [12%]) and use of communication strategies to address misinformation and raise awareness (n = 76 [10%]). For example, in Lao People's Democratic Republic, community leaders and village health volunteers have been targeting mothers in known high-risk villages by engaging them to understand their own personal views and potential hesitancy regarding immunization. Moreover, in Indonesia, a communication campaign was developed to advocate for measles and rubella immunization through short films, SMS blast messages, art/graphic design and communication channels (Facebook, Twitter, WhatsApp, etc.).

Strategies related to step 3 (Preparation, Cost, and Effort) targeted the determinants Utilization (n = 69 [9%]) and Management and Coordination (n = 29 [4%]). Strategies at that step were most commonly related to the theme: reminders and strategies to reduce time, costs and opportunity barriers (n = 39 [5%]). For example, in Eritrea, mothers and caregivers were encouraged by healthcare providers to bring defaulter children to sites for vitamin A supplementation and immunization during the African Vaccination Week and Child Health and Nutrition Week activities.

Strategies used at step 5 (Experience of Care) were most often related to the theme: adjusting service delivery approach and engaging community to ensure acceptability (n = 44 [6%]). A strategy under this theme was implemented in Ethiopia with the use of community outreach agents to perform the community-based monitoring of children eligible for vaccinations, thus engaging community leaders and volunteers. Moreover, strategies at step 2 (Intent) were most often related to the theme: financial and non-financial incentives to improve staff motivation and performance (n = 41 [5%]). For example, in South Sudan, 465 vaccinators and 24 supervisors were trained in interpersonal communication (IPC) skills. Lastly, we found fewer strategies targeting step 6 (After-Service), where the most common themes were: strengthening accountability, trust and communication for mobilization (n = 12 [2%]), including AEFI training conducted in multiple countries (Nicaragua, Eritrea, Mozambique and Myanmar, among others).

The least frequently identified themes among all JTHI steps were as follows: health workers being from the communities they serve (n = 6 [1%]), taking stock of post-care successes and failures (n = 6 [1%]), performance rewards for healthcare workers (n = 2 [0.2%]) and security initiatives to allow services to happen (n = 1 [0.1%]).

3.2. Strategies Targeting Key Populations and Gender

Our approach allowed the identification of strategies targeting special populations, including the key geographical contexts identified by the Equity Reference Group for Immunization and reflected in both IA2030 and Gavi's strategy 2021–2025: poor urban areas, remote rural communities and populations affected by conflict [3,8–10]. Additionally, gender was identified as a cross-cutting theme and influencing factor for immunization and was incorporated in the data interpretation process. The UNICEF searchable database allows filtering of results based on their relevance to key populations and the consideration of gender [17]. Given the volume of data, a few select examples related to the most common theme identified in the mapping (engaging local leaders to address misinformation and raise awareness) are highlighted here.

For example, in Malawi, mother care groups (village head chiefs, women volunteers) were created by Malawi Health Equity Network (MHEN) in hard-to-reach areas, urban slums and refugee camps. The groups' activities involve defaulter tracing (door-to-door), health education, interpersonal communication and advocacy at the community level.

Additionally, in Pakistan, a prototype on immunization in slums of one union council in Lahore was developed and implemented locally. Through this approach, twelve slum health committees were established with participation from local community notables, religious leaders, teachers and local government representatives for advocacy and social mobilization among slum communities.

Moreover, in Nigeria, the Women Advocates for Vaccine Access (WAVA), a coalition of women-focused civil society organizations, was formed to advocate for increased routine immunization and sustainable vaccine financing.

4. Discussion

We summarize pro-equity immunization strategies employed in 61 Gavi-supported countries between 2016 and 2020, as reported in JA reports. This mapping provides an overview of what is being done to improve immunization equity and reach the most disadvantaged communities in Gavi-supported LMICs. Moreover, we offer a thematic synthesis of strategies in the form of a searchable database, informed by the JTHI and GRISP frameworks [17].

Countries are using various strategies to tackle immunization challenges at each JTHI step. While there is an abundance of strategies targeting Point of Service (step 4); Knowledge, Awareness and Beliefs (step 1); and Preparation, Cost and Effort (step 3), we found gaps in addressing immunization Intent (step 2), Experience of Care (step 5) and After-Service (step 6). Mapping strategies against the JTHI and GRISP frameworks allowed the identification of common practices among countries, as well as opportunities for strategy development and future investments to improve immunization outcomes.

Strategies focused on leveraging communication strategies and engaging local leaders to raise awareness and address misinformation were common among countries. These strategies shape knowledge, awareness and beliefs about immunization among caregivers and health workers and influence the first step of the JTHI framework. Efforts aligned with this theme also support the IA2030 strategic priority to increase commitment and demand by improving public trust and confidence, acceptance and value of vaccination, and addressing the reluctance to vaccinate [8]. Vaccine hesitancy remains a key challenge in LMICs and was identified by the WHO as one of the top global health threats in 2019 [18,19]. While the prevalence of vaccine hesitancy in LMICs can vary, prioritizing efforts to influence caregiver knowledge and confidence about the importance, safety and effectiveness of vaccines can have a significant impact on vaccine uptake globally [20,21]. However, given that the causes for vaccine hesitancy can be complex and context-specific, understanding how Gavi-supported countries are addressing these challenges can inform future efforts to increase immunization coverage and equity, particularly in countries with similar socio-cultural contexts. [16,18,19].

Strategies targeting the logistics of service delivery, such as tailoring the location of services, were also common. These include efforts to provide tailored services for hard-to-reach communities, microplanning, Reach Every District (RED)/Reaching Every Child (REC) initiatives and other "bottom-up" approaches, which have previously been supported by the literature [22,23]. Additionally, countries reported strategies focused on reminders and strategies to reduce time, costs and opportunity barriers and on conducting coverage and equity assessments (CEAs). These strategies directly address the IA2030 strategic priority of improving coverage and equity as they focus on identifying barriers to vaccination due to age, location, social and cultural and gender-related factors [8]. Moreover, prioritizing CEAs can further contribute to bridging equity gaps by promoting the identification of under-served communities, the selection and prioritization of pro-equity strategies and the monitoring of pro-equity strategies, interventions and outcomes [24].

Furthermore, countries reported a variety of strategies focused on addressing systemic elements of the immunization process, such as strengthening healthcare systems, improving information and data management systems; strengthening supply chains and logistics; and investing in the healthcare workforce. These strategies demonstrate an alignment with GRISP transformative investments, including building vaccinator capacity, modernizing vaccine supply chains and investing in information systems [16].

Opportunities for strategy development can be found in the least common themes identified: health workers are from the communities they serve and security measures to allow immunization services to happen safely in conflict-affected areas. Strategies to address these themes can be guided by the GRISP areas targeting the mobilization of people (through engaging communities) and maximizing reach (through designing services to effectively deliver vaccines to all target groups and improve equity), respectively [16].

Lastly, there are opportunities for strategy development at the JTHI steps for which we found fewer strategies (Intent, Experience of Care, and After-Service). Immunization intent is related to the caregiver's decision-making power and self-efficacy, which is influenced by societal gender norms and roles [15]. Although women are traditionally the primary caregivers in households, they often lack the decision-making power to influence the health of their children [25–27]. Moreover, the link between maternal education and child immunization has been thoroughly documented in the literature and can be an important contributor to the "social distance" between caregivers and health workers, which is a key component of addressing the experience of care [4,7,15]. An emphasis on improving maternal health literacy can be an important consideration to address this gap [25–27]. Further, an ecological framework can be useful in identifying gaps and interventions targeting individual and household factors affecting women's decision-making process, including health literacy and capacity for negotiation within households and within healthcare settings [25].

Given that step 6 feeds back into the JTHI cycle and can influence other dimensions of the care-seeking process, more attention should be brought to assessing the opportunities at that step. JTHI step 6 strategies focus on clients' access to information about the after-effects following immunizations (AEFI), knowledge about follow-up appointments and when to return for services [15]. At that step, very few strategies targeted performance rewards and processes for evaluating programs (taking stock of post-care successes and failures). Opportunities for strategy development addressing these themes can be informed by two of the GRISP areas of action. Firstly, in the area of maximizing reach, there are opportunities for transformational investments related to building the capacity of vaccinators, including the provision of performance rewards for healthcare workers [16]. Secondly, in the area of monitoring progress, there are opportunities to develop strategies related to the evaluation of programs through surveys and review, which includes taking stock of post-care successes and failures [16].

4.1. Strengths and Limitations of the Mapping

Our synthesis builds on and reinforces previous work to describe pro-equity strategies for immunizations in Gavi-supported countries (13). Moreover, we demonstrate the utility of using JA reports to characterize and understand country-level practices to improve immunization coverage and equity. The mapping of strategies to multiple key dimensions and themes, including JTHI steps, systemic factors emphasized by GRISP and relevance to key populations, allowed us to create a searchable database which can be used for knowledge sharing among countries, as well as inspiration for addressing gaps and developing targeted approaches [17].

An important limitation of the mapping is that it considers only the strategies that are being reported by countries in the JA and MSD reports. Therefore, the data extracted from these reports might not include all strategies used at the national or subnational levels. Additionally, data might be incomplete for the countries where only one or two data points were available. Moreover, the review represents a snapshot of the strategies that are currently being implemented in all countries, without evaluating the implementation process or the efficacy of these strategies directly. Therefore, the recommendations that can be made from the data are limited to "what" is being done, without being able to explain "how" these strategies are implemented or how well they worked. This is an important evidence gap that needs attention.

4.2. Implications for Policy and Practice

An equity-driven approach is necessary to identify immunization gaps and opportunities to reach underimmunized and zero-dose children in LMICs. The awareness of current strategies and gaps can inform equity-driven immunization programs, policies and decision making targeting zero-dose and underimmunized children in LMICs. The dissemination of these findings can also promote knowledge and expertise sharing between countries and can serve as a base for strategic planning and scale-up of interventions promoting equitable immunization programs, particularly between countries in similar socio-political or cultural contexts. Future directions for this work could include an analysis of the country-level impact of these strategies on immunization inequities. An emphasis on monitoring and evaluation activities could further characterize the areas where investments are justified and desired.

Given that Gavi-supported countries submit JA or MSD reports yearly, it would be beneficial to continuously update the data and searchable database on a yearly basis, as reports become available [17]. Moreover, given the disruption of services that occurred due to the COVID-19 pandemic, we recommend a detailed analysis of the pro-equity mitigation strategies deployed in 2020 since the start of the pandemic. Lastly, continued work to categorize strategies based on key dimensions, such as relevance to key populations (urban, remote rural and conflict) and gender considerations, can provide opportunities for more targeted solutions to implementation challenges.

5. Conclusions

We conducted a targeted mapping and synthesis of pro-equity strategies for immunization in 61 Gavi-supported countries. Strategies were thematically mapped against the JTHI steps and the GRISP framework, which allowed us to identify common practices and opportunities for future investments. Findings have been incorporated into a learning tool and searchable database of pro-equity strategies, which can serve as a resource and a guide to other countries who want to improve their immunization coverage and equity [17].

Author Contributions: Conceptualization, V.I., A.S.M.S., A.S. and M.J.; methodology, V.I., A.S.M.S., A.S. and M.J.; formal analysis, V.I., A.S.M.S., A.S. and M.J.; data curation, V.I., A.S.M.S. and A.S.; writing—original draft preparation, V.I.; writing—review and editing, A.S.M.S., A.S. and M.J.; visualization, V.I.; supervision, A.S.M.S., A.S. and M.J.; project administration, A.S.M.S. All authors have read and agreed to the published version of the manuscript.

Funding: This research was funded through the UNICEF PHC-HSS Unit via the grant "Implementation Research Accelerator for Immunization Initiative" (SC210241) from Gavi, the Vaccine Alliance and through the Centre de recherche du Centre Hospitalier de l'Université de Montréal (CRCHUM) via a grant from the Canadian Institutes for Health Research (130280).

Data Availability Statement: The complete dataset for this study is available online in the UNICEF Immunization, Gender and Equity Solutions Library [17]. Data sources (Joint Appraisal and Multi-Stakeholder reports) can be found on the Gavi, the Vaccine Alliance website.

Acknowledgments: The authors would like to acknowledge colleagues Dadari et al., who led the initial project on which our work is built. Additionally, the authors would like to acknowledge the contribution of the Gavi Secretariat (Binay Kumar) for the acquisition of Joint Appraisal and Multi-Stakeholder Dialogue reports. Lastly, the authors would like to acknowledge Johanna Manga, who supported the validation of the data extraction method as part of the UNICEF PHC-HSS Unit.

Conflicts of Interest: The authors declare no conflict of interest.

List of Relevant Abbreviations

AEFI	Adverse Events Following Immunization
CEA	Coverage and Equity Assessment
CHW	Community Health Worker
CRVS	Civil Registration and Vital Statistics
CSO	Civil Society Organization
DHIS	District Health Information System
EPI	Expanded Programme on Immunization
GIS	Geographic Information System
GRISP	Global Routine Immunization Strategies and Practices
HeRAMS	Health Resources Availability Monitoring System
HSS	Health Systems Strengthening
IPC	InterPersonal Communication
IA2030	Immunisation Agenda 2030
IEC	Information, Education and Communication
JA	Joint Appraisal
JTHI	Journey to Health and Immunization
KAP	Knowledge, Awareness and Practices
MOU	Memorandum of Understanding
MSD	Multi-Stakeholder Dialogue
NGO	Non-Governmental Organization
RED	Reaching Every District
SDD	Solar Direct Drive
SMS	Short Message Service
SWAp	Sector Wide Approach
UNICEF	United Nations Childen's Fund
WHO	World Health Organization

Appendix A

Table A1. Gavi-supported countries included in phases I and II of the mapping.

Country	Phase I	Phase II
Afghanistan	✓	
Bangladesh		✓
Benin		✓
Burkina Faso		✓
Burundi		✓
Cambodia		✓
Cameroon		✓
Central African Republic	✓	
Chad	✓	
Comoros		✓
Cote d'Ivoire		✓
Democratic Republic of Congo	✓	
Djibouti		✓
DPR Korea		✓
Eritrea		✓
Ethiopia	✓	
Ghana		✓
Guinea		✓

Table A1. *Cont.*

Country	Phase I	Phase II
Guinea-Bissau		✓
Haiti		✓
India	✓	
Indonesia		✓
Kenya	✓	
Kyrgyzstan	✓	✓
Lao People's Democratic Republic		✓
Lesotho		✓
Liberia		✓
Madagascar	✓	
Malawi		✓
Mali		✓
Mauritania		✓
Mongolia		✓
Mozambique		✓
Myanmar	✓	✓
Nepal		✓
Nicaragua		✓
Niger		✓
Nigeria	✓	
Pakistan	✓	
Papua New Guinea		✓
Philippines		✓
Republic of the Congo		✓
Rwanda		✓
Sao Tome and Principe		✓
Senegal		✓
Sierra Leone		✓
Solomon Islands		✓
Somalia		✓
South Sudan		✓
Sudan		✓
Syria		✓
Tajikistan		✓
Tanzania		✓
Timor-Leste		✓
Togo		✓
Uganda	✓	
Uzbekistan		✓
Vietnam		✓
Yemen		✓

Table A1. *Cont.*

Country	Phase I	Phase II
Zambia		✓
Zimbabwe		✓

Appendix B

Table A2. Keywords used for data extraction.

Determinant of Immunization Coverage	Theme	Keywords (English)	Keywords (French)
Utilization	Adjusting time of immunization	schedule_change, time_change, extended_time, time_adjustment, weekend_immunization, service_delivery, weekend, event, period*	horaire*, changement_horaire, ajustement_horaire, prolong*, temps_supplémentaire, immunisation_weekend, fin_de_semaine, prestation_de_service, heur*_supplémentaire*
	Tailor location of service delivery to meet the needs of caregivers	marketplace_session*, mobile_session*, location*, service_delivery, urban, special_session*, marketplace, session*, rural, gender, transit_camp*, volunteer*, micro_plan, outreach, market*	prestation_de_service, urbain, marché, genre, place_du_marché, camp*_de_transit, service*_de_proximité, volontaire*, bénévol*
	Network of health workers	peer_support, network*, remote, rural, social_group, SMS, Whatsapp, text_message*, support	Support_par_les_pairs, réseau, éloigné, rural, groupe_social, SMS, messag*_texte, texto, Whatsapp, groupe*_de_soutien, soutien
	Reminder and recall systems	SMS, Whatsapp, reminder*, defaulter_tracing, defaulter_tracking, incomplete_vaccination, incomplete_immunisation, missed, unvaccinated, defaulter*	SMS, Whatsapp, rappel*, repérage, traçage, localisation, suivi, abandon*, décrochage, immunisation*_incomplète*
Social norms	Community leaders and multiple advocates to address misinformation/identify normative positions and match the messenger to the recipient	mistrust, misinformation, disinformation, influence, community, civil_society, NGO, religi*, shaman, clan_leader, tradition*, accepta*, rumo*, misconcept*	Désinformation, fausse_information, faux_renseignement*, influence*, communauté*, Communautaire, société_civile, ONG, religi*, organization_non_gouvernementale, rumeur*, idée*_fausse*
	Peer/women-support groups in communities	hesitancy, women_group*, women_support, peer_group, men's_group, peer_support, fem*	hésitation, groupe*_de_femme*, support_entre_femmes, groupe_de_pairs, groupe_d'hommes, support_par_les_pairs, soutien
	Leveraging social norms—using champions from the target population who are well-liked and influential to shape perceptions peers have of vaccines	champion*, mistrust, misinformation, disinformation, influence, community, NGO, civil_society, rumo*	champion, hésitation, fausse_information, faux_renseignements, influence, communauté, communautaire, ONG, société_civile, rumeur*
	Journalists as EPI champions	journal*, journalis*, news, media, print, radio*, social_media, channel*, Facebook, Twitter, Instagram, rumo*	journal*, journalis*, media*, radio, réseau*_socia*, chaîne*, Facebook, Twitter, Instagram, rumeur*
	Social structure household decision makers/widen the audience for IEC	decision_mak*, gender, empower*, mother*, father*, IEC, information_education_and_communication, KAP, Knowledge_attitudes_and_practices, daughter*, son*, girl*, boy*, teenag*	prise_de_décision*, décideur, genre, autonomisation, mère*, père*, IEC, information_éducation_et_communication, fill*, garçon*, adolescen*
	Gender transformative approaches: men as fathers	decision_make*, gender*, empower*, mother*, father*, daught*, son*, teenag*	décideur*, prise_de_décision, genre*, autonomis*, fill*, garçon*, adolescen*, père*, mère*

Table A2. *Cont.*

Determinant of Immunization Coverage	Theme	Keywords (English)	Keywords (French)
Management and coordination	EPI support groups for rural/urban populations	urban_immunization, rural, urban, slum*, communit*	immunisation_urbaine, rural, urbain, binonville*, communaut*
	Strategies for negotiating access to populations affected by conflict	conflict, safe_corridor*, corridor*_of_peace, safe_zone, change_agent, hard_to_reach, securit*	conflit*, corridor*_de_paix, sécurit*, zone_sécurit*, agent*_de_changement
	Communication chains amongst health providers	health_worker_communication, health/service_provider_communication, SMS, Whatsapp, messag*	travailleur_de_santé, prestataire_de_santé, communication, prestataire_de_services, SMS, Whatsapp
	Services monitoring system	monitoring_system, HeRAMS	système*_de_surveillance
	Alternatives to immunization records	microchip*, record*, registr*, bracelet	puce*, puce_électronique, dossiers, registr*, bracelet
	Population tracking	tracking, GIS, satellite, mobile_network, mapping	suivi, localisation, repérage, satellite, réseau_mobile, géolocalisation
	Linkages to registration systems	e-register, tracker, DHIS, DHIS2, CRVS, civil_registration_and_vital_statistics	registr*_numérique, tracker, état_civil_et_statistiques_démographiques, statistiques_de_l'état, DHIS, DHIS2
Human resources	Digital financial services	digital_money, digital_payment, mobile_money, electronic_payment, finance*, budget	argent_numérique, monnaie_électronique, paiement_électronique, argent_électronique, finance*, budget
	Health worker recognition	incentiv*, reward_system, motivation, recognition, pay-for-performance, training, capacity_building, reward	incitati*, motivation, encouragement, stimulus, valorisation, récompense, formation
Environment	Security to allow immunization services to happen	security, safe_access, late_hours, extended_hours	sécurité, accès_sécuritaire, heure_tardive, extension, horaire_prolongé, heures_supplémentaires
	Setting up overnight stay points to reach access-compromised areas	overnight, camping, night, mobile_team	nuit, pendant_la_nuit, camping, équipes_mobiles
Commodities	Cold chain technology	solar_direct_drive_refrigerator*, SDD, long_term_passive_cold_box, freeze_prevention, freeze_protetion, controlled_temperature_chain, outside_cold_chain, thermostable, cold_chain*, temperature*, freezer, fridge, refrigerator*	réfrigérateur_solaire, réfrigérateur, congélation, protection_contre_le_gel, prévention_du_gel, chaîne_de_température, thermostable, chaîne_de_froid, température*, réfrigérateur*, frigidaire*, congélateur
Budget and expenditures	Coordinated activity plans	one_plan, one_budget, one_system, MOU, joint_plan, SWAp, budget, expenditure, memorandum_of_understanding, sector_wide_approach	un_plan, un_budget, un_système, plan_conjoint, approche_sectorielle, budget, dépense

* Asterisks refer to truncated search terms used to extract relevant keywords and their variations.

References

1. UNICEF. Vaccination and Immunization Statistics: UNICEF Data 2022. Available online: https://data.unicef.org/topic/child-health/immunization/ (accessed on 18 December 2022).
2. WHO. Immunization Agenda 2030: Framework for Action—Annex 1. 2020. Available online: https://www.immunizationagenda2030.org/framework-for-action (accessed on 18 December 2022).
3. Chopra, M.; Bhutta, Z.; Chang Blanc, D.; Checchi, F.; Gupta, A.; Lemango, E.T.; Levine, O.S.; Lyimo, D.; Nandy, R.; O'Brien, K.L.; et al. Addressing the persistent inequities in immunization coverage. *Bull. World Health Organ.* **2020**, *98*, 146–148. [CrossRef] [PubMed]
4. Ali, H.A.; Hartner, A.M.; Echeverria-Londono, S.; Roth, J.; Li, X.; Abbas, K.; Portnoy, A.; Vynnycky, E.; Woodruff, K.; Ferguson, N.M.; et al. Vaccine equity in low and middle income countries: A systematic review and meta-analysis. *Int. J. Equity Health* **2022**, *21*, 82. [CrossRef] [PubMed]

5. Gavi, the Vaccine Alliance. The Zero-Dose Child: Explained. 2021. Available online: https://www.gavi.org/vaccineswork/zero-dose-child-explained (accessed on 18 December 2022).
6. Arsenault, C.; Johri, M.; Nandi, A.; Mendoza Rodríguez, J.M.; Hansen, P.M.; Harper, S. Country-level predictors of vaccination coverage and inequalities in Gavi-supported countries. *Vaccine* **2017**, *35*, 2479–2488. [CrossRef] [PubMed]
7. Arsenault, C.; Harper, S.; Nandi, A.; Mendoza Rodríguez, J.M.; Hansen, P.M.; Johri, M. Monitoring equity in vaccination coverage: A systematic analysis of demographic and health surveys from 45 Gavi-supported countries. *Vaccine* **2017**, *35*, 951–959. [CrossRef] [PubMed]
8. WHO. Immunization Agenda 2030: A Global Strategy to Leave No One Behind. 2020. Available online: https://www.who.int/teams/immunization-vaccines-and-biologicals/strategies/ia2030 (accessed on 18 December 2022).
9. Gavi, the Vaccine Alliance. Phase 5 (2021–2025). 2022. Available online: https://www.gavi.org/our-alliance/strategy/phase-5-2021-2025 (accessed on 18 December 2022).
10. Gavi, the Vaccine Alliance. Reaching Zero-Dose Children: The Vision for Leaving No-One Behind with Immunisation and Primary Health Care. 2021. Available online: https://www.gavi.org/our-alliance/strategy/phase-5-2021-2025/equity-goal/zero-dose-children-missed-communities (accessed on 18 December 2022).
11. Gavi, the Vaccine Alliance. How Our Support Works. 2022. Available online: https://www.gavi.org/programmes-impact/our-support (accessed on 18 December 2022).
12. UNICEF. Implementation Research for Immunization: Summary Report of Global Activities Supported by Gavi, the Vaccine Alliance (2015–2018). UNICEF Implementation Research and Delivery Science Unit. 2018. Available online: https://www.technet-21.org/media/com_resources/trl/4982/multi_upload/UNICEF%20Implementation%20Research%20for%20Immunisation%20Report%20to%20Gavi%20July%202018.pdf (accessed on 18 December 2022).
13. Dadari, I.; Higgins-Steele, A.; Sharkey, A.; Charlet, D.; Shahabuddin, A.; Nandy, R.; Jackson, D. Pro-equity immunization and health systems strengthening strategies in select Gavi-supported countries. *Vaccine* **2021**, *39*, 2434–2444. [CrossRef] [PubMed]
14. Gavi the Vaccine Alliance. Joint Appraisals. 2022. Available online: https://www.gavi.org/our-support/joint-appraisals (accessed on 18 December 2022).
15. UNICEF. Human Centered Design 4 Health. Resources: Journey to Health. Available online: https://www.hcd4health.org/resources (accessed on 18 December 2022).
16. WHO. Global Routine Immunization Strategies and Practices (GRISP): A Companion Document to the Global Vaccine Action Plan (GVAP). 2016. Available online: https://apps.who.int/iris/handle/10665/204500 (accessed on 18 December 2022).
17. UNICEF. Immunization, Gender and Equity: Solutions Library. 2022. Available online: https://www.ige.health/solutions/ (accessed on 18 December 2022).
18. WHO. Ten Threats to Global Health in 2019. Available online: https://www.who.int/news-room/spotlight/ten-threats-to-global-health-in-2019 (accessed on 18 December 2022).
19. Galagali, P.M.; Kinikar, A.A.; Kumar, V.S. Vaccine Hesitancy: Obstacles and Challenges. *Curr. Pediatr. Rep.* **2022**, *10*, 241–248. [CrossRef] [PubMed]
20. Dayton, J.M.; Edochie, I.N.; Newhouse, D.L.; Cojocaru, A.; Deudibe, G.B.; Kakietek, J.J.; Kim, Y.S.; Montes, J. COVID-19 Vaccine Hesitancy in 53 Developing Countries: Levels, Trends and Reasons for Hesitancy. World Bank. 2022. Available online: https://documents.worldbank.org/en/publication/documents-reports/documentdetail/099500109262235034/idu00dcb6062035fc0463008980026592b384da5 (accessed on 7 January 2023).
21. De Figueiredo, A.; Simas, C.; Karafillakis, E.; Paterson, P.; Larson, H.J. Mapping global trends in vaccine confidence and investigating barriers to vaccine uptake: A large-scale retrospective temporal modelling study. *Lancet* **2022**, *396*, 898–908. [CrossRef] [PubMed]
22. WHO. Microplanning for Immunization Service Delivery Using the Reaching Every District (RED) Strategy. 2009. Available online: https://www.who.int/publications/i/item/microplanning-for-immunization-service-delivery-using-the-reaching-every-district-(-red)-strategy (accessed on 18 December 2022).
23. WHO. Regional Office for Africa. In-Depth Evaluation of the Reaching Every District Approach in the African Region. 2007. Available online: https://cdn.who.int/media/docs/default-source/immunization/reaching-every-district-red/1-afro-1-red-evaluation-report-2007-final.pdf?sfvrsn=86869845_4 (accessed on 18 December 2022).
24. Equity Reference Group for Immunization. Guidance Note: Coverage and Equity Assessments for Immunization Programs. Available online: https://sites.google.com/view/erg4immunisation/related-resources (accessed on 18 December 2022).
25. Feletto, M.; Sharkey, A. The influence of gender on immunisation: Using an ecological framework to examine intersecting inequities and pathways to change. *BMJ Glob. Health* **2019**, *4*, e001711. [CrossRef] [PubMed]
26. WHO. Immunization Agenda 2030: Why Gender Matters. 2021. Available online: https://www.gavi.org/sites/default/files/2021-12/why-gender-matters-ia2030.pdf (accessed on 18 December 2022).
27. Equity Reference Group for Immunization. Discussion Papers: A Gender Lens to Advance Equity in Immunization. 2018. Available online: https://sites.google.com/view/erg4immunisation/discussion-papers (accessed on 18 December 2022).

vaccines

MDPI

Article

Comparing Multivariate with Wealth-Based Inequity in Vaccination Coverage in 56 Countries: Toward a Better Measure of Equity in Vaccination Coverage

Bryan N. Patenaude [1,2,*], Salin Sriudomporn [1,2], Deborah Odihi [1,2], Joshua Mak [1,2] and Gatien de Broucker [1,2]

1 International Vaccine Access Center, Johns Hopkins University Bloomberg School of Public Health, Baltimore, MD 21205, USA
2 Department of International Health, Johns Hopkins University Bloomberg School of Public Health, Baltimore, MD 21205, USA
* Correspondence: bpatena1@jhu.edu

Abstract: Introduction: Following a call from the World Health Organization in 2017 for a methodology to monitor immunization coverage equity in line with the 2030 Agenda for Sustainable Development, this study applies the Vaccine Economics Research for Sustainability and Equity (VERSE) vaccination equity toolkit to measure national-level inequity in immunization coverage using a multi-dimensional ranking procedure and compares this with traditional wealth-quintile based ranking methods for assessing inequity. The analysis covers 56 countries with a most recent Demographic & Health Survey (DHS) between 2010 and 2022. The vaccines examined include Bacillus Calmette–Guerin (BCG), Diphtheria–Tetanus–Pertussis-containing vaccine doses 1 through 3 (DTP1–3), polio vaccine doses 1–3 (Polio1–3), the measles-containing vaccine first dose (MCV1), and an indicator for being fully immunized for age with each of these vaccines. Materials & Methods: The VERSE equity toolkit is applied to 56 DHS surveys to rank individuals by multiple disadvantages in vaccination coverage, incorporating place of residence (urban/rural), geographic region, maternal education, household wealth, sex of the child, and health insurance coverage. This rank is used to estimate a concentration index and absolute equity coverage gap (AEG) between the top and bottom quintiles, ranked by multiple disadvantages. The multivariate concentration index and AEG are then compared with traditional concentration index and AEG measures, which use household wealth as the sole criterion for ranking individuals and determining quintiles. Results: We find significant differences between the two sets of measures in almost all settings. For fully-immunized for age status, the inequities captured using the multivariate metric are between 32% and 324% larger than what would be captured examining inequities using traditional metrics. This results in a missed coverage gap of between 1.1 and 46.4 percentage points between the most and least advantaged. Conclusions: The VERSE equity toolkit demonstrated that wealth-based inequity measures systematically underestimate the gap between the most and least advantaged in fully-immunized for age coverage, correlated with maternal education, geography, and sex by 1.1–46.4 percentage points, globally. Closing the coverage gap between the bottom and top wealth quintiles is unlikely to eliminate persistent socio-demographic inequities in either coverage or access to vaccines. The results suggest that pro-poor interventions and programs utilizing needs-based targeting, which reflects poverty only, should expand their targeting criteria to include other dimensions to reduce systemic inequalities, holistically. Additionally, a multivariate metric should be considered when setting targets and measuring progress toward reducing inequities in healthcare coverage.

Keywords: equity; vaccine; immunization; global health; LMICs; health equity; quantitative analysis; socioeconomic; measurement

Citation: Patenaude, B.N.; Sriudomporn, S.; Odihi, D.; Mak, J.; de Broucker, G. Comparing Multivariate with Wealth-Based Inequity in Vaccination Coverage in 56 Countries: Toward a Better Measure of Equity in Vaccination Coverage. *Vaccines* **2023**, *11*, 536. https://doi.org/10.3390/vaccines11030536

Academic Editors: Ahmad Reza Hosseinpoor, M. Carolina Danovaro, Devaki Nambiar, Aaron Wallace, Hope Johnson and Pedro Plans-Rubió

Received: 14 January 2023
Revised: 16 February 2023
Accepted: 21 February 2023
Published: 24 February 2023

1. Introduction

Routine vaccination coverage is an essential component of primary healthcare and assessing health systems' strength. Despite increases in national levels of coverage over time, sub-national inequities in coverage and vaccination status across individuals persist due to multiple structural and socio-demographic barriers to access [1]. Despite this, most metrics used for measuring the degree of inequity in health outcomes, such as vaccine coverage, only allow for measuring disparities along one dimension at a time, such as wealth or urban/rural location [2]. Such measures mask persistent disparities correlated with multiple dimensions. This study utilizes the Vaccine Economics Research for Sustainability and Equity (VERSE) measurement toolkit [3] to compare inequity in full immunization status using both traditional concentration indices and absolute equity gaps (AEG) employing wealth-based ranking with concentration indices and AEGs derived from a multivariate ranking procedure. The analysis is conducted separately for 56 countries utilizing their most recent Demographic and Health Survey (DHS) between 2010 and 2022.

The focus on measuring equity in vaccination coverage derives from a 2017 call by the World Health Organization (WHO) for new methodologies to monitor immunization coverage equity in line with the 2030 Agenda for Sustainable Development. To fill this evidence gap, the Vaccine Economics Research for Sustainability and Equity (VERSE) toolkit was created to provide a standardized approach for measuring and tracking multivariate equity in vaccination coverage, economic impact, and health outcomes [4,5]. The methodology of the VERSE project builds upon existing equity methodologies and toolkits, such as the United Nations Development Programme (UNDP) Global Dashboard for Vaccine Equity, as well as the WHO Health Equity Assessment Toolkit (HEAT) [2,3,6], by expanding the outcomes assessed and by providing a standardized approach for ranking individuals across multiple factors influencing equity including socioeconomic, demographic, educational, sex-based, and geospatial covariates. The metrics produced exhibit several desirable properties of equity metrics such as being comparable over time and between settings, while also being sensitive to the intersectional nature of health equity.

The VERSE toolkit's approach to assessing equity accounts for the intersectionality of individual and district-level correlates of disadvantage in becoming vaccinated is aligned with approaches taken by numerous governmental institutions and international organizations, including the European Commission [7], the United States Census Bureau [8], the government of the United Kingdom [9], and the United Nations [10], which have all begun expanding beyond a singular focus on income or wealth as the basis for measuring and tracking social equity. However, in examining equity in healthcare access, the measurement of equity remains limited to approaches employing either a single factor for ranking or a series of separate bivariate equity assessments [11–14]. While this type of sub-group comparison over specific factors is commonplace, a systematic approach for combining and measuring multivariate inequality over multiple groups is needed to produce numbers that better capture the combined magnitude of different types of inequities, while accounting for overlap and intersectionality. For example, urban/rural status and socioeconomic status may partially capture the same type of inequity, but an individual possessing both low socioeconomic status and living in a rural area may also face a higher aggregate degree of disadvantage compared with being of either low socioeconomic status or from a rural area alone [14,15].

In addition to generating comparable equity metrics across 56 countries, this study also compares both multivariate and traditional concentration indices and the corresponding absolute equity gaps for vaccination coverage within the same survey for each country in order to assess whether there are systematic differences in the magnitude of inequity captured between approaches. The analysis is conducted over coverage of 8 key routine vaccines against 4 antigens: Bacillus Calmette–Guerin (BCG), Diphtheria–Tetanus–Pertussis-containing vaccine doses 1 through 3 (DTP1–3), polio vaccine doses 1–3 (Polio1–3), and the measles-containing vaccine first dose (MCV1), as well as an indicator for being fully immunized for age with each of these vaccines.

2. Materials & Methods

The data for this study include the most recent DHS survey between 2010 and 2022 for 56 countries (see Appendix A). DHS surveys are nationally representative and all contain data at the individual-level on coverage for eight key routine vaccines against four antigens, which are utilized in this assessment. The vaccines assessed include: Bacillus Calmette–Guerin (BCG), Diphtheria–Tetanus–Pertussis-containing vaccine doses 1 through 3 (DTP1–3), polio vaccine doses 1–3 (Polio1–3), and the measles-containing vaccine first dose (MCV1), as well as an indicator for being fully immunized for age with each of these vaccines. Data on vaccination coverage, as well as socio-demographic covariates, are used alongside the VERSE multivariate vaccination equity assessment toolkit to measure both wealth-based and multivariate equity in vaccination coverage within each country over each vaccine outcome. A complete list of variables from the DHS surveys that are used in the multivariate equity assessment is presented in Appendix B.

The primary outputs of the VERSE toolkit and the featured outcomes of this study are a multivariate concentration index, a relative measure of equity, and an absolute equity gap in coverage, an absolute (level) measure of equity. These measures are derived from literature on the measurement of socioeconomic equity by Wagstaff and Erreygers, combined with measures of "direct unfairness"—a term borrowed from social choice theory, which has been applied to healthcare access in the works of Fleurbaey, Schokkaert, Cookson, and Barbosa [15–21]. The multivariate concentration index takes the form of a traditional concentration index over vaccination coverage where, instead of ranking individuals by income, individuals are ranked by multivariate unfair disadvantage in access. Multivariate unfair disadvantage, as parameterized in the VERSE model, is measured as an individual-level propensity score for unfair disadvantage, netting out the effect of fair sources of variation in coverage. For the purposes of this study, the only fair source of variation in coverage status is whether a child is underage to receive the vaccine according to the national immunization schedule of the country examined. Unfair sources of variation included in this assessment are the sex of the child, maternal education level, socioeconomic status derived from the DHS wealth index, coverage by health insurance, urban or rural designation, and geopolitical sub-unit of residence. These factors were chosen based on standardized and near-universal data collection across all demographic and health surveys (DHS) [22]. Complete mathematical details of the quantification of unfair disadvantage, as well as the multivariate equity metric produced by the VERSE toolkit, can be found in the VERSE toolkit's methodological publication [3].

In addition to the multivariate concentration index produced in the VERSE Toolkit, an absolute equity gap is also produced [19,20]. The AEG is a measure of the absolute difference in vaccination coverage achieved by the top 20% compared with the bottom 20% of the population, where the population is ranked based on their propensity score for unfair disadvantage. Mathematically, this is equivalent to isolating the top and bottom quintiles from the Lorenz curve used to estimate the Wagstaff (direct) concentration index [20]. In most equity studies, socioeconomic status as measured by either income or, in the case of the DHS surveys, wealth index, is the sole variable used to rank or group individuals prior to computing a concentration index, slope index, Gini coefficient, Kakwani index, Atkinson index, absolute equity gap, or relative equity gap. In keeping with this convention, we also compute the Wagstaff (direct) concentration index, as well as the AEG between the top and bottom quintile, utilizing the DHS's wealth index as the only criterion to rank individuals. Concentration indices and AEGs derived from both the multivariate and traditional approaches are computed for 56 countries utilizing the same DHS dataset. The concentration indices and AEGs are then compared directly within countries with one another to provide empirical evidence of the degree of inequity, stemming from multiple factors known to be related to disadvantage in being vaccinated, that is missed by using only the traditional approaches for equity measurement.

3. Results

3.1. Full Immunization for Age

Among the 56 countries included in the analysis, the average multivariate concentration index for the fully immunized for age status was 0.125 (95% confidence interval: 0.109, 0.140), not weighting by population size. Meanwhile, the average wealth-based concentration index was estimated only at 0.014 (0.004, 0.024)—a difference of 0.110, representing that traditional concentration indices captured, on average, 89% less inequity compared with multivariate concentration index (see Table 1).

Table 1. Average inequities among 56 studied countries, by vaccine.

Vaccine	Coverage	Multivariate Concentration Index	Wealth-Based Concentration Index	% Captured Inequity Difference	Coverage Gap Multivariate (Percentage Points)	Coverage Gap Wealth (Percentage Points)	Additional Coverage Gap (Percentage Points)
MCV1	0.772	0.079 (0.067, 0.090)	0.011 (0.002, 0.020)	86.1%	21.5 (17.8, 25.1)	11.4 (7.4, 15.4)	10.1
Polio1	0.860	0.049 (0.039, 0.059)	0.003 (−0.007, 0.013)	93.9%	19.0 (16.3, 21.8)	8.5 (5.5, 11.5)	10.5
Polio2	0.797	0.065 (0.053, 0.077)	0.006 (−0.004, 0.016)	90.7%	22.1 (18.9, 25.2)	9.7 (6.3, 13.2)	12.4
Polio3	0.684	0.087 (0.075, 0.100)	0.007 (−0.003, 0.016)	91.9%	24.0 (20.4, 27.5)	9.5 (5.6, 13.4)	14.5
BCG	0.868	0.058 (0.049, 0.068)	0.012 (0.002, 0.022)	79.3%	23.1 (20.7, 25.4)	14.3 (11.9, 16.6)	8.8
DTP1	0.844	0.063 (0.053, 0.072)	0.010 (−0.001, 0.020)	84.1%	22.8 (20.0, 25.5)	12.9 (9.9, 15.8)	9.9
DTP2	0.789	0.078 (0.066, 0.088)	0.012 (0.003, 0.022)	84.6%	25.0 (22.0, 28.1)	13.3 (9.9, 16.8)	11.7
DTP3	0.716	0.098 (0.086, 0.111)	0.014 (0.005, 0.024)	85.7%	27.1 (23.7, 30.4)	14.2 (10.4, 18.0)	12.9
FULL	0.559	0.125 (0.109, 0.140)	0.014 (0.004, 0.024)	88.8%	28.8 (25.1, 32.6)	13.8 (9.5, 18.2)	15.0

The countries with the most significant difference in concentration index between the two approaches were Chad (0.31), Gabon (0.26), Afghanistan (0.25), Angola (0.25), Ethiopia (0.24), Nigeria (0.22), Papua New Guinea (0.21), Yemen (0.20), Guinea (0.19), and Madagascar (0.18). These countries also have among the lowest full immunization coverage of countries with eligible DHS surveys, ranging from 16% to 50%, and the highest multivariate concentration indices, ranging from 0.205 to 0.331 (see Table 2). When considering wealth-based concentration indices, most of these countries either indicate very slight inequity, or none at all. However, comparing the two types of concentration indices illustrates that, among this group of countries, the traditional wealth-based concentration index misses between 67% and 107% of the coverage inequity for full immunization for age.

Furthermore, nine of these ten countries had the largest AEG values in the data set, ranging from a 33 to 59 percentage point gap in coverage between the most and least advantaged quintiles. The differences between the multivariate and wealth-based AEGs range from 3 to 36 percentage points, highlighting the importance of including multiple criteria when assessing disadvantage and equity.

Table 2. Inequities in fully immunized status, by country.

Country	Year	Coverage	Multivariate Concentration Index	Wealth-Based Concentration Index	Difference in Equity Levels (Concentration Indices)	Captured Inequity Difference (Percent)	Coverage Gap Multivariate (Percentage Points)	Coverage Gap Wealth (Percentage Points)	Additional Coverage Gap (Percentage Points)
Afghanistan	2015	41.0%	0.24 (0.23, 0.25)	−0.01 (−0.01, 0)	0.25	102.50%	54 (52, 55)	18 (16, 20)	35.7
Angola	2015	30.5%	0.32 (0.31, 0.34)	0.07 (0.07, 0.08)	0.25	77.1%	45 (42, 47)	42 (38, 46)	3.2
Armenia	2015	74.1%	0.06 (0.02, 0.10)	−0.09 (−0.13, −0.05)	0.15	244.0%	21 (14, 29)	−13 (−21.2, 4.8)	34.0
Bangladesh	2016	74.7%	0.04 (0.03, 0.05)	−0.01 (−0.02, 0)	0.05	125.6%	14 (10, 17)	10 (6, 13)	4.0
Benin	2017	60.7%	0.13 (0.11, 0.14)	0.08 (0.08, 0.09)	0.04	34.4%	38 (35, 41)	28 (25, 31)	10.2
Burkina Faso	2010	69.9%	0.08 (0.07, 0.09)	−0.02 (−0.03, −0.01)	0.09	119.0%	27 (23, 30)	16 (12, 20)	11.0
Burundi	2016	76.0%	0.05 (0.04, 0.05)	0 (−0.01, 0.01)	0.05	104.4%	17 (15, 20)	−2 (−5, 2)	19.0
Cambodia	2014	78.4%	0.07 (0.06, 0.09)	0.03 (0.01, 0.05)	0.04	58.1%	30 (27, 34)	17 (13, 20)	13.8
Cameroon	2012	47.7%	0.17 (0.15, 0.19)	0.05 (0.04, 0.06)	0.12	69.6%	37 (33, 41)	33 (29, 38)	4.0
Chad	2014	23.1%	0.33 (0.31, 0.34)	0.02 (0.02, 0.02)	0.31	93.9%	37 (34, 39)	13 (11, 16)	23.2
Comoros	2012	48.4%	0.18 (0.16, 0.20)	0.09 (0.08, 0.10)	0.08	47.0%	39 (34, 44)	25 (20, 31)	14.0
Congo (DRC)	2013	38.2%	0.20 (0.19, 0.22)	0.05 (0.05, −0.05)	0.15	77.0%	35 (32, 38)	26 (22, 29)	9.0
Cote d'Ivoire	2012	44.5%	0.19 (0.17, 0.21)	0.06 (0.05, 0.07)	0.13	70.2%	42 (37, 46)	30 (24, 35)	12.0
Dominican Republic	2013	60.4%	0.07 (0.06, 0.07)	0.01 (0, 0.02)	0.05	81.5%	19 (13, 25)	11 (4, 18)	8.0
Egypt	2013	49.0%	0.04 (0.03, 0.05)	−0.04 (−0.05, −0.04)	0.09	202.4%	10 (8, 13)	8 (6, 11)	2.1
Ethiopia	2016	38.2%	0.28 (0.25, 0.31)	0.04 (0.03, 0.06)	0.24	84.2%	59 (56, 63)	38 (34, 41)	21.9
Gabon	2012	15.9%	0.24 (0.19, 0.29)	−0.02 (−0.03, 0)	0.26	107.5%	21 (17, 24)	−1 (−6, 3)	22.0
Ghana	2014	73.9%	0.06 (0.04, 0.07)	0.02 (0.02, 0.03)	0.03	60.0%	18 (13, 23)	8 (3, 13)	9.8
Guatemala	2014	71.4%	0.04 (0.04, 0.04)	−0.07 (−0.07, −0.06)	0.10	275.7%	12 (10, 15)	6 (4, 9)	5.8

Table 2. *Cont.*

Country	Year	Coverage	Multivariate Concentration Index	Wealth-Based Concentration Index	Difference in Equity Levels (Concentration Indices)	Captured Inequity Difference (Percent)	Coverage Gap Multivariate (Percentage Points)	Coverage Gap Wealth (Percentage Points)	Additional Coverage Gap (Percentage Points)
Guinea	2018	33.2%	0.21 (0.19, 0.23)	0.02 (0.01, 0.03)	0.19	91.9%	33 (29, 38)	22 (18, 27)	11.0
Haiti	2016	33.6%	0.22 (0.2, 0.24)	0.04 (0.03, 0.05)	0.18	81.7%	33 (28, 37)	29 (24, 35)	3.7
Honduras	2011	83.1%	0.02 (0.01, 0.03)	−0.05 (−0.06, −0.04)	0.07	323.8%	9 (7, 11)	1 (−2, 3)	8.2
India	2020	48.0%	0.09 (0.08, 0.09)	0.02 (0.02, 0.02)	0.06	75.3%	22 (21, 23)	5 (4, 6)	16.8
Indonesia	2017	60.5%	0.11 (0.1, 0.12)	0.01 (0, 0.02)	0.10	89.6%	35 (32, 38)	14 (11, 17)	21.5
Jordan	2017	60.4%	0.05 (0.04, 0.06)	−0.05 (−0.07, −0.03)	0.09	202.2%	18 (14, 21)	−5 (−11, 1)	22.3
Kenya	2014	67.4%	0.07 (0.07, 0.07)	−0.03 (−0.03, −0.02)	0.10	135.2%	29 (27, 31)	13 (11, 16)	15.2
Kyrgyz Republic	2012	67.1%	0.09 (0.07, 0.11)	0.04 (0.03, 0.05)	0.05	60.0%	27 (22, 31)	−20 (−25, −15)	46.4
Lesotho	2014	70.9%	0.06 (0.06, 0.07)	0.04 (0.03, 0.04)	0.03	40.3%	22 (14, 29)	16 (9, 24)	5.5
Liberia	2019	53.3%	0.1 (0.08, 0.11)	0.03 (0.02, 0.03)	0.07	74.2%	27 (21, 32)	15 (8, 21)	12.2
Madagascar	2021	50.1%	0.21 (0.19, 0.22)	0.03 (0.02, 0.03)	0.18	87.8%	47 (44, 50)	31 (27, 34)	16.3
Malawi	2015	74.5%	0.04 (0.03, 0.04)	0.02 (0.01, 0.02)	0.02	56.4%	15 (12, 17)	7 (5, 10)	7.5
Maldives	2016	64.4%	0.04 (0.01, 0.07)	−0.09 (−0.12, −0.06)	0.13	317.5%	11 (4, 18)	5 (−6, 16)	5.6
Mali	2018	46.6%	0.11 (0.09, 0.13)	0.05 (0.04, 0.06)	0.06	57.7%	29 (25, 33)	20 (15, 24)	9.5
Mozambique	2011	55.6%	0.15 (0.14, 0.17)	0.1 (0.09, 0.11)	0.05	32.5%	38 (35, 41)	22 (19, 25)	16.3
Myanmar	2015	51.0%	0.15 (0.14, 0.17)	0.05 (0.04, 0.06)	0.11	68.2%	40 (35, 44)	26 (21, 30)	13.8
Namibia	2013	64.6%	0.07 (0.04, 0.09)	0 (−0.02, 0.01)	0.07	106.2%	19 (12, 26)	−10 (−18, −2)	28.9
Nepal	2016	67.7%	0.07 (0.05, 0.09)	−0.02 (−0.04, −0.01)	0.09	134.3%	25 (20, 30)	3 (−3, 9)	21.9
Niger	2012	48.0%	0.15 (0.13, 0.17)	0.06 (0.05, 0.07)	0.09	62.3%	37 (34, 41)	35 (31, 39)	2.4
Nigeria	2018	33.9%	0.33 (0.32, 0.34)	0.11 (0.11, 0.11)	0.22	67.1%	54 (52, 56)	39 (37, 42)	14.9

Table 2. *Cont.*

Country	Year	Coverage	Multivariate Concentration Index	Wealth-Based Concentration Index	Difference in Equity Levels (Concentration Indices)	Captured Inequity Difference (Percent)	Coverage Gap Multivariate (Percentage Points)	Coverage Gap Wealth (Percentage Points)	Additional Coverage Gap (Percentage Points)
Pakistan	2016	65.1%	0.15 (0.15, 0.16)	0.03 (0.02, 0.04)	0.12	80.9%	50 (47, 53)	35 (32, 39)	15.0
Papua New Guinea	2016	27.1%	0.26 (0.23, 0.28)	0.05 (0.04, 0.06)	0.21	81.6%	35 (31, 38)	28 (24, 31)	6.8
Peru	2012	63.2%	0.08 (0.07, 0.09)	0.02 (0.01, 0.03)	0.06	76.0%	27 (24, 30)	7 (3, 10)	20.5
Philippines	2017	58.9%	0.11 (0.09, 0.12)	−0.02 (−0.03, −0.01)	0.12	115.2%	37 (33, 41)	9 (4, 13)	28.2
Republic of Congo	2011	39.5%	0.20 (0.18, 0.22)	0.10 (0.09, −0.11)	0.10	50.0%	43 (39, 47)	16 (10, 22)	27.0
Rwanda	2019	92.1%	0.01 (0, 0.02)	0 (−0.01, 0.01)	0.01	80.0%	3 (1, 6)	2 (0, 5)	1.1
Senegal	2019	75.2%	0.06 (0.04, 0.08)	−0.06 (−0.08, −0.04)	0.12	200.0%	24 (19, 28)	17 (12, 22)	7.2
Sierra Leone	2019	63.3%	0.07 (0.05, 0.08)	0.01 (0, 0.01)	0.06	90.8%	20 (16, 24)	−1 (−5, 4)	20.3
South Africa	2016	48.0%	0.09 (0.06, 0.13)	0 (−0.01, 0.01)	0.10	103.2%	18 (11, 25)	−4 (−12, 4)	21.9
Tajikistan	2017	70.5%	0.07 (0.07, 0.07)	−0.05 (−0.05, −0.05)	0.12	173.2%	26 (22, 31)	−4 (−9, 1)	30.2
The Gambia	2020	48.0%	0.09 (0.08, 0.09)	0.02 (0.02, 0.02)	0.06	75.3%	22 (21, 23)	5 (4, 6)	16.8
Timor-Leste	2016	46.6%	0.16 (0.14, 0.17)	0.02 (0.01, 0.03)	0.14	86.0%	36 (32, 41)	19 (14, 24)	17.1
Togo	2013	61.7%	0.09 (0.07, 0.12)	0 (−0.01, 0.01)	0.09	103.3%	26 (21, 31)	5 (0, 10)	21.4
Uganda	2016	50.9%	0.09 (0.08, 0.11)	−0.04 (−0.06, −0.03)	0.14	147.8%	21 (18, 24)	−3 (−6, 1)	23.3
Yemen	2013	37.6%	0.24 (0.23, 0.25)	0.04 (0.03, 0.05)	0.20	83.3%	43 (41, 45)	39 (37, 41)	4.2
Zambia	2018	65.4%	0.06 (0.05, 0.07)	0.02 (0.02, 0.03)	0.03	58.6%	20 (16, 23)	8 (4, 12)	11.8
Zimbabwe	2015	68.0%	0.07 (0.05, 0.09)	0.02 (0.01, 0.03)	0.05	73.1%	22 (17, 27)	13 (8, 18)	9.0
Overall [a]			0.13 (0.12, 0.15)	0.01 (0.00, 0.02)	0.12	92.0%	0.30 (0.27, 0.34)	0.14 (0.10, 0.18)	16.4

Note: [a] 95% confidence intervals are presented in parentheses for estimated values. The overall averages in the last column are crude averages and not weighted by population size.

Countries presenting modest differences between concentration indices and equity gaps were typically also among those with the highest levels of coverage for the fully immunized for age status (ranging from 55.6% and 92.1%). While high coverage is likely to be correlated with higher levels of equity utilizing either wealth-based or multivariate approaches—due to fewer individuals missing out on vaccines—it is not always true that a higher performing country will have a higher degree of equity. For instance, Pakistan achieved a full immunization for age coverage level of 65.1% in 2016, yet its multivariate concentration index indicates significant inequity: 0.152, which is 0.123 points higher than its corresponding wealth-based concentration index. Additionally, low coverage does not always lead to inequity, depending on how that coverage is distributed with respect to the assessed characteristics. For example, Uganda achieved a full immunization coverage level of 50.9% in 2016, and yet presented significantly lower multivariate and wealth-based concentration indices, estimated respectively at 0.092 and −0.044, compared with Pakistan. This indicates that while there is a large proportion of children who did not receive the full course of immunization as per Uganda's immunization schedule, these children are more randomly distributed throughout the population in terms of both geographic and socio-demographic parameters (sex, wealth, education, insurance status) than in Pakistan.

Examining the absolute equity gaps using the multivariate metric, full immunization coverage among the bottom quintile of the population would need to increase by approximately 28.8 percentage points (95% confidence interval: 25.1, 32.6) to achieve a similar level of the fully immunized for age status as the most advantage quintile of the population (see Table 1). When utilizing only the wealth-based approach, the AEG for the fully immunized for age status was estimated as only a 13.8 percentage point gap (95% confidence interval: 9.5–18.2). This indicates that wealth-based measures significantly underestimate the fully immunized coverage gap between the most and least advantaged by 15.0 percentage points, on average, across all datasets (see Table 1).

3.2. *Individual Vaccines (BCG, DTP, Polio, and MCV)*

Focusing on BCG, the eight countries reporting the greatest difference between the multivariate and wealth-based concentration indices are the Maldives (0.178), Afghanistan (0.172), Chad (0.170), Senegal (0.133), Yemen (0.121), Guatemala (0.110), and Madagascar (0.117). However, absolute differences in the AEG vary widely from 1 to 42 percentage points. In contrast, countries with the lowest differences between multivariate and wealth-based concentration indices also had the lowest absolute differences between AEGs. For 44 of the 56 countries in this analysis, the multivariate concentration index is statistically significantly greater than that of wealth-only. For the remaining 12 countries, which include the Kyrgyz Republic, Republic of Congo, Mozambique, Comoros, Benin, India, The Gambia, Sierra Leone, Lesotho, Peru, Malawi, and Ghana, there is no statistical difference between multivariate and wealth-based concentration indices. When looking at total country averages for individual vaccines, BCG has the lowest difference between multivariate and wealth-based estimates with a concentration index difference of 0.046 and an AEG difference of 8.8 percentage points, suggesting that wealth accounts for a significant proportion of the total inequity in this birth-dose vaccine (see Table 1).

If we consider MCV1, the greatest differences in concentration index values are attributed to Guinea (0.230), Afghanistan (0.215), Madagascar (0.166), Angola (0.152), Nigeria (0.145), Ethiopia (0.145), and the Maldives (0.144). Again, we observe a wide range in the differences in AEG values between approaches, ranging from 4 to 39 percentage points. By evaluating inequity with a multivariate approach, it is revealed that the use of a wealth-only ranking metric results in a significant underestimation of inequity for 51 of the 56 countries considered. Countries for which the multivariate concentration index is not statistically different from the wealth-only concentration index include the Kyrgyz Republic, Mozambique, Republic of Congo, Comoros, and Lesotho. Using national averages, the difference between concentration indices as measured by each approach for MCV1 was 0.068 with an AEG difference between approaches of 10.1 percentage points.

For the three-dose vaccines DTP and Polio, the absolute difference between concentration indices generally increases for subsequent doses, though the same trend does not apply to differences in the AEG, suggesting that much of the inequity present after receiving the first dose occurs in the middle of the distribution rather than the tails of the distribution. The greatest difference in DTP concentration index values when comparing the multivariate and wealth-only methodologies are exhibited by Chad (DTP1: 0.192, DTP2: 0.216, and DTP3: 0.268) and Afghanistan (0.186, 0.204, and 0.224). Of all the vaccines included in this study, DTP3 has the highest national average absolute difference between concentration index types at 0.084 and experiences an AEG difference between approaches of 12.9 percentage points, on average. The concentration index differences for DTP1 and DTP2 are 0.053 and 0.066, respectively, with AEG differences between approaches of 9.9 and 11.7, respectively.

The greatest differences between multivariate and wealth-based concentration indices for Polio occur in the Maldives (0.160), Afghanistan (0.130), and Senegal (0.130) for dose 1; Gabon (0.150), Afghanistan (0.142), and Madagascar (0.135) for dose 2; and Angola (0.184), Chad (0.179), and Guinea (0.177) for dose 3. The average differences in concentration index over all countries for Polio doses 1, 2, and 3 are 0.046, 0.059, and 0.080, respectively, with differences in AEG between approaches estimated to be 10.5, 12.4, and 14.5, respectively.

4. Discussion

This case-study application of the VERSE toolkit to 56 countries demonstrates that using multivariate procedures for measuring vaccine coverage equity results in significantly larger values compared with traditional methods in most settings. The findings indicate that metrics which only utilize socioeconomic status as a basis for measuring inequity, in order to track whether or not access is pro-poor, will miss a significant amount of the variation in the overall equity in vaccination status that is directly correlated with observable characteristics such as education, sex, and geographic location [23,24].

In countries such as Chad, Afghanistan, or Guinea, if inequities in fully immunized status were only captured through the traditional wealth-based concentration indices or absolute equity gaps, the measures would show that there was no systematic inequity in vaccine coverage within the country (concentration indices between −0.006 and 0.020); however, the multivariate concentration index demonstrates otherwise.

Several recent studies on equity also support the empirical findings of this study. A 2022 systematic review by Ali et al. found that besides wealth, maternal education, sex, and geographic access can also systematically and independently affect vaccination coverage [25]. Additionally, a 2020 study by Acharya et al. comparing the inequalities in full vaccination coverage based on maternal education and wealth quintiles also found that in four of the six studied countries, the absolute inequalities arising from a metric using maternal education level were significantly larger than those measured using wealth quintile [26]. These studies further emphasize the importance of utilizing multivariate metrics to holistically measure and work toward reducing systemic inequality.

Multivariate indicators integrating these multiple socio-demographic parameters effectively quantify differences in coverage even in countries with more modest inequity, such as Uganda. Uganda achieved large increases in overall vaccination coverage during the 2000s with its immunization program through the implementation of Family Health Days and other regular health outreach initiatives, which made the coverage distribution significantly pro-poor. However, when considering the other factors included in the VERSE toolkit's approach, we can estimate a residual inequity driven by both supply- and demand-side factors such as the district of residence and maternal education [27]. Such an approach revealed aspects of access to vaccines, such as sufficient health literacy and adequate and timely supply across districts, which can help the country consider new approaches to continue to improve coverage equity [28,29].

While the VERSE approach and toolkit can yield a stable metric to track equity over time or between settings, it is also subject to several practical limitations common to all measures of equity and inequality [15]. The first is the inability to objectively state what a "good" or "bad" level of inequity is using the concentration index alone. Like all concentration indices, the results of the VERSE methods lend themselves more toward assessing relative performance than to categorizing objective performance. Although values closer to 0 are objectively preferred, whether a value of 0.1 is bad or good depends upon the circumstances of a specific setting, the mean level of coverage obtained in the setting overall, and the specific benchmarks associated with the rollout and distribution of each vaccine. For this reason, all equity metrics should be put into the context of the outcome or intervention they are evaluating. To assist with this contextualization, the VERSE toolkit produces an absolute equity gap alongside the concentration index to assist with interpretation. While the AEG is a measure of absolute inequity, and the concentration index measures relative inequity, they are both based on the same ranking procedure. They can therefore complement one another, with the AEG providing important coverage-level context to the concentration index.

Another limitation is the data used to populate the tool. While DHS surveys are designed to be nationally representative, evidence shows that settings like urban slums, conflict areas, and refugee settlements are significantly under-sampled, in addition to being more likely to be under-immunized [30]. As a result, estimates of vaccination coverage generated using the DHS are likely to be systematic overestimates of true immunization coverage, and estimates of coverage inequity are likely to be systematic underestimates of true coverage inequities.

5. Conclusions

Most measures of equity employed in healthcare equity analyses only examine inequities in outcomes across one dimension which is often decomposed into multiple dimensions. This approach results in the systematic underestimation of aggregate inequity in health outcomes and makes it impossible to measure aggregate inequity across multiple dimensions (e.g., sex, district, and socioeconomic status) in a manner that is comparable across time and place. The VERSE toolkit generates measures of multivariate inequity in vaccination coverage that allow for standardized measurement over time and between locations. Comparing the multivariate concentration indices and absolute equity gaps with traditional wealth-based measures of inequity demonstrates that wealth-based measures systematically underestimate the gap between the most and least advantaged in specific vaccination coverage, as well as fully-immunized coverage. Furthermore, these differences are directly attributable to differences in maternal education, geography, and sex. Not accounting for these multiple dimensions when measuring equity results in a missed vaccination coverage gap between the most and least advantaged of between 1.1–46.4 percentage points, depending on the country. As a result, closing the coverage gap between the bottom and top wealth quintiles is unlikely to eliminate the persistent socio-demographic inequities in both vaccination coverage and access to vaccines linked with other routinely measured covariates. The results suggest that pro-poor interventions, as well as campaigns and programs utilizing needs-based targeting which reflects poverty, should expand their targeting criteria to include other dimensions in order to reduce systemic inequalities, holistically. Additionally, a multivariate metric should be considered when setting targets and measuring progress toward reducing inequities over time and comparing inequity across settings.

Author Contributions: B.N.P. devised the project and analysis plan, interpreted the results, and reviewed the manuscript; S.S. ran analyses and wrote the manuscript; D.O. ran analyses and wrote the manuscript; J.M. ran analyses and wrote the manuscript; G.d.B. ran analyses, wrote the manuscript, and contributed to the interpretation of results. All authors have read and agreed to the published version of the manuscript.

Funding: This research was funded by the Bill and Melinda Gates Foundation under the Vaccine Economics Research for Sustainability and Equity grant (INV-003813). The funding agency had no influence over the analysis or decision to submit this manuscript for publication.

Institutional Review Board Statement: Not Applicable.

Informed Consent Statement: Not Applicable.

Data Availability Statement: The data used in this study are publicly available through the Demographic and Health Survey website.

Conflicts of Interest: The authors have no conflicts of interests to disclose.

Appendix A List of Countries and the Year of the Most Recent DHS

Country	Year
Afghanistan	2015
Angola	2015
Armenia	2015
Bangladesh	2016
Benin	2017
Burkina Faso	2010
Burundi	2016
Cambodia	2014
Cameroon	2012
Chad	2014
Comoros	2012
Republic of Congo	2011
Congo (DRC)	2013
Cote d'Ivoire	2012
Dominican Republic	2013
Egypt	2013
Ethiopia	2016
Gabon	2012
The Gambia	2020
Ghana	2014
Guatemala	2014
Guinea	2018
Haiti	2016
Honduras	2011
India	2020
Indonesia	2017
Jordan	2017
Kenya	2014
Kyrgyz Republic	2012
Lesotho	2014

Country	Year
Liberia	2019
Madagascar	2021
Malawi	2015
Maldives	2016
Mali	2018
Mozambique	2011
Myanmar	2015
Namibia	2013
Nepal	2016
Niger	2012
Nigeria	2018
Pakistan	2016
Papua New Guinea	2016
Peru	2012
Philippines	2017
Rwanda	2019
Senegal	2019
Sierra Leone	2019
South Africa	2016
Tajikistan	2017
Timor-Leste	2016
Togo	2013
Uganda	2016
Yemen	2013
Zambia	2018
Zimbabwe	2015

Appendix B List of DHS Variables Used in Multivariate Ranking

Variable Name	Code
Region	v101
Urban/Rural Status	v025
Maternal Education	v106
Wealth Quintile	v190
Sex of Child	b4
Health Insurance Coverage	v481

References

1. Olayinka, F.; Sauer, M.; Menning, L.; Summers, D.; Wonodi, C.; Mackay, S.; MacDonald, N.E.; Figueroa, J.P.; Andriamitantsoa, B.; Bonsu, G.; et al. Building and sustaining public and political commitment to the value of vaccination: Recommen-dations for the Immunization Agenda 2030 (Strategic Priority Area 2). *Vaccine* **2022**. [CrossRef] [PubMed]
2. Hosseinpoor, A.R.; Nambiar, D.; Schlotheuber, A.; Reidpath, D.; Ross, Z. Health Equity Assessment Toolkit (HEAT): Software for exploring and comparing health inequalities in countries. *BMC Med. Res. Methodol.* **2016**, *16*, 141. [CrossRef] [PubMed]

3. Patenaude, B.; Odihi, D.; Sriudomporn, S.; Mak, J.; Watts, E.; de Broucker, G. A standardized approach for measuring multivariate equity in vaccination coverage, cost-of-illness, and health outcomes: Evidence from the Vaccine Economics Research for Sustainability & Equity (VERSE) project. *Soc. Sci. Med.* **2022**, *302*, 114979. [CrossRef] [PubMed]
4. Arsenault, C.; Harper, S.; Nandi, A.; Rodríguez, J.M.; Hansen, P.M.; Johri, M. An equity dashboard to monitor vaccination coverage. *Bull. World Health Organ.* **2017**, *95*, 128–134. [CrossRef] [PubMed]
5. United Nations General Assembly. Transforming Our World: The 2030 Agenda for Sustainable Development. 25 September 2015. Available online: https://www.un.org/ga/search/view_doc.asp?symbol=A/RES/70/1&Lang=E (accessed on 12 October 2021).
6. Hosseinpoor, A.R.; Schlotheuber, A.; Nambiar, D.; Ross, Z. Health Equity Assessment Toolkit Plus (HEAT Plus): Software for exploring and comparing health inequalities using uploaded datasets. *Glob Health Action* **2018**, *11*, 1440783. [CrossRef] [PubMed]
7. European Commission. EU Multidimensional Inequality Monitoring Framework. European Commission—Joint Research Centre. 2021. Available online: https://composite-indicators.jrc.ec.europa.eu/multidimensional-inequality (accessed on 12 October 2021).
8. Glassman, B. *Multidimensional Inequality: Measurement and Analysis Using the American Community Survey*; U.S. Census Bureau: Suitland, MA, USA, 2019.
9. Vizard, P.; Speed, L. Examining Multidimensional Inequality and Deprivation in Britain Using the Capability Approach. *Forum Soc. Econ.* **2016**, *45*, 139–169. [CrossRef]
10. McKnight, A. *Multidimensional Inequality Framework*; London School of Economics: London, UK, 2018.
11. Millar, M.R.; Gourtsoyannis, Y.; Jayakumar, A. Ethics of vaccination: Should capability measures be used to inform SARS-CoV-2 vaccination strategies? *Br. J. Clin. Pharmacol.* **2022**, *88*, 47–55. [CrossRef]
12. Papageorge, M.V.; Evans, D.B.; Tseng, J.F. Health Care Disparities and the Future of Pancreatic Cancer Care. *Surg. Oncol. Clin. N. Am.* **2021**, *30*, 759–771. [CrossRef]
13. Portnoy, A.; Clark, S.; Ozawa, S.; Jit, M. The impact of vaccination on gender equity: Conceptual framework and human papillomavirus (HPV) vaccine case study. *Int. J. Equity Health* **2020**, *19*, 10. [CrossRef]
14. Bosch-Capblanch, X.; Zuske, M.-K.; Auer, C. Research on subgroups is not research on equity attributes: Evi-dence from an overview of systematic reviews on vaccination. *Int. J. Equity Health* **2017**, *16*, 95. [CrossRef]
15. Alonge, O.; Peters, D.H. Utility and limitations of measures of health inequities: A theoretical perspective. *Glob Health Action* **2015**, *8*, 27591. [CrossRef] [PubMed]
16. Barbosa, E.C.; Cookson, R. Multiple inequity in health care: An example from Brazil. *Soc. Sci. Med.* **2019**, *228*, 1–8. [CrossRef] [PubMed]
17. Fleurbaey, M.; Schokkaert, E. Unfair inequalities in health and health care. *J. Health Econ.* **2009**, *28*, 73–90. [CrossRef] [PubMed]
18. Fleurbaey, M.; Schokkaert, E. Chapter Sixteen—Equity in Health and Health Care11This chapter was written when Marc Fleurbaey was research associate at CORE. We thank Chiara Canta, Tom McGuire, Tom van Ourti and Fred Schrogen for their useful comments. In *Handbook of Health Economics*; Pauly, M.V., McGuire, T.G., Barros, P.P., Eds.; Elsevier: Amsterdam, The Netherlands, 2011; Volume 2, pp. 1003–1092.
19. O'Donnell, O.; van Doorslaer, E.; Wagstaff, A.; Lindelow, M. *Analyzing Health Equity Using Household Survey Data: A Guide to Techniques and Their Implementation*; World Bank Group: Washington, DC, USA, 2008.
20. Wagstaff, A. The concentration index of a binary outcome revisited. *Health Econ.* **2011**, *20*, 1155–1160. [CrossRef] [PubMed]
21. Williams, A.H.; Cookson, R.A. Equity-efficiency trade-offs in health technology assessment. *Int. J. Technol. Assess Health Care* **2006**, *22*, 1–9. [CrossRef] [PubMed]
22. Demographic and Health Surveys. The DHS Program—Quality Information To Plan, Monitor And Improve Population, Health, And Nutrition Programs. 2021. Available online: https://dhsprogram.com/ (accessed on 12 October 2021).
23. Patenaude, B.; Rao, K.; Peters, D. An Empirical Examination of the Inequality of Forgone Care in India. *Health Syst. Reform* **2021**, *7*, e1894761. [CrossRef]
24. Wahl, B.; Gupta, M.; Erchick, D.J.; Patenaude, B.N.; Holroyd, T.A.; Sauer, M.; Blunt, M.; Santosham, M.; Limaye, R.J. Change in full immunization inequalities in Indian children 12-23 months: An analysis of household survey data. *BMC Public Health* **2021**, *21*, 841. [CrossRef]
25. Ali, H.A.; Hartner, A.-M.; Echeverria-Londono, S.; Roth, J.; Li, X.; Abbas, K.; Portnoy, A.; Vynnycky, E.; Woodruff, K.; Ferguson, N.M.; et al. Vaccine equity in low and middle income countries: A systematic review and meta-analysis. *Int. J. Equity Health* **2022**, *21*, 82. [CrossRef]
26. Acharya, K.; Dharel, D.; Subedi, R.K.; Bhattarai, A.; Paudel, Y.R. Inequalities in full vaccination coverage based on maternal education and wealth quintiles among children aged 12–23 months: Further analysis of national cross-sectional surveys of six South Asian countries. *BMJ Open* **2022**, *12*, e046971. [CrossRef]
27. Ssebagereka, A.; De Broucker, G.; Ekirapa-Kiracho, E.; Kananura, R.M.; Driwale, A.; Mak, J.; Mutebi, A.; Patenaude, B. Equity in vaccine coverage in Uganda from 2000 to 2016: Revealing the Multifaceted Nature of Inequity. *Research Square* **2022**. [CrossRef]
28. World Bank. *Uganda Secures $180 Million to Accelerate Affordable and Equitable Access to Vaccines*; World Bank: Washington, DC, USA, 2021.

29. Babirye, J.N.; Engebretsen, I.M.S.; Rutebemberwa, E.; Kiguli, J.; Nuwaha, F. Urban settings do not ensure access to services: Findings from the immunisation programme in Kampala Uganda. *BMC Health Serv. Res.* **2014**, *14*, 111. [CrossRef] [PubMed]
30. Crocker-Buque, T.; Mindra, G.; Duncan, R.; Mounier-Jack, S. Immunization, urbanization and slums—A systematic review of factors and interventions. *BMC Public Health* **2017**, *17*, 556. [CrossRef] [PubMed]

vaccines

MDPI

Article

Mapping of Pro-Equity Interventions Proposed by Immunisation Programs in Gavi Health Systems Strengthening Grants

Joelle Ducharme [1,*], Gustavo Caetano Correa [1], Heidi W. Reynolds [1], Alyssa B. Sharkey [2], Virginia A. Fonner [3] and Mira Johri [4,5]

1 Measurement, Evaluation and Learning Department, Gavi, The Vaccine Alliance, 1218 Le Grand-Saconnex, Switzerland
2 School of Public and International Affairs, Princeton University, Princeton, NJ 08544, USA
3 Global Health Population and Nutrition, FHI 360, Durham, NC 27701, USA
4 Carrefour de l'Innovation, Centre de Recherche de l'Université de Montréal (CRCHUM), Montréal, QC H2X 0A9, Canada
5 Département de Gestion, D'évaluation, et de Politique de Santé, École de Santé Publique de l'Université de Montréal (ESPUM), Montréal, QC H3N 1X9, Canada
* Correspondence: jducharme@gavi.org

Abstract: Reaching zero-dose (ZD) children, operationally defined as children who have not received a first dose of the diphtheria, tetanus, and pertussis (DTP1) vaccine, is crucial to increase equitable immunisation coverage and access to primary health care. However, little is known about the approaches already taken by countries to improve immunisation equity. We reviewed all Health System Strengthening (HSS) proposals submitted by Gavi-supported countries from 2014 to 2021 inclusively and extracted information on interventions favouring equity. Pro-equity interventions were mapped to an analytical framework representing Gavi 5.0 programmatic guidance on reaching ZD children and missed communities. Data from keyword searches and manual screening were extracted into an Excel database. Open format responses were analysed using inductive and deductive thematic coding. Data analysis was conducted using Excel and R. Of the 56 proposals included, 51 (91%) included at least one pro-equity intervention. The most common interventions were conducting outreach sessions, tailoring the location of service delivery, and partnerships. Many proposals had "bundles" of interventions, most often involving outreach, microplanning and community-level education activities. Nearly half prioritised remote-rural areas and only 30% addressed gender-related barriers to immunisation. The findings can help identify specific interventions on which to focus future evidence syntheses, case studies and implementation research and inform discussions on what may or may not need to change to better reach ZD children and missed communities moving forward.

Keywords: immunization; vaccines; zero-dose; equity; health systems

Citation: Ducharme, J.; Correa, G.C.; Reynolds, H.W.; Sharkey, A.B.; Fonner, V.A.; Johri, M. Mapping of Pro-Equity Interventions Proposed by Immunisation Programs in Gavi Health Systems Strengthening Grants. *Vaccines* **2023**, *11*, 341. https://doi.org/10.3390/vaccines11020341

Academic Editor: Pedro Plans-Rubió

Received: 23 December 2022
Revised: 17 January 2023
Accepted: 1 February 2023
Published: 2 February 2023

1. Introduction

While global immunisation coverage has improved monumentally since the 1980s, progress in increasing coverage for different antigens has slowed or stalled over the last several years and has even declined during the COVID-19 pandemic [1,2]. Of particular concern are children who have not received any routine vaccination, referred to as zero-dose (ZD) children. These children are defined operationally by the Immunization Agenda 2030 (IA2030) as those who have not received a first dose of the diphtheria, tetanus, and pertussis (DTP1) vaccine in their first year of life [3]. With the COVID-19 pandemic straining health systems and severely impacting routine immunisation services in many countries, the number of ZD children—estimated at 14 million in 2019—increased by 34% globally in

2021, when there were approximately 18.2 million ZD children [4]. Of these, 12.5 million (68%) lived in one of the 57 Gavi-supported countries[1] [4]. Gavi-supported countries are countries that are eligible to apply for Gavi support, determined by their national income. In 2020, countries with a Gross National Income (GNI) per capita equal to or less than US $1630 over the last three years were eligible for support [5]. It is thus now more critical than ever to reverse this trend and reach the remaining unimmunised children. Reaching ZD children and missed communities, which are operationally defined as being home to clusters of ZD and under-immunized children, is a central component of both IA2030 and Gavi, the Vaccine Alliance's strategic plan for 2021–2025 (Gavi 5.0), with a vision of "leaving no one behind with immunisation" [3,6]. Reaching these populations is expected to bring more children to full immunisation and increase access to primary health care [7,8]. This, in turn, is an important component towards achieving universal health coverage, especially in low- and middle-income countries (LMICs) [9].

Even though the concept of equity has been guiding global immunisation efforts and was already a key principle of the Gavi 4.0 strategy (2016–2020), the stalled progress in recent years and backsliding of routine immunisation during the pandemic have highlighted the inability of traditional interventions to maintain high coverage and reach the approximately 15% of children worldwide who remain unvaccinated with DTP1 [2]. Adding to the complexity is that ZD children are among the world's most vulnerable populations and are believed to face complex and overlapping deprivations, with several proximal, distal and greater contextual determinants (e.g., gender, conflict, and health systems factors) at play. Indeed, they often have a lower socioeconomic status, belong to religious or ethnic minorities, suffer from childhood malnutrition and are children of mothers with lower levels of education and empowerment, making them more socially and economically disadvantaged [9–13]. Along these lines, the Equity Reference Group for Immunisation (ERG) has emphasized and called for a greater focus on four key areas to reach ZD children, namely conflict-affected, urban poor, and remote rural areas as well as gender-related barriers. While those overlapping vulnerabilities make it particularly challenging to reach ZD children with vaccination, the potential benefits to children's' health and development, to their families and communities, and to societies, are immense.

While the concept of "zero-dose" children has existed for several years [14], it only recently came to the forefront of the attention of the global health community and there is still an important lack of knowledge about which interventions can be implemented to best reach them, how much they cost, and how to sustain progress. Understanding which interventions are already being implemented is one step towards building this evidence base. To the best of our knowledge, only one study has been published that explores this question. Dadari and colleagues mapped pro-equity strategies being implemented in thirteen Gavi-supported countries through review of Joint Appraisal (JA) reports from 2016 to 2019 [15]. JA reports are documents submitted to Gavi by countries every year detailing all Gavi-supported activities implemented, progress and performance. The authors found that all thirteen countries had in place over 250 interventions aiming to increase vaccine equity and concluded that further efforts should be made to do a similar mapping with other types of Gavi documents and across more countries to establish a more complete picture [15].

Building on this foundation, the current paper presents findings from a similar mapping in Gavi Health System Strengthening (HSS) proposals. These documents are particularly relevant because they are focused on achieving equitable immunisation coverage and have by far the largest envelope of all Gavi cash grants [16]. Indeed, as of December 2021, commitments for HSS support from 2000 to 2025 for all Gavi-supported countries amounted to US $3005.4 million. In comparison, the next biggest funding lines were operational support with an envelope of US $935.5 m and immunisation services support with US $355.9 m [17]. In HSS proposals for the Gavi 4.0 strategy period, countries had to articulate how funds would be used and detail clear strategies to improve immunisation access and equity, though not specifically for zero-dose children since this only became a focus in Gavi

5.0. Proposals submitted to Gavi are reviewed and approved by an Independent Review Committee (IRC) comprising experts in different fields including public health, epidemiology, and economics. We reviewed these HSS proposals to document and learn more about the pro-equity interventions used by countries to improve immunisation equity and to understand how these investments can help us prioritise interventions moving forward.

2. Materials and Methods

2.1. Data Sources

All HSS proposals submitted by Gavi-supported countries from 2014 to 2021 inclusively were reviewed. The overall number of Gavi-supported countries during this period varied from 73 in 2014 to 57 in 2021 [5]. These proposals were most likely to have been developed and/or implemented during the Gavi 4.0 strategy period (2016–2020). Older proposals were excluded because they were written well before Gavi 4.0 and thus would likely not be focused on increasing equity. Two countries submitted two different HSS proposals during this period. In these cases, we included only the oldest one since 2014 in the analysis as those were more likely to have followed Gavi 4.0 recommendations and to have been implemented during that period. The documents were available through the "country documents" web pages on the Gavi website [18]. The final mapping included 56 HSS proposals from 55 countries (with two separate proposals for Syria related to different regions).

2.2. Analytical Framework Development

To collect relevant and useful information from the mapping, we developed an analytical framework based on the Gavi programmatic guidance [19] and the UNICEF mapping of JA reports [15]. Table 1 provides a list of the variables used to summarise the pro-equity strategies planned by each country to reach ZD/under-immunised children. Adapting the definition used by Dadari and colleagues [15], we defined a pro-equity intervention as any tailored or targeted approach designed to reach underserved/vulnerable populations or communities with immunisation. All other interventions planned to be implemented throughout the country or not targeted at the priority groups or areas identified as being most vulnerable were not included. We created categories of interventions by thematic areas (grouping interventions that were similar and had the same purpose) to analyse which types of pro-equity interventions countries planned to implement. We validated the categories against those used by UNICEF and the Gavi programmatic guidance to ensure they were comprehensive and aligned. When a thematic area was identified that did not fit in any of the existing categories, it was brought to an internal working group to determine whether to create new categories. A complete list of intervention categories and their definitions can be found in Table A1.

Table 1. Variables included in the analytical framework and their corresponding response type.

Variables	Response Type
Country	Open text
HSS proposal submission year	Open text
Is there at least one pro-equity intervention in the proposal?	Yes or No response
Intervention category (ies)	Open text [list all]
Description of intervention (s)	Open text
Partners engaged	Open text
Target population	Open text
Geographic areas	Open text
Involvement of civil society organisations?	Yes or No response
Are demand-side barriers addressed?	Yes or No response
Interventions addressing demand-side barriers	Open text
Are supply-side barriers addressed?	Yes or No response
Are gender barriers addressed?	Yes or No response
Gender transformative interventions	Open text

Table 1. *Cont.*

Variables	Response Type
Gender responsive interventions	Open text
Are funding strategies addressed/selected?	Yes or No response
Funding strategy details	Open text
Are supplemental immunisation activities (SIAs), including periodic intensification of routine immunization (PIRIs), discussed to reach vulnerable populations?	Yes or No response
What are key barriers and enabling factors?	Open text
Is sustainability discussed?	Yes or No response
Have other health/non-health sectors been integrated?	Yes or No response

2.3. Searching and Data Extraction

The search strategy consisted of a manual screening of specific sections of the HSS proposals and keyword searches. Data on interventions planned to reach the target populations were usually found in the "Objectives of the proposal" and/or "Description of Activities" sections. Different keywords were used to answer specific questions, such as "sustainability" and "gender" to identify whether those topics were addressed, for example. Relevant information was extracted into an Excel database, in which each row represented a different proposal and each column a variable of the analytical framework (see Table 1 for the variables included). One researcher extracted these data from all HSS proposals during February and March 2022. To run the correlation analysis in R, we also created a separate database listing all the pro-equity intervention categories included in the proposals.

2.4. Data Analysis

The quantitative analysis consisted of descriptive statistics (counts, proportions, and frequencies) and was conducted on Microsoft Excel PivotTables, version 2206. Furthermore, we performed a correlation matrix using the R expand function to find the correlations of interventions in each country. This was conducted to find which interventions are often planned to be implemented together in the countries. Lastly, we performed inductive and deductive thematic coding based on information and observations noted throughout data extraction for open-ended variables. The coding was conducted by constructing a matrix in Excel.

3. Results

Overall, 51 of the 56 HSS proposals reviewed (91%) included at least one pro-equity intervention. When ranked by frequency (Figure 1), we found that the 15 most common pro-equity intervention categories included a mix of supply-oriented, demand-oriented and multifaceted strategies (see Table A1 for a complete list of categories and their respective definitions). We found the most common category was "outreach/tailor location of service delivery and partnerships", with 46/56 proposals reviewed (82%) planning to implement this. This category included any activities that sought to increase immunisation coverage by either conducting outreach services or tailoring the location of service delivery to reach underserved populations. It also included mobile vaccination efforts, building new infrastructure, and creating or leveraging partnerships (e.g., with non-governmental organisations, private sector) to expand vaccine access. The second most common category was the development of microplans at the health facility or district level and/or the implementation of other "Reach Every District" (RED) strategies [20]. Microplans and RED strategies were often implemented together, but if proposals planned just one of the two, it was still included in this category.

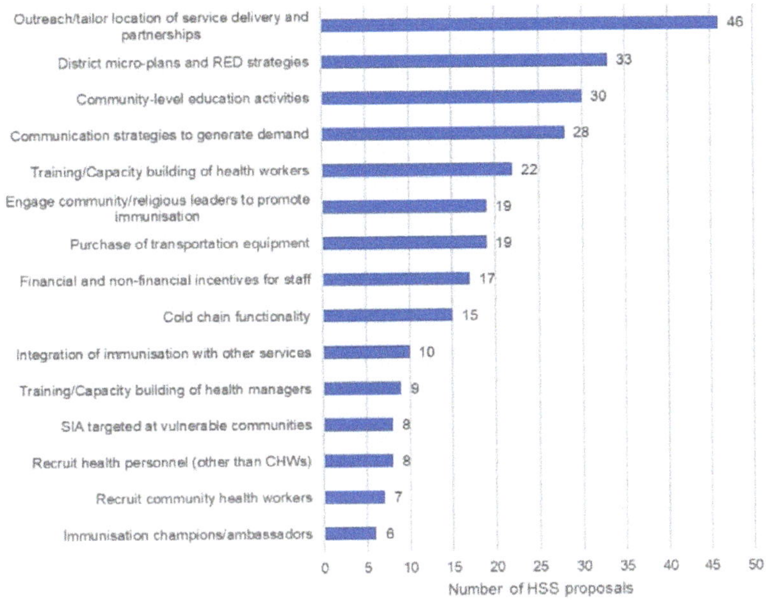

Figure 1. The 15 most common pro-equity intervention categories listed in the HSS proposals.

Three of the top six most common categories aimed to generate demand at community-level (community-level education activities, communication strategies to generate demand and engaging community and/or religious leaders to promote immunisation). On the supply-side, several countries invested in transportation (motorcycles, boats, etc.) and cold chain equipment for their most hard-to-reach districts.

Next, we looked at the proportion of HSS proposals addressing the close-ended variables of the analytical framework (Yes or No response type) as shown in Table 2. Of note, civil society organisations (CSOs) were often mentioned as key partners in implementing activities and reaching vulnerable populations. This was most often performed through implementing sensitisation and social mobilisation activities at community-level to generate demand.

Table 2. Number and proportion of HSS proposals (out of 56) which addressed the close-ended variables (Yes or No response type) of the analytical framework.

Close-Ended Variables	Number of Proposals with Answer "Yes"	Proportion of Proposals with Answer "Yes"
Is there at least 1 pro-equity intervention in the proposal?	51	91%
Involvement of civil society organisations?	47	84%
Are demand-side barriers addressed?	42	75%
Are supply-side barriers addressed?	51	91%
Are gender barriers addressed?	17	30%
Are funding strategies addressed/selected?	16	29%
Are SIAs, including PIRIs, discussed to reach vulnerable populations?	15	27%
Is sustainability discussed?	47	84%
Have other health/non-health sectors been integrated?	28	50%

Interventions addressing demand-side barriers included, for example, tailored immunisation sensitisation activities to different groups (women, religious, etc.) and conducting information, education, and communication (IEC) sessions in priority districts with communities, including educational chats, film showings, and outdoor theatres. Interventions addressing supply-side barriers, on the other hand, included conducting outreach and mobile sessions, investing in targeted infrastructure and procuring motorcycles, boats and other transportation equipment for health workers to access hard-to-reach areas.

Less than one third of the proposals (17/56) explicitly addressed gender-related barriers. Of those, sixteen included gender-responsive interventions and five proposed gender-transformative ones. Considering Gavi's gender policy, gender-responsive approaches "adopt a gender lens to consider individual needs of different gender identities without necessarily changing the larger contextual issues that lie at the root of the gender inequities and inequalities" [21]. For example, employing female health workers may facilitate enhanced immunisation service acceptance and uptake, but would not address the underlying cultural barrier that prevents female caregivers from seeking immunisation services from male health workers. Gender-transformative approaches, on the other hand, "attempt to re-define and change existing gender roles, norms, attitudes, and practices. These interventions tackle the root causes of gender inequity and inequality and reshape unequal power relations" [21]. For example, one country planned to have community health workers promote a gender approach with the involvement of fathers for the vaccination of children in households and another sought involvement of national and local leaders to promote, advocate immunisation and serve as 'role models' to help increase male participation.

Regarding geographic areas of focus, namely ERG settings, twenty-seven proposals selected remote-rural areas (including hard-to-reach areas) as a priority whereas only four prioritized urban poor areas (though twenty in total selected "urban") and four selected conflict-affected areas.

The correlation matrix of different interventions in each country showed that "outreach/tailor location of service delivery and partnerships" was very strongly correlated with other interventions. Indeed, this type of intervention was planned along with developing district microplans/RED strategies in 29 HSS proposals, with community-level education activities in 27 proposals and with communication strategies to generate demand in 25 proposals (Figure 2). Thus, this suggests that outreach sessions in countries were often planned along with microplanning and community engagement activities as a "bundle" of interventions. Figure 2 depicts the correlations between the eight most common categories and the complete correlation matrix can be found in Figure A1.

Interventions	Communication strategies to generate demand	Community-level education activities	District microplans and RED strategies	Engage leaders to promote immunisation	Financial and non-financial incentives for staff	Outreach/tailor location of service delivery and partnerships	Purchase of transportation equipment	Training/Capacity building of health workers
Communication strategies to generate demand								
Community-level education activities	17							
District microplans and RED strategies	18	20						
Engage leaders to promote immunisation	12	13	12					
Financial and non-financial incentives for staff	8	10	8	5				
Outreach/tailor location of delivery and partnerships	25	27	29	17	16			
Purchase of transportation equipment	9	12	11	6	9	19		
Training/Capacity building of health workers	14	14	14	11	7	20	7	

Figure 2. Correlation matrix representing the number of times the eight most common intervention categories were planned with each other in HSS proposals.

We additionally found that the theory, or rationale, behind the selection of specific pro-equity interventions in the HSS proposals was often not provided. When it was provided, it was generally for unique interventions that were not commonly used by countries, such as immunisation ambassadors programs and the tool "My Village My Home" implemented in a few countries, for example. Lastly, even though most countries included some pro-equity interventions, many activities listed in the HSS proposals overall were not targeted at the priority groups or areas identified as being most vulnerable but were instead planned to be implemented at the national level or in the other, non-priority areas. These were not included in the database, nor the analysis presented here.

4. Discussion

Our mapping confirmed that most countries have already been proposing pro-equity interventions using Gavi HSS funds for several years and is consistent with the results from UNICEF's mapping of JA reports [15]. It is the first time we are aware that such an analysis of pro-equity interventions in HSS proposals from all Gavi-supported countries was conducted. Importantly, we found that outreach and tailoring location of service delivery was very commonly presented in those proposals. This aligns with the observation that one of the main bottlenecks to getting children immunised reported in the proposals was the long distances to health facilities. This bottleneck is also well documented in the literature as a significant barrier to access to immunisation services [22]. Countries mostly addressed this bottleneck by conducting outreach and mobile sessions in hard-to-reach areas or areas with no health facility nearby. However, sustainability concerns and cost-effectiveness of conducting outreach and mobile sessions as compared to other long-term strategies were rarely discussed in the HSS proposals. One explanation for this might be the fact that outreach and mobile sessions have been used for a long time and are generally considered necessary to increase immunisation coverage in those contexts.

District microplans and RED strategies were also very common and were assembled into one category because they were frequently planned to be implemented concurrently and since microplanning is often the only component of RED that is implemented. The RED approach was developed by the World Health Organization (WHO), UNICEF and other partners in the Gavi Alliance to improve immunisation coverage and it includes five operational components aimed at improving vaccination coverage: re-establishment of regular outreach services, supportive supervision, on-site training, community links with service delivery, monitoring and use of data for action, and better planning and management of human and financial resources [20]. These components thus have a large span and since they were grouped together under "RED strategies" in the proposals, we could not have a clear vision on what was planned exactly in each country. It was interesting to see, however, how widespread this overall approach has become as a strategy to improve immunisation coverage and increase equity.

Interestingly, two categories were reported in the UNICEF pro-equity mapping of JA reports that were, however, not found in the HSS proposals. These were "peer support group for health providers" and "security to allow immunisation services to happen safely".

Additionally, the results showed that several proposals focused on reaching remote-rural and hard-to-reach areas, but few prioritised the other ERG settings, namely urban poor and conflict-affected areas. To note that only proposals that explicitly stated they would prioritise those areas and developed key interventions to improve coverage there were included in the results. It is possible that other planned pro-equity interventions would address barriers in those areas, but were not clearly acknowledged as doing so. These results were not surprising, however, as we analysed HSS proposals submitted starting from 2014, while the ERG priority areas were only defined in 2018. Furthermore, recent evidence shows that unlike what we might have expected, less than 50% of ZD children live in ERG settings worldwide, suggesting that although they are key areas for prioritisation, it is unlikely that we will make considerable progress by solely targeting those settings [23]. Still, many proposals did mention having large pockets of unimmunised children in large urban areas and slums. It is estimated that 28% of un- or under-vaccinated children lived in urban and peri-urban areas and up to 15% lived in conflict-affected areas in 2020 [24]. It would thus be beneficial to pay special attention to those populations. In this sense, it is worth noting renewed efforts to reach conflict-affected populations with the launch of the Zero-Dose Immunisation Programme (ZIP) in June 2022. This initiative led by Gavi in partnership with the International Rescue Committee and World Vision aims to identify and reach ZD children in the Horn of Africa and the Sahel regions, prioritising children living in conflict settings, mobile populations, and cross-border refugees [25].

Interestingly, the results of the correlation analysis suggest that "bundles" of interventions are commonly used at the country-level as part of the strategy to increase immunisation coverage in the priority areas. Indeed, we found that outreach sessions and tailoring location of immunisation services was often implemented along with developing district microplans/RED strategies, community-level education activities as well as communication strategies to generate demand. Conversely, the analysis revealed how often certain interventions were not bundled, potentially limiting their sustainability and effectiveness. This links to increasing evidence that there are no silver bullets but rather bundles, or packages, of evidence-based interventions tailored to local context that are needed to increase immunisation coverage [26,27]. Learning efforts exploring these bundles of interventions to better reach ZD children and how to use the interventions synergistically to build off one another would be worth exploring. Developing a theory of change, among other things, would be a useful exercise to justify the bundling of activities and validate their effectiveness through implementation research or other approaches [28].

The finding that the rationale, or theory, behind the selection of specific pro-equity interventions was seldom provided in the proposals does not suggest that there is no rationale, but only that it was not clearly formulated. This made it difficult to assess the relevance and intended effects of interventions in different contexts. The few instances when a rationale was presented were generally for interventions that were not commonly found in other countries' HSS proposals. One might reasonably assume that there was less established evidence supporting the implementation of these rarer interventions, thus the need to justify them in the proposals. Documenting the assumptions and reasoning for specific interventions, especially less common ones, would be beneficial to monitor and measure their effectiveness. For example, by developing a theory of change or a strong logical model based on evidence of good results from other similar programs.

Furthermore, in the case of bundles, theories of change would be helpful to articulate how different interventions are expected to work synergistically to produce change. It would also help with the monitoring and evaluation of programmes. Considering this, it would be highly useful to build an evidence base of interventions, namely through implementation research, that may be used in those bundles. This has been conducted, for example, in the field of family planning, where over sixty organisations have endorsed and participated in the development, dissemination and implementation of a repository of evidence-based interventions coined "High Impact Practices", or HIPs [29]. The group explores practices that have demonstrated impact and generate evidence around replicability, scalability, sustainability, and cost-effectiveness of the different interventions and disseminate information namely through evidence briefs. Building similar evidence on interventions aiming to reach ZD children would be extremely valuable and would help prioritisation and strategic planning for future investments. This work could also be used for advocacy, design and implementation of programs, development of policies and guidelines, and identify knowledge gaps for future research.

Furthermore, several of the interventions listed in the proposals were not considered pro-equity according to our definition (and were thus not included in the database nor analysis), but they could easily become so if they were targeted or tailored to specific populations. For example, social mobilisation activities to generate demand aimed at the entire population of a country through mass media could become pro-equity by adapting the messaging to specific target communities. Along the same lines, capacity building of health workers could become a pro-equity intervention if the health workers received adapted training on interpersonal relations with specific vulnerable groups such as refugees, for example, or if they served a low-performing area. In short, countries do not necessarily have to go back to the drawing board to design 'pro-equity' interventions but should build on existing interventions and tailor and target them to areas and/or populations with large numbers of ZD children. Accurately identifying who and where zero-dose children is evidently a critical pre-requisite to be able to do this effectively. This is not to say that innovative interventions are not needed to reach ZD children, but both strategies can be used coincidently. It is also not to say that simply targeting and tailoring an intervention to a subgroup will necessarily be effective. Understanding the context, including the different vulnerabilities and barriers faced by a particular community, as well as building human-centred designs will be critical to appropriately reach the remaining unimmunised children.

A crucial point at the centre of the ongoing work around zero-dose children is the lack of an agreed upon definition of what constitutes a "pro-equity" approach. Vega & Irwin first highlighted in 2004 that pro-equity health policy should not only consider socioeconomic status, but all other social and systemic factors that influence health [30]. Wagner more specifically referred to pro-equity approaches as promoting equity for women and girls, special education needs and "marginalized" populations [31]. In the current article, we defined pro-equity interventions as "tailored or targeted approaches towards un- or under-immunised children and missed communities". Dadari and colleagues, for their part, defined them as "strategies designed to reach underserved children and populations" [15]. However, there is no formal definition and none of the current ones explicitly address the intersectional nature of inequities. Intersectionality, a concept first coined in African American feminist literature, describes the ways in which different inequalities are linked together and are mutually reinforcing in perpetuating discrimination and disadvantage [32]. Promoting health equity has been a priority for a long time now and much effort has gone towards it. However, the fact that inequities remain today may in part be explained by the fact that even though research shows the importance of many social determinants on health, we often take a siloed view on how to address them. Policy and action have mostly failed to recognise their intersectional nature and have instead focused extensively on addressing inequities related to socioeconomic status or on specific programs without addressing social determinants, which may generate short-term results but may not promote sustainability [33]. Stakeholders should thus reflect on what can be completed differently, such as building packages of interventions addressing different, overlapping vulnerabilities for example, that might help us bridge the gap to promote equity and reach ZD children and missed communities. Having a clear and common definition of what constitutes a pro-equity intervention would be important to avoid working in silos and to help test the effectiveness of pro-equity approaches in reaching zero-dose children.

The limitations of this study must be acknowledged. First, the HSS proposals provided an incomplete picture of pro-equity interventions being implemented at the country-level. They were limited in scope and reflected what countries planned to do with Gavi HSS funds, but Gavi is not the only source of funds for programmes. This might have led to a loss of perspective of other sectors in the findings and analysis. Secondly, the documents analysed did not report on implemented activities, but rather on plans susceptible to change in the countries' dynamic contexts, and thus did not necessarily reflect what truly happened in the field. Furthermore, considering the length of each proposal, a search by keyword was performed. Even though we conducted a manual screening of sections likely to contain relevant information, it is likely that some information was missed. Finally, a number of subjective assessments had to be made during data extraction to decide the category of each intervention. However, inter-rater reliability was not assessed since there was only one analyst and steps were taken to maintain objectivity and avoid bias via building on the existing codes developed by UNICEF for the JA mapping and reviewing the findings with peers.

5. Conclusions

The findings from this mapping provide a portfolio analysis of HSS pro-equity programming in all Gavi-supported countries and can inform discussions on what may or may not need to change to better reach ZD children and missed communities in the future. Further mapping should be conducted to provide a more complete picture of pro-equity strategies being implemented in those countries beyond interventions funded by Gavi through HSS grants. The results can also help identify specific interventions that require further attention for further evidence synthesis, case studies and implementation research to learn more about their effectiveness, feasibility, acceptability, implementation cost and sustainability, among other factors. In addition to exploring new interventions, research should be conducted to investigate how to better design and implement commonly used interventions such as the ones identified in this mapping (e.g., outreach sessions, tailoring the location of service delivery, microplanning and community-level education activities) and adjust them to better reach the ZD children that are the key priority of Gavi 5.0 and IA2030.

Author Contributions: Conceptualization, J.D., G.C.C. and H.W.R.; data extraction, J.D.; methodology, J.D., G.C.C., H.W.R., A.B.S., V.A.F. and M.J.; analysis, J.D. and G.C.C.; writing—original draft preparation, J.D.; writing—review and editing, J.D., G.C.C., H.W.R., A.B.S., V.A.F. and M.J. All authors have read and agreed to the published version of the manuscript.

Funding: This research received no external funding.

Institutional Review Board Statement: Not applicable.

Informed Consent Statement: Not applicable.

Data Availability Statement: All data supporting reported results in this article are from HSS proposals publicly available on Gavi, the Vaccine Alliance's website gavi.org (accessed on 20 December 2022).

Acknowledgments: We would like to acknowledge the contribution and support provided by colleagues at Gavi including Hope Johnson, Esther Saville, Dan Hogan, Binay Kumar, Maria Patyna, Hamidreza Setayesh, Nilgun Aydogan and Patience Musanhu. We would also like to extend our gratitude for the feedback provided by Robert Scherpbier, Niklas Danielsson and Asm Shahabuddin at UNICEF.

Conflicts of Interest: The authors declare no conflict of interest.

Appendix A

Table A1. List of all pro-equity intervention categories found in HSS proposals relating to reaching ZD/under-immunised children and corresponding definitions.

Intervention Name	Definition
Immunization promotion activities: engage community/religious leaders to promote immunization	Any activities in which the explicit goal is to increase the engagement of community and/or religion leaders to promote immunization.
Immunization promotion activities: communication strategies (print, radio, TV, etc.) to generate demand	Any activities in which the explicit goal is to increase or improve communications to reach targeted groups, including through means such as local radio, theatre, skits, and mass media channels, to generate demand. This category can also include tailoring specific messages and/or translating existing material into local languages to reach certain groups/cultures.
Immunization promotion activities: immunization champions/ambassadors	Any activities that explicitly use immunization champions or ambassadors (or a similar title) to promote immunization.
Immunization promotion activities: community-level education and counselling activities	Any activities in which the explicit goal is to conduct community-based education or counselling activities to promote immunization.
Immunization promotion activities: health facility level education and counselling activities	Any activities in which the explicit goal is to conduct facility-based education or counselling activities to promote immunization.
Training/capacity building of health workers	Training or capacity building activities focused on health workers, including those providing clinical care and direct patient interaction.
Training/capacity building of health managers	Training or capacity building activities focused on health managers, including those involved with planning, directing, and coordinating nonclinical activities within health care systems.
Financial and non-financial incentives for staff	Interventions involving the use of incentives (either financial or non-financial) for staff involved in immunization programs to increase immunization coverage.

Table A1. *Cont.*

Intervention Name	Definition
Financial or non-financial incentives for users	Interventions involving the use of incentives (either financial or non-financial) for individuals receiving vaccinations and/or caregivers bringing in minors for vaccination. Incentives can include general improvements to the service and/or environment where immunizations occur (i.e., shaded waiting area, provision of snacks, improving service quality).
Reminder-recall systems	Interventions involving systems that either remind patients of upcoming immunization visits that are due (reminders) or are overdue (recall). Reminder and recall systems could be delivered through digital (e.g., email, text message) or non-digital (phone call, letter) means. [1]
Adjust hours/timing of immunization services	Any activities that seek to increase immunization coverage by altering, adjusting, and/or expanding the times of a healthcare facility or other location at which immunizations are offered, such as opening on the weekends or staying open later in the evenings.
Outreach sessions/tailor location of service delivery and partnerships for service delivery	Any activities that seek to increase immunization coverage by either providing outreach services to provide immunization or tailoring the location of service delivery. This category also includes mobile vaccination efforts, building new infrastructure (e.g., building new facilities or immunization centres), and creating or leveraging partnerships (e.g., with the private sector) to expand vaccine access.
Peer support groups for health providers	Any activities that seek to establish or strengthen peer support groups among health providers to provide a forum to share ideas and offer support to improve immunization programs.
Negotiating access to populations affected by conflict	Activities seeking to negotiate physical access to populations affected by conflict by identifying and negotiating secure access with all conflict participants, including state and nonstate actors, as well as their allies [2].
Recruit community health workers (CHWs)	Activities seeking to increase immunization coverage by recruiting community health workers to provide support to local immunization programs.
Recruit health personnel (other than CHWs)	Interventions seeking to increase immunization coverage by recruiting health personnel besides CHWs to provide or provide support to local immunization programs.
Recruit local HCWs who represent the communities they serve	Activities seeking to increase immunization by recruiting local healthcare workers who represent the communities they serve.
Security to allow immunization services to happen safely	Interventions seeking to provide security to allow immunization services to happen safety, such as by using military escorts or embedding vaccination program workers with military contingents [2].
Integration of immunization with other services to enhance convenience and strengthen Universal Primary Care	Interventions seeking to integrate immunization services with other healthcare services to increase coverage by enhancing convenience and strengthening Universal Primary Care.
Cold chain functionality	Interventions seeking to improve cold chain functionality, such as by identifying performance gaps, testing new equipment, etc. [3] This category also includes procurement of new cold chain equipment, or other interventions designed to improve the cold chain.
Rewards to communities/leaders for performance	Interventions that explicitly offer rewards to communities and/or community leaders for improvements in local immunization coverage.
Development of district microplans and RED strategies	The development of microplans (at the facility and/or district level), which consist of developing an integrated set of components prepared to support the activities performed during a health campaign [4]. RED (Reach Every District) strategies [5] include five operational components aimed at improving vaccination coverage: 1. re-establishment of regular outreach services; 2. supportive supervision: on-site training; 3. community links with service delivery; 4. monitoring and use of data for action; 5. better planning and management of human and financial resources Some interventions might include both microplans and REDs, whereas some might include microplans but not REDs or vice versa. Either scenario would still qualify for this intervention category.

Table A1. *Cont.*

Intervention Name	Definition
Purchase of transportation equipment	The purchase of transportation equipment (e.g., cars, motorcycles, boats, etc.).
PIRI, SIA targeted at vulnerable communities	Activities to support periodic intensification of routine immunization (PIRI) or disease specific supplementary immunization activities (SIAs) [6] such as campaigns
Redistribution of staff to areas where there is insufficient HR	Intentional plans to redistribute staff to areas where there are insufficient human resources to increase the capacity to carry out immunization programs.
Upgrading waste management/incinerators	Upgrading waste management and/or incinerators to improve the ability to carry out immunization programs.

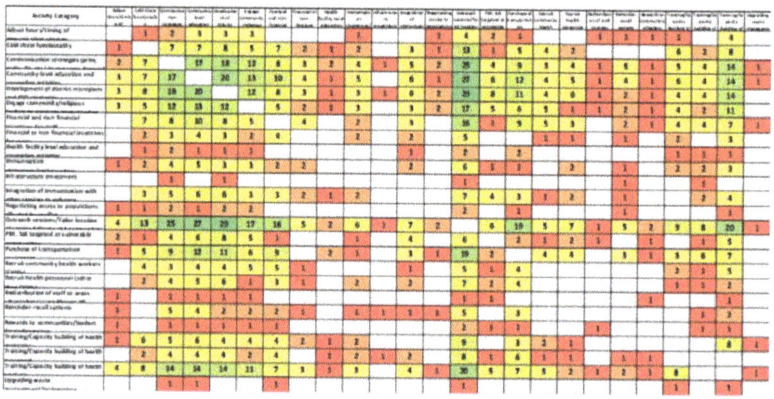

Figure A1. Complete correlation matrix (including all intervention categories).

References

1. Vaccination and Immunization Statistics [Internet]. UNICEF DATA. Available online: https://data.unicef.org/topic/child-health/immunization/ (accessed on 7 September 2022).
2. WHO Immunization Data Portal [Internet]. Available online: https://immunizationdata.who.int/ (accessed on 1 November 2022).
3. Immunization Agenda 2030 [Internet]. Available online: https://www.immunizationagenda2030.org/ (accessed on 30 November 2022).
4. Rachlin, A.; Danovaro-Holliday, M.C.; Murphy, P.; Sodha, S.V.; Wallace, A.S. Routine Vaccination Coverage—Worldwide, 2021. *MMWR. Morb. Mortal. Wkly. Rep.* **2022**, *71*, 1396–1400. [CrossRef] [PubMed]
5. Eligibility [Internet]. Available online: https://www.gavi.org/types-support/sustainability/eligibility (accessed on 6 September 2022).
6. Phase 5 (2021–2025) [Internet]. Available online: https://www.gavi.org/our-alliance/strategy/phase-5-2021-2025 (accessed on 6 September 2022).
7. Cata-Preta, B.O.; Santos, T.M.; Mengistu, T.; Hogan, D.R.; Barros, A.J.; Victora, C.G. Zero-dose children and the immunisation cascade: Understanding immunisation pathways in low and middle-income countries. *Vaccine* **2021**, *39*, 4564–4570. [CrossRef] [PubMed]
8. Santos, T.M.; Cata-Preta, B.O.; Mengistu, T.; Victora, C.G.; Hogan, D.R.; Barros, A.J.D. Assessing the overlap between immunisation and other essential health interventions in 92 low- and middle-income countries using household surveys: Opportunities for expanding immunisation and primary health care. *eClinicalMedicine* **2021**, *42*, 101196. [CrossRef] [PubMed]
9. Zero-Dose Children and Missed Communities [Internet]. Available online: https://www.gavi.org/our-alliance/strategy/phase-5-2021-2025/equity-goal/zero-dose-children-missed-communities (accessed on 19 August 2022).
10. Wendt, A.; Santos, T.M.; Cata-Preta, B.O.; Costa, J.C.; Mengistu, T.; Hogan, D.R.; Victora, C.G.; Barros, A.J.D. Children of more empowered women are less likely to be left without vaccination in low- and middle-income countries: A global analysis of 50 DHS surveys. *J. Glob. Health* **2022**, *12*, 04022. [CrossRef] [PubMed]
11. Vaccination: Helping Children Think, Learn and Thrive–VoICE [Internet]. Available online: https://immunizationevidence.org/featured_issues/vaccination-helping-children-think-learn-and-thrive/ (accessed on 19 August 2022).
12. The Zero-Dose Child: Explained [Internet]. Available online: https://www.gavi.org/vaccineswork/zero-dose-child-explained (accessed on 19 August 2022).
13. Johri, M.; Rajpal, S.; Subramanian, S.V. Progress in reaching unvaccinated (zero-dose) children in India, 1992–2016: A multilevel, geospatial analysis of repeated cross-sectional surveys. *Lancet Glob. Health* **2021**, *9*, e1697–e1706. [CrossRef] [PubMed]

14. Sissoko, D.; Trottier, H.; Malvy, D.; Johri, M. The Influence of Compositional and Contextual Factors on Non-Receipt of Basic Vaccines among Children of 12–23-Month Old in India: A Multilevel Analysis. *PLoS ONE* **2014**, *9*, e106528. [CrossRef] [PubMed]
15. Dadari, I.; Higgins-Steele, A.; Sharkey, A.; Charlet, D.; Shahabuddin, A.; Nandy, R.; Jackson, D. Pro-equity immunization and health systems strengthening strategies in select Gavi-supported countries. *Vaccine* **2021**, *39*, 2434–2444. [CrossRef] [PubMed]
16. Health System and Immunisation Strengthening Support Framework [Internet]. Available online: https://www.gavi.org/programmes-impact/programmatic-policies/hsis-support-framework (accessed on 19 August 2022).
17. Annual Progress Report 2021 [Internet]. Available online: https://www.gavi.org/progress-report (accessed on 30 November 2022).
18. All Country Documents | Gavi, the Vaccine Alliance [Internet]. Available online: https://www.gavi.org/country-documents/nigeria (accessed on 30 November 2022).
19. Gavi, the Vaccine Alliance. Zero-Dose Analysis Card [Internet]. Available online: https://www.linkedimmunisation.org/wp-content/uploads/2021/08/Gavi_Zero-dose_AnalysisCard.pdf (accessed on 30 November 2022).
20. Vandelaer, J.; Bilous, J.; Nshimirimana, D. Reaching Every District (RED) approach: A way to improve immunization performance. *Bull. World Health Organ.* **2008**, *86*, A–B. [CrossRef] [PubMed]
21. Gender Policy [Internet]. Available online: https://www.gavi.org/programmes-impact/programmatic-policies/gender-policy (accessed on 14 December 2022).
22. Yawson, A.E.; Bonsu, G.; Senaya, L.K.; Yawson, A.O.; Eleeza, J.B.; Awoonor-Williams, J.K.; Banskota, H.K.; Agongo, E.E.A. Regional disparities in immunization services in Ghana through a bottleneck analysis approach: Implications for sustaining national gains in immunization. *Arch. Public Health* **2017**, *75*, 10. [CrossRef] [PubMed]
23. Utazi, C.E.; Pannell, O.; Aheto, J.M.K.; Wigley, A.; Tejedor-Garavito, N.; Wunderlich, J.; Hagedorn, B.; Hogan, D.; Tatem, A.J. Assessing the characteristics of un- and under-vaccinated children in low- and middle-income countries: A multi-level cross-sectional study. *PLoS Glob. Public Health* **2022**, *2*, e0000244. [CrossRef]
24. Wigley, A.; Lorin, J.; Hogan, D.; Utazi, C.E.; Hagedorn, B.; Dansereau, E.; Tatem, A.J.; Tejedor-Garavito, N. Estimates of the number and distribution of zero-dose and under-immunised children across remote-rural, urban, and conflict-affected settings in low and middle-income countries. *PLoS Glob. Public Health* **2022**, *2*, e0001126. [CrossRef]
25. Gavi Launches New Partnership to Reach "Zero-Dose" Children across Marginalised Communities [Internet]. Available online: https://www.gavi.org/news/media-room/gavi-launches-new-partnership-reach-zero-dose-children-across-marginalised (accessed on 31 August 2022).
26. Uddin, M.J.; Larson, C.P.; Oliveras, E.; Khan, A.I.; Quaiyum, M.A.; Saha, N.C. Child immunization coverage in urban slums of Bangladesh: Impact of an intervention package. *Health Policy Plan.* **2010**, *25*, 50–60. [CrossRef] [PubMed]
27. Hu, Y.; Luo, S.; Tang, X.; Lou, L.; Chen, Y.; Guo, J.; Zhang, B. Does introducing an immunization package of services for migrant children improve the coverage, service quality and understanding? An evidence from an intervention study among 1548 migrant children in eastern China. *BMC Public Health* **2015**, *15*, 664. [CrossRef] [PubMed]
28. Skivington, K.; Matthews, L.; Simpson, S.A.; Craig, P.; Baird, J.; Blazeby, J.M.; Boyd, K.; Craig, N.; French, D.; McIntosh, E.; et al. A new framework for developing and evaluating complex interventions: Update of Medical Research Council guidance. *BMJ* **2021**, *374*, n2061. [CrossRef] [PubMed]
29. Homepage [Internet]. HIPs. Available online: https://live-jhu-hip-stage.pantheonsite.io/ (accessed on 31 August 2022).
30. Vega, J.; Irwin, A. Tackling health inequalities: New approaches in public policy. *Bull. World Health Organ.* **2004**, *82*, 482. [PubMed]
31. Wagner, D.A. Chapter 6. Pro-Equity Approaches to Monitoring and Evaluation: Gender, Marginalized Groups and Special Needs Populations. In *Monitoring and Evaluation of ICT in Education Projects: A Handbook for Developing Countries*; The International Bank for Reconstruction and Development/The World Bank: Washington, DC, USA, 2005; pp. 93–110.
32. Crenshaw, K. Mapping the Margins: Intersectionality, Identity Politics, and Violence against Women of Color. *Stanf. Law Rev.* **1991**, *43*, 1241–1249. [CrossRef]
33. Joe, W. Intersectional inequalities in immunization in India, 1992–1993 to 2005–2006: A progress assessment. *Health Policy Plan.* **2015**, *30*, 407–422. [CrossRef] [PubMed]

vaccines

MDPI

Article

Assessing Potential Exemplars in Reducing Zero-Dose Children: A Novel Approach for Identifying Positive Outliers in Decreasing National Levels and Geographic Inequalities in Unvaccinated Children

Nancy Fullman [1,*], Gustavo C. Correa [2], Gloria Ikilezi [1], David E. Phillips [1] and Heidi W. Reynolds [2]

1 Exemplars in Global Health, Gates Ventures, 2401 Elliott Ave, Seattle, WA 98121, USA
2 Gavi, the Vaccine Alliance, Chemin du Pommier 40, Le Grand-Saconnex, 1218 Geneva, Switzerland
* Correspondence: nancy.fullman@gatesventures.com

Abstract: Background: Understanding past successes in reaching unvaccinated or "zero-dose" children can help inform strategies for improving childhood immunization in other settings. Drawing from positive outlier methods, we developed a novel approach for identifying potential exemplars in reducing zero-dose children. Methods: Focusing on 2000–2019, we assessed changes in the percentage of under-one children with no doses of the diphtheria–tetanus–pertussis vaccine (no-DTP) across two geographic dimensions in 56 low- or lower-middle-income countries: (1) national levels; (2) subnational gaps, as defined as the difference between the 5th and 95th percentiles of no-DTP prevalence across second administrative units. Countries with the largest reductions for both metrics were considered positive outliers or potential 'exemplars', demonstrating exception progress in reducing national no-DTP prevalence and subnational inequalities. Last, so-called "neighborhood analyses" were conducted for the Gavi Learning Hub countries (Nigeria, Mali, Uganda, and Bangladesh), comparing them with countries that had similar no-DTP measures in 2000 but different trajectories through 2019. Results: From 2000 to 2019, the Democratic Republic of the Congo, Ethiopia, and India had the largest absolute decreases for the two no-DTP dimensions—national prevalence and subnational gaps—while Bangladesh and Burundi registered the largest relative reductions for each no-DTP metric. Neighborhood analyses highlighted possible opportunities for cross-country learning among Gavi Learning Hub countries and potential exemplars in reducing zero-dose children. Conclusions: Identifying where exceptional progress has occurred is the first step toward better understanding how such gains could be achieved elsewhere. Further examination of how countries have successfully reduced levels of zero-dose children—especially across variable contexts and different drivers of inequality—could support faster, sustainable advances toward greater vaccination equity worldwide.

Keywords: immunization; vaccines; zero-dose children; equity

Citation: Fullman, N.; Correa, G.C.; Ikilezi, G.; Phillips, D.E.; Reynolds, H.W. Assessing Potential Exemplars in Reducing Zero-Dose Children: A Novel Approach for Identifying Positive Outliers in Decreasing National Levels and Geographic Inequalities in Unvaccinated Children. *Vaccines* **2023**, *11*, 647. https://doi.org/10.3390/vaccines11030647

Academic Editors: Ahmad Reza Hosseinpoor, M. Carolina Danovaro, Devaki Nambiar, Aaron Wallace and Hope Johnson

Received: 2 February 2023
Revised: 9 March 2023
Accepted: 10 March 2023
Published: 14 March 2023

1. Introduction

The expansion of routine immunization is heralded as a global success story [1], enabling greater survival and improved child health worldwide [2]. Nevertheless, an estimated 25 million children were un- or under-vaccinated in 2021 [3], with many facing compounding barriers in vaccine access, availability, and demand. The ongoing COVID-19 pandemic has contributed to at least some of today's gaps in childhood vaccination [3], with estimates of under-one children without any doses of the diphtheria–tetanus–pertussis vaccine (no-DTP) rising from 10% prevalence in 2019 to 14% in 2021 [3]. Communities with high levels of unvaccinated or "zero-dose children" often face myriad vulnerabilities [4–7], such as residing in highly remote areas or informal settlements in cities [7–9]; being affected by displacement and/or prolonged conflict or unrest [7,8]; longstanding poverty and/or societal neglect [4]; or some constellation of these factors. Subsequently, optimally identifying where and how to better reach zero-dose children will likely require a combination of context-specific strategies and broader investments to address persisting structural challenges.

Over the last few years, a growing body of research has sought to assess characteristics of zero-dose children and their families or households, as well as potential drivers of high zero-dose prevalence at different geographic levels [4–8,10–17]. Past work has found that zero-dose children experience a higher odds of missing or lacking access to other types of primary care services [6,11,12], while their mothers were more likely to have no antenatal care visits and not deliver at a health facility [11,12]. Lower levels of household wealth, educational attainment, and measures of women's empowerment also have been associated with higher levels of zero-dose children [4,10,16,17]. Gender-based inequalities, which span from differential rates of immunization by infant gender and gender-related barriers related to who can seek or provide vaccination services [16,18], emphasize the complex yet crucial role that gender plays in a country and/or community [19]. Prior studies have found ethnic disparities [15], as well as differences by religious affiliation [13,20], among children who have received no doses of DTP, though the exact nature of these relationships varied by country. Quantifying these risk factors and determinants of zero-dose children can provide critical program inputs, spanning from identifying key barriers to service access [7,18] to honing in on what sociocultural forces may be negatively affecting vaccine sentiments and trust [18–20]. However, exclusively focusing on zero-dose risk profiles and factors associated with higher rates of unvaccinated children may miss important lessons around successful approaches to addressing inequalities in childhood immunization. Accordingly, also understanding what has worked to improve childhood vaccination can inform program and policy adaptations tailored for reaching zero-dose children.

Positive outlier, or so-called 'positive deviance', methodologies have been used at the unit or organizational level in healthcare settings [21–23], as well as for more population-level contexts [24–28], to generate or strengthen the evidence base around what works to improve key health priorities. While the exact approaches toward this type of research and synthesis vary, they usually espouse a shared premise: knowledge and implementation strategies around achieving success or progress exist from places or contexts where such success or progress have been previously attained [21]. As a result, identifying and then examining what contributes to exceptional performance or progress can offer actionable insights into what policies and practice could be adapted for similar impact elsewhere. For instance, the *Good Health at Low Cost* case studies first in 1985 [26] and then in 2013 [27], sought to synthesize how and why countries or regions achieved substantial advances in several health indicators compared to their peers with similar income and demographic profiles; in 2018, the World Bank took a similar approach for understanding rapid progress on universal health coverage measures and facilitating shared learning opportunities across countries [28]. In 2016, the Global Burden of Disease study developed analyses to compare country-level performance on various health metrics relative to changes in sociodemographic development [29–31]; such findings emphasized that important health program and policy lessons could be learned from countries where achievements exceeded expected levels or trends on the basis of sociodemographic improvements alone. Lastly, the Exemplars in Global Health (EGH) program has sought to synthesize key lessons and strategies used by countries that attained exceptional progress in health—exemplars—through mixed-methods research and engagement with partners [32–35]. As highlighted by past and current work on positive outliers, such analyses can foster opportunities for cross-country learning and exchange around successful policy or programmatic approaches for a given health challenge. With more learning agendas and priority-setting around zero-dose children for both national and global initiatives (e.g., Immunization Agenda 2030 [IA2030] [36] and Gavi 5.0 [37]), adopting a positive outlier lens toward country progress in reducing zero-dose children could further inform key immunization program and policy efforts.

With this study, we develop a novel approach for identifying positive outliers in reducing zero-dose children over time. This analysis currently takes a geographic focus, one of many important dimensions of inequality, by comparing patterns in both national and subnational declines in the percentage of under-one children with no doses of DTP (no-DTP) from 2000 to 2019 among 56 low- and lower-middle-income countries (LMICs). Based on this approach, identified 'exemplar' countries or subnational locations that substantially reduced zero-dose children could be targeted for further examination into the policy or program factors behind such gains.

2. Materials and Methods

2.1. Data

We used estimates of DTP1 among children under 1 year of age at the national and second administrative levels from the Institute for Health Metrics and Evaluation (IHME). The methods used to estimate DTP1 at different geospatial resolutions are detailed elsewhere [38]; in brief, DTP1 coverage estimates were derived from georeferenced household surveys and modeled using Bayesian geostatistical methods for 106 countries at the first and second administrative levels from 2000 to 2019. We opted to use these spatially modelled estimates over alternative sources (e.g., administrative data) to maximize both the potential number of countries included and comparability of estimates across locations. We subtracted DTP1 estimates from 100% to reflect the percentage of under-one children with no doses of DTP, or no-DTP prevalence—a commonly used indicator for zero-dose children [10,36].

For this analysis, we focused on 56 LMICs (Table 1). These countries were selected on the following criteria: (1) designation of low- or lower-middle income for fiscal year 2020 by the World Bank [39] or having received support from Gavi, the Vaccine Alliance as of 2018 [40]; (2) availability of both national and subnational no-DTP estimates at the second administrative level from 2000 to 2019; (3) not being classified as a post-transition middle-income country by Gavi and inclusion as part of Gavi's zero-dose segmentation country groups [41]. Supplementary Table S1 includes the full list of initially considered countries and those excluded from the current analysis.

Table 1. Included countries for identifying potential exemplars in reducing zero-dose children. * Gavi-supported indicates that the country received Gavi support as of 2018 or had a dedicated country hub page. ** Countries with national and subnational DTP1 estimates (for both first and second administrative units) as modeled by the Institute for Health Metrics and Evaluation. Supplementary Table S1 provides the list of initial countries considered but excluded due to not meeting inclusion criteria.

Country	World Bank FY20 Income Group	Gavi-Supported *	National and Subnational DTP1 Estimates Available, 2000–2019 **	Gavi zero-Dose Segmentation Grouping
Afghanistan	Low-income	Yes	Yes	Conflict/fragile
Angola	Lower-middle income	Yes	Yes	Core—ESA (Priority)
Bangladesh	Lower-middle income	Yes	Yes	Core—Rest of World (Priority)
Benin	Low-income	Yes	Yes	Core—WCA (Priority)
Burkina Faso	Low-income	Yes	Yes	Core—WCA (Priority)
Burundi	Low-income	Yes	Yes	Core—ESA (Standard)
Cambodia	Lower-middle income	Yes	Yes	Core—Rest of World (Standard)
Cameroon	Lower-middle income	Yes	Yes	Core—WCA (Priority)
Central African Rep	Low-income	Yes	Yes	Conflict/fragile

Table 1. *Cont.*

Country	World Bank FY20 Income Group	Gavi-Supported *	National and Subnational DTP1 Estimates Available, 2000–2019 **	Gavi zero-Dose Segmentation Grouping
Chad	Low-income	Yes	Yes	Conflict/fragile
Comoros	Lower-middle income	Yes	Yes	Core—ESA (Standard)
Congo	Lower-middle income	Yes	Yes	Core—WCA (Priority)
Côte d'Ivoire	Lower-middle income	Yes	Yes	Core—WCA (Priority)
Dem Rep of the Congo	Low-income	Yes	Yes	High impact
Djibouti	Lower-middle income	Yes	Yes	Core—ESA (Priority)
Eritrea	Low-income	Yes	Yes	Core—ESA (Standard)
Ethiopia	Low-income	Yes	Yes	High impact
Gambia	Low-income	Yes	Yes	Core—WCA (Standard)
Ghana	Lower-middle income	Yes	Yes	Core—WCA (Priority)
Guinea	Low-income	Yes	Yes	Core—WCA (Priority)
Guinea-Bissau	Low-income	Yes	Yes	Core—WCA (Priority)
Haiti	Low-income	Yes	Yes	Conflict/fragile
India	Lower-middle income	Yes	Yes	High impact
Kenya	Lower-middle income	Yes	Yes	Core—ESA (Priority)
Kyrgyzstan	Lower-middle income	Yes	Yes	Core—Rest of World (Standard)
Laos	Lower-middle income	Yes	Yes	Core—Rest of World (Priority)
Lesotho	Lower-middle income	Yes	Yes	Core—ESA (Standard)
Liberia	Low-income	Yes	Yes	Core—WCA (Standard)
Madagascar	Low-income	Yes	Yes	Core—ESA (Priority)
Malawi	Low-income	Yes	Yes	Core—ESA (Priority)
Mali	Low-income	Yes	Yes	Conflict/fragile
Mauritania	Lower-middle income	Yes	Yes	Core—WCA (Standard)
Mozambique	Low-income	Yes	Yes	Core—ESA (Priority)
Myanmar	Lower-middle income	Yes	Yes	Core—Rest of World (Priority)
Nepal	Low-income	Yes	Yes	Core—Rest of World (Priority)
Niger	Low-income	Yes	Yes	Conflict/fragile
Nigeria	Lower-middle income	Yes	Yes	High impact
Pakistan	Lower-middle income	Yes	Yes	High impact
Papua New Guinea	Lower-middle income	Yes	Yes	Conflict/fragile
Rwanda	Low-income	Yes	Yes	Core—ESA (Standard)
São Tomé and Príncipe	Lower-middle income	Yes	Yes	Core—WCA (Standard)
Senegal	Lower-middle income	Yes	Yes	Core—WCA (Standard)
Sierra Leone	Low-income	Yes	Yes	Core—WCA (Standard)
Somalia	Low-income	Yes	Yes	Conflict/fragile
South Sudan	Low-income	Yes	Yes	Conflict/fragile
Sudan	Lower-middle income	Yes	Yes	Conflict/fragile

Table 1. *Cont.*

Country	World Bank FY20 Income Group	Gavi-Supported *	National and Subnational DTP1 Estimates Available, 2000–2019 **	Gavi zero-Dose Segmentation Grouping
Tajikistan	Low-income	Yes	Yes	Core—Rest of World (Standard)
Tanzania	Low-income	Yes	Yes	Core—ESA (Priority)
Timor-Leste	Lower-middle income	Yes	Yes	Core—Rest of World (Standard)
Togo	Low-income	Yes	Yes	Core—WCA (Priority)
Uganda	Low-income	Yes	Yes	Core—ESA (Priority)
Uzbekistan	Lower-middle income	Yes	Yes	Core—Rest of World (Standard)
Vietnam	Lower-middle income	Yes	Yes	Core—Rest of World (Standard)
Yemen	Low-income	Yes	Yes	Conflict/fragile
Zambia	Lower-middle income	Yes	Yes	Core—ESA (Priority)
Zimbabwe	Lower-middle income	Yes	Yes	Core—ESA (Standard)

2.2. *Analysis*

We conducted three analyses to characterize potential exemplars in reducing zero-dose children over time, as summarized below. R version 4.2.1 was used for data processing, analyses, and visualizations [42].

Quantifying changes in zero-dose children across geographies. We assessed changes in the percentage of under-one children without any doses of DTP (no-DTP) between 2000 and 2019 across two geographic dimensions: (1) national levels; (2) subnational gaps among second-level administrative units. For the latter—subnational gaps—we used the 5th and 95th percentile values of the prevalence of no-DTP children estimated across second-level administrative units and computed the difference for a given country–year. We opted to use the 5th and 95th percentiles rather than absolute minimum and maximum values of no-DTP prevalence to offset the potential for undue influence of outliers for a given subnational unit–year. Furthermore, how countries define second-level administrative units widely varies (e.g., 10 or fewer units in Comoros, São Tomé and Príncipe, and Lesotho to 774 local government areas (LGAs) in Nigeria); using percentiles to define subnational gaps may also help mitigate the degree to which having more (or fewer) administrative units could affect measures of subnational inequality.

Identifying potential exemplars in reducing zero-dose children. Second, countries with the largest declines for *both* no-DTP metrics between 2000 and 2019 were considered as potential exemplars in reducing zero-dose children. Prior research conducted under the EGH program has typically used one progress measure per geographic unit [32,34,35], and then benchmarked changes against indicators of sociodemographic development. Because many locations with the highest levels of unvaccinated children face compounding vulnerabilities [4], any investments in reaching zero-dose children should also correspond with action to address disparities in immunization rates. Our approach to operationalizing this pro-equity lens from a geographic perspective was equally weighting reductions at the national level and subnational differences for no-DTP. In other words, a country that achieved marked national reductions in no-DTP prevalence without corresponding declines in subnational gaps should not be considered a potential exemplar in reducing zero-dose children.

We ranked each country ordinally, 1 to 56, based on their national and subnational reductions in no-DTP prevalence from 2000 to 2019, with 1 being the largest reduction and

56 being the smallest reduction or, if applicable, the largest increase since 2000. We took the mean of those rankings to identify which countries had achieved the most progress across both geographic dimensions. We applied these rankings and calculations for absolute and relative progress separately: computing percentage point changes for absolute progress from 2000 to 2019 and then percentage change from 2000 to 2019 for relative progress. We opted to consider both progress metrics—absolute and relative progress—as they could better represent a range of successful approaches used to reduce no-DTP prevalence from different starting points (i.e., higher and lower absolute levels of no-DTP children in 2000), and thus likely mirror different stages of immunization delivery needs and strategies.

Comparing divergent no-DTP trajectories since 2000 for select locations. Third, we conducted so-called "neighborhood analyses" for select countries, comparing them to other countries that had similar levels for both no-DTP measures in 2000 but different trajectories through 2019. Such analyses are thought to be supportive of potential cross-location learning and knowledge translation around what could work to address zero-dose challenges when starting from similar baseline levels of no-DTP prevalence. At the country-level, we focused on Nigeria, Mali, Uganda, and Bangladesh—the four countries selected for the Gavi Learning Hubs [43] and sought to match a "neighbor" exemplar to each country. Further detail on the Gavi's Learning Hub initiative is available elsewhere [43]; in brief, these four countries were selected on the basis of zero-dose metrics (i.e., high absolute numbers or prevalence of zero-dose children) as well as variations in zero-dose prevalence across geographic locations and among key populations that experience higher rates of no vaccination (i.e., rural, urban poor, refugeed, or conflict settings). A primary objective of the Learning Hubs is to support deeper assessment and engagement to improve monitoring and measurement systems, and to enable learning about what works programmatically to reach unvaccinated children and missed communities.

3. Results

3.1. Quantifying Changes in No-DTP Children from 2000 to 2019

Among the 56 LMICs included in this analysis, 44 (78.6%) had some kind of reduction in both national levels of no-DTP and subnational gaps in no-DTP prevalence between 2000 and 2019 (Figure 1; Table 2). In contrast, five countries—Benin, Kenya, Guinea, Papua New Guinea, and Uzbekistan—had at least some increase in both estimated national and subnational gaps in no-DTP prevalence. Five countries decreased national no-DTP levels between 2000 and 2019, but in tandem saw subnational gaps increase to some degree: Congo (an 8.4 percentage-point rise); Tajikistan (2.1 percentage points); Djibouti (0.7 percentage points); Central African Republic (0.6 percentage points); and São Tomé and Príncipe (0.4 percentage points). Two countries—Haiti and Myanmar– had the national percentage of under-one children with no DTP doses at least somewhat increase since 2000 while subnational gaps declined; this was particularly pronounced for Myanmar (a 6.1 percentage-point rise).

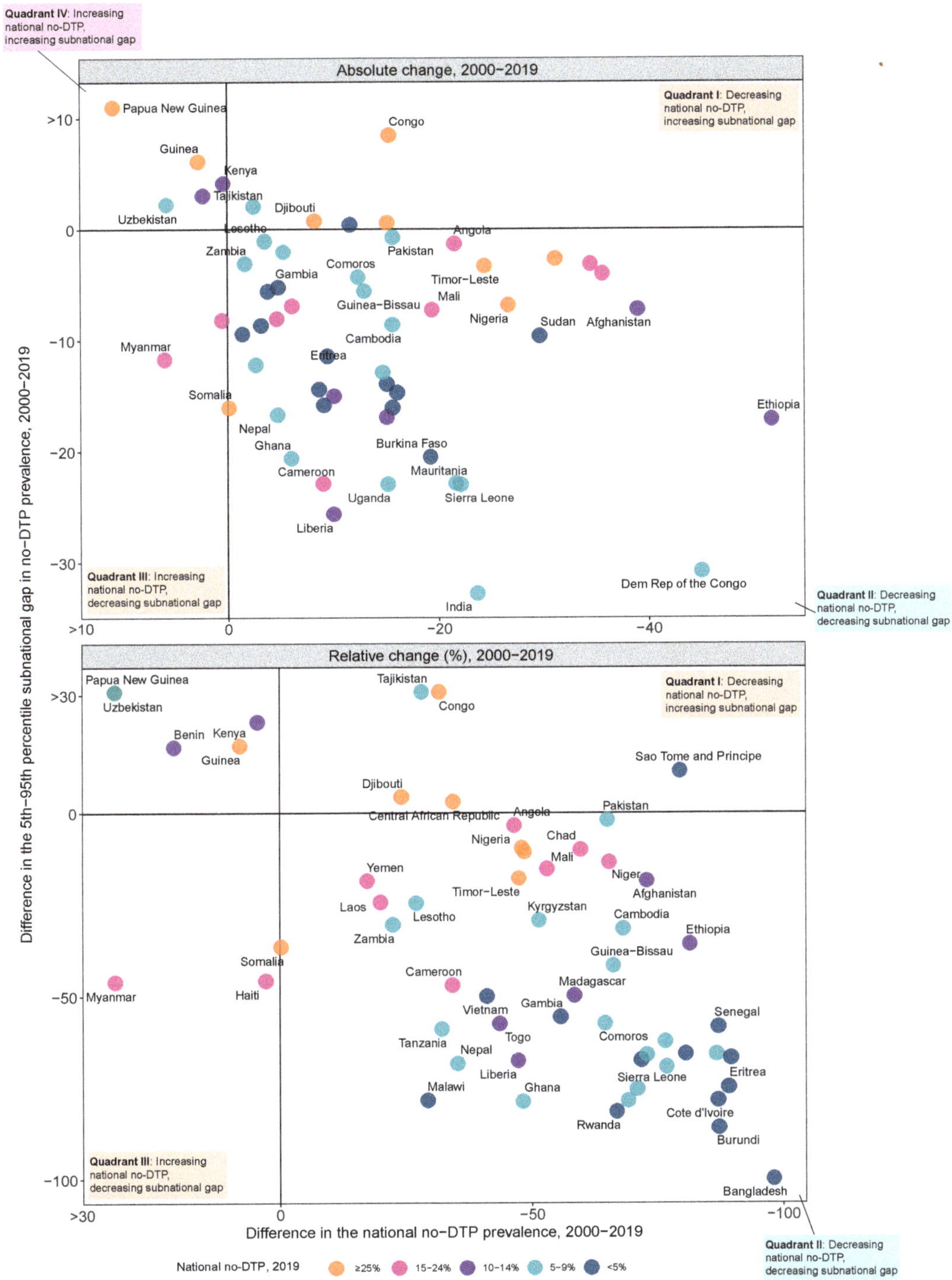

Figure 1. Comparing changes in no-DTP prevalence, nationally and for subnational gaps, from 2000 to 2019 for 56 LMICs. Countries are color-coded by national estimates of no-DTP in 2019.

Table 2. Comparing levels and changes in no-DTP prevalence, nationally and for subnational gaps, from 2000 to 2019 for 56 LMICs. Bolded countries are those with the largest progress in reducing zero-dose children for both national and subnational gaps, based on the difference between the 5th and 95th percentiles for no-DTP prevalence at the second-level administrative unit, for either absolute or relative declines from 2000 to 2019. pp = percentage-points.

Country	National Prevalence of No-DTP				Subnational Gap in No-DTP Prevalence (5–95th Percentile Difference across Districts)			
	2000 (%)	2019 (%)	Absolute Change, 2000–2019 (pp)	Relative Change, 2000–2019 (%)	2000 (pp)	2019 (pp)	Absolute Change, 2000–2019 (pp)	Relative Change, 2000–2019 (%)
Afghanistan	53.4	14.5	−39.0	−72.9	39.0	31.8	−7.2	−18.5
Angola	46.3	24.8	−21.5	−46.4	38.6	37.2	−1.3	−3.5
Bangladesh	**8.8**	**0.2**	**−8.6**	**−98.0**	**14.4**	**0.0**	**−14.4**	**−99.9**
Benin	11.3	13.6	2.4	21.1	16.9	19.9	3.0	18.0
Burkina Faso	23.8	4.6	−19.2	−80.6	31.2	10.7	−20.5	−65.8
Burundi	**18.4**	**2.3**	**−16.0**	**−87.3**	**17.1**	**2.4**	**−14.7**	**−85.9**
Cambodia	22.8	7.3	−15.6	−68.2	27.2	18.6	−8.6	−31.6
Cameroon	26.4	17.4	−9.0	−34.1	48.7	25.8	−22.9	−47.0
Central African Rep	44.0	28.9	−15.1	−34.3	19.1	19.7	0.6	3.1
Chad	59.7	24.0	−35.6	−59.7	40.4	36.4	−4.0	−10.0
Comoros	19.1	6.8	−12.3	−64.6	7.5	3.2	−4.3	−57.5
Congo	48.5	33.2	−15.3	−31.5	22.2	30.6	8.4	38.1
Cote d'Ivoire	17.9	2.3	−15.6	−87.1	20.5	4.4	−16.1	−78.4
Dem Rep of the Congo	**51.9**	**6.9**	**−45.0**	**−86.8**	**46.8**	**16.0**	**−30.8**	**−65.8**
Djibouti	34.3	26.1	−8.2	−24.0	17.2	18.0	0.7	4.4
Eritrea	10.6	1.1	−9.4	−89.2	15.3	3.8	−11.4	−74.8
Ethiopia	**63.4**	**11.7**	**−51.6**	**−81.5**	**47.9**	**30.8**	**−17.2**	**−35.8**
Gambia	8.6	3.8	−4.8	−55.7	9.4	4.2	−5.2	−55.7
Ghana	12.5	6.5	−6.0	−48.2	26.2	5.6	−20.6	−78.7
Guinea	35.6	38.4	2.8	7.9	33.2	39.3	6.1	18.4
Guinea-Bissau	19.5	6.6	−12.9	−66.3	13.4	7.8	−5.6	−41.7
Haiti	20.5	21.0	0.6	2.8	17.9	9.7	−8.2	−45.7
India	**30.9**	**7.2**	**−23.6**	**−76.5**	**52.5**	**19.7**	**−32.7**	**−62.4**
Kenya	9.6	10.0	0.4	4.4	16.6	20.8	4.1	24.8
Kyrgyzstan	10.3	5.0	−5.3	−51.5	7.0	5.0	−2.1	−29.3
Laos	30.8	24.6	−6.1	−19.9	28.4	21.5	−6.9	−24.4
Lesotho	13.1	9.6	−3.5	−26.9	4.3	3.3	−1.1	−24.6
Liberia	21.2	11.2	−10.0	−47.2	37.9	12.3	−25.6	−67.6
Madagascar	25.7	10.7	−15.0	−58.5	34.0	17.1	−16.9	−49.8
Malawi	4.8	3.4	−1.4	−29.2	12.0	2.6	−9.4	−78.4
Mali	36.4	17.1	−19.3	−53.1	47.8	40.5	−7.3	−15.2
Mauritania	28.1	6.5	−21.6	−76.8	33.0	10.1	−22.8	−69.3
Mozambique	12.7	3.6	−9.1	−71.8	23.5	7.6	−15.9	−67.5
Myanmar	11.5	17.6	6.1	52.9	25.4	13.7	−11.7	−46.0
Nepal	13.5	8.7	−4.7	−35.2	24.4	7.7	−16.7	−68.4
Niger	52.6	18.2	−34.5	−65.4	23.5	20.4	−3.2	−13.4
Nigeria	55.5	28.9	−26.6	−48.0	71.7	64.9	−6.8	−9.5
Pakistan	24.0	8.4	−15.6	−65.1	37.2	36.5	−0.7	−2.0
Papua New Guinea	17.3	44.4	27.1	156.4	13.7	32.5	18.8	137.7
Rwanda	5.7	1.9	−3.8	−66.9	6.9	1.3	−5.6	−81.5

Table 2. *Cont.*

Country	National Prevalence of No-DTP				Subnational Gap in No-DTP Prevalence (5–95th Percentile Difference across Districts)			
	2000 (%)	2019 (%)	Absolute Change, 2000–2019 (pp)	Relative Change, 2000–2019 (%)	2000 (pp)	2019 (pp)	Absolute Change, 2000–2019 (pp)	Relative Change, 2000–2019 (%)
São Tomé and Príncipe	14.6	3.0	−11.6	−79.5	3.6	4.0	0.4	11.4
Senegal	17.3	2.2	−15.1	−87.1	23.9	9.9	−14.0	−58.4
Sierra Leone	31.1	9.0	−22.1	−71.0	30.5	7.5	−23.0	−75.4
Somalia	51.2	51.1	−0.1	−0.2	44.0	27.9	−16.1	−36.5
South Sudan	64.1	33.0	−31.1	−48.5	25.2	22.5	−2.7	−10.6
Sudan	33.1	3.4	−29.7	−89.6	14.4	4.8	−9.6	−66.9
Tajikistan	8.9	6.4	−2.5	−28.0	6.3	8.4	2.1	32.7
Tanzania	8.3	5.7	−2.7	−32.0	20.7	8.5	−12.2	−59.0
Timor-Leste	51.3	27.0	−24.3	−47.4	18.6	15.3	−3.3	−17.9
Togo	23.1	13.1	−10.1	−43.5	26.1	11.1	−15.0	−57.5
Uganda	21.9	6.7	−15.2	−69.2	29.2	6.3	−22.9	−78.5
Uzbekistan	1.3	7.2	5.9	441.9	2.9	5.1	2.2	77.5
Vietnam	7.8	4.6	−3.2	−41.0	17.3	8.7	−8.7	−50.0
Yemen	27.1	22.4	−4.7	−17.2	43.4	35.4	−8.1	−18.5
Zambia	7.5	5.8	−1.7	−22.3	10.2	7.1	−3.1	−30.5
Zimbabwe	20.1	5.5	−14.7	−72.9	19.5	6.6	−12.9	−66.0

3.2. Identifying Potential Exemplars in Reducing Zero-Dose Children since 2000

Absolute progress. The DRC, Ethiopia, and India registered the largest absolute reductions in national no-DTP prevalence and subnational gaps from 2000 to 2019 (Figure 2; Table 2). Supplementary Figure S1A–C show both national and subnational no-DTP trends over time for each country.

In 2000, 51.9% of under-one children had no doses of DTP in the DRC nationally, with the country experiencing a 46.8 percentage-point gap between the territories with 5th and 95th percentiles for no-DTP prevalence (i.e., 28.5% to 75.3%). By 2019, national no-DTP prevalence levels fell to 6.9%, a 45.0 percentage-point decline. The DRC's subnational gaps narrowed by 30.8 percentage-points by 2019, decreasing to a total of 16.0 percentage points across the 5th and 95th percentiles of territories (i.e., 1.5% to 17.5%). As highlighted by Figrues 2 and S1A, subnational gaps started narrowing faster from 2015–2019 than in previous time periods.

For Ethiopia nationally, 63.4% of under-one children lacked any doses of DTP in 2000, but no-DTP prevalence fell 51.6 percentage points to 11.7% by 2019. Across its zones, Ethiopia had a 47.9 percentage-point gap between the 5th and 95th percentile levels of no-DTP prevalence in 2000, spanning from 39.6% to 87.5%. This subnational gap decreased by 17.2 percentage points by 2019, to a 30.8 percentage-point difference between the 5th and 95th percentile no-DTP levels across zones (i.e., 1.6% to 32.4%). However, amid such marked gains over the last 19 years, Ethiopia's reductions in subnational gaps have stagnated from 2016–2019 (Figure 2 and Figure S1B).

In India, national no-DTP prevalence was 30.9% in 2000 with a 52.5 percentage-point gap between the 5th and 95th percentile for no-DTP levels across districts (i.e., 7.2% to 59.7%). By 2019, 7.2% of under-one children had no doses of DTP in India nationally, a 23.6 percentage-point decline. Subnational gaps in India decreased 32.7 percentage points between 2000 and 2019, falling to 19.7 percentage-point difference in 2019 (i.e., 1.6% to 21.3%). Although overall subnational gaps have narrowed (Figure 2 and Figure S1C), several districts still exceeded 30% of under-one children with no doses of DTP in 2019.

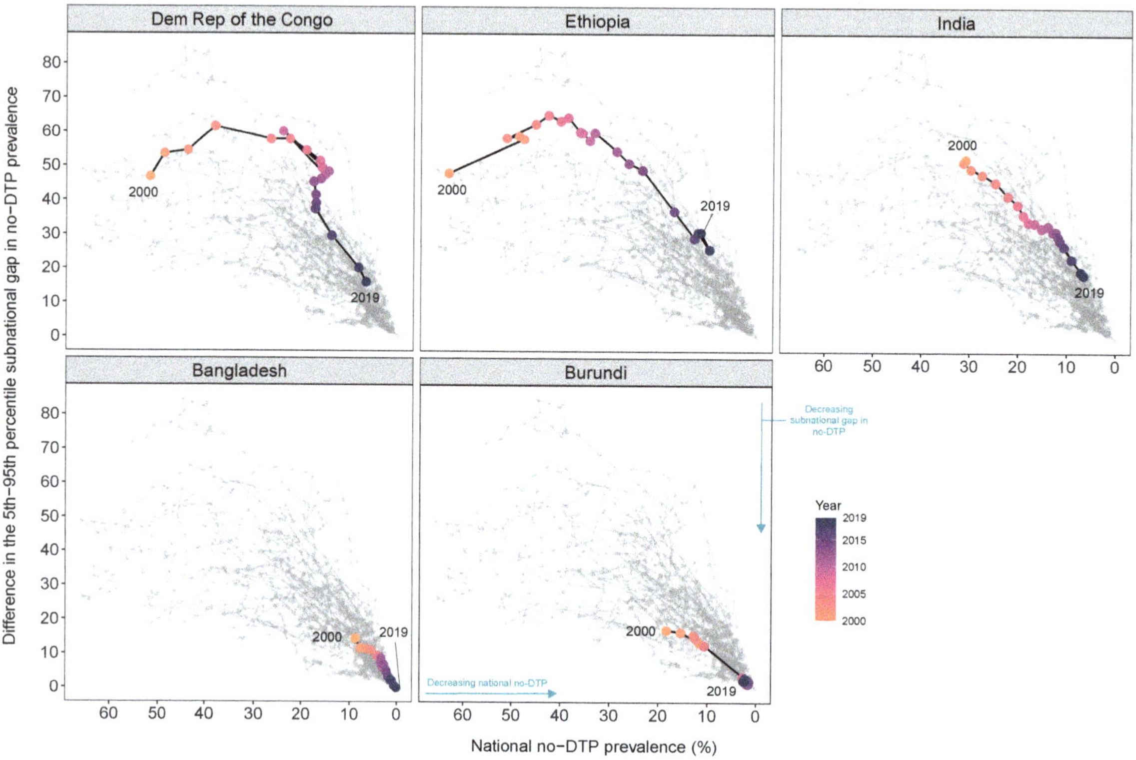

Figure 2. Comparing no-DTP trajectories for potential exemplars in reducing zero-dose children, 2000 to 2019. National no-DTP prevalence is represented on the x-axis and the subnational gap (as measured by the difference between the 5th and 95th percentile no-DTP prevalence across second-level administrative units) is represented on the y-axis. Each corner represents an extreme for each of these no-DTP metrics, with the lower right-hand corner—low national no-DTP prevalence and low subnational inequality—being the direction in which every location should strive to reach to equitably reduce no-DTP prevalence. Trends in the two no-DTP metrics for the potential exemplars are highlighted in black, with each circle representing a year from 2000 to 2019 that is color-coded from orange (2000) to blue (2019). The light gray trajectories represent the other 51 countries in this analysis.

Relative progress. As measured by the percentage change in no-DTP metrics between 2000 and 2019, Bangladesh and Burundi achieved the largest relative reductions in no-DTP prevalence (Figure 2; Table 2). National and subnational no-DTP trends are illustrated in Supplementary Figure S1D,E.

In 2000, estimated national prevalence of no-DTP was 8.8% in Bangladesh, already below the 10% target set forth by the Global Vaccine Action Plan for 2020 [44]. However, by 2019, the percentage of under-one children with no doses of DTP fell to 0.8% in Bangladesh, a 98.0% decline since 2000. Subnational gaps in Bangladesh fell by 99.9% since 2000, narrowing from a 14.4 percentage-point difference for the 5th and 95th percentiles across districts in 2000 (i.e., 3.3% to 17.7%) to approximately 0.01 percentage-points in 2019. Absolute subnational gaps began narrowing faster after about 2012 (Supplementary Figure S1D).

For Burundi, national no-DTP estimates were 18.4% in 2000, but decreased to 2.3% in 2019—an 87.3% reduction. Across Burundi's communes in 2000, there was a 17.1 percentage-point difference for the 5th and 95th percentiles in no-DTP prevalence (i.e., 10.2% to 27.3%). By 2019, this subnational gap fell to 2.4 percentage points, representing an 85.9% decline across communes at the 5th and 95th percentile (i.e., 1.5% to 3.9%). Progress accelerated after 2005 (Figure 2, Supplementary Figure S1E), when the country's 13-year civil war ended [45].

Table 2 details these estimates for 2000, 2019, and across change metrics for all 56 countries, while Figure 2 depicts trajectories for no-DTP across national levels and subnational gaps for potential exemplars in reducing zero-dose children for each year between 2000 to 2019.

3.3. Comparing Divergent No-DTP Trajectories since 2000 for Select Locations

Focusing on the four Gavi Learning Hub countries—Nigeria, Mali, Uganda, and Bangladesh—we mapped their no-DTP trajectories from 2000 to 2019 against potential exemplars in reducing zero-dose children (Figure 3); the exception was Bangladesh, which achieved among the largest relative reductions in national no-DTP prevalence and subnational gaps since 2000. Accordingly, Figure 3 excludes Bangladesh.

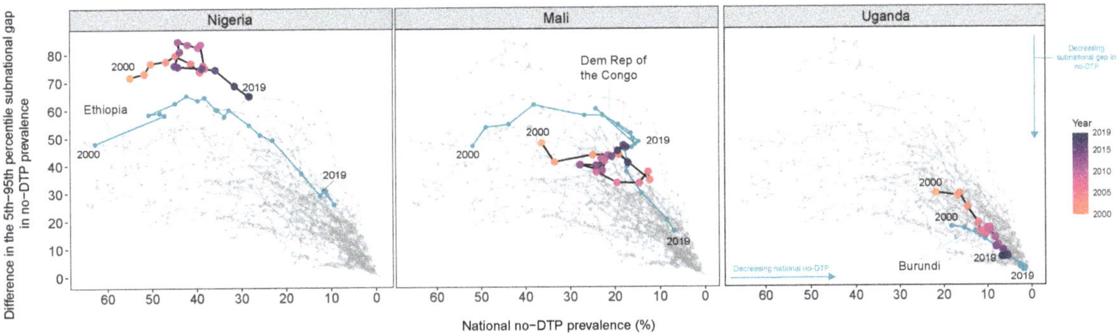

Figure 3. Comparing Gavi Learning Hub country no-DTP trajectories since 2000 to potential exemplars in reducing zero-dose children. Bangladesh, a Gavi Learning Hub country, was identified as potential exemplar based on its marked progress on relative no-DTP metrics of change (Figure 2). Accordingly, we focus on Nigeria, Mali, and Uganda here. National no-DTP prevalence is represented on the x-axis and the subnational gap (as measured by the difference between the 5th and 95th percentile no-DTP prevalence across second-level administrative units) is represented on the y-axis. Each corner represents an extreme for each of these no-DTP metrics, with the lower right-hand corner—low national no-DTP prevalence and low subnational inequality—being the direction in which every location should strive to reach to equitably reduce no-DTP prevalence. Trends in the two no-DTP metrics for the Gavi Learning Hub countries are highlighted in black, with each circle representing a year from 2000 to 2019 that is color-coded from orange (2000) to blue (2019). The teal trends represent trajectories for the potential exemplars in reducing zero-dose children based on their absolute or relative progress since 2000. The light gray trajectories represent the other countries in this analysis.

For Nigeria, Ethiopia was its closest 'neighbor' in terms of national no-DTP prevalence in 2000—55.5% in Nigeria and 63.4% in Ethiopia—with diverging no-DTP trajectories through 2019 (i.e., 28.9% in Nigeria and 11.7% in Ethiopia). From 2000 to 2019, Nigeria consistently had among the highest subnational no-DTP disparities in the world; even in 2000, when Ethiopia had the fourth highest subnational gap in no-DTP among included countries (47.9 percentage points; Table 2), Nigeria's subnational gap was more than 20 percentage points higher (71.7; Table 2). Nonetheless, given how Ethiopia markedly reduced no-DTP subnational gaps at the same time trends in Nigeria's subnational disparities more or less stagnated, they may be well-aligned for cross-country learning.

For Mali, the DRC was its closest 'neighbor' for subnational no-DTP prevalence gaps in 2000, with Mali experiencing a 47.8 percentage-point gap and the DRC having a 46.8 percentage-point disparity. By 2019, Mali still had a subnational gap exceeding

40 percentage points (40.5, Table 2) while the DRC reduced its subnational gap to 16.0 (Table 2). National no-DTP prevalence was more variable for Mali and the DRC, with Mali's national no-DTP levels registering far lower than the DRC's in 2000 (36.4% and 51.9%, respectively) but then only moderately declining to 17.1% by 2019. In contrast, the DRC's national no-DTP prevalence decreased to 6.9% in 2019. Yet the DRC's no-DTP metrics from 2010–2015—the time before the country accelerated no-DTP reductions—parallel Mali's 2019 no-DTP measures. Accordingly, this more recent time period may support optimal cross-country learning for Mali.

For Uganda, Burundi aligned most closely to its 2000 no-DTP measures but showed divergences by 2019. In 2000, national no-DTP prevalence was 21.9% in Uganda and 18.4% in Burundi; by 2019, their no-DTP estimates were 6.7% and 2.3%, respectively (Table 2). Subnational gap trends were less similar for these two countries, with Burundi's no-DTP subnational gap in 2000 being narrower (17.1 percentage points) than that of Uganda's (29.2 percentage points). Each country recorded sizeable declines in subnational no-DTP gaps, with Uganda's falling to 6.3 percentage points and Burundi's to 2.4. In many ways, both Uganda and Burundi could offer meaningful lessons around reducing subnational disparities among unvaccinated children.

4. Discussion

With this analysis, we offer a novel application of positive-outlier methods for identifying potential exemplars in reducing zero-dose children since 2000. The DRC, Ethiopia, and India showed among the largest absolute declines in both national no-DTP prevalence and subnational gaps between 2000 and 2019, while Bangladesh and Burundi demonstrated the largest percentage decreases in national no-DTP prevalence and subnational gaps during that time. Given the range of starting points, local contexts, and health system structures in these five countries, it is quite possible that the strategies used, and corresponding lessons learned in improving childhood vaccination—specifically around expanding service reach to unvaccinated children—may be applicable (or at least adaptable) to other settings. As highlighted by the so-called "neighborhood" analysis, comparing divergent no-DTP trajectories among peer locations could support deeper study around what catalyzed faster progress for some places—and how those lessons could be applied elsewhere. The combination of this positive outlier methodology and cross-country platforms supported by the Gavi Learning Hubs offers unique opportunities to better understand 'what works' for accelerating progress in reaching unvaccinated children worldwide.

Considering positive outliers—or potential exemplars—in reducing no-DTP prevalence for both absolute and relative progress can better reflect the range of successful strategies implemented from a range of different no-DTP prevalence starting points. After all, the types of programmatic and policy decisions that may occur when more than 30–50% of under-one children have had no doses of DTP could differ from those occurring when high zero-dose communities are more clustered and national levels of no-DTP are well below 10%. In health service delivery, these differences may unfold around more widespread intervention introduction and scale-up activities (e.g., addressing key infrastructure and personnel gaps that would otherwise impede adoption; mass mobilization and campaign-style outreach efforts) versus more tailored service provision to individuals or communities who still lack access to or demand for an intervention (e.g., hard-to-reach and hard-to-vaccinate populations [46]). For instance, in 2000, the DRC and Ethiopia started among the highest national levels of no-DTP observed across included countries in this study, as well as moderate-to-high levels of subnational gaps. Better understanding how the DRC and Ethiopia substantially reduced no-DTP metrics by 2019 could strengthen strategies adapted for countries that started at similar no-DTP measures in 2000 but had minimal or less pronounced reductions (e.g., Nigeria, Chad, Somalia).

Despite their marked progress since 2000, further improvements in vaccination reach and uptake are needed in the DRC, Ethiopia, India, and other countries still experiencing large populations of unvaccinated children. Accordingly, it is possible that lessons learned from countries with exceptional relative reductions from 2000 to 2019 could be applicable to countries such as the DRC, Ethiopia, and India today; after all, 2019 no-DTP estimates for the latter countries are quite similar to the 2000 estimates for countries such as Bangladesh and Burundi. For Bangladesh, reductions in national no-DTP and subnational gaps nearly paralleled each other time, charting a path toward nearly 0% no-DTP nationally and negligible subnational differences by 2019. These trends may reflect the country's concerted efforts to better reach rural communities with lower levels of vaccination [47], among other immunization and primary care strengthening interventions. For Burundi, levels of and subnational gaps in no-DTP markedly declined after the end of its civil war in 2005 [45]. From 2006 to 2010, Burundi adopted nationwide performance-based financing initiatives focused on improving child and maternal care [48], actions that have been associated with higher vaccination rates, particularly among the poor [49]. To better understand how different interventions and strategies may optimally align with current needs and barriers to vaccination, it is crucial to more deeply examine the programs and contexts in which past gains have occurred.

There is ample opportunity—and need—to characterize what drives successful vaccine delivery and uptake across the spectrum of past and current challenges, particularly around vaccination inequalities. One key consideration that emerged from this analysis involves the pathways by which no-DTP changed both nationally and sub-nationally from 2000 to 2019. Particularly among countries that started with higher levels of no-DTP (e.g., Nigeria and Mali; Ethiopia, and the DRC), subnational gaps often remained unchanged or increased while national no-DTP prevalence began improving. Such pathways suggest that explicit equity program targets and implementation practices may not occur until later. Other countries, including India and Bangladesh, had more consistent declines for both metrics from 2000 to 2019—a potential signal into the ways in which countries are concurrently addressing both national vaccination priorities and at least geographic inequalities. Nonetheless, it is also possible that countries such as India and Bangladesh experienced similar pathways of minimal changes in or rising subnational inequality amid decreasing national no-DTP prior to 2000. Developing a more formalized characterization or framework around 'pathways of progress' toward greater vaccination equity should be considered in future studies, both by geography and across other crucial factors (e.g., gender, wealth, education, religion, ethnicity).

While assessing progress metrics is a necessary first step to better identify potential exemplars in reducing zero-dose burdens, they alone cannot shed light on what countries have executed and how such actions were associated with further improvements. Formally applying methods such as that of the EGH program, with qualitative examination of policy and programs alongside quantitative analyses around drivers of progress [32], should be prioritized for countries and/or subnational locations with notable advances in reducing zero-dose children. Furthermore, the learning and evaluation platform offered through the Gavi Learning Hubs [43], wherein characteristics of immunization programs and factors contributing to their impact will be examined in prospective manner with country researchers and leadership, will enable greater cross-country or subnational engagement around what works to reach unvaccinated children across contexts. This is particularly important for larger countries where subnational locations started at similar starting points but experienced different trajectories over time. For instance, in Nigeria, bordering states Kaduna and Plateau had fairly high levels of no-DTP prevalence in 2000 (69.4% and 50.6%, respectively; Supplementary Figure S2A). By 2019, Plateau decreased its no-DTP prevalence to 14.5%, whereas Kaduna reduced no-DTP prevalence to 31.9%. Another pair of bordering states—Kogi and Enugu—had no-DTP prevalence of 48.1% and 40.7% in 2000; by 2019, Engu recorded a much larger decline by 2019 (to 7.5%) whereas Kogi still exceeded 20% no-DTP prevalence. In Ethiopia, three regions—Afar, Somali, Benshangual-Gomez—had the country's highest no-DTP prevalence in 2000, at 75% or higher, followed by Oromia (69.3%) (Supplementary Figure S2B). By 2019, Benshangual-Gomez and Oromia reduced regional levels of no-DTP to 8.3% and 11.1%. Although Afar and Somali also recorded substantive declines in overall no-DTP prevalence, each region still had no-DTP prevalence exceeding 25%—and experienced widening gaps in no-DTP among zones. Given these trends and patterns, it is likely that many countries—especially larger ones—could benefit from so-called neighborhood analyses and positive outlier research at the subnational level.

Past work has sought to synthesize and/or assess particular characteristics of successful immunization programs; nonetheless, few studies have expressly focused on both zero-dose children and incorporating mixed-methodologies with a positive outlier lens. For example, qualitative research in Senegal, Zambia, and Nepal points to factors including strong community engagement, integrated delivery, adaptive service provision, and robust data systems as central to improving and/or maintaining high levels of DTP1 and/or DTP3 [35,50–52]. However, the degree to which these approaches are fully transferable to communities with high zero-dose burdens remains unclear. Integrated service delivery, particularly for key primary care interventions for mothers and infants, may have an important role in addressing zero-dose burdens given the high overlap of missing vaccine doses with other essential health services [11]. Strengthening community engagement may require taking a longer-term lens and multifaceted investments, especially in areas of prolonged conflict and/or distrust of health systems and providers. Innovative programs such as the DRC's Mashako Plan, which was launched in 2018 and has sought to improve vaccination completion rates among select provinces through a mixture of supervision support, supply chain improvements, and monitoring efforts [53], may also provide valuable implementation lessons for countries with equally large and/or dispersed populations.

It is worth noting that declines in no-DTP prevalence—and thus increased coverage of DTP1, a marker of program reach—do not inherently equate to gains in broader program retention or complete immunization. For instance, in much of Ethiopia, DTP3 coverage has not improved in parallel amid sizeable increases in DTP1 [7,54,55]. This means that while more children are being reached by vaccination services—an unequivocally crucial milestone—an increasing percentage of them remain under-vaccinated and thus may still be vulnerable to preventable disease. Although some parts of immunization programs can support both vaccination initiation and completion well (e.g., sufficient availability of qualified health workers, strong supply, and cold chain systems), other factors can differentially affect how or whether children finish vaccination series after receiving their first doses [7,56,57]: the availability of defaulter tracking systems, provider-client relationships and trust, flexibility in scheduling for multiple vaccine doses and/or other health services, among others. As global immunization agendas such as IA2030 [36] and Gavi 5.0 [37] rightly bring more attention to zero-dose populations and programs strategies to reach them, it is crucial that political and funding commitments around addressing gaps in under-vaccination also are maintained.

Limitations

This analysis is subject to a number of limitations. First, this study focuses on changes in geographic inequalities at the second administrative level or higher, which results in representing only one of many critical factors that contribute to inequities in immunization delivery [19]. While geographic location can serve as a proxy for determinants also associated with location (e.g., district-level program funding levels, relative remoteness) [58], geography on its own cannot appropriately approximate the mechanisms by which gender, ethnicity, education, wealth, religious affiliation, and other individual, household, or community characteristics affect childhood vaccination [4,8,12–14,16,18]. It is also very possible that reductions in geographic inequalities do not consistently correspond with decreases in vaccination inequalities by these other key drivers of disparities across locations or do so consistently over time. Accordingly, it is critical to prioritize future research and analyses that explicitly assess how these trends in inequality may correlate with each other.

Second, focusing on the second-administrative level likely masks important differences experienced at more granular levels (e.g., within communities), [38,54] and thus potentially could obscure a more nuanced understanding of the localized sociocultural and/or economic contributors to higher levels of zero-dose children. Future analyses should explore alternative geographic levels or areal operationalizations (e.g., 5 × 5 km pixel estimates rather than administrative boundaries) to further characterize the distribution and magnitude of vaccination inequalities in a given location.

Third, country-to-country comparisons of subnational gaps and changes in these gaps over time may be affected by a country's total number of second-level administrative units rather than meaningful differences in vaccination equity at comparable areal units. For instance, subnational gaps in no-DTP may seem higher among in a country divided into more second-level administrative units than those with fewer units [59]. At least for the present analysis, having more (or fewer) second-level administrative units does not appear to be strongly related to 5th/95th percentile gap measures (i.e., $r = 0.47$ in 2000 and $r = 0.38$ in 2019) or change metrics from 2000 to 2019 (i.e., $r = -0.17$ for absolute change and $r = 0.03$ for percentage change). Since first- or second-level administrative units are often meaningful for health program implementation (e.g., district health authorities), we viewed using country administrative units as having more benefits and relevance than the potential drawbacks around variable subnational geographies. However, exploring alternative units of analysis (e.g., standardized pixel units) could be beneficial for future work.

Fourth, we opted to use estimates from IHME for this analysis rather than administrative data sources (e.g., DHIS2) or alternative sources (e.g., WUENIC estimates). Because the primary goal of this study was to be able to directly compare national and subnational levels and trends in no-DTP across countries, IHME estimates provided the greatest number of countries with subnational estimates for the full time period (2000–2019).

Fifth, DTP estimates draw from household surveys and other data sources in which groups or communities with higher rates of unvaccinated children may be systematically under-represented (e.g., displaced or highly mobile populations). Accordingly, current no-DTP estimates may not fully capture the 'true' magnitude or trends in zero-dose children among populations with disproportionately high vulnerabilities and risks for not being vaccinated.

Sixth, the time period of analysis focused on 2000 to 2019, and thus the identification of potential exemplars may be sensitive to estimated levels of childhood vaccination at either end of the 19-year range. Importantly, this analysis does not account for the ongoing effects of the COVID-19 pandemic, of which has had differential impacts across countries and communities since March 2020 [3,60,61]. Relatedly, these analyses do not reflect improvements in or worsening of conflict since 2019, such as in the Tigray region in Ethiopia [62].

Lastly, these analyses currently lack deeper contextual information from and by the communities most affected by higher rates of un- and under-vaccination. Our aim is to receive critical feedback on the potential applications of these positive-outlier methods for cross-country learning and synthesis around what works to reduce high rates of zero-dose prevalence, and to work with country and regional leadership to improve these approaches going forward.

5. Conclusions

Recognizing where exceptional progress in reducing zero-dose children has occurred is the first step toward better understanding what countries did to attain such improvements. Such insights then can inform strategy adaptions to other settings, and further reinforce successful strategies in places that achieved large reductions historically but still have large populations of unvaccinated children today. Characterizing pathways to greater vaccination equity, as well ensuring mechanisms by which effective knowledge translation and cross-country learning can be supported, will strengthen efforts toward ensuring all children can fully benefit from vaccines.

Supplementary Materials: The following supporting information can be downloaded at: https://www.mdpi.com/article/10.3390/vaccines11030647/s1, Table S1. Initial countries considered for the present analysis but were excluded for not meeting inclusion criteria; Figure S1. National and subnational trends in the prevalence of no-DTP children, 2000-2019, in the Democratic Republic of the Congo (A), Ethiopia (B), India (C), Bangladesh (D), and Burundi (E); Figure S2. Subnational no-DTP prevalence in Nigeria (A) and Ethiopia (B), 2000–2019.

Author Contributions: Conceptualization and Methodology: N.F., G.C.C., G.I., D.E.P. and H.W.R. Formal Analysis: N.F. Writing—Original Draft Preparation: N.F.; Writing—Review and Editing: N.F., G.C.C., G.I., D.E.P. and H.W.R. Visualization: N.F. and D.E.P. Supervision: G.I. and D.E.P. All authors have read and agreed to the published version of the manuscript.

Funding: This research received no external funding.

Institutional Review Board Statement: Not applicable.

Informed Consent Statement: Not applicable.

Data Availability Statement: Vaccine estimates used in this analysis are currently unpublished estimates from the Institute for Health Metrics and Evaluation (IHME). Data may be shared upon request to the corresponding author and IHME.

Acknowledgments: We thank Jonathan Mosser, Emily Hauser, Sam Rolfe, and Jason Nguyen from the Institute for Health Metrics and Evaluation for providing the estimates of childhood vaccination used in this study. We thank the following individuals from Gates Ventures, for their programmatic support and assistance: Patrick Y Liu, Jordan-Tate Thomas, Rowan Hussein, and Ryan Fitzgerald.

Conflicts of Interest: N.F., G.I. and D.E.P. are paid employees of Gates Ventures, which coordinates the Exemplars in Global Health (EGH) program. N.F., G.I., and D.E.P. previously worked at the Institute for Metrics and Evaluation (IHME): September 2008–2011 and February 2013–June 2022 for N.F.; August 2014–July 2020 for G.I.; and June 2009–February 2019 for D.E.P., G.C.C. and H.W.R. are employed by Gavi, the Vaccine Alliance. They had total freedom to express their views, which do not necessarily reflect those of Gavi.

References

1. Greenwood, B. The contribution of vaccination to global health: Past, present and future. *Philos. Trans. R. Soc. B Biol. Sci.* **2014**, *369*, 20130433. [CrossRef] [PubMed]
2. Li, X.; Mukandavire, C.; Cucunubá, Z.M.; Londono, S.E.; Abbas, K.; Clapham, H.E.; Jit, M.; Johnson, H.L.; Papadopoulos, T.; Vynnycky, E.; et al. Estimating the Health Impact of Vaccination against Ten Pathogens in 98 Low-Income and Middle-Income Countries from 2000 to 2030: A Modelling Study. *Lancet* **2021**, *397*, 398–408. [CrossRef] [PubMed]
3. WHO; UNICEF. *Progress and Challenges with Achieving Universal Immunization Coverage: 2021 WHO/UNICEF Estimates of National Immunization Coverage (WUENIC)*; WHO: Geneva, Switzerland, 2022.
4. Wendt, A.; Santos, T.M.; Cata-Preta, B.O.; Arroyave, L.; Hogan, D.R.; Mengistu, T.; Barros, A.J.D.; Victora, C.G. Exposure of Zero-Dose Children to Multiple Deprivation: Analyses of Data from 80 Low- and Middle-Income Countries. *Vaccines* **2022**, *10*, 1568. [CrossRef]
5. Wigley, A.; Lorin, J.; Hogan, D.; Utazi, C.E.; Hagedorn, B.; Dansereau, E.; Tatem, A.J.; Tejedor-Garavito, N. Estimates of the Number and Distribution of Zero-Dose and under-Immunised Children across Remote-Rural, Urban, and Conflict-Affected Settings in Low and Middle-Income Countries. *PLOS Glob. Public Health* **2022**, *2*, e0001126. [CrossRef]
6. Ozigbu, C.E.; Olatosi, B.; Li, Z.; Hardin, J.W.; Hair, N.L. Correlates of Zero-Dose Vaccination Status among Children Aged 12–59 Months in Sub-Saharan Africa: A Multilevel Analysis of Individual and Contextual Factors. *Vaccines* **2022**, *10*, 1052. [CrossRef]
7. Rainey, J.J.; Watkins, M.; Ryman, T.K.; Sandhu, P.; Bo, A.; Banerjee, K. Reasons Related to Non-Vaccination and under-Vaccination of Children in Low and Middle Income Countries: Findings from a Systematic Review of the Published Literature, 1999–2009. *Vaccine* **2011**, *29*, 8215–8221. [CrossRef]
8. Utazi, C.E.; Pannell, O.; Aheto, J.M.K.; Wigley, A.; Tejedor-Garavito, N.; Wunderlich, J.; Hagedorn, B.; Hogan, D.; Tatem, A.J. Assessing the Characteristics of Un- and under-Vaccinated Children in Low- and Middle-Income Countries: A Multi-Level Cross-Sectional Study. *PLOS Glob. Public Health* **2022**, *2*, e0000244. [CrossRef]
9. Soura, A.B.; Mberu, B.; Elungata, P.; Lankoande, B.; Millogo, R.; Beguy, D.; Compaore, Y. Understanding Inequities in Child Vaccination Rates among the Urban Poor: Evidence from Nairobi and Ouagadougou Health and Demographic Surveillance Systems. *J. Urban Health* **2015**, *92*, 39–54. [CrossRef]
10. Cata-Preta, B.O.; Santos, T.M.; Mengistu, T.; Hogan, D.R.; Barros, A.J.D.; Victora, C.G. Zero-Dose Children and the Immunisation Cascade: Understanding Immunisation Pathways in Low and Middle-Income Countries. *Vaccine* **2021**, *39*, 4564–4570. [CrossRef]
11. Santos, T.M.; Cata-Preta, B.O.; Mengistu, T.; Victora, C.G.; Hogan, D.R.; Barros, A.J.D. Assessing the Overlap between Immunisation and Other Essential Health Interventions in 92 Low- and Middle-Income Countries Using Household Surveys: Opportunities for Expanding Immunisation and Primary Health Care. *E Clin. Med.* **2021**, *42*, 101196. [CrossRef]

12. Santos, T.M.; Cata-Preta, B.O.; Victora, C.G.; Barros, A.J.D. Finding Children with High Risk of Non-Vaccination in 92 Low- and Middle-Income Countries: A Decision Tree Approach. *Vaccines* **2021**, *9*, 646. [CrossRef] [PubMed]
13. Santos, T.M.; Cata-Preta, B.O.; Wendt, A.; Arroyave, L.; Hogan, D.R.; Mengistu, T.; Barros, A.J.D.; Victora, C.G. Religious Affiliation as a Driver of Immunization Coverage: Analyses of Zero-Dose Vaccine Prevalence in 66 Low- and Middle-Income Countries. *Front. Public Health* **2022**, *10*, 977512. [CrossRef]
14. Bergen, N.; Cata-Preta, B.O.; Schlotheuber, A.; Santos, T.M.; Danovaro-Holliday, M.C.; Mengistu, T.; Sodha, S.V.; Hogan, D.R.; Barros, A.J.D.; Hosseinpoor, A.R. Economic-Related Inequalities in Zero-Dose Children: A Study of Non-Receipt of Diphtheria–Tetanus–Pertussis Immunization Using Household Health Survey Data from 89 Low- and Middle-Income Countries. *Vaccines* **2022**, *10*, 633. [CrossRef] [PubMed]
15. Cata-Preta, B.O.; Santos, T.M.; Wendt, A.; Hogan, D.R.; Mengistu, T.; Barros, A.J.D.; Victora, C.G. Ethnic Disparities in Immunisation: Analyses of Zero-Dose Prevalence in 64 Countries. *BMJ Glob. Health* **2022**, *7*, e008833. [CrossRef] [PubMed]
16. Johns, N.E.; Santos, T.M.; Arroyave, L.; Cata-Preta, B.O.; Heidari, S.; Kirkby, K.; Munro, J.; Schlotheuber, A.; Wendt, A.; O'Brien, K.; et al. Gender-Related Inequality in Childhood Immunization Coverage: A Cross-Sectional Analysis of DTP3 Coverage and Zero-Dose DTP Prevalence in 52 Countries Using the SWPER Global Index. *Vaccines* **2022**, *10*, 988. [CrossRef]
17. Wendt, A.; Santos, T.M.; Cata-Preta, B.O.; Costa, J.C.; Mengistu, T.; Hogan, D.R.; Victora, C.G.; Barros, A.J.D. Children of More Empowered Women Are Less Likely to Be Left without Vaccination in Low- and Middle-Income Countries: A Global Analysis of 50 DHS Surveys. *J. Glob. Health* **2022**, *12*, 04022. [CrossRef] [PubMed]
18. Tracey, G.; Olivia, B.; Jean, M.; Megan, H.; Sagri, S. Why Does Gender Matter for Immunization? *Vaccine* **2022**. [CrossRef] [PubMed]
19. Ali, H.A.; Hartner, A.-M.; Echeverria-Londono, S.; Roth, J.; Li, X.; Abbas, K.; Portnoy, A.; Vynnycky, E.; Woodruff, K.; Ferguson, N.M.; et al. Vaccine Equity in Low and Middle Income Countries: A Systematic Review and Meta-Analysis. *Int. J. Equity Health* **2022**, *21*, 82. [CrossRef]
20. De Figueiredo, A.; Simas, C.; Karafillakis, E.; Paterson, P.; Larson, H.J. Mapping Global Trends in Vaccine Confidence and Investigating Barriers to Vaccine Uptake: A Large-Scale Retrospective Temporal Modelling Study. *Lancet* **2020**, *396*, 898–908. [CrossRef]
21. Bradley, E.H.; Curry, L.A.; Ramanadhan, S.; Rowe, L.; Nembhard, I.M.; Krumholz, H.M. Research in Action: Using Positive Deviance to Improve Quality of Health Care. *Implement. Sci.* **2009**, *4*, 25. [CrossRef]
22. Lewis, T.P.; Aryal, A.; Mehata, S.; Thapa, A.; Yousafzai, A.K.; Kruk, M.E. Best and Worst Performing Health Facilities: A Positive Deviance Analysis of Perceived Drivers of Primary Care Performance in Nepal. *Soc. Sci. Med.* **2022**, *309*, 115251. [CrossRef] [PubMed]
23. Mabuchi, S.; Sesan, T.; Bennett, S.C. Pathways to High and Low Performance: Factors Differentiating Primary Care Facilities under Performance-Based Financing in Nigeria. *Health Policy Plan.* **2018**, *33*, 41–58. [CrossRef] [PubMed]
24. Bradley, E.H.; Byam, P.; Alpern, R.; Thompson, J.W.; Zerihun, A.; Abeb, Y.; Curry, L.A. A Systems Approach to Improving Rural Care in Ethiopia. *PLoS ONE* **2012**, *7*, e35042. [CrossRef]
25. Fetene, N.; Linnander, E.; Fekadu, B.; Alemu, H.; Omer, H.; Canavan, M.; Smith, J.; Berman, P.; Bradley, E. The Ethiopian Health Extension Program and Variation in Health Systems Performance: What Matters? *PLoS ONE* **2016**, *11*, e0156438. [CrossRef]
26. Halstead, S.B.; Walsh, J.A.; Warren, K.S. *Good Health at Low Cost: Proceedings of a Conference Held at Bellagio, Italy, 29 April–3 May, 1985*; Rockefeller Foundation: New York, NY, USA, 1985.
27. Balabanova, D.; Mills, A.; Conteh, L.; Akkazieva, B.; Banteyerga, H.; Dash, U.; Gilson, L.; Harmer, A.; Ibraimova, A.; Islam, Z.; et al. Good Health at Low Cost 25 Years on: Lessons for the Future of Health Systems Strengthening. *Lancet* **2013**, *381*, 2118–2133. [CrossRef] [PubMed]
28. *World Bank Business Unusual: Accelerating Progress Towards Universal Health Coverage*; World Bank: Washington, DC, USA, 2018.
29. Wang, H.; Naghavi, M.; Allen, C.; Barber, R.M.; Bhutta, Z.A.; Carter, A.; Casey, D.C.; Charlson, F.J.; Chen, A.Z.; Coates, M.M.; et al. Global, Regional, and National Life Expectancy, All-Cause Mortality, and Cause-Specific Mortality for 249 Causes of Death, 1980–2015: A Systematic Analysis for the Global Burden of Disease Study 2015. *Lancet* **2016**, *388*, 1459–1544. [CrossRef]
30. Wang, H.; Bhutta, Z.A.; Coates, M.M.; Coggeshall, M.; Dandona, L.; Diallo, K.; Franca, E.B.; Fraser, M.; Fullman, N.; Gething, P.W.; et al. Global, Regional, National, and Selected Subnational Levels of Stillbirths, Neonatal, Infant, and under-5 Mortality, 1980–2015: A Systematic Analysis for the Global Burden of Disease Study 2015. *Lancet* **2016**, *388*, 1725–1774. [CrossRef]
31. Lim, S.S.; Allen, K.; Bhutta, Z.A.; Dandona, L.; Forouzanfar, M.H.; Fullman, N.; Gething, P.W.; Goldberg, E.M.; Hay, S.I.; Holmberg, M.; et al. Measuring the Health-Related Sustainable Development Goals in 188 Countries: A Baseline Analysis from the Global Burden of Disease Study 2015. *Lancet* **2016**, *388*, 1813–1850. [CrossRef]
32. Carter, A.; Akseer, N.; Ho, K.; Rothschild, O.; Bose, N.; Binagwaho, A.; Hirschhorn, L.R.; Price, M.; Muther, K.; Panjabi, R.; et al. A Framework for Identifying and Learning from Countries That Demonstrated Exemplary Performance in Improving Health Outcomes and Systems. *BMJ Global. Health* **2020**, *5*, e002938. [CrossRef]
33. Exemplars in Global Health. Available online: https://www.exemplars.health/ (accessed on 28 January 2023).
34. Akseer, N.; Vaivada, T.; Rothschild, O.; Ho, K.; Bhutta, Z.A. Understanding Multifactorial Drivers of Child Stunting Reduction in Exemplar Countries: A Mixed-Methods Approach. *Am. J. Clin. Nutr.* **2020**, *112*, 792S–805S. [CrossRef]
35. Bednarczyk, R.A.; Hester, K.A.; Dixit, S.M.; Ellis, A.S.; Escoffery, C.; Kilembe, W.; Micek, K.; Sakas, Z.M.; Sarr, M.; Freeman, M.C. Exemplars in Vaccine Delivery Protocol: A Case-Study-Based Identification and Evaluation of Critical Factors in Achieving High

and Sustained Childhood Immunisation Coverage in Selected Low-Income and Lower-Middle-Income Countries. *BMJ Open* **2022**, *12*, e058321. [CrossRef] [PubMed]
36. World Health Organization (WHO). *Immunization Agenda 2030: A Global Strategy to Leave No One Behind*; WHO: Geneva, Switzerland, 2020.
37. Gavi, the Vaccine Alliance. *Gavi Strategy Phase 5 (2021–2025)*; Gavi: Geneva, Switzerland, 2019.
38. Mosser, J.F.; Gagne-Maynard, W.; Rao, P.C.; Osgood-Zimmerman, A.; Fullman, N.; Graetz, N.; Burstein, R.; Updike, R.L.; Liu, P.Y.; Ray, S.E.; et al. Mapping Diphtheria-Pertussis-Tetanus Vaccine Coverage in Africa, 2000–2016: A Spatial and Temporal Modelling Study. *Lancet* **2019**, *393*, 1843–1855. [CrossRef] [PubMed]
39. World Bank New Country Classifications by Income Level: 2019–2020. Available online: https://blogs.worldbank.org/opendata/new-country-classifications-income-level-2019-2020 (accessed on 28 January 2023).
40. Gavi the Vaccine Alliance. Gavi Country Hub. Available online: https://www.gavi.org/programmes-impact/country-hub (accessed on 28 January 2023).
41. Maphosa, T. Gavi Country Programmes Update. In Proceedings of the Gavi Board Meeting, Geneva, Switzerland, 7–8 December 2022.
42. R Core Team. *R: A Language and Environment for Statistical Computing*; The R Foundation: Vienna, Austria, 2018.
43. Gavi, the Vaccine Alliance. *Learning System Strategy: Responding to the Increased Evidence Needs Required to Successfully Implement Gavi's Strategy for 2021–2025*; Gavi: Geneva, Switzerland, 2022.
44. World Health Organization (WHO). *Global Vaccine Action Plan 2011–2020*; WHO: Geneva, Switzerland, 2013.
45. Cailhol, J.; Mathole, T.; Parsons, A.; Sanders, D.; Kandondo, D.; Ndayiragije, I.; Niyongabo, T. Burundi: Building a Health System Together with Global Health Initiatives, in the Aftermath of War. *Key Acron.* **2007**, *2*, 8.
46. Ozawa, S.; Yemeke, T.T.; Evans, D.R.; Pallas, S.E.; Wallace, A.S.; Lee, B.Y. Defining Hard-to-Reach Populations for Vaccination. *Vaccine* **2019**, *37*, 5525–5534. [CrossRef]
47. Uddin, M.J.; Saha, N.C.; Islam, Z.; Khan, I.A.; Shamsuzzaman; Quaiyum, M.A.; Koehlmoos, T.P. Improving Low Coverage of Child Immunization in Rural Hard-to-Reach Areas of Bangladesh: Findings from a Project Using Multiple Interventions. *Vaccine* **2012**, *30*, 168–179. [CrossRef]
48. Busogoro, J.F.; Beith, A. *Pay for Performance for Improved Health In Burundi*; P4P Case Studies; USAID: Washington, DC, USA, 2010.
49. Bonfrer, I.; Van de Poel, E.; Van Doorslaer, E. The Effects of Performance Incentives on the Utilization and Quality of Maternal and Child Care in Burundi. *Soc. Sci. Med.* **2014**, *123*, 96–104. [CrossRef]
50. Micek, K.; Hester, K.A.; Chanda, C.; Darwar, R.; Dounebaine, B.; Ellis, A.S.; Keskinocak, P.; Leslie, A.; Manyando, M.; Sililo Manyando, M.; et al. Critical Success Factors for Routine Immunization Performance: A Case Study of Zambia 2000 to 2018. *Vaccine X* **2022**, *11*, 100166. [CrossRef]
51. Sakas, Z.; Hester, K.A.; Rodriguez, K.; Diatta, S.A.; Ellis, A.S.; Gueye, D.M.; Matapano, D.; Mboup, P.S.; Ogutu, E.A.; Yang, C.; et al. Critical Success Factors for High Routine Immunization Performance: A Case Study of Senegal. *medRxiv* **2022**. [CrossRef]
52. Hester, K.A.; Sakas, Z.; Ellis, A.S.; Bose, A.S.; Darwar, R.; Gautam, J.; Jaishwal, C.; James, H.; Keskinocak, P.; Nazzal, D.; et al. Critical Success Factors for High Routine Immunization Performance: A Case Study of Nepal. *Vaccine X* **2022**, *12*, 100214. [CrossRef]
53. Gavi, the Vaccine Alliance. Democratic Republic of Congo Launches Major Vaccination Drive. Available online: https://www.gavi.org/news/media-room/democratic-republic-congo-launches-major-vaccination-drive (accessed on 29 January 2023).
54. Utazi, C.E.; Thorley, J.; Alegana, V.A.; Ferrari, M.J.; Takahashi, S.; Metcalf, C.J.E.; Lessler, J.; Cutts, F.T.; Tatem, A.J. Mapping Vaccination Coverage to Explore the Effects of Delivery Mechanisms and Inform Vaccination Strategies. *Nat. Commun.* **2019**, *10*, 1633. [CrossRef]
55. Kirkby, K.; Bergen, N.; Schlotheuber, A.; Sodha, S.V.; Danovaro-Holliday, M.C.; Hosseinpoor, A.R. Subnational Inequalities in Diphtheria–Tetanus–Pertussis Immunization in 24 Countries in the African Region. *Bull. World Health Organ.* **2021**, *99*, 627–639. [CrossRef] [PubMed]
56. Favin, M.; Steinglass, R.; Fields, R.; Banerjee, K.; Sawhney, M. Why Children Are Not Vaccinated: A Review of the Grey Literature. *Int. Health* **2012**, *4*, 229–238. [CrossRef] [PubMed]
57. Streefland, P.H.; Chowdhury, A.M.; Ramos-Jimenez, P. Quality of Vaccination Services and Social Demand for Vaccinations in Africa and Asia. *Bull. World Health Organ.* **1999**, *77*, 722–730. [PubMed]
58. Hosseinpoor, A.R.; Bergen, N. Area-Based Units of Analysis for Strengthening Health Inequality Monitoring. *Bull. World Health Organ.* **2016**, *94*, 856–858. [CrossRef] [PubMed]
59. Hosseinpoor, A.R.; Bergen, N.; Barros, A.J.D.; Wong, K.L.M.; Boerma, T.; Victora, C.G. Monitoring Subnational Regional Inequalities in Health: Measurement Approaches and Challenges. *Int. J. Equity Health* **2016**, *15*, 18. [CrossRef]
60. Causey, K.; Fullman, N.; Sorensen, R.J.D.; Galles, N.C.; Zheng, P.; Aravkin, A.; Danovaro-Holliday, M.C.; Martinez-Piedra, R.; Sodha, S.V.; Velandia-González, M.P.; et al. Estimating Global and Regional Disruptions to Routine Childhood Vaccine Coverage during the COVID-19 Pandemic in 2020: A Modelling Study. *Lancet* **2021**, *398*, 522–534. [CrossRef]
61. Shet, A.; Carr, K.; Danovaro-Holliday, M.C.; Sodha, S.V.; Prosperi, C.; Wunderlich, J.; Wonodi, C.; Reynolds, H.W.; Mirza, I.; Gacic-Dobo, M.; et al. Impact of the SARS-CoV-2 Pandemic on Routine Immunisation Services: Evidence of Disruption and Recovery from 170 Countries and Territories. *Lancet Glob. Health* **2022**, *10*, e186–e194. [CrossRef]

62. Gesesew, H.; Berhane, K.; Siraj, E.S.; Siraj, D.; Gebregziabher, M.; Gebre, Y.G.; Gebreslassie, S.A.; Amdeslassie, F.; Tesema, A.G.; Siraj, A.; et al. The Impact of War on the Health System of the Tigray Region in Ethiopia: An Assessment. *BMJ Global Health* **2021**, *6*, e007328. [CrossRef]

vaccines

MDPI

Opinion

Recovering from the Unprecedented Backsliding in Immunization Coverage: Learnings from Country Programming in Five Countries through the Past Two Years of COVID-19 Pandemic Disruptions

Anithasree Athiyaman *, Tosin Ajayi *, Faith Mutuku, Fredrick Luwaga, Sarah Bryer, Omotayo Giwa, Shadrack Mngemane, Nnang Nadege Edwige and Leslie Berman

Clinton Health Access Initiative (CHAI), Global Vaccines Delivery Team and Country Offices, Boston, MA 02127, USA
* Correspondence: aathiyaman@clintonhealthaccess.org (A.A.); tajayi@clintonhealthaccess.org (T.A.)

Abstract: Between 2020 and 2021, the COVID-19 pandemic severely strained health systems across countries, leaving millions without access to essential healthcare services. Immunization programs experienced a 'double burden' of challenges: initial pandemic-related lockdowns disrupted access to routine immunization services, while subsequent COVID-19 vaccination efforts shifted often limited resources away from routine services. The latest World Health Organization (WHO) and United Nations Children's Fund (UNICEF) estimates suggest that 25 million children did not receive routine vaccinations in 2021, six million more than in 2019 and the highest number witnessed in nearly two decades. Recovering from this sobering setback requires a united push on several fronts. Intensifying the catch-up of routine immunization services is critical to reach children left behind during the pandemic and bridge large immunity gaps in countries. At the same time, we must strengthen the resilience of immunization systems to withstand future pandemics if we hope to achieve the goals of Immunization Agenda 2030 to ensure vaccinations are available for everyone, everywhere by 2030. In this article, leveraging the key actions for sustainable global immunization progress as a framework, we spotlight examples of strategies used by five countries—Cambodia, Cameroon, Kenya, Nigeria, and Uganda—who have exhibited exemplar performance in strengthening routine immunization programs and restored lost coverage levels in the last two years of the COVID-19 pandemic. The contents of this article will be helpful for countries seeking to maintain, restore, and strengthen their immunization services and catch up missed children in the context of pandemic recovery and to direct their focus toward building back a better resilience of their immunization systems to respond more rapidly and effectively, despite new and emerging challenges.

Keywords: routine immunization; COVID-19 pandemic; coverage backsliding; recovery; Cambodia; Cameroon; Kenya; Nigeria; Uganda

Citation: Athiyaman, A.; Ajayi, T.; Mutuku, F.; Luwaga, F.; Bryer, S.; Giwa, O.; Mngemane, S.; Edwige, N.N.; Berman, L. Recovering from the Unprecedented Backsliding in Immunization Coverage: Learnings from Country Programming in Five Countries through the Past Two Years of COVID-19 Pandemic Disruptions. *Vaccines* **2023**, *11*, 375. https://doi.org/10.3390/vaccines11020375

Academic Editors: Ahmad Reza Hosseinpoor, M. Carolina Danovaro, Devaki Nambiar, Aaron Wallace and Hope Johnson

Received: 14 November 2022
Revised: 16 December 2022
Accepted: 26 December 2022
Published: 7 February 2023

1. Introduction

Between 2020 and 2021, the COVID-19 pandemic severely strained health systems across countries, leaving millions without access to essential healthcare services. Routine Immunization programs experienced a 'double burden' of challenges due to the COVID-19 pandemic and associated disruptions and to the subsequent COVID-19 vaccination efforts shifting often limited resources away from routine services. The latest World Health Organization (WHO) and United Nations Children's Fund (UNICEF) estimates suggest that 25 million children missed routine vaccinations in 2021, six million more than in 2019 and the highest number witnessed in nearly two decades.

Recovering from this sobering setback requires a united push on several fronts. Intensifying the catch-up of routine immunization services is critical to reach children left behind during the pandemic and bridge large immunity gaps in countries. At the same time, we must strengthen the resilience of immunization systems to withstand future pandemics if we hope to achieve the goals of Immunization Agenda 2030 to ensure vaccinations are available for everyone, everywhere by 2030.

2. Materials and Methods

This article spotlights examples of strategies used by five countries—Cambodia, Cameroon, Kenya, Nigeria, and Uganda—that have exhibited exemplar performance in strengthening routine immunization programs and that have restored lost coverage levels back to pre-pandemic levels to identify country-level learnings and inform and support other countries to adopt similar practices. No personal or patient-level health information was gathered for this work, and this work is not considered human subjects research. Coverage data was obtained from WHO-UNICEF and reported at the country-level.

3. Discussions

3.1. The Challenge: Historic Backsliding in Routine Immunization Coverage

Across the world, the COVID-19 pandemic has disrupted essential health services, adversely impacting significant gains in health outcomes achieved in recent decades. This is particularly so for routine immunizations, with recently published WHO-UNICEF estimates showing historic reductions in immunization coverage in 2021, with 25 million children missing out on life-saving vaccines, the highest number since 2006 [1]. The number of 'zero dose children' (those who did not receive any dose of Diphtheria, Tetanus and Pertussis (DTP) containing vaccines) [2] increased sharply from 13 to 18 million during the pandemic period, a shocking 37% increase since 2019. While immunization coverage dropped in all WHO regions, some regions were more affected than others, with coverage dips ranging between 1% in Europe to as high as 9% in South-East Asia.

As a result of this monumental drop in coverage, a disproportionate number of children in low- and middle-income countries are left most vulnerable to vaccine-preventable diseases. With rising immunity gaps, the risk of large outbreaks is imminent, with cases of measles already reported in Africa and Eastern Mediterranean, and wild polio virus 1 (WPV1) detected outside the endemic countries in Asia [3]. This threatens the lives of unprotected children and could be severely disruptive to already over-stretched health services. Furthermore, some specific newly introduced antigens like Human Papillomavirus (HPV) vaccines are also seen to be more adversely impacted and less resilient to these shocks. Over the last two years, HPV vaccine coverage dropped by 15% [1]. Since 2019, 3.5 million eligible girls have not yet received their first dose of HPV vaccine, the highest decline since 2010. The trend is compounded by the fact that 59% of cervical cancer cases occur in countries that have not yet introduced HPV vaccination into their national programs, leaving millions of adolescent girls unprotected against cervical cancer.

Routine immunization programs were impacted by a 'double burden' of managing the disruptive effect of the COVID-19 pandemic as well as the subsequent historic COVID-19 vaccination efforts to improve population immunity against the virus. Nearly all countries reported some form of disruption to routine immunization (RI) services in 2020 and early 2021, with primary and community care among the most affected service delivery settings [4]. In many countries, several planned outreaches and even Supplementary Immunization Activity (SIA) were either suspended or postponed. In early 2021, more than one third of countries (37%) participating in surveys monitoring pandemic impact on health systems still reported disruptions to their routine immunization services in comparison to early 2020 [4].

Despite these sobering trends, some countries improved vaccination coverage during the pandemic—39 countries recovered or almost recovered to pre-pandemic levels in 2021. But over two years, only 24 countries achieved higher coverage in 2021 than in 2019 [5]. This notable progress is attributable to the intensification and mitigation efforts of country programs to maintain and/or resume vaccine delivery to catch up on missed populations.

In some cases, these countries have managed to also attain high COVID-19 vaccination coverage—the fastest and one of the most complex global vaccine campaigns in history.

3.2. The Opportunity: Restoring Coverage and Strengthening Program Resilience

The vulnerability of global immunization systems demonstrates the urgent need to maintain, restore, and strengthen routine immunization systems in order to address the widening immunity gap in the context of the pandemic and build resilience for future shocks. Despite the complexities of managing immunization programs during a continually evolving pandemic, several countries have shown that improving immunization coverage is possible. Documenting and spotlighting learnings from these countries will help other countries to adopt similar practices to increase vaccination equity.

This article presents examples from five selected countries—Cambodia, Cameroon, Kenya, Nigeria, and Uganda—that have either maintained or increased their Diphtheria, Tetanus, and Pertussis–containing vaccine (DTP3) coverage rates in 2021 compared to 2019/20 (see Figure 1). Through strong partnership with the Ministries of Health in these countries, CHAI and immunization partners have witnessed and supported their journey to recovery. Using the key actions for sustaining global immunization progress [6], which highlight the urgent steps necessary for sustaining immunization activities globally as a conceptual framework, we outline several exemplary strategies adopted by these countries over the past two years that contributed to favorable immunization outcomes—also see [File S1].

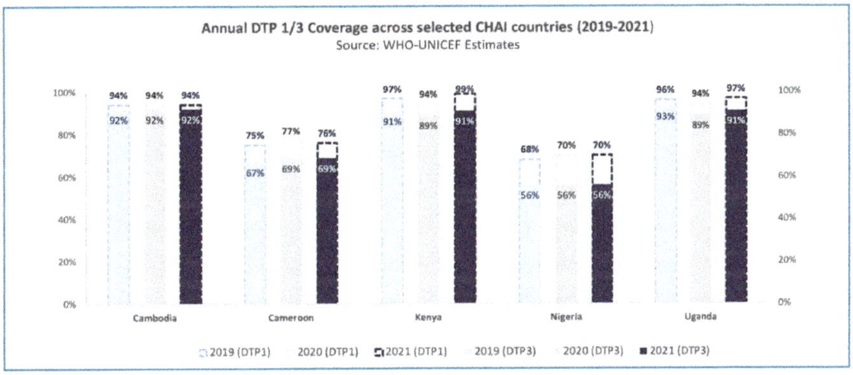

Figure 1. Graph representing DTP1/3 coverage levels in selected program countries—Cambodia, Cameroon, Kenya, Nigeria, and Uganda—between 2019 and 2021. It highlights that across these five countries, national coverage of DTP3 remained the same or increased between 2019 and 2021, showcasing the immunization systems' resilience to withstand shocks due to the COVID-19 pandemic. Source: 2021 WHO-UNICEF Estimates.

3.2.1. Conducting Frequent and Intensified Catch-up Activities

Closing immunity gaps and reaching missed communities require intensified efforts that are well planned and informed by evidence. In Cambodia, Kenya, Nigeria, Cameroon, and Uganda, multiple rounds of catch-up activities were conducted to service high-risk communities throughout the pandemic to address coverage gaps and inequities. These included a mix of intensified and targeted outreaches and campaign style periodic intensification of routine immunization (PIRIs) activities e.g., integrated child health days (ICHDs) and local immunization days (LIDs). In Cameroon, districts in conflict-affected regions were serviced through three rounds of periodic intensifications of routine immunizations (PIRI), which resulted in 28% improvement in DTP3 coverage in the South West Region in 2020/2021. To support with planning these outreach efforts, Clinton Health Access Initiative (CHAI) Cameroon helped track on a quarterly basis district level service delivery and immunization coverage indicators. We used an Excel/power BI-based dashboard, which enabled the rapid identification and prioritization of districts that required intensified catch-up activities. Similarly, in Cambodia, CHAI supported with data review and field assessments to assess and update the Expanded Programme for Immunization (EPI) list of high-risk communities with recent pockets of missed children, while in Kenya, CHAI supported the roll-out of tracking tools to monitor PIRI microplanning progress and review the accuracy and completion of immunization micro plans. In Nigeria, CHAI supported program planning for a catch-up campaign and identifying zero-dose children in 145 districts across the country, including redesigning microplanning and other data tools to accommodate infection prevention and control (IPC) needs in the context of the pandemic.

3.2.2. Strengthening Health Information Systems to Routinely Capture Immunization Coverage and Ongoing Disease Surveillance

Despite challenges brought on by the pandemic, these countries continued to strengthen health information system capacities to capture and use routine immunization data for planning and implementation. CHAI provided technical support to EPI across all levels in Cambodia, Uganda, and Kenya to strengthen data management and review capacities to promote immunization data use for planning and decision making. By promoting a systemic approach that leverages existing data, underserved communities can be identified and necessary resources allocated for rapid course correction. In Cambodia, CHAI supported the development of a new visualization dashboard that provided easy access and review of coverage gaps at all levels (national, provincial, district, and service delivery point) to enable prompt follow-up and action. The dashboard was made available in English and the local language, Khmer, for ease of access and user-friendliness. In Kenya, CHAI was instrumental in supporting the Health Management Information System (HMIS) team in separating PIRI and RI indicators within the DHIS2 platform to enable clear performance monitoring for supplementary immunization activities. In Cameroon, CHAI supported the identification and characterization of zero-dose communities using triangulation of demographic, geographic, and immunization data. Through this effort, health areas with the highest risk or probability of zero-dose children were prioritized for targeted action. CHAI also supported mentoring activities to improve data completeness, timeliness, and quality into DHIS2, resulting in an increase of 18% in timeliness, 5% in data quality, and 5% in completeness in the Adamawa region in Cameroon. In Nigeria, to inform decision making, CHAI was instrumental in the roll out of the PowerBI tool for the visualization of real-time campaign immunization coverage and reach. In Uganda, CHAI strengthened identification of underserved areas within health facility catchment areas through monthly reviews of health facility immunization registration data, resulting in in ~50% increase in the number of children from underserved villages vaccinated against DTP3 and MR1 [7].

3.2.3. Finding Synergies with the COVID-19 Vaccine Roll-out

Across the spectrum of activities undertaken to plan, implement, and monitor the COVID-19 vaccine roll-out, many of the countries who demonstrated resilience in the last two years capitalized on these activities for the mutual benefit of routine immunizations.

- To improve integrated delivery of services and promote a life course approach to vaccination, the Cambodian Ministry of Health, with support from CHAI and other partners, developed policies to integrate routine immunization into the COVID-19 outreach strategy in 2021, with a focus on prioritizing hard-to-reach communities. CHAI's support included the following:
    - The design and implementation of an integrated NCD screening and COVID-19 vaccination pilot in two provinces, which was initially implemented at mass vaccination sites and later shifted to health center fixed sites after the acute emergency phase (as booster dose delivery picked up pace). In the

first five months during implementation at mass vaccination sites, the pilot successfully resulted in the referral or linkage to care for approximately ~1600 adults with previously undiagnosed diabetes or hypertension. By the end of the second phase of the pilot (February 2022), which has now been transitioned to government implementation, a total of ~2700 adults had been referred for appropriate follow-up care.

    - To optimize healthcare worker capacity and national health budgets to provide hard-to-reach communities with immunization services, CHAI supported with analyzing COVID-19 and routine immunization coverage data at the provincial, district, and village levels to inform the implementation of such integrated outreach in previously underserved communities.

- The Ugandan Ministry of Health, with support from partners, developed and disseminated operational guidelines to support the symbiotic delivery of health services alongside COVID-19 vaccination, care, and treatment. This included models that encourage task shifting among healthcare workers and hybrid offsite and onsite approaches to supportive supervision to better balance workload and delivery of health services at the district level.
- Data reporting helped countries recognize and react to the cannibalistic effect COVID-19 vaccination was having on healthcare workers' ability to deliver other primary healthcare (PHC) services, including routine immunization. The government of Nigeria decided to separate the service delivery and data collection functions of COVID-19 vaccination to support front line healthcare workers to prioritize the dual duty of COVID vaccinations and other PHC services. CHAI provided guidance in developing strategies and adopting technical guidelines for the integration of COVID-19 vaccination with other PHC services, including immunization, Vitamin-A, and ante-natal care (ANC) services. Three main strategies were promoted, which combined to boost coverage by 70% by October 2022. The strategies included the following:
    - TEACH, which combines traditional microplanning methods with appropriate technology.
    - A family-centered integrated PHC approach that translates into the national strategy of improving access to basic health services.
    - SCALES 3.0 (Supervision, Communication, Accountability, Logistics, Immunization data and Service delivery), a strategy that incorporates integration of services, performance-based incentives, data use for action, and decentralized demand generation.
- In Cameroon, Kenya, and Nigeria, COVID-19 vaccination training was also used to refresh frontline healthcare worker knowledge on routine immunization and promote broader immunization best practices.
- In Kenya, through support from CHAI, several county-level EPIs leveraged COVID-19 vaccine outreach services, targeting teachers in schools to co-deliver HPV vaccinations to eligible adolescent girls enrolled in the schools.

3.2.4. Mobilizing Resources for Sustaining Immunization Services

Early intervention by governments to provide clear directives to health facilities was instrumental in minimizing service delivery disruptions. For example, the mid-2020 nationwide directive in Nigeria to continue routine outreach sessions resulted in an 11.6% increase [8] in service provision since the early disruptions. In Uganda, by engaging non-traditional health stakeholders, particularly at the district level, the immunization program was able to mobilize additional financing and resources, including human resources to support data management and operational aspects of delivering vaccinations, which tremendously eased pressure on system capacities and helped sustain routine immunization services.

3.2.5. Restructuring Health Systems to Build Resilience

Learning from the largest disruption to immunization service delivery in three decades and the largest vaccination rollout in history, a few countries are prioritizing investments in systems that enable multisectoral collaboration with strong community participation for agile decision making. For example, the Cambodian government is in the process of developing a PHC booster strategy to ensure all individuals can access a quality package of care in the public sector—from prevention to early diagnosis and management across the life course, encompassing maternal and child health, communicable diseases, selected non-communicable diseases, mental health, and other ageing-related illnesses. This strategy aims to emphasize stronger community engagement and new models of service delivery that could strengthen the resilience of health systems. CHAI is supporting by updating the community participation policy, which will redefine the governance, roles, and responsibilities for community heath workers within existing community structures. In Uganda, the government is adapting routine immunization for the use of Smart Paper Technology, which enables individual-level tracking of COVID-19 vaccine recipients and includes a reminder function for subsequent doses. CHAI is supporting the country to develop systems and processes that reduce missed opportunities for vaccination at every encounter with the health system, which has had a demonstrable impact on all antigens of note, including sustained increase in the number of vaccinated (11% in DTP3, 4% in MCV1, 72% in HPV2) in the supported districts in 2021 [7]. These health system capacities and processes will facilitate improved preparedness and operations to rapidly respond to emergent system shocks while maintaining the effectiveness of routine programs.

4. Conclusions

The importance of integrating routine immunization into primary healthcare systems has never been clearer. As countries continue to recover and adopt lessons from the last few years, to not only mitigate the effects of backsliding but to reach those who were previously unreached, integrated and holistic PHC systems offer the best way forward for supporting resilient and sustainable routine immunization programs. Investing in broader health system strengthening and improving linkages with communities will help advance immunization goals. With the future of the COVID-19 pandemic remaining uncertain, it is vital to focus on building back better the resilience of our immunization systems to respond more rapidly and effectively to challenges, and ensure all children continue to have access to lifesaving vaccinations despite new and emerging concerns. Learnings from the exemplary countries presented in this article provide insights into the various possibilities that can be unlocked with the right commitment and support.

Supplementary Materials: The following supporting information can be downloaded at: https://www.mdpi.com/article/10.3390/vaccines11020375/s1, File S1: Enablers for RI Recovery in CHAI focal countries.

Author Contributions: Conceptualization, writing—original draft preparation, A.A. and T.A.; Resources—F.M., F.L., S.B., O.G., S.M. and N.N.E.; Supervision—L.B. All authors have read and agreed to the published version of the manuscript.

Funding: The development of this commentary received no additional external funding, however the CHAI-supported work highlighted in this article was made possible through funding from Bill & Melinda Gates Foundation and Gavi, the Vaccine Alliance.

Institutional Review Board Statement: Not applicable. This work reports on country-level program policies and is not considered human subjects research.

Informed Consent Statement: Not applicable. This work reports on country-level program policies and is not considered human subjects research.

Data Availability Statement: No new data were created or analyzed in this study. Data sharing is not applicable to this article.

Acknowledgments: Many thanks to CHAI country team colleagues from Cambodia, Cameroon, Kenya, Nigeria, and Uganda, who provided insights during this commentary development. We extend our gratitude and appreciation to our Ministry of Health counterparts and health partners in countries who continue to make significant progress in immunization access.

Conflicts of Interest: The authors declare no conflict of interest.

References

1. 2021 WHO-UNICEF Estimates (WUENIC), as of 15 July 2022. Available online: https://www.who.int/teams/immunization-vaccines-and-biologicals/immunization-analysis-and-insights/global-monitoring/immunization-coverage/who-unicef-estimates-of-national-immunization-coverage (accessed on 25 January 2023).
2. Gavi, the Vaccine Alliance, *The Zero Dose Children: Explained*, April 2021. Available online: https://www.gavi.org/vaccineswork/zero-dose-child-explained (accessed on 25 January 2023).
3. GPEI. *Wild Polio (WP1) Remains Endemic Only in Two Countries Afghanistan and Pakistan. Malawi Confirmed Detection of WP1 in February 2022*, 17 February 2022. Available online: https://polioeradication.org/polio-today/polio-now/ (accessed on 25 January 2023).
4. WHO. *Third Round of the Global Pulse Survey on Continuity of Essential Health Services during the COVID-19 Pandemic*; WHO: Geneva, Switzerland, 2022.
5. Immunization Services Begin Slow Recovery from COVID-19 Disruptions, though Millions of Children Remain at Risk from Deadly Diseases. *WHO*, 26 April 2021. Available online: https://www.who.int/news/item/26-04-2021-immunization-services-begin-slow-recovery-from-covid-19-disruptions-though-millions-of-children-remain-at-risk-from-deadly-diseases-who-unicef-gavi (accessed on 25 January 2023).
6. Shet, A.; Carr, K.; Danovaro-Holliday, M.C.; Sodha, S.V.; Prosperi, C.; Wunderlich, J.; Wonodi, C.; Reynolds, H.W.; Mirza, I.; Gacic-Dobo, M.; et al. Impact of the SARS-CoV-2 pandemic on routine immunization services: Evidence of disruption and recovery from 170 countries and territories. *Lancet* **2021**, *10*, e186–e194. [CrossRef]
7. CHAI. *Review of Administrative Data for Immunization*; CHAI: Kampala, Uganda, 2021.
8. Ministry of Health. *Analysis of Weekly SMS Reporting*; Ministry of Health: Abuja, Nigeria, 2020.

vaccines

MDPI

Article

Evaluation of Container Clinics as an Urban Immunization Strategy: Findings from the First Year of Implementation in Ghana, 2017–2018

Anna Shaum [1,*], Melissa T. Wardle [1], Kwame Amponsa-Achiano [2], Raymond Aborigo [3], Joseph Opare [4], Aaron S. Wallace [1], Delia Bandoh [5], Pamela Quaye [2], Fred Osei-Sarpong [2], Francis Abotsi [2], George Bonsu [2] and Laura Conklin [1]

1 Center for Global Health, Global Immunization Division, Centers for Disease Control and Prevention, Atlanta, GA 30329, USA; ccu7@cdc.gov (A.S.W.)
2 Department of Disease Control and Prevention, Public Health Division, Ghana Health Service, Accra 00233, Ghana
3 Navrongo Health Research Centre, Health Research Division, Ghana Health Service, Navrongo 03821, Ghana
4 African Field Epidemiology Network, Kampala 10102, Uganda
5 Ghana Field Epidemiology and Laboratory Training Programme, School of Public Health, University of Ghana, Accra 00233, Ghana
* Correspondence: nla9@cdc.gov

Abstract: Background: In 2017, the Expanded Programme on Immunization in Ghana opened two container clinics in Accra, which were cargo containers outfitted to deliver immunizations. At each clinic, we assessed performance and clinic acceptance during the first 12 months of implementation. Methods: We employed a descriptive mixed-method design using monthly administrative immunization data, exit interviews with caregivers of children of <5 years (N = 107), focus group discussions (FGDs) with caregivers (n = 6 FGDs) and nurses (n = 2 FGDs), and in-depth interviews (IDIs) with community leaders (n = 3) and health authorities (n = 3). Results: Monthly administrative data showed that administered vaccine doses increased from 94 during the opening month to 376 in the 12th month across both clinics. Each clinic exceeded its target doses for the 12–23 month population (second dose of measles). Almost all (98%) exit interview participants stated that the clinics made it easier to receive child health services compared to previous health service interactions. The accessibility and acceptability of the container clinics were also supported from health worker and community perspectives. Conclusions: Our initial data support container clinics as an acceptable strategy for delivering immunization services in urban populations, at least in the short term. They can be rapidly deployed and designed to serve working mothers in strategic areas.

Keywords: vaccines; healthcare access; routine immunization

Citation: Shaum, A.; Wardle, M.T.; Amponsa-Achiano, K.; Aborigo, R.; Opare, J.; Wallace, A.S.; Bandoh, D.; Quaye, P.; Osei-Sarpong, F.; Abotsi, F.; et al. Evaluation of Container Clinics as an Urban Immunization Strategy: Findings from the First Year of Implementation in Ghana, 2017–2018. *Vaccines* **2023**, *11*, 814. https://doi.org/10.3390/vaccines11040814

Academic Editor: Pedro Plans-Rubió

Received: 17 February 2023
Revised: 3 April 2023
Accepted: 6 April 2023
Published: 7 April 2023

1. Background

Urbanization is rapidly increasing worldwide; it is estimated that by 2050, 66% of the world's population will live in an urban area [1]. Much of the increased urbanization is projected to occur on the African continent, where 56% of the population will be urban by 2050 compared to 37% in 2000 [1]. This vast transition to urban living has implications for health systems, and research has indicated significant health and immunization coverage disparities between the poorest urban communities and the wealthiest ones [2,3]. A systematic review of 63 studies conducted in 16 low- and middle-income countries (LMICs) identified that migration status, distance to health facilities, and a lack of parental awareness contribute to the low vaccination status of children living in urban areas [2]. Interventions designed to improve urban immunization coverage in LMICs have primarily focused on community outreach to improve the utilization of services through education, coordinating social mobilization activities, enhancing home visit services, or extending clinic hours [4]. However, urban populations encounter additional barriers to accessing services, highlighting a need for novel strategies to improve access for vulnerable urban communities [2,4].

"Access" can be challenging to define within low-resource contexts in which the overall availability of healthcare is low [5]. Peters et al. (2008) described a framework for accessing healthcare in low-income countries [5] and defined four primary dimensions of access: availability, geographic accessibility, financial accessibility, and acceptability. These dimensions account for the unique experiences in accessing healthcare in LMICs and highlight that the "local adaption and experimentation" of new strategies is critical for improving access. Thus, considering this framework in the initial development and small-scale evaluation of an innovative strategy can improve subsequent implementations and research to enhance access to health services [5].

Immunization services in Ghana are provided at fixed sites (permanent health structures), as well as outreach sites—designated locations where nurses bring vaccine carriers from larger central facilities to deliver immunization services for the day. In comparison to the rural setting, outreach services in many urban settings are frequently not planned or conducted under the assumption that since distance is not as great between fixed sites and households in the urban setting, parents can easily find their way to the existing fixed sites. However, in the urban setting, access to fixed sites can be very challenging due to transport time barriers, transport cost barriers, and busy work schedules. One potential strategy to improve access to immunization in urban settings is the provision of readily accessible, flexible, and convenient, service delivery sites located near urban workplaces or vulnerable urban communities. Container clinics are cargo containers that are converted to clinics and can be used to provide stationary or mobile medical services [6]. These clinics are relatively easy to build, can be easily placed in strategic locations (such as at front of urban markets), and can be adapted to community needs. Container clinics have been utilized to provide infrastructure where health systems are fragile or nonexistent in post-conflict or disaster settings [6–8]. However, to our knowledge, none of the published studies have evaluated the feasibility of using container clinics as a strategy to increase the reach of routine immunization services.

In Ghana, as in many LMICs, disparities between urban and rural immunization coverage exist. A study of Ghana's 2008 and 2014 Demographic Health Surveys (DHS) indicated that children living in urban areas of Ghana were less likely to be fully immunized than children living in rural areas [9]. Furthermore, an analysis of Ghanaian unimmunized children in 2017 found that the urban districts of Kumasi, Accra, and Sekondi-Takoradi had the most unimmunized children [10].

To address the unique urban barriers in accessing immunization services, the Expanded Programme on Immunization (EPI) in Ghana opened two container clinics in the Accra Metropolitan area in September 2017. The clinics were established in nearby locations where nurses previously provided outreach immunization services once per month. They were outfitted to provide daily child health services, including immunizations, home visits, and other forms of preventive and curative care. The container clinics were a small-scale feasibility/demonstration project that fit into a broader initiative known as the Ghana's Second Year of Life (2YL) project [11]. To inform future scale-up in Ghana and their use in other countries, we evaluated community acceptance and the performance of these container clinics during the first year of implementation.

2. Methods

2.1. Setting

The two container clinics were established in a large Accra sub-metro area of Ghana, with an overall population of 151,712 (2017 estimate). The sub-metro is divided into five zones that house several health clinics, including a polyclinic, maternity house, and hospital.

Two of the five zones in the sub-metro were purposively selected container clinic sites. These zones were selected because of expressed community interest, population mobility and vulnerability, limited health infrastructure, and low immunization coverage. For both sites, community advocacy was a key factor in their selection because it is a known indicator of the success of interventions in urban settings [2]. The first container clinic, referred hereafter as the "fishing community clinic," was placed in a zone with a slum community, directly on the Atlantic coast with a large fishing industry. The second container clinic, referred to hereafter as the "market clinic," was placed in a zone with a large market in Accra, primarily serving kayayei (informal laborers who carry goods for shoppers at markets) and seasonal migrant workers from the northern part of Ghana. Notably, the selection of this site was also informed by recent research that indicated significant social, cultural, and economic barriers among kayayei women [12,13]. Both clinics were implemented in coordination with the Accra Metropolitan Health Authorities and with the support of community leaders. The clinics were situated on gifted land provided by those same community leaders (see Figure 1 for a picture of the market clinic).

Figure 1. Image of the market container clinic prior to opening in Accra, Ghana, September 2017.

The container clinics were built near the previously designated outreach sites. The two sites planned services for an annual catchment child population of 310 children (0–23 months of age) at the fishing community clinic and 422 children at the market clinic.

2.2. Container Clinic Evaluation Design

We used a mixed-method design to evaluate the changes in the immunization services provided at the two locations between September 2017–September 2018. The following information was captured and triangulated to provide initial data on the clinics.

Infrastructure Assessment

To describe the evolving infrastructure of the clinics during implementation, we collected data on immunization infrastructure (e.g., cold chain capacity) and the services provided (e.g., vaccines offered) at the sites before or at the time of the clinics' opening (September 2017), and then six months (March 2018) and 12 months after opening (September 2018).

Monthly Number of Vaccine Doses

Every month, we prospectively collected the number of vaccine doses and the type of vaccines administered at each site using the monthly administrative reporting forms (September 2017 to September 2018). We captured the number of vaccine doses administered to children of 0–11 and 12–23 months of age for the pentavalent vaccine (diphtheria-tetanus-pertussis-hepatitis B-Haemophilus influenza type b) (Penta); oral poliovirus vaccine (OPV); measles rubella vaccine (MR), yellow fever vaccine (YF); meningococcal serotype A vaccine (Men A); rotavirus vaccine (Rota); pneumococcal conjugate vaccine (PCV); and inactivated poliovirus vaccine (IPV). Historical administrative records for these sites of when they were outreach posts were largely unavailable, although records from the fishing community site were available for the month prior to opening. Information on target populations for the catchment areas of both clinics were collected from administrative records and the nurses who worked at the outreach vaccination sites. These data were imported, aggregated, and tabulated using Microsoft Excel Office 365 Version 2208.

Caregiver Exit Interviews

At 12 months after container clinic implementation (September 2018), we conducted caregiver exit interviews. These were conducted to understand the characteristics of the populations being served and the acceptability of the clinics among the caregivers, and to compare those experiences to the health services they received prior to the clinics' implementation. We set the convenience sample to a target size of 60 exit interviews per clinic—calculated based on monthly attendance data—or until four weeks of data collection had passed (whichever occurred first). The criteria for participation in the exit interviews included being at least 16 years of age and a caregiver of a child under five. Attending the clinic for immunization was not a criterion for participation.

Information collected from the caregiver exit interviews included demographic variables such as the caregiver's age (years), child's age (months), whether or not they were a resident of the community (yes/no), profession (head porter/merchant/hairdresser/seamstress/unemployed/cleaner/other), and educational attainment (none/primary/junior high secondary/senior high secondary/university/unknown). Then, the interviewers proceeded to ask the caregivers about their experiences in accessing services at the container clinics using a structured questionnaire. The questions were aligned with the four dimensions of access including the availability of child health services provided by the container clinics (e.g., the ease of receiving child health care), geographic accessibility (e.g., the convenience of the location, location traveled from, and time spent traveling to the clinic), financial accessibility (e.g., missing work to come to the clinic for child health services), and acceptability (e.g., satisfaction and intention to return). We conducted interviews using tablets with forms programmed in Open Data Kit [14] and uploaded them to SurveyCTO [15].

Qualitative Focus Group Discussions and In-Depth Interviews

In September 2018, we also conducted caregiver and nurse focus group discussions (FGDs) and community leader and health authority in-depth interviews (IDIs) at both sites. Caregivers were selected using convenience sampling. The eligibility criteria included living in the catchment area of the container clinic and being a caregiver for a child under five, regardless of if they had attended the clinic. Groups were further stratified based on the caregiver having a child who was 0–23 months old or 24–59 months old. Nurses were eligible if they worked at the clinics before container clinic implementation. Community leaders were invited to participate if they held an authority role in their community and played a key role in setting up the clinic or its operations. Health authorities were selected if they were in a management role or had a unique historical background on the clinic. Guides for FGD and IDIs focused on themes related to access and the group or individual's perceived change in community access to childhood immunization services.

2.3. Statistical and Thematic Analysis

We computed descriptive statistics (counts/percentages, means/standard deviations, or medians/interquartile ranges) for the quantitative variables. The results were examined overall and then stratified by each community area where the container clinics were implemented. We summarized the number of all vaccine doses and the number of MR doses administered each month to monitor changes in the number of vaccine doses administered. For qualitative data, we used deductive codes from the study guides and objectives and added inductive codes as coding progressed. We created themes and sub-themes from the codes generated. We then integrated and organized the data using the conceptual framework described below.

2.4. Conceptual Framework

We present our results organized into the dimensions of healthcare access, as described in Peters et al.'s conceptual framework [5]. Recent studies, including those conducted in Ghana and Kenya, have used the framework to understand urban access to care [16,17]. We used the framework's four dimensions (availability, geographic accessibility, financial accessibility, and acceptability) during the analysis, in addition to the framework's determinant of 'individual and household characteristics of users'. Although immunizations are provided free of charge in Ghana, we assessed financial accessibility by examining the direct and indirect costs associated with a clinic visit.

2.5. Ethical Considerations

This project was determined to be non-research by the CDC Human Subjects Office, and approval was obtained from the Ghana Health Service's Ethics Review Committee, as it was evaluated under Ghana's Second Year of Life project [11]. The purpose of the evaluation was outlined for all participants. Verbal consent was obtained before the data collection, including consent to audio-record the FGDs and IDIs.

3. Results

We received monthly administrative immunization data from the clinic sites from September 2017 to September 2018. A total of 107 caregivers participated in the exit interviews across the two sites. We held six caregiver and two nurse FGDs (n= 28 FGD participants) and had IDIs with three community leaders and three health authorities; except for an additional community leader and health authority IDI at the market clinic, an equal number of FGDs and IDIs were held at each site.

3.1. Individual and Household Characteristics of Clinic Users

Our findings reflect the different urban populations served at the two container clinics. The exit interview responses revealed that approximately half of the caregivers attending the market clinic lived in the area (n = 25/45; 56%) in contrast to almost all the respondents from the fishing community clinic (n = 61/62; 98%) (Table 1). A higher percentage (13%; n = 8/62) of the caregivers attending the fishing community clinic were unemployed than the market clinic attendees; most women attending the market clinic were traders or head porters (71%; n = 32/45), and none reported unemployment. Additionally, maternal education levels differed at each site; almost half of the market clinic respondents (n = 22/45; 49%) reported receiving either no formal education or only primary school education compared to 20% (n = 13/62) of the fishing community caregivers. Caregivers at the market clinic were of a median age slightly older than that of the caregivers in the fishing community clinic (32 vs. 28 years old). The median age of the children attending was the same across both clinics (12 months).

For the qualitative portion of the evaluation, 34 individuals participated in the interviews and discussions, with 17 participants being from the fishing community, 14 from the market community, and three from the sub-metro health authority.

Table 1. Exit interview responses among caregivers of children 0–5 years of age from container clinics in two urban communities on the accessibility and acceptability of services offered 12 months post-implementation, September 2018 (N = 107).

		Total		Market Community		Fishing Community	
		N = 107		n = 45		n = 62	
Exit Interview Question	**Response**	N	%	n	%	n	%
Do you live in this community?	Yes	86	80.4	25	55.6	61	98.4
	No	21	19.6	20	44.4	1	1.6
What is your profession?	Head porter, trader, merchant	57	53.3	32	71.1	25	40.3
	Hairdresser	9	8.4	2	4.4	7	11.3
	Seamstress	9	8.4	3	6.7	6	9.7
	Unemployed	8	7.5	0	0.0	8	12.9
	Cleaner	5	4.6	1	2.2	4	6.5
	Other *	19	17.8	7	15.6	12	19.3
What is the highest level of education for this child's mother?	None	22	20.6	16	35.6	6	9.7
	Primary	13	12.1	6	13.3	7	11.3
	Junior High Secondary	51	47.7	18	40.0	33	53.2
	Senior High Secondary	19	17.8	5	11.1	14	22.6
	University	1	0.9	0	0	1	1.6
	Unknown	1	0.9	0	0	1	1.6
Is this location convenient for you?	Yes	106	99.1	44	97.8	62	100
	No	1	0.9	1	2.2	0	0
Did you come here today from home, work, or another location?	Home	69	64.5	13	28.9	56	90.3
	Work	28	26.2	23	51.1	5	8.1
	Home and work are the same	10	9.3	9	20	1	1.6
Did you have to miss work today to come to this container clinic?	Yes	19	17.8	5	11.1	14	22.6
	No	75	70.1	39	86.7	36	58.1
	DK/NA	13	12.1	1	2.2	12	19.3
If no, and this container clinic was not here, would you have had to miss work to get care today? ^	Yes	32	42.7	23	59.0	9	25.0
	No	40	53.3	15	38.5	25	69.4
	DK	3	4.0	1	2.5	2	5.6
Has the new container clinic made it easier to receive medical care for your child/children?	Yes	105	98.1	44	97.8	61	98.4
	No	0	0.0	0	0.0	0	0.0
	DK	2	1.9	1	2.2	1	1.6
If yes, in what ways has it made it easier? ^**	Container clinic is easier for me to get to than other clinics	98	93.3	40	90.9	58	95.1
	The hours are more suitable for my schedule	27	25.7	11	25.0	16	26.2
	Immediate attention	23	21.9	10	22.7	13	21.3
	No charge for service	2	1.9	2	4.5	0	0.0
	Other	5	4.8	1	2.3	4	6.6
How do services you received at clinics before compare to services you receive at the container clinic?	Container clinic is better	40	37.3	18	40.0	22	35.5
	Services are about the same	52	48.6	19	42.2	33	53.2
	Other clinic(s) were better	2	1.9	1	2.2	1	1.6
	Don't Know	13	12.2	7	15.6	6	9.7

Table 1. *Cont.*

Exit Interview Question	Response	Total N = 107 N	%	Market Community n = 45 n	%	Fishing Community n = 62 n	%
When you or your child need health services in the future, do you plan to return to this container clinic or go to a different clinic?	Return to the container clinic	97	90.7	43	95.6	54	87.1
	Go to a different clinic	6	5.6	1	2.2	5	8.1
	Don't Know	4	3.7	1	2.2	3	4.8
What recommendations do you have to improve the container clinic? **	No recommendations	41	38.3	28	62.2	13	21.0
	Add prescription services	29	27.1	4	8.9	25	40.3
	Add ANC services	25	23.4	11	24.4	14	22.6
	Expand size of clinic and seating	10	9.3	1	2.2	9	14.5
	Add other services	8	7.5	0	0.0	8	12.9
	Staff a physician/doctor	7	6.5	0	0.0	7	11.3
	Improve advertising	6	5.6	5	11.1	1	1.6

* Other responses included laborer, cook, housewife, artisan, apprentice, sanitation worker, teacher waitress, laundry worker, pedicurist, and binding shop worker. ^ Denominators are determined by responses to a preceding question. ** Responses may exceed sample sizes as participants could provide more than one answer. Abbreviations: Do not know (DK), not applicable (NA).

The average age of caregivers who participated in the FGDs was 29 years for non-attendees and 26 years for attendees. Most participating caregivers were traders (62%) and head porters (19%). The average age of children whose caregivers were in the 0–23-month FGDs was 10.8, while that of children whose caregivers were in the 24- to 59-month group was 33.5 months.

3.2. *Infrastructure and Availability of Services at Container Clinics*

The infrastructure and services provided by both clinics evolved within the first 12 months. Each clinic was developed from an outreach post that provided immunization services once a month by vaccine carriers to an expanded clinic with official EPI reporting tools and EPI refrigerators on-site; full-time staff including 2–6 nurses offered daily routine immunization services. Moreover, at six months, both clinics offered two additional routine vaccines—the rotavirus vaccine (Rota) and pneumococcal conjugate vaccine (PCV)—to their catchment populations, and the newly introduced inactivated polio vaccine (IPV) at 12 months post-implementation (Table 2). This infrastructure improvement was noted during the nurse FGDs:

> *… we used to suffer. Before we were doing the outreach without the container, you will be sitting there, sometimes before you even come, the rain has taken all your things, spoilt your registers, dust and all that; so when the container came it was really good.*—Nurse, the fishing community clinic

> *At first, we used to go and carry it (vaccines) from the polyclinic before we come here. And so, by the time the mother will come, the vaccine is not here yet because they come here very early. Now, the moment you come, you just pick your vaccine into your carrier and start working.*—Nurse, the market clinic

The increase in the availability of services was matched by an increase in utilization. Over the first year, the number of monthly vaccine doses administered increased consistently. When comparing the first to last month of doses administered, we observed a 442% increase at the market clinic (28 to 152 doses) and a 239% increase at the fishing community clinic (66 to 224 doses). This change included doses of IPV (introduced in June 2018) and the newly offered PCV and Rota (Figure 2).

Table 2. Summary of services and clinic infrastructure offered by two container clinics pre-implementation, and six months and twelve months post-implementation in the Accra Sub-Metro, 2017–2018.

Services and Infrastructure Offered	Pre-Implementation	6 Months Post-Implementation	12 Months Post-Implementation
Routine immunization services	Outreach	Fixed	Fixed
Frequency of routine immunization sessions	1 session/month	1–2 sessions/week	5 sessions/week
Types of Vaccines	Penta, OPV, MR, YF, Men A	Penta, OPV, MR, YF, Men A, **Rota**, **PCV**	Penta, OPV, MR, YF, Men A, Rota, PCV, **IPV**
Cold chain capacity	Vaccine carrier	Vaccine carrier	Refrigerator Refrigerator tags
Recording and reporting tools	Improvised with notebook Combined with other outreach sites	Improvised with notebook Official immunization recording tools DHIMS	Official immunization recording tools DHIMS
Staff	1–3 staff	2–6 staff	2–6 staff

Bold signifies new vaccines being offered at clinics. Abbreviations: Penta vaccine (diphtheria-tetanus-pertussis-hepatitis B-Haemophilus influenza type b vaccine); OPV (oral polio vaccine); MR (measles rubella vaccine), YF (yellow fever vaccine); Men A (Meningococcal Serotype A vaccine); Rota (rotavirus vaccine); PCV (pneumococcal conjugate vaccine); IPV (inactivated polio vaccine); DHIMS (district health information management system).

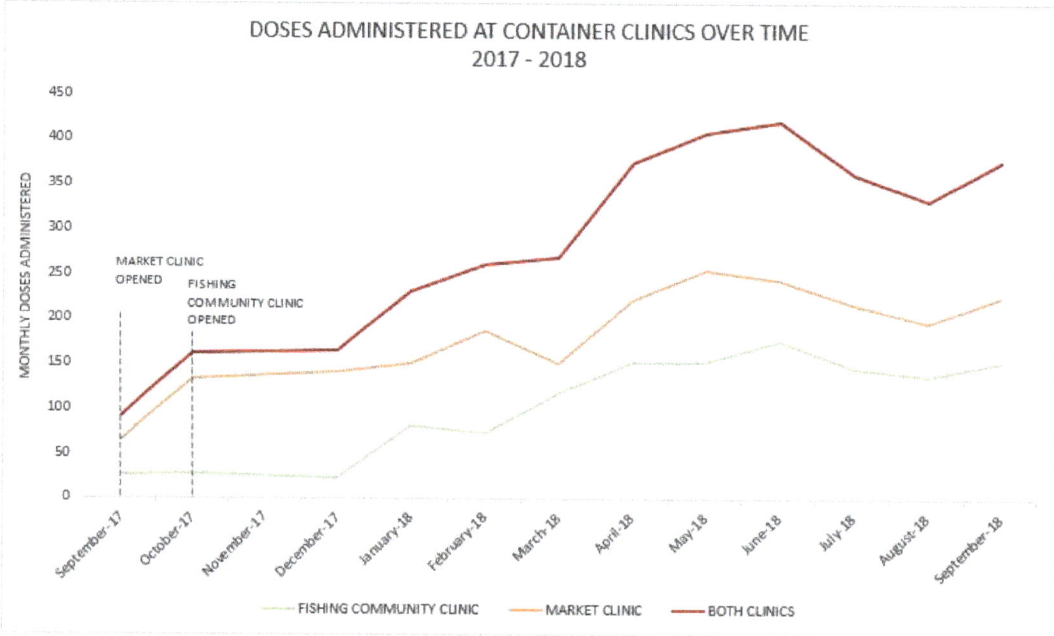

Figure 2. Panel line graph displaying total vaccine doses administered in two container clinics providing immunization services in Accra, Ghana, September 2017–September 2018. Total doses include Penta1-3, PCV1-3, Polio1-3, Rota1-2, MR1, YF, MR2, MenA, and IPV (introduced in June 2018). Abbreviations: "Penta" or Pentavalent vaccine (diphtheria-tetanus-pertussis-hepatitis B-Haemophilus influenza type b vaccine); OPV (oral poliovirus vaccine); MR (measles rubella vaccine), YF (yellow fever vaccine); Men A (Meningococcal Serotype A vaccine); Rota (rotavirus vaccine); PCV (pneumococcal conjugate vaccine); IPV (inactivated poliovirus vaccine).

When assessing measles-rubella dose 1 (MR1) and MR2 specifically, both container clinics exceeded their annual target population for MR1 and MR2. For example, at the market clinic, the target population for 12–23 months was 150 children, and 180 doses of MR2 were administered. At the fishing community clinic, the target population for 12–24 months was 110 children, and 153 doses of MR2 were administered (Figure 3). The nurses also described an increase in vaccine uptake among the target population and improved immunization service utilization for traditionally underserved populations:

> *It has really increased because we are actually now getting more than what we used to get. Like now, what we get in a week is more than the number we used to get for a month.*—Nurse, the fishing community clinic

> *... let's take the kayayei, they sleep here unless festive seasons before they go to their places but some people too those who are from northern region, their vaccination is very poor because sometimes a five year old hasn't taken Penta 3, no vitamin A at 6 ... when you go for visit you can look out for them and give them the vaccines.*—Nurse, the market clinic

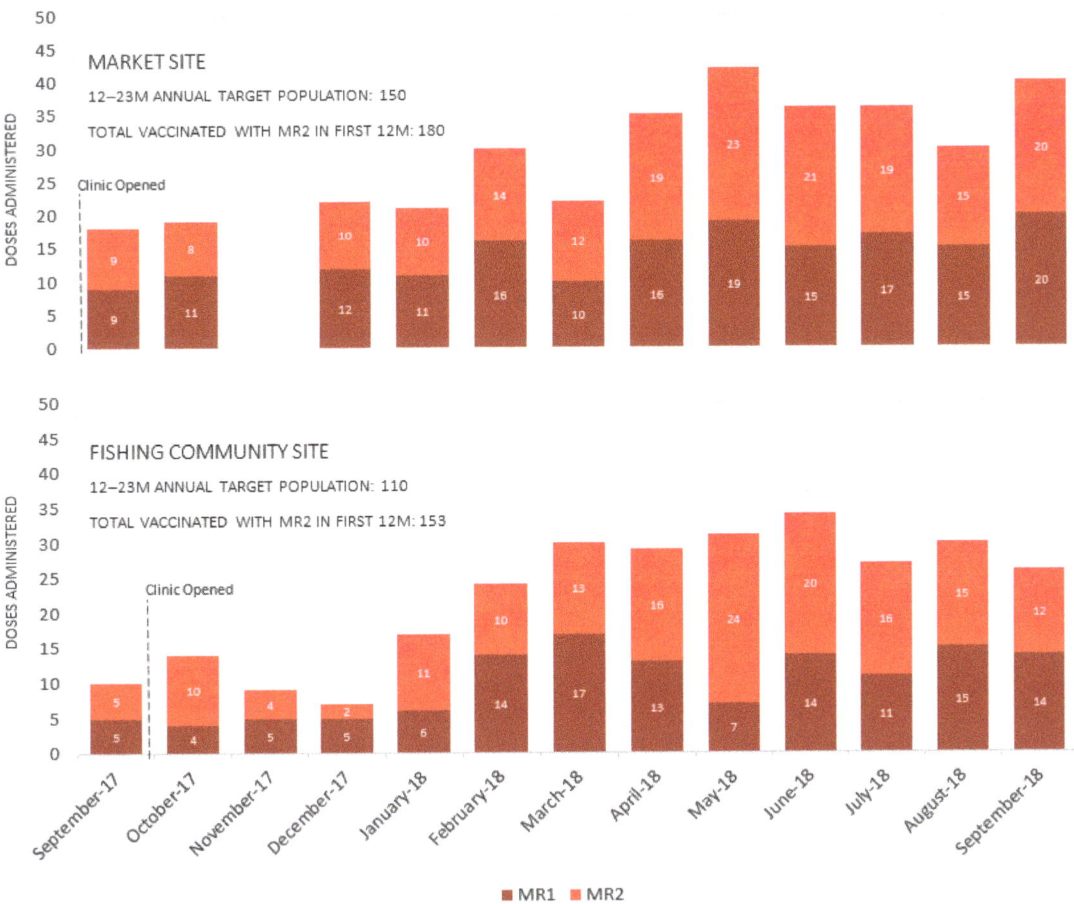

Figure 3. Stacked bar graphs displaying doses administered over time for measles-rubella-1 (MR1) and measles-rubella-2 (MR2) at both container clinic sites from 2017–2018. Abbreviations: MR1 (measles rubella vaccine dose 1); MR2 (measles rubella vaccine dose 2). Note: missing data for the market site in November 2017.

3.3. Geographic and Financial Accessibility of Clinics

On average, it took caregivers (N = 107) five minutes to reach the clinic, with the majority (71%; n = 32/45) in the market community traveling to the clinic from work, and the majority (90%; n = 56/62) in the fishing community coming from home. Almost all (99%; N = 106/107) caregivers said that the container clinic was in a convenient location. The theme of geographic accessibility also emerged from the qualitative data:

> *But this container clinic here, excuse me to say, it has helped me a lot, because I have a child that is 3 years, but I still bring him for weighing, now the container services, it is close to our houses.*—Caregiver, the fishing community

> *... I won't risk this for anything so I will try to always take my child but at first, I always felt lazy to go because I was always here [at the market] so going to the community clinic ... but now that this one is closer, why not? I can even send someone to bring the child.*—Caregiver, the market community

The container clinics appear to improve the financial "accessibility" of receiving an immunization, as almost all caregivers walked to the clinics (97%; N = 104/107) in an average of five minutes (see above). Additionally, among caregivers who did not miss work to attend the container clinics, 59% (n = 23/45) of the caregivers interviewed at the market clinic reported they would have missed work without the container clinic, and 25% (n = 9/62) of the caregivers at the fishing community clinic reported they would have missed work (Table 1). This finding was also seen in the FGDs and IDIs:

> *And then the immunization and everything goes on here so it has reduced their transportation in a way so it is a benefit to them, so they don't complain of not having money to go to the clinic again.*—Nurse, the market clinic

> *... I think that, those that take cars to far places before or walk far distance before going to the clinic has reduced. There is someone who also has to walk before going, she will get tired, container clinic has saved all that hassle.*—Community leader, the fishing community

3.4. Acceptability of Clinics

Approximately 96% (n = 43/45) of caregivers interviewed at the market clinic and 87% (n = 54/62) of caregivers interviewed at the fishing community clinic reported that they planned to return for future services. Additionally, 98% (N = 105/107) of exit interviewees stated that the container clinics made it easier to receive child health services. The top reasons mentioned for why services were easier to receive included: "the clinic is easier to get to than other clinics" (98%), "more suitable hours" (27%), and "immediate attention" (22%). Over three-quarters (86%; N = 92/107) of the caregivers across both sites reported that the container clinic services were either better or equal to those received at other clinics (Table 1).

Despite the high levels of acceptability among the exit interviewees, caregivers reported the need for more services. Among the market clinic caregivers, 24% (n = 14/45) reported that the clinics should provide antenatal care (ANC) services. Of the caregivers attending the fishing community clinic, 23% (n = 14/62) also suggested the addition of ANC services and many recommended that the clinic adds prescription services (40%; n = 25/62). Among the nurses, language barriers were also noted, which may affect the acceptability of services. The desire for expanded services and the challenge of language barriers were corroborated in the qualitative findings:

> *So since it is a clinic I think if it is expanded a bit, bring in more workers and increase the facilities so that it won't be a small place that only dishes out para [cetamol] for a headache then you have to go again to Polyclinic; but it should be a permanent place where if I have stomach pains I can be treated, admitted and if I need infusion I should be given so, if it is expanded a bit it will help us.*—Caregiver, the market community

> *Language barrier because most of them are from these French countries and the north. So they don't speak English and they don't understand the Twi too unless their hometown language or sign language and when you do the sign language they understand or sometimes they come along with other people who understand the Twi and their language.*—Nurse, the market clinic

4. Discussion

Our results suggest container clinics are an acceptable strategy to improve access to routine immunization services for the two urban communities in Ghana, and possibly in other similar urban areas. Following Peters et al.'s (2008) conceptual framework [5], we found that the placement of the container clinics within these communities addressed the availability, geographic and financial accessibility, and acceptability of routine immunization services. During the first 12 months of implementation, immunization sessions increased from monthly (when the clinics were only outreach sites) to daily; all recommended vaccines and supporting supplies and tools were stored on-site, and caregivers reported high satisfaction with both clinics. Improvements in geographical and financial accessibility were observed by minimizing commuting distance, time, and the indirect costs of lost wages for caregivers.

Implementing the container clinics required transforming the locations from outreach posts to fixed routine immunization sites. Transforming the sites into functioning clinics was essential because the outreach sites where the container clinics were built would cancel services due to poor weather that impacted vaccination sessions. Lack of resources, supplies, and tools are well-documented barriers to fully vaccinating children and also have implications for building trust with caregivers to return for future vaccination services, as well as the ability of health workers to effectively trace defaulters [17–20].

The utilization of vaccination services gradually increased as the container clinics became more established over the 12 months. In addition to the three-fold increase in vaccine doses administered during the first 12 months, both clinics exceeded their annual target population for the administration of MR1 and MR2 vaccine doses. Vaccine utilization is driven by a combination of demand and access factors, which this evaluation was not designed to disentangle. However, it is important to note that, in other studies, strategies for increasing demand include improving service frequency, design, and delivery [17–19,21]—factors that the container clinics addressed. Thus, we hypothesize that increased community demand for services due to the availability of a geographically proximate, brand new clinic was likely a key factor underlying the observed increase in the utilization of services at these sites.

While most studies have assessed geographical accessibility in the rural poor, recent studies have identified how urban caregivers experience limited access, especially when the distance to the health facility is more than 1–2 km from their home [20,22]. We found that container clinics can provide immunization services to previously hard-to-reach urban populations—nearly every exit interviewee stated that the clinic made receiving care for their child easier compared to accessing previous health service sites. Most caregivers from the exit interviews reported that they walked to the clinics, and data from the caregiver FGDs indicated that the proximity of the clinics was favorable.

Previous studies have found that employed caregivers faced higher opportunity costs when bringing their children to the clinic for vaccinations because of the loss of potential daily earnings [9,20,21,23,24]. In our evaluation, the market community was chosen to provide services to a notably vulnerable group, the kayayei, or head porters. Typically, these head porters are young, rural-urban migrants from the northern part of Ghana [12,25,26] who may forgo accessing health services due to cultural discrimination [26] or because of financial barriers related to lost wages [12]. Our results showed that the majority of the caregivers at the market clinic were indeed head porters or other migrant traders. Interestingly, more market caregivers reported they would have had to miss work if not for the container clinic than mothers in the fishing community did. Thus, placing container clinics near markets may address unique barriers faced by working caregivers, including head porters and migrant traders.

Finally, our results support the growing literature on how the urban poor are not a monolith and require tailored urban immunization strategies to achieve success [2,4,16,21,27]. The fishing community clinic served a stationary population with higher levels of unemployment and education, while the market clinic served a highly mobile population of working mothers with very little education. These differences influenced not only caregiver expectations of the clinic but also the overall acceptability of the clinic; we observed an almost 10% difference in acceptability when caregivers were asked if they planned to return to the container clinic or seek services elsewhere, with more market caregivers indicating they planned to return.

Acknowledging the diversity of urban contexts is important because although timely, the current focus on urban health is in danger of overlooking the nuances and unique challenges faced by the multitude of urban populations in Africa. A recent paper highlighting the diverse urban contexts in Johannesburg also argues that 'place matters':

> *Whilst the challenge of addressing the health of urban populations within developing countries is acknowledged, the diverse urbanisation experiences of different urban groups remain under-explored ... for action to improve the health of poor urban populations to be successful, urban policy makers and programmers need to understand the complexity of the urban context* [28]

5. Limitations

This evaluation had several limitations, including the method of convenience sampling in the exit interviews and FGDs, as well as the small size of the clinics' catchment populations, which impacted our ability to make inferences about caregivers who were not utilizing the clinics with the exit interview data. To overcome these limitations, we sought to increase the richness of the data by integrating our qualitative and quantitative findings. Additionally, exit interviews are subject to response bias, which can shift responses toward positive feedback. We also relied on administrative records to monitor changes in immunization doses administered over time, which may subject those results to the limitations of written and improvised records in low-resource settings [29]. Finally, while the results provide initial evidence about the success of container clinics in improving urban access to immunization, they are not generalizable to other urban settings in Ghana. We suggest that the lessons learned from this initial implementation inform future scale-up and full impact evaluations of container clinics as an urban immunization strategy.

6. Conclusions

Our initial data support that container clinics were an acceptable method for delivering immunization services to urban populations, at least in the short term. Our findings also highlight the importance of community engagement and context-tailored strategies to improve urban access to immunization; container clinics may be a more acceptable strategy when designed to serve working mothers and built-in strategic areas (e.g., urban markets). Further studies to understand the potential role of container clinics as an urban immunization strategy are needed, including studies on their cost-effectiveness, long-term sustainability, impact on immunization coverage, and ability to expand services to meet other community needs.

Author Contributions: Conceptualization, A.S., M.T.W., K.A.-A., R.A., J.O., D.B., P.Q., F.O.-S., F.A., G.B. and L.C.; formal analysis, A.S., M.T.W., R.A. and D.B.; methodology, A.S., M.T.W., R.A., A.S.W., D.B. and L.C.; project administration, M.T.W., K.A.-A., J.O., P.Q., F.O.-S., F.A. and G.B.; supervision, K.A.-A., J.O., A.S.W., P.Q., F.O.-S., F.A. and G.B.; writing—Original draft, A.S., M.T.W., R.A., A.S.W., D.B. and L.C.; writing—Review and editing, A.S., M.T.W., K.A.-A., R.A., J.O., A.S.W., D.B., P.Q., F.O.-S., F.A., G.B. and L.C. All authors have read and agreed to the published version of the manuscript.

Funding: Global Health Security Agenda funded the Centers for Disease Control and Prevention Immunization Second Year of Life project.

Institutional Review Board Statement: This work was determined to be a non-research evaluation by CDC.

Informed Consent Statement: Informed consent was obtained from all persons involved in the evaluation.

Data Availability Statement: The datasets used and/or analyzed during the current project may be available upon reasonable request.

Acknowledgments: We would like to thank Mawuli Nyaku and Neetu Abad, the Ghana Field Epidemiology and Laboratory Training Program, the nurses at the container clinics, and the Accra Metropolitan Health Authorities for their contributions to this evaluation.

Conflicts of Interest: The authors declare no conflict of interest. The findings and conclusions in this report are those of the authors and do not necessarily represent the views of the Centers for Disease Control and Prevention.

References

1. United Nations Department of Economic and Social Affairs and Population Division. *World Population Prospects: The 2014 Revision*; Population Division, United Nations: New York, NY, USA, 2015.
2. Crocker-Buque, T.; Mindra, G.; Duncan, R.; Mounier-Jack, S.L. Immunization, urbanization and slums—A systematic review of factors and interventions. *BMC Public Health* **2017**, *17*, 556. [CrossRef] [PubMed]
3. World Health Organization and UN Habitat. *Hidden Cities: Unmasking and Overcoming Health Inequities in Urban Settings*; World Health Organization: Geneva, Switzerland, 2010.
4. Nelson, K.N.; Wallace, A.S.; Sodha, S.V.; Daniels, D.; Dietz, V. Assessing strategies for increasing urban routine immunization coverage of childhood vaccines in low and middle-income countries: A systematic review of peer-reviewed literature. *Vaccine* **2016**, *34*, 5495–5503. [CrossRef] [PubMed]
5. Peters, D.H.; Garg, A.; Bloom, G.; Walker, D.G.; Brieger, W.R.; Rahman, M.H. Poverty and access to health care in developing countries. *Ann. N. Y. Acad. Sci.* **2008**, *1136*, 161–171. [CrossRef] [PubMed]
6. Morikawa, M.J.; Schneider, S.; Becker, S.; Lipovac, S. Primary care in post-conflict rural northern Afghanistan. *Public Health* **2011**, *125*, 55–59. [CrossRef]
7. Barmania, S. Typhoon Haiyan recovery: Progress and challenges. *Lancet* **2014**, *383*, 1197–1199. [CrossRef] [PubMed]
8. Sworo, G.D.; Kam, M.; Juan, E.J. Design of a Telemedicine-based system for Clinic-In-A-Can. In Proceedings of the 2012 IEEE Global Humanitarian Technology Conference, Seattle, WA, USA, 21–24 October 2012; IEEE Computer Society: Washington, DC, USA.
9. Asuman, D.; Ackah, C.G.; Enemark, U. Inequalities in child immunization coverage in Ghana: Evidence from a decomposition analysis. *Health Econ. Rev.* **2018**, *8*, 9. [CrossRef] [PubMed]
10. Ghana Health Service. Accra, Ghana. 2017. Available online: https://ghs.gov.gh/ (accessed on 16 February 2023).
11. Nyaku, M.; Wardle, M.; Eng, J.V.; Ametewee, L.; Bonsu, G.; Larbi Opare, J.K.; Conklin, L. Immunization delivery in the second year of life in Ghana: The need for a multi-faceted approach. *Pan Afr. Med. J.* **2017**, *27* (Suppl. S3), 4. [CrossRef]
12. Nyarko, S.H.; Tahiru, A.M. Harsh working conditions and poor eating habits: Health-related concerns of female head porters (Kayayei) in the Mallam Atta Market, Accra, Ghana. *BioMed Res. Int.* **2018**, *2018*, 6201837. [CrossRef]
13. Ahlvin, K. The burden of the Kayayei: Cultural and socio-economic difficulties facing female porters in Agbogbloshie. *Pure Insights* **2012**, *1*, 4.
14. Hartung, C.; Lerer, A.; Anokwa, Y.; Tseng, C.; Brunette, W.; Borriello, G. Open data kit: Tools to build information services for developing regions. In Proceedings of the 4th ACM/IEEE International Conference on Information and Communication Technologies and Development, London, UK, 13–16 December 2010; pp. 1–12.
15. Dobility Inc. *SurveyCTO*; Dobility Inc.: Cambridge, MA, USA, 2017.
16. Edusei, J.; Amoah, P. Appreciating the complexities in accessing health care among urban poor: The case of street children in Kumasi Metropolitan Area, Ghana. *Dev. Country Stud.* **2014**, *4*, 69–88.
17. Arnold, C.; Theede, J.; Gagnon, A. A qualitative exploration of access to urban migrant healthcare in Nairobi, Kenya. *Soc. Sci. Med.* **2014**, *110*, 1–9. [CrossRef] [PubMed]
18. Agarwal, S.; Bhanot, A.; Goindi, G. Understanding and addressing childhood immunization coverage in urban slums. *Indian Pediatr.* **2005**, *42*, 653–663. [PubMed]
19. Favin, M.; Steinglass, R.; Fields, R.; Banerjee, K.; Sawhney, M. Why children are not vaccinated: A review of the grey literature. *Int. Health* **2012**, *4*, 229–238. [CrossRef]
20. Babirye, J.N.; Engebretsen, I.M.; Rutebemberwa, E.; Kiguli, J.; Nuwaha, F. Urban settings do not ensure access to services: Findings from the immunisation programme in Kampala Uganda. *BMC Health Serv. Res.* **2014**, *14*, 111. [CrossRef] [PubMed]
21. Cutts, F.T. Strategies to improve immunization services in urban Africa. *Bull. World Health Organ.* **1991**, *69*, 407.

22. Ghei, K.; Agarwal, S.; Subramanyam, M.A.; Subramanian, S.V. Association between child immunization and availability of health infrastructure in slums in India. *Arch. Pediatr. Adolesc. Med.* **2010**, *164*, 243–249. [CrossRef]
23. Wadgave, H.V.; Pore, P. Missed opportunities of immunization in under-fives in adopted area of Urban Health Centre. *Ann. Trop. Med. Public Health* **2012**, *5*, 436. [CrossRef]
24. Egondi, T.; Oyolola, M.; Mutua, M.; Elung'ata, P. Determinants of immunization inequality among urban poor children: Evidence from Nairobi's informal settlements. *Int. J. Equity Health* **2015**, *14*, 24. [CrossRef]
25. Opare, J.A. Kayayei: The women head porters of southern Ghana. *J. Soc. Dev. Afr.* **2003**, *18*, 33–48. [CrossRef]
26. Lattof, S.R.; Coast, E.; Leone, T. Priorities and challenges accessing health care among female migrants. *Health Serv. Insights* **2018**, *11*, 1178632918804825. [CrossRef]
27. Jankowska, M.M.; Weeks, J.R.; Engstrom, R. Do the most vulnerable people live in the worst slums? A spatial analysis of Accra, Ghana. *Ann. GIS* **2012**, *17*, 221–235. [CrossRef] [PubMed]
28. Vearey, J.; Palmary, I.; Thomas, L.; Nunez, L.; Drimie, S. Urban health in Johannesburg: The importance of place in understanding intra-urban inequalities in a context of migration and HIV. *Health Place* **2010**, *16*, 694–702. [CrossRef] [PubMed]
29. Dunkle, S.E.; Wallace, A.S.; MacNeil, A.; Mustafa, M.; Gasasira, A.; Ali, D.; Elmousaad, H.; Mahoney, F.; Sandhu, H.S. Limitations of using administratively reported immunization data for monitoring routine immunization system performance in Nigeria. *J. Infect. Dis.* **2014**, *210* (Suppl. S1), S523–S530. [CrossRef] [PubMed]

vaccines

MDPI

Review

Achieving the IA2030 Coverage and Equity Goals through a Renewed Focus on Urban Immunization

Ibrahim Dadari [1,2,*], Rachel V. Belt [3], Ananya Iyengar [1,4], Arindam Ray [5], Iqbal Hossain [6], Daniel Ali [4], Niklas Danielsson [1], Samir V. Sodha [7] and The Global Urban Immunization Working Group †

1 Coverage & Equity Unit, Immunization Section, PG-Health, UNICEF Headquarters, 3 UN Plaza, New York, NY 10017, USA
2 College of Public Health, University of South Florida, Tampa, FL 33612, USA
3 Nuffield Department of Women's and Reproductive Health, University of Oxford, 75 George Street, Oxford OX1 2JD, UK
4 Johns Hopkins Bloomberg School of Public Health, International Vaccine Access Center (IVAC), Baltimore, MD 21231, USA
5 New Vaccines and Immunization Systems, Bill and Melinda Gates Foundation, New Delhi 110067, India
6 John Snow, Inc., 2733 Crystal Drive, Arlington, VA 22202, USA
7 Department of Immunization Vaccines and Biologicals, WHO Headquarters, Avenue Appia 20, 1211 Geneva, Switzerland
* Correspondence: idadari@unicef.org
† N.B. This Paper was written through the Global Urban Immunization Working Group.

Abstract: The 2021 WHO and UNICEF Estimates of National Immunization Coverage (WUENIC) reported approximately 25 million under-vaccinated children in 2021, out of which 18 million were zero-dose children who did not receive even the first dose of a diphtheria-tetanus-pertussis-(DPT) containing vaccine. The number of zero-dose children increased by six million between 2019, the pre-pandemic year, and 2021. A total of 20 countries with the highest number of zero-dose children and home to over 75% of these children in 2021 were prioritized for this review. Several of these countries have substantial urbanization with accompanying challenges. This review paper summarizes routine immunization backsliding following the COVID-19 pandemic and predictors of coverage and identifies pro-equity strategies in urban and peri-urban settings through a systematic search of the published literature. Two databases, PubMed and Web of Science, were exhaustively searched using search terms and synonyms, resulting in 608 identified peer-reviewed papers. Based on the inclusion criteria, 15 papers were included in the final review. The inclusion criteria included papers published between March 2020 and January 2023 and references to urban settings and COVID-19 in the papers. Several studies clearly documented a backsliding of coverage in urban and peri-urban settings, with some predictors or challenges to optimum coverage as well as some pro-equity strategies deployed or recommended in these studies. This emphasizes the need to focus on context-specific routine immunization catch-up and recovery strategies to suit the peculiarities of urban areas to get countries back on track toward achieving the targets of the IA2030. While more evidence is needed around the impact of the pandemic in urban areas, utilizing tools and platforms created to support advancing the equity agenda is pivotal. We posit that a renewed focus on urban immunization is critical if we are to achieve the IA2030 targets.

Keywords: zero-dose; urban immunization; catch-up and recovery; un-immunized; under-immunization; routine immunization

Citation: Dadari, I.; Belt, R.V.; Iyengar, A.; Ray, A.; Hossain, I.; Ali, D.; Danielsson, N.; Sodha, S.V.; The Global Urban Immunization Working Group. Achieving the IA2030 Coverage and Equity Goals through a Renewed Focus on Urban Immunization. *Vaccines* **2023**, *11*, 809. https://doi.org/10.3390/vaccines11040809

Academic Editor: Davide Gori

Received: 25 February 2023
Revised: 24 March 2023
Accepted: 3 April 2023
Published: 6 April 2023

1. Background

The most dramatic declines in routine immunization coverage in the last 30 years occurred in part due to the COVID-19 pandemic. There were approximately 25 million un-vaccinated or under-vaccinated children in 2021, out of which 18 million were zero-dose, based on the proxy indicator of the number of children who did not receive the first dose of a diphtheria-tetanus-pertussis-(DPT) containing vaccine [1]. This drop in coverage has resulted in an increase in the number of zero-dose children globally, from 13 million in 2019 to 18 million in 2021 (approximately 40% more zero-dose children) [2].

A greater focus on strategies to reach un- and under-vaccinated children in urban, rural, and conflict settings is encouraged by the Equity Reference Group on Immunization (ERG), as these populations are facing acute inequities [1]. Due to rapid global urbanization, the world's population is at least 56% urbanized as of 2020 and expected to reach 70% by 2050 [2]. This fast urbanization is not devoid of complications, especially in low- and middle-income countries (LMICs) where the numbers of large informal settlements and urban-poor populations are growing, resulting in huge inequalities in access to basic primary healthcare services, including immunization [3], as such a shift in the distribution of zero-dose and under-vaccinated children towards urban environments is envisaged [3].

The COVID-19 pandemic was declared a public health emergency of international concern in early 2020, and as of February 2023, over 755 million cases and 6.8 million deaths were reported [4]. Routine immunization faced backsliding of coverage due to the pandemic with more than 5 million additional zero-dose and under-vaccinated children added to the 2019 baseline globally. Disruptions to routine immunization occurred on a global scale, with low- and middle-income countries being the hardest hit, due to less resilient routine immunization systems. National lockdowns and restrictions of movements interrupted the provision of medical services and resulted in large swaths of the population either not having access to services or feeling nervous to access these services due to fear of COVID-19 transmission. Pakistan and India are said to have reported major drops in immunization coverage, with Pakistan reporting a substantial coverage decline in all childhood immunization services during the pandemic lockdown [5,6]. Due to data limitations, the extent of decrease in service coverage in some African countries has not been fully elucidated. However, the trend appears to indicate that countries with lower pre-pandemic immunization coverage trends saw more significant drops in performance than countries with higher immunization rates [5]. The routine immunization coverage trajectories as of the end of 2021 indicate some level of recovery but still show warning signs that without concerted efforts to strengthen immunization systems, gaps in coverage will persist [5,7]

A 2022 estimation of the number and distribution of zero-dose and under-immunized children within remote-rural, urban, and conflict-affected locations from 99 LMICs, showed approximately 30% of zero-dose children are in urban and peri-urban areas, compared with remote-rural areas which have about 11% [8]. A substantial proportion of these zero-dose or under-vaccinated children in urban settings are in slums and informal settlements, and these numbers are projected to increase with the current trends of rapid urbanization. These urban settings have their own context-specific challenges needing distinct approaches, including a larger proportion of transient or migrant populations, unclear catchment areas for health facilities, lack of appropriately disaggregated data, disenfranchised communities, increase in informal settlements, insecurity, and satisfying multiple stakeholders including private providers [3].

A major indicator of the Immunization Agenda 2030 (IA2030) [9,10] is a reduction in the number of zero-dose children by 50% by 2030, but this indicator is off-track in large part because of routine immunization backsliding. A total of 20 high-burden countries (Appendix A.1) are home to over 75% of the world's zero-dose children as of 2021 [11]. These countries are largely urbanized, with a considerable proportion of their zero-dose children localized in urban settings, as exemplified by 4 of these 20 focus countries accounting for over 50% of the global population of zero-dose children. These countries include Brazil, Mexico, Indonesia, and Nigeria, with 87%, 81%, 57%, and 53% urbanization, respectively [12]. Many countries have developed urban-specific immunization strategies or highlighted urban approaches in their comprehensive multi-year plan for immunization (cMYP) or national immunization strategies (NIS). Some of these countries attribute their quick recovery from the COVID-19 pandemic to an active urban approach being implemented in their countries.

To address issues of urban immunization, the Urban Immunization Working Group (UIWG) was established. The UIWG is an extra-organizational group comprising policy, program, and academic experts, representing their respective organizations, created to inform global, regional, and national/subnational discussions on immunization equity in urban areas [13]. The group meets virtually or in person 2–4 times every year, facilitated by UNICEF, and has broad membership across key immunization stakeholders. In addition to fostering collaboration and alignment among partners working to improve immunization coverage in urban settings, the urban immunization toolkit, which is now being used by many, is one of the group's products. The urban diagnostic research across several countries was also supported by the working group. The group continually discussed emerging issues and defined a trajectory for future engagement to strengthen the focus on immunization in urban settings.

To facilitate getting countries back on track toward achieving the IA2030 goals, this paper highlights the importance of a renewed focus on addressing the idiosyncrasies of immunization in urban settings through a review of existing data and information on (i) the estimated magnitude of coverage backsliding in urban and peri-urban settings in a select set of countries, (ii) key issues affecting routine immunization in urban and peri-urban settings, and (iii) effective pro-equity strategies for routine immunization recovery in urban settings. The outcome of this study will be shared with global and national immunization stakeholders to provide evidence on effective strategies to vaccinate children in urban-poor communities.

2. Methods

We conducted a systematic search of the published literature to identify relevant information and data on backsliding of immunization coverage in urban settings during the COVID-19 pandemic, the predictors and challenges of routine immunization and pro-equity strategies relevant to urban and peri-urban settings. Priority was given to the 20 high-burden zero-dose countries, per the 2021 WHO and UNICEF Estimates of National Immunization Coverage (WUENIC). This study has the following research questions prioritized for the review:

1. To what extent did COVID-19 pandemic interrupt routine immunization performance and other related services in urban and peri-urban settings in focus countries?
2. What were the predictors of decline or backsliding in immunization coverage in these settings?
3. What was done to recover immunization coverage?

The literature reviewed were from 2 databases, namely, PubMed and Web of Science, due to their broad coverage of health sciences, and inclusive of published literature in the 20 high-burden zero-dose countries for the period between March 2020 and January 2023, to cover the period of COVID-19 pandemic. Search terms used were "immunization coverage" and "urban" and were limited to twenty countries and the period of March 2020 to January 2023. The paper types include ecological studies, cross sectional, interventional, and pre- and post-studies. The full search strategy is available in Appendix A.2.

A total of 608 articles were identified from both databases (PubMed = 321 and Web of Science = 287), which were imported into Rayyan (rayyan.ai). Screening of records detected and removed 227 duplicates. The title and abstract screening of 318 articles based on our inclusion criteria was conducted by 2 authors, ID and RB. The blind decisions by both authors for inclusion were 90% aligned. The reviewers reviewed the misaligned articles and agreed on the final decision according to the criteria in Table 1. Thirty-seven articles were identified for inclusion after the title and abstract review. The remaining articles were screened and excluded if the papers fell outside the designated time period, did not contain references to urban populations or areas, and did not contain references to COVID-19. A flow chart for the literature review is included in Figure 1. A final 15 articles were included in the review, analyzed, and presented in this study.

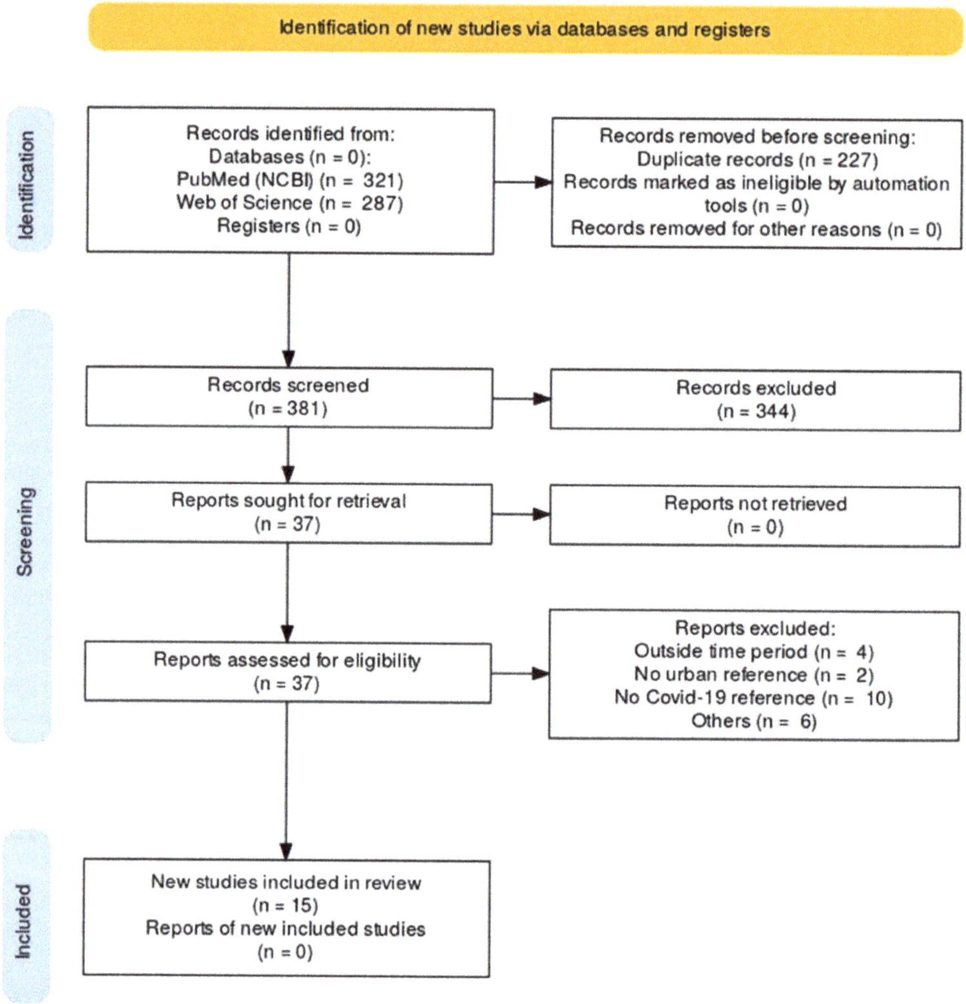

Figure 1. PRISMA Flow chart for the review of papers.

Table 1. Inclusion and exclusion criteria for literature search.

Criteria	Inclusion	Exclusion
Language	English, Spanish, French	Other languages
Dates	March 2020–January 2023	Before March 2020, unless analysis reviews general immunization trends pre-March 2020 to post-March 2020
Database	PubMed (NCBI), Web of Science (Clarivate)	Other databases

Table 1. *Cont.*

Criteria	Inclusion	Exclusion
Vaccines	All routine vaccines administered to children up to age of 18 years.	Exclude COVID vaccines and vaccines administered to adults >18 years.
Topic	COVID-19 impact on routine immunization and recovery	Articles which do not focus on the COVID-19 impact on routine immunization and recovery
Geographic Location (Countries)	India, Nigeria, Indonesia, Ethiopia, Philippines, Democratic Republic of the Congo, Brazil, Pakistan, Angola, Myanmar, United Republic of Tanzania, Mozambique, Afghanistan, Somalia, Mexico, Madagascar, Cameroon, Democratic People's Republic of Korea, Chad, Vietnam	All other countries
Geographic Location (Urban)	Urban and peri-urban, cities, Urban vs. rural analysis	Rural

3. Results

The findings from this study are organized according to the study objectives, which are (i) the backsliding of immunization in urban, (ii) immunization challenges and predictors in urban and peri-urban settings, and (iii) identified pro-equity strategies.

3.1. Backsliding of Immunization in Urban

Some papers provided an estimation of the magnitude of coverage backsliding in country contexts that are mostly urbanized or in context of urban and peri-urban settings. A nationwide ecological study in Brazil looked at the coverage figures of yellow fever vaccination before and during the COVID-19 pandemic. This study was conducted between April 2019 and March 2021 and found a 48.55% decline in the median yellow fever vaccination doses administered nationwide 1 year after pandemic control measures were instituted (April 2020–March 2021) compared to the pre-pandemic period (April 2019–March 2020) [14]. Some of the states with substantial decline rates included Paraná (49.97%), Sao Paulo (43.25%), and regions such as the North (34.71%), Midwest (21.72%), South (63.50%), and Southeast (34.42%). Brazil is a largely urbanized country with urbanization between 65% and 90% across the states.

A 2022 multi-city phenomenological qualitative study in India by Sahoo et al. documented the experiences of urban slum-dwelling women with maternal and child health services during the COVID-19 pandemic [15]. This study was conducted in four cities (one city with a dense slum population per state) across four states: Bhubaneswar Municipal Corporation (Bubaneswal, Odisha, India), Rishikesh Municipal Corporation (Rishikesh, Uttarakhand), Bhilai Municipal Corporation (Chetis Gerbilee, Chhattisgarh, India), and North Lakhimpur Municipal Board (North Lakhimpur, Assam, India). All participants reported getting their children vaccinated during the pandemic with little or no backsliding reported.

Manzoor and colleagues conducted a cross-sectional study to document the impact of the COVID-19 pandemic on routine childhood immunization in Mirpur, Azad Kashmir, Pakistan [16]. The study found that the COVID-19 pandemic had a major impact on the timing of routine immunization for children in Pakistan, where about 80% of caregivers had scheduled vaccinations for their children, 18% had delayed vaccination schedules, while 2% missed vaccination during the COVID-19 pandemic. The fear of contracting the COVID-19 virus was a key factor that resulted in delaying vaccination mentioned by about 65% of participants, and 40% reported that home is the preferred location to get their children vaccinated.

A comparative cross-sectional study in Wolaita of southwest Ethiopia documented the disparities in full immunization coverage among urban and rural children aged 12–23 months [17]. The study found that knowledge of and attitude towards immunization and fear of COVID-19 at the health facility and place of delivery were predictor variables for full vaccination coverage and that urban children had a higher full vaccination than rural children by a 15% point estimate.

A natural experiment, which assessed the impact of the COVID-19 pandemic on coverage of Reproductive, Maternal, and Newborn Health interventions in Ethiopia at the early stages of the pandemic, showed a significant reduction in coverage of BCG vaccination and chlorohexidine use in urban areas amongst the cohort impacted by COVID-19 outbreaks with little or no significant reductions in women seeking either preventative or curative health services [18].

A descriptive and retrospective cross-sectional study conducted in Yaoundé, Cameroon, showed a decline in the number of pediatric consultations by 52% in April and by 34% in May 2020, compared with rates during the same periods in 2019 ($p < 0.01$), following the partial confinement recommended by the government [19]. The demand for BCG vaccines, third dose of DPT, polio, and MMR in children, as well as tetanus vaccines in childbearing women showed a decline [19].

A 51% decline in the daily average total number of vaccinations administered during lockdown compared to the baseline was found throughout the Sindh province in Pakistan from a pre- and post-study analyzing provincial electronic immunization data; the paper examined the impact of the COVID-19 pandemic response on the uptake of routine immunizations with the highest decline seen in BCG vaccines at fixed sites [6]. It was also noted that slum union councils had a slightly larger decrease in immunization coverage than non-slum urban areas (53.8% vs. 51.3%). Some of the predictors of getting vaccinated included children born at health facilities and children of mothers with higher education levels.

Based on a study that analyzed routine statistics and a national household survey in Brazil, a decline of about 20% in vaccines administered to children aged 2 months or older was seen during March and April 2020, when social distancing was at the highest level compared to January and February of the same year [20]. This study also showed that children from poor households and the least developed regions of the country were most affected compared to other children.

3.2. Immunization Challenges and Predictors in Urban and Peri-Urban

A study in four cities of India identified some issues such as no first-time registration for childhood vaccination in Uttarakhand and children not receiving an associated package of health services such as child weighing in Chhattisgarh [15]. Despite the positive outlook for childhood vaccination, other maternal and child health services, including treatment of the sick child, and postnatal care suffered due to the COVID-19 pandemic.

A population-based longitudinal study was conducted by Meckonnen and colleagues in Kersa [21]. Through face-to-face interviews, data was collected from caregivers of over 14,000 children. Harar city children had a 45% coverage rate for full vaccination, while conversely, other towns classified as semi-urban showed the lowest level of full vaccination coverage. Overall, 39% of children were found to be fully vaccinated. Being in a semi-urban residence, older maternal age, rural residence, maternal education, and unemployment were associated with not being vaccinated. Some of the barriers responsible for low routine immunization coverage in urban settings included poor defaulter tracking mechanisms for urban children, unfriendly immunization service delivery in urban public health facilities due to overstretched human resources, lack of effective strategies to reach the most vulnerable and marginalized urban communities with vaccines, and private service provider barriers, to name a few.

A community-based cross-sectional mixed-method study conducted in Toke Kutaye district, central Ethiopia, assessed vaccination timeliness and associated factors among children [22] and found an overall timeliness of childhood vaccination of only 23.9 percent among children aged 12 to 23 months, making other children who did not receive timely vaccines vulnerable. Urban residence, participation of pregnant women in conferences, and institutional delivery are among the independent predictors associated with the timeliness of childhood vaccination.

A descriptive cross-sectional survey of adolescent girls' parents conducted in two urban and two rural secondary schools in Lagos, Nigeria, documented parental acceptance of human papillomavirus vaccination for adolescent girls [23]. Urban residence among other factors such as tertiary level of education in the mother, skilled occupation of both parents, and knowledge of HPV were all positively associated with getting vaccinated with HPV vaccines.

Tadesse and colleagues explored associated factors related to second-dose measles vaccination among under-five children in urban areas of North Shewa Zone, Oromia, Ethiopia, using a community-based cross-sectional study [24]. The study found a low (42.5%) level of second-dose measles vaccination (MCV2) among children in urban areas of the study area. Some of the predictors of MCV2 uptake included maternal age, average time mothers had been waiting for vaccination at the health facility, awareness about vaccine-preventable diseases, awareness around recommended age for the last MCV vaccine in the series, and knowledge of the recommended number of MCV doses. A lack of information was the major reason for children not getting the MCV2 vaccination.

Findings from a study in Cavite, the Philippines, which assessed hesitancy towards vaccines among caregivers using in-depth interviews, documented that among the reasons for delay or refusal of childhood vaccinations, fear of side effects emerged as the most salient concern, exacerbated by previous negative experiences (including trauma) from a dengue vaccine controversy in 2017. Respondents also highlighted religious, cultural, and health system factors, including appointment scheduling and waiting times as predictors of childhood vaccination [25].

3.3. *Identified Pro-Equity Strategies*

Some strategies to ensure full vaccination during the pandemic were also highlighted in some of the papers reviewed. In one such paper, parents from multiple states in India chose to use private hospitals for child immunization due to the fear of themselves or their kids getting infected with the COVID-19 virus [15]. Some of the facilities in these cities considered shortening the waiting time for routine childhood vaccination service delivery, while others changed their vaccination timing schedule to reduce the spread of infection during the COVID-19 pandemic.

Meckonnen and colleagues conducted a phenomenological qualitative study to document strategies to revitalize immunization service provision in urban settings of the cities of Addis Ababa, Dire Dawa, and Mekele in Ethiopia [26]. Their study found that the immunization service provision strategies existing during the study period in urban settings were not adequate to reach all children and are mostly static (fixed) sessions. Some of the proposed strategies included expanding routine immunization service access to marginalized populations through outreach services, strengthening the public–private partnership, engaging the private health facilities for vaccination services, and integrating technological innovations (such as digitalization of the EPI program and application of mHealth reminders) to facilitate inter-facility linkage.

Balogun and colleagues conducted a pre- and post-interventional study in seven urban slum communities in Ibadan, Nigeria, in 2020–2021 to document the effect of intensive training in improving older women's knowledge and support for infant vaccination in Nigerian urban slums [27]. Identified older women received training through participatory learning methods over an 8-month period with a manual and short video on the importance of immunization timeliness and completion, how vaccines work, and how to be advocates and supporters of infant vaccination. It was shown that participatory learning improved the knowledge of these older women who provide support and supervision for childcare in urban slums about vaccination and how to better support infant vaccination.

The study from Oromia (Tadesse et al.) also recommended some strategies for increasing the uptake of MCV2, including shortening the waiting time for vaccination at the health facility to within half an hour, intensifying awareness for parents and caregivers, and paying particular attention to mothers who are older than 36 years of age [24].

4. Discussion

With the rapid globalization seen in many countries, it is imperative to proactively identify and address urban-specific challenges to routine immunization, including mapping and reaching zero-dose children and missed communities. This renewed focus will assist efforts toward extending the reach of vaccines in urban settings and contribute to achieving the IA2030 targets. Already, it is estimated that about 30% of zero-dose children live in urban and peri-urban areas [8], and these numbers could grow rapidly without sufficient focus and proactive interventions. A key step, which this paper has taken, is to review evidence on the backsliding of coverage and routine immunization performance in urban settings and select focus countries harboring more than 75% of zero-dose children globally, documenting predictors of coverage and pro-equity strategies. Findings from this review show evidence of backsliding and disruption across the globe in urban and peri-urban contexts; major urbanized countries from around the world, such as Brazil, Pakistan, Ethiopia, India, and Cameroon, show various levels of immunization performance disruption in multiple urban contexts [6,15,18,19,28]. The disruptions to immunization affected multiple vaccines in each country's routine immunization schedule, including BCG, yellow fever (YFV), and DPT. Many challenges varied across the different global contexts, including no first-time immunization registration for children, poor tracking mechanisms for urban children, unfriendly delivery, and lack of effective urban-immunization-specific strategies; similarly, varied determinants of higher immunization coverage included institutional delivery of children, higher maternal education, lower maternal age, and positive knowledge and attitudes around immunization. Of the identified pro-equity strategies, shortening waiting time for service delivery, improved outreach services, and promotion of maternal and female figure education were associated with higher levels of immunization coverage. The predictors of childhood vaccination in urban settings, as well as noted pro-equity strategies, as documented in these studies, are consistent with what has been documented pre-pandemic [29–31].

These results suggest several potential areas for effective interventions to accelerate inroads into urban immunization. The identified pro-equity strategies above link to challenges on immunization and higher immunization coverage levels, and while there is a lot of diversity in backsliding issues, successful pro-equity strategies were also tailored to specific contexts, which emphasizes the need to contextualize interventions to address specific idiosyncrasies in each context [32]. Some results were contradictory to the idea that urbanized populations can be associated with poorer vaccination coverage, but most of the studies supported this idea. Additionally, this is not surprising as the world population transitions to become more urbanized [12], especially with the limited studies focusing on the peculiarities of essential vaccination in urban and peri-urban contexts.

This review contributes to a clearer understanding of the post-pandemic landscape of urban immunization in low- and middle-income countries, including challenges, immunization coverage determinants, and most importantly, pro-equity strategies. These pro-equity strategies are essential to ensuring that vaccines reach under-served populations and missed communities, and in examining these strategies more closely, we can better generate a starting point for a roadmap to longer-term urban immunization information. These are consistent with earlier documentation of pro-equity strategies in Gavi-supported countries [33].

Contextualized pro-equity urban immunization interventions will result in faster advances toward the IA2030 targets, and work to halt and slow down current backsliding and fragility in immunization systems. Additionally, many of the results point to the room for multisectoral and integrated interventions, as many of the determinants related to low immunization coverage point to potential interventions on gender barriers, education barriers, and systems strengthening [32,34,35]. Tools such as the urban immunization toolkit are being used by several countries to complement existing immunization guidelines by tailoring immunization planning, implementing, and monitoring approaches to meet challenging contexts in urban areas, especially in slum environments; many such tools are available to support these efforts globally [35].

There are some limitations to the data reviewed, including its quantity, generalizability, and whether urban-specific immunization challenges and contexts can be differentiated from generalized immunization challenges and contexts. There were a limited number of studies examining the post-pandemic urban immunization landscape, and the evidence was limited to a relatively small number of countries. Studies that concentrated on the slums were included alongside other peri-urban and urban settings across many different countries, and due to the evidence being contextualized, it may not be possible to generalize these findings. Additionally, many of the studies reviewed were only conducted in urban settings, so evidence of uniquely urban-related challenges is somewhat limited, as these challenges could apply in other settings. Furthermore, the definitions of urban and peri-urban used across the studies may have varied, which could have affected the findings and interpretation.

Because there is a relative dearth of information about urban immunization occurring after the acute phase of COVID-19, and much more information about the acceleration of global immunization and backsliding, it is essential that more studies be conducted on this intersection, as it is crucial to have more disaggregated data around urban backsliding, immunization performance evidence, and pro-equity strategies. Issues specific to the urban context need to be differentiated from generalized data in order to contextualize and prioritize the necessary correlated interventions and pro-equity strategies.

4.1. Policy Suggestions

(a) Multisectoral innovations: many of the drivers of immunization performance highlighted from this and other reviews transcend 'traditional' determinants of immunization performance (such as vaccine supply or trained community health worker availability). Addressing other social issues such as maternal education, access to water, sanitation, and hygiene (WASH) services, and (maternal and child) education is pivotal in improving immunization performance in urban settings [32], especially governance in the immunization space around urban and should be inclusive of these sectors for more robust programming.

(b) Strengthen partnerships: leveraging the comparative strengths and expertise of partners across immunization, health, and other sectors such as planning and sanitation will be valuable. For instance, the Mission Indradhanush (MI) in India, which worked across sectors, recorded significant gains in immunization coverage in both urban and rural settings [36]. Considering the diversity of non-government actors in urban areas, a purposeful policy shift to further incorporate private service providers and non-governmental organizations into immunization service delivery is needed.

(c) Monitoring and Data: The typical immunization data built upon traditional subnational administrative boundaries may not suffice to effectively monitor, measure, and track children in urban settings [13,35]. The urban population is fast growing and in motion most of the time. Modern innovations in digital registries and data tracking systems could provide answers on how to effectively track these inherently transient and migratory populations or populations that may not have access to the traditional identifications used in accessing government health services. Periodic routine micro census and the use of geographic information system (GIS) enable data to have shown great promise [8,37]. More enhanced disaggregation of immunization data by urban in routine data systems, such as the WHO and UNICEF joint reporting form (JRF), as well as in coverage surveys will support monitoring and tracking of immunization services in urban areas.

The above and other context-specific policy adjustments should be considered to make improvements and tend toward achieving the IA2030 goals.

4.2. Future Studies

The limited studies available and reviewed in this review point to the need for more evidence generation and documentation, including documenting and sharing tested innovations within the urban context. These are not only essential but also have the potential to be incredibly innovative and informative. Many countries included in the search have not performed or reported studies on immunization performance in urban contexts during or after the pandemic. Future studies could consider examining the efficacy and effectiveness of innovations, urban settlement micro plans and micro tracking mechanisms, GIS mapping, the intertwining of conflicts, displacements and urban immunization, digital registry systems, and how urban immunization plans can be combined with other social sector innovations.

5. Limitations

The literature search was limited to the top 20 zero-dose countries based on 2021 WUENIC data; these, however, may not be fully representative of other countries. Only 15 papers were eligible after screening, and some of the 20 countries were not represented at the conclusion of the literature review, indicating a limitation of existing literature on the subject. Grey literature and other non-published reports were not included in this review. Some of the studies did not fully elucidate the nuances of challenges faced in urban or peri-urban settings.

6. Conclusions

The findings presented clearly demonstrate the evidence of a decline in routine immunization coverage in urban and peri-urban settings; as such, the need to target and focus context-specific catch-up and recovery strategies to bring back routine immunization performance on track. However, they also elucidate the need to further explore and examine determinants of low immunization coverage in urbanized areas, particularly in low- and middle-income countries. There are relatively few papers that estimate the magnitude of backsliding caused by COVID-19 in urban and peri-urban settings, in these priority countries, as well as a dearth of papers focusing on key issues affecting routine immunization in these settings and effective pro-equity strategies to address those keys issues in immunization recovery. While the COVID-19 pandemic has only been affecting immunization coverage in these areas for almost three years, the backsliding caused by this international disruption has proved detrimental, particularly toward reaching the goals set by IA2030.

Over the many different contexts explored through the review, different factors have been shown to affect immunization coverage in urban and peri-urban areas. It is essential that each context is specifically examined for services to be designed and tailored to the communities affected by the lack of access to these services. Innovations in interventions will be needed to build a better pro-equitable system of immunization for these areas. Rapid global urbanization makes addressing urban immunization challenges an essential and immediate priority in order to keep up with the demands placed on global immunization systems in the 21st century.

Author Contributions: I.D. conceived the initial idea and drafted the frame of the paper. I.D. and R.V.B. conducted the review of the literature. I.D., R.V.B. and A.I. completed various sections of the paper. A.R., I.H., D.A., N.D. and S.V.S. provided input and critical review to various sections of the paper and in the finalization of the paper. All authors have read and agreed to the published version of the manuscript.

Funding: This research is funded in part by the Gavi, the Vaccine Alliance through Grant SC220417 to UNICEF.

Institutional Review Board Statement: Not applicable.

Informed Consent Statement: Studies included in this review obtained informed consent from subjects where applicable.

Data Availability Statement: All data and publications used are referenced and available in the related databases.

Acknowledgments: The Urban Immunization Working Group is an extra-organizational group facilitated by UNICEF, comprising experts and academics from several different organizations. Thanks go to staff from UNICEF, WHO, University of Oxford, Bill and Melinda Gates Foundation, John Snow, Inc. and Johns Hopkins Bloomberg School of Public Health, who contributed to this review. Additionally, thanks to other members of the working group for their contributions towards improving immunization in urban contexts.

Conflicts of Interest: The authors declare no conflict of interest.

Appendix A

Appendix A.1. Immunization Coverage Performance for the 20 Highest Burden Zero-Dose Countries

Rank	Country	DTP1 (%)	DTP3 (%)	MCV1 (%)	Number Zero-Dose Children
1	India	88	85	89	2,711,000
2	Nigeria	70	56	59	2,247,000
3	Indonesia	74	67	72	1,150,000
4	Ethiopia	70	65	54	1,134,000
5	Philippines	57	57	57	1,048,000
6	Democratic Republic of the Congo	81	65	55	734,000
7	Brazil	74	68	73	710,000
8	Pakistan	90	83	81	611,000
9	Angola	57	45	36	553,000
10	Myanmar	45	37	44	492,000
11	United Republic of Tanzania	82	81	76	402,000
12	Mozambique	67	61	84	372,000
13	Afghanistan	74	66	63	361,000
14	Somalia	52	42	46	338,000
15	Mexico	83	78	99	317,000
16	Madagascar	65	55	39	304,000
17	Cameroon	76	69		219,000

Rank	Country	DTP1 (%)	DTP3 (%)	MCV1 (%)	Number Zero-Dose Children
18	Democratic People's Republic of Korea	42	41	42	197,000
19	Chad	73	58	55	191,000
20	Viet Nam	87	83	89	187,000

Appendix A.2. Full Search Strategy

Keywords: "Routine Immunization"[TIAB] OR "Vaccination*"[TIAB] OR "Vaccination Coverage"[TIAB] OR "Childhood Vaccination"[TIAB]

AND

Urban OR Peri-urban OR City OR "Urban center" OR "urban slum"

AND

India OR Nigeria OR Indonesia OR Ethiopia OR Philippines OR "Democratic Republic of the Congo" OR Brazil OR Pakistan OR Angola OR Myanmar OR United Republic of Tanzania OR Mozambique OR Afghanistan OR Somalia OR Mexico OR Madagascar OR Cameroon OR Democratic People's Republic of Korea OR Chad OR Viet Nam

PubMed

(("Routine Immunization"[Title/Abstract] OR "vaccination*"[Title/Abstract] OR "Vaccination Coverage"[Title/Abstract] OR "Childhood Vaccination"[Title/Abstract]) AND ("Urban"[Title/Abstract] OR "Peri-urban"[Title/Abstract] OR "City"[Title/Abstract] OR "Urban center"[Title/Abstract] OR "urban slum"[Title/Abstract]) AND ("India"[Title/ Abstract] OR "Nigeria"[Title/Abstract] OR "Indonesia"[Title/Abstract] OR "Ethiopia"[Title/ Abstract] OR "Philippines"[Title/Abstract] OR "Democratic Republic of the Congo"[Title/ Abstract] OR "Brazil"[Title/Abstract] OR "Pakistan"[Title/Abstract] OR "Angola"[Title/ Abstract] OR "Myanmar"[Title/Abstract] OR "united republic of tanzania"[Title/Abstract] OR "Mozambique"[Title/Abstract] OR "Afghanistan"[Title/Abstract] OR "Somalia"[Title/ Abstract] OR "Mexico"[Title/Abstract] OR "Madagascar"[Title/Abstract] OR "Cameroon" [Title/Abstract] OR "democratic people s republic of korea"[Title/Abstract] OR "Chad" [Title/Abstract] OR "viet nam"[Title/Abstract])) AND (2020/3/1:2023/2/3[pdat])

Result = 321

Web of Science

AB = ("Routine Immunization" OR "Vaccination*" OR "Vaccination Coverage" OR "Childhood Vaccination") AND AB = (India OR Nigeria OR Indonesia OR Ethiopia OR Philippines OR "Democratic Republic of the Congo" OR Brazil OR Pakistan OR Angola OR Myanmar OR United Republic of Tanzania OR Mozambique OR Afghanistan OR Somalia OR Mexico OR Madagascar OR Cameroon OR Democratic People's Republic of Korea OR Chad OR Viet Nam) AND AB = (Urban OR Peri-urban OR City OR "Urban center" OR "urban slum") March 2020 to Feb 2023

Result = 287

Appendix A.3. Summary Table for Search Results

Title	Year	Type of Study	Location	Summary
Yellow fever vaccination before and during the COVID-19 pandemic in Brazil [14].	2022	Ecological, time series study	Brazil (Nationwide)	A 48.55% reduction in the median number of yellow fever vaccine doses administered in Brazil and in its regions 1 year before the pandemic as compared to 1 year during the pandemic: North (−34.71%), Midwest (−21.72%), South (−63.50%), and Southeast (−34.42%)

Title	Year	Type of Study	Location	Summary
Child Vaccination Coverage, Trends and Predictors in Eastern Ethiopia: Implication for Sustainable Development Goals [21].	2021	A population-based longitudinal study	Kersa, Eastern Ethiopia (incl. Harar town)	A little more than a third (39%) of children were fully vaccinated; with highest proportion (45%) seen in 2020 and the lowest (32%) in 2019. Other towns classified as semi-urban had the lowest fully vaccinated proportion even as Harar city saw 45% full vaccination for its children.
Experiences of Urban Slum-Dwelling Women with Maternal and Child Health Services During COVID-19 Pandemic: A Multi-City Qualitative Study From India [15].	2022	A phenomenological study to document MCH experience during COVID-19 pandemic	India: Four states Odisha, Uttarakhand, Chhattisgarh, and Assam. One slum city per state	All participants in this study mentioned that their children were vaccinated during the pandemic with little or no issues. Fear that the child may get infected with COVID-19 was highlighted by caregivers. A few choose a private hospital for child immunization due to fear of COVID-19.
Strategies to revitalize immunization service provision in urban settings of Ethiopia [26].	2021	A qualitative study with a phenomenological study design	Ethiopia: Addis Ababa, Dire Dawa and Mekele	The highlight of the study is that existing immunization service delivery strategies within urban contexts which are mostly fixed sites are not adequate to effectively reach children with vaccines in these settings.
Impact of COVID-19 pandemic on routine immunization of children [16].	2022	Cross-sectional study	Pakistan: Mirpur, Azad Kashmir,	The fear of COVID-19 infection was highlighted as an important factor for delayed vaccination in 65% of respondents.
Disparities in full immunization coverage among urban and rural children aged 12–23 months in southwest Ethiopia: A comparative cross-sectional study [17].	2022	A comparative cross-sectional	Ethiopia: Wolaita zone	Children in urban areas had a higher prevalence of full vaccination than their rural counterparts with a 15.10% (95% CI; 0.102–0.192) point estimate for the difference but still below WHO recommendation. Knowledge and place of delivery were predictor variables.
Effect of intensive training in improving older women's knowledge and support for infant vaccination in Nigerian urban slums: a before-and-after intervention study [27].	2021	Pre- and post-study	Nigeria: Seven urban slums communities in Ibadan	Participatory learning improved the knowledge about and support for infant vaccination among older women supervising childcare in these urban slum communities.
Assessment of vaccination timeliness and associated factors among children in Toke Kutaye district, central Ethiopia: A Mixed study [22].	2022	A community-based cross-sectional mixed-method study	Ethiopia: Toke Kutaye district, central Ethiopia.	Timeliness of childhood vaccination was 23.9 percent among children aged 12 to 23 months. Urban residence (AOR: 3.15, 95% CI: 1.56–6.4), participation of pregnant women in conferences (AOR: 2.35, 95% CI: 1.2–4.57), institutional delivery (AOR: 2.5)
Parental acceptance of human papillomavirus vaccination for adolescent girls in Lagos, Nigeria [23].	2020	A descriptive cross-sectional survey of adolescent girls' parents	India: 2 urban and 2 rural schools in Lagos	Tertiary level of education in the mother (cOR = 67.41; 95% CI = 15.25–297.97; p = 0.0000), skilled occupation in the mother (cOR = 11.55; 95% CI = 5.55–24.04; p = 0.0000), skilled occupation in the father (cOR = 4.10; 95% CI = 2.31–7.28; p = 0.0000), are predictors of HPV vaccination.
Second-dose measles vaccination and associated factors among under-five children in urban areas of North Shoa Zone, Central Ethiopia, 2022 [24].	2022	A community-based cross-sectional study	Ethiopia: urban areas of North Shewa Zone, Oromia	With a 90.1% response rate in 372 participants, the coverage of measles second-dose vaccination (MCV2) among children in urban areas was low (42.5%).

Title	Year	Type of Study	Location	Summary
Impact of COVID-19 pandemic response on uptake of routine immunizations in Sindh, Pakistan: An analysis of provincial electronic immunization registry data [6].	2020	Quantitative: Secondary data analysis of daily immunization coverage	Pakistan: Sindh urban and rural	The average daily vaccination rate during the COVID-19 lockdown saw a 52.5% decline. Bacille Calmette Guérin (BCG) vaccines saw the highest decline of 40.6% (958/2360). An estimated 8438 children per day missed their vaccines during the lockdown. Areas mostly affected included rural districts, urban sub-districts with large slums, and polio-endemic super high-risk sub-districts.
Impact of the Early Stages of the COVID-19 Pandemic on Coverage of Reproductive, Maternal, and Newborn Health Interventions in Ethiopia: A Natural Experiment [18].	2022	A nationally representative cross-sectional survey	Ethiopia: Addis Ababa	Significant reductions in coverage of BCG vaccination and chlorohexidine use in urban areas were observed in the COVID-19-affected cohort.
Impact and projections of the COVID-19 epidemic on attendance and routine vaccinations at a pediatric referral hospital in Cameroon [19].	2021	A descriptive and retrospective cross-sectional study	Cameroon: Yaoundé	There was a decline in vaccination demand including BCG vaccines, DPT, polio, and MMR in children as well as tetanus vaccines in women of childbearing age, all dropped significantly.
Scared, powerless, insulted and embarrassed: hesitancy towards vaccines among caregivers in Cavite Province, the Philippines [25].	2021	Qualitative: In-depth interviews (IDIs)	Philippines: Cavite Province	Among the reasons for delay or refusal of childhood vaccinations, fear of side effects emerged as the most salient concern, exacerbated by previous negative experiences (including trauma) from a dengue vaccine controversy in 2017.
Missed childhood immunizations during the COVID-19 pandemic in Brazil: Analyses of routine statistics and a national household survey [20].	2021	Qualitative: Ecological, time series study	Brazil: National with subnational statistics	About 20% decline in vaccination rates was seen in children 2 years or older during the months of March and April 2020 during the lockdown in comparison with January and February 2020. The least developed regions of the country were the most affected by missed immunization

References

1. Equity Reference Group. Who We Are/What We Do. Zero-Dose Community of Practice. Available online: https://www.zero-dose.org/services (accessed on 4 April 2023).
2. UN-Habitat. World Cities Report 2022. Available online: https://unhabitat.org/sites/default/files/2022/06/wcr_2022.pdf (accessed on 4 April 2023).
3. Equity Reference Group. Tackling Inequities in Immunization Outcomes in Urban Contexts. Available online: https://drive.google.com/file/d/1qB__5YAhyQiponTlL50a8y7h5LiTG_Kb/view (accessed on 4 April 2023).
4. World Health Organization (WHO). WHO Coronavirus (COVID-19) Dashboard. Available online: https://covid19.who.int/ (accessed on 4 April 2023).
5. Ota, M.O.C.; Badur, S.; Romano-Mazzotti, L.; Friedland, L.R. Impact of COVID-19 pandemic on routine immunization. *Ann. Med.* **2021**, *53*, 2286–2297. [CrossRef] [PubMed]
6. Chandir, S.; Siddiqi, D.A.; Mehmood, M.; Setayesh, H.; Siddique, M.; Mirza, A.; Soundardjee, R.; Dharma, V.K.; Shah, M.T.; Abdullah, S.; et al. Impact of COVID-19 pandemic response on uptake of routine immunizations in Sindh, Pakistan: An analysis of provincial electronic immunization registry data. *Vaccine* **2020**, *38*, 7146–7155. [CrossRef] [PubMed]
7. Causey, K.; Fullman, N.; Sorensen, R.J.D.; Galles, N.C.; Zheng, P.; Aravkin, A.; Danovaro-Holliday, M.C.; Martinez-Piedra, R.; Sodha, S.V.; Velandia-González, M.P.; et al. Estimating global and regional disruptions to routine childhood vaccine coverage during the COVID-19 pandemic in 2020: A modelling study. *Lancet* **2021**, *398*, 522–534. [CrossRef] [PubMed]
8. Wigley, A.; Lorin, J.; Hogan, D.; Utazi, C.E.; Hagedorn, B.; Dansereau, E.; Tatem, A.J.; Tejedor-Garavito, N. Estimates of the number and distribution of zero-dose and under-immunised children across remote-rural, urban, and conflict-affected settings in low and middle-income countries. *PLOS Glob. Public Health* **2022**, *2*, e0001126. [CrossRef]

9. Immunization Agenda. (IA2030). Scorecard. Available online: http://scorecard.immunizationagenda2030.org/ (accessed on 4 April 2023).
10. World Health Organization. Implementing the Immunization Agenda 2030. 2021. Available online: https://www.who.int/publications/m/item/implementing-the-immunization-agenda-2030 (accessed on 7 January 2021).
11. UNICEF. Catch-Up | Restore | Strengthen: Immunization Recovery Plan 2023–2025. 2022. Available online: https://apps.who.int/gb/MSPI/pdf_files/2023/03/Item1_24-03.pdf (accessed on 4 April 2023).
12. World Bank. Urban Population (% of Total Population). Available online: https://data.worldbank.org/indicator/SP.URB.TOTL.IN.ZS (accessed on 4 April 2023).
13. UIWG. Urban Immunization Working Group Terms of Reference. Available online: https://www3.paho.org/hq/index.php?option=com_content&view=article&id=14086:tag-onvpd-tor&Itemid=0&lang=en#gsc.tab=0 (accessed on 4 April 2023).
14. Silva, T.M.R.D.; Sá, A.C.M.G.N.D.; Prates, E.J.S.; Rodrigues, D.E.; Silva, T.P.R.D.; Matozinhos, F.P.; Vieira, E.W.R. Yellow fever vaccination before and during the COVID-19 pandemic in Brazil. *Rev. Saude Publica* **2022**, *56*, 45. [CrossRef]
15. Sahoo, K.C.; Doley, C.; Negi, S.; Das, S.; Verma, P.; Kanungo, S.; Pati, S. Experiences of Urban Slum-Dwelling Women with Maternal and Child Health Services During COVID-19 Pandemic: A Multi-City Qualitative Study From India. *Int. J. Public Health* **2022**, *67*, 1604348. [CrossRef]
16. Manzoor, A.; Abbasi, N.B.; Khizar, N.; Khalil, M.; Anjum, S.; Iqbal, A. Impact of COVID-19 pandemic on routine immunization of children. *Rawal Med. J.* **2022**, *47*, 45–48.
17. Asmare, G.; Madalicho, M.; Sorsa, A. Disparities in full immunization coverage among urban and rural children aged 12–23 months in southwest Ethiopia: A comparative cross-sectional study. *Hum. Vaccines Immunother.* **2022**, *18*, 2101316. [CrossRef]
18. Carter, E.D.; Zimmerman, L.; Qian, J.; Roberton, T.; Seme, A.; Shiferaw, S. Impact of the Early Stages of the COVID-19 Pandemic on Coverage of Reproductive, Maternal, and Newborn Health Interventions in Ethiopia: A Natural Experiment. *Front. Public Health* **2022**, *10*, 778413. [CrossRef]
19. Chelo, D.; Nguefack, F.; Enyama, D.; Nansseu, R.; Tefoueyet, G.F.; Awa, H.M.; Nkwelle, I.M.; Nguefack-Tsague, G.; Ndenbe, P.; Ndombo, P.K. Impact and projections of the COVID-19 epidemic on attendance and routine vaccinations at a pediatric referral hospital in Cameroon. *Arch. Pediatr.* **2021**, *28*, 441–450. [CrossRef]
20. Silveira, M.F.; Tonial, C.T.; Maranhão, A.G.K.; Teixeira, A.M.; Hallal, P.C.; Menezes, A.M.B.; Horta, B.L.; Hartwig, F.P.; Barros, A.J.; Victora, C.G. Missed childhood immunizations during the COVID-19 pandemic in Brazil: Analyses of routine statistics and of a national household survey. *Vaccine* **2021**, *39*, 3404–3409. [CrossRef]
21. Dheresa, M.; Dessie, Y.; Negash, B.; Balis, B.; Getachew, T.; Mamo Ayana, G.; Merga, B.T.; Regassa, L.D. Child Vaccination Coverage, Trends and Predictors in Eastern Ethiopia: Implication for Sustainable Development Goals. *J. Multidiscip. Healthc.* **2021**, *14*, 2657–2667. [CrossRef]
22. Dirirsa, K.; Makuria, M.; Mulu, E.; Deriba, B.S. Assessment of vaccination timeliness and associated factors among children in Toke Kutaye district, central Ethiopia: A Mixed study. *PLoS ONE* **2022**, *17*, e0262320. [CrossRef]
23. Rabiu, K.A.; Alausa, T.G.; Akinlusi, F.M.; Davies, N.O.; Shittu, K.A.; Akinola, O.I. Parental acceptance of human papillomavirus vaccination for adolescent girls in Lagos, Nigeria. *J. Fam. Med. Prim. Care* **2020**, *9*, 2950–2957. [CrossRef]
24. Tadesse, A.; Sahlu, D.; Benayew, M. Second-dose measles vaccination and associated factors among under-five children in urban areas of North Shoa Zone, Central Ethiopia, 2022. *Front. Public Health* **2022**, *10*, 1029740. [CrossRef]
25. Landicho-Guevarra, J.; Reñosa, M.D.C.; Wachinger, J.; Endoma, V.; Aligato, M.F.; Bravo, T.A.; Landicho, J.; Bärnighausen, K.; A McMahon, S. Scared, powerless, insulted and embarrassed: Hesitancy towards vaccines among caregivers in Cavite Province, the Philippines. *BMJ Glob. Health* **2021**, *6*, e006529. [CrossRef]
26. Mekonnen, Z.A.; Nigus, M.; Assefa, S.; Biru, A.; Teklu, A.; Feletto, M.; Gera, R.; Ba-Nguz, A.; Tilahun, B. Strategies to revitalize immunization service provision in urban settings of Ethiopia. *Ethiop. J. Health Dev.* **2021**, *35*, 98–110.
27. Balogun, F.; Bamidele, O.; Bamgboye, E. Effect of intensive training in improving older women's knowledge and support for infant vaccination in Nigerian urban slums: A before-and-after intervention study. *BMC Public Health* **2021**, *21*, 266. [CrossRef]
28. Baroni, L.; Alves, R.F.S.; Boccolini, C.S.; Salles, R.; Gritz, R.; Paixão, B.; Boccolini, P.D.M.M. Database on the coverage of the "Bolsa-Familia" conditioning cash-transfer program: Brazil, 2005 to 2021. *BMC Res. Notes* **2021**, *14*, 435. [CrossRef]
29. Larkin, H.D. Backslide in Global Childhood Vaccinations. *JAMA* **2022**, *328*, 1029. [CrossRef]
30. Maina, L.C.; Karanja, S.; Kombich, J. Immunization coverage and its determinants among children aged 12–23 months in a peri-urban area of Kenya. *Pan. Afr. Med. J.* **2013**, *14*, 3. [CrossRef] [PubMed]
31. Tefera, Y.A.; Wagner, A.L.; Mekonen, E.B.; Carlson, B.F.; Boulton, M.L. Predictors and Barriers to Full Vaccination among Children in Ethiopia. *Vaccines* **2018**, *6*, 22. [CrossRef] [PubMed]
32. Crocker-Buque, T.; Mindra, G.; Duncan, R.; Mounier-Jack, S. Immunization, urbanization and slums—A systematic review of factors and interventions. *BMC Public Health* **2017**, *17*, 556. [CrossRef] [PubMed]
33. Dadari, I.; Higgins-Steele, A.; Sharkey, A.; Charlet, D.; Shahabuddin, A.; Nandy, R.; Jackson, D. Pro-equity immunization and health systems strengthening strategies in select Gavi-supported countries. *Vaccine* **2021**, *39*, 2434–2444. [CrossRef]
34. Siddiqui, F.A.; Padhani, Z.A.; Salam, R.A.; Aliani, R.; Lassi, Z.S.; Das, J.K.; Bhutta, Z.A. Interventions to Improve Immunization Coverage Among Children and Adolescents: A Meta-analysis. *Pediatrics* **2022**, *149* (Suppl. 5), e2021053852D. [CrossRef]
35. United Nations International Children's Emergency Fund. *Urban Immunization Toolkit*; UNICEF: New York, NY, USA, 2018.

36. Gurnani, V.; Haldar, P.; Aggarwal, M.K.; Das, M.K.; Chauhan, A.; Murray, J.; Arora, N.K.; Jhalani, M.; Sudan, P. Improving vaccination coverage in India: Lessons from Intensified Mission Indradhanush, a cross-sectoral systems strengthening strategy. *BMJ* **2018**, *363*, k4782. [CrossRef]
37. WorldPop and National Population Commission of Nigeria. *Bottom-Up Gridded Population Estimates for Nigeria*, Version 2.0; WorldPop, University of Southampton: Southampton, UK, 2021.

vaccines

MDPI

Review

Equity-Informative Economic Evaluations of Vaccines: A Systematic Literature Review

Chanthawat Patikorn [1,2], Jeong-Yeon Cho [1,3], Philipp Lambach [4], Raymond Hutubessy [4] and Nathorn Chaiyakunapruk [1,5,*]

1 Department of Pharmacotherapy, College of Pharmacy, University of Utah, Salt Lake City, UT 84112, USA
2 Department of Social and Administrative Pharmacy, Faculty of Pharmaceutical Sciences, Chulalongkorn University, Bangkok 10540, Thailand
3 School of Pharmacy, Sungkyunkwan University, Suwon 16419, Republic of Korea
4 Department of Immunization, Vaccines and Biologicals (IVB), World Health Organization, 1211 Geneva, Switzerland
5 IDEAS Center, Veterans Affairs Salt Lake City Healthcare System, Salt Lake City, UT 84112, USA
* Correspondence: nathorn.chaiyakunapruk@utah.edu; Tel.: +1-801-585-3092

Abstract: The Immunization Agenda 2030 prioritizes the populations without access to vaccines. Health equity has been increasingly incorporated into economic evaluations of vaccines to foster equitable access. Robust and standardized methods are needed to evaluate the health equity impact of vaccination programs to ensure monitoring and effective addressing of inequities. However, methods currently in place vary and potentially affect the application of findings to inform policy decision-making. We performed a systematic review by searching PubMed, Embase, Econlit, and the CEA Registry up to 15 December 2022 to identify equity-informative economic evaluations of vaccines. Twenty-one studies were included that performed health equity impact analysis to estimate the distributional impact of vaccines, such as deaths averted and financial risk protection, across equity-relevant subgroups. These studies showed that the introduction of vaccines or improved vaccination coverage resulted in fewer deaths and higher financial risk benefits in subpopulations with higher disease burdens and lower vaccination coverage—particularly poorer income groups and those living in rural areas. In conclusion, methods to incorporate equity have been evolving progressively. Vaccination programs can enhance equity if their design and implementation address existing inequities in order to provide equitable vaccination coverage and achieve health equity.

Keywords: equity; inequality; disparity; economic evaluation; cost-effectiveness analysis; vaccine; immunization

Citation: Patikorn, C.; Cho, J.-Y.; Lambach, P.; Hutubessy, R.; Chaiyakunapruk, N. Equity-Informative Economic Evaluations of Vaccines: A Systematic Literature Review. *Vaccines* **2023**, *11*, 622. https://doi.org/10.3390/vaccines11030622

Academic Editor: Davide Gori

Received: 10 February 2023
Revised: 1 March 2023
Accepted: 2 March 2023
Published: 9 March 2023

1. Introduction

The number of children not receiving a single dose of routine vaccine (defined as the first dose of diphtheria, tetanus, and pertussis (DTP1) non-receipt), also referred as "zero-dose children", increased by 5 million in 2021 compared with 2019, going from 13 to 18 million. More than 60% of these children live in extremely poor conditions facing a lack of access to reproductive health services, water, and sanitation [1]. Health equity has been increasingly incorporated into economic evaluations of vaccines to foster equitable access. The Immunization Agenda 2030 prioritizes populations that are not being reached through current immunization efforts—particularly the most marginalized communities, those living in fragile and conflict-affected settings, mobile populations, and those moving across borders [2]. Robust and standardized methods are needed to evaluate the health equity impact of vaccination programs to ensure monitoring and effective addressing of inequities.

The Immunization Agenda 2030, through its Strategic Priority 3, addresses equity by defining key areas of focus and objectives to reach the goal of protecting everyone with full immunization, regardless of location, age, socioeconomic status, or gender-related barriers [2]. The World Health Organization's "Guide for Standardization of Economic Evaluations of Immunization Programmes" also recommends that the health equity impact be included if it is considered an important factor for decision-making [3]. These recommendations emphasized the need to explore and summarize how health equity was incorporated and evaluated in the existing literature on economic evaluations of vaccines.

Health technology assessment has been employed in many countries to inform healthcare decision-making [4]. This is especially relevant to countries aiming to provide accessible, affordable, equitable, and high-quality healthcare services to their populations while ensuring the sustainability of health systems in place. Equity-informative assessments can provide data on the health equity impact of health technologies and public health policies and the inherent tradeoff between total coverage and equitable coverage. Based on these data, decision-makers can better balance the efficient use of limited budgets and foster equitable access to healthcare. Health equity impact analysis has been increasingly incorporated into the economic evaluations of health technologies and public health policies, including vaccines [5–13]. Health equity impact analysis is conducted to estimate the distribution of impact of alternative policy options, broken down by one or more variables of concern to policymakers from an equity perspective [14]. Nevertheless, varying methods to evaluate the health equity impact can affect the application of findings to inform policy decision-making.

Several systematic reviews summarize equity-informative economic evaluations in terms of methodological aspects and the application of the methods in general [5,15–19]. However, no systematic review comprehensively describes how health equity is incorporated into the economic evaluations of vaccines. In addition, economic evaluations of vaccines differ from other health technologies given the unique characteristics of vaccines, such as program deployment costs, vaccination coverage, and herd protection [3]. Therefore, we conducted a systematic literature review to identify economic evaluations of the health equity impact of vaccines and immunization programs, focusing on the methods and applications.

2. Materials and Methods

The protocol of this review was registered with PROSPERO (CRD42022382729). We reported this review following the 2020 Preferred Reporting Items for Systematic Reviews and Meta-analyses (PRISMA) [20]. The PRISMA checklist table of this review is provided in Table S1 in the Supplementary Materials.

2.1. Search Strategy and Eligibility Criteria

We searched for equity-informative economic evaluations of vaccines in electronic databases, including PubMed, Embase, Econlit, and Cost-Effectiveness Analysis (CEA) Registry by Tufts Medical Center from database inception to 15 December 2022. The search terms used included a combination of vaccine, economic evaluation, and equity terms, which were modified to match the search techniques of each database. No language restriction was applied. We also screened reference lists of eligible articles to identify further potentially eligible articles. A full search strategy is presented in Table S2 in the Supplementary Materials.

We included articles that met the following eligibility criteria: full-text articles of economic evaluations estimating costs, outcomes, and health equity impact of vaccines across equity-relevant subgroups in any context. After duplicates were removed, identified articles were independently screened and selected by two reviewers (C.P. and J.-Y.C.) using the eligibility criteria. Article selection was performed using EndNote 20.3. Disagreements were resolved with consensus by discussing with the third reviewer (N.C.)

2.2. Data Extraction

Two reviewers (C.P. and J.-Y.C.) independently extracted data from the selected studies using the data extraction form developed and pilot-tested based on five randomly chosen articles to finalize the form. Discrepancies in data extraction were resolved with consensus by discussing with the third reviewer (N.C.).

The following data were extracted from the selected articles: first author, year of publication, country, vaccine, equity-relevant subgroups, existing inequities, intervention(s) and comparator(s), perspective, measurement of health and non-health benefits, model type, the inclusion of herd protection, and study findings, including cost-effectiveness and health inequity impact of vaccines.

2.3. Quality Assessment

Two reviewers (C.P. and J.-Y.C.) independently performed reporting quality assessment using the Consolidated Health Economic Reporting Standard (CHEERS) 2022 statement [21]. Any disagreements during the reporting quality assessment were resolved by consensus upon discussion with the third reviewer (N.C.).

2.4. Data Synthesis

Following data extraction, we summarized how health equity was incorporated and evaluated in the selected economic evaluations of vaccines, including methodological characteristics, characteristics of vaccines and immunization programs, existing inequities in the health systems, characteristics of equity-relevant subpopulations, and study findings. Equity-relevant subpopulations were categorized following the PROGRESS-Plus framework, including (1) place of residence, (2) race/ethnicity/culture/language, (3) occupation, (4) gender/sex, (4) religion, (5) education, (6) socioeconomic status, (7) social capital, (8) personal characteristics associated with discrimination (e.g., age, disability), (9) features of relationships (e.g., smoking parents, excluded from school), and (10) time-dependent relationships (e.g., leaving the hospital, respite care, other instances where a person may be temporarily at a disadvantage) [22].

3. Results

3.1. Study Selection

A database search identified 613 records, of which 19 articles met the eligibility criteria [6–13,23–33]. Citation searching of the eligible articles further identified two articles [34,35]. Thus, twenty-one articles were included in this review. These articles were published in 2011 and later. The study selection flow is presented in Figure ??. Excluded studies based on full-text assessment are shown with reasons for exclusion in Table S3 in the Supplementary Materials.

3.2. Study Characteristics

Characteristics of the included studies are summarized in Tables 1 and 2, as well as Table S4 in the Supplementary Materials. Studies were performed in many regions of the world, with most studies conducted in Sub-Saharan African countries (n = 8, 38%) [6–8,11,12,23,24,33], and six of them were performed in Ethiopia [6–8,11,12,33]. A large proportion of studies focused on vaccination programs in low- and middle-income countries (LMICs) (n = 17, 81%) [6–13,23,24,27–30,33–35]. These studies included a total of 11 antigens, of which rotavirus was commonly evaluated (n = 11, 52%) [10,11,13,23,27–30,33–35], followed by human papillomavirus (HPV) (n = 5, 24%) [9,12,25,26,35] and *Streptococcus pneumoniae* (n = 4, 19%) [8,31,32,35]. Rotavirus vaccine was the most commonly studied in LMICs (11 out of 17 studies, 65%) [10,11,13,23,27–30,33–35], while HPV vaccines [25,26] and pneumococcal vaccination [31,32] (two out of four studies, 50% each) were the most commonly studied vaccines in HICs. The breakdown of antigen by income economy is shown in Table S5 in the Supplementary Materials.

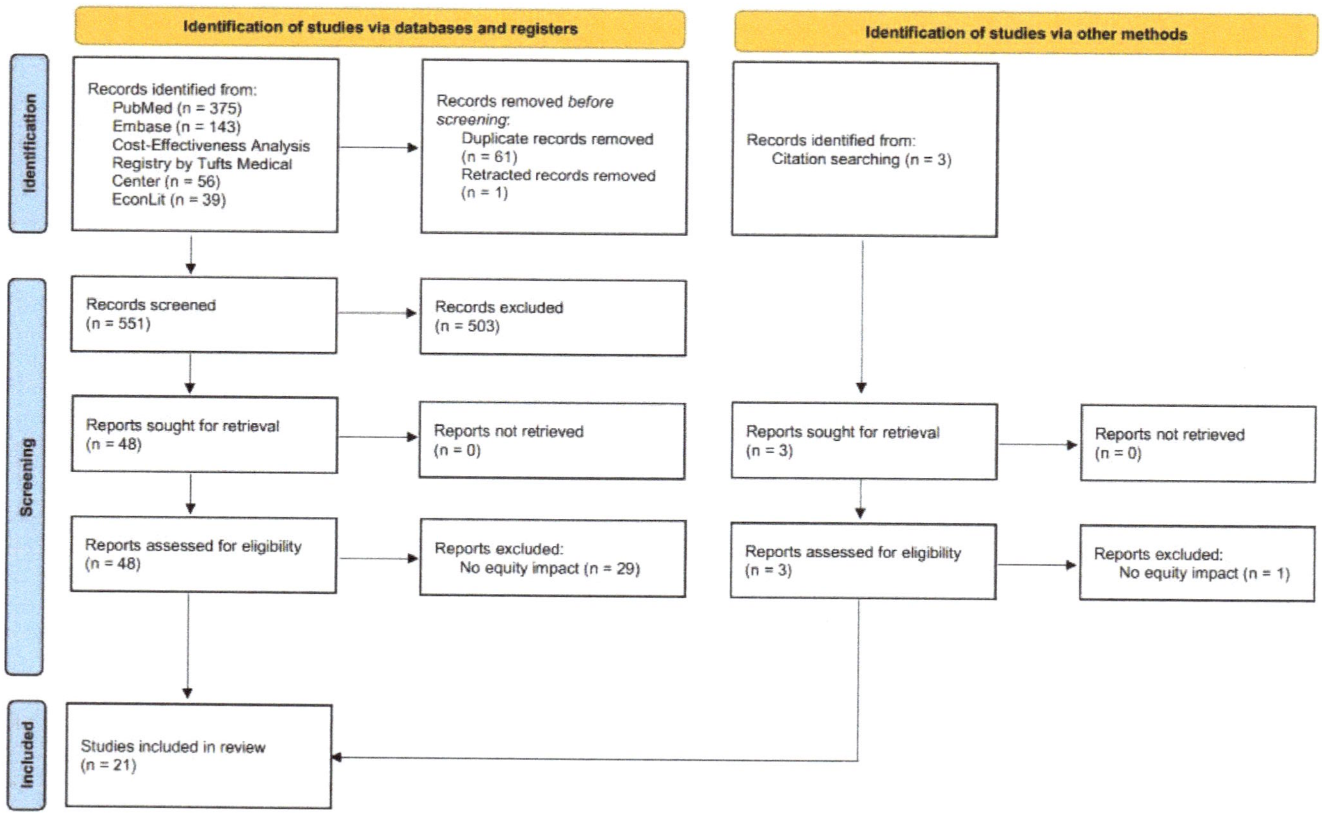

Figure 1. Study selection flow diagram.

Table 1. Summary of included studies.

	Health Equity Impact Analysis (n = 11)	Health Equity Impact Analysis with Financial Risk Protection (n = 9)	Health Equity Impact Analysis with Equity Weighting (n = 1)	Total (n = 21)
Region				
Sub-Saharan Africa	2	5	1	8 (38%)
East Asia and Pacific	2	2	-	4 (19%)
North America	3	-	-	3 (14%)
South Asia	2	-	-	2 (10%)
Latin America and Caribbean	1	-	-	1 (5%)
Multiple countries	1	2	-	3 (14%)
Income economy				
High-income	4	-	-	4 (19%)
Low- and Middle-income	7	9	1	17 (81%)
Antigen *				
Rotavirus	6	4	1	11 (52%)
Human papilloma virus	2	3	-	5 (24%)
Streptococcus pneumoniae	2	2	-	4 (19%)
Malaria †	1	1	-	2 (10%)
Measles	-	2	-	2 (10%)
Hepatitis B	-	1	-	1 (5%)
Hemophilus influenzae type b	-	1	-	1 (5%)
Yellow fever	-	1	-	1 (5%)
Rubella	-	1	-	1 (5%)
Neisseria meningitidis serogroup A	-	1	-	1 (5%)
Japanese encephalitis	-	1	-	1 (5%)

Note: * Number of studies may not add up, as some included multiple vaccines. † Malaria vaccine (RTS,S/AS01).

Table 2. Methodological characteristics of included studies.

	Health Equity Impact Analysis (n = 11)	Health Equity Impact Analysis with Financial Risk Protection (n = 9)	Health Equity Impact Analysis with Equity Weighting (n = 1)	Total (n = 21)
Equity-relevant subgroups				
Socioeconomic status	1	9	1	11 (52%)
Race/Ethnicity	3	-	-	3 (14%)
Place of residence	2	-	-	2 (10%)
Combination of characteristics	5	-	-	5 (24%)
Existing inequities *				
Mortality	10	6	1	17 (81%)
Vaccination coverage	6	5	1	12 (57%)
Disease incidence/prevalence	6	4	1	11 (52%)
Financial risk	-	9	-	9 (43%)
Intervention(s) vs. Comparator(s)				
Introduction vs. No vaccination	5	7	-	12 (57%)
Introduction vs. Introduction with improving vaccination coverage vs. No vaccination	3	-	-	3 (14%)
Improving vaccination coverage vs. Status quo	1	2	1	4 (19%)
Improving vaccination coverage vs. Status quo vs. No vaccination	2	-	-	2 (10%)
Perspective of analysis †				
Societal (Health system and household)	1	8	-	9 (43%)
Health system	10	-	1	11 (52%)
Household	-	1	-	1 (5%)
Costs *				
Direct medical costs	11	9	1	21 (100%)
Direct non-medical costs	1	8	-	9 (43%)
Indirect costs	1	3	-	4 (19%)

Table 2. *Cont.*

	Health Equity Impact Analysis (*n* = 11)	Health Equity Impact Analysis with Financial Risk Protection (*n* = 9)	Health Equity Impact Analysis with Equity Weighting (*n* = 1)	Total (*n* = 21)
Measurement of health benefits *				
Outcomes averted				
Deaths averted	8	7	1	16 (76%)
DALYs averted	6	-	-	6 (29%)
Cases averted	4	1	-	5 (24%)
Hospitalizations and outpatient/clinic visits averted	1	1	-	2 (10%)
Outcomes gained				
QALYs gained	3	-	-	3 (14%)
HALYs gained	-	-	1	1 (5%)
Years of life saved	1	-	-	1 (5%)
Measurement of financial risk protection *				
Household OOP expenditures averted	-	8 ‡	-	8 (38%)
Catastrophic health expenditures averted	-	3	-	3 (14%)
Money-metric value of insurance (risk premium)	-	2	-	2 (10%)
Impoverishments averted	-	2	-	2 (10%)
Model type				
Dynamic	-	-	-	0 (0%)
Static	11	9	1	21 (100%)
Herd protection				
Included in base-case analysis	1	-	-	1 (5%)
Included in scenario analysis	2	2 §	-	4 (19%)
Not included	8	7	1	16 (76%)

Abbreviations: DALY—disability-adjusted life year; HALY—health-adjusted life year; OOP—out-of-pocket; QALY—quality-adjusted life year. Note: * Number of studies may not add up, as some used multiple approaches. † Perspective was categorized based on authors' statements in the articles or reviewers' judgment based on methodologies of the studies. ‡ Two studies also estimated financial risk protection as household OOP expenditures averted as a percentage of household income. § Distributional effect of herd protection was estimated across subpopulations.

3.3. *How Equity Has Been Incorporated into Equity-Informative Economic Evaluations of Vaccines*

3.3.1. Overall Methods

All studies were cost-effectiveness analyses that performed health equity impact analyses to estimate the distributional impact of vaccines across equity-relevant subpopulations of interest (Table 2, with details in Table S4 in the Supplementary Materials). Eleven studies performed only health equity impact analysis as part of cost-effectiveness analyses to estimate the distributional impact and subpopulation incremental cost-effectiveness ratios (ICERs) of vaccines [23–32,34]. Nine studies are Extended Cost-Effectiveness Analyses that performed health equity impact analysis of vaccines with an estimation of the distributional financial risk protection [6–13,35]. One study is a Distributional Cost-Effectiveness Analysis that performed a health equity impact analysis of vaccines, incorporating equity-weighting and opportunity costs as the money was displaced to be spent on vaccines instead of other health services [33]. All studies used static models, of which herd protection of vaccines was considered in a base-case analysis in one study [25] and in a scenario analysis in four studies [10,13,32,34].

3.3.2. Existing Inequities across Equity-Relevant Subpopulations

These analyses were designed to simulate the distributional impact of vaccines within the existing health inequities across the equity-relevant subpopulation in the context of interest, where there were differences between more or less socially disadvantaged subpopulations. Existing inequities in these studies were inequities in disease mortality (*n* = 17, 81%) [7–9,11,13,23,25–35], vaccination coverage (*n* = 12, 57%) [7,8,11,12,23,25,27–30,33,35], disease incidence/prevalence (*n* = 11, 52%) [6,7,12,24–26,31–35], and financial risk (*n* = 9, 43%) [6–13,35].

Equity-relevant subpopulations of interest were socioeconomic status (*n* = 11, 52%) [6–13,27,33,35], race/ethnicity (*n* = 3, 14%) [26,31,32], and place of residence (regions, states, or rural/urban areas) (*n* = 2, 10%) [24,34]. The other five studies assessed the combination of characteristics of equity-relevant subpopulations (socioeconomic status, race/ethnicity, place of residence, and gender) [23,25,28–30], such as estimating the distributional effect of rotavirus vaccine across rural/urban areas, regions, gender, and income quintiles in India [28].

Socioeconomic status was categorized as income quintiles [6–13,23,27–30,33,35] or tertiles [25], ranging from the poorest to the richest. Income quintiles were defined using an asset index [23,28–30], gross domestic product per capita, Gini coefficient [8,13,35], and the National Demographic Health Survey [10,12]. However, some studies did not report how socioeconomic status was defined [6,7,9,11,25,27,33]. Regions were categorized following the National Demographic Health Survey [23,28,30]. There was no clear description of how rural and urban areas were defined [24,28,29].

3.3.3. Vaccination Programs Evaluated

Intervention(s) and comparator(s) assessed in the economic evaluations were mostly between the introduction of a vaccination program vs. no vaccination (n = 12, 52%) [6,8–11,13,24,26,28,31,34,35]. The remaining studies were modeled to evaluate the distributional impact of improving vaccination coverage of the vaccination programs across equity-relevant subpopulations. These included the introduction of a vaccine into a routine vaccination program vs. the introduction of a vaccine into a routine vaccination program with improving vaccination coverage vs. no vaccination (n = 3, 14%) [23,29,30], improving vaccination coverage vs. status quo of the currently implemented vaccination program (n = 4, 19%) [7,12,32,33] and improving vaccination coverage vs. status quo vs. no vaccination (n = 2, 10%) [25,27].

Strategies to improve equitable vaccination coverage described in four studies can be categorized into two broad approaches. Firstly, strategies specifically designed to improve vaccination coverage in the more socially disadvantaged groups, including investing additional resources into rotavirus vaccine delivery in rural areas [33], providing financial incentives for those who received measles vaccine as part of routine immunization with the aim to increase vaccination coverage by 10% in the bottom two income quintiles [7], and revising the eligibility criteria of receiving pneumococcal vaccination to increase the number of eligible vaccine recipients, especially in the Black population in the US [32]. Secondly, strategies designed to achieve equal vaccination coverage across equity-relevant subpopulations, including providing supplemental doses of measles vaccine in addition to the doses prescribed in the standard vaccination schedule (i.e., supplementary immunization activities (SIAs) or mass campaigns) with the aim to achieve 90% vaccination coverage in all income quintiles [7] and providing HPV vaccine as a school-only program or implementing a new mandatory law requiring active opting-out of HPV vaccination with equal coverage across ethnicity and income tertiles [25].

Potential benefits of achieving equitable vaccination coverage were also estimated in four studies, of which two studies estimated the impact of incremental reductions in vaccine under-coverage from current to full coverage [23,29]. The other studies investigated the impact of a scenario when all equity-relevant subpopulations had the same vaccination coverage as the highest coverage subpopulation [27,30]. However, these studies did not describe how to achieve the said equitable vaccination coverage.

3.3.4. Health and Non-Health Benefits of Vaccination Programs

Outcomes captured in these studies were chosen according to the health and non-health benefits of a particular vaccine to demonstrate the distributional impact of vaccination programs across equity-relevant subpopulations. The health benefits of vaccines included the prevention of deaths [6–9,11,13,23,27–35], cases [12,24,26,31,32], hospitalizations and outpatient/clinic visits [10,34], disability-adjusted life years (DALYs) [23,27–30,34], the gain in years of life saved [26], quality-adjusted life years (QALYs) [25,31,32], and health-adjusted life years (HALYs) [33].

Non-health benefits of vaccines, captured specifically in extended cost-effectiveness analyses, were quantified as financial risk protection in terms of household out-of-pocket

(OOP) expenditures averted [6–13], catastrophic health expenditures (CHE) averted [6,10,12], the money-metric value of insurance [8,13], and impoverishment averted [10,35]. The definitions and components of financial risk protection differed across studies. For example, CHE was defined differently across three studies. CHE was defined as a proportion of disease-related expenditure exceeding a specific threshold of household income or expenditures, including 10% of monthly household income [10], 40% of total household consumption expenditures [12], and 10% of total household consumption expenditures or 40% of non-food total household consumption [6]. Impoverishment was defined as household income falling below the World Bank poverty line [35] or country-specific poverty line due to medical expenditures [10]. The money-metric value of insurance or risk premium was defined as the difference between the expected value of the individual's income and the income the individual is willing to have in order to have an outcome that is certain [8,13].

3.4. Summary of Study Findings on Cost-Effectiveness and Health Equity Impact

The cost-effectiveness and health equity impact findings of vaccines are summarized in Table S6 in the Supplementary Materials. Subpopulation ICERs were estimated in ten studies that found similar findings of better cost-effectiveness results (lower ICERs) in equity-relevant subpopulations with higher disease burdens, especially the poorer-income groups and rural areas [23–25,27–32,34]. This demonstrated that introducing vaccines or improving vaccination coverage, compared to no vaccination, was more cost-effective in the more socially disadvantaged groups.

We found similar findings of more deaths averted and higher financial risk protection benefits in subpopulations with higher disease burdens, such as poorer income groups and those living in rural areas, across 21 studies [6–13,23–35]. However, higher household OOP expenditures were averted more in the wealthier income groups due to the aversion to private healthcare utilization [8,9,11].

Studies estimating the distributional impact of improving [7,25,31,33] or achieving [23,28–30] equitable vaccination coverage found that more deaths were averted in the more socially disadvantaged groups with higher disease burdens and lower vaccination coverage. Furthermore, one distributional cost-effectiveness analysis demonstrated that the pro-poor vaccination strategy of the rotavirus vaccine compared to the currently implemented program was a "lose-win" strategy as it showed a negative impact on total health despite a positive impact on health equity, which required a trade-off between efficiency and equity [33]. Interestingly, one study found that introducing rotavirus vaccine in the context of existing inequities in vaccination coverage across regions and socioeconomic subpopulations resulted in introducing disparities in the mortality reduction [23].

3.5. Reporting Quality

Reporting quality of the included studies, assessed using the CHEERS 2022 statement [21], is presented in Table S7 in the Supplementary Materials. Overall, most topics were adequately reported in the included studies. However, the health economic analysis plan and engagement with patients and others affected by the study were not reported in any study.

4. Discussion

Economic evaluations are typically performed to estimate the average incremental costs and effectiveness of interventions of interest. Equity-informative economic evaluations further provide a spectrum of impact across equity-relevant subpopulations to inform policy prioritization. This systematic review identified 21 equity-informative economic evaluations of vaccination programs to date, with progressively evolving methods to incorporate equity. The health equity impact of vaccines has been incorporated into economic evaluations by estimating the distributional health and non-health benefits of vaccination programs across equity-relevant subpopulations to better understand where and to whom more efforts and support should be provided. Extended cost-effectiveness analyses of vaccines were generally performed in LMICs to reflect the importance of financial risk protection, which is one of the goals of the health system for achieving universal health coverage [6–12,36,37]. Distributional cost-effectiveness analyses of vaccines were performed to estimate the distribution of health opportunity costs [33,38]. Since a vaccination program generally involves a large cohort of the population, distributional cost-effectiveness analyses could inform the trade-offs between improving total population health and reducing health inequities.

Existing inequities related to vaccines were shown in the included studies, where disease burden and financial risk were generally higher in more socially disadvantaged groups. There was usually lower vaccination coverage in poorer income quintiles, along with higher disease incidence and mortality compared to richer income quintiles. Successfully implemented equitable vaccination programs could help decrease diseases, deaths, and costs to health systems and households, as we found that immunization programs informed by equity-informative economic evaluations of vaccines generally resulted in more deaths averted and higher financial risk protection benefits in socially disadvantaged subpopulations compared to regular immunization programs [7,25,31,33]. Thus, equity-informed vaccination programs could enhance access to life-saving immunization for disadvantaged populations and ultimately help achieve health equity, if specifically designed to address existing inequities in health systems.

Forceful national and global decision-making on how best to adapt and optimize the implementation of immunization programs to reach all vaccination target groups needs to be underpinned by robust and standardized equity-informative economic evaluations. To ensure the ubiquitous application of such evaluations, global guidance is needed to incorporate health equity into economic evaluations and to ensure standardization in conducting, reporting, and interpreting the analyses. In this review, we highlight a few methodological considerations on how to shape future equity-informative economic evaluations of vaccines. Firstly, the health equity impact of improving vaccination coverage should be conducted to provide information on the potential benefits of moving towards achieving equitable vaccination coverage across equity-relevant subpopulations. Many studies were conducted to estimate the impact of vaccines introduced to contexts with existing inequities in vaccination coverage without consideration of the potential benefits of equitable vaccination coverage. Hence, models should be developed considering improving vaccination coverage as a gradual change rather than an instantaneous change to fully capture the marginal benefits of improving vaccination coverage. Different levels of target vaccination coverage should also be explored to develop evidence-informed optimal implementation strategies, as attempts to improve coverage early on (e.g., from 10% to 20%) are expected to have higher marginal benefits compared to boosting coverage in contexts with existing higher vaccination coverage (e.g., from 75% to 85%).

Secondly, we emphasize the importance of incorporating and reporting all relevant aspects of equity, as improving equity in one aspect could potentially lead to inequities in other aspects. For example, a pro-poor vaccination program that improved equitable vaccination coverage can introduce disparities in mortality reduction given the existing inequities in the mortality risk at baseline. Thus, policy decision-makers will be well-informed about both the positive and negative impacts of the vaccination programs.

Thirdly, a dynamic model should be developed to fully capture the distributional impact of most vaccination programs on the force of infection in susceptible individuals and indirect transmission-dependent effects [3]. Nevertheless, it is challenging to model herd protection between equity-relevant subpopulations—for example, modeling how higher vaccination coverage among the richer income groups will translate to herd protection for the unvaccinated in the poorer income groups.

Lastly, as highlighted by the CHEERS 2022 statement [21], stakeholder engagement is important to ensure that the studies align with needs of local stakeholders and policy decision-makers. De facto, none of the included studies reported the inclusion of stakeholder engagement. Thus, advocacy is needed to ensure that stakeholder engagement is included and transparently reported in future equity-informative economic evaluations of vaccines. Likewise, the inclusion of stakeholder engagement in economic evaluations, especially local stakeholders, is highly encouraged to gain a better understanding of their needs, opinions, and perceptions of how health equity and inequities are defined, measured, monitored, interpreted, and achieved. This is particularly important as we found that assessment and measurement of health equity impact were affected when equity was not clearly defined.

We accentuated a few limitations of our review that are worth mentioning. First, no specific guidelines or checklists are available to directly evaluate the equity-relevant methodological quality of equity-informative economic evaluations. Thus, quality assessment of the included studies could be carried out only in terms of reporting quality. Furthermore, the implications and applications of this review should be carefully interpreted since its findings and conclusions were based on a limited number of equity-informative economic evaluations of vaccines published since 2011. Analytical techniques of incorporating health equity in economic evaluations are continuously evolving, and we expect more studies to be published in the future.

5. Conclusions

The health-equity impact of vaccination programs has been increasingly estimated in economic evaluations across equity-relevant subpopulations to portray and/or address existing health inequities in health systems. Vaccines can enhance equity if the design and implementation of vaccination programs incorporate the effort and strategies to address existing health inequities to provide equitable vaccination coverage and achieve health equity. Guidelines on incorporating health equity into economic evaluations need to be developed to ensure standardization in conducting, reporting, and interpreting the analyses.

Supplementary Materials: The following supporting information can be downloaded at https://www.mdpi.com/article/10.3390/vaccines11030622/s1. Table S1: PRISMA 2020 Checklist. Table S2: Full search strategy. Table S3: Excluded studies with reasons. Table S4: Characteristics of the included studies. Table S5: Summary of antigen by income economy. Table S6: Summary of findings of included studies. Table S7: Reporting quality assessment using CHEERS 2022 statement.

Author Contributions: Conceptualization, C.P. and N.C.; methodology, C.P. and N.C.; validation: C.P., J.-Y.C. and N.C.; formal analysis, C.P. and N.C.; investigation, C.P. and J.-Y.C.; data curation, C.P. and J.-Y.C.; writing—original draft preparation, C.P.; writing—review and editing, C.P., J.-Y.C., P.L., R.H. and N.C.; visualization, C.P.; supervision, N.C.; project administration, N.C.; funding acquisition, C.P. and N.C. All authors have read and agreed to the published version of the manuscript.

Funding: This study is funded by the Department of Immunization, Vaccines and Biologicals (IVB), World Health Organization, Geneva, Switzerland (No: 2022/1307097).

Institutional Review Board Statement: Not applicable.

Informed Consent Statement: Not applicable.

Data Availability Statement: The data presented in this study are available within this article and its Supplementary Materials.

Conflicts of Interest: P.L. and R.H. work for the World Health Organization. The authors alone are responsible for the views expressed in this publication and do not necessarily represent the decisions, policies, or views of the World Health Organization. The other authors declare no conflict of interest.

References

1. World Health Organization; UNICEF. Progress and Challenges with Achieving Universal Immunization Coverage 2021 WHO/UNICEF Estimates Geneva: World Health Organization. 2022. Available online: https://cdn.who.int/media/docs/default-source/immunization/wuenic-progress-and-challenges-15-july-2022.pdf?sfvrsn=b5eb9141_7&download=true (accessed on 3 February 2023).
2. World Health Organization. Immunization Agenda 2030: A Global Strategy to Leave No One Behind Geneva: World Health Organization. 2020. Available online: https://cdn.who.int/media/docs/default-source/immunization/strategy/ia2030/ia2030-draft-4-wha_b8850379-1fce-4847-bfd1-5d2c9d9e32f8.pdf?sfvrsn=5389656e_69&download=true (accessed on 3 February 2023).
3. World Health Organization. *WHO Guide for Standardization of Economic Evaluations of Immunization Programmes*; World Health Organization: Geneva, Switzerland, 2019.
4. Kristensen, F.B.; Mäkelä, M.; Neikter, S.A.; Rehnqvist, N.; Håheim, L.L.; Mørland, B.; Milne, R.; Nielsen, C.P.; Busse, R.; Lee-Robin, S.H.; et al. European network for Health Technology Assessment, EUnetHTA: Planning, development, and implementation of a sustainable European network for Health Technology Assessment. *Int. J. Technol. Assess. Health Care* **2009**, *25*, 107–116. [CrossRef]
5. Ward, T.; Mujica-Mota, R.E.; Spencer, A.E.; Medina-Lara, A. Incorporating Equity Concerns in Cost-Effectiveness Analyses: A Systematic Literature Review. *Pharmacoeconomics* **2022**, *40*, 45–64. [CrossRef] [PubMed]
6. Assebe, L.F.; Kwete, X.J.; Wang, D.; Liu, L.; Norheim, O.F.; Jbaily, A.; Verguet, S.; Johansson, K.A.; Tolla, M.T. Health gains and financial risk protection afforded by public financing of selected malaria interventions in Ethiopia: An extended cost-effectiveness analysis. *Malar. J.* **2020**, *19*, 41. [CrossRef] [PubMed]
7. Driessen, J.; Olson, Z.D.; Jamison, D.T.; Verguet, S. Comparing the health and social protection effects of measles vaccination strategies in Ethiopia: An extended cost-effectiveness analysis. *Soc. Sci. Med.* **2015**, *139*, 115–122. [CrossRef] [PubMed]
8. Johansson, K.A.; Memirie, S.T.; Pecenka, C.; Jamison, D.T.; Verguet, S. Health Gains and Financial Protection from Pneumococcal Vaccination and Pneumonia Treatment in Ethiopia: Results from an Extended Cost-Effectiveness Analysis. *PLoS ONE* **2015**, *10*, e0142691. [CrossRef]
9. Levin, C.E.; Sharma, M.; Olson, Z.; Verguet, S.; Shi, J.F.; Wang, S.M.; Qiao, Y.L.; Jamison, D.T.; Kim, J.J. An extended cost-effectiveness analysis of publicly financed HPV vaccination to prevent cervical cancer in China. *Vaccine* **2015**, *33*, 2830–2841. [CrossRef]
10. Loganathan, T.; Jit, M.; Hutubessy, R.; Ng, C.W.; Lee, W.S.; Verguet, S. Rotavirus vaccines contribute towards universal health coverage in a mixed public-private healthcare system. *Trop. Med. Int. Health* **2016**, *21*, 1458–1467. [CrossRef]
11. Pecenka, C.J.; Johansson, K.A.; Memirie, S.T.; Jamison, D.T.; Verguet, S. Health gains and financial risk protection: An extended cost-effectiveness analysis of treatment and prevention of diarrhoea in Ethiopia. *BMJ Open* **2015**, *5*, e006402. [CrossRef] [PubMed]
12. Portnoy, A.; Sweet, S.; Desalegn, D.; Memirie, S.T.; Kim, J.J.; Verguet, S. Health gains and financial protection from human papillomavirus vaccination in Ethiopia: Findings from a modelling study. *Health Policy Plan.* **2021**, *36*, 891–899. [CrossRef]
13. Verguet, S.; Murphy, S.; Anderson, B.; Johansson, K.A.; Glass, R.; Rheingans, R. Public finance of rotavirus vaccination in India and Ethiopia: An extended cost-effectiveness analysis. *Vaccine* **2013**, *31*, 4902–4910. [CrossRef]
14. Cookson, R.; Mirelman, A.J.; Griffin, S.; Asaria, M.; Dawkins, B.; Norheim, O.F.; Verguet, S.; Culyer, A.J. Using cost-effectiveness analysis to address health equity concerns. *Value Health* **2017**, *20*, 206–212. [CrossRef] [PubMed]
15. Avanceña, A.L.; Prosser, L.A. Examining Equity Effects of Health Interventions in Cost-Effectiveness Analysis: A Systematic Review. *Value Health* **2021**, *24*, 136–143. [CrossRef] [PubMed]
16. Dukhanin, V.; Searle, A.; Zwerling, A.; Dowdy, D.W.; Taylor, H.A.; Merritt, M.W. Integrating social justice concerns into economic evaluation for healthcare and public health: A systematic review. *Soc. Sci. Med.* **2018**, *198*, 27–35. [CrossRef] [PubMed]
17. Johri, M.; Norheim, O.F. Can cost-effectiveness analysis integrate concerns for equity? Systematic review. *Int. J. Technol. Assess. Health Care* **2012**, *28*, 125–132. [CrossRef] [PubMed]
18. Lal, A.; Moodie, M.; Peeters, A.; Carter, R. Inclusion of equity in economic analyses of public health policies: Systematic review and future directions. *Aust. N Z J. Public Health* **2018**, *42*, 207–213. [CrossRef]
19. Yang, F.; Katumba, K.R.; Griffin, S. Incorporating health inequality impact into economic evaluation in low-and middle-income countries: A systematic review. *Expert Rev. Pharm. Outcomes Res.* **2022**, *22*, 17–25. [CrossRef]
20. Page, M.J.; McKenzie, J.E.; Bossuyt, P.M.; Boutron, I.; Hoffmann, T.C.; Mulrow, C.D.; Shamseer, L.; Tetzlaff, J.M.; Akl, E.A.; Brennan, S.E.; et al. The PRISMA 2020 statement: An updated guideline for reporting systematic reviews. *BMJ Clin. Res. Ed.* **2021**, *372*, n71.
21. Husereau, D.; Drummond, M.; Augustovski, F.; de Bekker-Grob, E.; Briggs, A.H.; Carswell, C.; Caulley, L.; Chaiyakunapruk, N.; Greenberg, D.; Loder, E.; et al. Consolidated Health Economic Evaluation Reporting Standards (CHEERS) 2022 explanation and elaboration: A report of the ISPOR CHEERS II good practices task force. *Value Health* **2022**, *25*, 10–31. [CrossRef]
22. Welch, V.A.; Petkovic, J.; Jull, J.; Hartling, L.; Klassen, T.; Kristjansson, E.; Pardo, J.P.; Petticrew, M.; Stott, D.J.; Thomson, D.; et al. Equity and specific populations. In *Cochrane Handbook for Systematic Reviews of Interventions*; Wiley: Hoboken, NJ, USA, 2019; pp. 433–449.
23. Anderson, I.V.J.D.; Pecenka, C.J.; Bagamian, K.H.; Rheingans, R.D. Effects of geographic and economic heterogeneity on the burden of rotavirus diarrhea and the impact and cost-effectiveness of vaccination in Nigeria. *PLoS ONE* **2020**, *15*, e0232941. [CrossRef]

24. Bell, G.J.; Loop, M.; Topazian, H.M.; Hudgens, M.; Mvalo, T.; Juliano, J.J.; Kamthunzi, P.; Tegha, G.; Mofolo, I.; Hoffman, I.; et al. Case reduction and cost-effectiveness of the RTS,S/AS01 malaria vaccine alongside bed nets in Lilongwe, Malawi. *Vaccine* **2020**, *38*, 4079–4087. [CrossRef]
25. Blakely, T.; Kvizhinadze, G.; Karvonen, T.; Pearson, A.L.; Smith, M.; Wilson, N. Cost-effectiveness and equity impacts of three HPV vaccination programmes for school-aged girls in New Zealand. *Vaccine* **2014**, *32*, 2645–2656. [CrossRef] [PubMed]
26. Goldie, S.J.; Daniels, N. Model-based analyses to compare health and economic outcomes of cancer control: Inclusion of disparities. *J. Natl. Cancer Inst.* **2011**, *103*, 1373–1386. [CrossRef] [PubMed]
27. Rheingans, R.; Atherly, D.; Anderson, J. Distributional impact of rotavirus vaccination in 25 GAVI countries: Estimating disparities in benefits and cost-effectiveness. *Vaccine* **2012**, *30*, A15–A23. [CrossRef] [PubMed]
28. Rheingans, R.; Anderson, I.V.J.D.; Anderson, B.; Chakraborty, P.; Atherly, D.; Pindolia, D. Estimated impact and cost-effectiveness of rotavirus vaccination in India: Effects of geographic and economic disparities. *Vaccine* **2014**, *32*, A140–A150. [CrossRef]
29. Rheingans, R.; Anderson, I.V.J.D.; Bagamian, K.H.; Pecenka, C.J. Effects of geographic and economic heterogeneity on rotavirus diarrhea burden and vaccination impact and cost-effectiveness in the Lao People's Democratic Republic. *Vaccine* **2018**, *36*, 7868–7877. [CrossRef]
30. Rheingans, R.; Anderson, I.V.J.D.; Bagamian, K.H.; Laytner, L.A.; Pecenka, C.J.; Gilani, S.S.; Ahmed, M. Effects of geographic and economic heterogeneity on the burden of rotavirus diarrhea and the impact and cost-effectiveness of vaccination in Pakistan. *Vaccine* **2018**, *36*, 7780–7789. [CrossRef]
31. Wateska, A.R.; Nowalk, M.P.; Lin, C.J.; Harrison, L.H.; Schaffner, W.; Zimmerman, R.K.; Smith, K. Cost-effectiveness of adult pneumococcal vaccination policies in underserved minorities aged 50-64 years compared to the US general population. *Vaccine* **2019**, *37*, 2026–2033. [CrossRef]
32. Wateska, A.R.; Nowalk, M.P.; Lin, C.J.; Harrison, L.H.; Schaffner, W.; Zimmerman, R.K.; Smith, K.J. Cost-effectiveness of revised US pneumococcal vaccination recommendations in underserved minority adults < 65-years-old. *Vaccine* **2022**, *40*, 7312–7320.
33. Dawkins, B.R.; Mirelman, A.J.; Asaria, M.; Johansson, K.A.; Cookson, R.A. Distributional cost-effectiveness analysis in low- and middle-income countries: Illustrative example of rotavirus vaccination in Ethiopia. *Health Policy Plan.* **2018**, *33*, 456–463. [CrossRef]
34. Urueña, A.; Pippo, T.; Betelu, M.S.; Virgilio, F.; Hernández, L.; Giglio, N.; Gentile, Á.; Diosque, M.; Vizzotti, C. Cost-effectiveness analysis of rotavirus vaccination in Argentina. *Vaccine* **2015**, *33*, A126–A134. [CrossRef]
35. Chang, A.Y.; Riumallo-Herl, C.; Perales, N.A.; Clark, S.; Clark, A.; Constenla, D.; Garske, T.; Jackson, M.L.; Jean, K.; Jit, M.; et al. The equity impact vaccines may have on averting deaths and medical impoverishment in developing countries. *Health Aff.* **2018**, *37*, 316–324. [CrossRef] [PubMed]
36. Verguet, S.; Woldemariam, A.T.; Durrett, W.N.; Norheim, O.F.; Kruk, M.E. Is the sustainable development goal target for financial risk protection in health realistic? *BMJ Glob. Health* **2017**, *2*, e000216. [CrossRef] [PubMed]
37. Verguet, S.; Kim, J.J.; Jamison, D.T. Extended cost-effectiveness analysis for health policy assessment: A tutorial. *Pharmacoeconomics* **2016**, *34*, 913–923. [CrossRef] [PubMed]
38. Asaria, M.; Griffin, S.; Cookson, R. Distributional cost-effectiveness analysis: A tutorial. *Med. Decis. Mak.* **2016**, *36*, 8–19. [CrossRef]

vaccines

MDPI

Commentary

Addressing Determinants of Immunization Inequities Requires Objective Tools to Devise Local Solutions

Siddhartha Sankar Datta [1,*], Federico Martinón-Torres [2], Nino Berdzuli [3], Niyazi Cakmak [1], Michael Edelstein [4], Simon Cottrell [5] and Mark Muscat [1]

[1] Vaccine-Preventable Diseases and Immunization Programme, World Health Organization Regional Office for Europe, DK-2100 Copenhagen, Denmark
[2] Translational Pediatrics and Infectious Diseases, Hospital Clínico Universitario and Universidad de Santiago de Compostela, 15706 Galicia, Spain
[3] Division of Country Health Programmes, World Health Organization Regional Office for Europe, DK-2100 Copenhagen, Denmark
[4] Azrieli Faculty of Medicine, Bar-Ilan University, Ramat Gan 5290002, Israel
[5] Vaccine Preventable Disease Programme, Public Health Wales NHS Trust, Cardiff CF10 4BZ, UK
* Correspondence: dattas@who.int

Abstract: Universal immunization substantially reduces morbidity and mortality from vaccine-preventable diseases. In recent years, routine immunization coverage has varied considerably among countries across the WHO European Region, and among different populations and districts within countries. It has even declined in some countries. Sub-optimal immunization coverage contributes to accumulations of susceptible individuals and can lead to outbreaks of vaccine-preventable diseases. The European Immunization Agenda 2030 (EIA2030) seeks to build better health in the WHO European Region by ensuring equity in immunization and supporting immunization stakeholders in devising local solutions to local challenges. The factors that influence routine immunization uptake are context specific and multifactorial; addressing immunization inequities will require overcoming or removing barriers to vaccination for underserved individuals or populations. Local level immunization stakeholders must first identify the underlying causes of inequities, and based on this information, tailor resources, or service provision to the local context, as per the organization and characteristics of the health care system in their countries. To do this, in addition to using the tools already available to broadly identify immunization inequities at the national and regional levels, they will need new pragmatic guidance and tools to address the identified local challenges. It is time to develop the necessary guidance and tools and support immunization stakeholders at all levels, especially those at the subnational or local health centre levels, to make the vision of EIA2030 a reality.

Keywords: immunization; inequities; local determinants; pragmatic; operational guidance; European Immunization Agenda 2030

Citation: Datta, S.S.; Martinón-Torres, F.; Berdzuli, N.; Cakmak, N.; Edelstein, M.; Cottrell, S.; Muscat, M. Addressing Determinants of Immunization Inequities Requires Objective Tools to Devise Local Solutions. *Vaccines* **2023**, *11*, 811. https://doi.org/10.3390/vaccines11040811

Academic Editor: Pedro Plans-Rubió

Received: 28 February 2023
Revised: 28 March 2023
Accepted: 3 April 2023
Published: 6 April 2023

1. Introduction

Immunization is one of the most cost-effective ways to protect populations from vaccine-preventable diseases. Consequently, ensuring universal access to immunization promotes population health and long-term prosperity [1,2]. Childhood immunization plays a key role in achieving 14 of the 17 United Nations Sustainable Development Goals (SDGs) [3], particularly SDG 3, 'Ensure healthy lives and promote well-being for all at all ages'. However, universal access to immunization should not be interpreted as a 'one size fits all approach'. There are population groups or individuals who will require local tailoring of services; failure to identify, acknowledge and address the barriers they face can lead to systematic inequities in immunization coverage. Immunization inequities contribute to accumulations of susceptible individuals in communities and thereby lead to outbreaks of vaccine-preventable diseases [4–6].

Monitoring and addressing immunization inequities are embedded in every regional and national immunization strategy in the World Health Organization (WHO) European Region (hereafter the Region). However, the countries in the Region nevertheless have difficulties in reaching and sustaining the 95% coverage target for the third dose of diphtheria-pertussis-tetanus containing vaccine (DTP3) established by European Vaccine Action Plan 2015–2020 (EVAP) [7]. The factors that influence immunization uptake and those responsible for sub-optimal vaccination coverage at subnational or national level, are multiple and often context specific [8–11]. The European Immunization Agenda 2030 (EIA2030) seeks to build better health tomorrow in the Region through stronger immunization programmes today, by ensuring equity in immunization, providing immunization across the life course and devising local solutions to local challenges [12].

It is critical that the national and subnational health systems systematically address the local factors influencing the immunization inequities, and thereby achieve and sustain high vaccination coverage in the countries. Such an approach should include a continuous process of reviewing local-level immunization coverage data, which can guide national and subnational health systems in identifying areas of sub-optimal coverage and inform national immunization policy. However, to successfully address the reasons for sub-optimal vaccination in certain areas or populations, it is critical that local-level immunization stakeholders undertake measures through use of the available tools to identify who is not vaccinated and gather information on the local drivers of and barriers to immunization uptake by the population. Tailored, local-level interventions are needed to address the identified barriers that lead to local immunization inequities. To develop these interventions, immunization stakeholders at all levels, but especially at subnational or local health centre levels, need pragmatic guidance and tools. Aligned to the core principle of EIA2030 to devise local solutions to local challenges, we outline what can be done to empower especially the subnational immunization managers and functionaries of a health system to address immunization inequities and thereby contribute to the ethos of the SDGs: "leaving no one behind".

2. Discussion

2.1. *Suboptimal Immunization Coverage and Risks of Disease*

Relatively high immunization coverage in the Region over the past two decades has allowed it to sustain polio-free status since 2002 [13] and achieve significant progress in reducing the burden of measles, rubella, tetanus, diphtheria and other vaccine-preventable diseases [6]. However, routine immunization coverage still varies considerably among the Region's 53 countries, and among different populations and districts within them. In 2021, while the regional coverage with DTP3 was 94%, 25 countries (47%) reported DTP3 vaccination coverage of more than 95%, 15 (28%) reported coverage between 90% and 95%, 11 (21%) reported coverage between 80% and 90% and 2 (4%) countries reported coverage below 80% [14]. During the same year, 13 (25%) countries reported that between 1% and 52% of their subnational administrative units attained DTP3 coverage of less than 80% [15]. A similar pattern was observed for the first dose of measles-containing vaccine (MCV1) in the Region in 2021: while the regional coverage was 94%, 28 countries (53%) reported less than 95% MCV1 coverage. These variations in immunization coverage between, and within, countries indicate that the unvaccinated and under-vaccinated populations in the Region are at high risk of vaccine-preventable diseases; where there are higher numbers of unvaccinated individuals concentrated in populations or groups, there is a higher potential for outbreaks or the re-emergence of vaccine-preventable diseases.

2.2. *Factors Influencing Vaccination Uptake*

National programmes and policymakers often attribute sub-optimal vaccination coverage to refusal to vaccinate based on concerns about vaccines, but this is only one of numerous possible contributing factors. The factors influencing vaccination coverage at local level are complex and can range from individual socio-economic conditions to issues around healthcare systems and accessibility of services [8–11]. Formative research and behavioural analysis of a Charedi Orthodox Jewish community of the London borough Hackney showed that critical issues related to sub-optimal immunization uptake were linked to access to and convenience of immunization services, both for the service providers and the population, while the assumption before the study was that under-vaccination was linked to cultural or religious anti-vaccination sentiment [16]. Several countries have shown that children living in poorer households, children born to mothers with lower levels of education and those residing in rural areas are more likely to be left behind in immunization uptake [17]. Vaccination coverage has also been found to be lower in specific population groups like asylum seekers, refugees, migrants and deprived communities in comparison to the general population [17–19]. In addition, studies have also demonstrated the role ethnicity can play as a cultural factor in influencing completion of scheduled vaccination doses [20,21]. Indeed, certain ethnic communities such as Roma and Sinti have often been disproportionately affected by outbreaks of measles [22]. Careful consideration of factors such as area of residence, living conditions and characteristics including age, gender, economic status, ethnicity, religion, migration status, education or disability will help national and subnational immunization programme managers to develop appropriate immunization delivery strategies that yield more equitable uptake.

2.3. Immunization Inequity and Regional Immunization Strategies

EVAP suggested that countries in the Region ensure that every individual is eligible to receive all appropriate vaccines, irrespective of their geographic location, age, gender, educational level, socioeconomic status, ethnicity, nationality or religious or philosophical affiliation [7]. EIA2030 builds on the successes and lessons learned through implementation of EVAP, with a vision and strategy for achieving the full benefits of immunization in the Region for the next decade, seeking to attain stronger and more resilient immunization programmes by focusing on three key principles: ensuring equity in immunization, providing immunization across the life course and devising local solutions to local challenges [12]. By ensuring that national immunization strategies have an equity-based approach to reach unvaccinated and under-vaccinated populations, EIA2030 aims to address the inequities in immunization coverage between and within countries through the use of innovative programming, better understanding of the concept of immunization equity and local-level interventions to identify and address barriers.

2.4. Identifying and Addressing Immunization Equity

In addition to determining the administrative areas of sub-optimal coverage by evaluating the routinely reported annual immunization coverage data, it is critically important for subnational immunization stakeholders to identify which populations groups in these areas have lower vaccination uptake and understand why they are not vaccinated. These will allow the stakeholders at the local level to devise tailored strategies to improve the vaccination coverage and thereby also reduce inequity.

Inequities are reflective of population groups in communities being left behind. As a starting point, understanding immunization inequities will require good-quality, robust disaggregated immunization coverage data at every level of a health system together with systematic monitoring. Since 2016, tools [23–25] developed by WHO have supported countries to illustrate socio-economic, demographic and geographic variation in uptake, enable comparisons of data about immunization (and other health parameters) within and across countries and devise analytical approaches to determine the factors associated with immunization coverage. Every country, through its network of national and subnational immunization programmes, should examine its local-level immunization uptake data to identify the presence or absence of inequities. Once population groups with low immunization coverage are identified, understanding the contextual issues they face is the next step toward improving vaccine equity and averting future outbreaks, especially among those who are also often at higher risk of severe but preventable outcomes. During EVAP implementation, the WHO Regional Office for Europe supported countries in the Region through implementation of the "Tailoring immunization Programmes" (TIP) initiative to diagnose vaccination barriers and motivators in populations with low vaccination coverage and design tailored interventions to address these barriers [26]. Whilst TIP provided a framework for countries to understand the perspective of populations with low vaccination coverage, an external review of TIP implementation in four countries in the Region in 2016 suggested that the efforts should go beyond identification of susceptible groups and diagnosis of challenges [27].

The organization and delivery of vaccination programmes vary widely in the Region, [28] thus preventing or reducing inequities in immunization coverage will inevitably require local-level tailoring of resources or service provision for underserved individuals or populations to overcome or remove barriers to vaccination. Immunization programme monitoring must now go beyond national or regional estimates of immunization coverage and additional efforts should be made to understand how vaccination uptake varies according to socioeconomic, demographic and geographic factors within a country. It is time that simple and pragmatic guidance and tools are developed for the immunization stakeholders at all levels especially for those at the local health facility levels, to identify and understand barriers to immunization uptake. This will pave the way for the subnational immunization managers to develop and implement successful interventions addressing these immunization inequities coupled with periodic evaluation of the targeted interventions and mid-course corrections, if need be.

2.5. Characteristics of Guidance and Operational Frameworks

Across the Region, while countries and immunization programmes vary widely in their immunization service delivery systems, they are also at different stages of recognizing, considering and addressing issues of immunization inequity. Thus, guidance and tools should contain pragmatic operational frameworks for all levels of the healthcare system, from the local health facility to the Ministry of Health.

The operational frameworks should be cohesive, implementable and relevant to the immunization stakeholders at national, sub-national, regional and local health facility levels. With a primary focus on "how to", pragmatic guidance and tools should focus on the following stakeholders to achieve a local demonstrable impact on immunization inequity:

a. decision- and policy-makers who can advocate for equity within immunization programmes, to ensure the required political support is maintained to tackle immunization inequity as part of the broader heath policy agenda;
b. immunization programme managers at the national and subnational levels who are developing and implementing immunization strategies, to embed equity in planning, delivery and monitoring of the immunization programmes;
c. immunization programme managers and their staff who are tasked with identifying, addressing and monitoring health inequities, to gather and use information on local determinants of inequities and make informed decisions on interventions.

The TIP tools and guidance developed by the WHO Regional Office for Europe are already available to support the immunization programme managers and their staff in identifying and characterizing population groups with lower immunization uptake and to diagnose vaccination behaviour barriers, system barriers and motivators.

An operational guide which contains pragmatic, cohesive and implementable operational frameworks relevant to the immunization stakeholders for all levels of health system and relevant, simple and action-oriented tools to address immunization inequity at the local health facility level is being developed by the WHO Regional Office for Europe in consultation with the countries in the Region, to empower subnational immunization managers to address determinants of immunization inequities closer to the location where the immunization inequity exists. Together with developing these pragmatic tools to address immunization inequity at the local health facility level, the WHO Regional Office for Europe will support capacity building of the national and subnational immunization programme managers on the use of these tools. Successful implementation of interventions to reduce or prevent immunization inequities at the local levels will require multipronged actions involving the stakeholders who have roles in vaccine programme planning and delivery and those involved in advocating for immunization equity in underserved groups. Only through developing and implementing robust local-level interventions will countries in the Region be able to achieve EIA2030′s strategic priority on immunization equity: namely, ensuring that routine immunization coverage is high in every community and that all individuals have equitable access to and adequately utilize all vaccines in national immunization schedules.

Addressing immunization inequity between population groups within a country will have an impact on the healthcare delivery and population health as a whole. Like immunization coverage, achieving equity should be viewed as a systematic and continuous process.

3. Conclusions and Future Directions

Attaining and maintaining high and equitable immunization coverage in every subnational administrative unit in the Region will contribute to better population health by expanding protection to those who are currently at most risk of acquiring vaccine-preventable diseases. Such an approach will reduce the risk of outbreaks of vaccine-preventable diseases and help address wider inequities in health. Achieving the health-related SDGs requires urgent attention to close the health inequity gap through collection and use of data and information at the local health facility level. Reducing inequity should be embedded as a core aim of national immunization programmes; accordingly, reducing local level inequalities in immunization service delivery and utilization must be a critical cornerstone of every national immunization strategy. Identifying, addressing and monitoring inequity within immunization programmes should become a systematic and ongoing process, with solutions tailored to the context of each country and population. A simple, effective, action-oriented and pragmatic operational guide designed especially for subnational immunization programme managers with appropriate linkages to all levels of health systems is critical in achieving the strategic immunization priorities outlined in EIA2030. This will ensure everyone everywhere in the Region reaps the benefits of the vaccines in national immunization schedules.

Author Contributions: S.S.D. designed the draft outline of the manuscript. F.M.-T., N.B., N.C., M.E., S.C. and M.M. provided their critical reviews to the intellectual content of the paper. All authors have read and agreed to the published version of the manuscript.

Funding: This research received no external funding.

Institutional Review Board Statement: Not applicable.

Informed Consent Statement: Not applicable.

Data Availability Statement: Data sharing not applicable.

Acknowledgments: The authors extend their gratitude to Catharina de Kat for her suggestions in the preparation of this manuscript.

Conflicts of Interest: The authors declare no conflict of interest.

References

1. Gavi, the Vaccine Alliance. Value of Vaccination. Cost-Effective. 2021. Available online: https://www.gavi.org/vaccineswork/value-vaccination/cost-effective (accessed on 23 February 2023).
2. World Health Organization. *Inequality Monitoring in Immunization: A Step-by-Step Manual*; WHO: Geneva, Switzerland, 2019; Available online: https://apps.who.int/iris/handle/10665/329535 (accessed on 3 April 2023).
3. Gavi, the Vaccine Alliance. Sustainable Development Goals. Global Health and Development. 2018. Available online: https://www.gavi.org/about/ghd/sdg/ (accessed on 23 February 2023).
4. Crocker-Buque, T.; Edelstein, M.; Mounier-Jack, S. Interventions to reduce inequalities in vaccine coverage in children and adolescents aged <19 years: A systematic review. *J. Epidemiol. Community Health* **2017**, *71*, 87–97. [CrossRef] [PubMed]

5. Bocquier, A.; Ward, J.; Raude, J.; Peretti-Watel, P.; Verger, P. Socioeconomic differences in childhood vaccination in developed countries: A systematic review of quantitative studies. *Expert Rev. Vaccines* **2017**, *16*, 1107–1118. [CrossRef] [PubMed]
6. World Health Organization Regional Office for Europe. *A Report on the Epidemiology of Selected Vaccine-Preventable Diseases in the European Region*; WHO EpiBrief No. 1; WHO Regional Office for Europe: Copenhagen, Denmark, 2020. Available online: https://www.euro.who.int/__data/assets/pdf_file/0006/431745/EpiBrief_1_2020_EN.pdf (accessed on 3 April 2023).
7. World Health Organization Regional Office for Europe. *European Vaccine Action Plan 2015–2020*; WHO Regional Office for Europe: Copenhagen, Denmark, 2014. Available online: https://www.euro.who.int/__data/assets/pdf_file/0007/255679/WHO_EVAP_UK_v30_WEBx.pdf (accessed on 3 April 2023).
8. Brearley, L.; Eggers, R.; Steinglass, R.; Vandelaer, J. Applying an equity lens in the Decade of Vaccines. *Vaccine* **2013**, *31* (Suppl. S2), B103–B107. [CrossRef] [PubMed]
9. Tauil, M.C.; Sato, A.P.; Waldman, E.A. Factors associated with incomplete or delayed vaccination across countries: A systematic review. *Vaccine* **2016**, *34*, 2635–2643. [CrossRef] [PubMed]
10. Boyce, T.; Gudorf, A.; de Kat, C.; Muscat, M.; Butler, R.; Habersaat, K.B. Towards equity in immunisation. *Euro Surveill.* **2019**, *24*, 1800204. [CrossRef] [PubMed]
11. Tiley, K.; White, J.M.; Andrews, N.; Ramsay, M.; Edelstein, M. Inequalities in childhood vaccination timing and completion in London. *Vaccine* **2018**, *36*, 6726–6735. [CrossRef] [PubMed]
12. World Health Organization Regional Office for Europe. *European Immunization Agenda 2030*; WHO Regional Office for Europe: Copenhagen, Denmark, 2021. Available online: https://www.who.int/europe/publications/i/item/9789289056052 (accessed on 23 February 2023).
13. World Health Organization Regional Office for Europe. Commemorating 20 years of polio-free status in the European Region in Proceedings of the Special Report on the 36th Meeting of the European Regional Certification Commission for Poliomyelitis Eradication, Copenhagen, Denmark, 19–20 October 2022: Twenty Years of Polio-Free Status in the WHO European Region (pp. 27–31). WHO Regional Office for Europe: Copenhagen, Denmark, 2022. Available online: https://www.who.int/europe/publications/i/item/WHO-EURO-2023-6967-46733-68044 (accessed on 3 April 2023).
14. World Health Organization. Immunization Dashboard European Region. Vaccination Coverage for the WHO European Region. Available online: https://immunizationdata.who.int/pages/profiles/eur.html (accessed on 23 February 2023).
15. World Health Organization. Immunization Analysis and Insights. Subnational Immunization Coverage Data. Available online: https://www.who.int/teams/immunization-vaccines-and-biologicals/immunization-analysis-and-insights/global-monitoring/immunization-coverage/subnational-immunization-coverage-data (accessed on 23 February 2023).
16. Letley, L.; Rew, V.; Ahmed, R.; Habersaat, K.B.; Paterson, P.; Chantler, T.; Saavedra-Campos, M.; Butler, R. Tailoring immunisation programmes: Using behavioural insights to identify barriers enablers to childhood immunisations in a Jewish community in London, U.K. *Vaccine* **2018**, *36*, 4687–4692. [CrossRef] [PubMed]
17. World Health Organization. *State of Inequality: Childhood Immunization*; WHO: Geneva, Switzerland, 2016. Available online: https://www.who.int/publications/i/item/9789241511735 (accessed on 23 February 2023).
18. Ekezie, W.; Awwad, S.; Krauchenberg, A.; Karara, N.; Dembiński, Ł.; Grossman, Z.; Del Torso, S.; Dornbusch, H.J.; Neves, A.; Copley, S.; et al. Access to Vaccination among Disadvantaged, Isolated and Difficult-to-Reach Communities in the WHO European Region: A Systematic Review. *Vaccines* **2022**, *10*, 1038. [CrossRef] [PubMed]
19. Godoy-Ramirez, K.; Byström, E.; Lindstrand, A.; Butler, R.; Ascher, H.; Kulane, A. Exploring childhood immunization among undocumented migrants in Sweden—Following qualitative study and the World Health Organizations Guide to Tailoring Immunization Programmes (TIP). *Public Health* **2019**, *171*, 97–105. [CrossRef] [PubMed]
20. Afolabi, R.; Salawu, M.; Gbadebo, B.; Salawu, A.; Fagbamigbe, A.F.; Adebowale, A.S. Ethnicity as a cultural factor influencing complete vaccination among children aged 12–23 months in Nigeria. *Hum. Vaccin. Immunother.* **2021**, *17*, 2008–2017. [CrossRef] [PubMed]
21. Forster, A.S.; Rockliffe, L.; Chorley, A.J.; Marlow, L.A.; Bedford, H.; Smith, S.G.; Waller, J. Ethnicity-specific factors influencing childhood immunisation decisions among Black and Asian Minority Ethnic groups in the UK: A systematic review of qualitative research. *J. Epidemiol. Community Health* **2017**, *71*, 544–549. [CrossRef] [PubMed]
22. Muscat, M. Who gets measles in Europe? *J. Infect. Dis.* **2011**, *204* (Suppl. 1), S353–S365. [CrossRef] [PubMed]
23. World Health Organization. Health Inequality Monitor. Health Equity Assessment Toolkit (HEAT). Available online: https://www.who.int/data/health-equity/assessment_toolkit (accessed on 23 February 2023).
24. Health Inequality Monitor. National Health Inequality Monitoring: A Step-by-Step Manual. Available online: https://www.who.int/data/inequality-monitor/manual (accessed on 23 February 2023).
25. World Health Organization. Explorations of Inequality: Childhood Immunization. 2018. Available online: https://apps.who.int/iris/handle/10665/272864 (accessed on 23 February 2023).
26. World Health Organization Regional Office for Europe. *The Guide to Tailoring Immunization Programmes (TIP)*; WHO Regional Office for Europe: Copenhagen, Denmark, 2013; Available online: https://apps.who.int/iris/bitstream/handle/10665/329448/9789289054492-eng.pdf (accessed on 3 April 2023).

27. Dubé, E.; Leask, J.; Wolff, B.; Hickler, B.; Balaban, V.; Hosein, E.; Habersaat, K. The WHO Tailoring Immunization Programmes (TIP) approach: Review of implementation to date. *Vaccine* **2018**, *36*, 1509–1515. [CrossRef] [PubMed]
28. European Observatory on Health Systems and Policies; Rechel, B.; Richardson, E.; McKee, M. *The Organization and Delivery of Vaccination Services in the European Union: Prepared for the European Commission*; WHO Regional Office for Europe: Copenhagen, Denmark, 2018. Available online: https://apps.who.int/iris/handle/10665/330345 (accessed on 3 April 2023).

vaccines

MDPI

Opinion

Addressing Immunization Inequity—What Have the International Community and India Learned over 35 Years?

Lora Shimp [1], Raj Shankar Ghosh [2] and Katharine Elkes [1,*]

[1] JSI Research and Training Institute, Arlington, VA 22202, USA
[2] Public Health Consultant, Delhi 201301, India
* Correspondence: katharine_elkes@jsi.com

Abstract: Countries around the world established immunization programs over 40 years ago to reach all infants. The maturity of these preventive health programs offers some useful learning on the importance of, and components needed for, population-based services to reach all communities. A public health success, ensuring equity in immunization, requires a multi-faceted approach that includes sustained government and partner commitment and human, financial, and program operational resources. Evidence from India's Universal Immunization Program (UIP) across stabilizing vaccine supply and services, enhancing access, and generating demand for vaccines in the community provides a useful case study. The political leadership in India took advantage of the two decades of learning from polio eradication and focused initiatives, such as the National Health Mission and Intensified Mission Indradhanush, to reach populations with immunization services. With a goal of leaving no one behind, India's UIP and partners are bringing essential rotavirus and pneumococcal vaccines nationwide, upgrading vaccine cold chain and supply systems with technologies, such as the electronic Vaccine Intelligence Network (eVIN), and optimizing funding for local needs through the Program Implementation Plan (PIP) budgetary processes and building health worker capacities through training, awareness, and e-learning.

Keywords: immunization; equity; inequity; India

Citation: Shimp, L.; Ghosh, R.S.; Elkes, K. Addressing Immunization Inequity—What Have the International Community and India Learned over 35 Years? *Vaccines* **2023**, *11*, 790. https://doi.org/10.3390/vaccines11040790

Academic Editors: Ahmad Reza Hosseinpoor, M. Carolina Danovaro, Devaki Nambiar, Aaron Wallace and Hope Johnson

Received: 14 February 2023
Revised: 22 March 2023
Accepted: 30 March 2023
Published: 4 April 2023

1. Introduction

The international community can debate equality and equity definitions and terminology, but fundamentally, are we considerate of individuals and their rights, needs, and convenience to access trustworthy and quality preventive health services, such as immunization? Are our health workers confident, satisfied, and sufficiently and proactively resourced in their work to provide these services to each individual, notably in rural, dense urban, fragile, or emergency settings with limited or no modern technology? These questions are explored in this article, including what it takes to sustain and expand a large-scale public health program, such as immunization, to ensure coverage, quality, equity, and inclusiveness. We reflect on this in the context of India's Universal Immunization Program (UIP) and the stewardship, policies, and initiatives for vaccine supply and program advances, technology innovations, and the legacy of learnings (such as from the Polio Eradication Initiative) to boost coverage and reduce inequities in routine immunization.

2. Background

The global Expanded Program on Immunization (EPI) was established in 1974, with remarkable planning and technology advances with countries, particularly over the last two decades [1]. However, how much of what is on paper or electronic forms or collected via our robust global immunization tracking system, referred to as "WUENIC", has been proven to consistently reach and incorporate inputs and feedback loops from all users [2]? These users include clients, caregivers, and all cadres of health workers, notably those who are community-based and may be more informally linked with the health system. Immunization programs in countries can incorporate biometrics and machine learning, but are full equity and human interface assured with these technologies to every individual whose data is collected or who uses the data? For sustainability, the backend technology management and access—and the data collected—must be owned, archived, and accessible over many years and as technology advances. This includes access not only for the health system but also by clients, such as parents or caregivers, to show verifiable immunization records for their child's school entry or by a refugee or immigrant in a stressful transient situation. Are we also addressing the behavioral science and economics of individuals in their decision-making to seek and access immunization services and their ability and comfort to act on those decisions to have themselves and those in their household and communities vaccinated?

The further one is removed from a problem, the easier it may seem to address. We need to check those assumptions, consider the people-side, and triangulate with qualitative measurements and process indicators, beyond the coverage figures, reporting milestones or quantitative data [3]. This is particularly relevant in the face of weak vaccine-preventable disease surveillance systems that can help to inform immunization program reach in communities. The vast majority of people around the world participate in vaccination services, as shown in WUENIC. However, several decades of polio eradication, the need for repeated measles campaigns in areas with pockets of unvaccinated clusters of people, and the global urgency of the COVID-19 pandemic have shown us that there are no quick fixes. Technology that is not fit-for-purpose nor singular vertical interventions fully meet public health needs of the most vulnerable populations. The global health community and donors need to refocus and sustainably resource preventive health interventions as a collective 'global good' for each birth cohort and over the life course, well beyond shortsighted annual funding. Governments and donors also need to reflect collectively on previously agreed upon recommendations, such as those of the Ministerial Conference on Immunization in Africa, to assess and revisit their own commitments [4].

While it helps to have universal terminology, such as the recent use of 'zero dose' for infants who have not received their first dose of DPT-containing vaccine, words do not guarantee action, and one year's success is not indicative of what it takes to maintain and grow a robust system [5,6]. The Immunization Agenda 2030 is ambitious and holistic, but we have learned from the over 35 years of EPIs and previous studies that local operational resources are critical for optimal performance every year [7–9].

3. Success of Routine Immunization in India

Two critical components for addressing equity and moving towards assured immunization program sustainability are the commitment and incorporation of local resources (particularly at subnational levels), and engagement and partnerships with civil society. India provides an interesting case study.

India's routine immunization program success to date can be summarized around six major milestones:

India's Universal Immunization Program (UIP) was launched in 1985 by the Indian Government, with prioritized (and annually budgeted and planned) local financial and logistics resources from federal, state, and district levels. This established the system for delivering essential vaccines (such as those preventing diphtheria, pertussis, tetanus, polio, and measles) to infants around the country and tetanus vaccine to pregnant women to prevent neonatal tetanus. Over the years, system strengthening has also increased focus on the following: supply chain to ensure availability of quality vaccines at every level; vaccine safety by augmenting adverse events following immunization (AEFI) surveillance; and data quality and accessibility. Two-way communication between the service provider and the beneficiaries also must be augmented through digital web-based platforms like the Mother Child Tracking System and availability and use of Maternal and Child Health cards that include all antigens and reminder dates. Additionally, particularly in the last 10 years,

UIP has collaborated with Gavi, the Vaccine Alliance, and partners to augment skills of health workers and front-line program managers, such as via initiatives like Routine Immunization Skills Enhancement [10].

In 1995, India launched the nationwide pulse polio immunization program, including National Immunization Days for supplemental polio vaccination. These efforts, linked with routine vaccination that also emphasized birth dose polio vaccination, encouraged multi-stakeholder coordination, program innovation, and community mobilization and engagement at every level of program planning and implementation. This included important collaboration with civil society partners, such as Rotary and the multi-partner Social Mobilization Network led by UNICEF and the Core Group Polio Partners [11]. India's recognition of being polio free in 2014 also elevated the value of vaccination and contributed to a shift in focus on routine immunization [12].

To further address equity in reaching often missed or underserved communities, India launched the National Health Mission in 2013 [13]. The National Health Mission was a bold step towards integration of immunization with other program deliverables in Primary Health Care. The program also integrated two previously vertical and siloed initiatives that began in 2006: National Rural Health Mission and National Urban Health Mission.

The Mission Indradhanush (MI) Program, launched in 2014, and the subsequent launch of Intensified Mission Indradhanush (IMI), launched in 2017, were designed to address vaccine inequity in a subset of districts and facility clusters across geography and gender, based on evidence from data collected from districts. Important within both initiatives is the role of civil society as key partners, including engaging the accredited social health activist (ASHA) program for linking missed communities with immunization services [14]. These initiatives have also contributed to surveyed fully immunized coverage (FIC) increases, as shown in Figure 1 and Table 1, with national FIC coverage at 76.4% for 12–23-month-olds from the most recent NFHS-5, 2019–2021 [15].

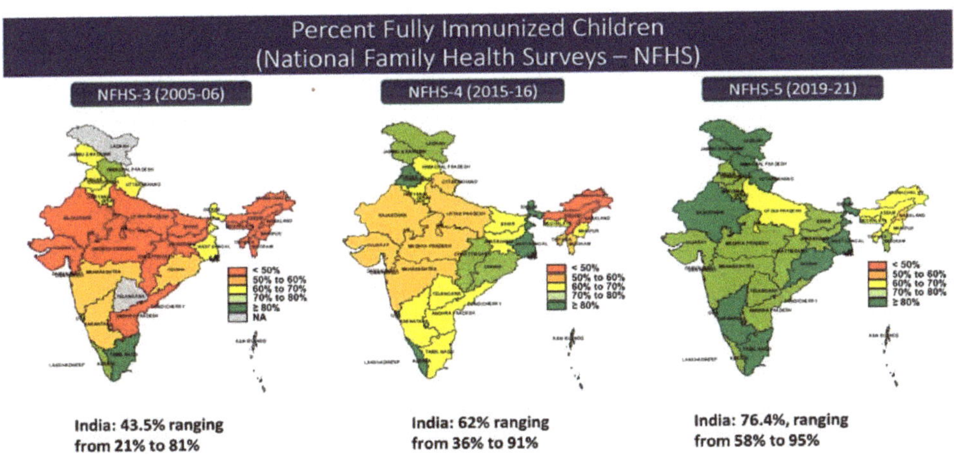

Figure 1. Percent of Fully Immunized Children (National Family Health Surveys—NFHS).

Table 1. India fully immunized coverage (12–23-month-olds, card and maternal recall) by state from National Family Health Surveys.

Fully Immunized Coverage	NFHS-3 (2005–2006)	NFHS-4 (2015–2016)	NFHS-5 (2019–2021)
Average	43.5%	62%	76.4%
Range (by state)	21–81%	36–91%	58–95%

In recent years, the UIP has expanded to include rotavirus vaccine, pneumococcal conjugate vaccine, inactivated polio vaccine, measles-rubella vaccine, and the Japanese

Encephalitis vaccine (for adults). Political and bureaucratic administrator interest has been high at all levels, including from the Prime Minister. UIP and several donor and resource partners supported these introductions at a national scale through sophisticated epidemiology, investment evidence and technical support, and civil society partner engagement for communications and confidence and trust building. For example, donors, such as the Bill and Melinda Gates Foundation, Gavi, and the Vaccine Alliance, provided complementary support for the vaccine rollouts, including additional technical assistance via the Immunization Technical Support Unit and partners, such as UNDP, UNICEF, WHO, John Snow Inc/India, Clinton Health Access Initiative, and others. Additionally, the program was emboldened by domestic manufacturing of the vaccines and a committed supply for scale up. The new vaccine rollouts also provided opportunity for strengthening health systems with technologies, such as the electronic Vaccine Intelligence Network (eVIN), Vaccine Safety Monitoring, and the National Cold Chain Management Information System (NCCMIS) for real time cold chain monitoring and management decisions.

COVID-19 vaccination necessitated rapid, wide-scale digital technology to facilitate vaccine access across the majority of India's population. The COVID-19 vaccination tracking software, known as CoWIN, enabled citizens to choose their vaccination place and time at their convenience with strong community acceptance as evidenced in the high COVID-19 vaccination rates in India [16]. Expansion of the tool with Indian resources is anticipated to benefit routine immunization equity and coverage, enabling health workers and citizens to track routine immunization through the digital application known as UWIN.

As the COVID-19 pandemic response shifts, India is reviving and sustaining its routine immunization coverage improvement program with experience, equity, evidence, and empowerment.

India has gained extensive experience from large scale polio and measles vaccination campaigns and conducting the world's largest routine immunization program (Universal Immunization Program) to reach approximately 26 million infants and 30 million pregnant women. As noted, Intensified Mission Indradhanush and COVID-19 vaccination have also contributed to equity in previously under-served communities and populations. The experiences gained from these programs cut across vaccine supply, access, and community mobilization and have been institutionalized in India's immunization and health systems. A few examples of this institutionalization include vaccination microplans that are part of annual health performance implementation planning, alternate vaccine delivery systems, house-to-house immunization campaigns, and community radio for peer-to-peer conversation in the community.

To address the equity gap, India is tailoring efforts across geographies, gender, and socio-economic strata. During COVID-19 waves in India, some of the most heavily disrupted populations were remote, economically challenged people with specific needs (such as the differently-abled), the transgender community, and populations that migrated from their workplaces. These populations also deserve attention as primary health care programs, such as immunization, adjust in the post COVID-19 phase. States are partnering with community-based organizations and civil societies to tailor services that will enable better access to populations with specific and special needs. Examples of such initiatives are the iHEAR project of Sangath that generated evidence around challenges faced by the disabled and transgender communities during COVID-19 vaccination and the Vaccine on Wheels project of Jivika that provided doctor-supervised mobile medical units for immunization.

To inform and mobilize evidence-based action by generating high-quality digital data, India is strengthening its laboratory-supported Vaccine Preventable Disease (VPD) surveillance with the help of domestic institutions, such as the National Centre for Communicable Diseases and the National Public Health Support Program of the World Health Organization, India Country Office. The data generated from an empowered VPD Surveillance will, in turn, help health workers to take strategic, timely action to address coverage inequity and improve the quality of immunization services.

A key lesson from COVID-19 vaccination was the ability to integrate the use of digital technology, such as via CoWIN and its mobile app, for empowering clients with vaccination information and records. CoWIN generated high-quality real-time data for communities to make informed choices about where and when to organize and receive services; for health workers to track, record, and report vaccination; and for health authorities to take timely action. With lessons from the wide acceptance of CoWIN by the community for COVID-19 vaccination, India is planning to empower its communities with digital UWIN technology. The technology will empower service providers with digitalization of immunization records for tracking, recording, and reporting immunization coverage. For the community, the application will provide flexibility by allowing them to choose the location where they want to receive vaccination services and to have a digital record of their data and vaccination history that can be downloaded and saved. The digital record of citizens will be directly linked to their Ayushman Bharat Health Account (ABHA). The ABHA account will uniquely identify every registered individual as a participant in India's digital healthcare system.

4. Discussion

Despite the remarkable achievements in India's vaccination efforts over the last several years, equity challenges remain to consistently and sustainably reach the most underserved populations. This is not unique to India. Shifts in immunization program focus and strategy, as outlined in the Immunization Agenda 2030, need to align with what immunization data are showing us on continuing inequities. These shifts include addressing disparities across countries and within large countries, such as India, through tailored approaches that are designed with and resourced to the specific fragile and conflict-affected, rural (remote and non-remote), and urban populations.

How can public health programs and donors adapt learning from the Indian immunization evolution and apply the latest equity approaches and tools, particularly in lower-resource settings? A key priority is to foster coordination and long-term resourcing with local institutions that are best placed to generate workable solutions with their populations. This can be achieved through supporting and partnering with civil society networks, particularly those that are established and have a track record of managing resources. As noted earlier with Rotary's involvement in polio eradication, civil society networks are more likely to garner local support, including for day-to-day operational funding, if they are part of planning and monitoring. This includes having access to data and opportunities for regular review meetings with health service representatives. The broader public and private sector health practitioner networks, such as the International Pediatric Association and the International Council of Nurses, also play a critical role in linking people with services for a positive experience of care.

Why is this important? As the COVID pandemic demonstrated, health workers are not only essential for preventing and managing outbreaks but they are also clients themselves. However, oftentimes health systems are not meeting their basic needs for a positive service experience, such as balanced workloads and sufficient supplies. In their delivery of immunization and primary health care, health worker networks will benefit from further adaptation of existing resources that have shown potential across many countries, such as the Reaching Every District and Tailoring Immunization Programmes guidance [17,18]. Pre-service and in-service training and on-the-job learning and mentoring can integrate the fundamentals of immunization service planning and service experience [19,20]. Figure 2 provides a visual example of service experience components that consider the needs of both health worker and service recipient clients.

As mentioned previously, funding for operational resources is also critical and requires a paradigm shift back to the fundamental platform of a functional public health program. Donors should require—and hold themselves accountable—in building health systems, such as USAID's commitment to championing global health and the health workforce in their 2024 budget allocation. This includes funding and monitoring innovations that embody frameworks for local ownership and equity analyses that involve sufficiently representative populations that lack technology access. Indicators, such as consistent availability of data minutes and evidence of use of a mobile device, should be required, not just ownership of a mobile device. Equitable sustainability also requires partnering with local institutions and engaging with communities, which often takes more time and investment but is arguably more likely for public health programs to be able to maintain, particularly in lower income countries.

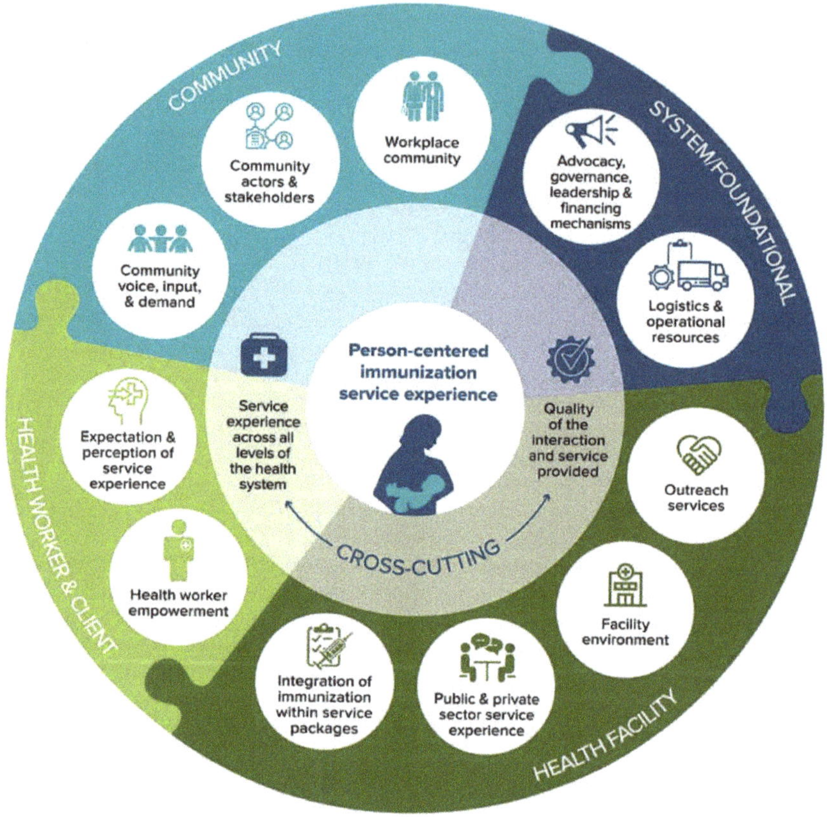

Figure 2. Person-centered immunization service experience graphic.

5. Conclusions

The various technical, operational, and resourcing approaches noted in this article take time to implement and to demonstrate impact on reducing inequity, as also shown in the evolution of India's immunization program. Nonetheless, important learnings can be adapted now for incrementally improving immunization services, quality, and access with populations. As annual coverage data provide a time-limited snapshot, immunization programs and donors will benefit from triangulating coverage data with process indicators and trend analyses. In addition, sustained immunization program success requires continuing political and administrative buy in, technical quality, program review at the district level upwards, and community partnerships. As the Immunization Agenda 2030 progresses, the global immunization community and countries can benefit by tailoring their immunization equity strategies from previous experiences, such as the components shown in the India example, and incorporating approaches that include behavioral science and person-centered care to support and empower health workers and clients.

Author Contributions: Conceptualization, L.S. and R.S.G.; writing—original draft preparation, L.S. and R.S.G.; writing—review and editing, L.S., R.S.G. and K.E. All authors have read and agreed to the published version of the manuscript.

Funding: This research received no external funding.

Institutional Review Board Statement: Not applicable.

Informed Consent Statement: Not applicable.

Data Availability Statement: No new data were created or analyzed in this study. Data sharing is not applicable to this article.

Conflicts of Interest: Author Raj Shankar Ghosh is a member of the scientific advisory board for the iHEAR Project of Sangath and the VaccineOnWheels project of Jivika. Both of these projects are mentioned in this article as examples of routine immunization work in India.

References

1. Keja, K.; Hayden, G.; Henderson, R.H. Expanded programme on immunization. *World Health Stat. Q* **1988**, *41*, 59–63. [PubMed]
2. WHO/UNICEF Estimates of National Immunization Coverage. Available online: https://www.who.int/news-room/questions-and-answers/item/who-unicef-estimates-of-national-immunization-coverage (accessed on 13 February 2023).
3. Generation, Quality, and Use of Routine Immunization Process Indicators in Strengthening Immunization Systems. Available online: https://publications.jsi.com/JSIInternet/Inc/Common/_download_pub.cfm?id=22952&lid=3 (accessed on 13 February 2023).
4. Ministerial Conference on Immunization in Africa | WHO | Regional Office for Africa. Available online: https://www.afro.who.int/publications/ministerial-conference-immunization-africa (accessed on 13 February 2023).
5. The Zero-Dose Child: Explained | Gavi, the Vaccine Alliance. Available online: https://www.gavi.org/vaccineswork/zero-dose-child-explained (accessed on 13 February 2023).
6. Bednarczyk, R.A.; Hester, K.A.; Dixit, S.M.; Ellis, A.S.; Escoffery, C.; Kilembe, W.; Micek, K.; Sakas, Z.M.; Sarr, M.; Freeman, M.C. Exemplars in vaccine delivery protocol: A case-study-based identification and evaluation of critical factors in achieving high and sustained childhood immunisation coverage in selected low-income and lower-middle-income countries. *BMJ Open* **2022**, *12*, e058321. [CrossRef] [PubMed]
7. Rainey, J.J.; Watkins, M.; Ryman, T.K.; Sandhu, P.; Bo, A.; Banerjee, K. Reasons related to non-vaccination and under-vaccination of children in low and middle income countries: Findings from a systematic review of the published literature, 1999–2009. *Vaccine* **2011**, *29*, 8215–8221. [CrossRef] [PubMed]
8. Favin, M.; Steinglass, R.; Fields, R.; Banerjee, K.; Sawhney, M. Why children are not vaccinated: A review of the grey literature. *Int. Health* **2012**, *4*, 229–238. [CrossRef] [PubMed]
9. Addressing Insufficient Operational Funding to Reach Zero-Dose Children and Missed Communities—USAID MOMENTUM. Available online: https://usaidmomentum.org/resource/addressing-insufficient-operational-funding-to-reach-zero-dose-children-and-missed-communities/ (accessed on 13 February 2023).
10. Rapid Immunization Skill Enhancement (RISE) in India—JSI. Available online: https://www.jsi.com/project/rapid-immunization-skill-enhancement-rise-in-india/ (accessed on 13 February 2023).
11. Deutsch, N.; Singh, P.; Singh, V.; Curtis, R.; Siddique, A.R. Legacy of Polio-Use of India's Social Mobilization Network for Strengthening of the Universal Immunization Program in India. *J. Infect. Diseases* **2017**, *216* (Suppl. S1), S260–S266. [CrossRef] [PubMed]
12. WHO Director-General Celebrates Polio-Free India. Available online: https://www.who.int/director-general/speeches/detail/who-director-general-celebrates-polio-free-india (accessed on 13 February 2023).
13. Home: National Health Mission. Available online: https://nhm.gov.in/ (accessed on 13 February 2023).
14. Agarwal, S.; Curtis, S.L.; Angeles, G.; Speizer, I.S.; Singh, K.; Thomas, J.C. The impact of India's accredited social health activist (ASHA) program on the utilization of maternity services: A nationally representative longitudinal modelling study. *Hum. Resour. Health* **2019**, *17*, 1–13. [CrossRef] [PubMed]
15. National Family Health Survey (NFHS-5). Available online: http://rchiips.org/nfhs/factsheet_NFHS-5.shtml (accessed on 13 February 2023).
16. India: WHO Coronavirus Disease (COVID-19) Dashboard With Vaccination Data | WHO Coronavirus (COVID-19) Dashboard With Vaccination Data. Available online: https://covid19.who.int/region/searo/country/in (accessed on 13 February 2023).
17. Reaching Every District (RED)—A Guide to Increasing Coverage and Equity in All Communities in the African Region. WHO, Regional Office for Africa. Available online: https://www.afro.who.int/publications/reaching-every-district-red-guide-increasing-coverage-and-equity-all-communities (accessed on 21 February 2023).
18. Tailoring Immunization Programs (TIP). WHO, Regional Office for Europe. Available online: https://apps.who.int/iris/handle/10665/329448 (accessed on 21 February 2023).

19. Quality Immunization Services: A Planning Guide. WHO, Iris. Available online: https://apps.who.int/iris/handle/10665/354403 (accessed on 21 February 2023).
20. ervice Experience. Vaccination Demand Hub. Available online: https://demandhub.org/service-experience/ (accessed on 21 February 2023).

vaccines

MDPI

Perspective

Why Reaching Zero-Dose Children Holds the Key to Achieving the Sustainable Development Goals

Dan Hogan [1,*] and Anuradha Gupta [2]

[1] Gavi, The Vaccine Alliance, 1218 Le Grand-Saconnex, Switzerland
[2] Sabin Vaccine Institute, Washington, DC 20037, USA
* Correspondence: dhogan@gavi.org

Abstract: Immunization has one of the highest coverage levels of any health intervention, yet there remain zero-dose children, defined as those who do not receive any routine immunizations. There were 18.2 million zero-dose children in 2021, and as they accounted for over 70% of all underimmunized children, reaching zero-dose children will be essential to meeting ambitious immunization coverage targets by 2030. While certain geographic locations, such as urban slum, remote rural, and conflict-affected settings, may place a child at higher risk of being zero-dose, zero-dose children are found in many places, and understanding the social, political, and economic barriers they face will be key to designing sustainable programs to reach them. This includes gender-related barriers to immunization and, in some countries, barriers related to ethnicity and religion, as well as the unique challenges associated with reaching nomadic, displaced, or migrant populations. Zero-dose children and their families face multiple deprivations related to wealth, education, water and sanitation, nutrition, and access to other health services, and they account for one-third of all child deaths in low- and middle-income countries. Reaching zero-dose children and missed communities is therefore critical to achieving the Sustainable Development Goals commitment to "leave no one behind".

Keywords: zero-dose children; underimmunized children; equity; multiple deprivation; Immunization Agenda 2030

Citation: Hogan, D.; Gupta, A. Why Reaching Zero-Dose Children Holds the Key to Achieving the Sustainable Development Goals. *Vaccines* **2023**, *11*, 781. https://doi.org/10.3390/vaccines11040781

Academic Editor: Eduardo Osuna

Received: 28 February 2023
Revised: 24 March 2023
Accepted: 29 March 2023
Published: 31 March 2023

1. Introduction

The Sustainable Development Goals (SDGs) place great emphasis on equity with a shared commitment to "leave no one behind". However, surveying the SDG indicators and related targets reveals that they place their measurement focus on national averages rather than disadvantaged or marginalized populations. Reducing child and maternal mortality, ending the epidemics of AIDS, tuberculosis, malaria, and neglected tropical diseases, and raising the coverage of essential services will all require health systems to reach disadvantaged and hard-to-reach populations suffering from a disproportionately high burden of morbidity and mortality. Therefore, direct measures of, and focus on, communities left behind are critical for the design of equitable health programs and for the success of the SDGs.

Immunization has one of the highest coverage levels of any health intervention [1] and therefore can be a pathfinder for other services and interventions. Immunization also provides substantial health and economic benefits, with an estimated 50 million future deaths averted through immunization activities in 2000–2019 [2], and USD 26 in economic benefits through averted costs of illness for every USD 1 spent on immunization between 2011 and 2020 [3] in low- and middle-income countries (LMICs). However, globally, in 2021, over 18 million infants failed to receive even the first dose of the basic diphtheria-tetanus-pertussis-containing vaccine (DTP1). These zero-dose children are markers of missed communities facing multiple deprivations, with two-thirds of zero-dose children living below the international poverty line of USD 1.90 per day [4]. Reaching them with immunization services can connect them and their families to the health system and other services, and all the health, economic, and social benefits that come with that. This includes poverty reduction (SDG1), better nutrition (SDG2), improved educational outcomes (SDG4), and reductions in inequalities (SDG10). In this Perspective, we explain how a focus on zero-dose children offers a pragmatic entry point for designing and reinvigorating programs and systems to achieve immunization commitments made by countries through the Immunization Agenda 2030 (IA2030) [5], including a 50% reduction in zero-dose children by 2030, and more broadly, to ensure that the aspiration of SDGs to leave no one behind is achieved.

2. Definition of a Zero-Dose Child

The term "zero-dose child" refers to a child who has failed to receive any routine immunizations. For monitoring purposes, it is a measure of whether a surviving infant has received at least one dose of the DTP vaccine. The focus on routine immunization as opposed to doses received through immunization campaigns is intentional, as the indicator aims to measure the reliable reach of immunization services, extended sustainably to reach all communities to achieve universal coverage. The choice of the lack of DTP as the indicator is a pragmatic one. While surveys can measure whether a child has received no doses of any vaccines, most administrative data systems report aggregated data that do not allow for the joint measurement of the receipt (or lack of receipt) of different vaccines. Vaccines other than DTP could also be considered as proxy indicators. DTP is preferred for global IA2030 monitoring, as the measurement of measles and polio vaccine coverage through household surveys may contain a mix of routine and campaign-delivered doses, and the BCG vaccine is not in every country's national schedule and is delivered through diverse platforms. At the population level, low coverage of the DTP, BCG, MCV, or polio vaccine tends to be highly correlated with the prevalence of children who have received no immunizations, and therefore, the choice of the metric is less important than the programmatic aim of identifying and reaching missed communities with dependable immunization services [6].

3. Reaching Zero-Dose Children to Accelerate Equitable Immunization

National immunization programs have made impressive gains in the past two decades, as many children, including those in low- and middle-income countries, are now protected against the leading causes of pneumonia, diarrhea, meningitis, and liver disease. Breadth of protection, defined by WHO to be the average coverage across 11 vaccines, doubled from 34% in 2000 to 68% in 2021 [7], meaning an increased number of children in the world are now protected against an array of vaccine-preventable diseases. However, while many life-saving vaccines have been added to national immunization schedules, some children continue to be deprived of the benefits of even the most basic vaccines in almost all countries.

In 2021, there were 25 million underimmunized infants worldwide, as measured by the lack of three doses of the DTP-containing vaccine (DTP3) (Figure 1), which is the standard measure of the strength of routine immunization systems [8]. However, of these 25 million children, 18.2 m (73%) were zero-dose children, highlighting how essential it will be to reach zero-dose children to improve routine immunization coverage. The importance of focusing on zero-dose children is apparent when considering trends over the past decade. Coverage with three doses of the DTP-containing vaccine (DTP3) rose by 11 percentage points between 2000 (72%) and 2010 (83%) but then by only 3 percentage points between 2010 and 2019 (86%) [8]. The modest increase in DTP3 coverage in the decade prior to the COVID-19 pandemic was largely driven by a reduction in the percentage of children who had received their first dose of DTP but failed to receive their second or third doses of DTP; i.e., DTP drop-out decreased by about one-third (6.7% to 4.4%). In comparison, the coverage of DTP1 increased by only 1 percentage point between 2010 (89%) and 2019 (90%), meaning 1 in 10 children were zero-dose children prior to the pandemic [8]. Increasing

DTP3 coverage will therefore be dependent on reaching zero-dose children and ensuring they are fully immunized.

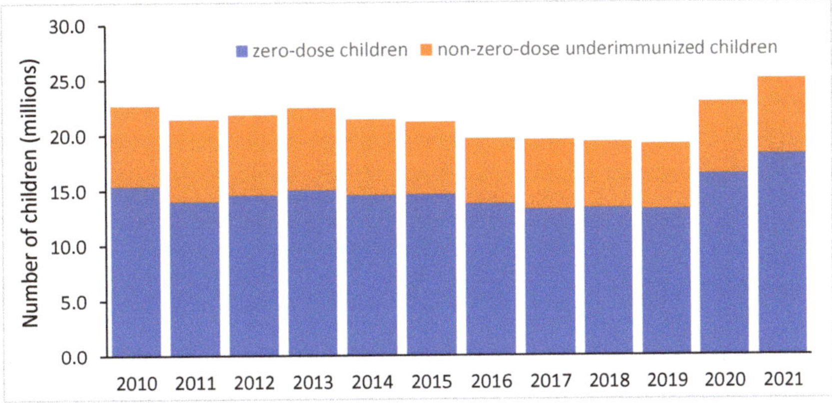

Figure 1. Annual number of zero-dose children and non-zero-dose underimmunized children globally, 2010–2021. Data source: WHO/UNICEF Estimates of National Immunization Coverage (WUENIC), July 2022 [8].

There is also evidence that reaching a zero-dose child may catalyze a cascade of further vaccinations. In an analysis of household survey data from 92 LMICs considering four basic vaccines, most children had either received no doses of any vaccines or received doses of three or more different vaccines [6]. This finding suggests that reaching zero-dose children should be a major focus of immunization programs seeking to increase full immunization coverage, as children who receive one dose almost always move on to receive several other vaccinations.

4. Where Are Zero-Dose Children?

Most zero-dose children live in low- and lower-middle-income countries, accounting for 87% of the global total of 18 million [8]. In 2021, six large-population countries, namely, India (2.7 m), Nigeria (2.2 m), Indonesia (1.1 m), Ethiopia (1.1 m), Philippines (1 m), and the Democratic Republic of the Congo (0.7 m), accounted for half of all zero-dose children. There are also smaller countries that have chronically low coverage and a very high proportion of zero-dose children who are zero-dose even without COVID-related disruptions, for example, Papua New Guinea (56%), South Sudan (49%), Somalia (48%), and Central African Republic (46%) as of 2019 [8]. All of these countries face fragility and conflict, which lead to weaker and less predictable immunization delivery.

High rates of zero-dose children in fragile and conflict settings also play out at the subnational level across countries. An analysis that combined conflict data from the Armed Conflict Location & Event Data Project (ACLED) with subnational coverage estimates from the Institute for Health Metrics and Evaluation (IHME) found that nearly 20% of zero-dose children in 99 LMICs live in conflict-affected settings [9]. The same analysis also concluded that roughly 40% of zero-dose children live in settings highlighted by the Equity Reference Group on Immunization (ERG), namely, urban, remote rural, and conflict-affected settings, with the remaining living in non-urban rural settings. In related work, Utazi et al. found high rates of zero-dose children in conflict-affected and remote rural regions, which are common in parts of the Sahel and the Horn of Africa [10].

More data are needed to quantify the sizes of zero-dose populations in urban slums at the global level, as they are often not captured by household surveys and are geographically too small for vaccine coverage levels to be estimated with geostatistical models. Work that has been conducted suggests that children living in slums may have better access to services than those in rural areas but still face large inequalities compared to wealthier urban households [10,11].

Overall, zero-dose children live in every country in the world. In many countries, the prevalence of zero-dose children can vary substantially across subnational areas. For example, geospatial modeling of subnational DTP1 coverage in Africa found that Angola, Chad, the Democratic Republic of the Congo, Ethiopia, Kenya, Mali, and Nigeria all had mean disparities in DTP1 coverage of 50% or more at the second administrative level [12]. The geographic targeting of resources to support the expansion of routine immunization services to reach missed communities is therefore critical. However, while geographic information can help target resources to reach chronically missed children, in many countries, other factors may be more important than just the geographic setting in determining why children are unvaccinated [10]. As zero-dose children often face multiple barriers to immunization, understanding the social, political, and economic contexts of zero-dose children and their families is key for program design.

5. Who Are Zero-Dose Children and What Barriers Do They Face?

Recent empirical studies by the International Center for Equity in Health and others have confirmed what most public health practitioners have long known: zero-dose children and their families face multiple barriers to obtaining immunization, and their presence in a community is often an indicator of compounded inequities. Moreover, stigma and discrimination are likely factors in determining whether a child benefits from vaccines.

Gender-related barriers to immunization are a key driver of children missing out on vaccinations. Children with empowered mothers, as defined by the Survey-based Women's emPowERment (SWPER) index, are much less likely to be zero-dose. In particular, in the domain of social independence, children whose mothers were measured to have low or medium levels of social independence were 3.3 times more likely to be zero-dose than children of mothers with high levels of social independence [13]. Although the analysis was not causal, the suggested effect sizes are enormous; theoretically, if barriers to immunization related to women's empowerment could be overcome, there would be 4.7 million fewer zero-dose children globally.

Consistent with the literature on inequalities in access to various health services [14,15], children from poorer households are more likely to be zero-dose than children from wealthier households. Unfortunately, there appears to have been little progress in reducing this gap over the past ten years, and the greatest absolute inequalities occur in the poorest countries, with low-income countries having a 14 percentage point difference in median zero-dose prevalence when comparing the poorest to wealthiest household quintiles [16]. Zero-dose children are often poor, with roughly two-thirds living below the poverty line of USD 1.90 per day [4].

Recent studies suggest that ethnicity and religion may contribute to disparities in immunization in some countries. In a study of 64 LIMCs, the median gap in the prevalence of zero-dose children between ethnic groups with the lowest vs. highest prevalence was 10 percentage points (pp), and gaps of 50 pp were observed in five countries [17]. Importantly, differences in zero-dose prevalence by ethnicity persisted even after controlling for wealth, maternal education, and area of residence, suggesting that other factors linked to ethnicity are key drivers of immunization inequalities in some countries. It is concerning that children from smaller ethnic groups in a country are more likely to be zero-dose than children in the dominant ethnic group [17]. The relationship between religion and immunization status appears to be significant in some countries but not consistently across countries [18]. In 27 of 66 countries studied, zero-dose prevalence varied by religious group, with children from the majority religion tending to be less likely to be zero-dose than children from minority religions, with the exception of countries where Muslims were the majority religion.

One significant gap in the evidence base about zero-dose children is in understanding patterns among refugee, migrant, and nomadic populations. A recent review by the World

Health Organization cited 26.4 million refugees in 2020 and 41.3 million internally displaced people due to violence and conflict in 2021, and while some of these populations experience lower immunization rates, it is context-specific with unclear patterns overall [19]. The size of nomadic, displaced, and migrant populations is dynamic and can be exacerbated by conflicts, climate shocks, food shortages, natural calamities, and loss of income. This in turn can increase the number of children who are missed by immunization services as well as household surveys designed to measure immunization coverage [20].

In addition to inequalities associated with accessing immunization, zero-dose children and their families face multiple deprivations related to health and development. Considering other child and maternal health services, zero-dose children and their mothers are roughly two times as likely to miss out on antenatal care and access to an institutional delivery, although interestingly, only about 20% less likely to access care for childhood illnesses or symptoms [21]. In an expanded analysis considering broader development indicators at the individual level, a lack of vaccination was strongly associated with lower access to improved water (prevalence ratio (PR) = 2.60) and sanitation (PR = 1.35), higher rates of childhood stunting (PR = 1.32), lower levels of maternal education (PR = 2.27), and lower levels of maternal demand for family planning satisfied with modern methods (PR = 1.42) [22]. Similar patterns were also observed in ecological analyses looking across countries and across subnational regions within countries, and a principal component analysis looking at these deprivation variables found that nearly all zero-dose children are in the highest deprivation quintile: i.e., if a zero-dose child is found, it is highly likely that they are facing multiple deprivations [22]. A geospatial analysis of time trends in zero-dose children in India from 1992 through 2016 found similar results, with zero-dose children more likely to be poor, have mothers with no education, suffer from severe stunting, and live in less developed states and districts [23].

6. What Is Needed to Sustainably Reach Zero-Dose Children?

The Immunization Agenda 2030 and the supporting Gavi 2021–2025 Strategy [24] have ambitious targets to reduce the number of zero-dose children by 25% by 2025 and 50% by 2030 as compared to 2019 levels. These targets are even more challenging following two years of backsliding in vaccination coverage during 2020 and 2021, resulting in an additional 5 million zero-dose children globally. Moreover, coverage disruptions due to COVID-related lockdowns in 2020 illustrated that gains in coverage among zero-dose children can be tenuous, as 95% of the increase in the number of underimmunized children in low- and lower-middle-income countries was due to an increase in zero-dose children [8]. Population growth presents another challenge. The 15 countries that had a zero-dose prevalence of 30% or more in 2021, accounting for 40% of all zero-dose children globally, are expected to see nearly a 10% increase in their birth cohorts in 2030 as compared to 2021 [8,25]. Thus, it will be important to design robust programs to sustainably reach zero-dose children to reach 2030 targets while avoiding a "one size fits all" approach.

The Identify-Reach-Monitor-Measure-Advocate (IRMMA) framework offers a way to develop strategies to reach zero-dose children and missed communities [26]. The IRMMA framework involves diving deeper into subnational- and community-level inequities and identifying where unvaccinated children live and what barriers to immunization they face. As the majority of zero-dose children tend to live in countries still developing their health information systems, data triangulation is often necessary, though imperfect. Tailored strategies appropriate for the local context then need to be designed and operationalized to overcome identified barriers. For example, strategies to sustainably reach zero-dose children with immunization services in urban slums would be different from those for nomadic populations or for children in cross-border settings. This will often require addressing gender barriers to immunization, and opportunities for integrated service delivery should be sought out to increase efficiency and sustainability and to take advantage of opportunities opened by vaccination. Supplemental immunization activities should also include the purposeful linking of newly reached zero-dose children back to the routine immunization system to ensure children go on to receive a full complement of vaccines. Such approaches also provide an opportunity to improve the data systems that enable the program's ability to monitor and measure progress. Robust monitoring and measurement are critical for refining delivery approaches and advocating for pro-equity investments. Political will is necessary to initiate and sustain the program and should be secured with a purposeful and inclusive advocacy approach.

Several data and evidence gaps also warrant attention. These include the need for investment in improved demographic and immunization coverage data to enable the identification and monitoring of efforts to reach zero-dose children. To the extent that data from household surveys are used to quantify the distribution and characteristics of zero-dose children, in cases where survey sampling frames are outdated, the picture may be incomplete, and new methods relying on gridded population survey sampling warrant consideration [27]. New innovative methods to overcome barriers to immunization should also be tried, documented, and shared. This should include information on program costs. While there are estimates of average immunization delivery costs [28], data on the incremental costs associated with expanding the reach of immunization systems are very limited [29] but likely higher for hard-to-reach populations [30].

7. Impact of Reaching Zero-Dose Children and Missed Communities

Reaching zero-dose children with a full complement of vaccines has the potential to substantially reduce child mortality, as nearly half of all vaccine-preventable deaths in LMICs occur among zero-dose children [26]. The impact of vaccination is potentially highest in zero-dose children, as they would otherwise be receiving no protection against vaccine-preventable diseases, be more susceptible to infection, and be the least likely to benefit from timely and high-quality treatment if they fall ill. In an analysis conducted by Gavi, the Vaccine Alliance based on data from the Vaccine Impact Modelling Consortium [2], immunizing zero-dose children would account for 53% of incremental impact in Gavi-supported countries through routine immunization between 2021 and 2025, with the remainder of the impact coming from scaling up new childhood vaccines among non-zero-dose children and HPV vaccination (Figure 2) [31]. A modeling study focused on 41 LMICs from 2021 to 2030 estimated that vaccination among the two poorest wealth quintiles would avert 1.2 to 3.8 times as many future deaths per person vaccinated as compared to vaccination in the two wealthiest quintiles [32]. The same study projected that vaccination would avert 24 million cases of medical impoverishment in 2021–2030, with more than 40% of the impact occurring within the poorest wealth quintile for many vaccines. Sustainably reaching communities currently missed by immunization would also help prevent future outbreaks, including the resurgence of measles and polio, and remove the need for repeated disease-specific supplemental immunization activities.

The potential impact of reaching zero-dose children and their communities goes beyond vaccine-preventable diseases. Nearly one-third of all-cause under-five child deaths in LMICs occur in households with a zero-dose child [33], so they must be a focus as countries strive for the SDG child mortality target of fewer than 25 under-five deaths per 1000 live births. Achieving the SDGs thus requires addressing the multiple deprivations faced by zero-dose children and missed communities through strengthened and integrated primary care, as well as improved water, sanitation, nutrition, and education.

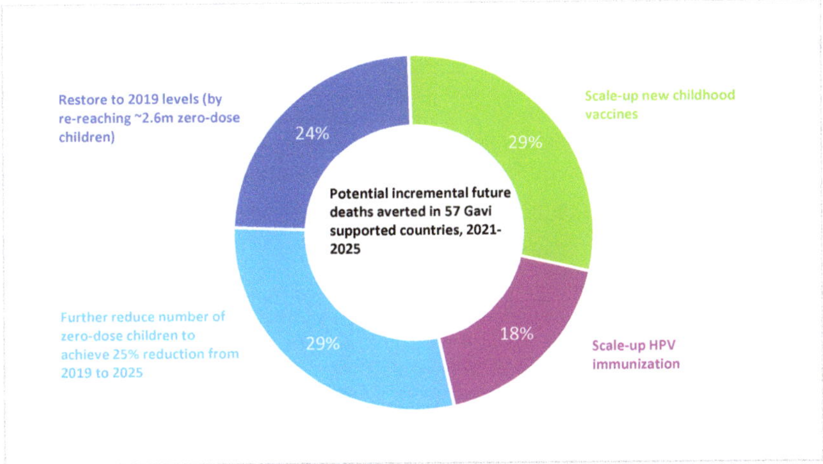

Figure 2. Potential incremental future deaths averted in 57 Gavi-supported countries through routine immunization, 2021–2025. Analysis based on Vaccine Impact Modeling Consortium impact ratios and immunization coverage as estimated in the WUENIC July 2021 release, ignoring the impact of maintaining coverage at 2020 levels and assuming Gavi 5.0 targets are met.

8. Conclusions

Zero-dose children account for over 70% of underimmunized children and must be reached with sustainable immunization services to meet ambitious targets for 2030. Identifying and understanding zero-dose children and missed communities will be key for designing effective interventions to reach them, which will often require tailoring to the local context. As zero-dose children and their families face multiple deprivations, with a high burden of morbidity and mortality, the potential for impact is great if they can be reached. By doing so, countries would be taking a key step toward ensuring no one is left behind in the Sustainable Development Goal era.

Author Contributions: Conceptualization, D.H. and A.G.; Analysis, D.H. and A.G.; writing—original draft preparation, D.H.; writing—review and editing, D.H. and A.G. All authors have read and agreed to the published version of the manuscript.

Funding: This research received no external funding.

Institutional Review Board Statement: Not applicable.

Informed Consent Statement: Not applicable.

Data Availability Statement: Data sharing not applicable.

Acknowledgments: The authors thank Taylor Holroyd, Joshua Lorin, and Todi Mengistu for data analysis support.

Conflicts of Interest: The authors declare no conflict of interest.

References

1. World Health Organization; The World Bank. *Tracking Universal Health Coverage: First Global Monitoring Report*; World Health Organization: Geneva, Switzerland, 2015.
2. Toor, J.; Echeverria-Londono, S.; Li, X.; Abbas, K.; Carter, E.D.; Clapham, H.E.; Clark, A.; de Villiers, M.J.; Eilertson, K.; Ferrari, M.; et al. Lives Saved with Vaccination for 10 Pathogens across 112 Countries in a Pre-COVID-19 World. *eLife* **2021**, *10*, e67635. [CrossRef] [PubMed]
3. Sim, S.Y.; Watts, E.; Constenla, D.; Brenzel, L.; Patenaude, B.N. Return On Investment From Immunization Against 10 Pathogens In 94 Low- And Middle-Income Countries, 2011–2030. *Health Aff.* **2020**, *39*, 1343–1353. [CrossRef] [PubMed]

4. Gavi, the Vaccine Alliance. *Prevent, Protect, Prosper: 2021–2025 Investment Opportunity Technical Appendix*; Gavi, the Vaccine Alliance: Geneva, Switzerland, 2019.
5. World Health Organization. Immunization Agenda 2030. Available online: https://www.who.int/teams/immunization-vaccines-and-biologicals/strategies/ia2030 (accessed on 21 March 2023).
6. Cata-Preta, B.O.; Santos, T.M.; Mengistu, T.; Hogan, D.R.; Barros, A.J.; Victora, C.G. Zero-Dose Children and the Immunisation Cascade: Understanding Immunisation Pathways in Low and Middle-Income Countries. *Vaccine* **2021**, *39*, 4564–4570. [CrossRef] [PubMed]
7. WHO; UNICEF. *Progress and Challenges with Achieving Universal Immunization Coverage. 2021 WHO/UNICEF Estimates of National Immunization Coverage (WUENIC)*; World Health Organization: Geneva, Switzerland, 2022.
8. WHO; UNICEF. *WHO/UNICEF Estimates of National Immunization Coverage (WUENIC) 2021 Revision*; World Health Organization: Geneva, Switzerland, 2022.
9. Wigley, A.; Lorin, J.; Hogan, D.; Utazi, C.E.; Hagedorn, B.; Dansereau, E.; Tatem, A.J.; Tejedor-Garavito, N. Estimates of the Number and Distribution of Zero-Dose and under-Immunised Children across Remote-Rural, Urban, and Conflict-Affected Settings in Low and Middle-Income Countries. *PLoS Glob. Public Health* **2022**, *2*, e0001126. [CrossRef]
10. Utazi, C.E.; Pannell, O.; Aheto, J.M.K.; Wigley, A.; Tejedor-Garavito, N.; Wunderlich, J.; Hagedorn, B.; Hogan, D.; Tatem, A.J. Assessing the Characteristics of Un- and under-Vaccinated Children in Low- and Middle-Income Countries: A Multi-Level Cross-Sectional Study. *PLoS Glob. Public Health* **2022**, *2*, e0000244. [CrossRef] [PubMed]
11. Fink, G.; Günther, I.; Hill, K. Slum Residence and Child Health in Developing Countries. *Demography* **2014**, *51*, 1175–1197. [CrossRef] [PubMed]
12. Mosser, J.F.; Gagne-Maynard, W.; Rao, P.C.; Osgood-Zimmerman, A.; Fullman, N.; Graetz, N.; Burstein, R.; Updike, R.L.; Liu, P.Y.; Ray, S.E.; et al. Mapping Diphtheria-Pertussis-Tetanus Vaccine Coverage in Africa, 2000–2016: A Spatial and Temporal Modelling Study. *Lancet* **2019**, *393*, 1843–1855. [CrossRef] [PubMed]
13. Wendt, A.; Santos, T.M.; Cata-Preta, B.O.; Costa, J.C.; Mengistu, T.; Hogan, D.R.; Victora, C.G.; Barros, A.J. Children of More Empowered Women Are Less Likely to Be Left without Vaccination in Low-and Middle-Income Countries: A Global Analysis of 50 DHS Surveys. *J. Glob. Health* **2022**, *12*, 04022. [CrossRef]
14. Hosseinpoor, A.R.; Victora, C.; Bergen, N.; Barros, A.; Boerma, T. Towards Universal Health Coverage: The Role of within-Country Wealth-Related Inequality in 28 Countries in Sub-Saharan Africa. *Bull. World Health Organ.* **2011**, *89*, 881–890. [CrossRef]
15. Barros, A.J.; Ronsmans, C.; Axelson, H.; Loaiza, E.; Bertoldi, A.D.; França, G.V.; Bryce, J.; Boerma, J.T.; Victora, C.G. Equity in Maternal, Newborn, and Child Health Interventions in Countdown to 2015: A Retrospective Review of Survey Data from 54 Countries. *Lancet* **2012**, *379*, 1225–1233. [CrossRef]
16. Bergen, N.; Cata-Preta, B.O.; Schlotheuber, A.; Santos, T.M.; Danovaro-Holliday, M.C.; Mengistu, T.; Sodha, S.V.; Hogan, D.R.; Barros, A.J.D.; Hosseinpoor, A.R. Economic-Related Inequalities in Zero-Dose Children: A Study of Non-Receipt of Diphtheria–Tetanus–Pertussis Immunization Using Household Health Survey Data from 89 Low- and Middle-Income Countries. *Vaccines* **2022**, *10*, 633. [CrossRef] [PubMed]
17. Cata-Preta, B.O.; Santos, T.M.; Wendt, A.; Hogan, D.R.; Mengistu, T.; Barros, A.J.D.; Victora, C.G. Ethnic Disparities in Immunisation: Analyses of Zero-Dose Prevalence in 64 Countries. *BMJ Glob. Health* **2022**, *7*, e008833. [CrossRef] [PubMed]
18. Santos, T.M.; Cata-Preta, B.O.; Wendt, A.; Arroyave, L.; Hogan, D.R.; Mengistu, T.; Barros, A.J.D.; Victora, C.G. Religious Affiliation as a Driver of Immunization Coverage: Analyses of Zero-Dose Vaccine Prevalence in 66 Low- and Middle-Income Countries. *Front. Public Health* **2022**, *10*, 977512. [CrossRef] [PubMed]
19. World Health Organization. *Ensuring the Integration of Refugees and Migrants in Immunization Policies, Planning and Service Delivery Globally*; World Health Organization: Geneva, Switzerland, 2022.
20. Wild, H.; Mohammed Ali, S.; Bassirou, B.; Tschopp, R.; Barry, M.; Zinsstag, J. Mobile Pastoralists in Africa: A Blind Spot in Global Health Surveillance. *Trop. Med. Int. Health* **2020**, *25*, 1328–1331. [CrossRef] [PubMed]
21. Santos, T.M.; Cata-Preta, B.O.; Mengistu, T.; Victora, C.G.; Hogan, D.R.; Barros, A.J.D. Assessing the Overlap between Immunisation and Other Essential Health Interventions in 92 Low- and Middle-Income Countries Using Household Surveys: Opportunities for Expanding Immunisation and Primary Health Care. *eClinicalMedicine* **2021**, *42*. [CrossRef] [PubMed]
22. Wendt, A.; Santos, T.M.; Cata-Preta, B.O.; Arroyave, L.; Hogan, D.R.; Mengistu, T.; Barros, A.J.D.; Victora, C.G. Exposure of Zero-Dose Children to Multiple Deprivation: Analyses of Data from 80 Low- and Middle-Income Countries. *Vaccines* **2022**, *10*, 1568. [CrossRef]
23. Johri, M.; Rajpal, S.; Subramanian, S.V. Progress in Reaching Unvaccinated (Zero-Dose) Children in India, 1992–2016: A Multilevel, Geospatial Analysis of Repeated Cross-Sectional Surveys. *Lancet Glob. Health* **2021**, *9*, e1697–e1706. [CrossRef]
24. Gavi, the Vaccine Alliance. 2021–2025 Strategy. Available online: https://www.gavi.org/our-alliance/strategy/phase-5-2021-2025 (accessed on 21 March 2023).
25. World Population Prospects—Population Division—United Nations. Available online: https://population.un.org/wpp/ (accessed on 28 February 2023).
26. Gavi, the Vaccine Alliance. *Programme Funding Guidelines, October 2022*; Gavi, the Vaccine Alliance: Geneva, Switzerland, 2022.
27. Thomson, D.R.; Rhoda, D.A.; Tatem, A.J.; Castro, M.C. Gridded Population Survey Sampling: A Systematic Scoping Review of the Field and Strategic Research Agenda. *Int. J. Health Geogr.* **2020**, *19*, 34. [CrossRef]

28. Portnoy, A.; Vaughan, K.; Clarke-Deelder, E.; Suharlim, C.; Resch, S.C.; Brenzel, L.; Menzies, N.A. Producing Standardized Country-Level Immunization Delivery Unit Cost Estimates. *PharmacoEconomics* **2020**, *38*, 995–1005. [CrossRef]
29. Portnoy, A.; Resch, S.C.; Suharlim, C.; Brenzel, L.; Menzies, N.A. What We Do Not Know About the Costs of Immunization Programs in Low- and Middle-Income Countries. *Value Health J. Int. Soc. Pharm. Outcomes Res.* **2021**, *24*, 67–69. [CrossRef]
30. Chatterjee, S.; Das, P.; Pinheiro, A.; Haldar, P.; Ray, A.; Brenzel, L.; Resch, S. The Incremental Cost of Improving Immunization Coverage in India through the Intensified Mission Indradhanush Programme. *Health Policy Plan.* **2021**, *36*, 1316–1324. [CrossRef] [PubMed]
31. Gupta, A. Gavi 5.0: Progress, Risks & Challenges. Presentation to the Gavi, the Vaccine Alliance Board, December 2021. Available online: https://www.gavi.org/sites/default/files/board/minutes/2021/30-nov/presentations/06%20-%20Strategy%2C%20Programmes%20and%20Partnerships.pdf (accessed on 15 February 2023).
32. Chang, A.Y.; Riumallo-Herl, C.; Perales, N.A.; Clark, S.; Clark, A.; Constenla, D.; Garske, T.; Jackson, M.L.; Jean, K.; Jit, M.; et al. The Equity Impact Vaccines May Have On Averting Deaths And Medical Impoverishment In Developing Countries. *Health Aff.* **2018**, *37*, 316–324. [CrossRef] [PubMed]
33. International Center for Equity and Health; Gavi, the Vaccine Alliance. *Proportion of Under-Five Deaths Occurring in Zero-Dose Households: An Analysis of DHS/MICS Household Survey Data from 81 Countries*; Gavi White Paper (in preparation). Gavi, the Vaccine Alliance: Geneva, Switzerland, 2021.

MDPI
St. Alban-Anlage 66
4052 Basel
Switzerland
Tel. +41 61 683 77 34
Fax +41 61 302 89 18
www.mdpi.com

Vaccines Editorial Office
E-mail: vaccines@mdpi.com
www.mdpi.com/journal/vaccines

www.ingramcontent.com/pod-product-compliance
Lightning Source LLC
Chambersburg PA
CBHW061558220926
51850CB00005B/364